MONEY, BANKING, AND THE FINANCIAL SYSTEM

MONEY, BANKING, AND THE FINANCIAL SYSTEM

CONCEPTUAL EXPLANATIONS OF THE NATURE AND FUNCTIONS OF MONEY, OF FINANCIAL INSTITUTIONS, INSTRUMENTS AND MARKETS, AND OF MACRO-MONETARY THEORY AND POLICY

ELBERT V. BOWDEN

Chair of Banking

Appalachian State University

West Publishing Company
St. Paul • New York • Los Angeles • San Francisco

Composition: *Polyglot*
Art: *Rolin Graphics*
Indexing: *Sandy Schroeder*

Copyright © 1989   By WEST PUBLISHING COMPANY
50 W. Kellogg Boulevard
P.O. Box 64526
St. Paul, MN 55164-1003

Printed in the United States of America

Library of Congress Cataloging-in-Publication Data

Bowden, Elbert V.
   Money, Banking, and the Financial System.
   Includes index.
   1. Money.   2. Banks and banking.   3. Monetary policy.
4. Financial institutions.   5. Money—United States.
6. Banks and banking—United States.   7. Financial
Institutions—United States.   8. Monetary policy—
United States.   I. Title.
HG221.B63   1989   332.1   88-33804
ISBN 0-314-72626-8

PREFACE

FOREWORD

These days it seems that every textbook in this field claims to be easily understandable and "student oriented." And while it's true that in recent years many books have become significantly better in this respect, unfortunately the readability/understandability seems to break down just when the subject matter gets most difficult.

Beyond that, I have been searching for a book which is thorough and which would help *all of the students in the class*—not just the top 20 or 30 percent—to gain an intuitive (common sense) understanding of the subject matter. Memorized definitions, formulas, and anything else which is just memorized—not conceptually understood—is not likely to be remembered for very long after the final exam. But I have not yet found a book which offers the kinds of conceptual explanations and the level of clarity and ease of exposition which I desire for my students, together with a thorough and solid coverage of the subject matter. Since I couldn't find a book which was completely satisfactory, I decided to try to write one. It has not been a quick and easy task.

The developmental stage and class testing of this evolving manuscript has given ample opportunity for both reviewers and students to comment and suggest improvements. A total of 39 academic colleagues, five bank officers, and 84 students have participated in this review process. Although this is a first edition of this book, it is a "thoroughly revised" first edition.

I hope this final product is successful in achieving my objective: **to cover the entire subject in a manner which fosters interesting and efficient learning** so that all students who honestly try will gain a thorough and precise **conceptual understanding** of every segment of the subject. If the book succeeds in achieving this objective then it will be a unique contribution to student understanding in this field, and all of my efforts and those of my many reviewers will have been justified.

DISTINGUISHING CHARACTERISTICS OF THIS BOOK

The key distinguishing characteristics of this book are:

1. The easy, user-friendly, non-mathematical communication of ideas, maintained throughout—from the easiest introductory ideas and concepts to the most complex theories; and

2. The careful, patient, conceptual explanations, designed to generate interest and give the reader a clear understanding and an intuitive "feel" in every sector of this broad subject area.

In addition, there are some substantive differences.

Substantive Difference

- Chapter one presents an overview of the entire subject area—the forest, before the trees.

- This book clearly explains the unique meaning of the term "demand for money" and the distinction between **demand for money** and **quantity of money demanded**. This important distinction is precisely maintained throughout the book. I know of no other book which does that.

- In chapter three the important concept of the **time value of money** is integrated with the relationship between bond prices and interest rates, and all of this is thoroughly (conceptually) explained—in words.

- The appendix to chapter one, *Guide to Information Sources*, plus extensive end-of-chapter lists of suggested readings will provide students—and instructors as well—with all of the sources needed for going deeper into any part of this subject, for staying current in the field, and for doing research and writing papers.

- The book maintains a constant awareness of the **revolutionary changes** now going on in the U.S. and worldwide money-banking-financial system, including a recognition at all times of the **globalization** of the system.

- Throughout the book I have tried to capture some of the often missed excitement of what is happening in all sectors of this rapidly changing field—in the institutional framework, in institutional practices, as well as in macro-monetary theory and policy.

Simple English—Not Math—Is the Communications Medium

All of the algebra in this book is located in appendixes and all of the appendixes are located on the blue-edged pages at the back of the book. Many years of experience tells me that most students will not gain much **conceptual understanding** when math is used as the communications medium. Students can memorize equations and manipulations with no awareness of the principles—the cause and effect relationships—illustrated.

There are many instances when algebra and calculus are more efficient communications media than is the English language—that is, more efficient for those who are adept at communicating in this medium. But the fact is that I have never had a class in which most of the students had this kind of math capability.

The Instructor Can Introduce As Much Math As Desired

For those instructors who wish to translate the theoretical interrelationships into equations, there's no reason not to do that. The students will gain conceptual understanding from reading the book. Then they can be assigned the math appendixes and see the simple algebra explained very patiently in simple English. Instructors who wish to go beyond that will have plenty of time to introduce additional math illustrations and applications in class.

For those instructors who wish to introduce a significant amount of math, the careful, patient explanations of the basic algebra presented in the appendixes will help poorly-prepared students to attain the basic level of proficiency needed to understand the classroom presentations.

The bottom line: The instructor who uses this book can have it either way—can teach a completely non-mathematical course, or can introduce as many math applications as desired, while secure in the knowledge that the students are gaining sound conceptual understanding from the textbook.

Prior Knowledge in the Subject is Not Required

This book does not take anything for granted regarding the prior knowledge and understanding of the student. Those who are well prepared will find the going easier. But those who are not well prepared will not be lost, either. They will just need to put in more study/practice/self-testing time to overcome their deficiencies. Everything they need is here in the book, explained so that they can understand. But *learning it well* is up to them.

Designed for Non-Frustrating, Efficient Learning

The book throughout is designed for an efficient learning experience—i.e., maximum comprehension and retention per unit of study time. Throughout the book—in even the most complex topics—I have done my very best to keep the discussion clear and interesting and to eschew scholarly exposition.

Using this book, "ordinary students" can understand the subject matter and can get interested in and feel some of the excitement in this field. Classes will be more alive, and there will be much less resistance to the more complex topics.

I have tried to limit the number of ideas introduced in each chapter so that each is short enough to be read and understood at one sitting. Although some chapters are more than 15 pages long, I believe the careful, patient explanations and the non-frustrating, non-boring style, will enable most students to make it through without fatigue and to understand it in one sitting. However, it needs to be emphasized that *reading and understanding is not enough. Thorough learning* requires practicing, reviewing, and self-testing. And that takes much longer than just "reading and understanding."

THIS BOOK CAN SERVE THE BASIC NEEDS OF A VARIETY OF COURSES

As you read through the Table of Contents you will see that this could serve as a basic textbook in several different courses, depending on how it is used. It is a thorough treatment of money and banking and the financial system, whether the emphasis is on theory, or institutions, or a balanced treatment of both. In addition, it also thoroughly explains (conceptually, understandably) the basics of several other subject areas:

- macro-monetary theory and policy
- financial institutions, instruments, and markets,
- intermediation, and the flow of funds system
- commercial banking and risk management, portfolio theory, GAP management, bond duration, futures, options, and swaps

This book does not provide everything needed for a full-term course in each of these subjects. But it offers the basic conceptual understanding which many students who take these courses never get. An enterprising instructor could use this book to ensure that the students will get this basic understanding.

The desired additional information could be brought in using sources listed in the *Guide to Information Sources* (appendix 1A) and in the end-of-chapter *Suggested Readings*.

Some instructors may want to use this book together with one or more carefully chosen paperbacks and/or books on library reserve. Any one of these approaches might result in a more successful course than would result from just assigning "the standard sequence of chapters" in one of the standard textbooks in the subject area.

TO THE INSTRUCTOR

This book is designed for flexibility. The sequence of chapters and the number of chapters to be covered is the instructor's choice. So your course design and emphasis is up to you.

Please Don't Feel Compelled to Assign All of the Chapters!

It would be impossible for an average student to *thoroughly learn* all of the material in this book in one semester. But some instructors may choose to move rapidly through the book and cover all of the chapters so that the students can at least "see it all go by one time." Because of the clear, easy exposition, that approach might be a viable alternative. But it isn't the approach I would choose.

My preference is for less breadth and more depth—for having the students cover less material and requiring that they *learn it well*. If that's also your objective, then you will not want to assign all of the chapters. The question of how many to assign, and which ones, will depend on the desired emphasis of your course and how much additional work (outside the text) you plan to assign.

The Instructor's Manual Offers Many Suggestions

The Brief Table of Contents (the first of the blue-edged pages, coming up soon) offers several alternative course outlines. The *Instructor's Manual* offers a much greater number of alternative course outlines. Also the *Manual* gives many suggestions for interesting class activities and outside assignments and gives suggested answers to all of the end-of-chapter questions.

Be As Eclectic As You Wish

Please feel free to be as eclectic as you wish. Include in your course whatever chapters you wish, in whatever order seems most appropriate to you. Choose whatever supplementary materials, kinds of outside assignments, etc. appear most likely to carry your students toward your chosen objectives.

No matter what you do, I think you will find that, because of the way the subject matter is treated in this text, your students will be attracted to it, enthusiastic about it, and consider this subject to be one of the highlight courses of their college career. I think this book will help to attract students to your course—and majors to your department.

Learning Aids Available: Study Guide, and Computer Software

Practice and self-testing is an essential part of gaining a permanent conceptual understanding of any complex subject. Both the *Study Guide* and the computer software are designed to give the students plenty of opportunity to do that. Also, most students need to do some self-testing to discover the difference between "reading and understanding," and *thoroughly learning* the subject.

The Study Guide. Each chapter of the **Study Guide**, in addition to further explanations of the more difficult topics, includes about 50 questions—fill-in, true-false, multiple choice, essay, and problems with graphs—for thorough self-testing on everything covered in the text. The answers to all of the questions—including the essays and graphs—are included at the end of each chapter.

Computer Software. The **computer software** consists of Lotus templates illustrating tabular and graphic examples of many concepts and principles from the text. The templates can be used in class demonstrations and/or as a tutorial and self-testing device. Each template provides the student the opportunity to practice shifting parameters and to observe the results both in tabular and graphic form. With some templates the student can observe the different results depending on the theoretical model chosen: modern monetarist, Keynesian, or new classical.

With the *Study Guide* and the computer software, students will have ample opportunity to really "dig in" on this subject—to learn it *thoroughly* and *permanently.*

ACKNOWLEDGEMENTS

I willingly acknowledge my debt and express my sincere appreciation to the many people who have helped to make this a better book.

Thanks to my Colleague-Reviewers

My colleague-reviewers have helped most on the substantive characteristics of the book—in helping me to make sure that everything that should be included, is included, that every topic is given proper treatment—the correct amount of depth and emphasis—and that on all issues where there are alternative theories or views, the treatment is carefully balanced among the alternatives.

Box 1 presents a list of the names of all of those to whom I owe a great debt of gratitude. My sincerest thanks to all of you. You have enabled me to produce a final product which is *far superior* to anything which I could have produced entirely on my own.

Thanks to my Bank Officer-Reviewers

The banking chapters have been made thoroughly up-to-date and accurate as the result of careful reviews and many suggestions by the following bank officers whose thoughtful assistance is hereby acknowledged and greatly appreciated:

John McNair, First Wachovia Bank, Winston-Salem, NC

Norman Potter, Avery County Bank, Newland, NC

Don Redding, NCNB National Bank, Charlotte, NC

Steve Salisbury, Triangle Bank, Raleigh, NC

Steve Woody, First Union National Bank, Charlotte, NC

Thanks to my Student-Reviewers

During the period 1985-1988 my students in both the money and banking course and the course on commercial bank management have been reading and writing comments on various evolving chapters. They were asked to make specific suggestions for improving the BMS chapter and cash prizes were offered for the best ideas for improvements. I received *literally hundreds* of suggestions—and found myself obligated for considerable sums in prize money! But it was worth it.

In response to these student suggestions, in many places the exposition has been fine-tuned and several real-world-type examples—the kinds students can relate to—have been introduced. I express my sincere appreciation to all of those students who have helped to make this book a more efficient (non-frustrating) teaching/learning tool.

Thanks to My In-House Reviewer/Study Guide Co-Author: My Wife

A special note of appreciation goes to my wife, economist and educator Judith L. Holbert (Bowden), formerly economics instructor at Appalachian State University, currently full-time mother, in-house reviewer, and writer.

Box 1

Special Thanks Go to the Following Individuals

Paul L. Altieri
Central Connecticut State College

Peter D. Anthony
Castleton State College

Yoktone Benjauthrit
Washington State University

Michael T. Bond
Cleveland State University

Kathleen Brook
New Mexico State University

Donald T. Buck
Southern Connecticut State College

Roger M. Clites
St. Mary's College (MN)

Jean-Pierre Courbois
Appalachian State University

Donna Kay Dial
Indiana University-Purdue

Richard J. Dowen
Northern Illinois University

Garey Durden
Appalachian State University

Marwan El Nasser
State University of New York-Fredonia

Gerald Evans
Monroe Community College (NY)

James Fackler
University of Kentucky

Richard Followill
Appalachian State University

William F. Hellmuth
Virginia Commonwealth University

James P. Hoban, Jr.
Ball State University

Thomas A. Johnson
William Rainey Harper College

Frank W. Jones
Mankato State University

Walter H. Kemmsies
Memphis State University

Benjamin J. C. Kim
University of Nebraska-Lincoln

Serpil Sisik-Leveen
Montclair State College

Felix R. Livingston
Troy State University

Robert W. McLeod
University of Alabama

Edward T. Merkel
Troy State University

Richard Miller
Pennsylvania State University

John A. Orr
California State University-Chico

Joseph M. Perry
University of North Florida

Dennis Andrew Petruska
Youngstown State University

Jack H. Rubens
Cleveland State University

Daniel Rubenson
Southern Oregon State College

Richard Schimming
Mankato State University

Larry J. Sechrest
University of Texas-Arlington

Guy A. Schick
California State University-Fullerton

Naim Sipra
University of Colorado

Neil T. Skaggs
Illinois State University

M. Dudley Steward, Jr.
Stephen F. Austin State University

Paul B. Trescott
Southern Illinois University

Howard Whitney
Franklin University

Douglas Wilson
University of Massachusetts-Boston

In addition to reading and making helpful suggestions on the manuscript, Judy has helped greatly in seeking out and identifying up-to-date sources and in many other ways, including at times bearing more than her fair share of the child-rearing task.

Thank you Judy for your help and for your cooperation and support. You have played a vital role in helping me to bring this project to fruition. Also, I am happy to have you as my co-author in the preparation of the *Study Guide*.

Thanks to My Excellent Secretaries

During the course of this project I have had the good fortune to have had the help of three excellent secretaries: Candy Hall, Betty Webb, and Sandy Hicks. To all three of you I express my sincerest appreciation for making this project less difficult, and the end result better than it otherwise might have been. Thank you Candy, Betty, and Sandy for your cheerful cooperation and your excellent work.

TO THE STUDENT

As you study this book you'll discover that this is an interesting, sometimes even *exciting* area of study. But to enjoy it you must study it carefully and learn it *well* as you go along.

Understanding is Only the First Step

Usually, as you read this book you won't have to struggle to understand anything. But understanding is only the first step. Learning it well, for a *thorough and permanent understanding*, requires much more than just "reading and understanding."

Learning Requires Practice and Self-Testing

You aren't going to be able to learn this subject just by reading—no matter how clear it may seem to you at the time. A lot of thinking and rethinking is required. And that's the hard part. But no matter how hard, if you're going to succeed in learning this, you must *practice explaining everything*. Frequent self-testing is absolutely necessary. Do it this way:

- After reading a chapter, go back and read the headings and subheadings and see what you can say about each topic.
- As you encounter graphs, practice with each graph until you can draw and explain it.
- Look at the end-of-chapter list of terms and see what you can say about each.
- Do the same for each of the end-of-chapter questions.

As you do these exercises you'll find out how much you have really learned and what topics you need to re-read, and study more. A *Study Guide* and computer software are available for even more practice and self-testing.

The Study Guide and Computer Software May Help

The *Study Guide* has a chapter corresponding to each chapter in the text. Each study guide chapter begins with further explanations of major topics in the chapter. Several of these "further explanations" consist of edited transcriptions of recordings of my classroom lecture/discussions. Then the remainder of the chapter consists of fill-in, true/false, multiple choice, and essay questions, and exercises with graphs.

The answers to all of the questions and exercises are given at the end of the chapter. The answers to the essay questions and the graph explanations provide concise summary explanations of the most important concepts and principles in the chapter. Perhaps you should go to your bookstore and take a look at the *Study Guide*. Also, if you enjoy playing games on computers, you may find that our Lotus templates offer you a "most-fun" way to practice with several of the concepts and principles

Learn It Well! It's Worth the Effort

Try to follow these suggestions: Read and study and practice and self-test. Then do more of the same until you can answer all of the questions and understand everything *thoroughly*. And do all of this *regularly*.

I'm urging you to do it the hard way. Even if you do, this subject will not always be easy. But you will find that it is understandable and interesting—sometimes even something to be excited about.

I can't guarantee that all this effort will make you rich and famous. But if you really do it well, you'll get an A in the course. And your efforts will guarantee you a lifetime of understanding of some very important things—things which most people never understand.

And about the rich and famous part? Knowledge in this field won't guarantee it. But it certainly won't hurt your chances. So *press on!* And my very best wishes for your *outstanding success.*

Brief Table of Contents With Suggested Alternate Course Outlines Depending on Desired Emphasis

NOTES
1. These are only *selected alternatives* among *many* alternatives. This is a very flexible book. Use it as best serves the objectives of your course.
2. The number of chapters assigned can be adjusted as appropriate to reflect assignments of supplementary materials, library work, student reports, outside papers, and/or other required activities.
(Optional Chapter Nos. are printed in Color.)

CONTENTS

PART II. OVERVIEW OF THE EVOLUTION OF AND THE 1980s REVOLUTION IN THE BANKING AND FINANCIAL SYSTEM

PART III. FINANCIAL INTERMEDIARIES, INSTRUMENTS AND MARKETS: THE FLOW OF FUNDS FROM SURPLUS ECONOMIC UNITS (SEUs) TO DEFICIT ECONOMIC UNITS (DEUs)

PART IV. PORTFOLIO THEORY AND COMMERCIAL BANKING: THE LENDING FUNCTION, AND THE MANAGEMENT OF ASSETS, LIABILITIES AND CAPITAL

PART V. THE MONEY SUPPLY PROCESS: THE BANKING SYSTEM, THE FED, THE MONETARY BASE, AND MONEY MULTIPLIERS

PART VI. OVERVIEW OF MONETARY THEORY AND POLICY: AN INTRODUCTION TO THE ISSUES, IDEAS AND PAST EXPERIENCE

PART VII. MONETARY THEORY I: THE BASIC MODELS AND THE IS-LM FRAMEWORK

PART VIII. MONETARY THEORY II: DEVELOPING AND USING THE AD-AS FRAMEWORK TO ANALYZE THE MACROECONOMY IN THE MODERN MONETARIST, MODERN KEYNESIAN AND OTHER RECENT MODELS

PART IX. INTERNATIONAL BANKING AND FINANCIAL MARKETS: RAPID GLOBAL INTEGRATION INTO A ONE-WORLD SYSTEM

CHAPTER 1

The Study of Money and Banking and the Financial System: What This Subject Includes, and Why

Chapter Objectives

Many students consider this subject to be *one of the most interesting and most educationally valuable courses* in their entire college career. In this chapter you will find out why this might be true.

This chapter provides an overview of the subject—what it contains, and why. When you finish this chapter you'll know very well the vital importance of this subject in understanding (1) the functioning of the money-banking-financial system, and (2) the functioning of the modern-day U.S. and world economy.

After you study this chapter you will have an initial understanding of, and be able to explain:

1. That **understanding money** is a key element in understanding the economy.

2. The **macroeconomic role** of money, and how this can be illustrated in the circular flow diagram.

3. What is meant by **monetary theory** and by **monetary policy** and the relationship between the two.

4. The vital role of **the banking system** in the functioning of **the money system** and **the economy**.

5. The functions of **central banks**, and the U.S. **Federal Reserve system**.

6. The meaning and importance of **financial institutions, financial instruments**, and **financial markets**.

7. Some characteristics of the "new world" of banking and finance: **globalization**, and the 1980s **revolution in banking**.

8. Some **desired characteristics** of a "good" money-banking-financial system.

9. The **major subject areas** included in this course.

1

UNDERSTANDING MONEY: KEY ELEMENT IN UNDERSTANDING THE ECONOMY

You have heard that money is the root of all evil. Maybe there's more than a grain of truth in that. But don't forget this: *Money is also the root of a lot of good.* Money is a very important determinant of what goes on in people's individual lives. It's also an important determinant of what happens in the nationwide and worldwide economy.

The healthy functioning of a modern economic system—whether we have good times or bad, economic growth or decline, prosperity or recession—depends very much on what's happening with *money*. Many of the important theoretical disagreements among economists hinge on money. Many of the nation's most important policy decisions are centered on questions about money.

Think of the importance of the circulatory system in the functioning of the human body. Now consider this: The money and financial system actually functions as *the circulatory system of the economy.* How important is money in the functioning of the economic system? Indispensable. A modern economic system could not exist without money.

Surely there is no one "magic key" which will unlock the door to total understanding of how a modern economic system functions. But money comes as close to being such a key as anything else you're likely to find.

Now take a minute to study figure 1-1: the **circular flow diagram**. There you'll see a simplified overview of the macroeconomy and an illustration of the vital role of the circulatory system—the total spending flow—in supporting the flows of inputs and outputs in the economy.

MONETARY THEORY, MONETARY POLICY, AND MACROECONOMICS

What will be the most important contribution of this course to your understanding of economics, finance, and the economy? No one can say for sure. But what you'll learn about **monetary theory** and **monetary policy** will be (at least) one of the most important.

Monetary Theory: How Money Influences the Economy

What's monetary theory? It's a part of economic theory, to be sure—a part of macroeconomic theory. Just as any other theory, it is concerned with trying to explain why things happen: "What causes what?" "What would happen if ...?"

Specifically, monetary theory tries to explain the relationships between what's happening with *money* and what's happening in the economy. Suppose we let the money supply expand. Or suppose we don't. What difference will that make in the economy? And how? You can't answer these questions without *monetary theory.*

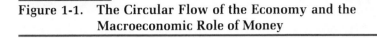

**Figure 1-1. The Circular Flow of the Economy and the
Macroeconomic Role of Money**

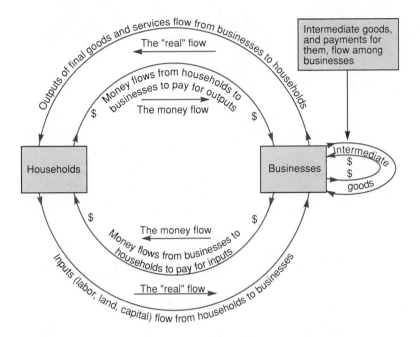

Money flows to households to pay for inputs, and it flows back to businesses to
pay for outputs.

The dollar value of the money flow is always exactly equal to the dollar value
of the "real" flow. If the money flow increases, the real flow increases by the
same amount—either because (a) there are more inputs and outputs being sold
(and bought), or (b) the prices of inputs and outputs go up (inflation), or (c) some
combination of a and b.

This circular flow diagram is a simple macroeconomic overview of the economy. It provides a conceptual framework in which various theories of macroeconomics can be visualized. Monetary theory, for example, is concerned with
understanding the factors which influence the money flow, and the ways in
which the money flow influences the real flow—that is, how a change in the
money supply can cause a change in real outputs and/or prices.

As you go more deeply into this subject, try to visualize the effects of various
macroeconomic influences within the context of the circular flow diagram. You
will be seeing various versions of this diagram and reading references to it at
various places throughout this book.

The question of how money influences the economy is *the basic question of
monetary theory.* You can't go far in money and banking without understanding
some monetary theory.

There isn't time in this one course for you to become an accomplished
monetary theorist. But it is essential that you learn the basics of monetary theory.
This book will help you to do that. Box 1-1 explains the meaning and role of
"theory" and why it is so important.

Box 1-1

Question: Exactly What is Meant by the Word *Theory*, As in the Phrase: *Economic Theory* or *Monetary Theory*?

In high school we all learned the meanings of the terms *hypothesis, theory,* and *scientific law.* We learned that all of these terms refer to cause-and-effect relationships among variables. What change will occur in the *dependent variable* as the result of a change in the *independent variable*?

We learned that which term you should use depends on your *degree of confidence* in the cause-and-effect statement. A "theory" is more likely to be true than an hypothesis, but is less certain than a "law." But here the focus is different.

When the term *theory* is used in the phrase "economic theory" or "monetary theory," degree of confidence in the stated cause and effect relationship isn't the focus.

The phrase "economic theory" means exactly the same as "principles of economics," or "economic laws," or "economic models." All of these terms refer to statements of *cause-and-effect relationships among economic variables.* Economists refer to "the law of demand," to "the *theory* of the firm," to "the *principle* of diminishing marginal productivity," and to "the neoclassical supply and demand *model*." All of these are examples of "economic theory."

The term *theory* in "economic theory" or "monetary theory" means "a statement of cause-and-effect relationships among variables." "What would happen if ...?" "What change in variable x would result from a given change in variable y (or vice versa)? And why?" That's theory.

Theory is concerned with understanding how and why things happen as they do.

Now you can understand why you sometimes hear the comment: "The only thing really worth learning is *theory*." Facts and events are temporal—only temporary. But an understanding of cause-and-effect relationships—of how and why things happen—is likely to be as applicable in the future as in the past and present.

In this book you'll be reading about many things which are not theory. You need to know some "institutional" material—some specifics about money, and about financial institutions, instruments, and markets. But throughout the institutional explanations, theory will be intertwined. At all times you will be finding out not only the *what*, but also the *how* and *why*. Theory is not "all there is," to be sure. But simple descriptive facts, without theory, have only limited, short-run value.

Monetary Policy: Regulating Money to Try to Regulate the Economy

When you understand **monetary theory**, then you know how money influences the economy. Once you understand this, then you can see how **monetary policy** can be used to influence economic conditions.

*Monetary policy means decisions and actions by the central bank (in this country, the Federal Reserve System—***the Fed***) in regulating the money supply and/or the financial markets to try to achieve desired conditions in the economy.* In terms of the circular flow diagram (figure 1-1), monetary policy is designed to influence the rate of the spending flow and thereby to influence the quantity and/or the prices of the goods and services in the input and output flows.

Successful monetary policy depends on accurate and reliable monetary theory. When economists disagree about monetary theory, then they also disagree on the question of appropriate monetary policy.

The Fed is constantly dealing in the nation's financial markets, but not for the purpose of trying to make a profit (as are the private financial institutions). The Fed influences supply and demand in the financial markets to try to have a desirable influence on **interest rates** and on the rate of growth of the **money supply**. Soon you'll know all about how this works.

Monetary Theory, Monetary Policy, and Macroeconomics

When you're studying monetary theory, you're working right in the middle of the field of **macroeconomic theory**. In fact, monetary theory is an important part— many economists would say *the most important part*—of macroeconomic theory. And all decisions regarding monetary policy are based—must be based—on monetary (and therefore macroeconomic) theory.

You can see that in this course you're going to need some understanding of the principles of macroeconomics. If you already have a good understanding of macroeconomics, good. But just in case you don't, this book includes a thorough explanation of all the macroeconomic theory you will need. This course will improve your understanding of macroeconomics.

THE BANKING SYSTEM: INTEGRAL PART OF THE MONEY SYSTEM

Money plays a vital role in the functioning of the economy. But what's so important about banking? Just this: *The money system is absolutely inseparable from the banking system.*

It is the **banking system** which actually creates most of the nation's money supply. And the banking system holds and transfers money and thereby permits money to perform its vital functions in the economy. So to understand the **money system** you must understand the banking system. The two are inseparable.

The Banking System and the Management of Financial Institutions

There are several ways of defining "the banking system," as is explained in box 1-2. The banking system, broadly defined, includes all of the many different kinds of financial institutions: commercial banks, plus all of the other institutions involved in the buying, holding, and selling of financial assets and in performing various other financial services. As banks and other financial institutions perform their functions, they influence (1) the quantity of money in the economy, (2) the rate of turnover of money, and (3) the cost of borrowing and the income from lending—the interest rate.

Banking activities have a significant influence on both microeconomic and macroeconomic conditions in the economy. But remember that these financial institutions are private, profit-motivated businesses. So you can't understand how the monetary system works unless you understand how these businesses operate—why they do what they do, and how their actions influence financial markets and the economy. So in this course you'll be learning about *the management of financial institutions.*

The Leading Role of Commercial Banks

In the broadly defined banking system, the leading financial institutions are **commercial banks**. Commercial banks play a predominant role in the nation's monetary and financial system. Aggregate assets of commercial banks exceed (by a

---

Box 1-2

Question: **Exactly What is the Banking System?**

"The banking system" can be defined in various ways. The narrowest definition might include only commercial banks—excluding all other financial institutions. But since 1980 this narrow definition is no longer realistic. The other depository institutions—the so-called thrift institutions (savings and loan institutions, mutual savings banks, and credit unions) were permitted to offer checkable accounts by the *Depository Institutions Deregulation and Monetary Control Act* (DIDMCA) of March 1980.

A realistic definition of the banking system now must include the commercial banks and all of the other depository institutions—the thrifts. All of these institutions offer checking accounts, savings accounts, and a broad range of financial services.

An even broader definition would include all the other financial services businesses such as insurance companies, brokerage firms, and even Sears-Roebuck because all of these firms are selling financial services and therefore are in the broadly defined "business of banking."

In this chapter and throughout this book, the term "the banking system" or "the banking industry" will always refer to the commercial banks, plus all of the thrift institutions. All of these are "depository institutions." All of them hold checkable accounts—immediately spendable money—and all of them participate in the money-creation process.

When a broader definition of "the banking system" is required, the term "the financial services industry" will be used.

---

significant margin) those of any other kind of financial institution. So commercial banks deserve (and will receive) some special attention.

Commercial banks are businesses, more or less like other businesses. Essentially they are in the business of *buying and selling current dollars*.

When banks take deposits, they "buy" current dollars from their depositors and others in exchange for their promises to pay (a greater number of) future dollars. Then when banks make loans they "sell" the current dollars in exchange for the borrowers' promises to pay (an even greater number of) future dollars. As the commercial bankers "buy and sell current dollars" in exchange for "promises to pay future dollars" they have an important influence on money and on the economy. Box 1-3 explains the distinction between current dollars and future dollars.

CENTRAL BANKING AND THE U.S. FEDERAL RESERVE SYSTEM

At the center of the banking system of every modern nation is the **central bank**. While the private financial institutions are operating in the money markets they are influencing the nation's money system and the economy—but not on purpose. They are just trying to operate efficiently and profitably and to generate some returns for their stockholders. But that isn't true for the central bank.

In every nation the central bank (e.g., the U.S. Fed) performs the important function of deciding on and carrying out monetary policy. The central bank serves as banker for the private banks. It controls the amount of **reserves** available to the banking system and thereby controls the size of—and changes in the size of—the

Box 1-3

Question: Exactly What is the Difference between "Current Dollars" and "Future Dollars"?

This distinction between *current dollars* and *future dollars* may seem strange to you. It's thoroughly explained in chapter 3 on "The Time Value of Money." But for now, here's a brief explanation.

A current dollar is worth more than a dollar to be received at some time in the future. So these "current" kinds of dollars are in fact quite different from "future" dollars.

It takes more than one future dollar to buy a current dollar. How much more? That depends on (1) how far in the future, and (2) the current rate of interest. You'll find out all about this in chapter 3.

nation's money supply.[1] Also, as mentioned a few pages back, the central bank can have a significant influence on the nation's financial markets. It can purposely influence supply and demand conditions (and therefore prices—i.e., interest rates) in those markets.

In this course you will gain a thorough understanding of central banking and the U.S. Federal Reserve System—what it is, what it does, and why and how. You'll find out how the Fed's monetary policies and actions work their way through the banking system and exert their influence on the economy. And you'll find out about the increasingly important role of the U.S. Fed and the central banks of other nations in influencing **international financial conditions and relationships**.

STRUCTURE OF THE FINANCIAL SYSTEM: MONEY, PLUS FINANCIAL INSTITUTIONS, INSTRUMENTS, AND MARKETS

What is the structure of this money-banking-financial system which plays the vital role of "circulatory system of the economy"? Quite simply, the overall system consists of *money, plus financial institutions, financial instruments, and financial markets*.

Financial Institutions

There are many kinds of financial institutions operating in the U.S. (and world) economy. Banks are one kind. But there are many others.

All financial institutions are involved in some way with the buying and selling of financial instruments in the financial markets. But different kinds of financial institutions perform significantly different functions in these markets.

Different financial institutions perform the broker function of bringing together buyers and sellers, the dealer function of buying, holding, and selling

---

[1] The total amount of checkable deposits which a bank can hold is legally limited by the amount of reserves it holds. Reserves consist of the bank's deposits in its Federal Reserve bank account plus its vault cash holdings. All this will be thoroughly explained in the chapters coming up.

existing financial instruments, and the financial intermediary function. **Financial intermediaries** are unique in that they *issue financial claims against themselves* to acquire "current dollars"; then they use those current dollars to buy the financial instruments issued by others.

The depository financial intermediaries—banks, savings and loan institutions, and credit unions—mostly take deposits, and make loans. The nondepository financial intermediaries—insurance companies, pension funds, investment companies (mutual funds) and business and consumer finance companies—do not actually "take deposits." But they all issue claims against themselves in exchange for the current dollars of savers. Then they use these funds to buy financial instruments—debt obligations of others.

By the late 1980s, many financial firms were performing several different functions—broker, dealer, depository and contractual intermediary, mutual fund, and others—all within the same corporation.

Banks and other financial institutions play a key role in the functioning of the national and worldwide financial and economic system. So in this course you should expect to find out a lot about financial institutions. And, to be sure, you will.

Financial Instruments

From the previous discussion of the functions of financial institutions, you already know something about the functions of financial instruments. **Financial instruments** are the claims to *future dollars* which their issuers use to acquire (to buy) current dollars.

Financial instruments include such things as government and corporate bonds, promissory notes, commercial paper, Treasury bills (T-bills), certificates of deposit (CDs), corporate stocks, insurance policies, and many others. In fact *money itself* consists of financial instruments. But, as explained in box 1-4, it's useful to make a distinction between "money" and "other financial instruments."

Financial instruments are evidences of **debt**, or (in the case of corporate stocks) evidences of **ownership**, or (in the case of insurance policies) evidences of **contractual obligations** involving the payment of future dollars. Financial instruments are always evidences of claims to future dollars. A financial instrument is a financial asset of the one who owns it and a liability (or capital obligation) of the one who issued it—the one who is obligated to pay future dollars.

Billions of dollars worth of financial instruments are being created (issued) and destroyed (paid off) every day. *The nation's money-banking-financial system operates on the creation, exchanging, and destruction of financial instruments.* In this course you'll be finding out exactly why and how it all happens.

Financial Markets

Financial markets are where current dollars are bought and sold in exchange for financial instruments. Or you might say that financial markets are where financial instruments are bought and sold in exchange for current dollars. Either way it means the same thing.

All over the nation and all over the world, every day people and businesses and financial institutions are buying and selling billions of dollars in the financial

---

Box 1-4

Question: **Exactly What is the Distinction between Money, and Other Financial Instruments?**

In every modern nation, money consists almost entirely of various kinds of financial instruments—*evidences of debt* issued by government and/or by the banking system. However it usually is helpful to conceptualize "money" (i.e., those financial instruments which serve as the immediately spendable medium of exchange) as different from other kinds of financial instruments.

This distinction lets us think of money as immediately spendable **current dollars**, and think of all other financial instruments as **claims to future dollars**. So "money" is current dollars and "other financial instruments" are "the owner's right to receive" (and the issuer's promise to pay) future dollars. As you go further into this subject you will find this conceptual distinction between money and other financial instruments helpful.

---

markets. Current dollars are being demanded. The demanders of funds create and issue (pay out) their financial instruments. The suppliers of the funds receive payment in the form of financial instruments.

As this demanding and supplying of billions of dollars is going on, interest rates are moving up and down to reflect changes in the demand for and supply of these funds (current dollars). Funds flow automatically (often instantaneously via electronic funds transfers) from surplus economic units and surplus areas to deficit economic units and deficit areas. That's how financial markets and interest rates are kept constantly in balance throughout the country and the world.

Basically, financial markets work just like other markets. They respond to *demand* and *supply* and to *the functions of price* (interest rates). For example, an increase in the demand for funds in a market tends to push interest rates up, and to attract more funds into that market. And *in financial markets the price (interest rate) responds very rapidly—almost instantaneously—to changes in supply and demand conditions.*

In this course you'll be finding out a lot about financial markets and how they work. And now, before you go on into the next section, take a minute and read box 1-5 and find out about "buying and selling money."

THE "NEW WORLD" OF BANKING AND FINANCE

In recent years the U.S. and world financial system has been the scene of explosive changes. In this book you'll be reading about those changes. This section highlights some of them.

The Globalization of the Financial System

Not long ago it was possible to study the American money/banking/financial system more or less independently—without constant concern for what was happening in the rest of the world. But not now! During the past two decades—especially since the mid-1970s—there has been explosive growth in international economic and financial activity and interrelationships.

Box 1-5

Question: Do Financial Intermediaries Really Buy and Sell Money?

When a bank takes a deposit from a customer, is the bank actually "buying" the money? Or only renting it? For example, when a person rents a house or a car, the renter only acquires the temporary use of the asset. Ownership of the asset doesn't actually change hands. What about when a bank takes a deposit? Is it buying the money from the depositor? Or only renting it?

It's quite all right to look at it either way. At first glance it may seem more logical to think of the bank as renting the money from the depositor. After all, the depositor certainly can get it back, either on demand or at some specified future date. Doesn't that mean that the money still belongs to the depositor? And not to the bank? Yes, that's one way to look at it.

But it's just as logical to look at it the other way. Think of it from the point of view of the individual depositor's personal balance sheet. Before the depositor makes the deposit, the balance sheet shows an asset item "cash." After the deposit, the cash is no longer there. The asset item becomes "bank deposits."

If the bank deposit happens to be in a non-checkable savings account, then the deposit is no longer spendable money. The depositor has actually sold the money to the bank in exchange for the bank's promise to pay money in the future.

Different books treat this subject differently. In this book, the subject will be treated as follows: When banks take deposits, they are buying money—buying current dollars—in exchange for their **promises to pay future dollars**. The future dollars may be promised either on demand, or at some definite future date.

Also, when banks lend, the loaned money no longer belongs to the bank. It no longer shows up on the bank's balance sheet. It is replaced by an item called "loans" or "securities"—borrowers' promises to pay future dollars. From this perspective it is true that banks do indeed buy and sell money (current dollars). And the "currency" used in each of these money-buying and money-selling transactions is a **financial instrument**—a promise to pay future dollars.

American dollars and U.S. financial instruments have been poured into the international financial markets by the hundreds of billions. By the late 1980s, foreign ownership of dollars and dollar-denominated financial assets amounted to more than $2 trillion. That was about three times the value of the entire U.S. domestic money supply (the M1 money supply: currency and checking accounts, plus travelers checks). Supply and demand conditions in international financial markets now exert a constant effect on domestic financial markets—so much so that the two have become, in fact, integrated and inseparable.

Throughout this book you will be kept constantly aware of the international nature of money and banking, and of **the globalization of financial markets**. Never will you be left with the feeling that the U.S. economy is an isolated "economic and financial island." By the late 1980s, that view had become totally unrealistic.

The 1980s "Revolution in Banking"

During the 1980s, revolutionary changes occurred in the banking (financial) industry. The relationships among banks and between banks and other financial institutions were dramatically altered. Sweeping (revolutionary!) legislative changes were made in the banking acts of the 1980s.

During the 1980s the development of new kinds of financial institutions and financial instruments proceeded at a rapid pace. And the rapid expansion of electronic funds transfer systems (EFTS) has had a profound impact.

Deregulation—the elimination of government restrictions—permitted greater competition among different kinds of financial institutions: in the "products" and services they provide, in the kinds of financial markets in which they compete, and in the geographic areas in which they do business. We made great strides toward a system of *nationwide and worldwide interstate and international banking*.

These recent changes in our financial system were the most radical since the Great Depression of the 1930s—and they aren't over. In fact they are continuing at whirlwind velocity. One result: The number of bank failures has increased dramatically—more than 100 per year in 1986 through 1988—more each year than at any other time since the deep depression year of 1933.

Truly, banking has become an exciting field of study, and also an exciting career path for alert people who enjoy challenges. In this course you will get a realistic picture of this very different and rapidly evolving modern-day U.S. and worldwide banking and financial system.

WHAT DO WE WANT FROM OUR MONEY-BANKING-FINANCIAL SYSTEM?

What are the characteristics of a "good" money-banking-financial system? What functions do we want it to perform? Here are some desiderata:

1. Efficient Exchange, and Funds Flowing Easily from Savings into Investment

As a society, from the **microeconomic** point of view, we want a system which will permit efficient exchange—the efficient flow of resources into their most productive and most desired uses. Also we want a system which will permit savings to flow smoothly and efficiently into investment—from the "net savers" (surplus economic units) to the "net borrowers" (deficit economic units) of the society.

2. A Stable "Full-Employment" Spending Flow

From the **macroeconomic** point of view we want a money and banking system which will promote a healthy circular flow of the economy. We want a spending flow which will support the overall rate of economic activity at desirable levels, with incomes, outputs, production, and employment at levels which meet the objectives of the society. And we want stability of the price level, and a desirable rate of growth of employment, production, outputs, and incomes.

3. A Variety of Financial Instruments for Savers

From the point of view of the savers we want a system which will provide a variety of opportunities to "invest" our savings—places where the savings will be safe and sufficiently liquid (easily reconvertible into spending money), and where we will receive a good rate of return (interest rate). Savers desire a broad variety of financial instruments, with various levels of safety, liquidity, and earnings.

4. A Variety of Financial Instruments for Borrowers

From the point of view of the borrowers—borrower consumers and borrower businesses—the money and banking system needs to provide a variety of financial instruments to let each borrower obtain the desired funds, under the desired terms, and at an interest cost which is kept low by competition and by the efficiency of the "transfer mechanism" whereby the current dollars of savers are channeled to borrowers.

5. An Efficient "Least-Cost" System

The desired system should be one in which the banks and other financial institutions are forced by competition to operate efficiently—where the spread between the cost of funds bought and revenue from funds sold accurately reflects the economic costs of these financial intermediation services. In such a system, profitability for each financial institution results from its efficiency in responding to market conditions and meeting the society's needs for financial intermediation services

6. An Understandable, Predictable System

It's very desirable to have an *understandable* system. It would be nice to be able to look at the financial system and see our monetary theories—cause and effect relationships between money-banking-financial conditions and other variables in the economy—operating *understandably and predictably*. It would be nice to be able to say: "If we permit the following change in the money supply (or in the financial markets, or the banking system, etc.) then we can confidently predict the following changes in the following variables. ..."

How well does the modern-day U.S. and worldwide money-banking financial system meet these desired conditions? Not perfectly. But for the most part, reasonably well. That's one of the things you'll be finding out about, throughout this book.

The Money-Banking-Financial System: Circulatory System of the Economy

How important is the banking system in the functioning of our economy? It's absolutely critical. It is the banking system—this broad array of private financial institutions, plus some government ones—which pumps in and circulates the money and supports the flows of spending throughout the economy. It is the flow of money through the banking system which supports the flows of inputs and outputs and keeps the economy alive and functioning. The "circular flow" again? Exactly.

Here's an example. Did you ever see a building under construction on which suddenly, for some reason, the construction stops and the half-built building just stands there? You wonder why. Chances are that for some reason the financing was cut off. That's a stark, real-world example of what happens to economic activity when something blocks the circulatory system of the economy. Without the financial flow, the real flow (production, and output) stops.

SUMMARY

This chapter has given you an introductory overview of the study of money and banking—of monetary theory and policy, and of banks and other financial institutions, of financial instruments, and financial markets. Now you know what's coming up in this course, and why.

In a nutshell:

- The money/banking/financial system is **the circulatory system of the economy**.

- The system consists of **money**, plus **financial institutions** (those called banks, and others), **financial instruments** (claims on future dollars which are used to obtain current dollars) and **financial markets**—the places where the financial institutions, businesses, governments, and the public exchange money for financial instruments, and vice versa.

- The system operates on basic market principles—**supply and demand, prices**, and **the profit motive**.

- The **central bank** plays the important role of controlling the size of the money supply and influencing conditions in financial markets.

- What the central bank does is called **monetary policy**, and it is based on **monetary theory**—that is, on our understanding of how money influences the economy.

- All of these financial institutions, instruments, and markets have become **internationalized** so that we now have, in effect, a global, **one-world financial system**.

- In this course you will be developing some depth of understanding in each of these subject areas.

Why Study This Course?

Now that you have an overview, what do you think? Why should you want to learn about money and banking and the financial system? First, all of this is going to have an important impact on your own personal life.

Will there be lots of job opportunities for you in the year you graduate? That will depend significantly on how you've chosen to spend your time while in college (of course!). But it also will depend very much on what the inflation rate, the interest rate, and the Fed's monetary policy stance is at the time.

If you're planning a career in the banking/financial field, the past, present, and future directions of the **revolutionary changes** now going on in the financial services industry will be of great interest to you. These changes are very much influencing the kinds of abilities required and the career opportunities available in this industry. In this course you'll get in touch with all that. And that isn't all.

Many business management and planning decisions require the kind of knowledge to be gained from this course. And you *absolutely cannot* understand the functioning of the economy without an understanding of money and banking and the financial system.

This course deals with many things you need to know—ranging from the practical business of banking to the basic cause-and-effect relationships of monetary theory. When you finish the course you'll know a lot more about relationships between *money and the economy* and about *the role that banks and other financial institutions play* in all of this. Also you'll know something about how bank managers make their decisions, and how these decisions (a) determine the success of the bank, and at the same time (b) influence the flows of money and therefore influence conditions in the U.S. and world economy.

It's obvious that in this course you're going to be learning much that's important to you personally, and much that's essential in economics and in banking and finance. If you can give it the time and effort it deserves, this course will turn out to be one of the most educationally valuable courses in your college career. And if you will approach it *seriously* and with a *positive attitude* you'll find it always *interesting*—perhaps sometimes even **enjoyable**. Surely that's enough to make it worth the effort!

Suggestions Regarding the Review Exercises

A word of warning: This book is purposely written to be easy to read and understand. Most students seem to appreciate that. But there is a danger. After you read and easily understand the material you may assume that you have learned it. But you haven't. Only when you begin to test yourself will you find out how much you have *really learned*. If you complete this chapter (or any chapter) without working carefully through the review exercises, thinking about and trying to recall the material in the chapter, you may be lulled into a false sense of security.

Many complex and difficult concepts and principles are explained in this book. But you may not be aware of the depth and complexity because "it's so easy to read and understand." Then the first exam will blow you away!

When you try to explain this material—or to distinguish between the close choices on a multiple choice exam—you'll find that it takes a lot more than just "reading and understanding." To master this subject you must **practice recalling** and **explaining** these concepts and principles. *If you don't do that you will not succeed in learning it.*

Each chapter ends with review exercises. Most students need to spend at least as much time *working with the review exercises* as in the initial reading of the chapter itself. (Believe it or not.) That's the only way to really understand everything and to be sure you're ready for the exams.

The *Study Guide* which accompanies this text gives **further explanation** of the more difficult concepts and it contains many more **questions for self-testing**. You may find that the *Study Guide* can help you to increase your speed and efficiency in mastering this subject and earning your A in the course. So please take a look at it. And now here are the review exercises for chapter 1—your first opportunity to practice all this good advice.

Important Principles, Issues, Concepts, Terms

The role of money in the economy	Monetary policy
The circular flow diagram	The meaning of "theory"
Monetary theory	What's so important about banking?

Why study financial institution management?

Importance of the commercial banks

Buying and selling current dollars

Central banking

The Federal Reserve System (the Fed)

The Fed's role in monetary policy

"Circulatory system of the economy"

Financial institutions

The financial intermediary function

Depository intermediaries

Nondepository intermediaries

Contractual intermediaries

Financial instruments

Financial markets

Supply and demand in financial markets

The globalization of the financial system

The 1980s "revolution in banking"

Desiderata for our money-banking-financial system

Specific topics to be learned in this course

Questions

1. Draw and label a circular flow diagram. Then explain this statement: "The circular flow diagram gives a simple overview picture of the entire macroeconomy."

2. Explain the macroeconomic role of money in terms of the circular flow diagram.

3. Explain what is meant by *theory* in the phrase, *monetary theory*. Then explain as much as you can about what is meant by monetary theory.

4. Explain what is meant by *monetary policy*. Then explain the relationship between monetary policy and monetary theory.

5. From the point of view of understanding the functioning of the economy, why is it essential to understand the banking system and how it works?

6. In the chapter you read that "financial instruments" are the medium of exchange used for buying and selling something. What? Explain exactly what all this means.

7. What are some of the characteristics of the "new world" of banking and finance?

8. Explain some of the things we would like to achieve from—some desiderata of— our money-banking-financial system.

Suggested Readings

Each chapter in this book lists at the end some suggested readings. In addition, appendix 1-A at the end of the book is "A Guide to Information Sources." It gives detailed instructions on how to find money and banking and financial information and current data. I think that when you get a chance to read it you will find that appendix helpful. Meanwhile you should at least be in touch with *The Wall Street Journal*, with the business /financial section of your local newspaper, with some of the business/financial programs on radio and TV, and with the *Federal Reserve Bulletin* published by the Board of Governors of the Federal Reserve System. Appendix 1-A tells much more.

PART I

Introduction and Basic Concepts of Money, Interest Rates, Monetary Theory and Monetary Policy

THE purpose of Part I is to establish right up front very clearly and thoroughly a conceptual understanding of the most basic concepts and principles in this subject area. Many students never really understand these basics, and for that reason, never thoroughly understand the subject matter of the course. To insure that a student gets the basics, the purpose of Part I is limited. It explains very carefully and patiently, and does not go into destracting detail on anything.

Part I contains just enough depth and detail to provide a thorough conceptual understanding. The greater depth and detail will be found throughout the book. But that depth and detail won't have great meaning to a student who doesn't have these basics explained in Part I.

Advice to the Student: If you will learn everything in Part I *very thoroughly*, it will help you throughout this book. And it will help you in all of your other courses in economics, banking, and finance.

Some of the concepts and theories explained in Part I are usually considered to be among the most difficult and confusing in the entire subject. But nothing is difficult or confusing once it is explained so as to be clearly understood. The purpose of these chapters in Part I is to accomplish that objective.

There are in fact many subtle meanings and distinctions concerning concepts and principles in this subject area which in most books are never explicitly addressed—never explained so the students really understand them. It seems to be assumed that these subtle distinctions either are already known, or are not significant. But with my students it doesn't seem that way.

You'll be seeing explicit explanations of many of these (usually implicit) subtleties throughout this book. But I think it's important in the early part of the course to get some of these concepts thoroughly and conceptually understood to serve as a sound base to build upon. Part I tries to do that.

CHAPTER 2

The Nature and Functions of Money: What It Is and What It Does and How

Chapter Objectives

This chapter introduces you to **the nature of money**—what it is and how it works—and its **critical role** in the functioning of the economic system. When you finish this chapter you'll know **what money is** and **what it does**, and **how**.

Specifically, after you study this chapter you will understand and be able to explain:

1. The essential **microeconomic** (efficient-resource-allocating) **role** which money plays in the economy.
2. Exactly what **money** is.
3. The **basic functions** of money and the importance of each.
4. The **evolution of money**, from the bulky commodity monies of ancient times to the **accounting figures** and **electronic impulses** of today.
5. The components of the present **U.S. money supply**.
6. How the modern domestic and international **payments systems** work, and how they have been changing rapidly in recent years.

THE NATURE AND IMPORTANCE OF MONEY

Throughout history, in every society something always has evolved to perform the functions of money. The reason? Because money lets people do things they couldn't do very well without money. Most important: *Money facilitates exchange.*

Money Lets Markets Work Efficiently

Of course it is possible to exchange things without using money. Some **barter** (trading things for things without the use of money) has always been going on. It still is. High income taxes may convince the dentist to fix the plumber's teeth in exchange for getting the plumber to fix the dentist's pipes. And maybe you will cut my grass if I will give you a bushel of apples off my tree.

But suppose I was trying to buy everything with bushels of apples? Or you, by cutting grass? How limited would be our ability to exchange things if barter were the only way!

Barter Exchange Is Very Inefficient

It is intuitively obvious (common sense) that exchange without the use of money would not be very efficient. Barter requires a **double coincidence of wants**. Each of us must find someone else who both (a) wants the goods we have, and (b) has the goods we want. Not an easy task! And what about trying to figure out how much to "pay" (the exchange ratios) for all of these goods? Impossible.

The Inefficiency of Barter: A Numerical Example

A barter economy would work just fine if there were only two goods to be exchanged. But as more goods are introduced, the system rapidly becomes very complicated. In an economy with only 10 goods there would need to be 45 different exchange ratios (prices). With 1000 goods the number of different exchange ratios (prices) would be almost half a million!

Box 2-1 shows how to calculate the number of prices required in a barter economy. Look at that box and you'll see how rapidly the number of prices must increase as the number of goods increases.

Why Exchange Things? To Survive!

We couldn't have much trading going on without something to serve as money. But what's so good about trading things anyway? Think of it this way. What if you had to be completely self-sufficient?

Box 2-1

Feature: Calculating the Number of Different Prices Required in a Barter Economy

In a barter economy, as the number of goods increases, the number of different prices required increases much more rapidly. For any given number of goods (N goods) in a barter economy, the number of different prices required can be calculated using the standard statistical formula for the number of possible combinations of N things, taken two at a time. Using Pn as the number of different prices required here's the formula:

$$Pn = \frac{N(N - 1)}{2}$$

For example, in an economy with 1000 goods, the number of different prices would be calculated as follows:

$$Pn = \frac{1000 \times 999}{2} = \frac{999,000}{2} = 499,500.$$

So you can see that with only one thousand different goods in the economy, almost five hundred thousand different prices (price ratios, goods-for-goods) would be required.

Suppose the economy had 10,000 goods. You can work it out yourself and you'll see that the number of different prices required would be almost fifty million!

What if all the food you had to eat was food that you yourself had produced? And your only housing was something you had built? Your only transportation was in something you had made? And you produced all of your own books and music and medical care and everything else? Inconceivable.

Only the most primitive kind of lifestyle could exist without exchange. And only the most primitive kinds of trade could occur without something to serve as money. So from mankind's point of view how important is money? It's absolutely essential. Down through the ages our survival has depended upon it.

The Microeconomic (Efficient-Resource-Allocating) Role of Money

The existence of an efficient medium of exchange (money) is essential to permit each of us to specialize in what we're relatively most efficient in producing—that is, our "comparative advantage" product—and then to exchange that product for the other things we want. Money is essential in the efficient functioning of markets and the price mechanism.

In its **microeconomic role**, money permits the society to achieve a more efficient allocation of resources. Money facilitates the flow of resources into their most efficient uses. The ultimate result is increased efficiency of the economy and increased economic welfare for the society. Box 2-2 explains the meanings of the microeconomic and macroeconomic functioning of the economy.

With specialization we can all become more efficient and enjoy higher standards of living. And savings can flow smoothly—either directly or through financial intermediaries—into investment. The high productivity of the modern world couldn't exist without a high degree of **specialization**. And all this specialization couldn't exist without money.

Box 2-2

Question: Exactly What Is Meant by the Microeconomic and Macroeconomic Functioning of the Economy?

The **microeconomic functioning** of the economy has to do with the alternative ways resources are allocated, and with the ways the market process and the price mechanism direct resources (inputs and outputs) so as to achieve the objectives of the society. *Microeconomics is concerned with choices among alternative outputs and choices among alternative inputs.* So the microeconomic functioning of the economy is concerned with whether or not we are producing the desired quantities of each output product—not too much of one product and too little of another—and whether or not we are using the most desirable (least cost) combinations of inputs—not too much of one and too little of another.

The **macroeconomic functioning** of the economy is concerned with the rate, or speed, at which the economy is operating. It deals with total production, total resource use, total employment, output, and income. Macroeconomics is not concerned with the shifting of resource flows from one product to another, or with the efficiency of the "input mix." It only deals with the factors which influence the size of the total employment-output-income flow. In short, *macroeconomics is concerned with what causes the circular flow of economic activity to speed up or slow down, and/or what causes changes in the price level.*

It wouldn't be an overstatement to say that money is (to borrow a French expression) the *elan vitale* of all market-directed economic systems.[1] Without the development of specialization and exchange and the evolution of something to serve as money, our modern civilization could never have evolved. You can be certain that if money didn't exist, neither would you, nor I!

Exactly What Is Money?

Money is *anything that performs the functions of money*. The key function is **medium of exchange**. The one essential characteristic which money has (and which nothing else has) is this: It is *immediately exchangeable* for all other kinds of marketable assets—goods and services, real estate, stocks and bonds, or whatever.

The term **liquidity** refers to the ease with which an asset can be exchanged for other assets. A highly liquid asset is one which can be exchanged for other assets (or for money), *quickly*, and *without loss of value*. Different assets (houses, cars, government bonds, etc.) have different degrees of liquidity. But **money** is the only asset that has **perfect liquidity**.

People Must Believe in Its General Acceptability

Why do you accept money in exchange for the things you want to sell? Because you are completely confident that other people will accept the money in exchange for the things you want to buy. This complete confidence in its **general acceptability** is an essential characteristic of money. Without this confidence, nothing could function as money.

So this leads us to a definition of money: *Money is anything which is generally acceptable as a medium of exchange* for goods and services and for other assets. Anything which meets this definition is money. Anything which does not, is not.

What is money made of? How does it look? It makes no difference. As long as it is performing the functions of money—as long as it is being used as a generally accepted medium of exchange—it is money.

THE BASIC FUNCTIONS OF MONEY

In every society, money performs four basic functions. All of these functions play significant roles in the operation of the economy.

The Medium of Exchange Function

The most basic function of money is to serve as the medium of exchange. But anything which is performing this function will automatically perform three other functions: standard of value, store of value, and standard of deferred payments.

---

[1] The term *elan vitale* has no exact equivalent in the English language. Sometimes it is loosely translated to mean "the life blood." More accurately, it means "the essence of," or "that indispensable characteristic or property of a thing without which it couldn't exist." Truly, money is the *elan vitale* of every market-directed economic system.

The Standard of Value (Unit of Account) Function

Anything used as the exchange medium will automatically be used as the "value standard" or the "accounting unit" in the society. Is my Toyota worth more than your Jeep? Put a dollar value on each and then we'll know.

How do I know if my business is making profits? Or losses? It's easy. Just add up the costs and the revenues. How impossible it would be to achieve maximum efficiency in a business (or in an economic system) without some **unit of account** to compare costs and prices of inputs and outputs!

The standard of value and medium of exchange functions are sometimes called the **primary functions** of money. These are the two functions which money performs in the present time.

The other two functions of money (standard of deferred payments and store of value) serve the purpose of transferring value from one time period to another. These two "future" functions are sometimes called the **secondary functions** of money.

The Standard of Deferred Payments (Borrowing and Lending) Function

Money lets you buy now and pay later. Or it lets you lend now and collect later. When people save money, that money can be borrowed and channeled into investments.

It is the **deferred payments** function of money which permits this transfer of spending power from earner-savers to borrower-spenders. As the borrowers spend, the economy's resources flow from those who do not wish to use them now, to those who do. This deferred payments function greatly increases the efficiency of the economic system. It permits the easy transfer of resources out of their less desired (less productive, less profitable) uses and into their more desired (more productive, more profitable) uses.

The Store of Value (Wealth-Holding) Function

Your wealth consists of all of the valuable assets which belong to you. Do you own a car? A watch? School supplies? A government bond? If so, then you have some wealth. Your wealth is your **store of value**. Probably some (at least a little) of your store of value is in the form of money.

What's the advantage of holding some of your wealth in the form of money? **Liquidity!** Of course. You can exchange it for anything else you want, whenever you wish. But you can't do that with your watch or your car.

So why don't you hold all of your wealth in the form of money? Because money (in the form of money) doesn't bring you the kind of personal satisfaction (utility) that you can get from your watch or your car. And although some forms of money (some checking accounts) pay interest, money doesn't bring you as much interest income as you could earn (for example) on a government bond. Also, money loses value over time by the amount of the inflation rate.

So money certainly is not the perfect way to store up value. But we all like to hold some of our assets in the form of money because of its liquidity. We can spend it whenever we please.

A Fifth Function of Money? Temporary Store of Purchasing Power

Sometimes it may be useful to split the "store of value" function into two separate functions. Some of the money being held at any moment is being held because the person expects to spend it soon, while some of it may be being held as a more permanent store of value.

Sometimes it may be useful to take the view that only the money in this more permanent "pool of money" is really performing the store of value function. If we take that view, then we need to add a fifth function of money: to serve as *a temporary store of purchasing power*—a pool of money which soon will be needed to support the medium of exchange function.

The next section describes the evolution of money. But before you go on into that, take a minute to read box 2-3 and find the answer to the question: "What is money worth?"

A BRIEF HISTORY OF THE EVOLUTION OF MONEY

Money existed in all of the ancient societies. But How? Who decided what would be used as the exchange medium? Usually no one decided. Money automatically evolved.

Money Usually Begins As a Useful Commodity

Usually money starts out as some useful commodity or tool—something that most people want for its own sake. If most people want it "for its own sake," then it's reasonable to assume that most people would accept it in exchange for other things. As soon as everyone becomes aware that everyone else is willing to accept this useful thing, the thing begins to perform the medium of exchange function. So, just automatically, it becomes money in that society.

Throughout history many different kinds of useful (and some not-so-useful) things have served as money at various times and places. The list includes: fish hooks, cattle, goats, salt, bullets, beer, wood, cigarettes, silver, gold, copper, other metals, grain, shells, whales' teeth, big wheels of stone and much more—even human beings. Obviously the substance or form of money isn't critical.

If it is generally acceptable as a medium of exchange then it is money—no matter what it may be made of—and no matter what other useful functions it may perform.

From Full-Bodied Money to Paper Money

Modern societies don't usually use these "commodity" kinds of money. More efficient kinds of money have evolved. Here are the major steps in that evolutionary process.

At first the commodity money must be **full-bodied**, which means that its **intrinsic value** must be equal to its **monetary value**—it must be worth as much as a thing (a commodity) as it is worth as money. Otherwise, in the beginning no one would accept it. But it isn't very convenient lugging around goats or cattle or big

Box 2-3

Question: What Determines the Value of Money? What is a Unit of Money (Say One Dollar) Worth?

There are two ways to go about answering this question:

1. The first way is to ask: "What quantity of **goods** can I **buy** with it?"

   Using this approach, the value of money is equal to its **purchasing power** —the real value of goods it will buy. So its value depends on—and moves opposite to—changes in—the price level. Higher prices mean lower value of money.

2. The second approach is to ask: "How much **interest cost** would I have to pay to borrow someone else's money?"

   Using this approach, the cost of borrowed money (and the return on loaned money, and the opportunity cost of holding cash) varies directly with the interest rate. As interest rates rise, money becomes more "valuable" in the financial markets.

Both ways of valuing money are accurate and useful;

- Using the first way (#1) you get the **purchasing power value** of money—what it's worth in buying things in the **goods markets**.

- Using the second way (#2) you get the **market value** of money—the "going price" when buying and selling (borrowing and lending) money in the **financial markets**.

---

wheels of stone when you want to buy something. So the next step is to develop paper money backed by (exchangeable into) the full-bodied commodity money.

As recently as the early 1900s, much of the money in the modern world consisted of paper money backed by (exchangeable "on demand" into) full-bodied coins made of gold or silver. Everyone was confident that they could exchange the paper money (gold certificates or silver certificates) for gold or silver coins whenever they wanted to. So they were perfectly willing to accept the paper money. Exhibit 2-1 shows some examples of paper money.

Paper money is much more convenient and efficient than full-bodied commodity money. But these days most money changes hands even more efficiently than with paper money.

From Paper Money to Checking Accounts

During the late 1800s, checking accounts began to become an important method of making payments. That trend has continued right up to the present. Today most of the money in the United States and in the other modern nations is "checking account money."

Almost 75 percent of the U.S. money supply now consists of "checkable deposits." People and businesses leave their money in the bank and transfer it to other people and businesses by writing checks and by electronic funds transfers. The only form in which this "checking account money" exists is in the accounting books (and computer memories) of the depository financial institutions.

In the world's modern economic systems there's no full-bodied commodity money anymore. There's no fully-backed paper money. And representing most of the (intangible) checking account money there's absolutely *no tangible kind of money at all*—not even dollar bills.

Exhibit 2-1.   The Evolution of Currency in the United States

Continental Currency, 1778

State Bank Note, 1837

Silver Certificate, 1891

continued

Exhibit 2-1. *Continuing*

National Bank Note, 1900

Federal Reserve Bank Note, 1914

Source: Federal Reserve Bank of Dallas, *Business Review*, December, 1975.

Checking Account Money Is More Efficient

Why do we let our money exist in such a seemingly flimsy form? Because, for all but the very small transactions, this intangible form of money is the form which functions best. Checking account (deposit balance) money permits the financial system to work much more efficiently.

In terms of *dollar value*, about 90 percent of total expenditures in the United States are made using checking account money—no currency, no coins. But in terms of the *number of individual transactions*, the great majority still are carried out using paper money and coins. Most people spend their pocket money (currency and coins) for their many small transactions and write checks and/or use electronic funds transfers for the few larger ones.

THE SIZE AND COMPONENTS OF THE U.S. MONEY SUPPLY

In the United States in the late 1980s the total money supply—according to the **M1** definition of money—amounts to about $800 billion. (Box 2-4 discusses M1 and the various other definitions of money.)

Most of Our Money Consists of "Checkable Deposit Balances"

Some three-fourths of the M1 money supply (about $600 billion) consists of checkable deposits—regular checking accounts, plus NOW accounts and other kinds of checkable accounts. These checkable deposits are located in the commercial banks and in the thrift institutions: mutual savings banks, savings and loan institutions (S&Ls) and credit unions.

The remaining part (about one-fourth) of the U.S. money supply (about $200 billion) consists of all of the currency in the hands of the public, plus travelers checks. Our currency consists of paper money issued by the Federal Reserve banks (about $183 billion) and some currency (mostly coins) issued by the Treasury (about $17 billion).

Our Currency Consists of Fiat Money and Token Coins, plus Travelers Checks

All of our official paper money these days is **fiat money**—meaning that it is declared by the government to be **legal tender** so that everyone is legally required

---

Box 2-4

Question: Of All of the Money Supply Definitions, Which One Is Really Money?

There are several definitions of money which are used when calculating the size of the U.S. money supply. The narrowest definition—the one which includes the smallest number of and the most highly liquid components—is called **M1**. This is the only definition which consists entirely of **true money**—that is, **immediately spendable** components.

The other definitions of the money supply (M2, M3, etc.) include somewhat less liquid components—components which are not true money because they are not immediately spendable in their present form. However, these non-spendable components are highly liquid and can be turned into "spendable money" at a moment's notice. For example, deposits in a passbook savings account or a money market mutual fund are included in M2 but not in M1.

The M3 definition includes some less-liquid components than M2.

These broader definitions of the money supply (M2, M3, etc.) sometimes give a better indication of the total **spending power** in the hands of the public than does the M1 definition. That's why we use several different "definitions" of the money supply. The Fed can monitor changes in each one and get a better estimate of what's happening to the amount of spending power in the economy—better than if it monitored only M1, which includes only immediately spendable components: checkable deposits, currency (including coins), and travelers checks.

The various "monetary aggregate" definitions of the money supply (M1, M2, M3, etc.) are explained thoroughly in Chapter 5.

to accept it as money. If you look on a dollar bill (or any other Federal Reserve note) you will see the inscription, "this note is legal tender for all debts, public and private." This fiat (government-decreed) money is the only official kind of paper currency we have.

Our paper currency is not exchangeable into any other form of currency—except other forms of fiat money, and coins. All of our circulating coins are **token coins**—meaning that they are **not full-bodied**. There aren't any coins in the U.S. money supply in which the *market value* of the metal is equal to the *face value* of the coin. The monetary value of all of our coins is greater (much greater!) than the market value of the metals contained therein.

The travelers check component of the U.S. M1 money supply really consists of privately issued currency. There are about $8 billion of travelers checks outstanding—about 1 percent of the M1 money supply.

Gold Is Not a Part of Our Money Supply

You will notice that in this discussion of the U.S. money supply nothing has been said about **gold**. That's because there hasn't been any really close relationship between the U.S. money supply and gold since the early 1930s. Since the 1960s there hasn't been any specific relationship at all.

Now take a few minutes and study figures 2-1 and 2-2, and table 2-1. There you'll get an overview of the changing size and components of the U.S. M1 money supply.

THE MODERN PAYMENTS SYSTEM

The **payments system** is the systematic way that money flows from buyers to sellers—from payers to receivers. If all payments were made in cash then the payments system would be very simple. A generally acceptable exchange medium (some form of currency) would be used. People buying things would pay with that medium; people selling things would accept that medium. And in fact most small transactions are carried out this way. Payment is made using paper money and coins and that's the end of it. But for most large transactions, it isn't quite that simple.

Check Clearing

When payments are made by check, funds must somehow be transferred from the buyer's account to the seller's account. Frequently these accounts are in different banks. Often the banks are located in different cities—sometimes in different countries throughout the world.

When the buyer's check is deposited in the seller's bank, the buyer's bank must transfer funds to the seller's bank. So there needs to be some means of "interbank settlements." If the two banks are located in the same city the settlement can be made through the local clearinghouse where (each day) each bank presents its claims against all the others. Then they settle up the differences.

Figure 2-1.   The Erratic Growth of the M1 Money Supply in 1987–88

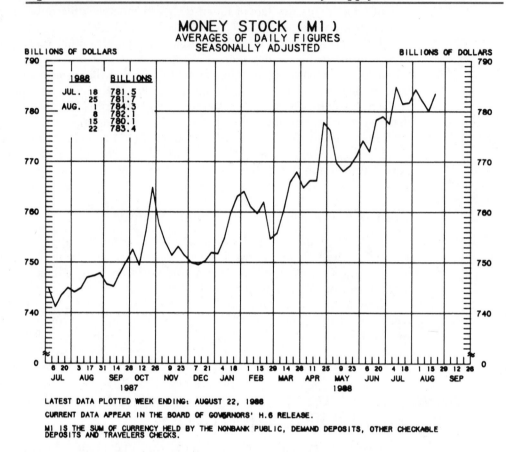

MONEY STOCK (M1)
AVERAGES OF DAILY FIGURES
SEASONALLY ADJUSTED

1988	BILLIONS
JUL. 18	781.5
25	781.7
AUG. 1	784.3
8	782.1
15	780.1
22	783.4

LATEST DATA PLOTTED WEEK ENDING: AUGUST 22, 1988

CURRENT DATA APPEAR IN THE BOARD OF GOVERNORS' H.6 RELEASE.

M1 IS THE SUM OF CURRENCY HELD BY THE NONBANK PUBLIC, DEMAND DEPOSITS, OTHER CHECKABLE DEPOSITS AND TRAVELERS CHECKS.

This chart shows the recent fluctuations in the size of the M1 money supply. As you can see, in 1987–88 it was growing, and fluctuating between $730 and $770 billion.

Historically, M1 has grown significantly. It grew from about $20 billion during the Depression of the 1930s, to more than $100 billion in 1945—a five-fold increase in about one decade.

After that it wasn't until the late 1960s that M1 doubled—to $200 billion. By 1976 it had passed $300 billion, and it passed $400 billion in the early 1980s. In the mid-1980s it passed the $600 billion mark and the above chart shows the more recent picture.

Source: *U.S. Financial Data*, The Federal Reserve Bank of St. Louis, St. Louis, MO 63166. Weekly.

Settlements with out-of-town banks (both domestic, and foreign) are made (a) through interbank deposits among correspondent banks, and (b) through bank deposits in the Federal Reserve banks.

The entire U.S. and worldwide banking system is tied together through a network of interbank correspondent relationships and deposit balances. If NCNB National Bank in Charlotte, N.C. receives for deposit a check drawn on Manufacturer's Hanover Bank in New York, NCNB may clear the check either through the Federal Reserve System or through its correspondent bank in New York.

Figure 2-2.   Fluctuations in Total Checkable Deposits, 1987–88

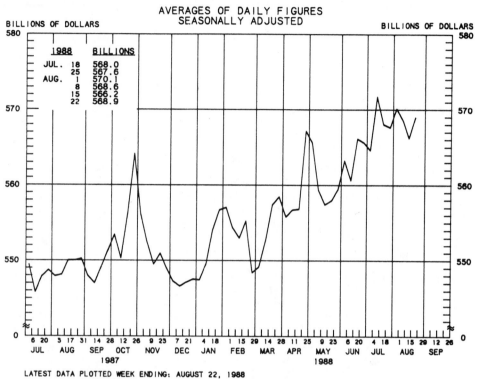

AVERAGES OF DAILY FIGURES
SEASONALLY ADJUSTED

BILLIONS OF DOLLARS

1988		BILLIONS
JUL.	18	568.0
	25	567.6
AUG.	1	570.1
	8	568.6
	15	566.2
	22	568.9

LATEST DATA PLOTTED WEEK ENDING: AUGUST 22, 1988

TOTAL CHECKABLE DEPOSITS IS THE SUM OF DEMAND DEPOSITS AND OTHER CHECKABLE DEPOSITS AT ALL DEPOSITORY INSTITUTIONS.

This figure explains the erratic changes in M1 which were occurring in the late 1980s: volatile shifts in total **checkable deposits**.

Over the past decades the growth rate of checkable deposits has been responsible for much of the growth of the M1 money supply. Prior to the 1980s the growth rate was fairly constant and steady. But during the 1980s several new kinds of checkable deposits were introduced, checkable deposits increased rapidly, and their growth rate became unstable. And that's why the M1 money supply during the 1980s has been unstable.

Source: U.S. Financial Data, The Federal Reserve Bank of St. Louis, P.O. Box 442, St. Louis, MO 63166. Weekly.

Clearing Through The Federal Reserve System

NCNB may send the check to the Federal Reserve bank of Richmond (actually to the Richmond Fed's Charlotte branch) which will add the money to NCNB's account there. Then the Charlotte branch will send the check to the Federal Reserve Bank of New York (FRBNY) which will subtract the money from the account of Manufacturer's Hanover there. Then the FRBNY will send the check to Manufacturer's Hanover where it will be deducted from the account of the person who wrote the check.

Table 2-1.   Currency in Circulation (Paper Money, and Coins) Plus Travelers Checks, 1930–1988

Year	Amount (Billions of Dollars)
1930	4
1935	6
1945	26
1955	31
1965	42
1975	87
1980	136
1983	172
1985	198
1988	208

This table shows that the value of currency in circulation has increased from $4 billion in 1930 to more than $200 billion in 1988. But the growth rate of currency in circulation has not been smooth over this period.

From 1930 to 1935, currency in circulation increased by about 50 percent. Then there was a more than 400 percent increase between 1935 and 1945 as the economy moved from serious depression to wartime boom.

From 1945 to 1965 the growth of currency in circulation was slow, with the stock of currency less than doubling during this 20-year period. After 1965 the currency-stock growth rate accelerated. The supply of currency more than doubled between 1965 and 1975, and more than doubled again between 1975 and 1985.

Since 1965 the currency growth rate has exceeded the growth rate of the M1 money supply. Some of this growth has been caused by the growth of the underground economy. The illegal drug trade which operates on cash, of course has played a role. But no one knows just how much.

Source: The Federal Reserve System: Purposes and Functions (7th edition), Publications Services, Board of Governors of the Federal Reserve System, Washington, D.C. 20551 (December, 1984), p. 106, and *U.S. Financial Data* (cited above).

Clearing Through a Correspondent Bank

The other method would be for NCNB to send the check for deposit to its own account in its correspondent bank in New York. The correspondent bank in New York then would get the funds from Manufacturer's Hanover through the New York clearinghouse, and Manufacturer's Hanover would then deduct the amount of the check from the account of the person who wrote the check. Figure 2-3 shows a diagram of this check-clearing process.

In the late 1980s the number of individual checks cleared each year continued to grow, and was approaching **50 billion**. That's 50 billion individual pieces of paper! More than 60 percent of these checks were cleared through clearing houses and the correspondent banking network. But that still left 35 to 40 percent— almost 20 billion checks—to be cleared through the Federal Reserve banks.

Electronic Funds Transfers

During the past thirty years there has been a steady increase in the use of electronic impulses to transfer funds from one bank to another and from one account (one owner) to another. These electronic transfers are made through what are now called "electronic funds transfer systems" (EFTS). There are local, statewide, regional, nationwide, and international EFT systems.

Figure 2-3.   A Graphic Illustration of the Check-Clearing Process

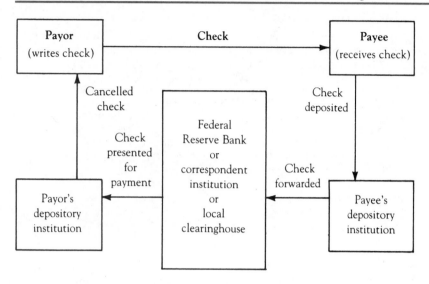

Transactions are settled at the Federal Reserve or a correspondent institution by crediting the deposit account of the payee's depository institution and debiting the deposit account of the payor's depository institution.

Source: *The Federal Reserve System: Purposes and Functions* (7th edition), Publication Services, Board of Governors of the Federal Reserve System, Washington, DC 20551 (December, 1984), p. 107.

Nationwide EFT Systems. There are now two nationwide electronic interbank funds transfer systems operating in the United States. One is **Fed Wire**, operated by the Federal Reserve. The other is the **Bank Wire** system which directly connects about 200 large banks. The Bank Wire system is owned and operated by the banks which are members of the system. These sophisticated electronics systems permit funds to be transferred instantaneously among banks throughout the country.

International EFT Systems. For worldwide funds transfers there are now three major systems. One is **CHIPS**—Clearinghouse Interbank Payments System— which has computer terminals in large banks in the United States and Europe and a central computer located in New York. Another international network is **SWIFT**—Society for Worldwide Interbank Financial Transactions. SWIFT is similar to CHIPS and is headquartered in Belgium.

London is the world center of the Eurodollar market. In 1983 another clearinghouse interbank system was initiated to serve this London interbank market. Its functions are essentially the same as CHIPS, and it has adopted the name **CHAPS**. All of these international EFT systems permit instantaneous funds transfers, worldwide.

Box 2-5

Feature: The Cashless and Checkless (Credit Card) Society? Not Yet!

In 1984 the Board of Governors of the Federal Reserve System commissioned a study called the "Survey of Currency and Transaction Account Usage," to obtain data on the payments habits of American families. This survey collected information on the use of checks, credit cards, and cash.

The survey found that:

- About 58 percent of the dollar value of total family expenditures are made by check.

- About 36 percent are made by currency (paper money and coins).

- Only 6 percent by credit card.

An interesting finding of the study was that less than 15 percent of the total stock of currency in the hands of the public was being held for transactions purposes. It makes one wonder who is holding the other 85 percent of our currency—and for what purposes!

Note: For the detailed results of this study, see: "The Use of Cash and Transaction Accounts by American Families," *Federal Reserve Bulletin,* vol. 72, no. 2 (February, 1986), pp. 87–108.

These national and international interbank payments systems—Fed Wire, Bank Wire, CHIPS, CHAPS, and SWIFT—have greatly increased the efficiency of the modern payments system. Through these systems money moves across the country and around the world with the speed of light—sometimes in amounts totaling more than $500 billion in one day!

Automated Clearinghouses (ACHs). Many payments are now being made through automated clearinghouses (ACHs) which are systematic arrangements for electronically transferring funds among banks and among accounts. These ACHs are being increasingly used for settlements of accounts among banks and to make preauthorized payments such as salary payments, social security payments, utility bill payments, and others.

ATMs and POS Terminals. At the "consumer contact" end of the EFTS network are the automated teller machines (ATMs)—now a familiar sight everywhere in the country—and point-of-sale (POS) terminals which are beginning to appear at some supermarket checkout counters. At the POS terminal a "debit card" is used to automatically subtract money from the buyer's bank account and add it to the seller's account.

The Worldwide "Payments Revolution"

The American economy and the world economy have undergone and are still undergoing a *payments revolution.* The modern payments system permits money to perform its functions with a speed and efficiency which would have been unbelievable only a few decades ago. This payments revolution is continuing at a rapid pace.

In the coming years, more bills and more salaries will be paid automatically through the ACH systems. Home banking, where people use their home computers to transfer funds automatically, will play an increasing role. And it won't be long before *worldwide financial markets* for stocks, bonds, futures contracts, other financial instruments, and commodities also—together with worldwide payments mechanisms—will permit instantaneous exchanges and payments worldwide, 24 hours a day.

[The payments system of] the future will be based more on EFTS and less on the [ch]ecks. But for many years, most of us will continue to [pay] for day-to-day transactions by transferring paper bills [arou]nd. And we will continue to use handwritten paper [checks], and for paying most of our monthly bills. Now read [the findings] of a recent Federal Reserve study which investigated [the payme]nts habits of American consumers.

```
      THANK YOU FOR SHOPPING AT
          BOB'S GARDEN CENTER
             (609) 641-6306

  4/07/91  11:16  DH        02 SALE
     THANK YOU FOR SHOPPING AT BOBS
   SORRY NO GUARANTEE ON HOUSE PLANTS
  -------------------------------------
  291004            1          .99 /EA
  VEGETABLE PLANTS 6 PK.          .99
  F99               2          .50 /EA S
  FERRY-MORSE SEED PACK        1.00
  F119              5          .60 /EA S
  FERRY-MORSE SEED PACK        3.00
  B179              1          .90 /EA S
  BURPEE SEED PACKS 1.79 RETAIL    .90
  B109              3          .55 /EA S
  BURPEE SEED PACKS 1.09 RETAIL   1.65
  B119              3          .60 /EA S
  BURPEE SEED PACKS 1.19 RETAIL   1.80

  SUB-TOTAL:     9.34    TAX:       .65
                        TOTAL:     9.99
  CASH TEND:    10.04 CHANGE:       .05

  ====)) JRNL# A20027           ((====
         CUST # *5
```

—the very essence, or "life-blood"—of the market

[?] money enables the price system to function to [?] resource allocation in the economy.

[?] is performing the functions of money, which are: [?], (2) standard of value, (3) standard of deferred [?]alue, and sometimes (5) "temporary store of pur-chasing power.

[?]ly has started out as a useful tool or commodity, [?]. Then it has evolved into more efficient forms— [?]king accounts.

[?] money supply amounts to about $800 billion. [?] is checkable deposits. The remaining one-fourth is currency.

[?]ernment-decreed, fiat money. None of it is backed by gold.

- The modern payments system now depends heavily on electronic funds transfers, nationally and internationally via Fed Wire, Bank Wire, CHIPS, CHAPS, and SWIFT and regionally and locally via ACH, ATMs, POS, and home banking EFT systems.

- EFT systems in recent years have touched off a worldwide payments revolution which is still proceeding rapidly.

Checklist of Important Principles, Concepts, Terms

The inefficiency of barter

The importance of exchange

The nature of money: What it is

The importance of "general acceptability"

The functions of money: What it does

The microeconomic role of money

Medium of exchange

Standard of value

Primary (present-time) functions of money

Standard of deferred payments

Store of value

Secondary (future) functions of money

Liquidity

Temporary store of purchasing power

The evolution of money

Full-bodied money

The U.S. M1 money supply

Depository financial institutions

Fiat money

Token coins

The modern payments system: How it functions

Check clearing through the Fed

Check clearing through a correspondent bank

Nationwide EFT systems

Fed Wire

Bank Wire

International EFT systems

CHIPS

CHAPS

SWIFT

Automated clearinghouses (ACHs)

ATM and POS terminals

The worldwide "payments revolution"

Questions

1. Explain what is meant by the comment, "money lets markets work efficiently."

2. Explain why living conditions in a barter economy would necessarily be very primitive.

3. Mention each of the basic functions of money, and explain why all of these functions perform roles which are essential to the efficient functioning of a modern economic system.

4. In every society, money has a tendency to evolve automatically. Explain why this is true, and then describe the process, or steps, in the evolution of a modern monetary system.

5. In our various "definitions" of the money supply, M1 (the narrowest) has only three components. What are those components?

6. Explain the process of check clearing, first through the Federal Reserve system, and then through a correspondent bank.

7. The textbook talks about the worldwide "payments revolution." What are the characteristics of this "revolution?" What is happening that is so revolutionary?

Suggested Readings

Alchian, Armen, "Why Money?" *Journal of Money, Credit and Banking* 9 (February 1977), part 2: 133–41.

Bequai, August. *The Cashless Society: EFTS at the Crossroads.* New York: John Wiley and Sons, 1981.

Federal Reserve Bank of Atlanta, *The Future of the U.S. Payments System* (Proceedings of Conference), Atlanta, 1981.

Federal Reserve Bank of Dallas, "Evolution of Money and Banking in the United States," *Business Review,* December 1975.

Galbraith, John Kenneth. *Money: Whence It Came, Where It Went.* Boston: Houghton Mifflin, 1975.

Radford, R. A. "The Economic Organization of a P.O.W. Camp" *Economica* 12 (November 1945): 189–201.

Spengler, Joseph J. "Coin Shortage: Modern and Premodern." *National Banking Review,* December 1965, pp. 201–216.

CHAPTER 3

The Time Value of Money, and Interest Rates and Bond Yields

Chapter Objectives

The purpose of this chapter is to give you a basic understanding of **the time value of money** and of interest rates and bond yields. In this chapter you will learn the formulas for compounding and discounting and for calculating bond values and yields. But the purpose is not so much to teach the formulas as to answer these questions: "What do these formulas mean? Why are they true? And why is all this so important in a course on money and banking and the financial system?"

After you study this chapter you will understand and be able to explain:

1. The importance of **the time value of money**.
2. The powerful effect of **compounding**.
3. The **magic rules** of **70**, and **72**.
4. How to find:
   a. **the future value of a present sum.**
   b. **the present value of a future sum.**
   c. **the present value of a bond.**
5. How to calculate the present value of:
   a. **a flow of income** to be received over a number of years, and of
   b. **a perpetual flow of income.**
6. The relationships between market interest rates, bond coupon rates, bond prices, and interest yields.
7. The meaning of **current yield** and **yield to maturity** and how to calculate each of these.
8. How the concept of **the time value of money** underlies the functioning of all financial markets.

MONEY: THE SOONER IT'S RECEIVED, THE MORE IT'S WORTH

In the last chapter you were reading about the speed with which payments are made through the modern payments system. Why is there so much emphasis on the speed of funds transfers? One reason is because of the time value of money. Box 3-1 gives an example.

Box 3-1

Feature: The Time Value of $500 Billion for One Day

In the previous chapter you read that the EFTS networks sometimes transfer as much as $500 billion in one day. Suppose these networks permit this $500 billion to arrive in the hands of the recipients only one day sooner than otherwise would be possible. How much is that worth to the recipients? It's worth a fortune! At an interest rate of 10 percent, $500 billion is worth a cool $138.9 million per day!

To calculate the daily interest earnings on $500 billion you can either calculate the annual earnings (10% × $500 billion = $50 billion)

and then divide by 360 (the number of days in the "banker's year"). Or you can divide the interest rate by 360 to get the daily rate of interest (10% ÷ 360 = .027778%) and then multiply this by $500 billion. Either way you come out with $138.9 million. That's a lot of interest earnings!

Later you'll be reading about financial institutions lending their surplus funds overnight. Now you can understand that when the sums are large, overnight lending can generate significant income.

Financial Markets Exist Because of the Time Value of Money

The concept of **the time value of money** underlies—in fact, justifies the existence of—all financial markets. The time value of money refers to *the earnings which invested money can generate over time.* The longer the money is invested, the greater the earnings can be. This is especially true because of the effect of compounding.

THE EFFECT OF COMPOUNDING

Suppose you have $100 and you invest it at the (very low) interest rate of 1%. Your interest income for one year will be $1. So at simple interest (no compounding) it would take 100 years for your $100 to double to $200. But it wouldn't *really* take that long because the **compound effect** shortens that time considerably.

Compounding: Earning Interest on Prior Years' Interest

At the beginning of the first year you have $100. If the 1% interest is paid at the end of the first year, then at the beginning of the second year you have $101. So you will earn interest on $101 during the second year.

At the beginning of the third year you will have $102.01. The "1 cent" is interest you earned during the second year on the $1 of interest that you earned in the first year. The compounding effect is beginning.

At the beginning of the fourth year you will have $103.0301. The compounding effect begins to accelerate. Box 3-2 shows why. When the interest rate is only 1%, the compounding effect doesn't take off like a drag race! But as the years go by, it adds up.

At an interest rate of 1% compounded once each year, $100 would double to $200 in 72 years. Or to say it differently, at 1%, $100 today is equal in value to $200 to be received 72 years hence. And conversely, $200 to be received 72 years in the future is worth (today) only $100.

Box 3-2

Feature: How the Compounding Effect Begins

Suppose you deposit $100 at an interest rate of 1%, compounded annually. At the beginning of the fourth year your deposit will be worth $103.0301. Here's why:

- Your initial sum $100.00
- Interest @ 1% ($1/yr) for years 1, 2, and 3   3.00
- Interest in the 2nd year on the $1 earned in the 1st year
  (one cent)   .01 ◄——— *This*
- Interest in the 3rd year on the $2 earned in the 1st and 2nd year
  (two cents)   .02
- Interest in the 3rd year on the one cent earned in the 2nd year   *generated*
  on the $1 of interest earned in the 1st year (1/100th of a cent)   .0001 ◄——— *this*
                                                     Total   103.0301

Each year in the future, more digits will be added to the right of the decimal point as more interest is earned on the interest earnings of each previous year.

The "Magic Rule of 72"—Compounding Once a Year

Suppose the interest rate is not 1%, but 10%. Then invested money will double 10 times as fast! It will double in 1/10th of 72 years, or 7.2 years. So at an interest rate of 10%, $100 today will be worth $200 in only 7.2 years. Conversely, a piece of paper (financial instrument) that gives you the right to receive $200 7.2 years from now, is worth $100 today.

You have just learned **the magic rule of 72**. When you invest money at a fixed interest rate compounded once each year, to find out how long it will take your money to double in value, divide the interest rate into 72. For example, if the interest rate is 3% it takes 24 years for money to double (72 ÷ 3 = 24). At 6% it doubles every 12 years. At 12% it doubles every 6 years.

The "Magic Rule of 70"—Continuous Compounding

What if the interest had been compounded, not once each year, but daily (continuously)? Then, at an interest rate of 1% it would take only 70 years for money to double in value. So the magic number for **continuous compounding** is 70.

Note: The answer obtained by dividing the number 72 or 70 by the interest rate is not precisely accurate. To get the precise answer you need to use the compounding or discounting formulas, explained in a few minutes. First, here are some illustrations of the explosive effect of compounding.

An Illustration of the Explosive Compounding Effect

Suppose you invest $100 at a fixed interest rate of 10%, compounded once each year. In 7.2 years your money would double, to $200. In another 7.2 years it would double again, to $400. And it would keep doubling every 7.2 years, to $800, $1,600, $3,200, $6,400, $12,800, and on and on it goes.

Figure 3-1.   **The Explosive Effect of Compouding: Arithmetic-Scale**

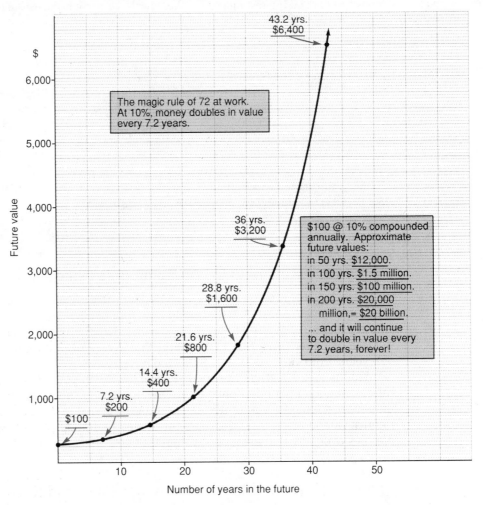

The future value of $100 @ 10%, compounded once each year.

In 100 years your $100 would have grown to $1.5 million. In 200 years, it would be up to $20 billion—and it would continue to double every 7.2 years, forever! Figure 3-1 illustrates this explosive effect of compounding.

Using a Ratio (Semi-Logarithmic) Scale For Compounding

As you look at figure 3-1 you can see what a tall piece of paper (or a microscopic vertical scale!) would be required to show the compounding effect very far into the future. That's why, on graphs dealing with the compounding effect of percentage changes, a "ratio scale" (logarithmic scale) is usually used on the vertical axis.

In Part III of this book you'll see ratio-scale graphs showing the growth of financial institutions, of the money supply, and of other financial magnitudes. Also, many of the historical charts in the various Fed publications (see Appendix 1-A) are ratio-scale charts. So it's important for you to take time right now to understand ratio-scale graphs.

On a ratio-scale graph the numbers on the vertical axis double to reflect the doubling effect of compounding. For example, the arithmetic scale on the vertical axis of figure 3-1 is marked off 10-20-30-40-50, etc. On a ratio scale the vertical axis begins at 1—100%—the initial value. Then the scale is marked off 2-4-8-16-32-64, etc.

Anything which is growing at a constant rate will show up as a straight line on a semi-log graph. This straight line graph can illustrate compound interest, population growth, or anything else which has a constant rate of change. And, for whatever application, as you project the straight line farther into the future, it always illustrates the explosive effect of compounding. From this projected straight line you can read the magnitude of the growing variable, any number of years in the future. Box 3-3 explains why.[1]

Figure 3-2 illustrates exactly the same explosive compounding effect that you saw in figure 3-1. The only difference is that the compounding effect is illustrated on a semi-log (ratio scale) graph. After you have studied this graph, go on to the next section and read about the formula for calculating exactly the same thing.

Box 3-3

Feature: How to Read Constant-Growth Future Values from a Ratio-Scale Graph

Since a constant rate of growth shows up as a straight line on the ratio scale graph, the graph can be used to calculate the size of future values. The value at the origin is always "100%"—it's the value you begin with. If the growth rate is 10%, compounded annually, the value will become 200% (will double) in 7.2 years.

When the rate of growth is constant, you only need to calculate this one point. Then draw a straight line from the origin through the point and extend the line as far as you wish. From this line you can read the future values.

What if the rate of change is not constant? Then the line in the graph will not be straight. An increasing rate of increase will produce an upward curving (increasingly steep) curve in the semi-log graph. If the rate of increase is decreasing then the curve will become progressively less steep.

FINDING THE FUTURE VALUE OF A PRESENT SUM

Suppose you deposit $100 in a savings account on January 1st of this year at an interest rate of 5%, compounded once each year. Then on January 1st of next year

---

[1] On a "semi-logarithmic" graph, only the vertical scale is logarithmic. The horizontal scale is arithmetic. On a "full-log," or "log-log" graph, both the vertical and the horizontal scales are logarithmic.

   Note: On a logarithmic (ratio) scale, equal intervals represent equal differences, *not in the numbers themselves, but in the logarithms of the numbers.*

Figure 3-2.   The Explosive Effect of Compouding: Ratio (Semi-Log) Scale

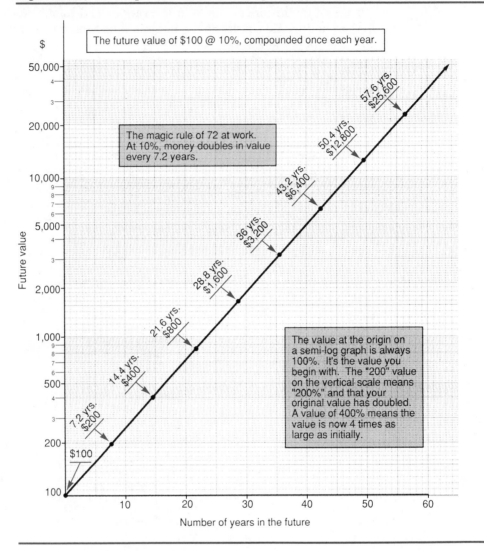

your account balance will be $105 (the initial $100, plus $5 interest earnings): $100 × 1.05 = $105.

On January 1st of the following year your balance will be $110.25—the initial $100, plus two years of interest on the $100 at 5% ($10), plus one year of interest on the $5 earned in the first year ($.25): $105 × 1.05 = $110.25.

If you have a calculator it would not be difficult (but it would be tedious!) to keep figuring this out, year by year, to find out how much total value $100 would generate at the end of 5 years, or 10 years, or whatever number of years you might choose. But fortunately there's an easier way.

Understanding the "Future Value" (Compounding) Formula

There's a simple formula for calculating the future value of a present sum. First, the symbols:

P = principal: the present value of the initial sum.

r = the interest rate.

$F1, F2, \ldots Fn$ = the future value, 1 yr, 2 yrs, ... n yrs hence.

Suppose the initial principal is $100 and the interest rate is 5 percent. Then the interest earned in the first year will be $P(r)$, which is $100(.05) = $5. So the future value at the end of one year (F1) is P + $5, or $100 + $5 = $105. So the formula for calculating F1 is:

$$F1 = P(1 + r). \tag{1}$$

What this formula says is this:

   The future value at the end of one year is equal to one times the value of the principal: $100, plus the interest rate times the value of the principal: .05 × $100. Using the above figures in the formula, it works out as follows:

$$F1 = \$100(1 + .05) = \$100 \times 1.05 = \$105.$$

For a future value two years hence, the formula is

$$F2 = P(1 + r)^2, \tag{2}$$

which works out as follows:

$$F2 = \$100(1 + .05)^2 = \$100 \times (1.05)^2$$
$$= \$100 \times 1.1025 = \$110.25,$$

which you will recognize as the same result obtained a moment ago when the problem was worked out the long way, not using the formula.

The General "Future Value" Formula

The general equation for the **future value** formula (also called the **compound interest** or **compounding** formula) is:

$$Fn = P(1 + r)^n. \tag{3}$$

   This formula will give an accurate future value for any sum of money invested today at interest rate r, for n years, compounded once each year.

   A word of warning: Be careful to interpret the future value formula correctly. It *does not* deal with a *flow* of income to be received over a period of future years. It only deals with a specific sum of money, to be received at some specific time in the future. It answers the question: "If I invest $100 today, what will be the specific value of that investment five years hence? Or ten years hence? Or on any other future date I might choose to cash out my investment?"

   Of course it is the flow of interest income over the years which causes the value of an investment to grow. But what this formula gives is the final result.

FINDING THE PRESENT VALUE OF A FUTURE SUM

If $100 today is going to be worth $105 one year from now, then $105 to be received a year from now must be worth $100 today. So calculating *the present value of a future sum* is just the reverse of calculating *the future value of a present sum.*

The "Present Value" (Discounting) Formula

The equation for calculating the present value (discounted value) of a future sum can be derived from the future value (compounding) formula (equation [3]).

Divide both sides by $(1 + r)^n$, and you have it:

$$\frac{Fn}{(1 + r)^n} = \frac{P(1 + r)^n}{(1 + r)^n},$$

which works out to

$$\frac{Fn}{(1 + r)^n} = P.$$

Arranged more conveniently

$$P = \frac{Fn}{(1 + r)^n}, \text{ or } P = \frac{1}{(1 + r)^n} \times Fn. \qquad [4]$$

You can see that equation [4] is algebraically the same as equation [3]. The only difference is that equation [3] is arranged to solve for *the future value of a present sum,* while equation [4] is arranged to solve for *the present value of a future sum.*

Now you see that the reciprocal of the **compound factor** $(1 + r)^n$, is the **discount factor**:

$$\frac{1}{(1 + r)^n}.$$

The discount factor gives the present value—also called the **discounted value**—of any sum of money to be received any number of years in the future. Here's an example.

Find the present value (P) of the financial instrument which will pay its owner $100(Fn) two years from now, when the interest rate is 5%: Fn = $100, $n = 2$, $r = .05$. Using equation [4]:

$$P = \frac{1}{(1 + .05)^2} \times \$100 = \frac{1}{(1.05)^2} \times \$100 = \frac{1}{1.1025} \times \$100 = \$90.70.$$

This tells you that when the market rate of interest if 5 percent, the right to receive this specific sum ($100) two years from now is worth (today) $90.70. This answer also tells us that if we invest $90.70 today at an interest rate of 5% compounded annually, the $90.70 investment will be worth exactly $100 two years from now.

Tables and Calculators are Used Instead of the Formulas

As you might have guessed, nobody in the financial world these days actually takes the time to calculate future values and present values using these formulas.

Present value and future value tables, and also preprogramed financial calculators give the answers immediately. The appendix to this chapter shows and explains the present and future value tables.

The Present Value of a Future Flow of Income

Now we come to the question of future **flows of income**. Suppose you're going to receive $100 per year for three years, beginning one year from now. What is the present value of that future flow of income? If you think about it, it's obvious. Just use equation [4], three times. Then add up the results:

$$P = \frac{100}{1.05} + \frac{100}{(1.05)^2} + \frac{100}{(1.05)^3}$$

$$= \frac{100}{1.05} + \frac{100}{1.1025} + \frac{100}{1.157625}$$

$$= 95.24 + 90.70 + 86.38 = \$272.32$$

The general equation for finding the present value (P)—also called **capitalized value**—of a future flow of income is as follows:

$$P = \frac{F1}{(1+r)} + \frac{F2}{(1+r)^2} + \frac{F3}{(1+r)^3} + \cdots + \frac{Fn}{(1+r)^n}. \qquad [5]$$

The Present Value of a Bond

Now, a minor complication. Suppose you're considering buying a bond which pays its owner $100 per year, and which will pay off its face value of $1,000 at the end of three years. (This is obviously a 10% bond because its face value is $1,000 and it pays interest of $100 per year.)

In this example we will continue to assume that the market rate of interest at the present time is 5%. So you know that this 10% bond is going to be worth more than its face value of $1,000. But how much more? Here's how to find out.

To find the present value of the bond we must discount the three annual income payments of $100. Also we must discount the face value of $1000 which will be received when the bond is paid off three years in the future. Here are the calculations:

$$P = \frac{100}{1.05} + \frac{100}{(1.05)^2} + \frac{100 + 1000}{(1.05)^3}$$

$$= \frac{100}{1.05} + \frac{100}{1.1025} + \frac{1100}{1.157625}$$

$$= 95.24 + 90.70 + 950.22 = \$1,136.16.$$

In this case, if you buy this bond you are going to receive a total of $1300: three payments of $100 each, plus the final payoff of $1000. But the present value of this $1,300 to be received in the future is only $1,136.16. What this means is, you could invest $1136.16 today at an interest rate of 5%, and receive $100/yr for the next two years and $1,100 the third year—a total of $1,300.

Here is the general formula for determining the present value (P) of a bond which pays a fixed interest return (F) each year, and then pays face value (Z) at maturity:

$$P = \frac{F1}{(1 + r)} + \frac{F2}{(1 + r)^2} + \frac{F3}{(1 + r)^3} + \cdots + \frac{Fn + z}{(1 + r)^n}. \qquad [6]$$

THE PRESENT VALUE OF A PERPETUAL INCOME

What about an asset which will pay $100 per year *in perpetuity* (forever)? Perhaps this is one of the "consolidated debt" bonds of the British government, called **consols**. Consols have no maturity date and pay a fixed annual return, in perpetuity. What would be the present value of a consol (or any other asset) which brings its owner a perpetual annual income of, say $100?

You could work it out using formula [5], where n would approach infinity. But after a few tedious hours working with your calculator you would discover that your answer was approaching the quotient of:

$$\frac{\$100}{.05}.$$

And sure enough, for a perpetual income stream for which the annual payment (F) is the same size each year, formula [5] reduces to:

$$P = \frac{F}{r}. \qquad [7]$$

So in this example the present value is:

$$P = \frac{100}{.05} = \$2,000.$$

At an interest rate of 5% the present value of a perpetual income of $100 per year is $2000. Or you can say it the other way: Anyone who invests $2,000 today in a perpetual bond (or any other perpetual fixed income investment) at an interest rate of 5%, will earn an annual income of $100 on that investment, forever. Why? Because $2,000 × 5% = $100.

UNDERSTANDING AND MEASURING
INTEREST RATES AND BOND YIELDS

By now you know that the time value of money is a very important concept. And you know that *the interest rate is the measure of the time value of money.* So it makes a great difference whether the interest rate is high or low.

What Is "The Interest Rate?"

In real-world financial markets there is not "an interest rate" but a **structure of interest rates**. Rates vary systematically with the riskiness of the borrower and the length of time to maturity.

For example the interest rate on long-term bonds is different from the rate on

---

Box 3-4

Feature: **Examples of Different Interest Rates on Alternative Investments**

In financial markets "the" interest rate is actually a great variety of different rates, depending on the kind of investment and reflecting especially **degree of risk** and **term to maturity**.

This "Key Interest Rates" box is published each Tuesday in *The Wall Street Journal* on the page which (daily) carries articles and data on recent interest rate developments.

Key Interest Rates

Annualized interest rates on cetain investments as reported by the Federal Reserve Board on a weekly-average basis.

	Week Ended:	
	Apr. 22, 1988	Apr. 15, 1988
Treasury bills (90 day)-a	5.83	5.89
Commrcl paper (Dealer, 90 day)-a	6.92	6.81
Certfs of deposit (Resale, 90 day)	7.01	6.87
Federal funds (Overnight)-b	6.93	6.81
Eurodollars (90 day)-b	7.08	6.99
Treasury bills (one year)-c	7.03	6.92
Treasury notes (three year)-c	7.88	7.75
Treasury notes (five year)-c	8.25	8.12
Treasury notes (ten year)-c	8.81	8.63
Treasury bonds (30 year)-c	9.05	8.85

a-Discounted rates. b-Week ended Wednesday April 20, 1988 and Wednesday April 13, 1988. c-Yields, adjusted for constant maturity.

Source: The Wall Street Journal, Tuesday, April 26, 1988, p. 55.

---

short-term securities. And there are different rates on different kinds of debt instruments—government securities, corporate securities, home mortgages, automobile loans, etc. Box 3-4 gives examples of some different interest rates.

Here's another interesting fact. The interest you will earn if you buy a debt security usually is not the interest rate stated on the face of the security—not unless you happen to buy the security at its **par value**—the exact **face value**. And that would be unusual. Here's why.

Bond Prices—and Therefore Interest Yields—Rise and Fall

When a bond is printed it has a stated par value—usually $1,000 or some multiple of that. Also it has a fixed interest rate, called the **coupon rate** stated as a percentage of the face value. After the bond is printed it is sold in the market, but not necessarily for its face value. Its market price depends on the supply and demand at that time for that kind of bond.

Suppose the stated coupon rate on the bond happens to be below the current market rate. Then no one will buy the bond until its market price falls below its face value.

Here's an example. Suppose General Motors has isued some long-term $1,000 bonds with a coupon rate of 4%. And suppose the market rate on that kind of bonds is now 10%. Then those $1,000 bonds are going to be selling in the market for a price of less than $1,000. Obviously! The price must fall to where it is low enough to let the GM bond-buyers earn 10% on their investment—on the amount they pay for the bond. Otherwise no one would buy. (For an explanation of the different meanings of the term "investment," see Box 3-5.)

Box 3-5

Question: Suppose You Buy a $1,000 Bond. Is That Really an Investment? Or Not?

The answer to this question depends on your perspective. In the language of the financial community (and of the general public), **yes**. But in economic theory, **no**.

It's unfortunate that one word must carry the burden of two different meanings. But this one does. It means:

1. In finance: exchanging money for some other asset—financial, or real—usually seeking a return on the "investment" (the amount paid for the asset).

2. In economic theory: an expenditure to buy **capital** (a three-meaning word!). An injection into the income-spending flow created by business purchases of capital goods— buildings, machinery, equipment, inven-

tories, etc.—the size of which has an important influence on the operating rate of the macroeconomy.

When you buy a bond in the "stocks and bonds" market you're just transferring ownership of that bond from someone else—some other "bond investor"—to yourself. From your point of view, it's an investment. But from the point of view of the spending-output-income flow of the macroeconomy, it isn't an investment at all.

Throughout this book both meanings of the word "investment" will be used. If you are careful to remember about these two different meanings, then from the context you will always be able to see which meaning applies.

Bond Prices Adjust to Equalize Interest Yields

Through the interaction of supply and demand in the financial markets, the prices of all debt instruments adjust—move up or down—to where identical **interest yields** exist on all identical debt instruments.

Suppose there is a very-long-term (say 50-year) bond paying a coupon rate of 10% and another identical security paying only 5%. Even though both securities have a stated face value of $1,000, the market value of the 10% bond will be about double that of the 5% bond. If the 10% bond is selling at par ($1,000), then the 5% bond will be selling for about $500. If the 5% security is selling at par ($1,000) then the 10% security will be selling for about $2,000.

What if yields on identical bonds were not the same? Then investors, speculators, and dealers would be buying the higher-yield bonds and selling the lower-yield bonds. That would cause prices of the higher-yield bonds to go up and push their yields down. Prices of the lower-yield bonds would go down and yields, up. This adjustment would proceed very quickly to move the market to equilibrium where the yields on all identical securities would be identical.

Current Yield? Or Yield to Maturity?

Investors, speculators, and dealers in the bond markets are constantly looking for opportunities to maximize the yield on their securities holdings. But what "yield" is that? Are we talking about how much return you get on your money if you buy the bond and hold it until maturity? In that case you have to calculate yield based on (a) the interest income to be received during the life of the bond, plus (b) the amount of the principal, repaid at maturity. Yield calculated in this way is called **yield to maturity**.[2]

---

[2] The term "internal rate of return" on any investment means the same thing as "yield to maturity" on a bond.

But suppose you aren't planning to hold the bond to maturity. Most bond buyers do not. And suppose the "yield" you're interested in is the coupon payments you will receive while you're holding the bond. Then you're interested in **current yield**.

Current Yield

Suppose you buy a long-term bond with a face value of $1,000 and a coupon rate of 5%. You are going to receive a **coupon payment** of $50 per year. Suppose you pay $1,000 for the bond. Then you will receive a current yield of 5%.

But suppose interest yields in the market are now 10% for this kind of bond. Then the market price of this bond will be less than $1,000. Suppose it's down to $500. If you buy the bond for $500, you're still going to receive a coupon payment of $50 per year. A $50 coupon payment on your $500 investment brings you a current yield of 10%. If you can buy a bond for one-half of its face value then your current yield will be double the coupon rate stated on the bond.

From what you've just read you could figure out the very simple formula for calculating current yield. It's the annual coupon payment divided by the price paid for the bond. In the above example, if you paid "par" for the 5% bond (annual coupon payment $50) your current yield would be 5% ($50 ÷ $1,000 = .05 = 5%). But if you paid $500 for the bond your current yield would be 10% ($50 ÷ $500 = .10 = 10%).

Yield to Maturity

Yield to maturity is different from current yield because it must reflect both the **coupon payments** and the **principal payment** at maturity. For a perpetual bond (a consol) there never will be a principal repayment. So current yield and yield to maturity are identical.

Or suppose you happen to pay exactly the face value for a bond. If you hold the bond to maturity you will get your money back—exactly the amount you paid and no less and no more. In this case current yield and yield to maturity are identical.

But suppose you bought a bond for less than its face value—say a $1,000, 5% bond for only $500. Your current yield is 10%. But what about yield to maturity? It will be more than 10%. In this case you're going to receive (1) a 10% current yield on your $500 investment throughout the life of the bond, then (2) at maturity you're going to receive a $500 **capital gain**.

Yield to Maturity Considers the Coupon Rate Plus or Minus Gains or Losses on the Principal

When the bond matures you're going to get back, not the $500 that you paid for the bond, but the $1,000 par value. So in this case, yield to maturity must be greater than current yield. How much does this "capital gain effect" push yield to maturity above current yield? It depends on (1) the amount of the capital gain, (2) how far in the future the capital gain is to be received, and (3) the present market rate of interest.

The present value of the capital gain to be received at maturity is the *discounted value* of that gain. Suppose it's a long time to maturity. And suppose the current market rate of interest is high. Then the discounted value of the future gain will not be very great.

The longer the *term to maturity* and the higher the *market rate of interest*, the greater the *discount* will be and the smaller the present value of the future gain will be. So the smaller the effect of the gain will be on yield to maturity.

Suppose the $1,000 bond that you bought for $500 matures in 50 years. The present (discounted) value of your $500 capital gain—to be received 50 years hence—is very small. So in this case, current yield and yield to maturity are almost identical. But what if that bond is paying off *next year*? Then you are going to double your money very soon!

The bottom line: When you buy a bond at more or less than par, the shorter the term to maturity, the greater will be the difference between current yield and yield to maturity. *The shorter the term to maturity, the more the price of the bond will reflect its face value (and yield to maturity) and the less it will reflect the size of the coupon payment (and current yield).*

Calculating Yield to Maturity

Calculating yield to maturity is the same as calculating current yield except that adjustments must be made to account for (1) the gain or loss which occurs at maturity and (2) the fact that your "average investment over the life of the bond" lies somewhere between your original investment in the bond, and the face value of the bond. Here's the formula for calculating the approximate yield to maturity:

$$\text{Yield to Maturity (YTM) (approximate)} = \frac{\text{Annual Coupon Payment (F)} \quad \dfrac{+\text{ Amount of discount or} - \text{ Amount of premium paid}}{\text{Years to maturity (n)}}}{\text{Average investment over the life of the bond}}$$

$$\text{Average investment (approximate)} = \frac{\text{Face value (Z)} + \text{price paid (Po)}}{2}$$

so the formula becomes:
$$\text{YTM (approx.)} = \frac{F + \dfrac{(Z - Po)}{n}}{\dfrac{(Po + Z)}{2}} \qquad [8]$$

Note: When a bond is bought at a discount (for less than face value) Z − Po will be a positive number and yield to maturity will be greater than current yield. When a premium (more than face value) is paid for the bond, Z − Po will be a negative number and yield to maturity will be less than current yield.

Example: Suppose you buy a bond with a face value of $1,000, at a coupon rate of 5%, and with 10 years to maturity. And suppose you pay only $500 for this bond. What would be your approximate yield to maturity? Using formula [8]:

$$\text{YTM} = \frac{50 + \dfrac{(1000 - 500)}{10}}{\dfrac{(500 + 1000)}{2}} = \frac{50 + \dfrac{500}{10}}{\dfrac{1500}{2}} = \frac{50 + 50}{750} = \frac{100}{750} = 13.3\%$$

Your yield to maturity would be approximately 13.3%.

Figure 3-3.   Selected Figures from a "Yield to Maturity" Bond Table

Coupon Rate: 10%

Yield to Maturity (%)	Remaining Years to Maturity					
	2 yrs	4 yrs	6 yrs	8 yrs	10 yrs	
10.0	100.00	100.00	100.00	100.00	100.00	
10.5	99.12	98.40	97.82	97.34	96.95	Price Paid
11.0	98.25	96.83	95.69	94.77	94.02	per $100
11.5	97.39	95.30	93.63	92.29	91.22	of Face
12.0	96.53	93.79	91.62	89.89	88.53	Value
12.5	95.69	92.31	89.66	87.58	85.95	

This table shows that:

1. Regardless of years to maturity, as the price you pay for the bond goes down, yield to maturity always goes up.

2. The shorter the term to maturity the greater the effect of the bond price on the yield to maturity. If the time to maturity is short, a small price discount has a large effect on yield to maturity.

Look at the 12.5% yield to maturity. If only two years are remaining to maturity, a discount of less than $5 per $100 can push YTM up from 10% to 12.5%. But if 10 years are remaining to maturity, a discount of almost $15 per $100 is required to push YTM up from 10% to 12.5%.

This is an easy calculation. But the members of the investment community don't usually use this formula. In the past, yield-to-maturity bond tables were used. (Figure 3-3 gives an example.) But now bond tables have been largely replaced by preprogramed calculators. With one of these you just enter the coupon rate, years to maturity, the price paid, and the present market rate of interest. Yield to maturity automatically appears.

In the bond markets, buyers and sellers are constantly watching current yields and yields to maturity on all of the various bonds—buying or selling whenever the yields appear high or low. This keeps yields on all bonds in line with changing supply, demand, and interest rate conditions in the financial markets. Box 3-6 tells more about the relationship between interest rates and the market prices of bonds and stocks.

THE TIME VALUE OF MONEY: KEY TO FINANCIAL MARKETS

Financial markets exist for the purpose of transferring current (present-time) dollars from those who wish to lend (sell current dollars) to those who wish to borrow (buy current dollars). It all happens because of the time value of money.

It is because of the time value of money that people are willing to pay for the use of money. Depository institutions "buy" *current dollars* from their depositors. They "pay" with promises to pay a greater number of *future dollars*. Then the financial institutions "sell" these current dollars to borrowers who promise to pay back an even greater sum of future dollars.

Box 3-6

Question: **Exactly Why Is It True That When Interest Rates Go Down, Bond Prices Go Up? And When Bond Prices Go Up, Interest Rates Go Down?**

There are two ways to answer this question:

1. First, there is a **mathematically precise inverse relationship** between the **price** you pay for a bond or any other fixed-coupon debt instrument, and the **interest yield** you receive on your investment. The fixed coupon rate guarantees the payment of a specific number of dollars per year.

Suppose the coupon pays $100. Then if you pay $1,000 for the bond your interest yield will be 10%. If you pay $500 your yield will be 20%; if you pay $2,000 your yield will be 5%. As the bond price goes up, the interest yield goes down. It must be so!

Yields on all financial instruments tend to move together. Asset managers constantly seek opportunities to buy financial instruments with higher yields. As they buy relatively high-yielding instruments that pushes their prices up and their yields down. As they sell relatively low-yielding instruments that pushes their prices down and their yields up. The result? Identical yields on identical instruments—and it all happens very quickly in the computerized, electronically linked U.S. and worldwide financial markets.

2. Another way to explain this relationship is to say that when market rates of interest are rising so that **newly issued bonds** are carrying higher coupon rates, no one will pay par value for **previously issued bonds** which carry lower coupon rates. If new 10% bonds are selling for $1,000, would you pay $1,000 for an old 8% bond? Not likely! The only way to get you to buy the 8% bond is for its price to drop low enough so that it will yield 10% on the amount you actually pay for it. So as interest rates rise, prices of existing bonds must fall.

In the case of equity securities (corporate stocks) this relationship is not as easily observable or as precise because most equities are held in the hope of capital appreciation—capital gains. So the expected return can't be calculated precisely. But rising interest rates (*ceteris paribus*) tend to depress stock prices as well as bond prices, partly because as bond prices fall and yields rise, *bond yields rise relative to stock yields*. So some investors sell stocks and buy some of the lower-priced, higher yielding bonds. That tends to push stock prices down along with bond prices (and push stock yields up). So when interest rates are rising, don't be surprised to see falling prices (and rising yields) of both bonds, and stocks.

Every bond or promissory note or other debt instrument exists for the purpose of transferring one person's current dollars to someone else. Depositors, bond-buyers, and others give up (sell) their current dollars in exchange for someone else's promise to pay a greater number of future dollars. Borrowers (bond-issuers, etc.) acquire present dollars in exchange for their promises to pay a greater sum of future dollars. All of these debt instruments—promises to pay future dollars—serve as the "currency" for buying current dollars.

Our entire system of financial markets, financial instruments, and financial institutions exists because of **the time value of money**. So a basic understanding of this concept is essential. This concept, learned well, will provide a sound conceptual base for much that you'll be reading throughout this book. Box 3-7 tells more about that.

SUMMARY

- **Financial markets** exist because of, and their functioning is determined by, **the time value of money**.

Box 3-7

Question: Why Does Money Have Time Value? And Do Financial Markets Really Exist Because of This?

The basic reason why *money* has time value is because *goods* have time value. Almost all consumers, at one time or another, want to acquire and have the use of goods *in the present time* rather than waiting until they have earned and saved enough to pay for those goods. Very few people wait to buy a house or a car until they can pay cash for it!

Businesses want to buy capital goods because they are *productive*. The sooner they can buy productive capital, the sooner they can begin to enjoy the profits. So capital goods have *time value*.

If nobody had any desire to spend any more than their current earnings, then money would have no time value. It's only because people and businesses want to spend more than their current incomes that there is a demand for borrowed funds. And that gives money **time value**. If money had no time value, that would mean that goods had no time value. A ridiculous idea!

It would be hard to conceive of a world where money has no time value. But in such a world there would be no borrowing or lending, and no need for financial instruments, financial institutions, or financial markets. All of these exist because of the **time value of money** and people's desire to transfer purchasing power between the future and the present, and vice versa.

- **Compounding**—earning interest on interest earnings from prior years—significantly increases the growth of a sum of money, over time.

- To find the number of years it would take for a sum of money to double in value, divide the interest rate into, for annual compounding, 72, and for continuous compounding, 70.

- The future value of a present sum can be calculated using the **compounding formula**: $Fn = P(1 + r)^n$.

- The present value of a future sum can be calculated using the *discounting formula*: $P = \dfrac{1}{(1 + r)^n} \times Fn$.

- The present value of a future **flow of income** is calculated by discounting each of the future annual payments, using the discounting formula.

- The **present value of a bond**, is calculated by discounting both the future interest income and the future principal payment.

- The present value of a **perpetual flow of income** can be calculated using the formula $P = \dfrac{F}{r}$.

- **Current yield** is the annual rate of return on the amount paid for the bond.

- **Yield to maturity** takes into account both (1) annual rate of return and (2) capital gains or losses on the principal.

- A basic understanding of **the time value of money** is an essential conceptual base for understanding the U.S. and worldwide financial system.

List of Principles, Concepts, Terms

Importance of a speedy payments system
Meaning of the time value of money
Importance of the time value of money
Compounding effect
Magic rules of 72, and 70
Explosive effect of compounding
Ratio scale (semi-log) graph
"Compounding factor"
Future value (compounding) formula
"Discount factor"

Present value (discounting) formula
Relationship between the compounding formula and the discounting formula
Present value of a future flow of income
Present value of a bond
Present value of a perpetual flow of income
Par value
Coupon rate
Current yield
Yield to maturity

Questions

1. Explain as thoroughly as you can what is meant by the statement: "Financial markets exist because of the time value of money."

2. In the "magic rules of 70, and 72," why are those numbers 70, and 72? Why not 50? Or 100? Explain.

3. On an arithmatic-scale graph, the effects of compound interest show up as a curve which is getting constantly steeper. But on a ratio-scale graph, a constant rate of increase shows up as a straight line. Explain why.

4. The "compounding effect" results from interest earnings on money which was earned as interest in prior years. Explain

this, and illustrate with an arithmetic example.

5. Write down the general "future value" (compounding) formula, and then explain exactly what it means. Do the same for the "present value" (discounting) formula.

6. Explain how to find the present value of a bond which pays a fixed annual return and then repays the principal at maturity.

7. The shorter the term to maturity, the less effect current yield will have on the market value (price) of a bond. Explain why.

8. Explain this statement: "Financial institutions, instruments, and markets exist because of the time value of money."

Suggested Readings

Clayton, Gary E. and Christopher B. Spivey. *The Time Value of Money.* Philadelphia: W. B. Saunders, Co., 1978.

Federal Reserve Bank of Chicago. *The ABC's of Figuring Interest.* 1984.

Federal Reserve Bank of New York. *The Arithmetic of Interest Rates.* 1984.

Federal Reserve Bank of Dallas. *Selected Interest Rates.* 1984.

Fisher, Irving. *The Theory of Interest.* New York: Macmillan, 1930.

CHAPTER 4

The Demand for Money and Velocity: An Introduction to Macro-Monetary Theory

Chapter Objectives

Why do people want to hold some of their assets—their wealth—in the form of money? And what determines how much money (instead of other assets) people will want to hold? And how do these decisions influence macroeconomic conditions? In this chapter you will begin to learn the answers to these questions.

Specifically, when you complete your study of this chapter you will understand and be able to explain:

1. The **liquidity preference motives** which cause people to want to hold some of their assets in the form of money: the **transactions, precautionary** and **speculative** motives.
2. The importance of **expected interest rate changes** in influencing the size of **speculative balances**.
3. The special meaning and importance of the term **demand for money**, and the distinction between the **demand for money (Md)** and the **quantity of money demanded (Mqd)**.
4. The important distinction between **stocks** and **flows**.
5. The **Cambridge k** which expresses Mqd as a fraction (k) of national income (Y), and its relationship to the **velocity of circulation of money (V)**, which also reflects Mqd.
6. Some basics of **monetary theory**: factors which influence the demand for money (Md) and the quantity of money demanded (Mqd), and how these can influence macroeconomic conditions.

LIQUIDITY PREFERENCE: MOTIVES FOR HOLDING MONEY

The desire to hold *money* (instead of some other asset) is called the **demand for money**. It is also called **liquidity preference**. People and businesses have various motives for demanding (desiring to hold) money.

Why do people prefer to "remain liquid"?—that is, why do they want to hold some of their wealth (assets) in the form of money? Most modern models of the macroeconomy assume that there are three reasons: For transactions (to buy things), and for precautionary and speculative reasons.

The Transactions Motive

The first and foremost reason for holding money is for transactions: because we're planning to use it as a **medium of exchange**. The more we're planning to spend (per day, week, etc.), the more money we're likely to want to have on hand. People with more wealth and more income tend to spend more and to have a greater **transactions demand** for money.

Frequency of Income Payments. Also, the less frequently people receive their income payments, the greater their average desired money balances are likely to be. If we all got paid daily we wouldn't feel the need to hold very much money for transactions purposes. But if we only get paid on Fridays we will want to hold at least enough money to carry us through the following week.

The Size of National Income. The aggregate quantity of money demanded in the entire economy at any moment (how much money all the poeple, businesses, etc., want to hold) is closely related to the size of the national income.

As national income increases, total transactions increase. So people's desired money balances increase. In fact there usually has been a fairly stable relationship between the size of the national income (Y) and the size of the total money balances (Mqd) desired by the public. Why? Mostly because of what we've just been talking about: *the transactions demand for money.*

The Precautionary Motive

Another motive for holding money is for *precautionary reasons.* You may want to have a few dollars on hand to meet unforeseen needs for liquidity. The $20 bill you keep folded up and tucked away in the secret compartment in your wallet is there "just in case"—because of the **precautionary motive**.

The size of the precautionary demand for money is influenced by exactly the same things that influence the transactions demand. As a person's wealth and income increase and as the length of time between income payments increases, desired precautionary balances increase. So it isn't unrealistic to combine the transactions and precautionary motives and consider both to be included under the transactions demand for money. This is usually done in modern monetary analysis.

The Speculative Motive

People also hold some of their assets in the form of money for speculative reasons—to try to profit from future price changes. For example, suppose you were planning to buy some government bonds but thought the prices of those bonds soon would be coming down. Would you hold *money* while waiting for (speculating on) lower bond prices? If so, that would be an example of the **speculative demand** for money.

When Interest Rates Are Expected to Rise, Hold Money! The speculative motive is mostly related to expected changes in interest rates. Suppose investors expect interest rates on bonds to rise. Instead of investing in today's low-interest bonds they will want to "stay liquid" (hold money) and wait. Nobody wants to buy low-interest-paying bonds today if they expect to be able to buy higher-interest-paying bonds tomorow!

When Interest Rates Are Expected to Fall, Buy Bonds! It also works the other way. Suppose investors expect interest rates to fall. They will use their speculative money balances to invest in today's high-interest bonds, hoping to "get locked in" before the rates come down.

Conclusion: When interest rates are expected to rise, speculative balances increase. When interest rates are expected to fall, speculative balances decrease. This relationship between expected interest rate changes and the desired size of speculative money balances plays a key role in some of the macroeconomic models coming up later.

THE SPECIAL MEANING OF THE TERM "DEMAND FOR MONEY"

Demand for money means *the desire to hold money balances.* That's a different meaning of the word "demand." In its usual meaning, the word "demand" means *quantities of something which would be purchased at various prices during some period of time.* In this usual meaning, demand is a "flow"—so much per day, week, or month.

In the phrase "demand for money" the word "demand" *does not* refer to a flow. It refers to a **stock of money**—to the **money balances** that people would want to hold at the present time. In box 4-1 and figure 4-1 you'll see some further explanation and some illustrations of the distinction between stocks and flows.

Box 4-1

Question: Exactly What is the Distinction between a *Stock* and a *Flow*?

A **stock** of something is *an existing quantity at a point in time, at rest.* It can be measured in pounds or gallons or cubic feet or dollars' worth or bushels or carloads or by any other measure. If you measure it this morning and then measure it again tonight, unless something has been added to or subtracted from it, the "stock" will be the same size. A stock is not "time related."

A **flow** is a measure of something in motion. It cannot be measured except in terms of **a period of time**. For example a "stock" (existing quantity) of water could be measured in gal-lons. But a flow of water must be measured in gallons per minute, per hour, or the like.

1. The size of a **stock** tells *how much* **exists** at *a* **point** *in time.*

2. The size of a **flow** tells *how much* **goes by** *in a period of time.*

Wealth is a *stock*. **Income** is a *flow*. If you have $10, that is a stock. If you are earning $10 per hour, that is a flow. Figure 4-1 gives some simple illustrations of all this.

Figure 4-1.　Illustrations of the Distinction between Stocks and Flows[1]

STOCKS	FLOWS
A stock is an *existing quantity* at a *point in time*. An inventory. A snapshot of the quantity on hand at the moment. The size of a stock is not related to the passage of time.	A flow is a quantity in motion. It is always expressed as a *rate—how many units go by per unit of time*. The size of a flow cannot be expressed without reference to a *time period*.

Five gallons	 5 gallons per minute
Inventory: 50 cars	Sales: 5 cars per week
Wealth (savings): $5,000	Income: $500 per week
Demand for money Quanity demanded: $240	Demand for goods Quantity demanded $400 worth per week

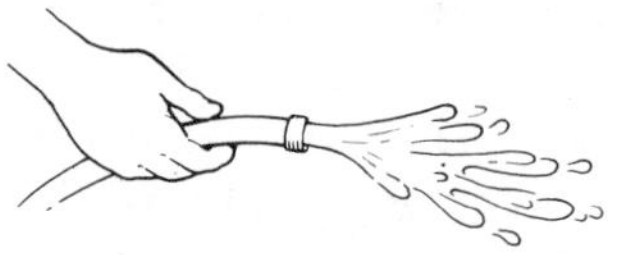

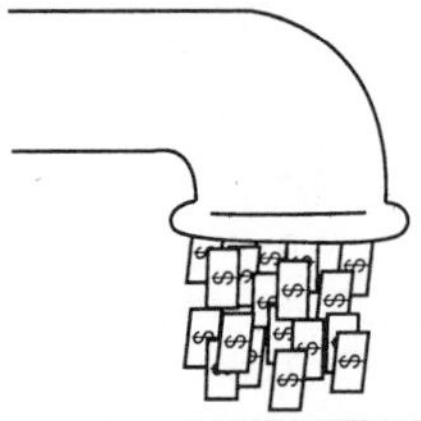

---

[1] This figure certainly won't challenge your mental capabilities so relax for a minute and enjoy looking at it. One of my students commented that these illustrations are "insulting to the intelligence of a junior-senior level college student." I tried to explain that a good bit of confusion in monetary theory and in macroeconomics in general results from a failure to clearly distinguish between stocks and flows—that some articles even appear in the professional journals where there is confusion on this issue. One reason why so many students have difficulty understanding IS-LM analysis (coming up later) is that they don't clearly understand that IS deals with flows and LM, with stocks. So please! Try not to be insulted by this simple illustration. Recognize that this is a *very important concept*, illustrated (admittedly!) in a *very simple way*. And try to spend enough time with the figure to make sure that you'll never forget—especially the bottom line: **demand for money** vs. **demand for goods**.

Demand for Money Refers to "Desired Stocks of Money"

Your own **demand for money** (Md) refers to the various (different) amounts of money (money balances) you would prefer to hold at various (different) costs of holding money. And your **quantity of money demanded** (Mqd) is your "desired inventory of money" of cash and checkable deposits—at any moment, *given the existing costs of holding money.*

On the asset side of your own personal balance sheet, how much would you like to be holding, right now, in the form of money? As compared with your holdings of stereo equipment or bonds or stocks or automobiles or clothing or whatever? *The amount of your total assets which you would like to be holding in the form of money at this moment indicates the quantity of money you demand (your Mqd) at this moment.* If we could add up your Mqd together with the Mqd of everyone else, we would arrive at *the aggregate quantity of money demanded in the economy* at this moment.

Throughout this book you will be seeing the terms "demand for money" (Md) and "quantity of money demanded" (Mqd). Remember that "demand" in this case is not the desire to acquire more money. It is not the desire to spend or receive money. It is only the desire to hold **money balances**—*the desire to have money on hand.*

Demand for Money: A Definition

The term "demand for money" may be defined as the various quantities of money (money balances) that people, businesses, other organizations—the entire society—would desire to hold (as balances in their checkable accounts, cash registers, wallets, etc.) at the various costs that might exist for holding money. The most important cost of holding money is the loss of the **interest income** that could be earned on alternative assets. The next section explains that. But before you go on you might want to read box 4-2 and see an entirely different way of looking at "the demand for money."

Box 4-2

Feature: The Demand for Money—Patinkin's "Other View"

It is possible, and under some circumstances useful, to define the demand for money as a flow. During the 1950s, the very highly regarded economist, Don Patinkin, using what he called "semantic liberty," developed the idea that "goods can be used to buy money" (as well as vice versa). Patinkin explains that it is possible to think of "trading goods for money" as the opposite of "trading money for goods."

Patinkin's unique conceptualization results in an aggregate demand function for money which is the obverse image of the aggregate demand for goods, and which is not a stock, but a flow—it happens over time. This unique conceptualization of "demand for money," although interesting and for some purposes useful, is not the usual meaning and is not the meaning used in this book.

For a thorough explanation of this interesting perspective on the demand for money, see: Don Patinkin, *Money, Interest, and Prices,* 2nd edition, Mathematical Appendix, "On Stocks and Flows," New York: Harper and Row Publishers, 1965, pp. 515–23.

INTEREST RATES INFLUENCE THE QUANTITY OF MONEY DEMANDED (MQD)

You know that the basic **demand for money** (the desire to hold money balances) is determined by the transactions motive, and also by precautionary and speculative considerations. But given this basic demand for money, what will be the actual **quantity demanded**?

How many dollars of money balances will the public actually desire to hold? That depends on the **opportunity cost** of holding money—on how much you lose by holding money. How much interest income must be forfeited when you hold money balances instead of holding some other (higher yielding) asset? Perhaps a government bond?

An Opportunity Cost Example

Suppose you're keeping $1,000 in cash as your average money balance. And suppose you could earn 8% interest on government bonds. If you would exchange your $1,000 (cash) for $1,000 worth of government bonds you would earn interest of $80 per year. So $80 is how much you're losing in forfeited interest income. That's the opportunity cost you are "paying" for the utility you get from holding your $1,000 in cash.

Now suppose the interest rate on government bonds goes up to 16 percent. Your opportunity cost (forfeited interest income) goes up to $160 per year. Maybe you'll decide to reduce your cash balance and put $400 into government bonds and earn some of that high interest income!

Why are you now willing to try to get along with a money balance of only $600? Your *basic demand for money* (Md—your desire for liquidity) hasn't changed. But your *quantity of money demanded* (Mqd) has decreased from $1,000 to $600. Why? Because *the implicit price you must pay* (the opportunity cost of holding money) went up from 8 percent to 16 percent. Box 4-3 further explains Md and Mqd, and if you'll look at figure 4-2 you'll see all this illustrated on a graph.

Interest Earned on Money Balances Reduces the Opportunity Cost

The above (government bond) example of the opportunity cost of holding money assumes that no interest is earned on money balances. During the 1980s there has been increasing use of NOW accounts and other **interest-bearing checking accounts**.

If you were holding all of your money balances in the form of interest-earning checkable deposits, and if the interest on those deposits was equal to (or near) market rates, then the opportunity cost to you of holding those money balances would be very small. But that isn't usually what happens.

Almost everyone holds some currency. No interest can be earned on that. And most people do not keep large enough balances in their checkable deposits to qualify for the highest available rates. Also, most people are required to pay some

---

Box 4-3

Question: Exactly What is the Distinction between Demand for Money (Md) and Quantity of Money Demanded (Mqd)?

In the literature on this subject, the distinction between the basic demand for money (Md) and the specific quantity of money demanded (Mqd) frequently is not made clear. The term "demand for money" often is used to mean "the quantity demanded at existing rates," ignoring the functional relationship between the level of interest rates and the quantity of money demanded. There is a logical explanation for this.

According to the assumptions and conclusions of the classical model, interest rate changes have no effect on the size of desired money balances. According to that model, the one and only factor which influences the size of desired money balances is the transactions motive. So the size of desired money balances is a function of income and nothing else.

In the classical model the money demand curve is vertical—absolutely inelastic with respect to interest rate changes. Therefore the demand for money (Md) is always the same as the quantity of money demanded (Mqd). So there is no need to distinguish between the *basic demand* and the *quantity demanded*. Do not be surprised when you read in the literature the phrase "demand for money" and find that this is in fact a reference to a specific quantity of money demanded.

Throughout this book, a point on the money demand curve will be referred to as "the quantity of money demanded" (Mqd). The term "demand for money" will be reserved for use only when the reference is to the entire money demand function—the entire Md curve.[2]

---

[2] Sometimes it is not easy to keep the "Md-Mqd" distinction precise. For example, when national income increases this causes the transactions demand for money to increase. It brings a rightward shift in the money demand curve. Clearly this is an increase in the demand for money (Md).

However, on this newly shifted demand curve, the quantity of money demanded (Mqd) still is but one point. And that point (given the Md curve) is determined by the oppor-

tunity cost of holding money (the interest earnings available on alternative assets). So the quantity represented by that point is accurately referred to, not as Md, but as Mqd. In this case the quantity of money demanded is larger than before, not because of a reduction in the opportunity cost of holding money, but because of an increase in the demand for money—a rightward shift in the curve, induced by an increase in national income.

---

service charges on their checkable accounts. So the opportunity cost of holding money balances still is, for most people, quite significant.[3]

Let's suppose you add up all of your money holdings of cash and checkable deposits, then you calculate all of your interest earnings and service charges and find that your average net return on your total money balance is 2 percent. That means that your opportunity cost of holding money is not equal to the rate of interest you could have been earning on alternative assets. It's 2 percentage points less than that.

For example, suppose the market rate on alternative investments is 8%. Since you're earning 2% on your money balances the opportunity cost to you of holding money is only 6%. So the quantity of money you will want to hold when market rates are 8% will be the same as if market rates had been 6% and earnings on your cash balances had been zero. Or suppose market rates are 16%. The size of your desired money balances will be the same as if market rates had been 14% and earnings on your money balances had been zero.

The Md curve in figure 4-2 will shift to the right to reflect the 2 percent earnings on your money balances. After the rightward shift, the new Md curve

---

[3] For a detailed analysis and data dealing with both the implicit and explicit costs of holding money balances, see: Kenneth C. Carraro and Daniel L. Thornton, "The Cost of Checkable Deposits in the United States," *Review of the Federal Bank of St. Louis.* vol. 68, no. 4 (April 1986), pp. 19–27.

Figure 4-2.   One Individual's Demand for Money

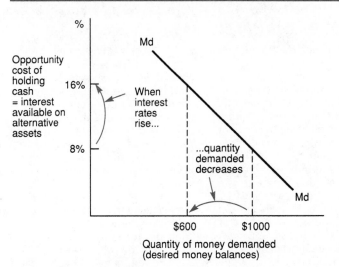

Quantity of money demanded
(desired money balances)

As The Opportunity Cost Of Holding Money Increases, The Quantity Demanded (Desired Quantity Of Money Balances) Decreases.

When interest earnings available on alternative assets increase from 8% to 16%, this individual's quantity of money demanded (desired money balance) decreases from $1,000 to $600. Or if the available return on alternative assets would drop from 16% to 8%, this individual's desired money balance would increase from $600 to $1,000.

The steepness of this curve indicates the interest-rate elasticity of this individual's demand for money. The steeper the curve, the less responsive the quanity demanded to changes in interest rates, so the less interest-rate elastic the individual's demand for money.

will indicate a quantity demanded for each interest rate equal to the quantity previously demanded for an interest rate 2 percentage points lower. Now look at figure 4-3 and that's what you'll see.

The rapid expansion of interest-bearing checking accounts since 1980 has reduced the opportunity cost of holding checking-account money. So looking at figure 4-3 you would expect that average money balances would have increased during the 1980s. And that is exactly what has happened.

The Entire Money Supply Is Always Being Held by Someone

Here's another interesting fact about money. All of the money in existence in the economy—the entire **money stock** or **money supply**—is always owned by (held by) people, businesses and other organizations. So *the quantity of money being held at any moment is always exactly equal to the size of the money supply.* Therefore, to say "an increase in the size of the money supply" is the same as to say *an increase in the quantity of money being held by the public.*

Alternatively, suppose that the size of the money supply decreases. That means that the people, businesses, and other economic units *are holding less*

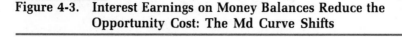

**Figure 4-3. Interest Earnings on Money Balances Reduce the
Opportunity Cost: The Md Curve Shifts**

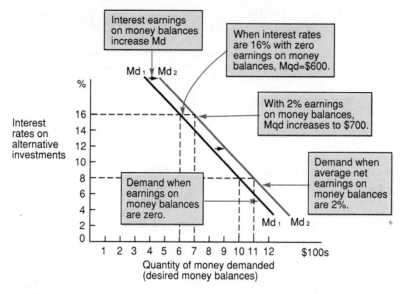

Interest earnings reduce the opportunity cost of holding money balances below
the rates shown on the vertical axis. That causes the public to increase their
money balances. The Md curve shifts to the right.

When the average net earnings on money balances are 2%, the Md curve shifts
to the right exactly far enough to indicate, for each level of interest rates, a
quantity demanded equal to that for interest rates two percentage points lower.

For example, the Md2 curve indicates, at an interest rate of 8%, desired money
balances of $1100. That's exactly the quantity which would be demanded on the
Md1 curve with an interest rate of 6%. At an interest rate of 16%, the Md2 curve
indicates a quantity of money demanded of $700. That's exactly the quantity
which would have been demanded on the Md1 curve at an interest rate of 14%.

If the average net earnings on money balances had been 4%, the Md 2 curve
would have shifted twice as far to the right. Then at market rates of 16%, the
quantity demanded would be equal to that when interest rates were 12% and
earnings on money balances were zero.

---

money than before. As you read the next section it's important for you to keep in
mind this equality (identity) between (a) the size of the money supply and (b) the
total amount of money balances being held by the public. But first, box 4-4 gives
some further explanation of this important equality (identity).

THE MACROECONOMIC ROLE OF MONEY

Now you can begin to see why **the demand for money** is a very important concept. Suppose that (at this moment) people are holding larger (or smaller) money
balances than they desire to hold. Are they likely to alter their spending and/or

---

Box 4-4

Question: **Where Is the Money Stock?**

All of the money in existence must be held (owned) by someone. That isn't surprising. It's that way with all assets: stocks and bonds, automobiles, houses, and everything else. Nothing of value just lies unclaimed in the streets! The money is in the wallets, cash registers and checking accounts of the public.

The more money in existence, the more being held by the public. Obviously! Suppose you read that the money supply (money stock) increased by 10% last year. Would that mean that the people, businesses, etc. increased their money balances by 10%? Exactly! That's the only thing it could mean. And it's true no matter whether the people want to be holding more money, or not.

---

asset-holding patterns to try to achieve their desired sizes of money balances? Of course they are.

Money Supply Changes Can Cause Spending and/or Asset (Portfolio) Adjustments

Suppose the money supply expands. People will find themselves holding more money than before and (*ceteris paribus*)[4] more than they want to hold. So to get rid of their excess money they will begin buying more goods and services or stocks and bonds or something.

Or suppose the money supply decreases and people find themselves holding smaller quantities of money than they desire to hold. They will cut back their spending and/or sell some assets to try to increase their money balances.

Now you can see how the relationship between (1) the size of the money supply and (2) the quantity of money demanded can have a significant influence on the macroeconomy. Changes in the money supply can cause changes in the rate of total spending, in the supply, demand, and prices of stocks and bonds, and in interest rates. So changes in either the money supply or money demand can influence the macroeconomy—employment, production, output, income, interest rates, and the price level.

People Adjust Their Spending and/or Asset Holdings to Attain Their Desired Money Balances

Whenever the money supply is greater than the total quantity demanded by the public (M > Mqd), people will begin spending more to try to reduce their money balances. Either total spending for goods and services will be speeding up or more financial assets will be demanded—or maybe both. But either way, total spending in the economy will be speeding up.

Suppose more **financial assets** are demanded. Then their prices will be pushed upward and interest rates will fall. (If you don't remember all about this relationship between financial asset prices and interest rates, it's explained in the previous chapter in Box 3-6.) As interest rates go down, that tends to stimulate

---

[4] *Ceteris paribus* means "other things being equal," or "holding everything else constant." It means "assuming that nothing else changes in the meanwhile." Remember?

Box 4-5

Question: When the M = Mqd Equilibrium Exists Does
That Mean That All of the People—
All Economic Units—Are in Equilibrium?

You probably could guess that the answer to this question is "No." And that "no" would hold true for any kind of macroequilibrium in the economy. There are always some economic units on one side of the equilibrium, and some on the other. Equilibrium occurs where the "disequilibrating effects" of these various economic units balance out.

Later you'll be reading about macroequilibrium where savings withdrawals (leakages) from the income stream are exactly equal to and offset by investment injections. In this case some economic units are making net withdraw-

als from the spending flow while others are making net injections. Equilibrium occurs where the withdrawals and injections are exactly equal and offsetting.

It works the same way in the equilibrium between M and Mqd. Some economic units always will be shifting out of money and into financial assets; others always will be shifting out of financial assets and into money. The M = Mqd equilibrium occurs where these two opposite actions are exactly equal and offsetting.

more investment spending. Either real employment and output and income will be increasing or there will be inflation.

But suppose the money supply is smaller than the total quantity demanded (M < Mqd). Then total spending will be slowing down for the opposite reasons. The economy will be slowing down. National employment and output and income will be decreasing and/or prices will be falling (deflation).

Conclusion: The only time when the economy can be in macroequilibrium (no forces pushing for a speedup or slowdown) is when the quantity of money demanded by the public is exactly equal to the existing size of the money supply (Mqd = M). Too much money in the hands of the public will cause increased spending and economic speedup and/or inflation; too little money will result in a spending slowdown, decreased employment, output, and income, and/or deflation. (Note: as explained later, Mqd = M is a *necessary* but not *sufficient* condition for macroequilibrium.) Box 4-5 tells more about this equilibrium.

THE DEMAND FOR MONEY (MD), THE MONEY SUPPLY (M), AND THE VELOCITY OF CIRCULATION (V)

How long is "the average dollar" held in someone's money balance before it is spent? That depends on the ratio of total money balances (the money supply, M) to total spending (the national income, Y).

The Greater the Mqd the Smaller the Velocity

The greater the size of money balances people want to hold (Mqd), the less frequently each dollar will be spent. So the slower the **velocity of circulation** (V) will be. Here's an example.

Suppose in some hypothetical economy the money supply (M) is $100 billion. And suppose the economy's total spending—national output and income (Y)— amounts to exactly $100 billion per year. Then the average dollar must be turning over once each year. When M = $100 billion and Y for the year = $100 billion then it's obvious that the average dollar is being spent only once each year. So it's obvious that *the velocity of circulation (V) is one.*

Now suppose that in this little economy, Y is still $100 billion. But now the size of the money supply (M) is only $10 billion. Then each dollar must turn over (be re-spent) ten times each year. That's the only way a money supply (M) of $10 billion could create a spending flow (Y) of $100 billion. *Now the velocity of circulation (V) must be 10.*

The bottom line: For any given level of Y, the smaller the quantity of money, the greater must be the velocity of circulation (V).

If M = (1)Y, then V = 1;

If M = (1/2)Y, then V = 2;

If M = (1/10)Y, then V = 10;

etc.

So the general equation is:

$$V = \frac{Y}{M}, \text{ or, expressed differently,}$$

$$V = \frac{1}{M} \times Y.$$

Example:

$$\text{If M} = \$100 \text{ and Y} = \$500, \text{ V} = \frac{1}{100} \times 500; \text{ V} = 5.$$

With a money supply of $100 and national spending and income of $500, it's obvious that each dollar is being spent to generate income 5 times during the year. So the income velocity of money is 5.

Now you know the relationships between the national income (Y), velocity of circulation (V), and the money supply (M). But so far nothing has been said about the *quantity of money demanded by the public (Mqd).* That's coming up now.

The Quantity of Money Demanded As a Function of National Income[5]

As national income (Y) increases, people desire to hold larger money balances. Md increases. So at each opportunity cost of holding money (at each interest rate r) Mqd increases. If Y increases by 10%, then *ceteris paribus,* if r doesn't change then Mqd would increase by 10%. Therefore we can say that

---

[5] *Note:* When national income changes, the transactions demand for money changes. So the entire demand function (the curve Md in figure 4-2) shifts. So in fact there is a change in *the demand for money:* Md = f(Y). But also, since this analysis deals with a *specific quantity of money demanded* at a specific interest rate (r)—a specific point on a shifting curve—it is appropriate to refer to this changing specific quantity as a change in *the quantity of money demanded.* Mqd = f(Y, r), and if we assume a given r($\bar{r}$) then Mqd = f(Y, $\bar{r}$), so Mqd = f(Y).

Md—and therefore Mqd at each given interest rate—is a function of Y. So at any given level of interest rates:

$$Mqd = f(Y, \bar{r}) = f(Y).$$

Now, if we can put a number (k) on this functional relationship, we can express the precise size of Mqd (given the level of r), as:

$$Mqd = kY.$$

This symbol "k" is referred to as the "Cambridge k" because this was the symbol used by Alfred Marshall, A. C. Pigou and other economists at Cambridge University in England in their version of the equation of exchange (to be explained later).

From the equation, if we know the number for k, then for each size of Y we can calculate immediately the size of the public's total desired money balances. For example, suppose k = 1/6. That means that people want to hold money balances amounting to 1/6th of the value of Y. If Y = $600, then Mqd = 1/6 × $600 = $100. If Y increases to $660, Mqd increases to 1/6 × $660 = $110. If Y increases to $1,200, Mqd increases to 1/6 × $1,200 = $200.

In Macroequilibrium Mqd Equals M

Since all of the money supply is always being held by the public, for the economy to be in macroequilibrium *the quantity of money in the money supply* must be exactly equal to *the quantity of money desired by the public.* So in macroequilibrium the following relationships must hold true:

If M = (1)Y, then Mqd = (1)Y. k = 1 and V = 1.

If M = (1/2)Y, then Mqd = (1/2)Y. k = 1/2 and V = 2.

If M = (1/4)Y, then Mqd = (1/4)Y. k = 1/4 and V = 4.

If M = (1/6)Y, then Mqd = (1/6)Y. k = 1/6 and V = 6.

etc.

It's obvious that as the quantity of money demanded (Mqd, or kY) falls, velocity increases. There is a precise inverse (reciprocal) relationship between k and V.

Example: If Mqd is $200 and Y is $1,200, since Mqd = kY:

$$200 = k\ 1200.\ k = \frac{200}{1200}.\ k = \frac{1}{6}.$$

What about velocity? Since MV = Y:

$$200V = 1200.\ V = \frac{1200}{200}.\ V = 6.$$

When M = 200, each dollar must be spent six times to generate total spending (Y) of $1,200. So V = 6. So k = 1/6th.

It's obvious that when:

$$MV = Y;\ then\ kY = M.$$

$$\$200 \times 6 = \$1,200;\ 1/6 \times \$1,200 = \$200.$$

Box 4-6 explains more about the relationship between k and V.

Box 4-6

Question: What Difference Does It Make Whether We Use k or V?

Why do we use both k and V? We always get the same results either way. But the focus of each is different. The focus of k is on the **money stock**. The focus of V is on the **spending flow**. Stocks vs. flows again? Exactly! And each focus has an advantage.

The advantage of k is that it focuses on *the desired size of M*. For any size of the national income, it tells us what size the money supply must be *to satisfy the public's desire to hold money balances*. So it tells us the **quantity of money** needed to maintain any given equilibrium level of Y.

Alternatively, the advantage of V is that it focuses on the size of the **total spending flow**. For any given change in the size of the money supply, V tells us the amount of change which will occur in *total spending* (Y). Both V and k give us useful ways of looking at exactly the same situation—but from two different perspectives.

Velocity, k, and the Macroeconomic Role of Money

We can't know how much spending will be generated with a given money supply—nor can we foretell the economic impact of a given change in the money supply—unless we know the velocity of circulation (V). Another way to say it is: To predict the effect of any change in the size of the money supply (ΔM) we must know *the size of the public's desired money balances*—Mqd, = kY.

Economists spend a great amount of time and effort analyzing and trying to understand the demand for money—trying to identify the factors which influence V (and k). All **monetary theory** requires an understanding of—and some assumptions regarding the specific nature of—the **demand for money**.

Much of our understanding of the macroeconomy depends on our understanding of the demand for money—the relationships expressed by V and k. You will be encountering these terms in the chapters coming up. It's important that you learn well the relationships among M, V, k, and Y explained in this chapter.

SUMMARY

- Understanding the **demand for money** is an essential step in understanding the macroeconomic role of money in the economy.

- People, businesses, and other organizations *demand money* because of their **liquidity preference** motives—i.e., for **transactions, and precautionary and speculative reasons**.

- The word **demand** in the phrase **demand for money** refers to **desired money balances**. It refers a **stock**, not a **flow**.

- In its **macroeconomic role** money supports **total spending** and thereby supports the flow of inputs and outputs and the level of prices in the **circular flow** of the economy.

- The larger the national income (*ceteris paribus*) the greater the **quantity of money demanded**. Mqd can be expressed as a fraction (k) of national income (Y). **Mqd = kY**.

- The larger the **quantity of money demanded** (k), the slower the **velocity of circulation** (V).
- The demand for money is an essential element of monetary theory. The functioning of the money and banking system and of the macroeconomy cannot be understood without a basic understanding of the **demand for money**.

Checklist of Principles, Issues, Concepts, Terms

Liquidity preference

Transactions motive

Precautionary motive

Speculative motive

Effects of expected changes in interest rates

Special meaning of "demand for money"

Distinction between Md and Mqd

Opportunity cost of holding money

Effect of interest rates on Mqd

Effect on Mqd when interest is earned on money balances

Total money supply is always being held by the public

How money supply changes can cause spending changes

People can alter spending or assets to adjust money balances

Relationships between M, Mqd, k, and V

In macroequilibrium, Mqd = M

How V and k determine the effects of M

Questions

1. The textbook says that when interest rates are expected to rise, asset managers will want to hold money. When rates are expected to fall they will want to hold bonds. Explain why this is true. Give a numerical example.

2. The word "demand" in the phrase "demand for money" has a different meaning than the usual meaning of the word demand. Explain what this means and why this distinction is important.

3. Explain this statement: "It is logical to assume that interest rate changes would influence the quantity of money demanded by the public."

4. Explain exactly what is meant by: "The macroeconomic role of money."

5. Explain and give some numerical examples of the relationship between the velocity of money (V), and the "Cambridge k."

6. Explain how the quantity of money demanded (Mqd) would be changed by *an increase* in each of the following:
   a. The interest rate
   b. Earnings on money balances
   c. The expected rate of inflation
   d. The price level
   In each case try to explain why, and illustrate with either a shift of or a movement along the Md curve.

7. Explain the meaning of and the differences between each of the motives for holding money balances.

Suggested Readings

Bowsher, N. N. "The Demand for Currency: Is the Underground Economy Undermining Monetary Policy?" Federal Reserve Bank of St. Louis, *Review.* (January 1980): 11–17.

Dotsey, Michael. "An Investigation of Cash Management Practices and Their Effects on the Demand for Money." Federal Reserve Bank of Richmond *Economic Review.* (September/October 1984); 3–11.

Goldfeld, Stephen M. "The Demand for Money Revisited." *Brookings Papers on Economic Activity.* no. 3, 1973.

Judd, John P. "The Recent Decline in Velocity: Instability in Money Demand or Inflation?" Federal Reserve Bank of San Francisco *Economic Review.* no. 2, spring 1983, pp. 12–19.

Judd, John P., and John L. Scadding. "The Search for a Stable Money Demand Function." *Journal of Economic Literature* 20. (September 1982); 993–1023.

Koskela, E and Viren M. "Inflation, Hedging and the Demand for Money: Some Empirical Evidence." *Economic Inquiry* 25(2). (April 1987): 251–65.

Laidler, David E. W. *The Demand for Money: Theories and Evidence,* 3rd ed. New York: Harper & Row, 1985.

McCallum, Bennet T. and Marvin S. Goodfriend. "Theoretical Analysis of the Demand for Money." *Economic Review* 74(1). Federal Reserve Bank of Richmond (January/February 1988): 16–24.

Radecki, L. J. and C. C. Garver. "The Household Demand for Money: Estimates from Cross-sectional Data." *Federal Reserve Bank of New York Quarterly Review* 12(1). (Spring 1987): 29–34.

CHAPTER 5

More About Money: The Aggregates, Velocity, and Issues of Monetary Policy

Chapter Objectives

This chapter continues from the previous one and goes more deeply into **macro-monetary theory**: *the role of money in the macroeconomy*. Here you'll read about the role of money in influencing the **circular flow** of the economy, about various **definitions** of the money supply (the monetary aggregates), and more about the importance (and sometimes the elusiveness) of **velocity**.

Specifically, when you complete your study of this chapter you will understand and be able to explain:

1. The meaning of **monetary aggregates** and the importance (and difficulty) of choosing and "targeting" the appropriate monetary aggregates.

2. The role of the **Federal Reserve** (the Fed) in defining and monitoring the monetary aggregates.

3. The relationship between the size of the **money supply** and the size of the **aggregate quantity demanded** (total spending for output) in the circular flow of the economy.

4. More about the critical role of **velocity of circulation** and the problems caused by **unexpected changes** in velocity during the 1980s.

5. **The key monetary policy issue**: Growth of the money supply must be restricted: but **how tightly**? And should the money-growth rate **be altered** to try to achieve desired conditions in the economy and in the financial markets? Or not?

CALCULATING THE SIZE OF THE MONEY SUPPLY: EXACTLY WHAT IS MONEY?

It's very easy to define money "in general." Money is anything which is serving as a generally acceptable **medium of exchange**. Money is any **perfectly liquid asset**—anything which is immediately exchangeable for other goods and services. Money is anything that people are completely confident that they can spend, to buy things.

Does "Money" Include All Immediately-Spendable Assets?

The general definitions are easy. But when we're trying to determine the size of the nation's money supply, what do we include? In general, we add together, or "aggregate," all of the *perfectly liquid* (immediately spendable) *assets* in the hands of the public. But *specifically*, it isn't so easy to decide where to draw the line—what to include and what to exclude.

Currency. There's no question about dollar bills and coins (currency).[1] All of that in the hands of the public (not in bank vaults) is included in the nation's money supply to be sure. But wait! What about all those silver coins that have disappeared from circulation and are being hoarded in safe deposit boxes? Those coins won't ever be used again as a medium of exchange. So they really aren't serving as money. The velocity of circulation of those coins will be permanently zero! Still they *could be* spent, and they are included as a part of the U.S. money supply.

"Demand Deposit" Checking Accounts (DDs). What about the money in "demand deposit" checking accounts (often called DDs, or DDAs)? That's immediately spendable. It can be spent in its present form just by writing checks. But it isn't quite as "perfectly liquid" as cash. How would you like to be running out of gas at 4:00 a.m. on a long, lonely out-of-state road and have only your checkbook (no cash) with you? I wouldn't! But that's the exception.

Most of the time and for most purposes, money in a checking account is immediately spendable. So when we're trying to add up all of the component parts and find out the size of the nation's money supply, we definitely must include checking account money. Sometimes it's slightly less liquid than cash, but certainly it's liquid enough to be called "money."

Other Checkable Deposits (OCDs). What about the money deposited in NOW accounts? And in "share draft" accounts at credit unions? And in all of the other kinds of accounts transferrable by check?

Several new kinds of checkable accounts became available in the early 1980s at banks, savings and loan institutions, mutual savings banks, and credit unions. Are the deposits in these checkable accounts a part of the nation's total money supply? Yes. These accounts are frequently called "OCDs" (other checkable deposits) and are just as liquid as the traditional "demand deposit" checking accounts. So of course we include these deposits as components of the money supply.

Where Do We Draw the Line?

Now we come to the tough part. What about the money market fund accounts offered by mutual fund companies, brokerage firms, and other financial institutions? Many of those accounts offer check-writing privileges. That makes the

---

[1] Sometimes you will see the term "currency and coins," where paper money is considered to be "currency" and "coins" are stated separately as though coins were not a part of currency. There is nothing wrong with this distinction. However, the term currency, standing alone, includes coins.

money in those accounts immediately spendable. So are those dollars—those "deposits"—a part of the nation's money supply? Or not?

And what about money in passbook savings accounts which are *not* transferable by check? And money in certificates of deposit (CDs)? And in government securities?—Treasury bills and bonds and such? All of those are very liquid assets. Most of them can be turned into "spendable money" at a moment's notice. So should the dollar value of those highly liquid financial instruments be included when we're adding it all up to find the size of the nation's aggregate money supply? Or not?

There are some good reasons for using a very narrow definition of the money supply—for including only the most immediately and freely spendable kinds of assets. What assets? (1) currency (including coins), and travelers checks—all immediately spendable, and (2) all deposits in depository-institution checkable accounts with unlimited check-writing privileges. As you know, those are the only components included in the present definition of the nation's M1 money supply.

We Have More Than One Definition of Money

What about the many other kinds of highly liquid (but not quite as liquid) assets?—assets which are sometimes called "near-money" because they can be turned into "cash money" at a moment's notice?—assets which people hold instead of money because these assets usually pay a higher return? Aren't there some good reasons for defining the money supply more broadly, to include these other highly liquid ("near-money") assets? Yes, there are. So what do we do? We do both. *We have more than one definition of the money supply.* The broader definitions include these additional "near money" components.

THE FED DEFINES AND MONITORS THE "MONETARY AGGREGATES"

The Federal Reserve System (the Fed—briefly described in box 5-1) has the responsibility of *defining the monetary aggregates*—that is, it must decide *which ones* of the highly liquid financial instruments will be included as component parts in each of its definitions of the money supply. The Fed also has the responsibility for *monitoring and exercising control over changes in the size of the money supply*—changes in the money supply as defined by its "monetary aggregate" definitions.

What are the Monetary Aggregates?

A *monetary aggregate* is a group of carefully selected, highly liquid assets which the Fed decides to call "money." The most narrowly defined monetary aggregate (the definition of the money supply which includes the smallest number of components) is M1.

You already know that the M1 definition includes only currency, travelers checks, and checkable deposits. This narrow definition doesn't even include all

Box 5-1

Feature: A Thumbnail Sketch of the Federal Reserve System (The "Fed")

The **central bank** in the United States is not a single bank, but a "system." It consists of twelve Federal Reserve banks, one in each of the twelve Federal Reserve districts. The system is unified by the **Board of Governors** in Washington which exercises control over the entire system.

When you see references to the Federal Reserve System or the Fed, this means the entire system of banks. They all act together to implement policies established for the entire system by the Board of Governors and the **Federal Open Market Committee** (FOMC).

The FOMC consists of the seven members of the Board of Governors plus the President of the Federal Reserve Bank of New York, plus four of the other eleven Federal Reserve District bank presidents, on a rotating basis. The FOMC is a very important deliberative body because it performs the central banking function of deciding the rate at which the nation's money supply will be permitted to expand.

You'll be reading all about the Fed and the FOMC later.

---

checkable deposits. Deposits with limited check-writing privileges and deposits at nondepository institutions (e.g., brokerage accounts) are excluded from M1 and included in M2.

M2 includes everything in M1 plus several additional highly liquid components such as deposits in noncheckable passbook savings accounts and money market mutual funds.

After the M2 aggregate there's the M3 aggregate which includes everything in M2 plus some additional (highly liquid but somewhat less liquid) assets. And there's "L" (for "liquid assets") which includes everything in M3, plus more. Finally, as a very broad indicator of changes in spending power in the economy, the Fed monitors the amount of (and changes in) total nonfinancial debt outstanding in the economy.[2]

Now look at box 5-2 and you'll see the specific definitions of each of these monetary aggregates and the changing size of each, from 1984 through 1988. For changes since that time you'll need to look at table 1.21 on page A-13 in a recent issue of the *Federal Reserve Bulletin*.[3]

Why So Many Monetary Aggregates?

Why does the Fed define and monitor all these different "monetary aggregates"? Because by monitoring the changes in several monetary aggregates it's sometimes possible to get a more balanced picture of what is really happening to the nation's money supply. As Fed Board Chairman Paul Volcker said in his report to

---

[2] The total debt which the Fed monitors is defined as "total domestic nonfinancial sector debt." It includes all outstanding debt of all households, all nonfinancial businesses, and all governmental units (federal, state, and local). All government and corporate bonds, promissory notes, mortgages, installment debt, and all other nonfinancial debts are included.

[3] As you study box 5-2 you will see references to various money supply components which you do not yet understand. All of those terms will be defined and explained at appropriate times in the chapters coming up.

Box 5-2

Feature: Definitions of the Money Supply: The Components of the Various Monetary Aggregates, and the Changing Size of Each, 1984–1988

1.21 MONEY STOCK, LIQUID ASSETS, AND DEBT MEASURES[1]

Billions of dollars, averages of daily figures

Item[2]	1984 Dec.	1985 Dec.	1986 Dec.	1987 Dec.	1988 Mar.	Apr.[r]	May[r]	June
22 M1	564.5	633.5	740.6	765.9	752.1[r]	778.2	763.6	778.5
23 M2	2,373.2	2,573.9	2,821.5	2,914.8	2,958.9	2,999.3	2,989.8	3,015.8
24 M3	2,991.4	3,211.0	3,507.2	3,677.7	3,737.6[r]	3,771.8	3,768.3	3,797.1
25 L	3,532.7	3,841.4	4,151.9	4,341.9[r]	4,417.0[r]	4,461.1	4,471.9	n.a.
26 Debt	5,927.1	6,740.6	7,593.3	8,289.3[r]	8,436.8[r]	8,498.0	8,555.0	n.a.
M1 components								
27 Currency[3]	158.5	170.2	183.0	199.4	199.2	201.6	203.6	205.8
28 Travelers checks[4]	4.9	5.5	6.0	6.5	6.9	6.9	7.1	7.6
29 Demand deposits[5]	253.0	276.9	314.4	298.5	279.9	291.9	282.8	290.8
30 Other checkable deposits[6]	148.2	180.9	237.3	261.6	266.1[r]	277.8	270.1	274.3
Nontransactions components								
31 M2[7]	1,808.7	1,940.3	2,080.8	2,148.9	2,206.8[r]	2,221.1	2,226.2	2,237.3
32 M3 only[8]	618.2	637.1	685.7	762.9	778.7	772.5	778.5	781.3
Money market deposit accounts								
33 Commercial Banks	267.4	332.8	379.6	358.2	360.9[r]	360.3	356.9	360.0
34 Thrift institutions	149.4	180.8	192.9	167.0	163.8	163.0	162.6	162.4
Savings deposits[9]								
35 Commercial Banks	121.5	123.7	154.2	176.7	182.5	185.1	187.1	189.6
36 Thrift institutions	161.5	174.8	212.9	233.3	236.1	239.5	241.3	244.1
Small denomination time deposits[10]								
37 Commercial Banks	386.9	384.0	365.3	385.2	397.2	399.5	401.4	405.3
38 Thrift institutions	498.2	497.5	489.7	529.3	556.6	560.9	562.8	565.2
Money market mutual funds								
39 General purpose and broker-dealer	167.5	176.5	208.0	221.1	234.9	236.1	232.7	229.8
40 Institution-only	62.7	64.5	84.4	89.6	97.4	91.9	90.0	86.3
Large denomination time deposits[11]								
41 Commercial Banks[12]	270.9	285.4	289.1	323.6	328.5[r]	325.6	329.6	334.2
42 Thrift institutions	146.8	151.9	150.7	161.8	165.3	165.6	167.1	166.8
Debt components								
43 Federal debt	1,364.7	1,583.7	1,803.9	1,954.1	1,993.2	2,001.6	2,005.2	n.a.
44 Nonfederal debt	4,562.4	5,156.9	5,789.4	6,335.1[r]	6,443.6[r]	6,496.4	6,549.8	n.a.

1. Latest monthly and weekly figures are available from the Board's H.6 (508) release. Historical data are available from the Banking Sections, Division of Research and Statistics, Board of Governors of the Federal Reserve System, Washington, D.C. 20551.

2. Composition of the money stock measures and debt is as follows:

M1: (1) currency outside the Treasury, Federal Reserve Banks, and the vaults of depository institutions; (2) travelers checks of nonbank issuers; (3) demand deposits at all commercial banks other than those due to depository institutions, the U.S. government, and foreign banks and official institutions less cash items in the process of collection and Federal Reserve float; and (4) other checkable deposits (OCD) consisting of negotiable order of withdrawal (NOW) and automatic transfer service (ATS) accounts at depository institutions, credit union share draft accounts, and demand deposits at thrift institutions.

M2: M1 plus overnight (and continuing contract) repurchase agreements (RPs) issued by all commercial banks and overnight Eurodollars issued to U.S. residents by foreign branches of U.S. banks worldwide, MMDAs, savings and small-denomination time deposits (time deposits—including retail RPs—in amounts of less than $100,000), and balances in both taxable and tax-exempt general purpose and broker-dealer money market mutual funds. Excludes individual retirement accounts (IRA) and Keogh balances at depository institutions and money market funds. Also excludes all balances held by U.S. commercial banks, money market funds (general purpose and broker-dealer), foreign governments and commercial banks, and the U.S. government.

M3: M2 plus large-denomination time deposits and term RP liabilities (in amounts of $100,000 or more) issued by commercial banks and thrift institutions, term Eurodollars held by U.S. residents at foreign branches of U.S. banks worldwide and at all banking offices in the United Kingdom and Canada, and balances in both taxable and tax-exempt, institution-only money market mutual funds. Excludes amounts held by depository institutions, the U.S. government, money market funds, and foreign banks and official institutions. Also subtracted is the estimated amount of overnight RPs and Eurodollars held by institution-only money market mutual funds.

L: M3 plus the nonbank public holdings of U.S. savings bonds, short-term Treasury securities, commercial paper and bankers acceptances, net of money market mutual fund holdings of these assets.

Debt: Debt of domestic nonfinancial sectors consists of outstanding credit market debt of the U.S. government, state and local governments, and private nonfinancial sectors. Private debt consists of corporate bonds, mortgages, consumer credit (including bank loans), other bank loans, commercial paper, bankers acceptances, and other debt instruments. The source of data on domestic nonfinancial debt is the Federal Reserve Board's flow of funds accounts. Debt data are based on monthly averages.

3. Currency outside the U.S. Treasury, Federal Reserve Banks, and vaults of depository institutions.

4. Outstanding amount of U.S. dollar-denominated travelers checks of nonbank issuers. Travelers checks issued by depository institutions are included in demand deposits.

5. Demand deposits at commercial banks and foreign-related institutions other than those due to depository institutions, the U.S. government, and foreign banks and official institutions less cash items in the process of collection and Federal Reserve float.

6. Consists of NOW and ATS balances at all depository institutions, credit union share draft balances, and demand deposits at thrift institutions.

7. Sum of overnight RPs and overnight Eurodollars, money market fund balances (general purpose and broker-dealer), MMDAs, and savings and small time deposits.

8. Sum of large time deposits, term RPs, and term Eurodollars of U.S. residents, money market fund balances (institution-only), less the estimated amount of overnight RPs and Eurodollars held by institution-only money market funds.

9. Savings deposits exclude MMDAs.

10. Small-denomination time deposits—including retail RPs—are those issued in amounts of less than $100,000. All individual retirement accounts (IRA) and Keogh accounts at commercial banks and thrifts are subtracted from small time deposits.

11. Large-denomination time deposits are those issued in amounts of $100,000 or more, excluding those booked at international banking facilities.

12. Large-denomination time deposits at commercial banks less those held by money market mutual funds, depository institutions, and foreign banks and official institutions.

Source: *Federal Reserve Bulletin*, p. A-13.

Congress on July 20, 1983:

> No single concept or definition of money or credit aggregates can reasonably be expected always to provide reliable signals about economic performance, or about the course of monetary policy .... all definitions of "money" necessarily involve at the margin a degree of arbitrariness ....[4]

During 1985–86, the different behavior of the various aggregates (M1, M2, and M3) underscored the necessity to monitor more than one aggregate. From the fourth quarter of 1985 to June '86, the M2 and M3 aggregates were growing at between 7% and 8%—well within the "target ranges" which had been set by the Federal Open Market Committee (FOMC). But M1 was growing at about 12%—far above the Committee's target range. The charts in figure 5-1 show the picture.

In its 1986 midyear report to Congress, the Federal Reserve Board commented as follows:

> The rapid rise in M1 over the first half of the year underscored the degree of uncertainty surrounding the behavior of the aggregate and, in particular, about its behavior relative to GNP. The nature of the relationship among M1, income, and interest rates appears to have been significantly altered by the changed composition of the aggregate in recent years, as well as by the prospects for greater price stability. The Committee decided that growth of M1 in excess of the previously established 3 to 8 percent range for 1986 would be acceptable ...[5]

In his testimony to Congress during July of 1986 Fed Chairman Paul Volcker again emphasized his unwillingness—and the unwillingness of the Fed Board and the FOMC—to base monetary policy entirely (or even *largely*) on the rate of growth of M1. Volcker said:

> Experience over the first half of 1986 underscored the difficulty—I would say the impossibility—of conducting monetary policy in current circumstances according to one or two simple, pre-set criteria.
>
> ... the weight of the evidence strongly suggests that M1 alone during this period of economic and institutional transition is not today a reliable measure of future price pressures (or indeed a good short-term "leading indicator" of business activity). The more restrained performance of the broader aggregates, as well as the performance of the economy and prices themselves, point in a different direction.[6]

From these quotes it's clear that in midyear 1986 the Fed did not have much confidence in the M1 aggregate as a guide to monetary policy. M1 velocity was exhibiting a significant and unexpected slowdown and the Fed's emphasis was shifting to the M2 and M3 aggregates which were showing much greater stability.

And after that? More of the same. In his testimony to Congress on February 23, 1988 Fed Board Chairman Alan Greenspan said:

> The setting for monetary policy for the year 1988 and beyond is more than normally complex.
>
> ... uncertainties persist about key indicators of policy—the monetary aggregates—and their relation to the performance of the economy. Our approach to monetary

---

[4] Paul A. Volcker, *Monetary Policy Report to the Congress*, Federal Reserve Board, Washington, D.C., July 20, 1983, Appendix, p. 1.

[5] *Monetary Policy Objectives for 1986*, Federal Reserve Board, Washington, D.C., July 18, 1986, p. 3.

[6] *Testimony of Paul A. Volcker, Chairman, Board of Governors of the Federal Reserve System*, Federal Reserve Board, Washington, D. C., July 23, 1986, p. 3.

Figure 5-1.   Different Growth Rates of the Monetary Aggregates, 1985–86

The rate of growth of M1 far exceeded the upper limit of the Fed's target range...

While the rates of growth of M2 and M3 were well within the target ranges.

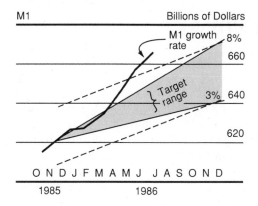

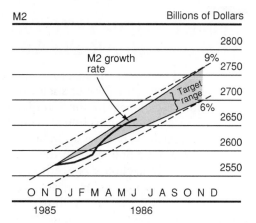

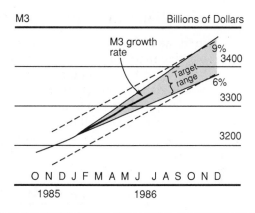

Source: *Monetary Policy Objectives for 1986*, Federal Reserve Board, Washington, D.C., July 18, 1986.

policy in 1988 will require a delicate balancing of considerations which must take account of ... the maintainence of sustainable growth in the U.S. and world economy in 1988 and beyond.

The annual ranges (target ranges for M2 and M3) are wider than in the past, recognizing that the linkage between money and credit growth and economic performance has become noticeably looser in recent years.[7]

By early 1987 the Fed had decided to stop using M1 as a target. In his testimony in February of 1987 Fed Chairman Paul Volcker explained to the Congress that the erratic behavior of M1 growth had caused this aggregate to become misleading.

---

[7] *Testimony of Alan Greenspan, Chairman, Board of Governors of the Federal Reserve System*, Federal Reserve Board, Washington, D. C., February 23, 1988, p. 2.

Now look at figure 5-2 and you'll see the different growth rates of the monetary aggregates in 1986–87. You will notice that there is no chart showing M1. That's because by 1986–87 the Fed had stopped targeting M1.

THE MONEY SUPPLY, TOTAL SPENDING, AND THE CIRCULAR FLOW

You know that the macroeconomic role of money is to support the flow of total spending. This **flow of spending** is what keeps the economy going and supports the price level. In the circular flow diagram, inputs (labor, land, capital) are flowing from households to businesses. Outputs (final goods and services) are flowing from businesses to households. That's the **real flow** of inputs and outputs. The **money flow** goes in the opposite direction to pay for the real flow.

As households are selling inputs to businesses they are receiving money in return. As businesses are selling outputs to households the money is flowing back, completing the circular flow. That's what you saw back in figure 1-1: The Circular Flow of the Economy and the Macroeconomic Role of Money.

Sometimes Increased Spending Can Generate More Output

In terms of the circular flow diagram, suppose the size of the spending flow would begin to increase—more money being paid by businesses to households and more being paid by households to businesses. The effect to this increase in spending would depend on whether or not the economy was already at *full employment*.

Suppose the economy was in a slump. Suppose households had more inputs and were ready to sell them to businesses, and businesses had excess capacity and

Figure 5-2. Different Growth Rates of the Monetary Aggregates, 1986–87

The rate of growth of M2 throughout 1987 fell far below the Fed's target range. But since the economy continued to expand it's clear that this indicator wasn't very reliable during 1987.

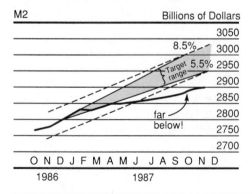

The rate of growth of M3 was also slow—barely within the target range for most of the year and falling below the range near the end of the year.

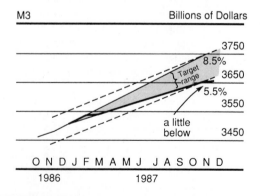

Source: *Monetary Policy Objectives for 1988,* Federal Reserve Board, Washington, D.C., February 23, 1988, p. 11.

were ready to produce and sell more outputs to households. Then the increased spending could result in increased employment and production. It could generate more real output and income.

Sometimes Increased Spending Can Only Cause Inflation

But suppose the economy was already at full employment. If the households didn't have any more inputs to sell and the businesses were already operating at full capacity, then the size of the *real flow* (the goods flow) could not increase. But you know that the dollar value of the spending flow must always be exactly equal to the dollar value of the real flow.

If total spending amounts to a million dollars that means that a million dollars is being spent. So a million dollars worth is being bought. Obviously. If spending increases and there's no increase in the quantity of real goods and services being produced, then prices must go up. The items in the existing goods flow are "revalued upward"—**inflation.**

As spending increases, output and/or prices must increase as much as necessary to keep the dollar value of the real flow equal to the dollar value of the spending flow.

How Large Should the Money Supply Be?

You already know that the size of the money supply has a lot to do with the size of the spending flow. So how large should the money supply be? It should be large enough to support a "large enough but not too large" spending flow.

The spending flow (money flow) should be large enough to support the **natural rate employment level** of the real flow. A spending flow any smaller would result in unemployment. A spending flow any larger would result in inflation. Box 5-3 explains what is meant by the "natural-rate employment level."

So the general answer to the question about the appropriate size of the money supply is easy: "Large enough to support just the right amount of spending, and no larger than that." But how large is that in terms of billions of "monetary aggregate" dollars? That question is not so easy to answer.

The companion question is: How fast should the money supply be permitted to increase? In general, that one's easy too: "Fast enough to support the natural-rate employment and output levels and a healthy rate of economic growth—but not fast enough to cause inflation." But when you try to answer the question in terms of specific rates of growth for the monetary aggregates, that isn't so easy to do either. It depends a lot on the stability (or instability) of the **velocity of circulation** (V).

The Appropriate Size of M Depends on V

The money supply influences total spending. But the money supply itself isn't spending at all. The money supply (monetary aggregate) figure is a measure of "a stock of dollars at rest." Only when people spend their dollars do they create the spending flow. And that's what generates economic activity and supports prices. The critical link between the *size of the money supply* and the *size of the*

Box 5-3

Question: Exactly What Is Meant by the "Natural Rate" of Employment, Output, and Income—and Unemployment?

In the past economists have stated as the objectives of macroeconomic policy: "Full employment, stable prices, and economic growth." All noble objectives, to be sure! But what do they mean? Does full employment mean absolutely zero unemployment at all times? And does stable prices mean absolutely zero inflation at all times? Of course not.

These days most economists refer to a **natural operating rate** for the economy—a rate fast enough so that unemployment is not a serious problem, but at the same time a rate slow enough so that there are no excess demand pressures which would cause inflation.

Most modern-day economists agree that there is some "most desirable, *long-run welfare-maximizing* operating rate" of the economy—and that when the economy operates either below or above this rate, long-run economic welfare will not be maximized, either because of too much unemployment or too much inflation.

Economists disagree about the rate of unemployment which indicates that we are at this "natural rate." Is it where unemployment is 7%? or 4%? or what? Also there is great disagreement about what, if anything, should be done if the economy moves below or above, this rate. But most economists agree that some such rate does exist—wherever it may be.

Throughout this book—and in most books these days—when you see the term "full employment," what it means is "the natural rate of employment, output and income." It means this **long-run welfare-maximizing rate**—the rate at which the economy is operating "fast enough, but not too fast"—where the employment rate is as high (and the unemployment rate as low) as it can be without causing inflation to accelerate.

spending flow, is **velocity**. So the critical question is: How fast are those money-supply dollars being spent?

If we knew exactly what the velocity of circulation (V) would be, then for each *money supply size* we'd know exactly how large the total spending flow would be. But unfortunately, most of the recent predictions about the size of and changes in velocity—especially during the "financial services revolution years" of the 1980s—usually have been far from the mark.

Money Supply Growth Must be Controlled—But How Tightly?

Should the Fed define "monetary aggregates" and try to keep the money supply growth rate within some "target range?"—even recognizing the uncertainties and arbitrary decisions required? Yes. They should, and they do.

Money supply growth definitely must be controlled. Just about everyone agrees on that. But what is the *appropriate rate* of money growth? That is the difficult and controversial question. You'll be going deeply into this question later. But meanwhile box 5-4 shows what Milton Friedman—leader of the monetarist school of thought—has to say about it.

Figure 5-3 shows how the velocity of the M1 money supply has changed since the early 1900s. From 1929 to 1946 it followed a downtrend. Then from 1946 to the early 1980s, it followed an uptrend. Throughout the 1980s the trend has been downward again.

Box 5-4

Feature: Milton Friedman's View: Give the Fed's Job to a Computer

The Fed Has No Clothes

By Milton Friedman

Every now and then a reporter asks my opinion about "current monetary policy." My standard reply has become that I would be glad to answer if he would first tell me what "current monetary policy" is. I know, or can find out, what monetary actions have been: open-market purchases and sales and discount rates at Federal Reserve Banks. I know also the federal funds rate and rates of growth of various monetary aggregates that have accompanied these actions. What I do not know is the policy that produced these actions.

Many alternative policies have been proposed. For example, undertaking monetary actions directed at attaining a specified steady numerical rate of growth of: (1) seasonally adjusted or (2) unadjusted monetary base, or (3) one or another broader monetary aggregate or (4) nominal gross national product. Or: stabilizing at a specified numerical level (5) one or another price index or (6) exchange rate or (7) index of exchange rates or (8) one or another nominal or real interest rate or (9) rate of unemployment.

However, the closest I can come to an official specification of current monetary policy is that it is to take those actions that the monetary authorities, in light of all evidence available, judge will best promote price stability and full employment—i.e., to do the right thing at the right time. But that surely is not a "policy." It is simply an expression of good intentions and an injunction to "trust us."

Examining Some Gobbledygook

The accuracy of this description can be readily documented. Consider the following excerpts from the nearly 1,000-word statement of "Monetary Policy Plans for 1988" in the Federal Reserve's Monetary Policy Report to Congress, submitted Feb. 24, 1988, in accordance with legislated requirements.

"For 1988, the [Open Market Investment] Committee set ranges of 4% to 8% for growth of M2 and M3. ... [W]hile the Committee at this time expects that growth of M2 and M3 will be around the middle of their ranges, the outcome could differ if significant changes in interest rates are required to counter unanticipated weakness in aggregate demand or an intensification of inflation. In carrying out policy, the Committee will continue to assess the behavior of the aggregates in light of information about the pace of business expansions and the source and strength of price pressures, with attention to the performance of the dollar on foreign-exchange markets and other indicators of the impact of monetary policy."

Is it inaccurate to summarize this gobbledygook as "doing the right thing at the right time"? Indeed, the one specific element—the numerical ranges for M2 and M3—is there only because Congress mandated it in 1975 over the vigorous objections of the Fed.

Such a "policy" can be used to judge present actions or anticipate future actions only through informed conjecture based on empirical extrapolation of past reactions of the Fed to a variety of stimuli, and analysis of the beliefs and attitudes of the participants in the decision-making process—that is, by statistical extrapolation and psychoanalysis. And of course there is a sizable and remunerative industry in the financial community engaged in reading the Federal Reserve tea leaves.

Contrast such a process with, at the one extreme, a policy of steady growth in the monetary base or of buying and selling gold at fixed prices; or, at the other, of stabilizing an index of basic commodity prices. The first two would yield precise predictions of monetary actions; the third would not, but at least it would provide a ready means of judging the success or failure of the monetary authorities in carrying out their stated policy and of anticipating their future actions.

I hasten to add that the present situation is not unique. On the contrary, it has persisted for nearly the entire 74 year life of the Federal Reserve System. The only exception was from the outbreak of World War II to 1951, when the Fed followed an announced policy of pegging interest rates on federal government securities. For the rest, the Fed has consistently resorted to statements of good intentions both with respect to the future and with respect to its past actions. It has claimed credit for good results and blamed forces beyond its control—generally fiscal policy—for any bad outcomes. And this avoidance of accountability has paid spectacular dividends. No major institution in the U.S. has so poor a record of performance over so long a period as the Federal Reserve, yet so high a public reputation.

To come down to cases, consider the past quarter-century, from 1962 to 1987. Growth in both monetary aggregates and prices fluctuated widely, averaging 8.5% a year in M2 and 5.5% in the GNP deflator; severe recessions occurred from 1972 to 1975 and again from 1980 to 1982; accelerating inflation reached more than 15% during the 1970s and was accompanied by stagflation, followed by drastic disinflation and wild gyrations in interest rates and economic activity.

During the prior decade (1952 to 1962), M2 grew at an average annual rate of 5.5%, and prices of 2.3%, suggesting, in line with much other experience, that monetary growth at about 3% a year was consistent with stable prices. Suppose that in 1962 the Fed had adopted a policy of increasing M2 at an annual rate of 3% to 5% year after year. It could not have stayed within that range week by week or even month by month. However, it clearly could have done so on a semi-annual or annual basis, if it had taken steady monetary growth as its overriding objective.

If monetary growth from 1982 to 1987 had averaged 4% a year instead of 8.5%, M2 currently would be roughly one-third its present level and so would the price level, implying that inflation would have averaged about 1% a year instead of 5.5%. Even more important, the country (and the world) would never have suffered the accelerating inflation of the '70s and the accompanying stagflation, or the subsequent disinflation and erratic movements in interest rates and exchange rates.

Ups and downs in the economy, in prices, interest rates and employment would still have occurred, but they would have been far milder. President Nixon would never have had occasion to impose price controls or President Carter to impose credit controls. Departure from Breton Woods would at the very least have been postponed. When it did occur, it would not have been followed by the revolution that occurred in financial markets and institutions.

[Continued on next page]

Not a Fanciful story

You can readily add to this story. And, though hypothetical, it is by no means fanciful—as is suggested by the experience of Japan, which adopted a very similar policy in 1971 under much less favorable circumstances. (Japan, under pressure from us, now appears to be departing from that policy in an inflationary direction, with, as usual, favorable initial effects. It remains to be seen whether it will revert to its earlier policy soon enough to avoid the later bad effects.

The hypothetical alternative policy would have had one other result: The news media would have paid far less attention to the Federal Reserve System. No poll would have designated the Chairman of the System as the second most powerful person in the country and far fewer people would know his name or the names of the other members of the board. The able people now earning high salaries reading the Fed tea leaves would be earning equally high salaries engaged in more productive activities. Similarly, it would be hard to attract individuals of the caliber of Arthur Burns or Paul Volcker or Alan Greenspan to serve as chairman. Why not, they might well say, turn such a boring job over to a computer? And, indeed, why not? It's my own favorite recipe for improving monetary performance.

_____

Mr. Friedman is a senior research fellow at the Hoover Institution.

_____

Source: The Wall Street Journal, Friday, April 15, 1988, p. 30.

During times when velocity is increasing (as it was most of the time between World War II and the early 1980s), money supply growth needs to be restricted enough to offset the effect of the increase in velocity. But during times when velocity is decreasing (as during the 1980s), the money supply can be permitted to grow somewhat more rapidly, without causing inflationary increases in total spending.

Figure 5-3.   The Changing Income Velocity of the M1 Money Supply, 1910–1987

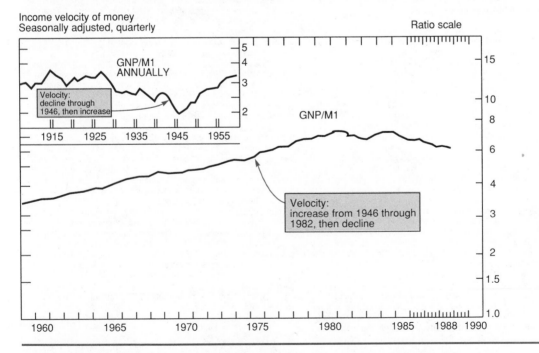

THE MONEY SUPPLY, FINANCIAL MARKETS, AND INTEREST RATES

Changes in the size of the money supply (ΔM) can influence total spending in various ways. One of the important ways is through the effect of ΔM on financial markets and interest rates.

Money supply changes have both **expectational effects** and **real effects** on financial markets. The expectational effects sometimes exert a great influence in the short run. But in the longer run, fundamental demand and supply conditions exert greater control.

Short-Run Expectational Effects of Money Supply Changes

Suppose the money supply is expanding more rapidly than members of the financial community think it should. And suppose the lenders (bond-buyers) and the borrowers (bond-sellers) both expect the expanding money supply to result in inflation.

Everyone knows that inflation reduces the real value of money. So lenders will require higher rates of interest to offset the effects of inflation. And borrowers will be willing to pay higher rates so that they can buy now before prices rise. So in the financial markets there is a reduced supply and an increased demand for **loanable funds**. Money gets tight. Interest rates rise. Now read box 5-5, and then look at figure 5-4 and you will see a supply-and-demand graph which illustrates expectational effects in the bond markets.

Here's another expectational effect of rapid money-growth. When the members of the financial community think the money supply is expanding too rapidly, they may expect the Fed to tighten money—to try to reduce the danger of inflation. If the Fed tightens, that will force interest rates up. When borrowers (bond-sellers) expect the Fed to push rates higher, they try to borrow now, before the rates rise. This creates a further increase in the demand for funds. The demand curve in figure 5-4 shifts to the right even more. Interest rates are pushed up even more.

At the same time, lenders (bond-buyers) also begin to expect the Fed to tighten and interest rates to rise. So they delay their lending (bond-buying) to wait for the

---

Box 5-5

Question: Is It Correct to Say Loanable Funds? Lendable Funds? Borrowable Funds? Or What?

The term "supply and demand for **loanable funds**" is commonly used to refer to the supply of and demand for funds in the financial markets. It would perhaps be more accurate to refer to the supply of **lendable funds** and to the demand for **borrowable funds**. But such terminology would be cumbersome and really isn't necessary. So throughout this book you will see the commonly-used terminology: "supply and demand for loanable funds."

Figure 5-4. Expectational Effects of Increasing the Money Supply

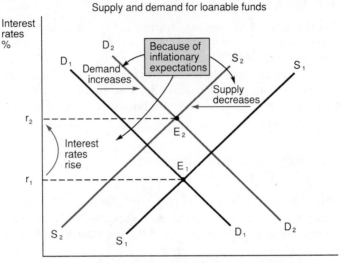

Supply and demand for loanable funds

Quantity of funds demanded and supplied

Inflationary expectations cause lenders to be less willing to lend, and borrowers, more eager to borrow. So the supply of loanable funds decreases while the demand increases. Money becomes tight and interest rates rise, even though (in fact, *because!*) the money supply is increasing.

Borrowers who expect inflation want to obtain more funds so that they can buy goods now before prices rise. So the demand for funds increases.

Lenders who expect inflation are less willing to lend at present nominal interest rates because **expected inflation** lowers expected real rates. So the supply of funds decreases.

Increased demand and decreased supply in the loanable funds market cause interest rates to rise from i1 to i2.

Note: Economists use both the letter "i" and the letter "r" to refer to the interest rate. Sometimes these letters are used interchangeably, but more frequently the letter "i" is used to refer to the *nominal* (market) rate of interest, while the letter "r" is used to refer to the *real* rate.

Nominal rate vs. real rate: The real rate, *ex ante* (before the fact) is the nominal rate minus the expected rate of inflation. *Ex post* (after the fact) the real rate is the nominal rate minus the actual observed inflation rate.

higher rates. This reduces the supply of available funds in the financial markets. The supply curve in figure 5-4 shifts leftward even more. Interest rates are pushed up even more.

During the late 1970s and early 1980s these *expectational effects* had a major influence on short-run interest rate fluctuations. This is one of the reasons why, during the early 1980s the "science" of predicting the future course of interest rates became extremely hazardous, and the results, often highly inaccurate.

The Fundamental Effects of Money Supply Changes on Interest Rates

Suppose we push aside the expectational effects and focus on the fundamentals. Then the results we get are completely opposite. Assuming no changes in expectations, an increase in the size of the money supply will tend to push interest rates lower—not higher.

When M increases, some people begin to find that the quantities of money they are holding are greater than the quantities they want to hold (M > Mqd). So they begin trying to get rid of their surplus dollars. Some of the dollars may be spend for goods and services. Some may be deposited and then lent through financial intermediaries (banks, savings and loans, etc.). Some may be spent as direct investments in financial instruments—for stocks, bonds, etc.

The ultimate result will be that a greater supply of funds will flow into the financial markets. The greater *supply of funds* will create a greater *demand for financial instruments* (securities). The prices of securities will be forced upward. As security prices rise, interest rates will fall.

The Loanable Funds Market and the Debt Securities Market: The Same Market!

Now study figure 5-5 and you'll see these **fundamental effects** of an increase in the money supply. Also you'll see that the supply and demand for **loanable funds** is exactly the same as the supply and demand for **debt securities**, looked at from the opposite point of view. These are *two different ways of looking at exactly the same financial market.*

The supply and demand graphs in figure 5-5 show what happens when M increases so that M is greater than Mqd. Immediately there is an increase in the supply of loanable funds—which means: an increase in the demand for debt securities. Interest rates for loanable funds go down; prices of debt securities go up.

The graphs in figure 5-5 illustrate the "fundamentally correct" response of financial markets to an increase in the money supply. During the last half of the 1980s these fundamentals had much more influence than in the late 1970s and early '80s. Why? Because by the mid-1980s inflationary expectations had subsided.

The indeterminance of the outcome of an expansion in the money supply—depending on whether or not the fundamental effects or the expectational effects dominate—can make interest rate forecasting a very hazardous occupation. And you can imagine the difficulty it adds to the Fed's task of deciding on and carrying out monetary policy.

During the 6-year period 1983–88 the U.S. inflation rate remained low and stable at less than 4 percent. The longer the economy maintains this low rate of inflation, the more likely it is that the **supply and demand fundamentals** will exert the major influence on financial markets and interest rates. And that' a desirable outcome because it will make interest rate forecasting and monetary policy decisions much more reliable than in the high-inflation environment of the late 1970s and early 80s. But when you read professor Alan Blinder's comments in box 5-6 you'll see that in 1988 inflationary expectations still were having a significant impact on the financial markets.

Figure 5-5.   Fundamental Effects of an Increase in M. The Supply of Loanable Funds Increases, Which Means That the Demand for Bonds Increases

A. The loanable funds market
Increased M brings increased
supply of loanable funds and
decreased interest rates

B. The debt securities market
Increased M brings increased
demand, higher prices, and
lower yeilds for debt securities
(bonds paying $100/yr)

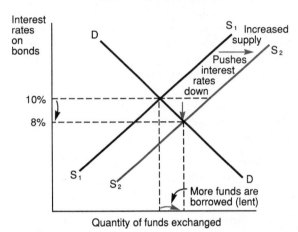

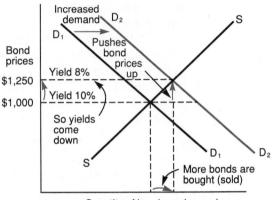

The interest rate begins at 10%. Then the increased supply of loanable funds creates a surplus of funds in the financial markets. So the "price" (interest rate) begins to fall. It continues to fall until the quantity demanded increases enough and the quantity supplied decreases enough to eliminate the surplus supply of loanable funds. The market reaches equilibrium when the interest rate falls to 8%.

These bonds pay $100 per year. So at the initial price of $1,000 they yield 10%. Then more loanable funds come into the financial markets. People begin buying up these bonds and create a shortage. Bond prices go up until the quantity supplied increases and the quantity demanded decreases enough to eliminate the shortage. The market reaches equilibrium at a price of $1,250, at which the $100/yr. bonds yield 8%.

These two graphs depict the same financial market, but from two different points of view. The **supplier of loanable funds** is the **demander** of debt securities. The **supplier of debt securities** is the **demander** of loanable funds. We can look at this market from either perspective. The results always must be the same. It's the same market!

Note: If you don't have a perfectly clear understanding of *why* these two graphs are saying exactly the same thing, and *why* the downward movement of interest rates from 10% to 8% is precisely equivalent to the upward movement of bond prices from $1,000 to $1,250, then please go back to chapter 3 and read the section "Understanding and Measuring Interest Rates and Bond Yields," and then go to chapter 4 and read the box titled, "Question: Exactly why is it that when prices of financial assets go up, interest rates fall?"

SUMMARY

- This chapter deals with *monetary theory*: the way in which changes in the size of the money supply influence the macroeconomy.

- Money is "the exchange medium." Money is "purchasing power." Money is "liquidity."

- M1 includes currency and coins, travelers checks, and checkable accounts at depository institutions.

Box 5-6

Feature: Alan Blinder's View of the "Natural Rate" of Unemployment

Balancing The Equation Between Inflation and Joblessness

By ALAN S. BLINDER

Reprinted from February 15, 1988 issue of *Business Week* by special permission, © 1988 by McGraw-Hill, Inc.

Like it or not, there is a point at which fuller employment tends to nudge inflation higher. Today that 'natural' rate may be around 5.5%—meaning the economy still has room to grow without strain

The U.S. economy quietly passed a landmark in December when the civilian unemployment rate dropped to 5.8% for the first time since 1979. The stock market celebrated the good news by plunging. More significantly, the decrease in joblessness gives practical importance to a question that has been strictly academic so far in the 1980s: How low can we push down the unemployment rate before we start to encounter serious capacity constraints and inflationary pressure? In economists' jargon, what is the "natural" rate of unemployment?

This question has been hotly debated in academia for years, but policymakers could safely afford to ignore it while the unemployment rate topped 7%. Now that we're finally below 6%, the issue demands attention, for it is fundamental to the proper conduct of macroeconomic policy. If the natural rate is 6% or more, we already may be stirring the slumbering inflationary dragon, and sluggish growth in 1988 would be welcome. But if the natural rate is 5% or less, we ought to push for more rapid economic growth.

I will argue shortly that the natural rate is probably 5.5% or a bit less. But first it is useful to clarify what the concept does and does not mean.

FLASH POINT? Milton Friedman coined the term "natural rate of unemployment" two decades ago to signify the level of joblessness at which inflation would neither rise nor fall in the absence of outside influences, such as a change in energy prices. The natural rate is not a magical flash point below which inflation surges and above which it drops precipitously. Rather, small departures from the natural rate in either direction lead to very gradual changes in inflation. Nevertheless, the natural· rate of unemployment is still a sensible—shall I say natural?—long-run target for macroeconomic

policy because no one wants inflation either to rise or to fall indefinitely.

Some people react negatively to the natural-rate concept as a conservative or defeatist notion because it suggests settling for an unemployment rate—say, 5.5%—that is uncomfortably high. But a theory is not false simply because its implications are unpleasant. When physicists assure us that we cannot build a perpetual-motion machine, we do not shun their advice as too pessimistic—we set about doing the best we can within the limits imposed by nature. Similarly, the validity of the natural-rate theory depends on scientific evidence, not on whether the idea is cheerful or doleful. At present, the weight of the evidence seems to favor the theory—at least for the U.S.

Others reject the natural-rate concept because the adjective suggests something foreordained and immutable. That is simply a misunderstanding. Most determinants of the natural rate—such as labor-force composition, unemployment insurance, unionization, education and training programs, the minimum wage, and the welfare system—are man-made and at least somewhat manipulable. If we find the natural rate too high for our liking, we can try to lower it. The natural rate is natural only in the limited sense that it cannot be lowered simply by increasing aggregate demand. More subtle labor-market policies are necessary.

HOW MANY FACTORS? The natural rate varies through time, and estimates of it are always uncertain. In the 1960s many people thought it was 4%, although subsequent research suggests that 4.5% or 5% might have been a better guess. The natural rate probably increased during the 1960s and 1970s because of an influx of inexperienced workers into the labor force, the spread of unemployment benefits, rising minimum wages, and other factors. By 1980 expert opinion held that the natural rate of unemployment was near 6%, with most dissenters favoring a higher number. My own estimate was 5.8%—the average unemployment rate actually attained in 1979.

If 5.8% was correct in 1979, today's natural rate should be somewhat less than 5.5%, mainly because the labor force has relatively fewer inexperienced teenagers than it did then. This factor shaves about a third of a point off the figure. Other factors, though more difficult to quantify, also point to a falling natural rate since 1979: Unemployment benefits reach a smaller fraction of the unemployed, the real minimum wage has fallen considerably, and labor unions are weaker than they were.

But wait. If the natural rate really is 5.5% or less, why did inflation accelerate in 1987? An outside influence, the cost of energy, provides most of the answer. After falling about 20% in 1986, energy prices rose approximately 8% in 1987—adding more than two percentage points to inflation. Most of the rest of the acceleration is traceable to higher import prices, a consequence of the lower dollar. Signs of inflationary pressures in the labor market are harder to find. For example, unit labor costs rose just 1.6% during the past four quarters, slower than in the previous two years.

If the natural rate is just less than 5.5% today, our economy still has some margin for expansion before it enters the inflationary danger zone. Wall Street should learn to stop fretting over each tidbit of good economic news.

- The other monetary aggregates (M2, M3, and L) include other highly liquid (but somewhat less liquid "near-money") assets. The Fed also monitors total debt.

- The money supply is the total stock of dollars in existence at a point in time. Total spending consists of the money supply (M) *times the velocity of circulation (V)*.

- During the 1980s, velocity (and the demand for money) has behaved in unpredicted ways. This has made the Fed's monetary policy task exceedingly difficult.

- **Financial markets** can be analyzed from the point of view of the supply and demand (1) for loanable funds, or (2) for debt securities. An increase in *the demand for loanable funds* is the same thing as an increase in *the supply of debt securities*.

- The interest-rate effects of an increase in the money supply depend on both **fundamental** and **expectational** influences. If money growth triggers inflationary expectations, interest rates may be pushed up—not down. That sometimes happened in the late 1970s and early 80s.

- There is general agreement that *the nation's money supply should be monitored and its growth limited*. But there is much disagreement about which **monetary aggregates** to target, and then **how tightly** the growth of this monetary aggregate should be restricted.

Important Principles, Issues, Concepts, Terms

General definitions of money

The monetary aggregates: M1, M2, M3, L, Total Debt

How large should the money supply be? Depends on V (or, Mqd).

Role of money in the circular flow of the economy

Effects of changes in the size of the money supply

Problems caused by changes in velocity

Problems of defining the monetary aggregates

Natural rate of employment, output, and income

Fundamental influences of ΔM on interest rates

Expectational influences of ΔM on interest rates

The supply and demand for loanable funds

The supply and demand for debt securities

Monetary theory

Monetary policy

Disagreements regarding appropriate monetary policy

Questions for Thought and Discussion

1. When you calculate the velocity of circulation of money for some past year, the figure you come up with depends a lot on which highly liquid assets you decide to include in your chosen "monetary aggregate." Explain.

2. The question of how large the money supply should be and of the rate at which it should be permitted to grow is easy to answer in general, but very difficult to answer in specific terms. Explain what all this means and why it is true.

3. If some of the monetary aggregates which the Fed monitors are not really "money" then why does the Fed monitor them? Explain.

4. Sometimes increased spending generates more output; at other times only inflation. Explain why this is true, in terms of the circular flow diagram and the "natural rate" idea.

5. When the money supply increases, this could cause interest rates to either go up or go down, depending on ... what? Explain, and use supply-and-demand graphs to illustrate.

6. In the explanation of figure 5-4 there is an explanation of the meaning of the *real rate* of interest: *ex ante*, and *ex post*.
   Can you explain these two different meanings of "real rate?" Try.

7. During the 1980s, the velocity of the M1 money behaved in unexpected ways. De-

scribe this behavior, then discuss some of the possible reasons for this.

8. In this chapter there is an article by professor Milton Friedman in which he recommends that the Fed's money supply control function be replaced by a computer, programmed to permit the money supply to grow at a constant rate, year after year, no matter what. But in this chapter you also read opposite statements by Paul Volcker, former Fed Chairman, and Alan Greenspan who was appointed to the Chairmanship in midyear 1987. Both Volcker and Greenspan said that in today's environment it would not be appropriate to follow Friedman's suggested "money growth rule." Volcker said that the relationships between the growth rate of the money supply and conditions in the macroeconomy were not sufficiently dependable to permit the money supply growth rate to serve as the only—or even the most important—guide to monetary policy.

   What do you think about this issue? It's very early in this book, and certainly premature for you to be thinking about the answer to such a complex issue. But it's a very important question today. Do you think the Fed should follow a "money growth rule" and let a computer do the job? Or should the day-to-day discretion of the Federal Open Market Committee continue to set monetary policy? Discuss.

Suggested Readings

Balbach, Anatol. "How Controllable is Money Growth?" Federal Reserve Bank of St. Louis, *Review* 63 (April 1981): 3–12.

Duprey, James N. "How the Fed Defines and Measures Money." Federal Reserve Bank of Minneapolis, *Quarterly Review* (Spring/Summer 1982): 10–19.

Friedman, Milton, and Anna J. Schwartz. *A Monetary History of the United States, 1867–1960.* Princeton, N.J.: Princeton University Press, 1963.

Kane, Edward J. "Selecting Monetary Targets in a Changing Financial Environment." Federal Reserve Bank of Kansas City, *Monetary Policy Issues in the 1980s* (1982).

Lane, Timothy D. "The Rationale for Money-Supply Targets: A Survey." *Manchester School of Economic and Social Studies* (June 1955); 179–207.

McMillin, W. D. and J. S. Fackler. "Monetary vs. Credit Aggregates: An Evaluation of Monetary Policy Targets." *Southern Economic Journal.* 53(3) (January 1987); 3–16.

Morris, Frank. "Do the Monetary Aggregates Have a Future as Targets of Federal Reserve Policy?" Federal Reserve Bank of Boston, *New England Economic Review* (March/April 1982): 5–14.

Simpson, Thomas D. "The Redefined Monetary Aggregates." *Federal Reserve Bulletin* (February 1980); 97–114.

Taylor, Herbert. "Interest Rates: How Much Does Expected Inflation Matter?" Federal Reserve Bank of Philadelphia, *Business Review* (July/August 1982): 3–12.

PART II

Overview of the Evolution of and the 1980s Revolution in the Banking and Financial System

PART II describes the evolution of, and more recently the ongoing revolution in the institutional structure of the U.S. banking system. The purpose of this part is to provide some depth of understanding about the past, present, and future outlook for the changing structure and functions of the depository financial institutions.

From this part you will gain an understanding of the way in which the U.S. banking system evolved, the important developments and changes, and especially the major (revolutionary!) changes which occurred (1) during the Great Depression of the 1930s, and again (2) during the turbulent years of the 1980s.

Chapter 6 traces the evolution of commercial banks, from the beginning up the end of the 1970s. Chapter 7 does the same for the thrift institutions.

Chapter 8 explains the conditions which led to, and then gives the highlights of the very significant changes which have occurred and which continue to occur in both the structure and functions of the depository financial institutions—that is, it explains the 1980s *Revolution in Banking*. Then chapter 9 gives an overview of the evolution of the structure and functions of the central bank of the United States—the Federal Reserve System.

After you complete your study of Part II you will have a good overview understanding of the U.S. banking system: how it evolved, its changing structure and functions, the important and changing role of the Federal Reserve System, and the revolutionary changes which have been rapidly transforming the U.S. banking system and the entire financial services industry.

CHAPTER 6

Evolution of the U.S. Banking System I: Focus on Commercial Banks

Chapter Objectives

The purpose of this chapter and the next is to present the historical highlights in the evolution of the U.S. banking and financial system. In this chapter the emphasis is on the commercial banks. After you study this chapter you will understand and be able to explain:

1. The origins of commercial banking.
2. The functions of the **First and Second Banks of the United States**.
3. Banking and currency conditions in the United States prior to the Civil War.
4. The **National Banking System**: Why it was set up, what it hoped to accomplish, what it achieved, and problems with the system.
5. How the "dual banking system" evolved.
6. The events leading to the establishment of the **Federal Reserve System**.
7. The aims, and major provisions of the banking legislation of the 1930s.
8. Different organizational forms of banks: Unit banks, branch banking, multibank holding companies, and one-bank holding companies.
9. The structure of bank regulation and supervision: Comptroller of the Currency, the Federal Reserve, FDIC, state regulators, and the issue of "regulatory consolidation."

THE EARLY DEVELOPMENT OF BANKING

Throughout recorded history someone has always been performing the banking (money-lending) function. Many times in many societies the money lenders have been condemned as **usurers** and outlawed or supressed. But they have never been permanently stamped out.

During the Renaissance period in western Europe, as trade and commerce grew, the role of bankers grew. Then as the Western world moved into the Industrial Revolution there was a great expansion in commerce. Money and banking expanded rapidly to facilitate that commerce.

Goldsmiths Become Bankers

During the Middle Ages, in several places in Europe goldsmiths evolved into bankers. People would leave their gold and silver coins for safekeeping. Soon the goldsmiths found that they could make money by lending these coins to other people. As long as they kept enough coins on hand to meet withdrawals, no problem!

As time went on, the goldsmiths discovered that they could issue receipts for gold and silver coins—for example the receipt might say "payable to the bearer on demand, one gold crown"—and people would use these receipts as money. So A-ha!

The goldsmiths can have large numbers of these "receipts" printed up and then lend these to borrowers. Earning interest on printed pieces of paper? What a way to get rich!. As the years passed, the **goldsmith bankers** flourished, and the money supply expanded to meet the needs of expanding trade.

Early Banking in North America

In the American colonies, as economic activity and trade expanded, banking also expanded. When the United States was established as a nation (in 1789) there were many banks in all of the thirteen states. There was great variety, in size, safety, and even *honesty* among these banks. (Sometimes the unscrupulous have been attracted to banking!)

Currency (paper money and coins) was issued by the government. But paper money was also issued by the banks. The goldsmith approach? Right! Earning interest on printed paper. But there's a catch.

The bank is supposed to have some gold coins in its vault to "pay off" those notes whenever anyone comes in and demands gold. But why would anyone do that? It's easier to carry around paper money than to carry gold coins.

As long as everyone is sure that the bank would give them the gold anytime they wanted it, then nobody asks for it. So a bank with a good reputation can keep a very small amount of gold in its vault and issue a very large amount of currency and make very large profits. Many banks did just that.

There Was No Nationwide Regulation of Banking

Under the common law *anyone could engage in banking*. It wasn't until after the 1800s that the states began to restrict banking by requiring corporate charters.

The first modern-type, incorporated bank in this country was the **Bank of North America**, which started doing business in Philadelphia in 1782. In 1790 there were only three incorporated banks in the country: the Bank of North America, plus the Bank of New York and the Bank of Massachusetts, both established in 1784.

The banks were regulated (if at all) by the states. In many cases there wasn't much regulation. So what could the federal government (which is charged by the U.S. Constitution with overseeing and controlling the nation's money) do about this lack of regulation? One approach would be to establish a government bank—a "Bank of the United States"—to perform some **central banking** functions. Ultimately that's what happened.

U.S. Banking Legislation: Reaction to Crisis

The history of banking in the United States is a very interesting history of economic, political, and philosophical conflict. It's a history of federalism vs. states rights, centralization vs. decentralization, industrialization vs. agriculture, big business vs. small business, concentration vs. dispersion of economic power—and is deeply involved with basic issues concerning the appropriate role of government in the economy.

These conflicts were very much in evidence as the Congress debated banking legislation in the 1790s. Many of these conflicts are still very much in evidence 200 years later as the Congress debates banking legislation for the 1990s.

Only when conditions get to the **near-crisis** stage—only when it is absolutely clear that *something must be done*—only then do we get major banking legislation. That was true in the 1790s. It is still true. (See Box 6-1.)

NATIONWIDE BANKS: THE FIRST AND SECOND BANKS OF THE UNITED STATES

In 1789–90, Alexander Hamilton and the Federalists and others who favored political centralization supported the establishment of a **Bank of the United States**. Many of them were in favor of denying the states the power to charter and supervise banks—but they lost this one.

Thomas Jefferson and the agrarianists who opposed the centralization of political power and were strong proponents of states rights were bitterly opposed to establishing a U.S. Bank. Their charge: Unconstitutional! But the Federalists won this one.

The First Bank of the United States: 1791–1811

The **First U.S. Bank** was a nationwide commercial bank which also performed some central banking (treasury-servicing and money-control) functions. This bank was partly owned by the federal government and partly by private stockholders. It held the deposits of and served as banker for the federal government and it acted as "watchdog over the nation's currency" by trying to keep the state banks honest.

The First U.S. Bank had ten branches, each located in one of the growing cities, mostly along the East Coast. All of these branches operated as regular commercial banks. So they were in competition with the (much smaller) state banks.

Also, as depositors brought state bank notes to the U.S. bank, the U.S. bank would present these notes to the state banks, demanding gold. This forced the state banks to *limit their note issues*, and to *keep adequate reserves*.

The state banks weren't happy about the competition from the U.S. bank. And they certainly weren't thrilled about having to limit their note issues and having to pay out their gold reserves!

When the first bank's 20-year charter came up for renewal in 1911, there was a storm of state-bank protest. The charter-renewal legislation was defeated by a narrow margin.

Box 6-1

Congressional Negotiations on Banking Legislation

Compromising Positions

When House and Senate negotiators this week meet to settle their differences over banking bills, they'll also add to a long and sometimes loony legacy that has shaped current banking law.

By JAY ROSENSTEIN

A Massive banking bill passed by the Senate in late 1979 proposed a modest increase in federal deposit insurance coverage from $40,000 to $50,000 per account, an intended adjustment for inflation. But the vastly different House-passed bill left the $40,000 insurance level untouched. When it came time to settle their differences, negotiators from the two sides "compromised" at $100,000.

That crucial decision came without hearings, without detailed research, and apparently without enthusiastic support from the Federal Deposit Insurance Corp. or the Federal Savings and Loan Insurance Corp.

Welcome to the wild, wonderful, rare, and unpredictable world of House-Senate conference committees.

Members of the House and Senate Banking Committees will start this year's major conference committee tomorrow to try to resolve differences between their respective chambers over major banking legislation. This includes a rescue plan for the ailing FSLIC—a situation some observers say was created in part by the 1980 decision to boost deposit insurance coverage—and proposed limits on the growth of commercial banks and their non-bank competitors.

It has been five years since the last of the big-time conferences was held. That was the 1982 session from which emerged the Garn-St Germain Act that bolstered the nation's savings and loan industry and gave some new powers to depository institutions.

"There's really one similarity running through conferences, and that is that they are very unpredictable," says Kenneth Guenther, executive vice president of the Independent Bankers Association of America. "I know, particularly when you're the outside people looking in, there are times of considerable anxiety."

Adds another banking industry lobbyist here who declined to be identified, "That move to $100,000 insurance in 1980 shows one thing. A lot of legislation is being written in conference, not in the committees."

Use of the conference committee as a device for ironing out differences between the House and Senate dates back to the beginning of Congress. The first, held in June 1789—just two months after the new Congress began lawmaking—was to settle differences over "laying a duty on goods, wares and merchandizes imported into the United States."

Many of the major banking bills of modern times were finalized in a conference when the House and Senate couldn't reach an agreement on key points. Among them: the creation of the Federal Reserve System in 1913; establishment of the Federal Deposit Insurance Corp. in 1933; the Glass-Steagall Act of 1933 that separated commercial banking from investment banking; limits on the ownership and powers of bank holding companies in 1970; and the phaseout of interest rate ceilings on deposits in 1980.

Not all differences get settled before or during a conference committee. Many still get settled the old fashioned way—over the telephone or in the hallway—and then go right to the floor of the House and Senate.

A classic example was the massive banking bill of 1978. A busy Congress was set to adjourn for the year, and most of the bets were for approving only another extension of deposit rate ceilings. But in a frantic 34-hour marathon that went back and forth from back rooms to the open chambers of the House and Senate, the weary-eyed law-makers at 7 a.m. on a Sunday morning finalized a major package. It included a two-year extension of deposit rate ceilings, new supervisory tools for federal regulators, and something for just about everyone.

. . .

Just how this week's conference committee will rank on the list of all-time banking conferences also is hard to size up.

. . .

The House is entering the negotiations with a limited bill; the Senate comes in with a much broader proposal. Which side will give in on what points, why, and what will the agreement mean? If history is any guide, we may never really know.

Source: BANKING WEEK June 22, 1987, p. 3.

Explosive Growth of State Banks and Bank Notes: 1811–1816

After 1811 the only banks were state-chartered banks and unchartered private banks. During the War of 1812 the number of state banks and the value of their note issues grew explosively. In the five-year period from 1811 to 1816 the number of state banks approximately tripled (from about 80 in 1811 to 246 in 1816) and the value of their outstanding notes more than doubled (from less than $50 million to more than $100 million).

By 1816 most of the state banks were refusing to redeem their notes in gold or silver. Some of the notes were worthless. Near-crisis conditions existed in the money and financial markets. So it was time for the balance to shift the other way—to charter the Second Bank of the United States.

The Second Bank of the United States: 1816–1836

The **Second U.S. Bank** was established in 1816—again with a 20-year charter. And again the legislation passed by a narrow margin.

The Second Bank performed the same functions as the First Bank, but it was much larger. It was truly a nationwide bank, with branches (25) located in all of the populated areas of the country. But it only lasted 20 years.

As the bank's charter was nearing expiration the opposition forces were strong. This time there was a political and personality clash between Nicholas Biddle, President of the Second Bank, and Andrew Jackson, President of the United States.

Biddle openly opposed Jackson's reelection in 1832, and the future of the bank became an important campaign issue. So when Jackson was reelected, the charter-renewal was dead. In 1836 the bank was rechartered as a state bank in Pennsylvania, but after that it only survived for a few years.

Exactly What Was a "Bank of the United States"?

Was a Bank of the United States a central bank? Or a commercial bank? Was it a government bank? Or a private bank? In fact it was all of these.

Each Bank of the United States during its 20-year period of existence was by far the largest commercial bank in the country. It was a nationwide bank which issued notes, took deposits, made loans, and tried to make profit for its stockholders.

The federal government held 20 percent of the stock, but the other 80 percent was held by private investors, both domestic and foreign. So it was a 20 percent government and 80 percent private bank. But it was also a **central bank**.

In addition to performing fiscal functions for the government, it tried to maintain the stability of the nation's currency by (1) issuing sound bank notes which were immediately convertible into gold or silver and (2) presenting state bank notes to the issuing banks and demanding gold or silver.

Should central banking powers have been exercised by a largely private, profit seeking enterprise? One which *competes with* (for profits) and at the same time attempts to *regulate* the other banks in the nation? Perhaps not. Economic historians disagree about that.

State Banking (Wildcat Banking? Banking Anarchy?) 1836–1863

Except in a few states, the essential "money and banking function" was poorly performed during the period from 1836 to the time of the Civil War.

In the early 1800s most of the states had tightened the rules so that private (unincorporated) banks were no longer permitted. After that, only banks with charters granted by the state could continue to operate. But charters were only granted by special act of the legislature. So you don't have any friends in the legislature? You haven't helped to support the party in power? And you want a bank charter? No chance!

The So-Called "Free Banking" Laws. First Michigan (in 1837) and soon thereafter New York and then other states enacted **general bank-incorporation laws**. These laws permitted any banking corporation which could meet the requirements of the law to apply for and receive a bank charter.

In some states (notably Massachusetts, New York, and Louisiana) the requirements were strict and well enforced. Note issues were limited and adequate capital and reserves were required. But in most states the requirements were either inadequate or poorly enforced.

Wildcat Banking. Under the circumstances what would you expect? Unscrupulous people established banks and tried to locate them in out of-the-way places (so its note-holders would have difficulty finding the bank to exchange the notes for gold and silver) and then issuing a flood of notes and getting very rich. Wildcat banking? Yes. Locate your bank so far out in the woods that only a wildcat can find it!

An Up-to-Date "Currrency Guide" Was Required. Suppose you were in a retail business at that time. You would need a *currency guide*, constantly updated, listing all of the thousands of different kinds of banknotes and indicating the latest value of each. Or you could insist on accepting only gold or silver coins. But if you do that you'll soon be out of business. Not everyone has gold and silver coins!

The states of New York, Massachusetts, Louisiana, and some others provided good examples for others to try to follow. But political pressures on both sides of the "bank regulation and control" question are always strong. And legislation depends more on politics than on economics.

The only nationwide answer would be for legislation at the federal level. That legislation finally came during the Civil War in the form of the **National Currency Act** in 1863. Then that act was significantly amended to become the **National Banking Act** in 1864.

THE NATIONAL BANKING SYSTEM: 1864–1914

The 1863–64 legislation was designed to accomplish two things:

1. Create **a new market for government bonds** to finance the Civil War.
2. Provide the nation with **a sound and dependable currency**.

Congress killed both these birds with one stone.

Federal Chartering and Supervision of Privately-Owned Banks

The National Banking Act was patterned after state banking laws, especially those of New York. The act did not establish a government bank. Nor did it establish (or permit) any nationwide bank. What it did was to establish *a system for chartering individual banks and then for supervising those banks by the federal government.* This was the first entry of the federal government into private bank chartering, supervision, and regulation.

The act established the office of **Comptroller of the Currency** in the Treasury Department to grant charters, to conduct bank examinations, and to administer all of the laws regarding national banks.

Note Issues Backed 100% by U.S. Government Bonds

The Act stated that these newly-chartered national banks could issue notes only up to 90 percent of the value of government bonds which the bank had bought and then deposited with the Comptroller of the Currency. So a bank with $1,000 in government bonds deposited with the comptroller was permitted to issue $900 in notes.

The new banks could print up $900 in notes, add in $100 of their own money and then buy a $1,000 government bond and leave it on deposit with the comptroller. The government got the money it needed (newly printed national bank notes) to finance the war, while the national banks earned interest on $1,000 when they only had to put up $100 plus some newly-printed paper.

The national bank notes were **guaranteed** by the Comptroller of the Currency. If a bank failed, the comptroller would sell that bank's bonds and use the proceeds to pay off the note-holders. So the notes were completely safe and circulated at par.

National Bank Requirements Were Fairly Stringent

Who was eligible to apply for and receive a charter to become a national bank? Anyone! All you had to do was to: (1) meet the requirements for *capital adequacy*, (2) maintain the *reserves* required both for your circulating banknotes and for your deposits, (3) *invest* in only those kinds of (safe and dependable) assets specified in the act, (4) *issue banknotes* only in accordance with the detailed regulations in the act, and (5) provide periodic *reports* on your financial condition and be open to *examination* by federal bank examiners.

State banks which met the requirements could apply for federal charters and become national banks. But why should they? Most of the state banking laws had lower capital requirements, lower reserve requirements, more liberal lending and asset-ownership powers and involved less supervision. It soon became evident that the national banking system was not going to fly without some additional push!

State Bank Notes Were Taxed Out of Existence

To get the state-chartered banks out of the note-issuing business—which, at the time, meant *out of the banking business*—the Congress passed an annual 10 percent tax on their notes. Needless to say, it wasn't very long before all of those notes disappeared. Finally the country had—really for the first time—a sound and uniform currency system: a system of **national bank notes**.

At first the number of state banks declined significantly. Many of them applied for and recieved national bank charters. Some, denied the note-issue privilege, went out of business. In general, if you couldn't issue notes, you couldn't make loans because borrowers wanted currency. And if you couldn't make loans, you couldn't make it in the banking business. But about that time, something was happening that was soon to change all that.

During the post–Civil War period, **demand deposits** (checking accounts) began growing rapidly, replacing currency as the medium of exchange in an increasing number of transactions. There was nothing to say that a state bank couldn't offer checking accounts! So they did—and it was on this basis that they survived and grew.

State Banks Survive and Grow: A "Dual Banking System"

There were more than 1000 state banks in 1864. Four years later (in 1868) the number was down to less than 300. And by 1868 the number of national banks was up to more than 1600. But then came the turnaround.

By 1990 there were more than 5000 state banks and only about 3700 national banks. By 1914 (the year the Federal Reserve System began operating) there were about 17,500 state banks and only about 7500 national banks.

Although it wasn't planned that way, the national banking system really resulted in a **dual banking system**—a system of nationally chartered and regulated banks side by side and intermeshed with a heterogeneous system of state-chartered and state-regulated banks. And this is the U.S. banking system which still exists today. And it's true not only of commercial banks. As you'll be reading in the next chapter, that's the pattern throughout the thrift industry, too.

NATIONAL BANKING CRISES LEAD TO THE FEDERAL RESERVE ACT

The national banking system certainly succeeded in doing what it was designed to do: finance the Civil War and provide the nation with a sound system of banks and a sound currency. But in the process of doing this, it severely limited the ability of the currency to expand during times of rapidly expanding demands.

Inelastic Currency

After the Civil War the government was no longer borrowing heavily. So there was no longer a flood of government securities to support currency expansion. In fact quite the opposite occurred. During the three decades after the Civil War the government paid off about two-thirds of its bonds. So the base for the national-bank-note currency was greatly eroded.

In addition, there is considerable seasonable variation in the demand for currency. When the public returns currency to the banking system, bank reserves increase. But whenever currency demands are especially high, bank reserves approach depletion.

Suppose the word gets out that bank reserves are getting very low. People get nervous and begin running to the banks to get their money. When that happens (unless there is some outside source available to pour currency into the system) banks must suspend payments. Then you have *a real panic!*

The Pyramiding of Reserves

In the national banking system, small banks kept their reserves in larger banks. The larger banks kept their reserves in the giant banks in the major financial centers—New York and Chicago. During times of heavy currency withdrawals, the smaller banks would call on the larger banks for cash. At the same time, the larger banks' customers also would be withdrawing cash.

Soon banks all over the country would be calling on the money center banks to provide currency. When everyone is asking at the same time, there is just no way!

Whenever a major currency demand would develop, a **financial panic** was almost sure to result. Such panics occurred in 1873, 1884, 1893, and 1907. And at many times in between there were "near-panics."

During the severe panics the usual thing was for banks to announce that no payments would be made until some future date. For some of these banks the "future date" never arrived. When banks stop payments, businesses can't function. The economy is hard hit.

The Panic of 1907 and the Federal Reserve Act

The panic of 1907 was particularly severe. Widespread public reaction brought pressure on Congress to do something to change the system. As a result the **Aldrich-Vreeland Act** was passed (in 1908) establishing the **National Monetary Commission** to investigate and make recommendations. Then the wrangling, positioning, lobbying, and in-fighting ensued. Ultimately the Commission recommended that a central bank be established.

Finally, in December of 1913 (again, by a narrow margin) Congress passed the **Federal Reserve Act**. Two days before Christmas it was signed into law by President Woodrow Wilson. The **Federal Reserve System** actually was set up and began functioning in 1914.

The new Federal Reserve System established a place where banks could keep their reserves *outside the commercial banking system.* Also it provided for **currency elasticity** by permitting banks to borrow from the Federal Reserve banks—the "lenders of the last resort."

All National Banks Were Required to Join the Fed

The Fed was established for several purposes. Perhaps the most important purpose was to provide currency (Federal Reserve notes) to the banking system whenever necessary to prevent a liquidity crisis. It was also supposed to be a regulator of the banks and to serve as fiscal agent for the federal government.

All national banks were required to become members of the Federal Reserve System. State banks could join if they wished, so long as they met the minimum requirements. Only a relatively small number of the (larger) state banks chose to join the Fed.

Finally, with the creation of the Federal Reserve System the United States had, for the first time, a **true central bank**. You'll be reading more about the evolution and activities of the Fed at various places throughout this book.

The Number of Banks, 1900–1933: Rapid Growth, Then Sharp Decline

From the early 1900s up until 1920 the number of commercial banks in the United States grew rapidly. In 1920 there were about 30,000 banks in the country. More than two-thirds of these banks were small and state chartered.

In many states it was easy to establish a bank. So in many places there were too many banks and many of the banks were too small to be profitable. During the 1920s, many failed.

In the more than 50-year period between the creation of the national banking system (1864) and 1920, there were less than 3000 bank failures in the country. Then in the nine-year period 1921–29, there were more than 5000 bank failures. And then: The Depression.

THE 1930s: DEPRESSED CONDITIONS AND REVOLUTIONARY CHANGES IN BANKING

The depression years were tough times for bankers, for individuals—for the entire nation. Whenever any business fails, someone gets hurt. But when a bank fails, many people get hurt. Before deposit insurance, depositors lost their money. So if enough banks fails, spending stops. The economy collapses.

During 1930 through 1933 more than 8000 banks failed. Of the 30,000 banks in 1920, in April, 1933 less than one-half remained. Thousands of people saw their money evaporate as one bank after another collapsed. Everyone was running to the bank and demanding cash. But there wasn't enough cash.

What was our new central bank—our "lender of last resort"—(the Fed) doing while all this was going on? Not much. You'll be reading about that in chapter 9 which focuses on the history of the Fed.

In March of 1933 President Roosevelt declared a **banking holiday** and closed all the banks. There was no more running to the banks and demanding cash because the banks were closed. The banks stayed closed until things calmed down a bit. Many of the closed banks never reopened. Although thousands of banks failed, the 1933 banking holiday succeeded in preventing the collapse of the entire banking system. Figure 6-1 provides dramatic evidence of what happened.

Aims of the 1930s Legislation

Out of this traumatic experience arose financial reform legislation—new laws designed (1) to alleviate the crisis and (2) to create a sound financial system. How? By restoring confidence in the banking system and by insuring its stability.

The Congress used three approaches:

1. **Limiting competition** among banks
2. Increasing **federal regulation** and supervision.

3. Establishing **deposit insurance** to assure depositors that they will not lose their money when a bank fails.

Most of the financial legislation of the 1930s dealt with commercial banks because they were by far the most prominent form of depository institution at that time. Then later (after the World War II), as the thrifts grew in importance, most of the 1930s regulations were extended to those depository institutions as well. These new 1930s laws had profound effects on our banking and financial system right up to the 1980s.

Figure 6-1. Commercial Banks in the United States 1915–1986

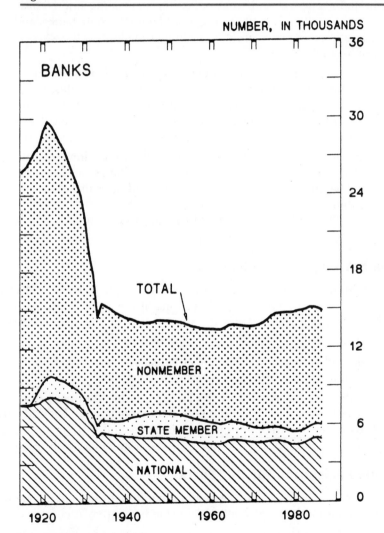

This chart clearly shows the effect of the financial collapse of the early 1930s. The state banks were hardest hit. But many national banks also went under.

Source: 1987 Historical Chart Book, Board of Governors of the Federal Reserve System, p. 82.

The Banking Act of 1933

The Banking Act of 1933—the **Glass-Steagall Act**—was really a "bundle" of acts. It revolutionized the business of banking. Here are the key provisions:

1. It established the **Federal Deposit Insurance Corporation** (FDIC) to insure demand, savings, and time deposits at commercial banks and at mutual savings banks. It was hoped that the FDIC would restore confidence in the banking system. As it turned out, it really did. The FDIC legislation has been referred to as one of the most successful, most effective pieces of legislation ever passed.

2. It supported the **McFadden Act** (1927) which (a) prohibits banks from branching across state lines unless the state being entered has passed legislation *specifically authorizing* entry by out-of-state banks, and (b) requires all national banks to observe the branching laws of the states in which they are located.

3. It separated the **banking business** from the **brokerage business**. Banks were prohibited from acquiring or underwriting corporate stock. This was to eliminate these "risky assets" from bank portfolios. This provision of the 1933 act requiring the banker-broker separation is usually what is being referred to when reference is made to the "Glass-Steagall Act."

4. It authorized the Federal Reserve Board to set **interest rate ceilings** on savings and time deposits at all member banks, and it prohibited banks from paying any interest at all on demand deposits. When the Fed issued regulations implementing this authorization—setting interest rate ceilings—it decided to call this "Regulation Q," which in the banking community soon became **Reg Q**.

The Banking Act of 1935

The Banking Act of 1935 wasn't "revolutionary" as was the 1933 Act. Mostly what it did was to extend the provisions of the 1933 Act to nonmember banks, and to *extend and to centralize the powers of the* **Federal Reserve System**. Specifically, the 1935 act did the following:

1. It extended Reg Q to nonmember banks and prohibited nonmember banks from paying interest on demand deposits.

2. It extended the powers of the Fed by giving the Board of Governors the power to set reserve requirements. And it created the **Federal Open Market Committee** (FOMC) which soon became and still is the nation's most powerful deliberative body on matters of monetary policy.

1930s Legislation for the Thrifts

Although commercial banks were the predominant form of depository institution at the time, the thrifts also attracted some legislative attention:

1. The 1930s legislation established the **Federal Home Loan Bank System**, headed by the Federal Home Loan Bank Board (FHLBB). This agency was created to perform for the S&Ls more or less the same kinds of functions (and exercise more or less the same kinds of supervision and controls) as the Fed does for the commercial banks.

2.   The 1930s legislation created the **Federal Savings and Loan Insurance Corporation** (FSLIC). The agency was created to provide deposit insurance for the S&Ls, as the FDIC provides deposit insurance for the banks.

Before we go any further into the discussion of what was happening with the thrifts in the 1930s and in the years following that, you need more background information on what the thrifts are, why they were created, and what they do. You'll be reading about that in the next chapter. Meanwhile the present discussion continues with an explanation of the evolution of the organizational structure of commercial banks, and of the regulatory framework in which they operate.

EVOLUTION OF THE ORGANIZATIONAL STRUCTURE OF COMMERCIAL BANKS

In 1933 when President Roosevelt's "bank holiday" ended, some 14,000 banks reopened. As you saw in figure 6-1, about one-third were national banks and the remainder were state banks. Since that time, right up to the present, the number of banks in the country has fluctuated between 14,000 and 16,000 and the ratio between national banks and state banks has remained approximately the same.

Several thousand new banks have been created since 1933. But several thousand have been eliminated, almost entirely by mergers of smaller banks with larger banks. So while the number of banking corporations hasn't changed significantly, the size of the average bank—and particularly the size of the major banking corporations—has grown explosively.

If you look at the number of banking offices, instead of the number of banking corporations, you see the great difference between 1933 and the 1980s. That's what is shown in figure 6-2.

That figure indicates that there are now around 15,000 banks. But in addition there are some 45,000 branch offices. Add these together and you come up with about 60,000 bank offices in the country—many more than ever before.

Size Diversity among Commercial Banks

There is great size diversity among the commercial banks. It would take more than 5,000 of the smallest banks to equal the assets of Citicorp. In fact, every bank in the "top 50" in the country has assets greater than the assets of the 1,000 smallest banks.

Figure 6-3 shows that the 100 largest banks hold about one-half of all of the bank deposits in the country. Now you can understand why, when banking legislation is being discussed, the question "What do the bankers want?" can't be answered until you answer this: "Which bankers?" It's almost certain that the view of the $10 million banker will be different from the view of the $10 billion banker.

Different Commercial Banking Structures

One reason for the great diversity in bank siize is that in some places banks are confined to one location—no branching. In other places, banks can branch

Figure 6-2.   Changes in the Number of Banks, and of
               Bank Branches, since 1915

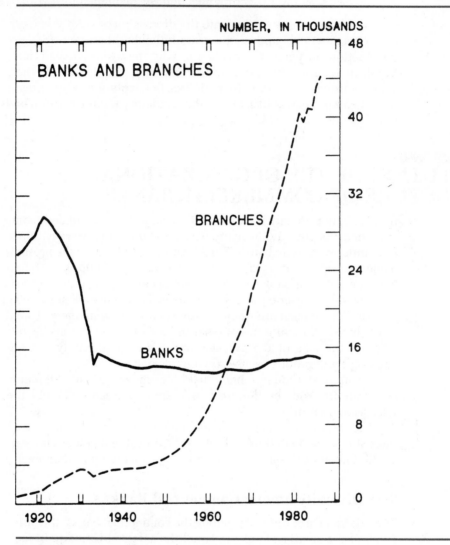

Source: *1987 Historical Chart Book*, Board of Governors of the Federal Reserve System, p. 82.

statewide, and in special cases, interstate. This diversity of legal environment
(together with some other causes) has resulted in several different kinds of banking structures.

Unit Banks. A unit bank is a banking corporation with only one office. More than
half of the banks in the country are unit banks. But most of them are small, so unit
banks account for only a small percentage of total bank assets.

   The reason for the large number (and small size) of unit banks is primarily
because of state laws prohibiting banks from establishing branches. Figure 6-4
indicates that even in the mid-1980s, many of the states were still either restrict-

**Figure 6-3.   Share of Commerical Bank Deposits
Held by the Largest 100 Banks**

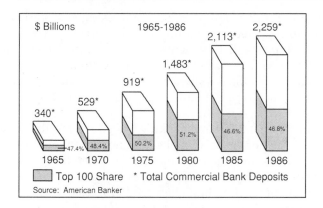

Source: *American Banker 1988 Year Book*, p. 136.

Figure 6-4.   Different State Laws Regarding Bank Branching

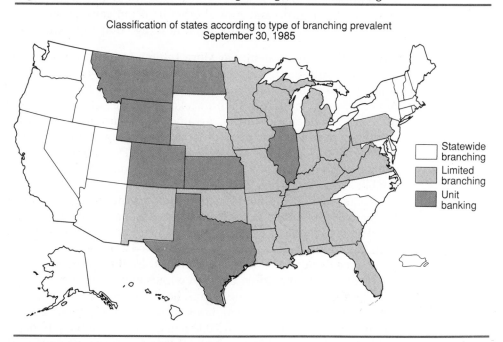

Source: *A Profile of State Chartered Banking*, 11th ed., The Conference of State Bank Supervisors, Washington, D.C., 1986, p. 84.

ing or prohibiting branch banking. But during 1986–88 as a result of much pressure on the state legislatures, some of the antibranching walls seemed likely to be tumbling down soon.

Branch Banking. In states where it is legal, a banking corporation can own and operate several banking offices in addition to the "home office." In many states banks are permitted to establish branches statewide, either by acquiring existing banks located throughout the state and operating these banks as branches, or through starting up new offices (called *de novo* branching). Some states permit only citywide or countywide branching, and some permit branching only into contiguous counties.

As you saw in figure 6-2, branch banking has grown rapidly since World War II. But in the 1980s the number of branches has not continued to grow as rapidly, and in some areas has declined as automated teller machines (ATMs) have replaced some branches. However, in the states which now are relaxing their past restrictions on branching, new branches are being established. Also, with the rapid growth of regional interstate banking (discussed later), many previously independent banks now are becoming the branches of out-of-state banks.

Multi-Bank Holding Companies (Sometimes Called "Group Banking"). A holding company is a corporation which owns stock in one or more other corporations. Suppose a holding company bought up the stock of Old National Bancorp (Spokane) and Union Commerce (Cleveland) and Century Banks (Ft. Lauderdale) and Fulton National (Atlanta) and First United BanCorp (Ft. Worth) and First Hawaiian (Honolulu) and several other banks in various states. That would be an example of an interstate multi-bank holding company. And it would be illegal!

The Douglas Amendment: No More Interstate Multi-Bank Holding Companies. Interstate multi-bank holding companies are illegal under the 1956 *Douglas Amendment* to the *Bank Holding Company Act of 1956*. In 1927 the McFadden Act outlawed **interstate branching** (except by special state legislative permission). But the McFadden Act didn't say anything to prohibit a holding company from owning banks in two or more different states. Big loophole? Yes!

In 1956 the loophole was plugged by the Douglas Amendment. So the interstate multi-bank holding companies in existence today are those which were established prior to the 1956 Act.

Some states prohibit branching, yet permit statewide multi-bank holding companies. So those states have "group banking" instead of branch banking. What's the difference? Only that under the multi-bank holding company structure each bank must have its own charter and exist as "a bank in its own right." But top-management and policy are exercised by the holding company which owns the bank, just as would be the case with branch banking.

There are about 300 multi-bank holding companies operating in the United States, but only 21 of them hold banks in more than one state. These 300 companies control more than 2000 banks with more than 10,000 branches. They hold more than one-third of the total value of banking assets in the nation.

One-Bank Holding Companies. The Douglas Amendment was specifically aimed at holding companies controlling at least 25 percent of the stock of two or more banks. It didn't say anything about a holding company which held the stock of only one bank.

Eureka! Banks are prohibited from being involved in various kinds of (profitable) businesses and from holding various kinds of (profitable) assets which they might like to hold. So why not establish a holding company (which is not a bank), let the holding company own the stock in the bank and let the holding company also hold whatever assets, issue whatever liabilities, and get involved in whatever business it might wish? A great idea! It really caught on during the 1960s.

A holding company can issue liabilities (e.g., commercial paper) to acquire funds, and with no Reg Q interest ceiling! So a holding company can acquire funds at market rates and lend those funds to the bank. (You will understand the importance of this when you read about "disintermediation" in the next chapter.)

The One-Bank Holding Company Movement. During the late 1960s most of the nation's largest commercial banks (and several which were not so large) formed one-bank holding companies. Then they began issuing liabilities to attract funds, and also acquiring non-bank businesses and other assets which the bank itself was not permitted to own. The **Bank Holding Company Act of 1970** plugged the one-bank-holding-company loophole.

Since 1970, one-bank holding companies are required to register with the Fed and to gain approval for the acquisition of any new businesses: either bank or non-bank businesses. Under the 1970 act, non-bank businesses owned by the holding company must be "closely related" to banking.

One-bank holding companies are permitted to own finance companies, equipment-leasing companies, credit life insurance companies, trust companies, and several others. It is through this holding company structure that the banks in the 1970s and 80s have been diversifying their operations geographically and by product line. They are getting into businesses and reaching into areas and competing in markets which would be closed to the bank itself but which are permitted to the holding company.

A holding company such as "Citicorp" or "BankAmerica Corp." can do many things which "Citibank" or "Bank of America" could not do. Look through the list of the top 50 U.S. commercial banking companies published each summer in *Fortune* magazine, or the top 200 published each spring in *Business Week*. You will see that the commercial banking corporations listed there are holding companies—not banks. Now you understand why.

BANK REGULATION AND SUPERVISION: THE OVERLAPPING BUREACRACY

You already know who the bank regulators are. The purpose of this section is to pull it all together in one place so that you get a picture of the overlapping authority.

Comptroller of the Currency

The Comptroller of the Currency charters, regulates, examines, authorizes mergers and branches, and performs other functions relating to *nationl banks*. There are less than 5,000 national banks, but their total assets amount to well over half of total commercial bank assets in the nation.

The Federal Reserve

The Federal Reserve exercises supervisory authority over all members: All national banks, plus state member banks. But in practice the Fed bank examiners concentrate on the state member banks, leaving the national banks to be examined by examiners from the office of the Comptroller of the Currency.

The Fed establishes regulations relating to all member banks, authorizes mergers and branches for member banks, and exercises control over all bank holding companies, members or not.

Fed Supervision of Nonmember Banks. Because the Fed enforces bank holding company legislation—which relates to *all banks*, both state and national, Fed-members and nonmembers—it exercises authority over all commercial banks which are holding companies. Also, as a result of banking legislation of the early 1980s, all banks which have transactions accounts (accounts on which unlimited check writing privileges are available) must hold reserves with the Fed (or with a correspondent bank which passes the reserves through to the Fed) and are subject to certain Fed regulations.

Fed Member Banks Hold About 75% of All Bank Assets. Fed member banks include all of the national banks (approaching 5000) plus all state-chartered banks which have chosen to become Fed members (about 1000) for a total of about 6000 banks. That's less than half of the total number of banks in the country, but these banks are the largest banks.

Fed member banks hold about 75 percent of all commercial bank assets in the country. And the Fed's regulatory arm, don't forget, extends to all of the other banks in the system which have checkable accounts, and also to all bank holding companies.

The Federal Deposit Insurance Corporation (FDIC)

More than 96 percent of the banks in the country, holding more than 99 percent of bank assets, are insured by FDIC. This gives the FDIC regulators access to virtually all of the state-chartered banks in the nation. In fact, the FDIC is the *only* federal government organization which has the power to examine and to influence the day-to-day activities and policies of the great majority of the state-chartered banks.

The FDIC admits state-chartered banks to membership in the insurance program, it examines those banks, establishes regulations which they must follow, and authorizes mergers and branches by these state-chartered banks. So in addition to its role in insuring deposits, the FDIC has been able to establish *nationwide standards* in bank procedures and practices. No bank wants to lose its FDIC insurance!

The FDIC also has the authority to exercise all of its controls over both the national banks and the state Fed-member banks. But in practice FDIC examiners concentrate most of their efforts on the banks which are chartered by the 50 states and which are not subject to examination by the Comptroller of the Currency or the Fed.

Chartering and Examination by the 50 States

Each state-chartered bank is subject to the chartering requirements of its home state, it is examined by, and subject to the regulations of the "banking commission" (or whatever the state supervisory-regulatory organization is called in that state).

All new banks, all acquisitions, mergers, or branches must be approved by the state regulators. Also, the states have regulations regarding the activities of bank holding companies.

Each state has its own banking laws and regulations, and its own approach to and methods of enforcement. However, through the Council of State Bank Supervisors and various other interstate associations, significant progress has been made in moving toward uniformity. Still, conditions from state to state are far from uniform. Each state's legislature must respond to political realities in that state.

State-Chartered Banks: How Many? How Large?

Look back at figure 6-1 and you'll see that the number of state-chartered banks amounts to about 70 percent of the total number of banks in the country (something over 10,000). But since all of the smallest banks are included in this category, the number belies the relative importance of state banks in the banking system.

Only 43 percent of total bank assets are held by state banks, and the largest of those banks are Fed members. There are about 9000 state-chartered non-Fed-member banks. Even though these banks amount to almost two-thirds of the total number of banks in the country, they only hold about 25 percent of total commercial bank assets.

A Bank Could Be Hounded by Regulators!

Pity the poor national bank. It is subject to regulations issued by and to examination by the Comptroller of the Currency, the Federal Reserve, and the FDIC. And reports must be sent to all three of these agencies. Isn't this "a little much"?

And what about the state member banks? They are subject to examination by both the Fed and the FDIC and also by the state bank examiners. And they are subject to the regulations of and must submit reports to all three. Their merging and branching activities must be approved both by the state regulators and by the Fed.

Even the state-chartered non-Fed-member banks are now required to submit reports to the Fed as well as to the FDIC and to the state. Also they must meet the Fed's reserve requirements as well as those which may be established by the state. They are subject to examination visits from the FDIC and from their own state supervisors.

Should the Regulatory Agencies be Consolidated?

For the past two decades, not a year has passed when there hasn't been some discussion of and/or proposed legislation calling for a consolidation or merging of the bank regulatory-supervisory bureaucracy. Critics argue: "This is not an efficient way to run a supervisory-regulatory program."

On the other side, the supporters of the status quo argue that the variety of regulatory-supervisory agencies, with the degree of coordination among them which has been achieved, is far more desirable than a singular, monolithic supervisory agency whose power and influence could, in the wrong hands, or when captured by the wrong philosophy, do great harm to the banking system and to the economy. As with most such questions, there is no "obviously correct" answer.

Figure 6-5 illustrates and summarizes the overlapping regulatory and supervisory structure which has just been described.

SUMMARY

- Modern banking grew up during the renaissance, and was speeded by the practice of **goldsmiths** issuing **deposit receipts** which circulated as currency.

- Early banks in the United States were either state chartered, or not chartered at all.

- The First and Second **Banks of the United States** (1791–1811, 1816–1836) were nationwide commercial banks which also performed some central banking functions—serving as the government's bank, and limiting state bank note issues by presenting these notes and demanding gold.

- In the period 1836–1863 when only state banks existed, there was no dependable nationwide currency. In many states there was very little effective regulation of banking or note-issues.

- During the Civil War, to raise funds and also to provide a stable nationwide currency, the **National Banking System** was set up. This system achieved its primary objectives, but the **inelastic currency** and **pyramiding of reserves**, contributed to repeated liquidity crises (panics).

- The 1907 panic resulted in the **Aldrich-Vreeland Act**, the **National Monetary Commission**, and (ultimately) the passage of the **Federal Reserve Act** in 1913.

- At the beginning of the 1920s there were some 30,000 banks in the country, but only about 15,000 remained in April of 1933.

- New banking legislation in the 1930s was aimed toward **limiting competition** among banks, increasing **federal regulation** and supervision, and establishing **deposit insurance.**

- Since the Depression, the total number of banks in the United States has remained at between 14,000 and 16,000, and the ratios of state to national banks, and of Fed-member to nonmember banks, have not changed significantly. Although the number of banks hasn't increased, the number of banking offices has increased greatly.

- There is great **size diversity** among the commercial banks, with each of the giant banks holding assets equal to the assets of several thousand of the

Figure 6-5. Regulation and Supervision of Commercial Banks

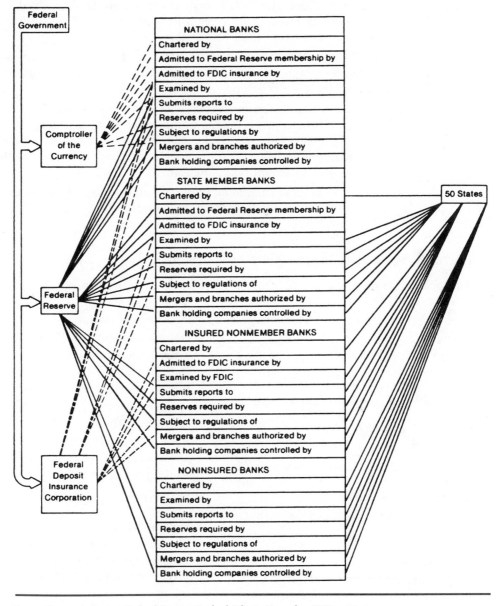

Source: *Economic Review*, Federal Reserve Bank of Atlanta, December 1982, p. 46.

smallest banks. The size diversity is somewhat related to different state laws regarding branch banking.

- Different **bank organizational forms** are: Unit banks, branch banking, multi-bank holding companies, and **one-bank holding companies**. Most large banks today are structured as one-bank holding companies, but the some 300 **multi-bank holding companies** hold more than 2000 banks with more than 10,000 branches, and hold more than one-third of total banking assets in the nation.

- The **McFadden Act** (1927) restricts interstate banking, and the **Douglas Amendment** (1956) prohibits multi-bank holding companies from acquiring banks in more than one state.

- In the late 1960s most banks turned to the one-bank holding company structure to avoid some of the restrictions which are placed on banks but not on bank holding companies.

- The bank regulation and supervision structure is overlapping and somewhat confusing, involving the Comptroller of the Currency, the Fed, FDIC, and (for state-chartered banks) the examining agencies of the 50 states. Between the Fed and FDIC examinations, almost all state-chartered banks are subject to federal examination.

- Some observers recommend that the examining agencies should be consolidated. Others disagree, fearing the concentration of power in the hands of one regulatory agency.

Important Principles, Issues, Concepts, Terms

Banking in ancient times

Usurers

Banking during the Renaissance and Industrial Revolution

How goldsmiths became bankers

"Goldsmith currency"

Early banking in North America

Economic, political, and philosophical conflicts on banking

Alexander Hamilton's view

Thomas Jefferson's view

First Bank of the United States: structure and functions

State banking, 1811–1816

Second Bank of the United States: structure and functions

Nicholas Biddle

Andrew Jackson

The U.S. banks: central banks? or not?

State banking

Wildcat banking

"Free banking" laws

National Currency Act (1863)

National Banking Act (1864)

National Banking System: structure and characteristics

National banks

Comptroller of the Currency

National bank notes

State bank-note tax

Dual banking system

Inelastic currency

Pyramiding of reserves

Panic of 1907

Federal Reserve Act (December, 1913)

Changing number of banks, 1900–1933

The 1933 "Banking Holiday"

Aims of the 1930s legislation

McFadden Act (1927)

Banking Act of 1933 (Glass-Steagall Act)

FDIC

"Reg Q"

Banking Act of 1935

Federal Reserve System changes

Federal Home Loan Bank System

Federal Home Loan Bank Board (FHLBB)

FSLIC

Present number and size of commercial banks

Different geographic structures of commercial banks

Unit banks

Branch banking

Multi-bank holding companies

Douglas Amendment (1956)

"Group banking"
One-bank holding companies

Overview of bank regulation and supervision
Proposals for regulatory reform

Questions and Problems

1. Explain how the goldsmiths became bankers "just automatically."

2. Describe the banking situation at about the time the United States became a nation.

3. Discuss the First and Second Banks of the United States. Why were they created? Why were they permitted to expire? What functions did they perform? Were they central banks? Or not? Discuss.

4. Describe the note-issue situation in the United States following the demise of the Second United States Bank in 1836.

5. Describe the National Banking System. Why was it created? And then why was the Federal Reserve System superimposed upon it?

6. Why do we now have a "dual banking system" in the United States? Was it planned that way? Or did the "forces of the marketplace" create it? Discuss.

7. Give the highlights of the banking legislation of the 1930s. What was the overall aim or purpose of this legislation?

8. Describe the present U.S. commercial banking system. Mention numbers and sizes, and both corporate and geographic organizational structures.

9. Describe the present setup for banking regulation and supervision in the United States.

Suggested Readings

Benston, George J. *Bank Examination*. New York University, Institute of Finance, 1973.

Cagan, Philip. "The First Fifty Years of the National Banking System—An Historical Appraisal." *Banking and Monetary Studies*. Homewood, Ill.: Richard D. Irwin, 1963.

Carson, Deane, ed. *Banking and Monetary Studies*. Homewood, Ill.: Richard D. Irwin, 1963.

Cocheo, Steve. "Anatomy of an Examination." *ABA Banking Journal*. February 1986.

Davis, Ricard. "The Recent Performance of the Commercial Banking Industry." *Quarterly Review*. Federal Reserve Bank of New York, Summer 1986.

Federal Deposit Insurance Corporation. *Annual Report*.

———. *Statistics on Banking*. Washington, D.C., annual.

Federal Reserve Bank of Chicago. *Bank Structure and Competition*, annual publication.

Federal Reserve System. *Functional Cost Analysis: 1984 Average Banks*. Washington, D.C.: Government Printing Office, 1984.

Friedman, Milton and Anna Jacobson Schwartz. *A Monetary History of the United States 1867–1960*. Princeton, N.J.: Princeton University Press, 1963.

Galbraith, John A. *The Economics of Banking Operations*. Montreal: McGill University Press, 1963.

Geographic Restrictions on Commercial Banking in the United States: The Report of the President. Washington, D.C.: Government Printing Office, 1981.

Gilbert, Milton. "Bank Market Structure and Competition: A Survey." *Journal of Money, Credit and Banking* 16. (November 1984): 617–644.

Golembe, Carter H. "The Deposit Insurance Legislation of 1933." *Political Science Quarterly* 75. (June 1960): 181–200.

Golembe, Carter H. and David S. Holland. *Federal Regulation of Banking 1983–1984*. Washington D.C.: Golembe Associates, 1983.

———. *Federal Regulation of Banking*. Washington, D.C.: Golembe Associates, 1981.

Heggestad, Arnold. "Market Structure, Competition and Performance in Financial Industries: A Survey of Banking Studies." Franklin Edwards (ed.), *Issues in Financial Regulation*. New York: McGraw-Hill Book Company, 1979.

Keeton, William. "Deposit Insurance and the Deregulation of Deposit Rates." *Economic Review*. Federal Reserve Bank of Kansas City, April 1984.

Klebaner, Benjamin J. *Bank Regulation*. Federal Reserve Bank of Kansas City, 1985.

———. *Commercial Banking in the United States: A History*. Hinsdale, Ill.: Dryden Press, 1974.

Kroos, Herman. *Documentary History of Banking and Currency in the United States.* New York: McGraw-Hill, 1969.

Mayer, Martin. *The Money Bazaar*, part 3. New York: E. P. Dutton, 1984.

Mote, Larry R. "Banks and the Securities Markets." *Economic Perspectives.* Federal Reserve Bank of Chicago, March/April 1979.

Robertson, Ross M. *The Comptroller and Bank Supervision.* Washington, D.C.: Office of the Comptroller of the Currency, 1968.

Savage. Donald T. "Developments in Banking Structure 1970–81." *Federal Reserve Bulletin* 68, (February 1982): 72–85.

Spong, Kenneth. *Bank Regulation.* Federal Reserve Bank of Kansas City, 1985.

———. *Banking Regulation, Its Purposes, Implementation, and Effects*, 2nd ed. Kansas City: Federal Reserve Bank of Kansas City, 1985.

Stevens, Edward J. "Composition of the Money Stock Prior to the Civil War." *Journal of Money, Credit and Banking* 2, (February 1971): 86–87.

Wallach, Henry C. "Reflections on Glass-Steagall." *Monetary Policy and Practice.* Lexington, Mass.: Lexington Books, 1982.

CHAPTER 7

Evolution of the U.S. Banking System II: Focus on the Thrifts

Chapter Objectives

This chapter continues from the previous one, first tracing the evolution of the thrift institutions up to the 1930s, then discussing the conditions of both banks and thrifts during the post World War II period. After you study this chapter you will understand and be able to explain:

1. The development and functions of
   a. The **mutual savings banks** (MSBs)
   b. The **savings and loan institutions** (S&Ls)
   c. The **credit unions** (CUs)
2. How all of the depository institutions (banks and thrifts) are a **close-knit system** so that the reach of the smallest local institution is worldwide.
3. The growing difficulties imposed on the depository institutions in the 1960s and '70s by the restrictions of the 1930s legislation, especially with **rising market interest rates** and **disintermediation**.
4. The recommendations for deregulation in the **Hunt Report** and the **FINE Study**.
5. Various actions taken by banks and thrifts to "**loophole free**" from the 1930s legislative restrictions.

THE THRIFTS HAVE SEVERAL THINGS IN COMMON

The three important kinds of thrift institutions in the United States are (1) savings and loan institutions, (2) mutual savings banks, and (3) credit unions. There are several similarities among the thrifts:

1. *The Origins.* The thrifts had their origins in the early 1800s except for the credit unions which began in the early 1900s. All of them were established to provide a place where small savers could place their savings and the pooled savings could be used to finance residential construction and, in the case of credit unions, low-cost consumer loans. During the 1800s the commercial banks were not interested in holding small savings accounts. (Some are not, even today.) So the thrift institutions encouraged people to

be thrifty and save by providing a safe place for and some return on small savings.

2. *Mutual Organizations.* All of the thrift institutions began as *mutual* organizations in which there are no stockholders and the organization is actually owned by the depositors. Top policy decisions are made by a board of trustees, and the board employs management and other personnel to operate and carry out the functions of the thrift. The purpose of the thrift is to serve the interests of its members (its depositors) and all profits belong to, and (beyond that which is used for reserves or for expansion) are paid out to the depositors.

3. *Limited Assets (Loans and Investments).* All of the thrifts were created with specific limitations regarding the kinds of assets they could hold—that is, the kinds of loans and investments they could make. Most of the assets of the thrifts are home mortgage loans, consumer loans, and government securities. (Thrift asset structures now are changing in response to the revolutionary banking acts of the 1980s.)

4. *State Charters at First.* All of the thrifts started out with state charters and under state supervision. But over the years, all kinds of thrifts have become eligible for federal charters and for federal deposit insurance. By the 1980s almost all thrifts were under some form of federal government supervision. The federal government first began chartering savings and loan associations and credit unions in the 1930s. But it was not until 1980 that the federal government issued the first federal charter to a mutual savings bank.

5. *New Powers in the 1980s.* Since the early 1980s all thrifts have been empowered to offer (and most of them are offering) checkable deposits. Also, thrifts now can hold (invest in) assets and make kinds of loans which previously were the private domain of the commercial banks.

   If the thrifts can offer checking accounts and make commercial-bank-type loans and hold other bank-type assets—all of which until recently were exclusively "commercial banking" functions—then what's the difference between a thrift institution and a commercial bank? In many cases, by the late 1980s there wasn't much difference. Still, most of the thrifts have chosen to continue to focus their efforts on their traditional lines of business: taking savings deposits and making home mortgage loans.

The following sections give some of the highlights of the development and current status of each of these kinds of thrift institutions: mutual savings banks (MSBs), savings and loan associations (S&Ls), and credit unions (CUs). But first, take a look at figures 7-1 and 7-2 and see an overview picture of the depository institutions. Figure 7-2 shows the recent growth of deposits in these thrift institutions. (Note: The figure uses a ratio—semi-log—scale which was explained in chapter 3.)

MUTUAL SAVINGS BANKS (MSBs)

Mutual savings banks were established to provide a "safe haven" for the deposits of small savers. The first mutual savings banks were established in Europe and in

Figure 7-1.   Overview of the Depository Institutions

Where Are the Nation's Deposits Held?

$ Billions

Credit Unions
$152.2 **4.3%**

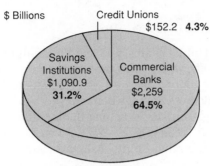

Savings Institutions
$1,090.9
31.2%

Commercial Banks
$2,259
64.5%

Total: $3,502.1

Note: Includes deposits gathered both domestically and internationally by U.S. institutions.

Source: American Banker

Number of Deposit-Taking Institutions in the U.S.

December 31, 1986

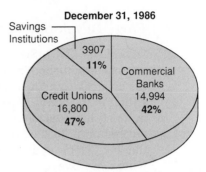

Savings Institutions
3907
11%

Credit Unions
16,800
47%

Commercial Banks
14,994
42%

Total Number: 35,701

Note: Savings institutions include savings banks and savings and loans.

Source: American Banker

Source: American Banker, as reported in *American Banker 1988 Yearbook*, p. 136.

Figure 7-2.   Thrift Institution Deposits Total Deposits by Type of Institution, 1950–1986

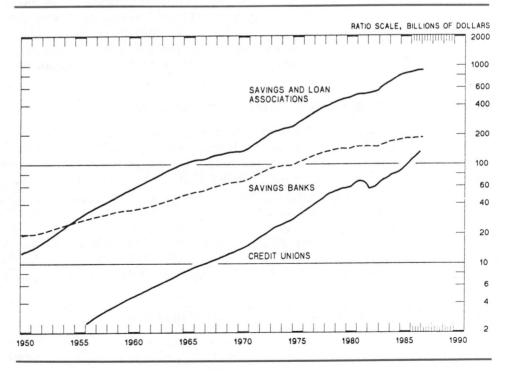

Source: *Historical Chart Book 1987*, Board of Governors of the Federal Reserve System, Washington, D.C., p. 8.

the United States between 1810 and 1820. The MSBs were usually organized by social groups (or sometimes by wealthy individuals) to encourage thrift as a way of helping the poor to better their lot.

Early Development in the United States

One of the first MSBs in the United States was the Philadelphia Savings Fund Society, established in 1816. That MSB is now the largest in the country with total assets great enough to place it among the 50 largest commercial banking companies in the nation. Also the Bowery Savings Bank in New York City (established in 1834) has assets large enough to place it among the top 50 commercial banks. Several other MSBs hold assets in the billions. "But," you may ask, "how could that be? I've never even seen or heard of a mutual savings bank!" It all depends on where you live.

Most States Don't Have MSBs

There are only 17 states in which MSBs have been chartered. About three-fourths of all of the MSBs in the United States are located in three states: Massachusetts, New York, and Connecticut. The remaining one-fourth are in the Northeast, Midwest, and in Oregon, Washington, and Alaska. Why this geographic distribution? Mostly because of historical accident.

The MSBs were the first thrift institutions in the country. They first developed in the industrializing, commercial areas of the country in the time that commercial banks were not accepting small savings. As industry and commerce spread all over the nation, MSBs had two formidable competitors: savings and loan associations, and the commercial bank—which soon discovered that small savings accounts could be profitable. In many states the chartering authorities didn't see any necessity for chartering MSBs. Did the already existing banks and S&Ls in the state help the state authorities to decide that MSBs were not needed? Of course.

In Some States, MSBs Are Dominant

In the early 1900s there were more than 600 mutual savings banks in the country. Since that time some have been consolidated and some have disappeared. In the late 1980s there were only 435 MSBs in the country. But their average size is much larger than the average for either commercial banks or any other form of depository institution. And in those areas in which they operate, especially in New York and Massachusetts, they dominate the savings and mortgage lending market.

Many of the MSBs have extensive branches, most now offer checkable accounts, and several are involved in the life insurance business. In the areas they operate they are formidable competitors to the commercial banks.

MSB Assets: Mostly Home Mortgages

Traditionally the *purpose* of the MSB was too encourage thrift among the poor and working class. But you can't pay interest on savings accounts unless you invest the money and earn enough to make the interest payments!

The MSBs generally were restricted in what kinds of assets they could buy with their savings deposits. Mostly they were permitted to make residential mortgages (and limited kinds of commercial loans) and to hold government securities. But a small amount of assets might be placed in corporate bonds, in the common stocks of "blue chip" companies, and in consumer loans. In the late 1980s, of the more than $200 billion in assets held by the mutual savings banks, about 60 percent was placed in home mortgages.

Federal Chartering of MSBs

Mutual savings bank deposits are covered by either state-sponsored or FDIC insurance. The *Financial Institutions Regulatory and Interest Rate Control Act of 1978* permits MSBs to convert to federal charters if they wish. In September of 1980 the first federal charter was granted to a mutual savings bank.

More than 90 percent of the MSBs in existence today were organized before 1900. Perhaps with federal chartering available we will see more MSBs, especially in view of the new powers granted them in the banking acts of 1980 and 1982 — powers which enable them to compete more effectively with commercial banks.

The MSBs have played an important role in home mortgage financing. In the beginning, home mortgage financing wasn't the primary purpose of the MSBs. But for the savings and loan associations, from the very beginning *home mortgage financing was their primary purpose*. That's what you'll be reading about in the next section. But first you might want to read box 7-1 and find out about the recent development of stock savings banks.

SAVINGS AND LOAN ASSOCIATIONS (S&Ls)

Savings and loan associations (S&Ls) began as "building societies" in the early 1800s, both in Europe and in the United States. The specific purpose was to finance residential housing. A society would be formed in which all of the

---

Box 7-1

Question: **What about Savings Banks Owned by Stockholders? The Stock Savings Banks (SSBs)**

During the "financial revolution years" of the 1970s and '80s, many new financial innovations occurred — some, in the nature of financial institutions themselves. In some states, SSBs have some regulatory advantages over the S&Ls, and several S&Ls have chosen to depart from their mutual "association" status, to sell stock, and to become SSBs.

An SSB looks like and operates like an S&L. The difference is that it is owned by stockholders, not by its depositors. An important advantage is that it can sell stock to acquire capital. Another factor of some significance in some cases, is that a stockholder-owned association can be sold to another firm which would like to acquire it. When this happens, it isn't unusual for the stockholders to enjoy capital gains.

Many S&Ls have become stock-owned, but haven't changed their names. They still call themselves S&Ls, not SSBs.

members agreed to contribute (deposit) a certain amount of money each week or month. Then when the pool of money got large enough it would be lent to one member of the society to finance a house.

The S&Ls Opened to the General Public and Grew Rapidly

The first of these cooperative home-financing societies in the United States was the Oxford Provident Building Association of Philadelphia, established in 1831. During the 1830s and 1840s several other neighborhood "building associations" were formed. But after the Civil War these closed societies changed their approach and began accepting savings deposits from everyone. With the mutual form of organization, anyone who made deposits became a share owner and received interest and the right to participate in earnings.

In the post–Civil War period, both MSBs and S&Ls grew rapidly—and at the same time that commercial banks also were growing rapidly and had become actively involved in attracting saving deposits. The MSBs were located in the areas of rapid growth and industrialization, and centers of trade and commerce. That explains why, during the late 1800s and early 1900s growth of the MSBs outstripped that of the S&Ls.

Until the time of World War I the S&Ls were coming from behind. The number of MSBs expanded from about ten in 1820 to more than 600 in the early 1900s. And the average MSB was much larger than the average S&Ls. In the period just prior to World War I, the commercial banks and MSBs had approximately equal amounts of savings deposits. The S&Ls were far behind with less than one-fourth as much as either MSBs or commercial banks.

Thousands of S&Ls Were Created in the 1920s

Following World War I there was a building boom. Thousands of new S&Ls were created during the 1920s and by 1929 there were more than 12,000 S&Ls. In 1929 they were holding about one-fourth of all non-farm residential mortgages in the country.

During the 1930s the S&Ls were hit hard. Homeowners defaulted on their mortgages. Many of the banks which were holding the cash reserves of S&Ls, failed. In spite of several federal government programs designed to support them, more than one-third of the S&Ls in the nation disappeared during the 1930s.

At the beginning of the Depression (in 1930) the S&Ls held assets and deposits approximately equal in size to that of the MSBs. But by 1945, S&L assets and deposits had dropped to half the size of the MSBs. Then after World War II as the economy expanded the S&Ls expanded rapidly—not in numbers, but in size. They soon became the largest source of home mortgage loans in the country.

Since 1960: Declining Numbers, Increasing Size

The actual number of S&Ls has been declining for the past three decades. There were 6300 in 1960, 4600 in 1980, and only about 3000 in 1988. But over this three-decade period the average asset-size increased from about $11 million to more than $150 million.

The holding company movement which swept commercial banking also occurred to a lesser extent in the S&L industry. During the 1970s and '80s many

S&Ls changed from mutual associations to stock companies as a means of acquiring additional capital (by selling stock), and to make the holding company form available to them. By the late 1980s, more than one-fourth of the S&Ls in the United States had converted from mutual (depositor-owned) associations to stockholder-owned corporations.

Federal Home Loan Bank Board (FHLBB): "The S&Ls' Fed"

The S&Ls are controlled by the Federal Home Loan Bank Board (FHLBB) in Washington. The Board consists of three persons appointed by the President. The supervisory and service role of the FHLBB for the S&Ls is comparable to that of the Fed for the commercial banks. There are 12 District Federal Home Loan Banks which provide services and make loans to the S&Ls in their districts. The geographic structure of the system is parallel to that of the Federal Reserve System. And the Federal Home Loan Banks even have a "discount window" through which the S&Ls can obtain advances.

About two-fifths of the S&Ls in the country are chartered by the federal government. The others are state chartered. The federally chartered S&Ls are insured up to $100,000 under the Federal Savings and Loan Insurance Corporation (FSLIC). State chartered S&Ls can also apply for FSLIC insurance, and in recent years most have done so.

The asset powers (those assets which can be held, loans made, etc.) of the S&Ls are now being expanded. In the past, the S&Ls have been required by law to be essentially *a single function industry: to take savings deposits and to make home mortgages.* At the end of the 1970s more than 80 percent of the assets of the S&L industry were held in the form of home mortgages. But that is rapidly changing as the S&Ls participate in the revolutionary changes now going on in the U.S. financial system.

The size structure of the S&Ls is very uneven, as is that of the commercial banks. For example, the largest 4 percent of the S&Ls hold some 40 percent of the total S&L industry's assets. There are several multi-billion-dollar S&Ls, while at the other end of the spectrum there are many with assets of only a few million dollars.

CREDIT UNIONS

There are now about 16,000 credit unions. So in terms of numbers, there are more credit unions than there are commercial banks. But most credit unions are very small. If all of the assets of all of the credit unions in the United States were added together the total wouldn't add up to the size of *one* of the nation's largest banking corporations. The 435 MSBs in the country have total assets considerably greater than the total of the some 16,000 credit unions.

The "Typical Credit Union" Is Very Small

You can see that the average credit union is small. But as in the case of the commercial banks and the other thrifts, the size-range is great. A few (very few) credit unions have assets in the neighborhood of $1 billion. But for more than half of the credit unions, total assets amount to less than $1 million.

Many of the credit unions are so small that they have no full-time personnel. They are manned by volunteers in office space provided by the company whose employees are members of the credit union. Employers sponsor credit unions and encourage thrift among their employees by providing free office space and free time for employees to serve as volunteers for the credit union.

A credit union is a nonprofit organization, chartered for the purpose of taking small savings deposits from and making loans to its members. To be a member you must have "something in common" with the other members. This "common bond" is usually "place of employment." In fact, more than 80 percent of the credit unions are occupation-related. Others are for members of social or religious organizations, common area of residence, common enjoyment of similar activities—would you believe common last name? Almost any "common bond" definition you can think of can be used.

The National Credit Union Administration (NCUA)

About 60 percent of the credit unions now have federal charters. All federally chartered credit unions have their deposits insured (up to $100,000) by the National Credit Union Share Insurance Fund (NCUSIF) which is administered by the National Credit Union Administration (NCUA), established in 1970. State-chartered credit unions which meet the requirements can also be covered by NCUSIF. About half of the state-chartered credit unions now have this deposit insurance coverage.

The first credit union was established in New Hampshire in 1909. The growth of credit unions was slow until 1934 when the Federal Credit Union Act offered federal charters, nationwide. Many new credit unions were established during the 1930s and '40s.

Diversification and Rapid Growth

In the 1950s some credit unions began to offer a broader range of services and began advertising to attract members. Since that time there has been aggressive competition by some of the credit unions for members, for savings deposits, and for consumer (and sometimes home mortgage) loans.

Some credit unions have pushed for payroll savings plans whereby a part of each person's income is paid into that person's CU account. Credit unions generally have offered higher interest rates on deposits, lower rates on loans, free insurance, and sometimes refunds on loan interest. Many CUs have offered "the best available financial deal" for the small saver and borrower.

The credit union industry, although still relatively small, has been the most rapidly growing depository intermediary since World War II. Total assets grew from about $1 billion in 1950 to more than $72 billion in 1980. That's a 7200 percent increase! By 1980, credit unions in the United States had more than 45 million members (one in every six people) and were offering an increasingly broad range of financial services, including "share drafts"—which really means interest-bearing checking accounts.

The recent trend is toward a smaller number of credit unions and larger size. In the late 1960s there were about 24,000 credit unions, and by the early 1980s, about 22,000. But some of those didn't survive the traumatic financial market conditions of the early 1980s.

Since it is a mutual organization and nonprofit, credit unions must pay out their earnings to their members (except those funds used for expansion, and for reserves). And they have one advantage over all other financial intermediaries. They are tax-exempt. As you can imagine, the competing financial intermediaries are not thrilled about this CU tax exemption!

Back-up Sources of Liquidity for Credit Unions

How do credit unions meet their needs for liquidity in case of unusually heavy withdrawal demands? The commercial banks can go to the Fed "discount window" and borrow. The mutual savings banks and the savings and loan associations can go to the Federal Home Loan Bank. Where can the credit unions go?

Credit Union Leagues, and the U.S. Central CU. The credit unions can always do as the banks and other thrifts frequently do. They can go into the money market and borrow at money market rates to meet their liquidity needs. But the credit unions have gotten together and worked out something better: Credit union leagues. These "leagues" provide clearing house services for making loans between credit unions. And in 1974 the Credit Union National Association (CUNA) established the "U.S. Central Credit Union" to provide interstate loans and to help the credit union leagues to obtain funds from outside the credit union industry.

The Central Liquidity Facility. In 1978, federal law authorized the creation of a Central Liquidity Facility (CLF) to provide funds for credit unions. The CLF can issue and sell debt securities to the public and then lend the funds to the credit union industry. The CLF is administered by the National Credit Union Administration (NCUA).

Credit Unions: Small, but Significant and Growing

Credit unions are not very big in the total financial services picture. But in the segment of the market which they target, they are certainly significant. Couple that with their growth rate, and you can see that the credit unions are not competitors to be taken lightly by the other financial intermediaries. Table 7-1 illustrates the rapid growth of credit union deposits, from $5 billion in 1960 to almost $200 billion in 1988.

The other depository intermediaries are not complacent about the competition (and some special advantages) of credit unions. But most depository intermediaries are more concerned about the rapidly increasing competition from outside—from nondepository firms. You'll be reading all about that in the next chapter.[1]

---

[1] On the increasing importance of credit unions, see: James R. Kraus, "Credit Unions Nibbling at Banks' Market," *Banking Week*, 3(8), May 2, 1988, p. 1.

Table 7-1.   The Growth of Savings Deposits by Type of Depository Institution, 1960–1987 (Billions of Dollars)

Yearend	Commercial Banks	Savings Assoc.	Savings Banks	Credit Unions	Total
1960	$ 67.1	$ 62.1	$ 36.3	$ 5.0	171.3
1965	130.8	110.4	52.4	9.2	303.1
1970	205.8	146.4	71.6	15.5	439.3
1975	393.4	285.7	109.9	33.0	822.0
1980	677.8	511.6	153.5	61.7	1,404.6
1982	921.0	568.0	155.2	74.8	1,719.0
1984	1,140.1	725.0	248.1	102.6	2,215.8
1986	1,325.0	740.9	346.1	152.2	2,564.2
1987*	1,389.0	768.4	373.5	167.6	2,698.5

*preliminary

Sources: Federal Home Loan Bank Board; Federal Reserve Board; as reported in: *A Profile of State Chartered Banking*, 11th ed., The Conference of State Bank Supervisors, Washington, D.C., 1986, p. 24; also, *Savings Institutions Sourcebook 88*, United States League of Savings Institutions, Chicago, 1988, p. 24.

THE INTERLOCKED U.S. AND WORLDWIDE SYSTEM OF DEPOSITORY INSTITUTIONS

Now that you know something about the thrifts—the non-bank depository institutions (from this chapter) and you know something about the commercial banks (from the previous chapter) it's time for some discussion about the *integration* that exists among all these institutions. Truly, this is a tightly interlocked system through which all kinds of financial arrangements and payments are made, U.S. and worldwide.

The American banking system is a closely knit, interlocked system. And it isn't just the commercial banks. All of the thrift institutions are locked into the same system. Each of the institutions provides certain services and performs certain functions. But each requires interlocking relationships with the remainder of the system in order to perform its functions.

Commercial Banks Usually Service the Thrifts' Checkable Accounts

For example, in 1974 the National Credit Union Administration authorized some credit unions to offer share-draft accounts—accounts on which checks could be written. How could a credit union let its customers write checks and send them all over the country, or all over the world? How would these checks be "cleared" and the money taken out of the check-writers account and transferred to the ultimate receipient? It would be impossible unless the credit union was somehow tied into the banking system.

Inter-Depository-Institution Deposits and Correspondent Relationships

Many S&Ls failed during the 1930s because they were closely tied into the banking system. They held their reserves in commercial banks which failed.

Small depository institutions (banks and thrifts) always hold some deposits in larger depository institutions. Ultimately most of these deposits wind up in major commercial banks. The intermediate-size banks may hold the deposits of the small banks and thrifts. Then these intermediate banks have deposits in the larger banks. Ultimately the smallest thrift in the system has access to the worldwide banking network, through this "spiderweb" correspondent system. There isn't much that the small banks and thrifts could do unless they were a part of this interlocked system.

Small Institutions Depend on Larger Ones, and Both Profit

Without the big banks, the small depository institutions couldn't really function. So why do the big banks want to help their small competitors—the little banks and thrifts? It isn't that they are "social minded." It's just that it's good business (profitable!) to sell banking services "wholesale" to other segments of the industry. If one big bank refused to do that, someone else would immediately step in and provide the service and earn the profit.

A Nationwide and Worldwide System

It is this "spiderweb of interlocking relationships"—including the commercial banks, the thrifts, and the many different kinds of nondepository financial institutions—which provides the efficient functioning of the U.S. and worldwide financial system. These interlocking relationships have produced the unified "nationwide and worldwide financial services system" which is absolutely essential to the functioning of the U.S. and world economy. And even the smallest of the thrifts is, through correspondent ties, a part of this worldwide system.

EVOLUTION OF THE U.S. FINANCIAL SYSTEM AFTER THE 1930s

From the previous chapter and this one you have a general view of the depository industry in the United States. Now it's time for a more specific look at developments and events following World War II. It's time to focus on the series of events which led to the **revolution in banking** of the 1970s and '80s.

The 1930s Legislation Was Successful For Awhile

During the 1940s, '50s, and early '60s the financial system functioned well enough within its depression-born regulatory framework. One obviously positive effect was that of **deposit insurance**. The FDIC did restore confidence in the system—no more "runs on the banks." Also the FSLIC helped to create confidence in the S&L industry.

In the years following World War II, bank failures were averaging only about six a year—much lower than in pre-FDIC years. And on the rare occasion when a bank did fail, depositors didn't lose their money.

Req Q Had Little Effect in the 1940s and 1950s. Until the mid-1960s, Reg Q had little effect on the industry—except perhaps to create some complacency among bankers. Market interest rates remained approximately equal to or below Req Q ceilings.

There was a "comfortable spread" between the interest rate paid for the *cost* of funds—zero for demand deposits and about 3 percent or less for savings deposits—and the interest rate earned on the *uses* of funds—about 6 percent for loans. This comfortable spread, plus the lack of substitutes for demand-deposit accounts, truly let the bankers relax. These comfortable years for bankers led to the term "3-6-3 bankers"—bankers who "pay 3% on deposits, charge 6% on loans, and are on the golf course by 3."

Distinctions between Banks and Thrifts

Under the 1930s legislation the banking industry was completely separate from the thrift industry. The banks had always had a monopoly in demand deposits. Then the 1930s legislation allowed banks significantly greater freedom than the thrifts in their uses of funds. The S&Ls were generally required to put most of their loans into home mortgages. They were prevented from making commercial loans or significant amounts of consumer loans, and from holding commercial paper.

This artificial heterogeneity resulted partly from the fact that the thrifts and the banks operated under completely different regulatory and supervisory agencies. The banks were under the Comptroller of the Currency, the Fed and the FDIC; the S&Ls were under the FHLBB and FSLIC.

Reg Q Is Extended to the Thrifts

It was not until 1966 that Reg Q interest rate ceilings were extended to cover the thrifts. In that year the FDIC was authorized to set interest rate ceilings on rates paid by the mutual savings banks and the FHLBB was authorized to do the same for the S&Ls. These agencies were supposed to get together with the Fed and coordinate their Reg Q ceilings.

The Reg Q ceilings for the thrifts were set slightly higher than those for commercial banks. This was to give the thrifts a little more power to attract deposits and thereby channel more money into home mortgage loans. The idea was also that the thrifts "deserved" this competitive edge, since the banks could offer checking accounts (and get *interest-free* money) while the thrifts were prohibited by law from doing this.

It was not until 1970 that the National Credit Union Administration (NCUA) was authorized to impose interest rate ceilings on credit union deposits. The NCUA ceilings were not tied to Reg Q and usually were set slightly higher than the S&L ceilings.

Problems with Reg Q in the 1960s and 1970s

Reg Q was originally imposed to prevent the banks from competing with each other by offering higher interest rates to attract deposits. What's supposed to be bad about that? It's just that as banks pay more for their deposits, they have to earn more on their loans (or go broke!).

Which loans can generate the highest interest income for the banks? Risky loans! But risky loans can lead to defaults—and sometimes to bank failures. So the Reg Q ceilings are supposed to give the banks a low-cost source of funds and thereby keep the banks out of the risky loan business—let those borrowers go to the factoring companies, to the consumer finance companies, or to other sources—perhaps to the pawn shops or the loan sharks.

At that time it was argued that in the absence of Reg Q ceilings, banks might be tempted to undertake risky loans to generate enough interest income to pay higher rates on deposits. Recent theories on banking dispute this argument. But nonetheless, we lived with Reg Q for half a century.

How well did it work? As long as market rates were low, the Reg Q ceilings really didn't have any effect. But what happened when market rates went up? *Disintermediation*. Lots of depositors pulled their money out of the depository intermediaries (banks and thrifts) and put their money where it would earn the market rate (not the Reg Q rate). The problem didn't become serious until the mid-1960s.

BY THE MID-1960s THE 1930s "SHOE" NO LONGER FIT

In 1965 the inflation rate accelerated. Interest rates rose rapidly. Market rates of interest in 1966 reached a 100-year high—significantly above the Reg Q ceiling rates. Did disintermediation occur? Of course.

The Disintermediation Problem of the 1960s and '70s

As interest rates on unregulated financial instruments (T-bills, commercial paper, etc.) increased rapidly, funds flowed out of time-, savings-, and demand-deposit accounts and into these higher paying alternatives. So what happened to the legislatively established "guaranteed low-cost source of funds" for the banks and thrifts? It disappeared.

Every time market rates of interest significantly exceeded Reg Q ceilings, funds flowed out of the depository intermediaries and into other kinds of financial assets—ones which paid the higher market rates. This **disintermediation** problem was repeated in 1969, 1974–75, and 1979–80. Problems with Reg Q seemed to multiply as time went on.

New Financial Institutions and Instruments

As disintermediation occurred because of Reg Q restrictions, more and more nonregulated intermediaries and nonregulated financial instruments began to appear. The power of "the free market" at work? Exactly!

The explosive growth of money market mutual funds (MMMFs) provides the best example of this financial innovation. The MMMFs pool the small deposits of many shareholders and invest this money directly in short-term money market instruments. Shareholders in MMMFs can "cash out" anytime they wish. So they have complete liquidity and earn market rates of interest. The best of all possible worlds!

The first MMMF was established in 1972. In 1978 the MMMFs held total assets of less than $4 billion. But by 1980 MMMF "deposits" had surged to over $60 billion. And in 1982? Would you believe to more than $230 billion? That's right: to (at that time) about half the size of the total U.S. M1 money supply![2] Where did all of those MMMF deposits come from? Most of it was "disintermediated" from the financial intermediaries—the banks and thrifts. So how did the intermediaries survive? Several hundred didn't. You'll be reading more about that soon.

Basic Problem of the Thrifts: Unbalanced Portfolios

Beginning in the mid-1960s the banks frequently had difficult times during periods of financial disintermediation. But the thrifts suffered even more. Their limited kinds of deposits (no demand deposits) and the structure of their loan portfolios (mostly home mortgages) made them more vulnerable to the credit crunches of the 1960s and 1970s.

By design, the S&Ls and mutual savings banks have always allocated most of their funds to long-term mortgage loans. So their asset portfolios have always been dominated by long-term, fixed-interest loans which earn rates that were set in low-rate times—perhaps 5, 10, or 15 years ago.

But their *sources* of funds (mostly savings deposits) are short term and must either (a) pay market rates, or (b) flow away via disintermediation. All this would be no problem during normal, stable, low-interest-rate times. But during the credit crunch, high-interest periods of the 1960s and 1970s? *A serious problem!*

During these times the thrifts lost deposits. So they had to go to the money markets (and pay high market rates) for funds. Often the rates they were paying were higher than the rates they were earning on their home mortgage portfolios. What happens when you pay out more than you bring in? You don't last very long. Many thrifts didn't.

The Rising Cost of Funds

The thrifts saw their cost of funds rising during the 1970s for several reasons:

1. *Reg Q ceilings were raised* at various intervals. So the thrift either paid the higher rate or experienced a large outflow of deposits to other thrifts—and/or to the new, nonregulated accounts and financial instruments which were rapidly appearing on the scene.

2. *The new unregulated kinds of deposit accounts*—for example, large CDs—carried higher interest cost than passbook savings accounts and other traditional sources of funds.

3. Even though institutions were prohibited from explicitly paying more to their depositors to compete for funds, they did compete by offering free services—by paying **implicit interest** to attract and hold customers. So their cost of funds increased as their *increased operating costs* (the costs of providing free services) became a part of their cost of funds.

---

[2] The M1 money supply includes currency, travelers checks, and most checkable accounts at banks and thrifts. The various "monetary agregates" (the different definitions of the money supply) were explained in chapter 5, box 5-2.

THE HUNT REPORT AND THE FINE STUDY CALL FOR DEREGULATION

In the late 1960s it was becoming obvious that some changes needed to be made. Several studies were conducted and reports prepared offering specific recommendations. The most important of these studies are the Hunt Report (1971) and the FINE Study (*Discussion Principles*, 1975; *Compendium of Papers*, 1976).[3]

Both Studies Offered Similar Recommendations

Both of these were very thorough studies. Both identified major structural problems of the financial industry and suggested sweeping—you might say *revolutionary*—changes in the American banking and financial services industry. The major recommendations of both of these studies are the same: *Deregulate the industry!* Specifically, both studies recommended:

1. Abolish Reg Q ceilings on savings and time deposits and remove the zero-interest ceiling on demand deposits.

2. Remove distinctions between banks and S&Ls. All depository institutions should be allowed to offer demand deposits, and all should have the same freedom in deciding on their uses of funds. That is, all should be permitted to make the same kinds of investments and to hold the same kinds of assets (loans and securities).

3. Remove the restrictions on branching, both intrastate and interstate.

4. Combine the regulatory and supervisory functions of the federal banking and thrift agencies to eliminate overlapping (and sometimes contradictory) authority.

Bills Were Introduced but No Acts Were Passed

Both of these studies recommended removing the anticompetitive restraints enacted in the 1930s. The recommendations of the Hunt Report led to the proposed Financial Institutions Act of 1973, but the act never passed. The FINE Study proposals were incorporated into a similar attempt at legislative reform in 1975, but this one didn't pass either.

Both legislative proposals were defeated largely as a result of intensive lobbying by S&Ls and small banks. They didn't want to lose their "umbrella of anticompetitive protection" to which they had become accustomed and under which they had grown and prospered. So financial reform was not accomplished in the 1970s despite widespread recognition of the need for it.

---

[3] The official title of the Hunt report is: *Report of the President's Commission on Financial Structure and Regulation* (U.S. Government Printing Office, Washington, D.C., 1971). For an overview of the Hunt Report, see "Policies for a More Competitive Financial System" (Federal Reserve Bank of Boston, Conference Series No. 8, 1972).

The full title of the FINE Study is: *Financial Institutions and the Nation's Economy, Discussion Principles* (U.S. Congress, House, Committee on Banking, Currency, and Housing, 94th Congress, 1st Session, 1975) and *Compendium of Papers* (2nd Session, 1976). For more information on the FINE Study, see William G. Dewald, "FINE Principles and Prospects for Financial Institutions Reform," Carnegie-Rochester Conference Series on Public Policy, vol. 7, Amsterdam (North-Holland Publishing Co., 1977), pp. 131–52.

Perhaps it's time to coin "the Law of U.S. Financial Legislation": *Only in times of crisis can the political process (the U.S. Congress) succeed in taking action on financial reform.* This may not be a "natural law." But it certainly seems to have been holding true for a long time.

It was not until near-crisis conditions developed in the early 1980s that the political obstacles were overcome and some of the much-needed reform legislation was passed.

THE UNLEGISLATED (MARKET-DIRECTED) FINANCIAL REVOLUTION BEGINS

The lack of financial reform legislation in the 1970s did not prevent financial innovation from occurring in the industry. The inflation rate was high and rising. So were interest rates. The banks and thrifts, in order to survive, had to somehow slow or stop the disintermediation process. But the problem wasn't just disintermediation.

Increasing Competition for Funds

The years of complacency in a protected environment of regulation were slipping away. Suddenly banks were competing against each other and against the thrifts for funds. And the thrifts were fighting back. The competitive game got tougher. Some bank and thrift managers forgot that they were supposed to be genteel "3-6-3 bankers."

The banks faced the problems of the growth of nonbank intermediaries and the growth of demand deposit substitutes. The thrifts suffered from their restrictions on sources and uses of funds—especially their lack of demand deposit accounts.

At the same time, all of the financial institutions were being hit by the computer-telecommunications revolution, by high and rising interest rates, and by serious inflation.

A few banks and thrifts failed. And many of the institutions that survived began to look quite different from the depository institutions of the 1960s. Thrifts were beginning to look more like banks. The barriers creating artificial differences between the thrifts and the banks were eroding—with or without Congressional approval. An example of the power of market forces, getting around obstacles? Yes.

Thrifts and Banks Offer Interest-Bearing Checking Accounts

In 1972 the first Negotiable Order of Withdrawal (NOW) account was offered by a savings bank in Massachusetts. A thrift institution was offering a checking account—and one that bears interest!

By 1978 the thrifts in six New England states and in New York were offering NOW accounts. In 1978 some credit unions began offering share draft accounts, which also are interest-bearing checking accounts. The thrifts were fighting for survival against the banks and against all of the new nonregulated financial instruments and institutions.

But the banks fought back. In 1978 automatic transfer service (ATS) accounts were introduced by commercial banks. With the ATS account, the depositor's money is held in an interest bearing savings account, and when the depositor writes a check the funds to cover the check automatically flow from the savings account to the checking account. So, from the point of view of the depositor, is the ATS account an interest-bearing checking account? Yes.

Brokers Offer Interest-Bearing Checking Accounts

Not only the thrifts and the banks were competing against each other. In the 1970s Merrill Lynch made headlines with its CMA (cash management account). In cooperation with a bank, Merrill Lynch had introduced an account offering money market interest rates and check-writing privileges. And it was available nationwide!

What Merrill Lynch started soon spread. Big cracks in the walls between bankers and brokers? Yes. What about the Glass-Steagall Act? Also big cracks in the walls preventing interstate banking? Yes. And what about the McFadden Act?

Were the brokers and banks and thrifts and others all ignoring the laws and doing illegal things? Maybe so. Sometimes it's hard to know what's legal and what isn't. That's the way it is when a major revolution is just getting started.

The Situation Becomes Increasingly Untenable

It was in the late 1970s that the situation for the banks and thrift became intolerable. They were entangled in an antiquated, depression-induced legal and regulatory framework that didn't allow them to meet the demands of a rapidly changing marketplace.

The high and increasing U.S. inflation rate and the seriously low international value of the dollar exacerbated the problem. As you might guess, OPEC's 1400 percent increase in the price of oil since the early 1970s had something to do with it. Oil in international markets is priced in U.S. dollars. When the oil price goes up 1400 percent, that means the value of the oil-purchasing dollar drops to about seven cents! Serious inflation? Yes. No wonder the dollar was weak.

Tight money policy was instituted in October 1979. What happened to the depository institutions when they were hit with very high and very volatile interest rates? While strapped with (or supported by, depending on your point of view) antiquated Reg Q interest rate ceilings? And with each Fed member bank required to forego millions of dollars of interest because of non-interest-bearing required reserves?

How did the depository institutions cope? And survive? Hundreds didn't. So what happened? The rules were changed. And the institutions changed. The introduction of new computer-telecommunications technology was greatly accelerated. A revolution was triggered in the financial services industry—a revolution that was destined to continue throughout the 1980s and beyond. The following chapter focuses on this "banking revolution of the 1980s"—on what happened, and why.

SUMMARY

- The three important kinds of thrift institutions in the United States are savings and loan associations (S&Ls), mutual savings banks (MSBs), and credit unions (CUs). The S&Ls and MSBs began in the early 1800s as mutual organizations, with state charters, for the purpose of providing a "safe haven" for small savers, and for financing home loans.

- Credit unions were first established in the early 1900s, and are focused more on consumer loans than home mortgage loans.

- Mutual savings banks only exist in 17 states. Most of them are located in Massachusetts, New York, and Connecticut. The average MSB is larger than either the average commercial bank or the average S&L institution. But none of these are anywhere near as large as the giant money center commercial banks. Prior to 1980 all MSBs were state chartered. The first federal MSB charter was granted in 1980.

- The S&Ls began as closed-membership "building societies" for financing residential housing. After the Civil War the S&Ls opened their membership to the general public and they grew rapidly. But the MSBs continued to be by far the largest form of thrift institution up to the 1920s.

- The S&Ls grew rapidly in the 1920s. In 1929 there were more than 12,000 S&Ls holding about one-fourth of all non-farm residential mortgages in the country. At that time the S&Ls held assets and deposits approximately equal in size to those of the MSBs. The Great Depression wiped out many of the S&Ls—leaving less than 6,000 by 1934.

- Over the past three decades the number of S&Ls has declined and the average size has increased significantly.

- The Federal Home Loan Bank Board (FHLBB) performs service functions for the S&Ls, administers the Federal Savings and Loan Insurance Corporation (FSLIC), and makes advances to the S&Ls.

- There are some 16,000 credit unions in the United States. The typical credit union is a small nonprofit organization taking small savings deposits and making consumer loans to its members. But a few are large and in recent years several have been growing rapidly and expanding their banking services.

- The National Credit Union Administration (NCUA) provides service functions for the credit unions, and administers the National Credit Union Share Insurance Fund (NCUSIF) which insures credit union deposits up to $100,000.

- Credit unions get a back-up source of liquidity from the credit union leagues, and the U.S. Central Credit Union established by the Credit Union National Association (CUNA) in 1974.

- The U.S. and worldwide system of depository institutions is tightly tied together through interbank deposits and correspondent relationships so that even the smallest depository institution can provide financial services on a worldwide basis.

- Following World War II, deposit insurance was very successful, and the other depression-born regulations were not restrictive.

- In the mid 1960s, Reg Q began to create disintermediation and the depository institutions were hurt. The thrifts were heavy with long-term low-interest fixed-rate mortgage loans. So as their cost of funds and operating costs rose, their loan revenues did not.

- The Hunt Report and the FINE Study of the early 1970s recommended deregulation, but Congress failed to act.

- During the 1960s and '70s the banks and thrifts began finding ways to use loopholes to avoid regulations. Holding companies were established to assist in attracting funds and to permit banks broader latitude in their activities.

- In the 1970s some of the thrifts, and then banks, and then stockbrokers began offering checking accounts which paid interest. The revolution was beginning. The following chapter focuses on this **banking revolution** of the 1980s.

Important Principles, Issues, Concepts, Terms

Different kinds of thrift institutions

Origins of the thrifts

Mutual organizations

Thrift asset limitations

Shift from state to federal charters

Development of MSBs

Geographic concentration of MSBs

Federal chartering of MSBs

Early history of S&Ls

S&Ls growth in the 1920s

Recent trends in S&L numbers and size

Role of the FHLBB

Asset powers of the S&Ls

Size structure of the S&Ls

Credit unions: number, size, and characteristics

History of the "Credit union movement"

The National Credit Union Administration (NCUA)

Recent developments in credit unions

Sources of liquidity for credit unions

Growth of credit unions

New powers for the thrifts in the 1930s

Interlocking relationships among depository institutions

The nationwide and worldwide financial system

Effects of FDIC legislation

Effects of Reg Q—at first, and then later

1930s legal distinctions between banks and thrifts

The disintermediation problem

New financial institutions of the 1970s and '80s

New financial instruments of the 1970s and '80s

Unbalanced portfolios of the thrifts

Rising cost of funds in the 1960s, '70s, and '80s

Recommendations of the Hunt Report

Recommendations of the FINE Study

Problems created by Reg Q in the 1960s and '70s

The "market-directed" financial revolution

Questions

1. Mention and explain some of the common characteristics of all of the thrift institutions.

2. Why are mutual savings banks in the United States so unevenly geographically distributed?

3. Describe the evolution and current condition of the savings and loan industry in the United States.

4. Describe the evolution and current condition of the credit unions in the United States.

5. Describe some of the correspondent relationships which exist among the depository institutions, U.S. and worldwide.

6. In the mid-1960s, the effects of the depression legislation began to create serious difficulty for depository institutions, especially the thrifts. Explain what happened, and why.

7. Give the highlights of the results of the Hunt Report and the FINE Study, and then try to explain why none of these recommendations were immediately enacted by the Congress.

8. The financial revolution of the 1970s and '80s was initiated, not through legislation, but through market developments in the financial system. Explain.

Suggested Readings

Barth, James R., Dan Brumbaugh, Jr., Dan Sauerhaft, and George H. D. Wang. "Insolvency and Risk-Taking in the Thrift Industry: Implications for the Future." *Contemporary Policies Studies.* (Fall 1985), 1–6.

Benston, George J. "Interest on Deposits and the Survival of Chartered Depository Institutions." *Economic Review.* Federal Reserve Bank of Atlanta (October 1984), 42–55.

———. "Savings Banking and the Public Interest." *Journal of Money, Credit and Banking.* (February 1972), 133–266.

Black, Robert P. and Doris E. Harless. *Nonbank Financial Institutions.* Federal Reserve Bank of Richmond, 1975.

Carron, Andrew. *The Plight of the Thrift Industry.* Washington, D.C.: The Brookings Institute, 1982.

———. *The Rescue of the Thrift Industry.* Washington, D.C.: The Brookings Institute, 1983.

Cox, William N. and Pamela V. Whigham. "What Distinguishes Larger and More Efficient Credit Unions?" *Economic Review.* Federal Reserve Bank of Atlanta (October 1984), 34–41.

Credit Union National Association. *Credit Union Report.* Madison, Wis., annual publication.

Fortier, Diana and Dave Philis. "Bank and Thrift Performance Since DIDMCA." *Economic Perspectives.* Federal Reserve Bank of Chicago (September/October 1985), 58–68.

Garsson, Robert M. "Shaky S&Ls May Stay Open to Keep Funds Afloat." *The American Banker.* (September 15, 1986), 10.

Goudreau, Robert E. "S&L Use of New Powers: Consumer and Commercial Loan Expansion." *Economic Review.* Federal Reserve Bank of Atlanta (December 1984), 15–33.

Gup, Benton E. *Financial Intermediaries, an Introduction.* Boston: Houghton Mifflin, 1976.

Hill, G. Christian. "Agencies that Insure Bank, Thrift Deposits Face Major Problems." *The Wall Street Journal.* May 23, 1984.

Kareken, John H. "Deposit Insurance Reform or Deregulation is the Cart, Not the Horse." *Quarterly Review.* Federal Reserve Bank of Minneapolis (Spring 1983), 1–9.

Keeley, Michael C. "The Health of Banks and Thrifts." *FRBSF Weekly Letter.* Federal Reserve Bank of San Francisco, February 21, 1986.

Kroos, Herman and Martin Byln. *A History of Financial Intermediaries.* New York: Random House, 1971.

Mahoney, Patrick J. and Alice P. White. "The Thrift Industry in Transition." *Federal Reserve Bulletin.* Board of Governors (March 1985), 137–56.

Marvell, Thomas. *The Federal Home Loan Bank Board.* New York: Praeger, 1969.

Moran, Michael J. "The Federally Sponsored Credit Agencies: An Overview." *Federal Reserve Bulletin.* (June 1985), 373–88.

———. "Thrift Institutions in Recent Years." *Federal Reserve Bulletin.* 68 (December 1982), 725–38.

National Council of Savings Institutions. *National Fact Book of Savings Institutions.* Washington, D.C., annual publication.

Pugh, Olin P. "Credit Unions: From Consumer Movement to National Market Force." *Bankers Magazine.* (January/February 1980), 19–27.

Shaw, Edward S. "Financial Intermediaries." *International Encyclopedia of the Social Sciences.* vol. 5, New York: Macmillan, 1968, pp. 432–38.

Teck, Alan. *Mutual Savings Banks and Loan Associations: Aspects of Growth.* New York: Columbia University Press, 1968.

United States League of Savings Associations. *The Federal Guide.* Chicago, Ill., Annual.

———. *Savings Institutions Sourcebook.* Chicago, Ill., Annual.

CHAPTER 8

The 1980s Revolution in Money and Banking: A New Financial System for the 1990s

Chapter Objectives

This chapter builds on the two previous chapters and explains the revolutionary changes in the U.S. banking and financial system. After you study this chapter you will understand and be able to explain:

1. How the high and volatile nominal interest rates of 1979–80 resulted in the dual crises of
   a. Fed membership and
   b. disintermediation.
2. The purposes and specific provisions of the early 1980s legislation: the Depository Institutions Deregulation and Monetary Control Act (DIDMCA) of 1980 and the Garn–St Germain Act of 1982.
3. The FSLIC crisis of 1986–87, and the provisions of The Competitive Equality Banking Act of 1987.
4. Developments in **interstate banking**, including **regional reciprocity** arrangements.
5. Reasons for and effects of the rapid growth of **non-bank banks**.
6. The rapid growth of **electronic funds transfer systems** (EFTS).
7. The **dissolving boundaries** between and among the various kinds of financial services institutions, and the newly developed **fiercely competitive** environment.
8. The important role of **loopholing** in speeding the revolution in banking.

FINANCIAL INDUSTRY TURMOIL IN 1979–80: THE CRISIS ARRIVES

By the end of the 1970s the banking and financial services industry was in **near-crisis conditions**. But (as always) there was widespread disagreement in the industry about what action should be taken. The great diversity of the financial services industry has always resulted in serious conflict and an inability to reach consensus.

The giant money-center banks, the small community banks, and the dozens of multi-billion dollar so-called "regional" banks in between—all were taking different positions. Then there was the Fed-member position and the non-Fed-member position. Consider also the thrifts, with their own points of view. It isn't surprising that "consensus" was (as always) impossible to achieve.

The Fed's "New Operating Procedures" (Monetarist Experiment?) of October 6, 1979

During 1978 and '79 the inflation rate increased significantly—to over 10 percent. In September of 1979 the international value of the dollar was plummeting. Emergency action was required.

On Saturday, October 6, 1979 the Fed announced strong money tightening measures—actions that came to be known to some as the Fed's "Saturday Night Special." But to the banks and thrifts it was the Fed's "Saturday Night Massacre." On that Saturday the Fed announced an increase of the discount rate to a record 12 percent. It also imposed an additional 8 percent reserve requirement on bank holdings of certain kinds of borrowed reserves.

In addition (and most important) the Fed announced that from then on they would stop being very concerned with how high short-term interest rates might go—that from then on they were going to concentrate on *limiting the amount of total reserves in the banking system* (and therefore the total amount of money in the economy).

The Fed promised to stick to this policy no matter if interest rates went much higher, and were unstable. In the days and weeks that followed, money market rates soared and fluctuated widely.

The Exodus of Banks from Fed Membership

In the late 1970s the number of Fed-member banks declined as banks exercised their option to withdraw. State banks were free to do that. National banks could get state charters, drop their national charters and then withdraw. An increasing number of banks were doing this as the costs of Fed membership were increasingly outweighing the benefits.

When interest rates are over 10 percent, holding non-interest-bearing required reserve deposits in the Fed banks becomes *very expensive!* Following the October 6 policy change the cost of being a Fed member increased dramatically. More banks (several hundred) announced their intention to withdraw from the Fed. This was one of the "crisis situations" which led to the revolutionary banking legislation in March of 1980.

A Sharp Wave of Disintermediation

The other crisis was disintermediation. As money market interest rates went into the teens, depositors were drawing their money out of the banks and thrifts (which were limited by Reg Q to paying less than 6%) and putting their funds where they could earn money market rates—sometimes 15 percent or more.

The S&Ls were particularly hard hit. Most of their assets consisted of long-term home mortgages which had been issued at much lower rates. Many of the thrifts were faced with paying more than 10 percent to obtain funds at the same time that many of their assets (home mortgages) were bringing in returns as low as 6 percent—sometimes even less.

For many institutions, current losses were large. Projected losses were even larger. The only question: "How long can we hold on?" When a crisis gets to be *a real crisis* the Congress usually acts. And clearly, this was a real one. After months of conflict, in March of 1980 the Congress acted.

THE DEPOSITORY INSTITUTIONS DEREGULATION AND MONETARY CONTROL ACT (DIDMCA) OF 1980

Under the constant urging of Fed Chairman Paul Volcker, the Congressional committees got together and worked out a compromise. The *Depository Institutions and Deregulation and Monetary Control Act (DIDMCA) of 1980* was finally passed by Congress and signed by President Carter on March 31, 1980. The next section describes the DIDMCA. But first, read box 8-1 for an overview of important banking legislation during this century.

Specific Provisions of the Act

This "omnibus act" contained nine titles, each of which was an act in itself. There were titles dealing with the simplification of financial regulations, foreign control

---

Box 8-1

Feature: Major Banking Legislation since 1900

Federal Reserve Act (1913)
  Established the Federal Reserve System

McFadden Act (1927)
  Prohibited branching across state lines without state legislative approval

Banking Act of 1933 (Glass-Steagall Act)
  Prohibited paying interest on demand deposits, established Reg Q, established the FDIC, prohibited banks from engaging in securities activities

Bank Holding Company Act (1956) and *Douglas Amendment* (1956)
  Regulated formation and expansion of new bank holding companies. Prohibited new multistate bank holding companies

Bank Merger Act (1966)
  Established merger guidelines

Amendments to Bank Holding Company Act (1970)
  Regulated one-bank holding companies

Depository Institutions Deregulation and Monetary Control Act (1980)
  Established uniform reserves, initiated Reg Q deregulation, and authorized checkable accounts for all thrifts

Garn–St Germain Depository Institutions Act (1982)
  Permitted banks and thrifts to offer a money market deposit account, continued Reg Q deregulation, and provided for emergency capital and mergers for thrifts.

Competitive Equality Banking Act (1987)
  Recapitalized the FSLIC, closed nonbank bank loophole, and required the Federal Reserve to speed the nation's check clearing process.

Source: Federal Reserve Bank of Dallas, *Annual Report 1987*, p. 12.

of U.S. financial institutions, truth in lending, state usury laws, and other matters. But the "revolutionary" titles dealt with:

1. Establishing the same **reserve requirements** for all depository institutions, whether state or national, bank or thrift, Fed-member of nonmember. (The only difference was that small institutions had lower requirements than large ones.) This modification stopped the Fed membership exodus.

2. Reg Q **interest rate ceilings** were to be phased out over a period of time. (That phase-out was finally completed in March, 1986.)

3. The commercial bank monopoly on checking accounts was ended as NOW accounts, ATS accounts, and share draft accounts became available nationwide. Now all depository institutions are authorized to offer interest-paying **checkable accounts**.

4. The thrifts were permitted to expand their asset holdings beyond home mortgages. The S&Ls were authorized to invest up to 20 percent of their assets in consumer loans, commercial paper, and corporate debt securities.

The DIDMCA of 1980 made the thrifts much more like commercial banks, and made nonmember banks (and all thrifts which had checkable accounts) a lot like Fed-members. All were required to hold the same reserves at the Fed banks.

Some Effects of the New Act

The DIDMCA was the first revolutionary change in the banking and financial services system since the 1930s. The act permitted thrifts to move into the banking business. But many of the small thrifts had been satisfied with their "niche" as it was. This new act threw them into a hostile competitive environment with no choice except to fight or die. Given their unbalanced portfolios—long-term low-interest assets (home mortgages) and short-term high-interest liabilities (forced by disintermediation of savings deposits)—it was not a fair fight. As it turned out, many fought and survived. But many did not survive.

The number of S&Ls declined from 4,600 in 1980 to less than 3,000 in 1988. Some decided to merge, more than 500 failed, and more than 400 became savings banks. The number of savings banks increased from 460 in 1980 to 984 in 1988. At the end of the 1980s, although many newly established thrifts are prospering, several of the older ones are still fighting for survival.

The non-Fed-member banks were required by the DIDMCA to hold reserves in the Fed banks. This requirement was phased in over a period of years. Also, the act lowered reserve requirements. For smaller institutions the reserve requirement on checkable deposits was only 3 percent, and for the very small ones it was zero.

THE 1980 ACT LEFT MANY PROBLEMS UNSOLVED

The act increased FDIC insurance coverage from a maximum of $40,000 to $100,000, and it dealt with other issues. But it did not address the interstate banking question which was high on the agenda for several bankers. Why no action? Because opinions on this issue were split right down the middle. No compromise was possible.

The scheduled repeal of Reg Q was of no immediate help. The flood of disintermediation continued. In mid-May of 1980 (less than two months after the new act was passed) it was estimated that some 40 percent of the nation's thrifts were losing money.

The 1980 Bond Market Crash

During the first few months of 1980, the bond market lost some $300 billion in value—its biggest crash since the Depression of the 1930s. And of course, the same thing was happening to the value of fixed-rate mortgage loans, and to all other long-term fixed-interest financial instruments. Why? Because of high (astronomical!) nominal interest rates. The prime rate reached a peak of over 20 percent in April of 1980. After that, rates came down and the bond markets recovered somewhat. But massive disintermediation continued.

The Unforgetable Lesson of the Early 1980s

The turbulent events in the money and bond markets during the early 1980s had a serious and lasting impact on the psychology of bank and thrift managers, and on all other portfolio managers and investors as well. The dangers of holding long-term fixed rate securities will never be forgotten.

Today, many financial institutions are not obligating themselves to any kind of long-term obligation which does not "reprice" at fairly frequent intervals and those who do are hedging their long-term fixed-rate instruments. How this hedging works will be explained later.

The Continuing Thrift Crisis: 1980–82

In 1981 some money market mutual funds (MMMFs) were paying rates of 15 percent and more. Passbook savings accounts at the S&Ls were paying 5-1/2 percent and at banks, 5-1/4 percent. The banks and thrifts were authorized to issue several new kinds of CDs on which money market rates could be paid. But all of these new instruments required minimum deposits (e.g., $10,000) and all imposed penalties for early withdrawal. The MMMFs were offering money market rates with very low minimum deposit requirements, and complete liquidity—you could withdraw your money anytime you wanted to. So disintermediation continued. Some banks and many thrifts were threatened by bankruptcy. Another crisis? New legislation required? Exactly!

In 1981 the Federal Home Loan Bank Board's list of "troubled S&Ls" increased from 121 in January to 404 (about 10% of the industry) in July. During this period many thrifts were closed. Most of these were merged with other thrifts or with banks with the help of funds from the FSLIC.

In July of 1981, the largest S&L in the state of New York (West Side Federal) was facing bankruptcy. FHLBB Chairman Richard Pratt said: "If Congress does not act in the short run to address this matter, there will be no long run for a very substantial segment of the thrift industry." But Congress did not act.

During 1981 losses by the S&Ls reached a record of $4.6 billion. During the first half of 1982 their losses were running at an annual rate of more than $6 billion.

In July of 1982 the net worth of the nations S&Ls was down by 20 percent from the year earlier. By the fall of 1982 S&L failures were averaging about *three per week.* That compares with an average of *less than three per year* prior to 1981.

THE GARN–ST GERMAIN ACT OF 1982

In 1981 and 1982 various bills were proposed to prevent the (not-so-slow) death of the thrift industry. Finally on October 15, 1982 *The Depository Institutions Act of 1982* (the Garn–St Germain Act) was passed.

The new act gave the banks and thrifts something they both had been pleading for: money-market-rate deposit accounts (MMDAs) with almost no-strings attached. Now they could compete openly with the MMMFs. Also, the act established "income capital certificates" (net worth certificates) to inject new equity into ailing thrifts to stave off the threat of immediate bankruptcy. And (over the objections of small bankers) it permitted the S&Ls to do some commercial lending and to perform some other commercial banking functions.

The New Money Market Deposit Accounts (MMDAs)

Banks and thrifts were authorized to offer the new money market deposit accounts beginning on December 14, 1982. The new accounts would have a minimum balance of $2,500 and would permit six transactions per month—three by check.

Assets of the money market funds had grown from less than $4 billion on January 1, 1978, to more than $230 billion in the fall of 1982. But after December 14, MMMF assets declined. By February of 1983, MMMFs had experienced withdrawals of more than $30 billion while the banks and thrifts had attracted deposits of more than $200 billion into their new MMDA accounts. Some of this inflow into the MMDAs was "reintermediation." But many billions of the dollars were merely shifted out of other (low paying) accounts at the same bank.

In January of 1983 banks and thrifts began offering super-NOW accounts paying close to money market rates, and with unlimited checkwriting privileges. Suddenly there was a sharp increase in the cost of funds. By early 1983 the new challenge for the depository institutions had become: "Where can we invest all this money and generate enough earnings to pay its high cost?"

The Ultimate Phase-Out of Interest Rate Ceilings

During 1984, '85, and '86, interest rate ceilings, minimum deposit requirements, and early withdrawal penalties all were progressively phased-out. The final stroke in the elimination of interest rate ceilings occurred on March 31, 1986, exactly six years after the DIDMCA was signed into law by President Carter.

The only restriction which remained (and on into 1989 still remains) is the prohibition of interest payments on demand deposits. Businesses are prohibited from holding interest-bearing checkable deposits, such as NOW accounts, so they still can't earn interest on their checking deposits.

The DIDMCA and Garn–St Germain Acts Didn't Solve All the Problems

When the DIDMCA was passed in March 1980, the act was called **revolutionary**—"the most far reaching, most important financial legislation in 50 years." But soon after the act was passed, it became clear that the thrift crisis was getting worse, not better. Something more was needed.

Finally, 2-1/2 years (and several hundred failed thrifts) later, in October of 1982 the Garn–St Germain Act was passed. This act was also hailed as "far reaching," "revolutionary"—"the most important financial legislation in 50 years."

Again, a few months after this act was passed, more major legislation was being called for. But no such legislation was forthcoming until 1987 when the FSLIC crisis made action imperative.

During the five-year period from 1982 to 1987 several comprehensive banking bills were prepared. Hearings were held and there was much heated discussion. But until midyear 1987, no action. The issues proposed and discussed (argued about) during this five-year period dealt with such things as:

- Securities activities by banks
- Insurance activities by banks
- Real estate activities by banks
- Fed payment of interest on required reserves
- Bank dealings in rentals and leasing
- Check-holding policies by depository institutions
- State usury ceilings on interest rates
- Payment of interest on demand deposit (regular checking) accounts
- Credit card regulations and disclosure information
- Interstate banking arrangements
- Non-bank banks and the definition of "a bank"
- Changes in the deposit insurance structure
- Changes in the regulatory and supervisory structure
- Emergency funding for FSLIC
- Capital requirements for banks and thrifts
- And several others

No Congressional action was taken on any of these issues for five years because no *crisis* developed. Then in 1987, a crisis! FSLIC (in governmentese, "fizz-lick") was going broke. Too many thrifts had failed and were failing. FSLIC didn't have enough funds either to bail them out or to pay off their depositors.

THE FSLIC CRISIS OF 1986–87 AND THE COMPETITIVE EQUALITY BANKING ACT OF 1987

Emergency legislation to bail out the FSLIC was introduced in the fall of 1986, and you know what that means: Time to pile on! Tie your pet objectives to the emergency FSLIC bill!

Amendments were added dealing with several of the issues listed above. The wrangling continued while FSLIC's funds drained. During 1987 a group of technically bankrupt thrifts were continuing to operate, losing millions of dollars each day. But FSLIC could not close them because it didn't have the funds to meet the "closing costs."

By June of 1987 some S&L depositors were getting nervous about the safety of their funds and about the soundness of the FSLIC. So the Congress was spurred into action. After about two months of negotiating, arguing, and horsetrading on issues, both Houses of Congress finally passed and on August 10, 1987, President Reagan signed the *Competitive Equality Banking Act of 1987*.

The act provided $10.8 billion for recapitalization of the FSLIC. It set a temporary moratorium on all new powers for commercial banks—securities, insurance, etc—until March 1, 1988. It closed the nonbank-bank loophole, permitted the some 160 existing nonbank banks to continue to exist, but limited the rate of their asset growth. It also limited the amount of time a depositor's bank can delay crediting a deposited check to the depositor's account. Box 8-2 discusses some of the effects of this provision.

The Legislative Outlook

Of all of the issues listed previously, the *Competitive Equality Banking Act of 1987* really only addressed three of them: the check-holding policies by depository institutions, the nonbank-bank loophole, and emergency funding for the FSLIC. Immediately after the passage of the 1987 act, Congress went to work on several of the other issues, notably the first three involving permission for banks to more freely enter the securities, insurance, and real estate businesses.

Senator Proxmire, Chairman of the Senate Banking Committee announced that when his term expires in early 1989, he will not seek reelection, and that in his last term he will make a major effort to see basic financial institution restructuring legislation enacted. Proxmire wants to repeal the Glass Steagall restrictions on banking activities, but now, as always, there is great disagreement on both sides of this issue. As this book goes to press in midyear 1988, there is no immediate crisis, and history tells us that major banking legislation in this country requires some kind of crisis. But with the efforts of the powerful Chairman of the Senate Banking Committee, and the powerful American Bankers Association lobby—it may be that this case will be an exception. But I wouldn't "bet the bank" on it.

Meanwhile, the banking regulators continue to call for Congressional action dealing with the restructuring of the financial services system.

Box 8-2

Feature: Speeding the Check-Clearing Process

Competitive Equality Banking Act of 1987

Now there is a new challenge to add to the evolution of the payments system. In 1987, legislation was passed that also will impact significantly the Federal Reserve and its operations as well as the relationship that financial institutions have with their customers. The Competitive Equality Banking Act of 1987 has many sections that cover a wide variety of banking topics—most notably the recapitalization of the Federal Savings and Loan Insurance Corporation (FSLIC) and the closing of the nonbank bank loophole.

The act most impacts Federal Reserve operations in the area of expedited funds collection, by specifying maximum time limits within which funds are to be made available to customers.

At the same time, the act gives very broad regulatory powers to the Federal Reserve to regulate the payments system and expedite the collection of checks. Because of reductions in the amount of time a depositor's bank will have before giving customers credit for their deposited checks, increased emphasis will be placed on the transmission of information to a depositor's bank regarding whether the deposited check will be paid.

The Board of Governors of the Federal Reserve System is directed to write regulations that will require the speedy return of a dishonored item to the depositor's bank, that all returned checks be eligible for return through the Federal Reserve banks, that institutions be permitted to return dishonored checks directly to the institution in which the check was first deposited, that endorsements be placed in specified positions, and that the requirements be expanded to notify a depositor's bank that a check will not be paid.

Simply putting a return item in the mail by midnight of the business day following receipt may no longer be an acceptable method of return. To meet the new requirements, new technology will be employed, new endorsement standards will be enforced, and the industry's very thinking on the check collection process will be altered. The Federal Reserve will have to put processes in place to help make this happen. The banking industry will have to do the same. A lot of work will have to be done in a relatively short time period—within the next three years.

Source: Federal Reserve Bank of Dallas, 1987 Annual Report, p. 13.

THE RAPID GROWTH OF INTERSTATE BANKING

The McFadden Act prohibits a bank from branching across a state boundary *unless* the state legislature permits such branching. The Douglas Amendment (1956) prohibits a bank holding company from acquiring banks in two different states. Both these laws are still on the books. Still the 1980s have seen the explosive growth of interstate banking. Interstate competition among the financial services institutions is intense.

The larger banks are offering almost all of their services on an interstate basis. About the only thing a bank can't do in any other state it wishes to, is to set up a branch office to take deposits. But some are finding ways to do that. Money market funds and brokers are taking deposits nationwide and are offering checking privileges to depositors nationwide.

No important new legislation regarding interstate banking has been passed by the Congress, nor is any such legislation expected. The opposition from some banks is too great. However, interstate activities by banks and other financial institutions continue to increase rapidly.

Nationwide Banking Already Exists

As far back as March 27, 1982, an article in *The Economist* said "Nationwide banking has already arrived in America without any change in the law. The nation's bankers have found loopholes in the law." The article gives several examples of nationwide banking, including deposit-taking, nationwide automated teller machine (ATM) networks, and others. The article concludes that by the time Congress changes the law, it won't make any difference.[1]

There have been a large number of interstate mergers involving failing savings and loan institutions. For example, one such merger permitted Citicorp of New York (the nation's largest bank) to acquire Fidelity Savings and Loan in California.

For many years banks have been setting up "loan production offices" (LPOs) in other states. You can't walk into an LPO and make a deposit, but you can arrange a loan. Banks solicit corporate treasurers all over the country offering them CDs, trying to attract deposit funds. Also foreign branches of American banks take deposits from all over the world.

Several banks have been issuing credit cards nationwide. So have the brokers and so has Sears Roebuck.

Bank holding companies have subsidiary finance companies which can establish branches anywhere in the country. Also under the Edge Act of 1919 banks are permitted to establish banking offices *for international purposes* in any state they wish.

Prior to the passage of the *International Banking Act of 1978* foreign banks were permitted to set up operations in several states, while domestic banks were prohibited by the McFadden Act from doing so. During the 1970s the number of foreign bank entities operating in U.S. domestic markets increased from about 200 to more than 300. The 1978 act changed all that. Those foreign operations which were already in place were permitted to remain, but from then on new foreign banks were required to declare a "home office" and subsequently be subject to the same branching constraints as the domestic banks in that state.

Summary of Interstate Activities by Individual Banks and Bank Holding Companies

Many banks operate offices in other states providing just about every banking service you can think of *except* accepting deposits. They arrange loans, finance consumer purchases, finance mortgages, sell insurance, provide credit card services, finance international trade transactions, provide trust services—just about everything but taking deposits. But that does not mean that banks do not gather deposits outside their own state. Aggressive banks are "beating the bushes" at corporate headquarters nationwide looking for deposits, which then are "received and recorded" by the bank in its home state.

Banks with "Grandfathered" Rights. A few banks already had branches in other states when the McFadden Act was passed in 1927. Those banks were permitted to keep those branches and (depending on state laws) perhaps expand the operations in the state or states in which it has this "grandfathered" position. There are

---

[1] "America's Nationwide Banking," *The Economist*, March 27, 1982, pp 16–17.

only two such banks: Heritage Bank of New Jersey, which has a bank in Pennsylvania, and Bank of California, which has branches in Oregon and Washington.

There are 21 bank holding companies which owned banks in two or more states at the time the Douglas Amendment was passed in 1956. So these banks are also "grandfathered" in their right to own banks in more than one state. Altogether there are more than thirty states interlinked through these "grandfathered" arrangements. And there are at least five foreign banks with "grandfathered" banks in at least two states—usually New York and California.

Interstate Mergers Involving Troubled Thrifts. In 1981 the Federal Home Loan Bank Board (FHLBB) adopted a policy of allowing interstate thrift mergers when necessary to bail out an ailing institution. Several such mergers have occurred, some of them involving the acquisition of a troubled thrift by an out-of-state bank. The most notable case of this occurred when Citicorp acquired Fidelity Federal of San Francisco as mentioned previously.

Interstate Financial Services of Nondepository Institutions. In 1977 the Fed approved the Merrill Lynch **Cash Management Account** (CMA), saying that it did not violate banking laws. This decision opened the door to the "almost banking" business for brokerage (and other) firms. And it opened the door to nationwide "special-account" banking.

As a CMA account customer you begin with a $20,000 minimum—in stocks, bonds, money market funds, cash, whatever. Dividends and interest on your stocks and bonds are paid into the account and automatically invested in money market funds. You receive a VISA card and a checkbook on which you can write checks on the balance in your money market fund. The checking and credit-card functions are carried out for Merrill Lynch by Banc One of Columbus, Ohio.

Following the overwhelming success of the CMA account, other brokers established similar accounts. Money flowed out of the banks and thrifts and into these broker-operated accounts. Nationwide "special account" banking? Yes.

The banks couldn't compete because Reg Q prohibited them from offering money market rates and they couldn't offer stockbroker services. But by 1983, all that had changed.

On October 21, 1983, the *Wall Street Journal* carried a half-page Citibank ad which said: "Once it was smart to have a CMA. Now it's smarter to be in FOCUS." The ad compared the Citibank FOCUS account with the Merrill Lynch CMA account. It wasn't long before several major banks were offering CMA-type accounts, with checkwriting and brokerage services, all operating nationwide.

The Explosive Growth of Nonbank Banks. A nonbank bank is a bank which does not meet the definition of "bank" as defined in the regulatory laws. As of midyear 1987, the law said that you are a bank if you are doing these two things: (1) making commercial loans and (2) taking deposits. Suppose you aren't making commercial loans. Or suppose you make commercial loans but you don't take deposits. Either way, under the law, you are not a bank. You don't fit the legal definition.

What's the big deal? Just this: A nonbank bank could be set up anywhere. Since it isn't a bank, it doesn't fall under the banking laws. So a corporation could set one up in each state! Goodbye Douglas Amendment!

Who owns nonbank banks? Many companies. Sears. Parker Pen. General Electric. Dryfus Corporation and other mutual fund companies. Stockbrokerage companies. Several bank holding companies. Some S&Ls too. Dimension Financial Corporation applied for permission to establish 31 of these nonbank banks, located in 25 different states.

Fed Chairman Paul Volcker throughout the mid-1980s, was calling on Congress for legislation changing the definition of "bank" to bring these nonbank banks under the banking laws. Volcker's proposed new definition was included in a banking bill as far back as 1983, and in several banking bills since that time. But it wasn't until August 10, 1987, when President Reagen signed the *Competitive Equality Banking Act of 1987* that the nonbank bank loophole was closed.

Interstate Financial Services Competition from Nonfinancial Firms. Clearly, the brokers have moved into the banking business and the bankers have moved into brokerage, cash management, and other financial services. Almost all of this is done on a complete nationwide basis—no state boundary restrictions.

Much the same is going on with many nonfinancial firms, including Sears, G.E., G.M., Ford, Chrysler, J.C. Penney, Exxon, and so many others. Interstate banking? I don't know what else you'd call it. Certainly during the 1980s interstate competition in financial services has been fierce.

Interstate Electronic Funds Transfer Systems. The nation is now linked with electronic funds transfer systems and nationwide automated teller machine (ATM) networks. You can go from Florida to Hawaii, and find an ATM where you can withdraw cash.

The sophisticated computer telecommunications networks are having a significant "dissolving effect" on barriers to interstate banking.

State Laws Permitting Out-Of-State Banks to Enter: Regional Banking Zones

In the early 1980s one of the hottest issues to burst on the revolutionary banking scene was state legislative action to permit interstate banking. Both South Dakota and Delaware invited outside banks to come in and set up limited-purpose banks. Citicorp set up a nationwide credit card operation through its South Dakota subsidiary. Delaware passed its law in February 1981, and by December of 1983, eleven out-of-state banks had been established there.

Before the end of 1983, fifteen states had passed some form of law to permit out-of-state banks to come in. Some states required reciprocity—your banks can come into our state only if our banks are permitted to go into your state.

The New England "Regional Reciprocity" Plan

Several of the New England States passed laws permitting banks in other New England states to enter. In 1983 there was a flurry of interstate merger activity in New England, especially between Massachusetts and Connecticut.

By the end of 1983, "regional reciprocity" interstate banking legislation was being considered in many states. But there was some strong opposition, especially from small banks, and from the large money-center banks which did not want to be "frozen out" of these regional areas.

Citicorp argued that it was unconstitutional for a state to permit banks from "selected other states" (instead of "all other states") to enter. The case went to the

U.S. Supreme Court which, on June 10, 1985, handed down the decision that such regional interstate banking arrangements were not unconstitutional. This decision has been referred to as "the most important legal decision for the future of American banking."[2]

By mid-1987 (two years after the Supreme Court decision) 45 of the 50 states, plus the District of Columbia had enacted laws permitting some form of interstate banking. Only Arkansas, Colorado, Hawaii, Kansas, and Montana had not passed such legislation. Many "superregional" banks had already (very rapidly!) developed. Several of the regional banks which in the early 1980s had assets in the $5 to $10 billion range suddenly found themselves merged with other banks, and with assets of more than $20 billion.

In 1987 the *American Banker* surveyed and identified 38 superregional banks and found that their assets, on average, increased by more than 23 percent in 1986. The fastest growing regions were New England and the Southeast, where assets of the superregional banks grew by some 34 percent. Truly, the structure of the American banking system forevermore will be significantly affected by the development of these regional interstate banking pacts.[3]

The U.S. Congress has been completely silent on this issue. It has played no role in these developments which are shaping the future structure of the nation's banking system.

On the inability of Congress to pass new major banking legislation for close to five years, in June of 1987, newly appointed Federal Reserve Board member Edward W. Kelley, Jr., said: "What's going on right now is really the worst of all worlds—deregulation by loophole and lawsuit. That is dangerous and it's unfair and it's inefficient and it's not the way to do things. Congress could make the Fed's job a lot easier if it would get off the fence and pass legislation clarifying what the different sectors of the financial services industry will be allowed to do."[4]

In this same vein. E. Gerald Corrigan, President of the Federal Reserve Bank of New York, in that bank's 1986 annual report gives an overview of the current situation and recommendations for deregulation and restructuring of the banking system. Corrigan's view of problems with the current situation is presented in box 8-3.

EFTS: THE ELECTRONIC BANKING REVOLUTION

During the 1970s the technology was fully developed for rapid expansion of electronic funds transfer systems (EFTS). Automated teller machines (ATMs) and point-of-sale terminals (POS) were ready. But there were several impediments.

One impediment was the legal environment: the question of the legality of establishing and operating remote units in places where a bank was prohibited from branching. Also, in attempting to work out shared systems, there was a question of breaking the antitrust laws.

---

[2] Gordon Matthews, "Two Years Later, Court Decision Reshaping Industry," *Banking Week*, June 15, 1987, p. 1.

[3] Ibid.

[4] Barbara A. Rahm, "Texan Kelley Learning the Ropes As Fed's New Governor," *Banking Week*, June 15, 1987, p. 23.

Box 8-3

Feature: E. Gerald Corrigan, President, FRB New York, Highlights the Current Situation

- Money and capital markets are now truly international in character.

- Barriers between classes of financial institutions are becoming increasingly blurred.

- The separation of "banking" and "commerce" more generally is also being increasingly challenged.

- The nature and incidence of interest rate, exchange rate, and credit risk are changing in ways that may have longer-term and cyclical implications that are not fully understood at the present time.

- The securitization of the liabilities of households and businesses is spreading very rapidly.

- At least for large banks, the rate of profitability in intermediation activities is under pressure.

- Spreads and fees associated with at least some financial services may not be providing returns that are commensurate with risks.

- We are seeing a virtual explosion in financial transactions and short-run volatility in the prices of most classes of financial instruments.

- Payment and settlement risk have increased sharply in recent years.

- Finally, it should also be recognized that many of the trends cited above have materialized in force over the past three or four years. As such, they have not been tested over one or more interest rate or business cycles—cycles which at some point surely will reappear.

The speed and scope of change we are seeing in our financial markets and institutions have taken on a revolutionary character. Innovation has fostered the application of very sophisticated forms of mathematics and computer technology to the financial marketplace, making possible the design of new techniques, new instruments, and worldwide trading and funding strategies. . . . While it is beyond debate that the process of change and innovation has brought with it important benefits, there persists a nagging sense of unease—a sense of unease that is prevalent among financial market practitioners themselves—that all is not well. To some considerable extent, that sense of unease seems of grow out of the concern that legitimate broad-based public interest considerations about the structure and stability of financial markets and institutions are being swept aside in a helter-skelter of events that lacks an underlying sense of direction and may be weakening the system.

Source: Federal Reserve Bank of New York, *Annual Report 1986*, pp. 6–10.

Also, in the beginning, customer resistence to these "electronics monsters" was strong. So during the 1970s, although automated clearinghouses for transferring funds among financial institutions developed rapidly, the customer-contact EFTS expansion proceeded very slowly.

Rapid Growth of ATMs and Shared Networks in the 1980s

It was during the early 1980s that the electronic banking revolution actually began to materialize. There was rapid growth of installed ATMs and rapid increase in customer acceptance. Regional ATM networks were established throughout the country.

Then these regional networks began joining and merging. By the mid-1980s virtually all of the banks and all of the thrifts were tied together through ATM networks, not just nationwide, but worldwide. Now, no matter how small your "local hometown" bank or thrift may be, chances are you can withdraw cash from your account at an ATM in New York or Honolulu, and maybe London or Paris!

Point-of-Sale Terminals, and Home Banking

By the mid-1980s in many places in the country there were point-of-sale terminals installed and operating at supermarkets, department stores, and in other retail establishments. And the installation of POS terminals was expanding rapidly.

During the early 1980s some 25 banks were testing and/or using some form of home banking system. The first commercial home-banking and information system was put into operation by Chemical Bank of New York in September of 1982. The system, called "PRONTO" allows customers to use home computers to obtain account information and to perform banking transactions. In 1983 Chemical Bank began licensing other banks to use the system.

Several other home banking systems soon appeared in various other parts of the country, and as we approach the end of the 1980s, home banking continues to expand.

A Mastercard-VISA Joint Nationwide Debit Card Program: Entree

After more than a year of planning, in October of 1987 the new nationwide debit card system began. The new debit card, Entree, can be used in point-of-sale (POS) terminals to pay for purchases, nationwide. This new system brings both POS and ATM into a truly nationwide customer-contact EFT system. Another revolutionary change in the banking and payments system? Yes. The Appendix to this chapter explains various kinds of EFTS devices and systems.

BATTLEGROUND OF THE REVOLUTION: EVERYBODY INTO BANKING AND BANKS INTO EVERYTHING

The competitive environment in the financial services industry in the United States during the 1980s has been truly revolutionized. As long ago as 1983, the May 16 issue of *U.S. News and World Report* (p. 69) carries the story: "Revolution in Banking: Has it Gone Too Far?" The subtitle of the article is: "The headlong rush by banks, brokers and others to be all things to all customers is causing worry in Washington."

The July 18, 1983 issue of *Newsweek* (p. 61) carries the story: "The Brave New World of Super Banks." The introductory paragraph of that article says:

> "Today it is the main street savings and loans. Tomorrow: superbank....
> ... you will be able to shop for stocks and bonds, insurance and real estate—even
> for a package deal for the family vacation. You may bank at home by personal
> computer borrowing money, say, to buy a refrigerator from the bank's department-
> store subsidiary next door. Superbank will be big, powerful, and more convenient
> than the neighborhood supermarket; keeping money there will seem easier than you
> could have dreamed."

James Robinson, III, Chairman and CEO of Shearson American Express, is quoted in the January 3, 1983 issue of *Forbes* (p. 71), saying:

> "The industry that once was known as banking, the industry known as insurance, and the industry known as brokerage—and a host of additional businesses—are all now evolving into a new industry called financial services."

Focus of the Revolution: The Financial Services Markets

The focus of the financial services revolution is in the financial services market place. The competition is fierce, both for the saver's dollar and for the borrower's loan.

Competition for the Saver's Dollar. Partly as a result of the very high interest rates of the late 1970s and early '80s, partly as a result of the heavy advertising by competing financial institutions trying to attract funds, and partly for other reasons, the users of financial services in the United States have become much better educated regarding alternatives. They have learned to look carefully and to make choices based on their own best interests.

The competition for the saver's dollar has become intense. And the competition is no longer limited to banks and thrifts competing among themselves. The brokerage companies, insurance companies, the credit card companies, Sears Roebuck, and many others are in the market trying to "buy the saver's dollar." The competition in this market is fierce. Every institution is constantly devising new kinds of accounts to try to attract funds.

Competition for the Borrower's Loan. Similarly, on the "money selling" side the competition is intense. It hasn't been many years since loan instruments—home mortgages, commercial and industrial (C&I) loans, and consumer loans—were all fairly standard. But not anymore. Financial institutions constantly are thinking of new kinds of instruments to use to attract borrowers.

By the end of the 1980s, the new generation of "financially aware" consumers of financial services are watching for the best deal. They will do business with whoever does the best job of offering them what they want. It doesn't have to be a bank or thrift. It can be an insurance company, brokerage firm, or General Electric, General Motors, Sears, J. C. Penney, Kroger, or any other of the new entrants into the (potentially lucrative) financial services market.

The Brokers Invade Banking

The Merrill Lynch CMA account made serious inroads into the banking business. The account was initiated in 1977. Before the end of 1982 Merrill Lynch had attracted almost one million depositors for its $20,000-minimum accounts, and had attracted some $50 billion into the accounts. Needless to say, by mid-1983 there wasn't a major brokerage firm in the country that was not offering some such account.

By 1983 several banks were establishing CMA type accounts. But the brokers were already entrenched in the business.

All of these so-called "asset-management" accounts offer a checking account, a brokerage account, money funds, a debit or charge card, and a comprehensive statement to the depositor on account activity. The account holder can choose to have the funds in regular money market funds, a government securities fund, a tax-exempt securities fund, or invested directly in stocks or bonds at the choice of the depositor.

All dividends and interest automatically are placed into the account in the money fund. Assets can be shifted, stocks or bonds can be bought or sold at any time. Checks written are drawn from the money fund balance. More money can be deposited or withdrawn at any time. And money can be borrowed at relatively low interest against the portfolio of stocks and bonds. All this, and you can call your instructions to your service representative *toll free*.

How do stockbrokers offer banking services? And how do bankers offer stockbroker services? It's easy. The brokers make arrangements to work through a bank (or acquire one). The bankers make arrangements to work through a broker (or acquire one).

The Banks Invade the Brokerage Business

At the beginning of 1982, no major bank in the United States offered discount brokerage services to its customers. By the end of 1982, almost 600 commercial banks and thrifts had announced plans to enter this business. Soon there were more than 1,000 banks and thrifts offering discount brokerage services.

Banks are prohibited by the Glass-Steagall Act of 1933 from underwriting or dealing in securities (except for general obligation municipal bonds). It had been assumed that the banks could not offer brokerage services. But in 1982, it turned out that they could.

In April of 1982, San Francisco's Crocker National Bank established its "working capital account"—a CMA-type account which offered its customers broker services. In May of 1982, the Federal Home Loan Bank Board permitted a group of S&Ls to establish a brokerage and investment services program called "Invest," (based in Tampa). Invest brokers located in participating S&Ls can trade stocks and bonds, offer mutual funds, and provide investment advisory services.

In 1982 and '83 several banks decided either to acquire broker firms or to set up their own discount brokerage services. The federal regulators permitted this action—a new interpretation of the Glass-Steagall Act. Bank-owned discount brokerage units continued to expand. In 1987 the Supreme Court held that the establishment of discount brokerage operations in various states does not violate the laws prohibiting interstate banking.

Brokers (and Others) Acquire or Establish Nonbank Banks

Since a nonbank bank is not a bank, anyone could own one. So at the same time that banks were acquiring and establishing brokerage firms, some brokerage, mutual funds, insurance, and several nonfinancial firms were acquiring existing banks and then turning them into "nonbank banks"—or establishing their own nonbank banks.

The movement started in 1982 with the Dreyfus Mutual Fund Company acquiring banks in New Jersey and New York and then disposing of their commercial lending function. At that time Fed Chairman Paul Volcker urged Congress to plug this loophole—this growth of unregulated banks—but, as you know, the Congress did not do that until August, 1987.

Insurance Companies, Credit Card Companies, and Nonfinancial Businesses Enter the Fray

During the early 1980s Prudential Insurance acquired the Bache (pronounced baysh) brokerage firm, and established a nonbank bank, "Prudential Bank & Trust Company." Other insurance companies—including Aetna, Metropolitan Life, Cigna, Travelers, and a number of others—have been diversifying into all of these financial services, including CMA-type asset management accounts and financial planning services. The same pattern has developed among the mutual funds, many of which are in the process of becoming full financial services businesses.

American Express and the other credit card companies have been doing the same thing. And you already know that Sears Roebuck, with more than 600 in-store financial centers across the country, is already one of the nation's largest consumer financial services firms.

The "Revolutionized" Financial Services Industry

What is the nature of this "revolutionized financial services industry"? How do you know when you're dealing with an insurance company or a brokerage house? Or a commercial bank? Or a real estate firm? Or a personal investment advisory service or a depository institution?

All of these "financial conglomerate firms" are involved in checking accounts, various kinds of savings accounts, time deposit accounts, real estate, financial planning, consumer and commercial loans, stock and bond brokerage—so trying to draw lines between them doesn't make much sense. All of them are responding in as many ways as they wish to the demands of the market, reaching out for those segments of the financial services business which they wish to engage in.

The management of each financial institution (or nonfinancial institution) decides what financial areas and geographic areas they wish to serve. Then they figure out ways to do it. If there are legal impediments, they figure out how to make it legal. Then they proceed to carry out their plans.

There are still some restrictions which the banks haven't been able to get around. None of them are actually buying and holding corporate stocks, for example. But several have expanded into consumer finance, insurance, real estate, and mutual fund activities.

Competition on the Lending Side of the Market

Competition on the lending side has also been fierce. Both American Express and Merrill Lynch, for example, are making home loans in more than 25 states. These nonbank businesses pioneered the "home equity loan," which spread throughout the bank and thrift industry in 1986–87 following the passage of the 1986 tax law which permits an interest deduction for home loans, but not for most other loans.

In consumer lending, none of the banks come close to the loan volume of General Motors Acceptance Corporation (GMAC), or Ford or Chrysler or Sears. GMAC is in fact the largest consumer lender in the United States and probably in the world. Banks have been getting a declining share of the consumer lending market. (But it should be mentioned in passing that several of the growing consumer-lending companies are owned by bank holding companies.)

In business lending, the banks still hold the lions share. But commercial lenders are a constant competitive threat. GMAC, Ford, Chrysler, GE Credit, and

Box 8-4

Question: What about the "Other Revolution"?—In Financial Instruments and Markets?

In addition to all of the revolutionary changes discussed in this chapter, during the 1980s another kind of revolution was occuring in the financial markets. There was previously unheard of **volume** and **volatility** in the financial markets. There was a bewildering array of new kinds of financial instruments introduced, and options and futures trading increased to the point where this sometimes seemed to dominate the markets.

At this point you only need to be aware of this "other ongoing revolution." It will be explained and discussed in part III of this book which deals with financial instruments and markets.

several others are moving aggressively into commercial and industrial (C&I) lending. Also many large corporations are now bypassing the intermediaries altogether and are getting their short-term funds by issuing and selling commercial paper just as they obtain their long-term funds by issuing bonds.[5]

"LOOPHOLING" PLAYS A MAJOR ROLE

As you look back over the revolutionary changes which have occurred in the 1980s, clearly the legislation of 1980 and '82 played an important role. But much of it has resulted from **loopholing**—aggressive responses to market demands and profit opportunities, without much regard for what the regulators might have to say.

Much of the deregulation process which has occurred during the 1980s has been initiated by aggressive firms in the industry—bankers, brokers, insurance companies, and even nonfinancial businesses—finding loopholes in the law, and stretching the loopholes until legislative action has become imperative.

Given the market forces for change, plus the rapid development of new technology, sooner or later near-crisis conditions develop and Congress is forced to take some kind of action. That's how it has happened so far. Don't be too surprised if that's the way it happens from now on.

SUMMARY

- Following the inititation of the Fed's new operating procedures in October 1979, high interest rates caused an exodus of banks from Fed membership and a sharp wave of disintermediation.

---

[5] In this discussion of "Everybody into Banking and Banks into Everything," what about the thrifts? For all practical purposes, the lines between the banks and thrifts have dissolved. Those thrifts that want to act like commercial banks are already doing so. Throughout this discussion, the word banks could just as well be replaced with "banks and thrifts," or with the term "depository institutions."

- The Depository Institutions Deregulation and Monetary Control Act (DIDMCA) of 1980:

  a. Set the same reserve requirements for all depository institutions.
  b. Called for the phase-out of Reg Q interest rate ceilings.
  c. Permitted of all of the thrift institutions to offer interest-bearing checkable accounts.
  d. Permitted the thrift institutions to engage in activities previously reserved for commercial banks.

- The Garn–St Germain Act (October 1982) permitted depository institutions to offer deposit accounts paying money market rates, and gave the S&Ls some financial support and more commercial banking powers.

- Many banks and thrifts continued to fail and in 1986–87, the funds of the Federal Savings and Loan Insurance Corporation (FSLIC) ran out. Crisis legislation—the *Competitive Equality Banking Act of 1987*—provided $10.8 billion for recapitalization of FSLIC, closed the nonbank bank loophole, and made a few other changes, but many key issues were not addressed.

- Interstate banking activity has existed for some years, but in the mid-1980s the Supreme Court approved "regional reciprocity interstate banking pacts." After that almost all states passed laws permitting interstate banking on a regional basis, and there was a flurry of interstate merger activity.

- The electronic funds transfer system (EFTS) revolution really began to occur in the 1980s. By the end of 1987 the entire nation was tied together through shared ATM and POS networks, and access to some of these networks was available in foreign countries.

- The boundary lines between and among financial services institutions have become increasingly blurred and this has brought fiercely competitive financial services markets—both in attracting and in lending funds.

- Much of the financial services revolution has resulted not so much from the revolutionary legislation, but from "loopholing" by aggressive and enterprising financial institutions, seeking higher profits by better serving the demands of the market.

Important Principles, Issues, Concepts, Terms

The Fed's "New Operating Procedures" of October 6, 1979

Financial industry turmoil in 1979–80

Interest rate developments in 1979–80

Fed membership exodus

Disintermediation crisis

DIDMCA of 1980: important provisions and effects fects

Problems unsolved by the DIDMCA

1980 bond market crash

Crisis of the thrifts, 1980–82

Garn–St Germain Act (1982)

Ultimate phase-out of Reg Q

Importance of the 1980 and 1982 acts

Problems with the FSLIC

Banking Act of 1987

Developments in interstate banking

"Grandfathered" interstate banking rights

Interstate mergers of "troubled" banks and thrifts interstate mergers

Interstate banking activities by nondepository institutions

Growth of nonbank banks

Competition from nonfinancial firms

Interstate EFTS

Regional interstate banking

The electronic banking revolution

Competitive revolution in financial services

Broker invasion into banking

Bank invasion into brokerage

Banking activities by nonbanking financial companies

Banking activities by nonfinancial companies

Characteristics of the "revolutionized" financial services industry

Competition on the lending side of the market

Role of "loopholing" in the banking revolution

Questions and Problems

1. Why were interest rates so high and volatile in the late 1970s and early '80s? And how did these high and volatile interest rates contribute to the revolution in the U.S. financial system?

2. What were the most important (revolutionary!) provisions of the DIDMCA of 1980 and the Garn–St Germain Act of 1982? Why do you think the Congress enacted these revolutionary provisions?

3. What was the 1981–82 crisis of the thrifts? And what were the provisions of the Garn–St Germain Act which tried to lessen the seriousness of this crisis?

4. What was the FSLIC crisis of 1986–87, and what new banking legislation resulted from that?

5. Describe the recent developments and current status of interstate banking in the United States.

6. Describe the competitive environment which now exists in the financial services industry in the United States. Mention nonbank banks, the growth of EFTS, and competition between the depository and nondepository financial institutions.

Suggested Readings

Bennett, Barbara. "Bank Regulations and Deposit Insurance: Controlling the FDIC's Losses." *Economic Review*. Federal Reserve Bank of San Francisco (Spring 1984), 16–30.

Benston, George. "Deposit Insurance and Bank Failures." *Economic Review* 68, Federal Reserve Bank of Atlanta. (March 1983), 4–17.

Bowden, Elbert V. and Judith L. Holbert. *Revolution in Banking*, 2nd edition. Reston, Va.: Reston Publishing Company, 1984.

Byrne, Harlan. "New Life at Sears." *Barron's.* January 27, 1986.

Cargill, Thomas and Gillian Garcia. *Financial Reform in the 1980s.* Stanford: Hoover Institution, 1985.

Cassasus, Barbara. "Deregulation Makes Its Impact." *The Banker.* (January 1986), 63–69.

Cooper, Kerry and Donald R. Fraser. *Banking Deregulation and the New Competition in Financial Services.* Cambridge, Mass.: Ballinger, 1986.

Council of Economic Advisors "Financial Market Deregulation." *Economic Report of the President 1984.* Washington, D.C.: U.S. Government Printing Office, 1984.

Dunham, Constance and Richard F. Syron. "Interstate Banking: The Drive to Consolidate." *New England Economic Review*. Federal Reserve Bank of Boston, May/June 1984.

Evanoff, Douglas and Diana Fortier. "The Impact of Geographic Expansion in Banking: Some Axioms to Grind." *Economic Perspectives.* Federal Reserve Bank of Chicago, May/June 1986.

Federal Reserve Bank of Atlanta. *The Future of the U.S. Payments System.* Proceedings of a conference, June 23–25, 1981, Atlanta: Federal Reserve Bank of Atlanta, 1981.

Federal Reserve Bank of Atlanta. "New Directions in Interstate Banking." *Economic Review.* Special issue January 1985.

Federal Reserve Bank of Chicago. "The Depository Institutions Deregulation and Monetary Control Act of 1980." *Economic Perspectives.* (September/October 1980), 3–23.

———. "The Garn–St Germain Depository Institutions Act of 1982." *Economic Perspectives.* (March/April 1983), 3–31.

———. *Toward Nationwide Banking, A Guide to the Issues. 1986.*

Felgran, Steven D. "Bank Entry into Securities Brokerage: Competitive and Legal Aspects." *New England Economic Review.* (November/December 1984), 12–33.

Frieder, Larry. "Toward Nationwide Banks." *Economic Perspectives*. Federal Reserve Bank of Chicago, special issue 1986.

Germany, J. David and John E. Morton. "Financial Innovation and Deregulation in Foreign Industrial Countries." *Federal Reserve Bulletin*. (October 1985), 743–753.

Garcia, Gillian, et. al. "The Garn–St Germain Depository Institutions Act of 1982." *Economic Perspectives*. Federal Reserve Bank of Chicago (March/April), 3–32.

Gross, Laura. "Diversified Financial Giants Gaining Consumer Approval." *American Banker*. September 25, 1986.

Kane, Edward J. *The Gathering Crisis in Federal Deposit Insurance*. Cambridge, Mass.: MIT Press, 1985.

Miller, Merton. "Financial Innovation: The Last Twenty Years and the Next." *Journal of Financial and Quantitative Analysis*. December 1986.

Moulton, Janice M. "Nonbank Banks: Catalyst for Inter-state Banking." *Business Review*. Federal Reserve Bank of Philadelphia, November/December 1985.

Pavel, Christine and Harvey Rosenblum. "Banks and Nonbanks: The Horse Race Continues." *Economic Perspectives*. Federal Reserve Bank of Chicago (May/June 1985), 15.

Savage, Donald T. "Interstate Banking Developments." *Federal Reserve Bulletin*. (February 1987), 79–92.

Sprague, Irvine H. *Bail Out, An Insider's Account of Bank Failures and Rescues*. New York: Basic Books, 1986.

U.S. Department of Commerce, National Commission on Electronic Fund Transfers. *EFT in the United States: Policy Recommendations and the Public Interest*. Washington, D.C.: U.S. Government Printing Office, October 28, 1977.

U.S. Government Accounting Office. *Deposit Insurance, Analysis of Reform Proposals*. September 30, 1986.

White, George C. Jr. "Electronic Banking and Its Impact on the Future." *Magazine of Bank Administration* 55 (December 1979), 39–42.

CHAPTER 9

Evolution, Structure, and Functions of the U.S. Central Bank: The Federal Reserve System

Chapter Objectives

The purpose of this chapter is to explain the evolution and the current structure and functions of the U.S. central bank—the Federal Reserve System. After you study this chapter you will understand and be able to explain:

1. How the Fed was originally set up, its functions, and its initially passive monetary policy role.

2. The meaning of the commercial loan theory (real-bills doctrine) and why it wasn't an adequate guide to monetary policy.

3. The importance of the leadership of the Federal Reserve Bank of New York (FRB-NY) and of Benjamin Strong it's president during the 1920s, the Fed's changing monetary policy role, and the lack of leadership and inability to deal with the crisis of the 1930s.

4. Changes made by the Banking Acts of 1933 and 1935 to unify the Fed and to separate it from the Administration.

5. The modern-day structure and functions of the Fed:
   a. The continuing special importance of the FRB-NY.
   b. The structure and importance of the Federal Open Market Committee (FOMC).
   c. The specific functions and responsibilities of the members of the Board of Governors.

A REAL U.S. CENTRAL BANK—FINALLY!

It was two days before Christmas in 1913 when President Woodrow Wilson signed the controversial and compromise-filled **Federal Reserve Act**. It called for not one, but for "not less than eight and not more than twelve" Federal Reserve banks geographically dispersed throughout the country. Each bank was to have its own Board of Directors and to have considerable automony in establishing and carrying out its policies.

Each Fed Bank Was Established as a Separate Corporation

Each bank was to be established as a corporation, and the stock was to be purchased and held by the member banks located in that Federal Reserve district. Each bank was to agree to purchase up to 6 percent of the value of its own capital and surplus, in Federal Reserve bank stock, but in fact, only one half of this amount of stock has been sold to the member banks. The sale of this stock provided the funds for the establishment of the individual Federal Reserve banks, so that no funds were required to be appropriated by Congress for the establishment and operation of the system. Throughout its history the Fed's income has come from its securities holdings and no government funds have ever been appropriated for its operation.

The stockholders of the individual Federal Reserve banks do not have the normal rights of ownership held by stockholders in private corporations. The stockholder banks participate in the selection of directors of the Federal Reserve bank according to a formula established by the Federal Reserve Act.

The Federal Reserve Board was to Supervise and Coordinate

The act created the **Federal Reserve Board** to be located in Washington and to consist of seven members, five appointed by the President for 12-year terms, and the other two to be ex-officio members: the Comptroller of the Currency and the Secretary of the Treasury. The board was not expected to "run the system" but to supervise and coordinate some of the functions. In addition, a Federal Advisory Council was established, consisting of 12 members, one from each Federal Reserve district, to make policy recommendations.

National Banks Must Join. Others May

All national banks were required to become Fed members and state-chartered banks could apply for membership if they wished. Based on the breakdown established in the National Banking Act (1864), member banks were classified into three groups: reserve city banks (banks located in New York and Chicago), city banks, (banks located in other large cities), and country banks (located in small cities and rural areas). Required reserves were set at 18 percent for reserve city banks 15 percent for city banks, and 12 percent for country banks. The higher reserves for the banks located in the larger cities were justified on the basis of "the pyramiding of reserves," explained in Chapter 6.

A Nationwide Check-Clearing System

Checks would move from one Federal Reserve District Bank to another, enroute to the member bank on which the check was drawn. The Federal Reserve also established a nationwide check-clearing system. This efficient clearing system was available at no charge to members, and also to nonmembers who agreed to meet the requirements established by the Fed.

Each Fed Bank was Authorized to Issue Currency

Each of the 12 Federal Reserve Banks was permitted to issue **Federal Reserve notes** (to circulate as currency) backed by a 40 percent reserve of gold or gold certificates. In addition, the act specified that these Federal Reserve notes were to be a full obligation of the federal government.

The Fed Banks Were Supposed to "Rediscount" Promissory Notes

Each bank was authorized to rediscount (that is, to buy) the promissory notes of its member banks in order to provide more reserves to those banks. But these promissory notes had to be short-term: no longer than three months for commercial loans (called "commercial paper") and six months for agricultural loans (called "agricultural paper").

This rediscounting function was intended to be the important provision which would provide the needed **elasticity of the currency**. The idea was that during times of expanding business activity the banks would make loans and receive promissory notes. Then, as their reserves grew thin, they would rediscount (sell) the promissory notes to their Federal Reserve bank. This would give them additional reserves so they could make more loans and avoid a "credit crunch."

Buying and Selling Government Bonds was Permitted

Almost as an afterthought, the act authorized the Federal Reserve banks to buy and sell government bonds. There was no thought at the time that this buying and selling of government bonds would eventually become, by far, the most important means of providing elasticity to and of exercising control over the nation's money supply.

CURRENCY ELASTICITY AND THE "REAL BILLS" DOCTRINE

One of the most important reasons why the Fed was set up was to provide currency elasticity. But how elastic should the nation's currency be?

Everybody remembered that the value of the currency issued by the Continental Congress during the Revolutionary War was seriously depreciated by over-issue. The phrase "not worth a Continental" is still used by some people who have no idea where it came from. Whenever a currency is issued in excess it will always depreciate in value. If unlimited issuance continues, ultimately it will become worthless.

The Fed's Guideline: The Commercial Loan Theory

At the time the Fed was set up, it was widely believed that the "commercial loan theory" or the "real-bills doctrine" gave the answer to the question "How much elasticity?" Responsible bankers (both commercial bankers and central bankers) considered it appropriate to follow this guideline. Box 9-1 explains the meaning of "real bills."

Box 9-1

Question: **Exactly What Is Meant by "Real Bills?"**

The term "real bills" goes all the way back to before Adam Smith. It means loan instruments (promissory notes) which are secured by physical assets (i.e., "real") which are going to be sold (and therefore the loans are self-liquidating) and which are short term (i.e., "bills"). When the "real goods" are sold, the money is automatically received to pay off the "bill"—the short-term debt obligation. "Bills" were usually thought of as being due in ninety days or less, except in the case of agricultural "bills" which were generally limited to maturities of about six months.

The commercial loan theory (the real-bills doctrine) says that banks should only make loans which are (1) short-term and (2) made for the purpose of financing commerce, inventories, goods in process, and agricultural production. Such loans are self-liquidating—that is, when the goods are sold, that automatically generates the funds to pay off the loans.

All loans of this type are *productive*. A money expansion to finance new goods production will not be inflationary because as the money supply expands, the output of goods expands. So says the theory.

Furthermore, banks making self-liquidating short-term commercial loans won't get into any "liquidity bind." Since the loans are self-liquidating, the banks will always be experiencing a return cash-flow from loans made previously. So there can't be a problem. So says the theory.

Suppose businesses are trying to borrow from the banks and the banks are already loaned up—no excess reserves to lend. Under the commercial loan (real bills) theory, the newly-created Federal Reserve banks would invite the commercial banks to sell them (to rediscount) some of their promissory notes. That way the Fed banks could provide more reserves for the banks to lend.

Problems with the Commercial Loan Theory

The real bills doctrine called for the central bank to be a passive participant in the expansion and contraction of the nation's money supply. In the early years that is generally the way the Federal Reserve banks saw their role. Whenever businesses wanted to borrow more, the Fed would freely rediscount the banks' promissory notes and provide additional reserves. Currency elasticity was assured.

As long as output was growing, the money supply could grow without danger of inflation. So says the theory. And it's certainly true in the long run. But what about the short run?

Suppose businesses all over the country get the idea that this is a good time to borrow and build more inventories of inputs so that in the future they can expand production. And suppose wholesalers and retailers decide to stock up, too. The banks are quite willing to finance these "short-term self-liquidating" commercial loans, and the Fed Banks are quite willing to rediscount the promissory notes and provide more funds so that the lending can continue. Then what happens?

Soon there's too much demand for the available supplies of goods in the economy. Shortages develop. Inflationary pressures mount. In this case, the real-bills doctrine didn't turn out to be an effective guideline.

In the early years the Fed banks "more or less" followed the real-bills doctrine. They looked at the function of rediscounting promissory notes as the important technique for providing money elasticity. But they didn't blindly follow the real-bills doctrine.

The Fed bankers could see when a money expansion was getting to be "clearly too much." Then they would raise the rediscount rate to discourage rediscounting. In those days the Fed banks' only active monetary policy instrument was adjusting the rediscount rate (now called the "discount" rate).

THE FED: FROM THE BEGINNING TO THE GREAT DEPRESSION

The full title of the Federal Reserve Act is:

> "An act to provide for the establishment of Federal Reserve banks, to furnish an elastic currency, to afford means of rediscounting commercial paper, to establish a more effective supervision of banking in the United States, and for other purposes."

A "Decentralized" Central Bank

What the Federal Reserve Act (with amendments in 1914) actually did was to establish 12 different central banks, each with a separate governing board and officers, and each to function more or less independently in supervising, providing banking services for, and rediscounting "real bills" for the commercial banks in its district. The Federal Reserve Board was established to exercise some supervisory and coordinating functions, but in fact, the system was a confederation of reserve banks with each retaining considerable autonomy in determining policy within its district. Figure 9-1 shows a map of our geographically decentralized central bank.

It wasn't quite clear exactly what the role of the board was to be in determining monetary policy for the nation. And in fact, following the real bills doctrine, the only significant monetary policy decisions had to do with adjusting the discount rates charged to member banks. The individual reserve banks were permitted to establish the discount rate in their district, subject to the approval of the Federal Reserve Board in Washington.

When you look back at the early structure and functioning of the Federal Reserve System, it's easy to see the compromises which were made to make the system politically acceptable to enough people to get it passed by Congress. The system was decentralized and the powers of monetary control were decentralized. Those who were involved in the decisions were both geographically and occupationally dispersed: bankers and nonbankers from all over the country, plus representatives of the federal government. Given the **dispersion of power** it's no surprise that the system lacked central direction. The early system was torn by disagreements and power struggles.

Leadership of the FRB-NY: The Benjamin Strong Era

It is not surprising that leadership within the system began to gravitate toward the Federal Reserve Bank of New York. The New York bank was by far the largest and

**Figure 9-1.   Map of the Geographic Structure of the
Federal Reserve System**

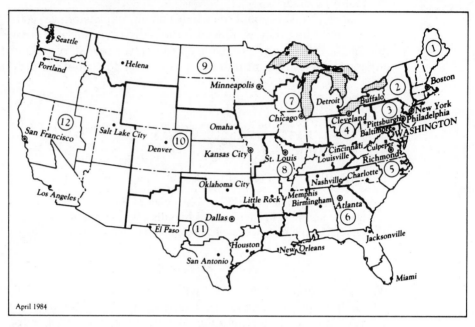

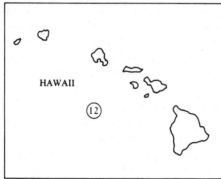

LEGEND

—— Boundaries of Federal Reserve Districts   ◉ Federal Reserve Bank cities

—— Boundaries of Federal Reserve Branch territories   ● Federal Reserve Branch cities

✪ Board of Governors of the Federal Reserve System   ■ Federal Reserve Bank facility

Source: *Federal Reserve Bulletin*, Board of Governors of the Federal Reserve System, Washington, D.C. (inside back cover).

most important bank in the system. And it was located in the financial center of the nation.

Another important factor contributing to the preeminence of the New York bank was the leadership ability and banking savvy of the highly respected president of that bank: Benjamin Strong. Strong was instrumental in forming the unofficial "Open Market Investment Committee" which met during the 1920s to determine open market policy. Strong's position as chairman of this committee permitted him to have considerable influence and coordinative effect over the other banks in the system.

Strong was also chairman of the Governors' Conference, which was an unofficial "coordinating committee" of the Federal Reserve bank presidents. For most of the 1920s, the functioning of the Fed System was significantly influenced and its effectiveness considerably increased by Strong's leadership. He was the first of a number of individuals whose abilities and leadership have played a decisive role in influencing the effectiveness of Fed policies.

It was during the 1920s, looking back at the disastrous effects of the "permissive" monetary policies during World War I that the Fed, under Strong's leadership, began moving away from the real bills doctrine and began to take an active role in regulating the quantity of money. To some extent, open market operations and discount policy were used during the 1920s to try to steady the economy.

The Post-Strong Era: No Decisive Policy

In 1928 Strong resigned his position as head of the New York bank shortly before his death, and his leadership was sorely missed. The disagreements and struggles among the banks—and especially between the New York bank and the board in Washington—left the nation without decisive monetary policy to deal with the stock market speculation of the late 1920s, or with the banking crises and the economic collapse of the 1930s. If Strong had lived or if some other equally capable leader had quickly arisen to replace him the history of the U.S. economy and of the banking system of the 1930s might have been written in a somewhat kindlier vein. Too bad it didn't happen that way.

From 1929 to 1933, as the economy decended into deep depression, there were three waves of bank failures. The money stock declined sharply. How did the Federal Reserve System meet this first serious liquidity crisis since 1907? It didn't—at least not very effectively.

It reduced the discount rate from 6 percent in 1929 to 1.5 percent in mid-1931. But then it raised it to 3.5 percent in late 1931 because of concern that low interest rates in this country might cause gold to flow overseas where it could earn a higher return. During 1932, for some months the Fed bought securities. But it did not follow this policy persistently. By 1933 it was obvious that some reforms were needed.

Unification and Leadership Were Clearly Needed

From the time the Federal Reserve began to operate in 1914 until the depression years of the 1930s, valuable functions were performed. Nationwide check clearing became much more efficient, the fiscal functions of the Treasury were more efficiently performed, and some of the problems associated with the inelastic currency of the pre-Fed days were overcome. But it wasn't until the mid-1930s, with the Banking Acts of 1933 and 1935 and new operating policies and procedures and new, centralized, vigorous and effective leadership that the Federal Reserve System began to function as a unified and purposeful central bank for the United States.

UNIFICATION OF THE FED: THE BANKING ACTS OF 1933 and 1935

Economic, monetary, and banking conditions throughout the United States deteriorated throughout 1930, '31, and '32. In March of 1933, newly inaugurated President Frandlin D. Roosevelt ordered all banks closed until something could be done to rebuild confidence in the banking system. It was obvious that something had to be done.

Also it soon became obvious that a decentralized central banking system wasn't the answer. The nation can't operate on 12 different monetary policies! The Banking Acts of 1933 and 1935 addressed this problem and accomplished a major restructuring of the Federal Reserve System. These acts (1) centralized the Fed in Washington and (2) separated it from the executive branch.

The Fed Board Was Restructured, with Expanded Powers. The two Treasury Department representatives were removed from the board. The name of the board was changed from "Federal Reserve Board" to "The Board of Governors of the Federal Reserve System." The new board consisted of seven members, appointed by the President, each with a fourteen-year term. The terms were staggered so that one would end every two years. One member of the board is appointed by the President to a four-year term as Chairman. This still is the structure of the Fed board.

In addition, the board was given the authority to set reserve requirements within a broad range, was given final say regarding discount rates for each of the 12 member banks, and was given additional regulatory powers over commercial banks.

The FOMC Was Established. The Federal Open Market Committee (FOMC) was established, made up of the seven members of the Board of Governors, plus five Fed Bank presidents. The FOMC was to determine open market policy for the system as a whole. Since that time the FOMC has become the deliberative body which determines the Fed's monetary policy.

Long-Term Board Chairmen Have Helped to Shape the System. Although the Federal Reserve Act was passed in 1913, it wasn't until the mid-1930s that the nation really had a unified central banking system. The unification was solidified by the appointment of a chairman who was an outstanding banker and who proved to be a strong and capable leader. Marriner S. Eccles served as Chairman of the Board of Governors from the depth of the depression (1934) until after World War II (1948).

There have been three other long-term board chairmen who have exercised effective leadership and have contributed significantly to the unification of the system and the stability of monetary policy. William McChesney Martin, Jr., 1951–1970 (twenty years!); Arthur F. Burns, 1970–1978; and Paul Volcker, 1979–1987. Volcker resigned the chairmanship and was replaced by Alan Greenspan in July, 1987. All of these long-term board chairmen have had a significant influence on the evolution of the Federal Reserve System and on its relationships with the administration and the Congress. All of them have played a very significant role in influencing monetary policy, and the economy.

THE MODERN-DAY STRUCTURE AND FUNCTIONING OF THE FEDERAL RESERVE SYSTEM

The modern-day structure of the Federal Reserve System is not very different from the system which began operation in 1914. The twelve Federal Reserve districts and Federal Reserve banks still look about the same. The 1930s restructuring of the Board of Governors and the official creation of the Federal Open Market Committee were very important changes. Still, the present Federal Reserve System looks very much like the original Federal Reserve System. But its functioning? That's something else!

In the beginning the system functioned as a confederation of twelve Federal Reserve banks, loosely coordinated by the board in Washington. Today, it is a tightly unified system, entirely controlled in all important respects from the top—by the Board of Governors and the Federal Open Market Committee.

Even more important, the focus is completely different. In the beginning the Fed saw its role as one of passive accommodation of the demands for short-term funds. The Fed now sees its role as one of active, purposeful, constant control over the money supply and/or financial market conditions. The Fed plays a planned and purposeful role aimed toward fostering the economic health and growth of the nation and stability in the U.S. and international financial markets. You can be sure that no one at the Fed considers "real bills" as a guide to policy anymore!

The formal policy-formation structure of the modern-day Federal Reserve System is illustrated in Figure 9-2.

WHO REALLY CONTROLS FED POLICY?

When you look at the formal structure of the Fed you see a lot of boards and committees. Each is made up of a diverse range of individuals. So where does the power of control actually reside? Is it as diffused, decentralized, and fragmented as the organizational structure appears to suggest? Definitely not.

In the beginning, power and control was diffused. Coordination, when it occurred, resulted from the leadership efforts of a few strong and able individuals. Then the Banking Acts of 1933 and 1935, while making only minimal changes on the organizational chart, centralized the power of the system in the Board of Governors. Those acts made all of the significant decisions and actions of the 12 Federal Reserve banks "subject to the approval of the Board of Governors." And ever since the 1930s *the Fed board has constantly exercised its powers of control over the system.*

The 12 Fed banks still have the legal authority to set the discount rate for their district, "subject to the approval of the board." But in practice, the board lets it be known what discount rate will be approved (the same rate for all 12 banks, of course). Then that's the rate the individual banks "choose to submit" for approval.

The board of directors of each of the 12 district banks has the power to choose the president of that bank. But again, this choice is "subject to the approval." The Federal Reserve board in Washington has not always been willing to approve the

**Figure 9-2.   Chart of the Organizational Structure of the
Federal Reserve System**

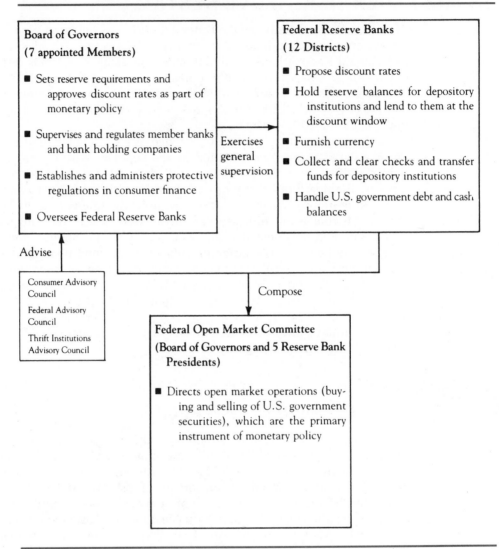

Source: *The Federal Reserve System: Purposes and Functions*, 7th Ed. Board of Governors of the Federal Reserve System (Washington, D.C., 1984) p. 5.

district bank's choice. So now, the usual procedure is for the district Fed bank to select a list of acceptable candidates, and the Fed board in Washington makes the final choice.

To be sure, there are many nitty-gritty details that must be handled on a day-to-day basis at the district level. The district banks and their governing bodies play an important role in taking care of all this. But in terms of control of the system and direction of system-wide functions—including most importantly establishing and carrying out national and international monetary policy—the power rests with the Fed board in Washington. The board's power is absolute and unchallengable, regardless of the apparent diffusion of power which the organizational structure might suggest.

The Special Position of FRB–New York

As the policy making powers of the 12 Federal Reserve banks have diminished, one of the Federal Reserve banks has continued to hold a position of singular importance. The Federal Reserve Bank of New York has developed (unofficially— you can't see it on the organizational chart) into what might be called "the central bank for the Federal Reserve System." Perhaps you could call it "the unofficial Board of Governors' bank."

As long as monetary policy consisted primarily of following the commercial loan theory (the "real-bills doctrine"), passively discounting commercial paper for member banks, each district bank could perform this monetary policy function in response to the needs of trade in the district. But what happens when we introduce the modern view of monetary policy?

When the central bank assumes the responsibility for controlling the size of the nation's money supply and/or interest rates, and when the primary tool for monetary control becomes the buying and selling of government securities in the open market, the policy must be unified. Twelve different "central banks" deciding on and carrying out their own policies? Ridiculous!

The FRB-NY Executes All Open Market Operations

What actually happens is this: The Federal Reserve Bank of New York does all of the buying and selling of securities. The System Open Market Account (SOMA) manager at the Federal Reserve Bank of New York is in charge of the "trading desk" which carries out all of the purchases and sales. The securities bought and sold by the FRB-NY are allocated among (and actually are owned by) the 12 Federal Reserve banks. Each bank's share of each security purchase (and sale) is allocated according to the relative size of that bank.

The SOMA manager plays the important role of carrying out the monetary policy decisions of the FOMC. The monetary policy decisions of the FOMC are transmitted by a directive to the SOMA manager, who is responsible for conducting day-to-day open market operations. The FOMC directive is stated in general terms. The SOMA manager must exercise considerable discretion regarding the specific kinds and quantities of securities to be bought and/or sold on any given day.

The preeminient position of the FRB-NY is further illustrated by the fact that the president of that bank has become the second most important person in determining the nation's monetary policy—second only to the chairman of the Board of Governors. You have already read about the important role played by Benjamin Strong, FRB-NY president during the 1920s.

The 1930s legislation formally establishing the FOMC recognized the special importance of the position of the presidency of the New York Fed bank. Permanent FOMC membership was granted to the holder of that key office. Today, the president of the New York Fed serves as vice-chairman of the FOMC.

OPERATIONS OF THE FOMC—THE EXPANDED BOARD OF GOVERNORS?

In actual fact, who is it that establishes monetary policy for the nation? The FOMC was set up to supervise the conduct of open market operations—one of the three tools for implementing monetary policy. The committee is not charged with implementing the two other tools: changing discount rates and reserve requirements. But how is it possible to decide anything about open market operations without first making decisions regarding over-all monetary policy? And without also deciding on discount rate and reserve requirement policies? You already know the answer. It isn't.

What all this means is that the Federal Open Market Committee in its meetings in Washington (about once every six weeks) functions as the supreme deliberative body for determining the nation's monetary policy. It decides what the monetary policy stance will be: What growth rates of the money supply will be fostered or permitted and what money market conditions should be strived for. And it decides what actions should be taken—on reserve requirements and discount rates as well as open market operations—to try to achieve its chosen objectives.

So the supreme function of the Board of Governors—that of deciding on and directing the implementation of monetary policy for the nation—isn't really performed by the board, but by the FOMC. It wouldn't be unrealistic to say that, in practice, the FOMC is "the expanded Board of Governors of the Federal Reserve System." There are 12 voting members: the seven members of the Board, the president of the New York Fed, and four other Federal Reserve bank presidents, on a rotating basis. In addition, there are many nonvoting participants in each of the FOMC meetings.

The FOMC: Twelve Voting Members, Plus Many Others

The seven nonvoting Federal Reserve Bank presidents attend the meetings and participate in the discussions. So do several of the senior staff members of the Board of Governors in Washington and also of the 12 Federal Reserve banks. Over the years, the Fed Board and the Fed banks have managed to attract to their senior staff positions some of the nation's most capable, most highly qualified economists with expertise in money, banking, and finance. The counsel of these highly qualified people is always available to the FOMC members as they deliberate and work toward their decisions.[1]

The role of the FOMC chairman (the Fed Board chairman) depends a lot on the personality of the individual and the leadership which he or she wishes to exercise. And the role of the vice-chairman (president of the FRB-NY) also depends a lot on the person who holds that position.

Ever since the mid-1930s, for most of the time the Fed and the FOMC have been extremely fortunate to have outstanding, highly capable leadership, both in the board chairman and in the FRB-NY president. Over the decades, power in the

---

[1] As an indication of the excellence of the staff personnel of the Board of Governors, it's interesting to note that three members of the staff have, in the past, received Presidential appointments to board membership. These were Robert Holland (1973), Charles Partee (1976), and Lyle Gramley (1980).

System has gravitated upward to the positions of those who have demonstrated their ability to use it intelligently and effectively.

The power of the Fed chairman and the Fed Board in influencing the decisions of the FOMC are considerable. The Fed Board, through its ability to choose the individuals who will become presidents of the individual Federal Reserve banks, has the power to, in effect, appoint the individuals who will become members of the FOMC. This power is particularly important in the choice of the person who will become the president of the FRB-NY—not an unlikely candidate to succeed the present chairman of the Board of Governors in Washington. Box 9-2 has something to say about that.

THE BOARD OF GOVERNORS: WHAT DOES IT DO?

Being a Fed Board member is a full-time job. The board members occupy offices in the Federal Reserve headquarters building at 20th and Constitution Avenue in Washington. That building also houses several hundred other Fed employees: economists, statisticians, lawyers, and other support personnel. Also, this is where the Federal Open Market Committee holds its meetings. But what do the board members do between FOMC meetings? Quite a lot.

Keeping an Eye on Changing Economic Conditions. Just keeping up with developments in the U.S. and world economy and the continuing analyses of these developments—to be ready to participate intelligently and effectively in the next FOMC meeting or in the next intermeeting telephone conference—would be a full-time job. Without their excellent staff support, it would be an impossible job. But the board members are required to do much more than that.

Reviewing and Deciding on Applications from Banks. In the last few years the number of banks applying for Fed approval to merge with other banks has grown explosively. Banks are applying for permission to form holding companies and acquire other banks, to expand their geographic range of operations, to perform a variety of new functions, including insurance, leasing, securities brokerage activities, and various other.

Box 9-2

Question: Would You Pay $60,000 for the Privilege of
     Being Fed Board Chairman?

Prior to his appointment as Fed Board chairman by President Carter in 1979, Paul Volcker was serving as president of the Federal Reserve Bank of New York. His salary at the New York Fed was more than $150,000. As Fed Board chairman his salary was less than $90,000. Would you be willing to do that?

It seems unfortunate that it's necessary for our outstanding citizens to make financial sacrifices for the privilege of providing services for the good of the nation. But that's the way it is.

The board must review all of these proposals and make the decisions. Without a highly competent staff to assist them, this flood of activity would be impossible for the board members to handle. Fortunately, many of these cases can be handled by the individual Federal Reserve banks and need not come to the attention of the board in Washington.

Taking and Explaining Positions on Legal Cases. The Board is always involved in many legal cases which challenge its decisions. The legal staff of the board carries out most of the detailed work on the 20 or so cases which are always going on. But the members of the board at some point must get involved and explain and support their positions on the legal issues.

Testifying to Congress. Some kind of legislation dealing with banking is always being considered in the Congress. The Congressional committees drafting legislation are continually calling on the members of the board to testify on various legislative proposals. This also is a time-consuming activity and one which lays the members of the Board open to attack by some of the outspoken members of Congress.

Reporting to Congress. Since the new legislation of the late 1970s (amendments to the Federal Reserve Act in 1977 and the Humphrey-Hawkins Act of 1978), the Fed Board has been required by law to make periodic reports to Congress. These reports must explain what the Fed's monetary policies are and the rationale underlying those policies and must set specific growth-rate targets for the money supply. So the Fed (actually the chairman) must justify the Fed's policies and actions to the Congress. This, too, could be a full-time job!

Clearly, Fed Board membership requires a lot of time and work on a continuing basis. You won't be surprised to know that most board members could earn a lot more money for their efforts by resigning from the board and doing something else. So it isn't at all unusual for board members to resign before their fourteen-year appointments are completed. In fact, in recent years the turnover has been quite high. It must take a lot of dedication to stick with it for the full 14-year term!

The Fed's Primary Function: Monetary Policy

You can see that the Board members are involved in many things. But their most important function (by far) is to serve as a majority on the FOMC and in establishing and conducting monetary policy. And the monetary policies of the board are largely determined at the FOMC meetings under the leadership and strong influence of the Chairman of the Board and (frequently) of the president of the New York Fed bank.

SUMMARY

- The compromise-ridden Federal Reserve Act of 1913 called for a geographically dispersed and lose-knit central banking system of 12 Fed banks, loosely coordinated by the Federal Reserve Board in Washington.

- Each District Fed bank was authorized to issue currency, and a nationwide check-clearing system was established.
- All national banks were required to join the system. State banks were permitted to do so.
- In the early years the Fed followed the real-bills doctrine and rediscounted promissory notes responding to the public's demand for funds. Sometimes this passive policy permitted overexpansion of the money supply.
- Most of the coordination which occurred during the 1920s resulted from "unofficial" leadership, especially that of Benjamin Strong, FRB-NY President.
- The uncoordinated Fed was not equipped to meet the liquidity needs of the financial crises of 1929–33.
- The Banking Acts of 1933 and 1935 (1) removed the administrative members (the Secretary of the Treasury and the Comptroller of the Currency) from the Fed Board, (2) expanded the powers of the board, and (3) officially established the Federal Open Market Committee (FOMC).
- Since the 1930s the development of the system and its policies has been significantly influenced by the personalities and leadership abilities of the few long-term board chairmen.
- Since the 1930s the Fed Board has exercised centralized control over the system. The board in Washington actually makes the decisions.
- The FOMC is the supreme deliberative body for deciding monetary policy for the nation. The president of the New York Fed bank serves as vice-chairman of the FOMC.
- The System Open Market Account (SOMA) manager, located at the New York Fed, interprets and carries out the monetary policy directives of the FOMC.
- Membership on the Board of Governors involves keeping in touch with changing economic conditions, reviewing applications from banks, taking positions on legal cases, testifying and reporting to Congress, and other functions. But the primary function is the determination of monetary policy.

Important Principles, Issues, Concepts, Terms

Initial structure of the Federal Reserve System

Purpose of the initial Fed Board

Functions of the new Fed System

Commercial paper (1914 definition)

Role of "rediscounting"

Importance of currency elasticity

"Real Bills" Doctrine

Commercial loan theory: meaning, and problems

Early functioning of the Fed

Early leadership of the FRB-New York

Benjamin Strong

Lack of Fed unification and leadership, 1928–33

Fed's performance after the '29 crash

Amendments to the Fed's structure—1933 and 1935

Role of long-term Fed Board Chairmen

Structure and functioning of the FOMC

Execution of open market operations

Special role of the FRB-New York

Activities of the Board of Governors

Congressional oversight committees

The Fed's primary function

Controversial monetary policy issues

Questions and Problems

1. Describe the structure and the intended functions of the Federal Reserve System as it was initially created.

2. Explain the meaning of the "real bills" doctrine, and the rationale for adopting this doctrine.

3. Describe the functioning of the Federal Reserve System during the 1920s, and explain the special role of the Federal Reserve Bank of New York during this period.

4. What changes in the Federal Reserve System occurred as a result of the banking acts of 1933 and 1935? Has the functioning of the Fed been significantly different since that time?

5. Who really is in control of Fed policy? Discuss.

6. Describe the Federal Open Market Committee: its structure, and its functions.

7. Discuss the functions of the Board of Governors of the Federal Reserve System.

8. There is now, and for more than two decades there has been, *one major issue* of serious controversy regarding monetary policy. What is that issue, and why is this a *very serious matter? Discuss.*

Suggested Readings

Brunner, Karl, ed. "Congressional Supervision of Monetary Policy: A Symposium." *Journal of Monetary Economics* 4 (April 1978), 325–88.

Burns, Arthur F. "The Independence of the Federal Reserve System." *Challenge.* (July/August 1976), 21–24.

Chandler, Lester V. *Benjamin Strong, Central Banker.* Washington, D.C.: The Brookings Institution, 1958.

Dewald, William G. "The National Monetary Commission, A Look Back." *Journal of Money, Credit and Banking* 4 (November 1972), 930–36.

Eccles, Marriner. *Beckoning Frontiers.* New York: Knopf, 1951.

Federal Reserve Bulletin. "Record of Policy Actions of the Federal Open Market Committee." (published periodically).

Flannery, Mark J. "Deposit Insurance Creates a Need for Bank Regulation." *Business Review.* Federal Reserve Bank of Philadelphia, January/February 1982.

Kane, Edward J. "External Pressure and the Operations of the Fed." in Raymone E. Lombra and Willard E. Witte, *Political Economy of International and Domestic Monetary Relations.* Ames, Iowa: Iowa State University Press, 1982, pp. 611–632.

Kettl, Donald F. *Leadership at the Fed.* New Haven: Yale University Press, 1986.

Maisel, Sherman. *Managing the Dollar.* New York: W. W. Norton, 1973.

Mayer, Thomas. "The Structure and Operation of the Federal Reserve system: Some Needed Reforms." U.S. Congress House Committee on Banking, Currency, and Housing, *Compendium of Papers Prepared for the FINE Study.* 94th Congress, 2nd session, 1976, 2:669–726.

Mengle, David. "The Discount Window." *Economic Review.* Federal Reserve Bank of Richmond, May/June 1986.

Taylor, Herb. "The Discount Window and Monetary Control." *Business Review.* Federal Reserve Bank of Philadelphia, May/June 1983.

Weintraub, Robert. "Congressional Supervision of Monetary Policy." *Journal of Monetary Economics* 4 (April 1978), 341–63.

Wooley, John. *Monetary Politics.* New York: Cambridge University, 1985.

PART III

Financial Intermediaries, Instruments and Markets: The Flow of Funds from Surplus Economic Units (SEUs) to Deficit Economic Units (DEUs)

PART III focuses directly on the functions which are the whole *raison d'etre* of the financial system. The financial system exists for the purpose of transferring funds from those who do not wish to spend now, to those who do. In Part III you will be reading about the net savers—the surplus economic units (SEUs)—and the net borrowers—the deficit economic units (DEUs)—and how funds flow from the surplus units to the deficit units.

In this part you will take an in-depth look at financial intermediation and at the financial intermediaries (FIMs)—at who they are and what they do and how. Also you will be reading about how the FIMs buy and sell and create and destroy financial instruments and how that results in a flow of funds from SEUs to DEUs. You will read about the various instruments of the money market and the capital market and the role which these play in the flow of funds from SEUs to DEUs.

Also in this part you will find out the important role of interest rates in the flow of funds process. And you will find out about factors which cause interest rates on different financial instruments to be different, depending on degree of risk and term to maturity. Then you will learn how to illustrate all this with term structure and risk structure yield curves. And you'll find out how to "read" these yield cures and draw conclusions about the relative riskiness of different financial instruments, and about the conditions and outlook in the markets.

After you finish studying Part III you will have a good understanding of the functions of the FIMs. And you will understand the role of financial instruments and markets in facilitating the flows of funds between the SEUs and DEUs. Also you will know how the structure of interest rates responds to and is determined by the interaction of the supply of funds (from SEUs) and the demand for funds (from DEUs).

CHAPTER 10

Financial Intermediation: Facilitating the Flow of Funds from Savers (SEUs) to Borrowers (DEUs)

Chapter Objectives

This chapter and the two following ones explain the theory and practice of financial institutions, instruments and markets.

This chapter explains **financial intermediation**: what it is, how it works, and its importance. From this chapter you will understand and be able to explain:

1. Exactly what is meant by **financial intermediation**, and the kinds of **financial institutions** involved in this.

2. The distinction between the **broker**, **dealer**, and **financial intermediary** functions.

3. The **relative asset size** of:
   a. Depository versus nondepository financial intermediaries
   b. Different kinds of depository intermediaries
   c. Different kinds of nondepository intermediaries

4. What is meant by **financial instruments** and their role in "the buying and selling of current dollars."

5. The **microeconomic role** of financial intermediation: increasing the efficiency of resource allocation in the economy, and the **macroeconomic role**: supporting the circular flow of the economy.

6. How financial intermediation **reduces investment risks** for earner-savers (surplus economic units—SEUs) and **reduces financing costs** for borrower-spenders (deficit economic units—DEUs).

7. How financial intermediation promotes the **efficiency**, **stability**, and **growth** of the economy.

THE "MIDDLEMAN" ROLE OF FINANCIAL INTERMEDIATION: "BUYING AND SELLING CURRENT DOLLARS"

Financial intermediaries (FIMs) function as "middlemen" in the financial markets. The "middleman role," in general, involves buying and then reselling something—hopefully reselling at a higher price. What the financial intermediaries buy and then resell is currently available funds—**current dollars**.

The Flow of Funds from Surplus Economic Units (SEUs) to Deficit Economic Units (DEUs)

Sometimes it's useful to think of the economy as consisting of a great number of individual economic units with each person, household, business, governmental unit, and nonprofit or other organization being one economic unit. Some of these economic units are always receiving more current income than they wish to spend, while others would like to spend more than they are receiving. So some are **surplus economic units—SEUs**: current income > expenditures. Others are **deficit economic units—DEUs**: expenditures > current income.

On balance, households are SEUs and businesses and governments are DEUs. But there are many exceptions. A household which decides to buy a house, certainly becomes a DEU during that spending period!

Revenues Usually Lag Behind Expenditures

From the point of view of the economy, it's very important that businesses (and sometimes governments) be DEUs. In the normal production process revenues lag behind expenditures. So funds must be provided "up front"—before the ultimate revenues are realized. Most of this financing is done by debt (credit).

Now you can see why, in a growing economy, the amount of productive debt outstanding tends to be always increasing. Fortunately that's exactly what has been happening in the American economy.

The Rapid Growth of Private Debt

At the end of World War II (1945) total private debt in the United States amounted to about $150 billion. By 1960 it was up to $600 billion. By the early 1970s it reached $1.5 trillion and by the early 1980s, $5 trillion. By the late 1980s it was approaching $10 trillion. Rapid growth of private debt!

In analyzing debt, it's important to distinguish between *debt for the purpose of production* and *debt for the purpose of consumption*. The more **productive debt** a business or the economy has, the more rapidly it can grow and the healthier it can be. But **consumption debt** can have the opposite effect. Debts for consumer goods are not self-liquidating. Instead, these debts are a drain on future income. An overload of consumer debt can dampen future spending—both for an individual or household, and for an economic system.

The DEUs Obtain Funds from the SEUs

As the surplus economic units (SEUs) are saving a part of their incomes, the deficit economic units (DEUs) are seeking funds to spend—mostly for investment. For the stable and efficient functioning of the economy the total amount saved by the SEUs must be offset by the spending of the DEUs.

Many SEUs lend *directly* to DEUs. But most of the nation's savings flow from savers to borrowers *indirectly*, via financial intermediaries (FIMs).

Financial Intermediaries Issue Financial Instruments to "Buy Current Dollars"

The function of **financial intermediation** is to facilitate the flow of funds from SEUs to DEUs. Financial intermediaries are always buying current dollars from their depositors and others and then selling these current dollars to their borrowers and others. When financial intermediaries enter the financial markets to acquire current funds, they issue claims to (promises to pay) future funds.

The **depository intermediaries** issue promises to pay interest (except on demand deposit accounts), and promises to repay the deposited funds either on demand or (with CDs) at some specified future date. The **contractual intermediaries** (e.g., life insurance companies and pension funds) issue promises of future payments under certain specified circumstances.

The DEUs Issue Primary Financial Instruments: Stocks and Bonds and Commercial Paper

As primary instruments are issued by the DEUs, some are bought by SEUs. But most are bought by financial intermediaries (FIMs).

The financial instruments issued by the DEUs for the purpose of obtaining funds which they wish to spend for capital investment (plant, equipment, inventories) are called **primary instruments**. The financial instruments issued by FIMs for the purpose of obtaining funds which then will be loaned to the DEUs can be called (for the lack of a better term) **intermediary instruments**.

The Intermediary Function Is Distinctly Different from the Broker and Dealer Functions

In chapter 1 you read about the distinctions between brokers, dealers, and financial intermediaries. Here's a brief review.

In the financial markets the **broker function** involves buying or selling financial instruments for someone else. *The broker never owns the security.* The broker only assists in the transfer of title from the former owner to the new owner. For someone who wishes to buy, the broker receives a commission for finding a seller. For someone who wishes to sell, the broker receives a commission for finding a buyer. A "broker" is not a financial intermediary. Neither is a "dealer."

The **dealer function** actually involves buying, holding, and selling financial instruments. Most stockbrokers are also dealers in some stocks. When their customers place buy (or sell) orders the broker-dealers may sell the stocks from (or buy them for) their own inventory. Dealer-brokers get more directly involved in the market than nondealer brokers. But dealers are not in the business of issuing (selling) their own financial instruments. They only buy, hold, and sell existing securities issued by someone else. That isn't financial intermediation.

The **financial intermediary function** means *acquiring funds by issuing "intermediary" instruments and then using the funds to buy primary instruments.* Anyone who performs this function of buying current funds from SEUs and selling them to DEUs is performing the financial intermediary role. Anyone who doesn't, is not.

Figure 10-1 illustrates the flows of funds from savers to borrowers in exchange for financial instruments—both the direct flow via direct investment and the indirect flow via financial intermediaries.

Many Financial Firms Perform All Three Functions: Broker, Dealer, and FIM

While the functions of broker, dealer, and financial intermediary are distinctly different, there's nothing to say that one firm can't be performing all three functions. And in fact most large financial firms in this country and abroad are heavily involved in performing all three functions—and in providing other financial services as well.

Figure 10-1.   The Flow of Funds from Surplus Economic Units (SEUs) to Deficit Economic Units (DEUs)

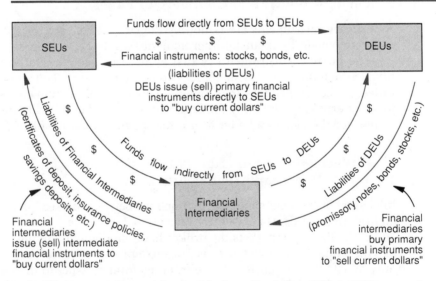

In the U.S. economy, about one-fourth of the flow of funds from SEUs to DEUs occurs **via direct finance**. The remaining three-fourths of the funds flow indirectly **via financial intermediaries**.

Financial intermediaries issue their own liabilities (deposits, etc.) in exchange for the surplus funds of the SEUs. Then they make those funds available to the DEUs in exchange for the DEUs' liabilities (promisory notes, etc.)

Financial intermediaries use **intemediary financial instruments** to obtain funds from SEUs. Then they use these funds to buy **primary financial instruments** from the DEUs.

During the 1980s there has been a rush of (1) brokerage firms into financial intermediation, (2) banks and thrifts into the brokerage business, and (3) non-financial corporations (e.g., Sears, Parker Pen, Montgomery Ward and many others) into both brokerage and financial intermediation. You can't be sure anymore who's doing what in the financial markets—not unless you take a close look to see what functions each firm is performing.

FINANCIAL INTERMEDIATION SERVES THE SEUs THE DEUs AND THE ECONOMY

From the point of view of **net savers** (SEUs), financial intermediaries provide a safe and convenient place to deposit savings and earn income. From the point of view of **net borrowers** (DEUs), financial intermediaries provide a readily available, low-cost source of funds. From the point of view of the functioning of the economy, financial intermediation plays some essential roles too, both **microeconomic** and **macroeconomic**. (If you aren't quite sure of the meanings of these terms, go back to chapter 2 and reread box 2-1.)

The Microeconomic Role: Increasing the Allocative Efficiency of the Economy

By saving (not consuming), the SEUs release resources (inputs) from the production of consumer goods. Then, mostly via financial intermediation, the DEUs acquire the saved funds and buy up the released inputs. *This is how the inputs released by the SEUs are redirected into the production of the kinds of goods demanded by the DEUs*—mostly investment (capital) goods.

The flow of funds from SEUs to DEUs—and the simultaneous action of the price mechanism—induces resources to flow away from less desired (less timely, less productive) uses and into more desired (more timely, more productive) uses. All of this results in increased efficiency and productivity of the economic system. Ultimately the effect is to increase the economic welfare of the society.

Money (the exchange medium) permits the price mechanism to function efficiently. And it's the price mechanism which brings about the efficient allocation of resources. But *this efficient outcome couldn't be achieved without the efficient transfer of funds from SEUs to DEUs*. Most of this transfer depends on the functions of the financial intermediaries.

In short, because it facilitates the flow of funds from SEUs to DEUs, financial intermediation facilitates the efficient allocation of society's inputs and outputs. Figure 10-2 uses supply and demand graphs to illustrate the **microeconomic** significance of the efficient flow of funds from SEUs to DEUs. This figure illustrates the microeconomic significance of financial intermediation.

The Macroeconomic Role: Supporting the Circular Flow of the Economy

Financial intermediation also plays an important macroeconomic role. As income is earned and saved (not spent for consumer goods), that tends to reduce total spending in the economy. Unless there is an offsetting spending injection (by

**Figure 10-2.   Supply and Demand Graphs Illustrate the Reallocative
Effects of the Flow of Funds from SEUs to DEUs**

Savings flow from SEUs to DEUs and reallocate some of the society's resources from the production of
SEU-demanded goods to the production of DEU-demanded goods.

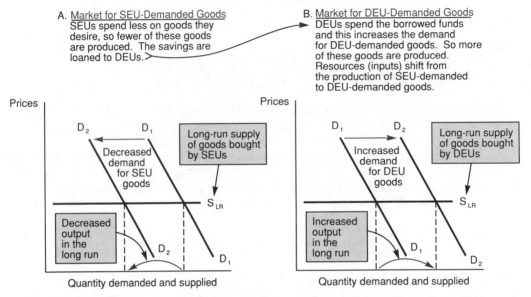

On balance, **households** are SEUs and **businesses** are DEUs. Therefore, on balance, the shift from SEU-
demanded goods to DEU-demanded goods amounts to a shift from **consumer goods** to **capital goods**, and on
balance this represents the flow of **savings** into **investment**.

There are always some households during some periods of time which are DEUs, and some businesses which
during some periods of time, are SEUs. Also, some of the savings of the SEUs flow into government spending and
result in increased production of **government-demanded goods**.

*The net effect of the transfer of spending from SEUs to DEUs results in decreased output of consumer goods
and increased output of capital goods.* But within this flow of funds, some households are (at some times) DEUs
so that their borrowing and spending resullt in increased output of consumer goods; while some businesses are
(at some times) SEUs, so that their savings result in reduced output of capital goods.

investors or someone) then the size of the spending flow will decrease. The
economy will slow down. Unemployment will increase as the economy goes into
recession.

Financial intermediation reduces the likelihood that savings outflows from
the spending stream will result in an economic slowdown. By channeling money
from savers to borrowers, *financial intermediaries provide an easy and efficient
way for the spending stream outflows caused by savers, to be offset by spending
injections by borrowers.*

When the savings withdrawals of the SEUs are offset by spending injections
by the DEUs, no decrease in spending occurs. So no economic slowdown occurs.
Figure 10-3 uses a spending flow diagram to illustrate this important **macroeconomic role** of financial intermediation.

Figure 10-3.   The Spending Flow Diagram: How DEU Injections Can Offset SEU Withdrawals

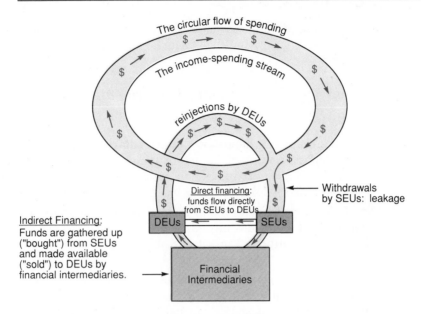

Funds withdrawn by the SEUs flow to the DEUs (via both direct and indirect financing) and are reinjected into the spending flow.

Financial intermediaries play a middleman role which facilitates the flow of funds from SEUs to DEUs and thereby helps to maintain the size of the spending flow.

The SEUs withdraw savings (drain off funds) from the circular spending flow. This tends to reduce the size of the spending flow. But when these savings are transferred to the DEUs and reinjected into the spending flow, the size of the spending flow is maintained.

In this diagram all of the withdrawals and reinjections are shown to occur at one place in the spending flow. Obviously this is unrealistic. Withdrawals by SEUs and reinjections by DEUs are occurring all the time in small amounts all around the spending flow circle.

Reinjections by DEUs may sometimes be either smaller or larger than withdrawals by SEUs. This is true both (1) because financial intermediaries can serve as a reservoir of funds, sometimes acquiring more than they are currently lending and at other times lending more than they are currently acquiring; and (2) because depository intermediaries can create and lend money in excess of the amounts being withdrawn by the SEUs and they can destroy money by reducing their lending at the times when loans are being repaid. Whenever the **savings withdrawals** are either greater than or less than the **reinjections**, the size of the spending flow will become smaller or larger.

AN OVERVIEW OF FINANCIAL INTERMEDIARIES IN THE U.S. ECONOMY

When you think of the importance of the financial intermediary function in the economy, it isn't surprising that financial intermediaries are numerous, and of great variety.

The Great Variety of Financial Intermediaries

Who are these financial intermediaries?

- First, there are the **depository intermediaries** which take deposits and "issue deposit liabilities," some of which are "checkable" and serve as money. The depository intermediaries are: Commercial banks. Savings and loan companies. Mutual savings banks. Credit unions.

- Then there are the **contractual intermediaries** which do not strictly "take deposits" but which do "buy current dollars" in exchange for various kinds of contracted future payments or obligations: Insurance companies and pension funds.

- There are the **investment companies** (mutual funds) which are somewhat similar to depository intermediaries. They don't "take deposits," but they "issue mutual fund shares" in exchange for current dollars. Then they usually do not lend directly to the DEUs, but use the funds obtained to buy existing DEU securities, mostly stocks, bonds, commercial paper and T-bills.

- Finally, there are the many different kinds of business and consumer **finance companies** which issue their own liabilities of various kinds to acquire funds—you might say they "buy current dollars in the wholesale market"—and then sell the funds in the retail market by lending these funds to businesses mostly to finance inventories and payrolls, and to consumers to buy cars, appliances, and other consumer goods.

More Than Half of the Financial Intermediary Assets Are Held by the Depository Institutions

Figure 10-4 shows the important kinds of financial intermediaries in the U.S. economy and indicates the relative asset size of each, as of 1987. You can see that the depository intermediaries were holding a little more than half of the total assets of all financial intermediaries. The nondepository intermediaries were holding about 42 percent of the assets, and money market mutual funds were holding about 3 percent.

Money Market Mutual Funds Are "Almost" Depository Intermediaries

Money market mutual funds (MMMFs) are shown separately because sometimes these funds are considered to be depository intermediaries. They "issue shares" to obtain funds and then use the funds to buy money market financial instruments (T-bills, etc.). They pay their "shareholders" money market interest rates and offer immediate withdrawal of "deposited" funds.

**Figure 10-4.   Overview of Financial Intermediaries in the
U.S. Economy in the Late 1980s**

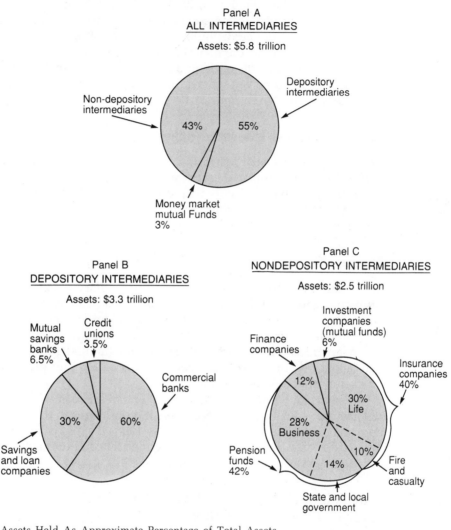

Panel A
ALL INTERMEDIARIES

Assets: $5.8 trillion

Non-depository
intermediaries

Depository
intermediaries

43%   55%

Money market
mutual Funds
3%

Panel B
DEPOSITORY INTERMEDIARIES

Assets: $3.3 trillion

Mutual   Credit
savings   unions
banks   3.5%
6.5%
                           Commercial
                           banks

30%   60%

Savings
and loan
companies

Panel C
NONDEPOSITORY INTERMEDIARIES

Assets: $2.5 trillion

Investment
companies
(mutual funds)
Finance   6%
companies
                        Insurance
                        companies
             12%   40%
                   30%
                   Life
          28%
          Business
                      10%
Pension
funds   14%   Fire
42%   and
                          casualty
State and local
government

Assets Held As Approximate Percentage of Total Assets

But the MMMFs are "not exactly" depository intermediaries, and they are not under the same regulatory controls as the banks and thrifts. If MMMFs are considered to be depository intermediaries, then the depository intermediaries were holding almost 60 percent of total intermediary assets in the late 1980s.

The Depository Intermediaries

In figure 10-4, panel B shows a breakdown of the total assets of the **depository intermediaries**—those which take deposits and all of which (nowdays) can offer checkable accounts. You can see that the **commercial banks** hold about 60% of the total.

The **savings and loan institutions** are next in relative size. They hold about half as much as the commercial banks—about 30% of the total. The remaining 10% of total depository intermediary assets are split between the **mutual savings banks** (MSBs) and the **credit unions**, with total MSB assets amounting to about twice as much as total credit union assets. But note this: In recent years the percentage growth rate of credit union assets has been much higher than for any of the others. By the time you are reading this, credit unions will have a larger slice of the pie than shown in figure 10-4.

The Contractual Intermediaries

Panel C shows a breakdown of the total assets of the **nondepository interme-diaries**. You can see that the **contractual intermediaries** (insurance companies and pension funds) hold more than 80% of the total. **Insurance companies** hold about 40% of the nondepository total and **pension funds** hold slightly more than that—about 42% of the total.

Finance Companies and Investment Companies (Mutual Funds)

The remaining 18% of nondepository intermediary assets are held by **finance companies** and **mutual funds**, with finance company assets amounting to about twice as much as mutual fund assets. The figure for finance companies (about 12% of the nondepository total) includes all kinds of both commercial and consumer loan companies. The **investment companies** (mutual funds) percentage of the total (about 6%) includes both open-end and closed-end investment companies, but excludes money market mutual funds.

Since the mid-1980s, investments in mutual funds have been growing rapidly. At some times during 1987 people were buying shares in these funds at the rate of more than $1 billion per day. By the early 1990s it's likely that the share of mutual fund assets (as a percentage of total nondepository intermediary assets), will be more than the 6% figure shown here.

Many Financial Services Firms Perform
Several Different Functions

Now that you have an overview picture of the financial intermediaries in the U.S. economy, here is a brief word of warning, "lest ye forget." Take care as you interpret the pie charts in figure 10-4. Examples:

Where is Citicorp? Certainly it's the largest in commercial banking. Also it owns one of the largest savings and loan institutions in the country. It is very involved in pension fund administration, it owns insurance companies, it owns finance companies, and some of its activities, although not defined as "mutual funds" are so close as to be, for practical purposes, indistinguishable from mutual funds.

Where is Ford Motor Company? It owns one of the largest savings and loan institutions in the country, and is in the top three in finance companies. And it is significantly involved in various kinds of banking and other financial services activities.

Sears Roebuck is into almost everything on the chart. And the list could go on and on. There is no sizeable bank in the country which is not represented in several of the slices both in panel B and in panel C.

The bottom line: The "pie slices" shown in figure 10-4 mostly indicate "functions" and not specific companies, or institutions. Most firms which operate in the financial services industry—both financial firms and nonfinancial firms as well—are involved in many of the functions indicated by these slices.

FINANCIAL INTERMEDIATION BENEFITS THE SEUs

Savers (SEUs) place their funds in financial intermediaries because it's easier. Less information, and fewer "tough decisions" are required. Also, its safer—less risky than direct investment. So why would SEUs sometimes make direct investments?—lend directly to borrower-spenders (DEUs) without going through a financial intermediary? Because with direct investment they have a chance to earn more income.

Most people, most of the time (with a little bit of luck) could earn a higher return by investing directly. Returns on government bonds or corporate bonds or corporate stocks are usually higher than on bank or thrift deposits. But is the greater return worth the trouble?

To many people, no it isn't. Without the safety (and peace of mind) afforded by financial intermediation, many people (SEUs) would be reluctant to make their savings available for investment by the DEUs.

Different Kinds of Risk Borne by SEUs

When SEUs lend directly to the DEUs, the savers face three kinds of risk. Two of these kinds of risk—default risk, and market risk (explained below)—could be avoided by placing savings in insured deposits at a bank or thrift. But with the third kind—purchasing power risk—financial intermediation doesn't necessarily solve the problem.

Default risk. A saver might buy a bond and the company that issued the bond might not be able to make the specified payments. Or it might go broke! But SEUs could lend directly and still avoid this **default risk** by investing in U.S. Government securities which have zero default risk.

Market risk (also called "price risk," and "capital risk"). The market values of all marketable securities (stocks, bonds, etc.) go up and down, reflecting changing market conditions. If you buy bonds (even U.S. Government bonds) and *then market rates of interest go up, the market value of your bonds will go down.* You will lose purchasing power as the market value of your portfolio of financial assets decreases. That's **market risk**.

Purchasing power risk. This is the risk of **inflation**. As prices rise, the real value of fixed-dollar-denominated financial assets decreases. For example, suppose the inflation rate is 9%. That means that the value of all of your dollar-denominated assets—checking accounts, savings accounts, cash, bonds, CDs, fixed-rate insurance policies, pension funds, accounts receivable, other debts owed to you, etc.—is decreasing at the rate of 9% per year.

Suppose the **nominal interest rate** on your savings account is 6%. Then on that account you are not even earning enough interest to offset the effect of inflation. You are in fact receiving a **real rate of return** on that account of minus 3%.

Figure 10-5 illustrates the potential seriousness of purchasing power risk. That figure indicates that during most of the 1970s and in the early 1980s most savers in the United States were receiving negative real rates of return on their

Figure 10-5.   Nominal and Real Interest Rates, 1950s–1980s

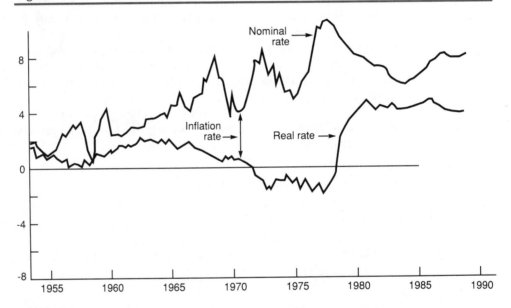

On this graph, the vertical distance between the two rates indicates the realized rate of inflation as measured by the consumer price index.

During the low-inflation years of the mid-1950s, both nominal and real rates were below 2%. Real rates were negative from 1973 to 1981 because of the high inflation rates during that period. But then, since the early 1980s, real rates have been fluctuating around 4%—higher than at any other time in the past 50 years.

When real rates are negative it pays to borrow and buy real assets (whose prices are rising) and then later pay off the loans with inflated dollars. So the demand for borrowed funds tends to be strong and the supply weak. Rates tend to rise.

Note: To update this chart, the easiest way is to use the statistical tables in the **Federal Reserve Bulletin**. The nominal T-bill rate can be found in the table "Interest Rates: Money and Capital Markets," p. A-24, and the inflation rate (as indicated by the rate of change in the consumer price index) can be found in the table "Consumer and Producer Prices," p. A-50. Just subtract the inflation rate from the nominal interest rate to find the real rate.

Source: *Federal Reserve Chart Book 1987.* Updated by the author from the *Federal Reserve Bulletin.*

savings. Since the inflation rate exceeded the nominal interest rate, on the average the actual purchasing power of the average person's savings was declining.

Intermediaries Can Eliminate Some Kinds (But Not All Kinds) of Risk

Financial intermediaries deal with default risk and market risk by (1) **prudent investment choices** and (2) **diversification**. The financial intermediaries have access to the kinds of information required to enable them to make well-informed investment choices—better choices than most SEUs could make. Also thay have total assets large enough so that they don't have to "put all their eggs in one basket." They can invest in a widely diversified portfolio of assets.

Most savers (SEUs) would rather not worry about prudent investment choices, or diversification. So they place their money in insured deposits at a bank or thrift and thereby completely eliminate both default risk and market risk—even though this means giving up the chance for higher returns from direct investment.

But on the third kind of risk—purchasing power risk—the financial intermediaries may not be of much help. When prices rise, the purchasing power of money in insured deposits goes down. Unless the interest income on those deposits goes up enough to offset the effect of inflation, the savers lose. And the safety-seeking depositors may not be able to protect themselves from that. (See box 10-1 on the so-called Fisher Effect.)

Financial Intermediaries "Manufacture" Safety and Liquidity to Attract Funds

You might say that the financial intermediaries "manufacture safety and liquidity" for the savers. Some of their liabilities are (1) highly liquid—redeemable on demand—and (2) have zero default risk because of deposit insurance. To attract

Box 10-1

Question: Will Interest Rates Rise to Protect Savers from the Effects of Inflation?—The "Fisher Effect"

Suppose everyone feels sure that the inflation rate over the next 12 months is going to be 9%. If interest rates are freely responsive to market conditions, then nominal market rates certainly will move above 9%.

Borrowers will be willing to pay more than 9%. They will want to borrow and buy now before prices rise by 9%. And surely savers will not supply funds to borrowers unless the offered rate is above the break-even rate of 9%!

The bottom line: An increase in the expected inflation rate will tend to force an increase in nominal interest rates. This is the so-called **Fisher Effect**, named for its founder, Irving Fisher.

The Fisher Effect offers to savers some protection against the effects of inflation. The Fisher Effect says: If financial markets are (1) completely free and (2) perfectly competitive and if (3) the rate of inflation is precisely and accurately expected—big ifs!—then interest rates automatically will rise by exactly enough to compensate for the effect of inflation and, in addition, will provide a "normal" market-determined real rate of return on savings. The Fisher Effect never has worked out very well in the past. But the tendency stated by the principle definitely has been observable.

funds the intermediaries create a great variety of financial instruments—their own liabilities—designed to meet the savers' needs. That's how they compete with each other for the "current dollars" of the savers.

Financial intemediation can't eliminate all of the risks. But it can provide savers more safety (and some earnings) for their savings. And the depository intermediaries offer a high degree of liquidity—you can get your money any time you wish. So the intermediaries attract savings from the SEUs which then flow to the DEUs and are spent.

The effects of financial intermediation are

a.   **microeconomic:** to help to bring about desired reallocations of resources via market-directed adjustments, and

b.   **macroeconomic:** to transfer idle funds from savers to spenders and thereby help to support total spending (the circular flow of the economy) and maintain a high level of employment, output, and income.

FINANCIAL INTERMEDIATION ALSO BENEFITS THE DEUs, AND THE ECONOMY

Without an efficient, safe, and dependable system of financial intermediation it's likely that many savers would just hoard their savings. And without financial intermediation most of the transfers of savings from SEUs wouldn't be carried out very efficiently.

Intermediation Holds Down the Cost of Borrowing

Without financial intermediaries it would be necessary for borrowers to try to induce savers to lend to them directly. But how much interest would the borrowers have to offer, to induce all of the savers to incur the risks of direct investment? For example, consider this: How many people do you suppose would be able to borrow enough money to buy their own home without the help of a financial intermediary?

A well-developed system of financial intermediation holds down interest costs throughout the economy by providing for the efficient transfer of funds from savers to borrowers. Financial intermediaries can pool the savings of many small SEUs and make these funds available for the purchase of big-ticket items by DEUS.

With financial intermediation, savers can have **safety** and **liquidity**—and without having to hoard cash. And this tends to increase the **propensity to save**. Borrowers can get the funds they want—and without having to pay the high costs which would be required to induce the SEUs to incur the risks of direct investment.

Financial Intermediaries Are Specialized and Efficient

Financial intermediaries can make funds available to DEUs at **low interest cost** because the intermediaries are specialized in performing their "middleman" role. They are expert at attracting the savings of SEUs. And they are specialists in gathering and analyzing the kinds of information needed to make lending decisions.

Also, as they make their loans and investments their costs of operation are reduced by their ability to take advantage of economies of scale and portfolio diversification. In today's competitive environment they are forced to perform their intermediary functions in a highly efficient way. Why? To survive!

Financial Intermediation Benefits the Economy

As financial intermediation reduces interest costs to borrowers it lowers the cost of real investments—and therefore, costs of production—throughout the economy. The **lower cost** stimulates profits, generates investment, fosters economic growth. More output and income to share. On the average, we all live better.

The Evidence of Benefits Are Everywhere. You see evidence of the effects of an efficient system of financial intermediation everywhere you look—both in the U.S. economy and throughout the world. Stop for a moment and look around you. How many of the things that you see would exist without the role of financial intermediaries? For example, without financial intermediation, how many people would own their own home? Or car? Refrigerator? T.V.? VCR?

What about business capital? How much of the physical capital—plant and equipment and inventories—would exist without financial intermediation? And what about the so-called "social overhead capital"—highways and water systems and schools and playgrounds and public buildings, etc., etc.—financial intermediation involved again? Yes. *Without the invention and widespread use of modern financial instruments and markets, most of these things would not— could not!—exist.*

Even much of our "human capital development" is now being financed through financial intermediaries. Student loans are bringing higher education within the reach of millions of people. The ultimate result will be a stronger, more efficient, more productive economy—and (we hope) a better society for all of us.

Intermediaries Foster Prudent Financial Management and Efficient Resource Allocation. Beyond their role of transferring funds from SEUs to DEUs, financial intermediaries provide several very important **fringe benefits** to the economy and the society. As businesses and households deal with financial intermediaries they are forced to learn some of the principles of prudent finance.

As the intermediaries make loans, they tend to channel funds toward those projects which are most likely to be successful—good for their owners, and good for the economy. So the intermediaries tend to improve the financial management of both households and businesses. And all of this improves the functioning of the economic system.

The contractual intermediaries play an important role in the financial system through their operations in the financial markets. They contribute significantly to risk management in the financial system. And the depository institutions, don't forget, are the ones who provide our monetary (payments) system, U.S. and worldwide.

The "Modern World" Could Not Exist Without It. How much of the growth of the U.S. and worldwide economy has resulted from financial intermediation? Nobody can answer that exactly. But you can be absolutely certain that *without financial intermediation the great allocative efficiency and productivity of the modern* *world economies could not have been achieved. In fact, the "modern world" as we know it could not exist.*

Direct Investment and Financial Intermediation in the U.S. Economy

The **flows of funds** between SEUs and DEUs, both directly and via financial intermediation, is constantly occurring in the financial markets. Some of this flow represents new savings. But most of it represents the reshuffling of accumulated savings as savers (asset holders) shift their funds in response to changing market conditions and/or outlook, and as loan repayments are turned over into new loans.

In the U.S. economy in the late 1980s, an amount greater than $1 trillion a year was flowing through the nation's financial markets between saver-lenders (SEUs) and borrower-spenders (DEUs). About one-fourth (some $250 billion) of that funds transfer occurred via **direct investment**. The other three-fourths (some $750 billion) flowed through **financial intermediaries**.[1]

Financial Intermediation Depends on Financial Instruments and Markets

The extent of **financial intermediation** would be very limited without the existence of a well-developed system of **financial instruments** and **markets**. And the functions of financial markets would be very limited without a well-developed system of financial instruments, and financial intermediation. It all ties together to form an efficient, integrated system.

The speedy and efficient flow of funds from SEUs to DEUs requires this **integrated system** of financial institutions, instruments, and markets. The system works to transfer funds speedily and efficiently from SEUs to DEUs throughout the United States and worldwide. It also serves to facilitate the "return flows" of these funds—the flow of loan repayments. And it works no matter who the SEUs and DEUs may be, and no matter where in the world they may be located.

You'll be reading more about all this in the two following chapters which deal specifically with financial instruments and markets—with what they are and how they work.

SUMMARY

- *The stable and efficient operation of the economy requires that the savings of surplus economic units (SEUs) be offset by the spending of deficit economic units (DEUs).*

---

[1] Information on the flows of funds through the financial markets and financial intermediaries (and on other flows of funds in the economy) is published by the Board of Governors of the Federal Reserve System in its *Flow of Funds Accounts*, available from Publications Services, the Federal Reserve Board, Washington, D.C. 20551. Some of this information is published in the "Flow of Funds" tables in the *Federal Reserve Bulletin* (monthly), pp. A42 and A43.

- The transfer of funds from SEUs to DEUs serves the purposes of
  a. reallocating the society's resources away from less desired and toward more desired current uses (microeconomic effects), and
  b. helping to offset the savings withdrawals of SEUs by funding the spending injections of DEUs (macroeconomic effects).

- **Financial intermediaries** perform the middleman role. They issue **intermediary instruments** (their liabilities) and use these to acquire funds from SEUs; then they use the funds to purchase **primary instruments** issued by DEUs. *In the U.S. economy about three-fourths of the flow of funds from SEUs to DEUs moves via financial intermediation.*

- The **broker** and **dealer** functions are not intermediary functions. But by the late-1980s most large broker-dealers were also acting as intermediaries, and many intermediary firms were offering a broad range of financial services—including brokerage services.

- There is a great variety of financial intermediaries, including both depository and nondepository intermediaries. In asset size, the **depository intermediaries** make up more than half of the total.

- **Commercial banks** are by far the largest of the depository intermediaries, holding some 60% of total depository intermediary assets. The remaining 40% of the depository intermediary assets are held by the so-called **thrift institutions**.

- Of the assets of the nondepository intermediaries, some 82% of the assets are held by the **contractual intermediaries**—the **insurance companies** and **pension funds**. The remaining 18% of the assets are held by **finance companies** and **mutual funds**.

- Depository intermediaries permit SEUs to escape both **default risk** and **market risk**. But in the past, financial intermediation has not protected against the "purchasing power risk" of inflation.

- Financial intermediaries can transfer funds from SEUs and DEUs very efficiently. They have expertise in **attracting savings** from SEUs and **making loans** to DEUs. Also they benefit from economies of scale and diversification.

- Financial intermediaries reduce **borrowing costs**, promote better **financial management** and facilitate the **shifting of resources** into their most productive uses. All this promotes the efficiency, productivity, and growth of the economy.

Important Principles, Issues, Concepts, Terms

Surplus Economic Units (SEUs)

Deficit Economic Units (DEUs)

Advantages and disadvantages of direct investment by SEUs

Definition of financial intermediation

The difference between broker, dealer, and intermediary functions

The "middleman" role of financial intermediaries

How intermediaries "buy and sell current dollars"

Primary financial instruments

Intermediate financial instruments

Kinds of financial intermediaries

Specific functions of different kinds of intermediaries

Microeconomic role of financial intermediation

Macroeconomic role of financial intermediation

How to use supply and demand graphs to illustrate the microeconomic role

How to use the circular flow diagram to illustrate the macroeconomic role

Relative asset sizes of various intermediaries in the U.S. economy

Relative size of the various kinds of depository intermediaries

Relative size of the various kinds of nondepository intermediaries

How financial intermediation benefits SEUs

Default risk

Market risk (capital risk)

Purchasing power risk

Real and nominal rates of interest, 1950s–1980s

How financial intermediation benefits DEUs

How financial intermediation fosters economic growth

How financial intermediaries "manufacture" safety and liquidity

How financial intermediation lowers the cost of borrowing

How low borrowing cost affects the economy

Real evidence of the benefits of financial intermediation

How intermediaries foster prudent financial management and efficient resource allocation

Why the modern world economy could not exist without financial intermediation

Questions

1. Explain this statement: "Financial intermediation consists of the creation, exchanging, and destruction of financial instruments."

2. Explain the importance of financial intermediation in the functioning of a modern economic system.

3. Many different kinds of financial institutions are involved in financial intermediation. Mention some, and explain their different functions.

4. Explain the distinction between the broker, dealer, and financial intermediary functions.

5. Discuss the relative asset size of the various kinds of financial intermediaries in the American economy.

6. Explain the microeconomic role and the macroeconomic role of financial intermediation.

7. Explain how financial intermediation reduces investment risks for savers at the same time that it reduces financing costs for borrowers.

Suggested Readings

American Council of Life Insurance. *Life Insurance Fact Book.* Washington, D.C., annual publication.

_____. *Pension Facts.* Washington, D.C., annual publication.

Benston, George J., ed. *Financial Services, the Changing Institutions and Government Policy, Banks, Savings and Loans, Finance, Insurance and Credit Card Companies, Brokerage Houses, Mass Retailers.* Englewood Cliffs, N.J.: Prentice Hall, 1983.

Carraro, Kenneth, and Daniel Thornton. "The Cost of Checkable Deposits in the United States." *Review.* Federal Reserve Bank of Philadelphia, November/December 1985.

The Consumers Union Report on Life Insurance, 4th ed. New York: Holt, Rinehart & Winston, 1980.

Eisenbeis, Robert. "Inflation and Regulation: The Effects on Financial Institutions and Structure." in Richard Aspinwall and Robert Eisenbeis (eds.) *Handbook for Banking Strategy.* New York: John Wiley & Sons, 1985.

Federal Deposit Insurance Corporation. *Bank Operating Statistics.* Washington, D.C.: U.S. Government Printing Office, annual.

Federal Reserve Bank of Atlanta. *Payments in the Financial Services Industry of the 1980s.* Proceedings of a conference, September 22–23, 1983. Westport, Conn.: Quorum Books, 1984.

Greenough, William C., and Francis P. King. *Pension Plans and Public Policy.* New York: Columbia University Press, 1976.

Gurley, John, and Edward Shaw. *Money in a Theory of Finance.* Washington, D.C.: Brookings Institution, 1960.

Harris, Maury. "Finance Companies as Business Lenders." *Quarterly Review* 4. Federal Reserve Bank of New York, (summer 1979), 35–39.

Hayes, Samuel L. III. "The Transformation of Investment Banking." *Harvard Business Review*. (January/February 1979), 153–171.

Insurance Information Institute. *Insurance Facts*. New York: Insurance Information Institute. annual.

Investment Company Institute. *Mutual Fund Fact Book*. Washington, D.C., annual publication.

Kessler, Ronald. *The Life Insurance Game*. New York: Holt, Rinehart & Winston, 1985.

McGill, Dan M. *Fundamentals of Private Pensions*, 5th ed. Homewood, Ill.: Irwin, 1984.

Meltzer, Allan. "Credit Availability and Economic Decisions." *Journal of Finance*. 29 (June 1974), 763–778.

Rosenblum, Harvey, Diane Siegel, and Christine Pavel. "Banks and Nonbanks: A Run for the Money." *Economic Perspectives* 4. Federal Reserve Bank of Chicago (May/June 1983), 3–12.

Wiesenberger Investment Companies Service. *Investment Companies, 1984*. New York: Wiesenberger Financial Services, 1984.

CHAPTER 11

Real Assets, Financial Assets, and the Economic Functions of Financial Instruments and Markets

Chapter Objectives

This chapter goes more deeply into the subject of the **flow of funds** from net savers (surplus economic units—SEUs) to net borrowers (deficit economic units—DEUs). Here the focus is on different kinds of **financial markets** and the various **financial instruments** traded therein. After studying this chapter you will understand and be able to explain

1. More about the **middleman role** of financial intermediaries (FIMs) as they "buy and sell" current dollars.
2. The role of **financial instruments**—financial assets other than money (OFAs)—as the "currency" for "buying and selling current dollars."
3. How financial intermediaries, instruments, and markets form an **integrated, interdependent system** which is essential to the healthy functioning of the U.S. and worldwide economic and financial system.
4. The general characteristics of and various kinds of financial instruments.
5. How financial instruments are created and destroyed by individuals, businesses, and governments.
6. **Financial markets:** how they function, and their essential role in the U.S. and world economy.
7. The characteristics of the **primary market**, and the role of **investment banks**.
8. The characteristics of the **secondary market**, and highlights of the major secondary markets.

THE DISTINCTION BETWEEN "REAL ASSETS" AND "FINANCIAL ASSETS"

Everything that you own is either **financial** or **real**. The money in your wallet is a financial asset. Your car or your calculator is a real asset. All of the assets in an economic system are either financial or real.

Real assets include all of the useful things: houses and cars and clothes and factories and machines and VCRs and every other valuable thing. Real assets are valued because they are useful. But not so with financial assets.

Financial assets are nothing more than claims to, or rights to acquire *real assets* or *other financial assets*—or sometimes, *services*. Financial assets—such as the dollar bills in your wallet or the funds in your savings account—have no inherent or intrinsic usefulness. Financial assets have value only because they represent claims to something real—present claims and/or future claims. The value of *a financial asset* rests on the existence of valuable real assets or services which the financial-asset owner ultimately will receive.

Financial Assets: "Money," Plus "Other Financial Assets" (OFAs)

The **liquidity** of any asset is a measure of how quickly, easily, and costlessly the asset can be exchanged for other assets. For any asset other than money, it's a question of how easily you can "liquidate" the asset—exchange it for money. Money is the only **completely liquid** asset. Money represents a claim to real assets—a claim which can be exercised at any moment.

Money: The Only Completely Liquid Asset. In conceptualizing financial assets, it is useful to think of money as a special kind of financial asset—the only one with the very special characteristic of **complete liquidity**.

Financial Instruments: All Other Financial Assets (OFAs). It wouldn't be conceptually incorrect to think of all nonmoney financial assets as *somewhat less liquid substitutes for money*. And we can define these other financial assets as **financial instruments** and refer to them as OFAs. With this definitional framework it's easy to focus on what happens in the flow of funds process.

The Flow of Funds from SEUs to DEUs. Using the distinction between *money* on one side and *financial instruments* (OFAs) on the other, it is easy to see how funds move from SEUs to DEUs, either through financial intermediaries, or directly.

The middleman **financial intermediaries** (FIMs) create and issue new liabilities—financial instruments (OFAs)—to buy funds from SEUs. Then they sell these funds to DEUs in exchange for DEU-issued financial instruments (OFAs). The funds-seeking DEUs create and issue new OFAs to buy funds—either from the FIMs or from the SEUs.

OFAs Shift the "Time-Period Availability" of Purchasing Power

When OFAs are created and used to buy funds, that shifts the time-period availability of purchasing power. *For the SEUs the purchasing power availability shifts from the present to the future. For the DEUs it shifts from the future to the present.*

In all of these **flow of funds** transactions, present purchasing power is being shifted from those to whom the time value of money (right now) is less, to those to whom the time value of money (right now) is greater. The SEUs are giving up their current dollars in exchange for promises of future dollars; the DEUs are giving their promises of future dollars, in exchange for current dollars.

OFAs are created and used as the means of payment for the current dollars acquired. And all of these OFAs (financial instruments) have one thing in common. They convey to their owners present or future claims: to funds, to real assets, or to services.

FINANCIAL INSTRUMENTS: CLAIMS ON (AND OBLIGATIONS TO PAY) FUTURE DOLLARS

The "financial instrument" is a very important (indespensable!) human invention. From the point of view of its owner, a financial instrument is *a future claim*. From the point of view of its issuer it's *a future obligation*.

These OFAs may be **debt instruments** (e.g., promissory notes, bonds, CDs, **contractual instruments** (e.g., insurance policies), or **ownership instruments** (e.g., shares of corporate stock). OFAs are assets to their buyer-owners. But they are liabilities to (or ownership claims on) their seller-issuers.

There Is a Great Variety of Financial Instruments

Each kind of financial instrument has its own set of specifications—its own rate of return, frequency and/or conditions of future payment, degree of safety, liquidity, term to maturity, etc., etc. In general, the lower its degree of safety and liquidity, the higher will be its rate of return.

Almost Anyone Can Create Financial Instruments

OFAs are created for the purpose of acquiring funds. Billions of dollars worth are being created and destroyed every day. Businesses, governments, FIMs, private individuals—almost everyone is involved in the creation and destruction of OFAs.

When Individuals Make Deposits, or Borrow. If you go to your bank and deposit $5,000 and receive in return a **certificate of deposit** (CD), that transaction will result in the creation of a new financial instrument—one $5,000 CD. Or if you sign a **promissory note** to borrow $5,000, that transaction will result in the creation of a new financial instrument—one $5,000 promissory note.

When Governments Borrow. When the government runs a deficit or when it needs money to pay off maturing securities, it prints up and sells new **government securities**—bonds, T-bills, etc. All of these are new financial instruments which the government uses as their "medium of exchange" to buy funds from the public.

When Businesses Borrow. When businesses want to obtain money they can borrow from the banks and sign promissory notes. Or if they're large and well respected in the financial community they can print up **bonds** (long-term debt instruments) or **commercial paper** (short-term debt instruments) or **stocks** (ownership shares in the corporation) and sell them to get the funds they want.

SEUs and FIMs Sell Current Dollars in Exchange for OFAs. The individuals and businesses—both direct investors and FIMs—who buy these government and corporate securities are giving up their current dollars and receiving in exchange these OFAs—these promises to pay future dollars. Clearly, the "financial instrument"—the "currency" which permits the transfer of purchasing power between the present and the future—must be one of mankinds greatest inventions!

Financial Instruments Expire and Are Paid Off (Destroyed) at Maturity

Many OFAs (almost all formal debt instruments) have a **maturity date**. That's when the face value of the instrument comes due and the creator-issuer is obligated to "pay off." Or to say it differently, that's when the *future dollars* promised by a debt instrument become *current dollars* and must flow back from the borrower to the lender.

When you pay off your promissory note at the bank, your banker stamps it PAID and gives it to you for a souvenir. It isn't good for anything else. It certainly isn't a valid financial instrument anymore!

When the term of your CD runs out, that's when your future dollars become current dollars. You return the certificate to your banker and receive the face value, plus interest. Another financial instrument expired? Yes.

The same thing happens with Treasury bonds, notes, and bills, with corporate bonds, notes, and commercial paper, and with home mortgages and almost all other debt securities. Many billions of dollars worth of financial instruments expire, and are paid off every week.

At the same time, new OFAs are being created and used to acquire more funds. Often, new OFAs are issued to get the funds to pay off the maturing OFAs. Many businesses do this, but the really big player in this rollover financing market is the federal government. Each week the U.S. Treasury refinances (rolls over) *several billion dollars* of OFAs.

Some Financial Instruments Have No Fixed Maturity Date

Some OFAs have variable maturity dates. An obvious example would be your deposits at the local bank or thrift. You can get "paid off" anytime you wish.

Some bonds and some loans are *callable* and some are automatically *renewable* so there is no definite payoff date. Some corporate bonds are *convertible*— can be exchanged for shares of stock in the corporation at the option of the bondholder. Insurance polices (contracts) obviously have variable maturity dates.

Consols. The "consols" (perpetual bonds) issued by the British government have no maturity date. People buy perpetual bonds to obtain the flow of interest income, and/or in the hope of capital gains from falling interest rates.

When you want your principal out of a perpetual bond you just sell the bond in the market for whatever it's worth at the time. If the coupon rate on your consol is above the current market rate, then you'll receive a premium. But if the coupon rate is below market you'll have to sell at a discount. (If this isn't clear, go back and read the explanation of bond prices and interest rates in chapter 3.)

Equities. Equity securities—i.e., corporate stocks—are ownership shares in the corporation. These do not have a maturity, or "payoff" date. So the way people get their money out of shares of stock is to sell the shares, just as in the case of perpetual bonds.

Values of OFAs Reflect the Value of Future Claims Conveyed

Stocks, bonds, mortgages—in fact almost all financial instruments—convey some kind of future-dollar claims to their owners. There is much variability among financial instruments regarding their promises of future payments. A U.S. government bond gives definite periodic payments and then pays off a definite amount at maturity. At the opposite extreme, shares of common stock convey a completely variable claim to future funds.

Between these two extremes there are all kinds of financial instruments, with all kinds of variations in the future claims conveyed. The *value of each financial instrument derives from and reflects the size, timing, and dependability of these promised future payments.* The present value of each instrument is determined in the financial markets where these instruments are bought and sold. Financial markets will be explained soon. But first, a brief look at derivative instruments: futures and options.

Derivative Financial Instruments: Options and Futures

Since the early 1970s, and especially during the 1980s, the U.S. and worldwide financial markets are in the process of a major transformation. A good bit of this transformation is related to the rapid (explosive!) growth of **derivative instruments**. Derivative instruments have no "intrinsic value" in themselves but derive their value from the underlying instruments to which they relate. Options and futures contracts are derivative instruments. All of these instruments offer financial managers opportunities to reduce risk. Here are some examples.

Futures Contracts. A futures contract is an instrument which fixes the price *now* for an exchange which is going to happen on a *future date*. Every futures contract has a buyer who agrees to pay the price which is set now and a seller who agrees to deliver and to accept the price set now.

Why would anyone want to enter into a futures contract agreement? Mainly either (a) to hedge, or (b) to speculate.

Hedging with a Futures Contract. Suppose you are a wheat farmer and you'd like to fix the price you're going to get for your wheat crop. You estimate the number of bushels, and then sell them for delivery at harvest time for a price which is set now. No matter what happens to the spot price of wheat between now and harvest time, you have your money locked in.

Suppose you are a miller, and a large bakery wants you to give them a contracted price for flour to be delivered next June. It's risky for you to enter into such a contract (that's a futures contract, too, of course) unless you can hedge your position by locking in a definite price for the wheat you will need. So the farmer sells wheat for future delivery, the miller buys wheat and sells flour for future delivery, and the baker buys flour for future delivery. All are futures contracts, and all are examples of **hedging**.

Using Futures Contracts for Speculation. Suppose you aren't a wheat farmer or a miller, but you're keeping a close eye on the size of the wheat crop and you think it's going to be much larger than expected. So you think when this big crop hits the market, the price will drop. How can you profit from this knowledge? Sell some wheat for future delivery!

You can sell at the current (high) futures price which reflects the current (high) price outlook for wheat. Then when the future arrives and the bumper crop hits the market and prices plummet, you can buy the low priced wheat and sell it at the high price specified in the contract. Actually what you'd do is sell the contract itself, because its value will have risen enough to reflect the difference between the price specified in your contract and the market price.

Example: If your contract specifies that you will sell the wheat and receive $100,000 and the market value of that wheat at the contracted time of delivery is only $60,000, then your contract is worth $40,000. Your speculation—attempt to profit from future price movements—in this case paid off.

Futures Contracts on Financial Instruments

Financial futures contracts were first traded on the organized exchanges during the 1970s and their growth has been explosive. Why? Because they permit financial asset-holders to reduce their risks.

By the mid-1980s you could buy for future delivery various kinds of money market instruments: T-bills, bank CDs, Eurodollar time deposits, and others. And you could buy or sell long term instruments: Treasury notes, Treasury bonds, Ginnie Mae (GNMA) mortgage contracts and others. Also you could buy or sell several different kinds of foreign currencies, indexes of stocks, and you could even hedge against (or speculate on) the inflation rate by buying or selling consumer price index futures.

When you Buy Futures, You Hope the Price Goes Up. When you buy one of these financial instruments for future delivery, if its price goes up, you win. At the delivery date you can buy the instrument for the lower price specified in the contract and then sell it in the market at the current (higher) price, for a profit. But in fact, as in the case of the wheat speculator, you wouldn't actually do that.

You would sell your futures contract for a price determined by the spread between the market price and the price stated in the contract. If the contract price is $100,000 and the present market price is $150,000, then the value of your contract is $50,000.

When you enter into a futures contract you *guarantee* that you will carry out your end of the deal. When the time comes, you will buy or sell whatever is specified, and at the specified price.

If the market price moves in a way unfavorable to you, you still must comply with the terms of the contract no matter how much you may loose. That's a disadvantage of futures contracts as compared with options contracts, coming up now.

Options Are Like "One Way Futures." An option contract gives the buyer the opportunity to either buy or sell something in the future at a price specified now. But the option-holder is not obligated to undertake that transaction.

If you hold an option to buy something for $50 and its market value goes up to $100, you certainly will exercise your option! But if you have an option to buy something for $50 and its market value goes down to $10, you certainly will not exercise the option. So with options, your loss is limited to the price you paid for the option contract.

Financial options are available on a broad range of individual stocks, T-notes, T-bonds, Eurodollars, stock indexes and stock index futures, on various foreign currencies and currency futures and other financial instruments.

These new kinds of financial instruments—derivative instruments—are widely and increasingly used by financial managers to hedge their portfolios, and by speculators and traders who try to "outguess" future price changes. Later in this chapter, and also in the chapters coming up you'll be reading more about these derivative instruments and the markets in which they trade. The appendix to chapter 17 explains how these derivative instruments are used by asset managers to reduce their interest rate risk. And now it's time to talk about the financial markets in which all of these various kinds of financial instruments are traded.

THE NATURE AND FUNCTIONS OF FINANCIAL MARKETS

Financial markets exist wherever financial instruments (OFAs) are being bought and sold. Financial markets can be viewed either as *the interaction of the demand and supply for* **OFAs**, or as *the interaction of the supply and demand for current dollars*—i.e., **loanable funds**.

Suppose you go to the bank and deposit $1,000 and get a $1,000 CD. You're selling your current dollars in exchange for their promise to pay you a larger sum of future dollars. You're buying an OFA (the CD) and selling current dollars in the financial market. Or suppose you borrow $1,000 and sign a promissory note. Then you're selling an OFA (the promissory note) and buying current dollars.

Suppose your mother wants more dividend income. So she decides to sell her 100 shares of IBM stock and buy utilities stocks which pay higher dividends. She is both selling and buying equity securities in the financial market.

If your local city council (or the U.S. Government or General Motors or anyone else) decides to sell bonds to obtain funds, they're operating in and are a part of the financial market. If Chrysler Corporation or Hewlett-Packard or Consolidated Edison or anyone else decides to issue and sell more shares of stock to get more current dollars, they're operating in and are a part of the financial market. And anyone who decides to buy some of those bonds or stocks is operating in and is a part of the financial market.

Financial Markets Are an Essential Component of Financial Intermediation

Financial markets perform essential functions for the economy. The micro and macroeconomic functions of money and of financial intermediation depend on the existence of efficient financial markets. The modern world economy depends on and in fact couldn't function without our well developed and efficient world-wide system of financial markets.

The Functions of Financial Markets

It is in the *financial markets* that the flow of funds from SEUs to DEUs actually occurs. The **ultimate borrowers** (DEUs) issue and sell their **primary securities** in the financial markets.

The **ultimate lenders** (SEUs) sometimes enter the financial markets and buy the primary securities issued by DEUs. But more often the SEUs buy the **"intermediary" instruments** issued by the FIMs. Then the FIMs enter the financial markets and buy the primary securities issued by the DEUs.

The Financial Markets Are Everywhere and Interlinked Worldwide

The **financial markets** are everywhere that OFAs are bought and sold—which means just about everywhere. The financial market center of the United States and of the world is the Wall Street area of New York City. But there are several other major market centers in the United States and throughout the world. And **financial transactions**—exchanges of current dollars for financial instruments—are going on even in the smallest villages.

Financial markets all over the world are closely tied together through intricate telecommunications and electronic funds transfer system (EFTS) networks. The communications links provide instant information on market conditions and prices and the instant transmission of buy and sell orders in all market centers worldwide.

A multimilliondollar sale or purchase can be executed on the New York, London, Tokyo, or some other exchange in response to a telex message or a phone call. And through this global information network and these speedy transactions, *changes in the demand, supply, and price conditions for each kind of financial instrument in any one market center are almost instantaneously transmitted to and reflected in other market centers throughout the world.*

THE PRIMARY (NEW ISSUES) MARKET

It is possible to categorize financial markets in several different ways. We can use as many different categories as are helpful in analyzing and understanding the financial system. One useful distinction is that between the "primary" (new issues) market and the "secondary" (resale) market.

The **primary market** is where new issues of securities are initially sold. When your local city council (or the U.S. Government or du Pont or Disney or anyone else) sells new bonds to acquire funds, those bonds are sold in the primary market. Also when a corporation issues and sells new shares of stock, shares are transferred from the issuer-seller to the investor-buyers through the primary market.

So-Called "Investment Banks" Deal in the Primary Market

When a corporation or a state or local government or a foreign government wants to raise money by issuing new securities, they contact an **investment banking** firm. If it's a large issue, usually several investment banking firms (sometimes as many as 40 or 50 or more) will enter into a temporary partnership agreement to form an **underwriting syndicate** to underwrite and market the new securities.

Look through the pages of almost any issue of *The Wall Street Journal* and you'll see announcements for the sale of new securities. The announcement always lists the investment bankers who are marketing the issue. Exhibit 11-1 gives an example.

Investment Bank: A Different Meaning of the Word "Bank"

The Glass-Steagall Act of 1933 prohibits commercial banks from underwriting new security issues, except for general obligation municipal bonds. So the (so-called) "investment banks" really are not banks at all. Mostly they are specialized departments of (sometimes subsidiaries of) major stockbrokerage firms. So who are our investment bankers? First Boston, Merrill Lynch, E.F. Hutton, and all those others whose names you see listed in Exhibit 11-1, plus many more.

Altogether there are some 3,000 financial firms involved in investment banking. But well over half of the business is transacted by the 20 largest firms. All of these firms provide stockbroker (and other) financial services, in addition to investment banking—i.e., in addition to the function of marketing new issues of securities.

Investment Bankers Are Dealers and Brokers in Newly Issued Securities

Investment bankers often (but not always) *underwrite* a new security issue. **Underwriting** involves the following:

1. First they investigate to determine the soundness (degree of default risk) of the new securities.
2. Then they set a price (in the case of a bond issue, a yield) which they consider appropriate, based on existing prices and yields on similar securities in the secondary (resale) markets.
3. Then they they quote a specific price and *guarantee that price* to the issuer. In effect, they buy the entire issue and become dealers in that security.
4. Then they sell the securities directly to final buyers (retail), and also in blocks to other dealers (wholesale).

Underwriting Involves Some Risk

When investment banks underwrite an issue they hope to profit by the spread between the price they pay to the issuer of the security and the price they charge the buyers. But what if financial market conditions worsen after the underwriting agreement has been made? Then the underwriter-dealer firms can suffer losses. That's exactly what happened in 1979 when a group of investment banking firms agreed to underwrite a $1 billion bond offering by IBM.

Exhibit 11-1 An Illustration of the Primary Market

This is a new-issue underwriting syndicate ad from *The Wall Street Journal*, September 30, 1988. Reprinted by permission.

This announcement is not an offer of securities for sale or a solicitation of an offer to buy securities.

New Issue   September 30, 1988

1,875,000 Shares

Associated Natural Gas Corporation

Common Stock

Price $10 per share

Copies of the prospectus may be obtained from such of the undersigned (who are among the underwriters named in the prospectus) as may legally offer these securities under applicable securities laws.

Dillon, Read & Co. Inc.

Bear, Stearns & Co. Inc.	The First Boston Corporation	Alex. Brown & Sons Incorporated
Drexel Burnham Lambert Incorporated	Goldman, Sachs & Co.	Hambrecht & Quist Incorporated
Kidder, Peabody & Co. Incorporated	Lazard Frères & Co.	Montgomery Securities

PaineWebber Incorporated   Prudential–Bache Capital Funding

Robertson, Colman & Stephens   Salomon Brothers Inc

Smith Barney, Harris Upham & Co.   Wertheim Schroder & Co.
                              Incorporated   Incorporated

Thomson McKinnon Securities Inc.   Arnhold and S. Bleichroeder, Inc.

Sanford C. Bernstein & Co., Inc.   Eberstadt Fleming Inc.   Fahnestock & Co. Inc.

First Albany Corporation   Interstate Securities Corporation

Janney Montgomery Scott Inc.   Ladenburg, Thalmann & Co. Inc.

C.J. Lawrence, Morgan Grenfell Inc.   Legg Mason Wood Walker
                                                                                              Incorporated

Neuberger & Berman   Raymond James & Associates, Inc.

The Robinson–Humphrey Company, Inc.   Wheat, First Securities, Inc.

Boenning & Scattergood Inc.   Mabon, Nugent & Co.

The IBM underwriting agreement was made on Wednesday, October 3, 1979. Then on Saturday, October 6 the Fed announced that it was severely tightening monetary policy. When the financial markets opened on Monday October 8, interest rates shot upward and bond prices tumbled. As a result the IBM bond-underwriting syndicate is estimated to have lost somewhere between $10 and $15 million.

Sometimes investment bankers avoid this risk by acting only as **brokers**—not as underwriter-dealers. They offer the new securities for sale to their customers (and charge a commission), but they do not actually take a position in the securities.

Almost all new issues of long-term securities are marketed through investment banks. The one important exception is U.S. Government securities, all of which are initially marketed by the Federal Reserve banks. If you want to buy a U.S. Government bond and don't want to pay a broker's commission, you can do that at any Federal Reserve bank, or branch.

New Short-Term Issues Often Are Sold Directly by the DEU Issuer to the SEU Buyer

New issues of short-term non-U.S. Government primary securities are mostly **commercial paper** issued by major corporations. Commercial paper is often sold in large blocks directly by the issuer to the ultimate buyers—insurance companies, money market funds, or any other funds managers with sizeable funds available for short-term investment.

Issuers who cannot find a direct buyer can sell their commercial paper (at a discount) to one of the several **commercial paper dealers**. These dealers resell the paper to ultimate buyers (financial institutions, and others) all over the country and the world.

The Primary Market Increases the Efficiency of the U.S. and World Economy

The modern, highly developed and efficient **primary market** reduces the cost and increases the speed of marketing new issues. So it reduces the cost of new investments in the economy. Also this nationwide and worldwide market increases the mobility of funds both geographically and among different firms and industries. This high mobility of funds nurtures the growth of expanding industries and tends to keep interest rates and returns on investments in balance throughout the U.S. and worldwide economy.

Via the primary market, the U.S. and world economy's real resources for capital investment are induced to flow into the most productive places and uses. *The ultimate result is increased efficiency and economic growth and higher levels of economic welfare throughout the nation and the world.*

THE SECONDARY (RESALE) MARKET

The secondary market is where existing securities (stocks, bonds, notes, etc.) are bought and sold. Securities are bought by people who want to invest in existing securities, from people who want to get cash for the securities they own. The greatest amount of securities trading (by far) occurs in the **secondary market**.

The secondary market is where the price of each security is established from moment to moment and that influences the prices of new issues in the primary market. *The price at which a newly issued security will be offered is mostly determined by current prices of comparable securities in the secondary market.*

The New York Stock Exchange and most other stock and bond exchanges trade only *existing long-term securities*. So they are entirely *secondary markets*. But it's different in the market for **short-term securities** (the money market). In the short-term securities markets, both existing securities and new issues are traded. So the primary and secondary markets are not distinctly separate.

The Stock Exchanges

There are several organized secondary markets for trading stocks and bonds. The **New York Stock Exchange** (NYSE—the "Big Board") lists some 2,000 different stocks. It is (both in dollar value of listed stocks and in dollar volume) the largest stock exchange in the world. The **American Stock Exchange** (ASE), also located in the Wall Street financial district a few blocks from the NYSE, is called the "curb market" because it started out as a specific place on the sidewalk where people got together to trade stocks.

There are several smaller (so-called) "regional" exchanges in other U.S. cities: Philadelphia, Chicago, Denver, San Francisco, Honolulu, and others. There are also major exchanges in London, Paris, Frankfurt, Amsterdam, Tokyo, Hong Kong, and in other foreign cities, and there are minor exchanges in many cities througout the world.

A Worldwide Communications System. The stock and bond exchanges in New York operate through a communications system which ties together thousands of brokers and dealers located in cities and towns—even little villages—all over the country and all over the world. These brokers take buy and sell orders for stocks and bonds and transmit them almost instantaneously to the trading floor where they are executed in a matter of minutes.

On the NYSE trading floor there is a **trading post** (specific location) where each stock is traded, and one or more **specialists**—major brokerage firms—dealing in each listed stock. As buy and sell orders arrive at the "trading post" they are executed.

A "Managed Auction" Market. The New York stock exchange operates as a **managed auction market**. If there are more buy orders, the stock price goes up. But the specialist is supposed to sell shares to keep the price from going up too fast. If there are more sell orders the price goes down. But in this case the specialist is supposed to buy shares to keep the price from falling too fast. But what happens if there's a sudden flood of buy or sell orders? Trading in that stock may be halted and not resumed until later—perhaps the next day—and perhaps at a significantly higher or lower price.

The major stock exchanges only list and trade the stocks and bonds of major corporations. So where are the so-called "unlisted" stocks and bonds traded? Some of them, nowhere.

The stocks of some small, little known, and/or closely-held corporations[1] have no developed secondary market. But the unlisted stocks of more than 30,000 U.S. corporations do have a well-developed secondary market. It's called the **over-the-counter** market.

The Over-the-Counter (OTC) Market

The **OTC market** is really a communications network among brokers. In principle, it's not too different from the "hot line" your local "used auto parts dealer" (junk yard) uses to find a transmission or a water pump for your 1939 Studebaker.

If you want to buy an OTC stock or bond, your broker can put your buy order into the communications network and very soon you'll have the stock. Or perhaps your broker is a dealer in (buys, sells, holds), and is **making a market** in that stock. If so you can buy shares out of your broker's inventory.

Most broker-dealers serve as *market makers* in several different securities. They hold an inventory of each, and stand ready to buy or sell at any time.

Or maybe your broker knows of some other broker who is making a market in the stock you want to buy. Market makers advertise their specialties. So everyone knows which dealers are making a market in which securities.

Given all the options, it's obvious that buying and selling stocks on the OTC market can be done almost as quickly and efficiently as on the organized stock exchanges. Trading on the OTC market has grown explosively during the 1970s and 80s. The development of the NASDAQ system (explained below) has had a lot to do with this rapid growth.

Almost all kinds of securities are traded in the OTC market—stocks, corporate and government (including foreign government) bonds, and various short-term instruments including commercial paper, negotiable CDs, and several others.

The NASDAQ Part of the OTC

The **NASDAQ** (pronounced NAZDAK) system of *computerized automated OTC quotations* was initiated in 1971. (NASDAQ is an acronym for "National Association of Securities Dealers Automated Quotations.")

By 1987 the NASDAQ system was listing more than 5,000 of the most actively traded OTC stocks, and many more stocks were being added. Information on each of these stocks is instantly available to dealers and brokers on their computer terminals. Several of the NASDAQ-listed stocks can be traded directly through the computer network. Not even a phone call is required.

By the mid-1980s some NASDAQ-listed OTC stocks were clearly eligible for listing on the NYSE. MCI Communications was an outstanding example. The efficiency of the NASDAQ system explains why the managements of these corporations were not hurrying to apply for NYSE listing. The point is that by the mid-1980s the Big Board (NYSE) was no longer the only game in town!

During the late 1980s there were several times that NASDAQ's daily volume of shares traded exceeded the volume on the NYSE. Perhaps this helps to explain

---

[1] A "closely-held" corporation is one in which all of the stock is held by only a few people—e.g., a family-owned corporation.

why "seats" (memberships) on the New York Stock Exchange, which sold for more than $500,000 in the 1920s, were going for less than $100,000—sometimes even less than $50,000—in the early 1980s.

But then why in December of 1986 did a NYSE seat sell for more than $600,000? And then in early 1987, for more than $1 million? Fixed supply and increased demand, of course. In early 1987 future profit opportunities for "Big Board" brokers were looking very bright! Then came the October crash and the outlook wasn't so bright anymore. You can read about that in the appendix to this chapter. And now, here's a brief look at the markets where futures and options contracts are traded.

The Markets Where Futures and Options Are Traded

As the trading in futures and options contracts has grown explosively, the markets in which these derivative instruments are traded have become the most rapidly growing financial markets, U.S. and worldwide. In the early 1970s, futures contracts began trading on some of the major stock and bond markets such as the NYSE, and several others. Also the organized futures markets which have been trading grain and other commodities futures for more than a century also began trading futures in financial instruments.

As the trading in options contracts exploded, the need for additional exchanges and trading facilities became increasingly urgent. By 1980, some of the organized exchanges were applying to the securities regulators for permission to establish separate exchanges just for the trading of options. But the regulators did not move with the speed of light.

It wasn't until 1982 that permission for these options exchanges was granted, and several of them were established. Figure 11-1 lists the major organized markets on which futures and options contracts now are traded. But in addition, don't forget, many kinds of financial futures and options are traded in the over-the-counter market, just as they were before the organized exchanges got involved.

As the growth of trading in options continued to grow, additional exchanges were being planned and applied for. So by the time you're reading this, it's likely that there will be several options exchanges not shown in figure 11-1.

Figure 11-1.   Examples of Exchanges on Which Futures and Options Contracts Are Traded

Futures and Options		Options, But Not Futures	
ACC	Annex Commodities Corp.	AMEX	American Stock Exchange
CBT	Chicago Board of Trade	CBOE	Chicago Board of Trade Options Exchange
CME	Chicago Mercantile Exchange		
CMX	Commodity Exchange		
CSCE	Coffee, Sugar, and Cocoa Exchange		
IMM	International Money Market of the CME		
KCBT	Kansas City Board of Trade		
LIFFE	London International Financial Futures Exchange		
MCE	Midwest Commodity Exchange		
NASD	National Association of Securities Dealers		
NYFE	New York Futures Exchange		
PBOT	Philadelphia Board of Trade		
SIMEX	Singapore International Monetary Exchange		

This list illustrates the global nature of the futures and options markets.

Self-Regulation of Futures and Options Markets

Just as in the case of the stock exchanges, the **commodity exchanges** impose fairly stringent rules on their members. All members must keep proper accounts, keep sufficient funds on deposit with the exchange and in general follow sound business procedures and practices. Each exchange also establishes rules regarding trading procedures, margin requirements, and contract terms, and each exchange establishes safeguards to try to prevent manipulation of the markets by speculators.

REGULATION OF THE SECURITIES MARKETS

Each of the exchanges on which stocks, bonds, futures, and options are traded impose regulations on their members. But in addition there are two important federal government commissions: The SEC and the CFTC.

The Securities and Exchange Commission (SEC)

The Securities and Exchange Commission (SEC) was empowered by the Securities and Exchange Act of 1934 to regulate trading in stocks and bonds for the primary purpose of keeping the markets and their participants honest and protecting the public. SEC regulations require full and honest disclosure by all brokers and dealers and issuers of financial instruments, in all markets. The SEC has authority to regulate all organized exchanges which trade securities. The Commission sets rules governing the conduct of brokers and dealers, and they review the rules of the exchanges and of the broker associations.

An important recent thrust of the SEC is to try to prosecute insider trading—that is, acting on insider (not publically known) information to buy or sell and profit at the expense of the other stockholders of the corporation. Insider trading prosecutions were very much in the news in the late 1980s.

The Commodity Futures Trading Commission (CFTC)

Government regulation of the futures and options exchanges is exercised by the **Commodity Futures Trading Commission** (CFTC). The CFTC was created in 1974 to regulate the trading of futures contracts, to guard against manipulation or other problems. CFTC members are appointed for five years by the President, with Senate approval.

New futures and options contracts require the approval of the CFTC which decides whether the proposed contracts are in the public interest. It also audits the brokerage houses and exchanges. And in general it enforces the federal laws regarding the commodities exchanges. A major purpose is to prevent misrepresentation or market manipulation. In recent years CFTC members have complained that their commission has not been sufficiently funded to enable them to undertake the necessary investigations to perform their functions as well as they should.

SUMMARY

- A financial instrument is a **liability** of its user, and an **asset** of its owner. It serves as "currency" for "buying current dollars." Billions of dollars worth of financial instruments are created and destroyed every day.

- **Financial markets** exist wherever financial instruments are being bought and sold. Interest rates in financial markets can be viewed either as resulting from *the interaction of demand and supply for financial instruments*, or as resulting from *the interaction of demand and supply for loanable funds (current dollars)*.

- The **primary market** for securities is the "new issues" market. New long-term securities, except U.S. Government bonds, are usually marketed by **investment bankers** who either **underwrite** and sell the new securities, or serve as **brokers** in marketing the new issue. New U.S. Government securities are marketed by the Federal Reserve banks.

- The price at which a newly issued security will be sold is mostly determined by *current prices of similar securities in the secondary market*.

- The primary market for non-U.S. Government short-term securities (e.g., commercial paper) is less formalized and is not distinctly separate from the secondary market. Frequently, **commercial paper** is sold directly by the issuing DEU to the purchasing SEU or intermediary.

- The primary market enables DEUs to acquire desired funds. It *increases the mobility of funds* and thereby keeps interest rates in balance, and it *improves the allocation of funds for new investments throughout the U.S. and world economy*.

- The **secondary market** involves the resale of existing securities. It includes the New York Stock Exchange, several other exchanges, and the over-the-counter (OTC) market for stocks and bonds.

- Futures and options contracts offer opportunities to (a) hedge asset or liability positions and thereby reduce risk, or (b) speculate and make big profits (or big losses). The creation of and trading in futures and options on financial instruments has grown explosively during the 1980s.

- Regulation of the securities markets is exercised by (a) the exchanges themselves, (b) the Securities and Exchange Commission (SEC), and (c) the Commodity Futures Trading Commission (CFTC).

Important Principles, Issues, Concepts, Terms

Distinctions between real assets and financial assets

The role of financial instruments in the financial intermediation process

Definition and general characteristics of financial instruments

How financial instruments are created and destroyed

Debt, contractual, and ownership instruments

Definition of financial markets

How to view financial markets as markets for "buying and selling loanable funds"

How to view financial markets as markets for "buying and selling other financial assets" (OFAs)

The functions of financial markets and their role in the intermediation process

The primary market

Investment banks

Commercial paper dealers

Role of the primary market in the U.S. and world economy

The secondary market

How secondary market prices influence primary market prices

The organized stock exchanges

The over-the-counter market

NASDAQ

Futures contract

Options contract

Futures and options exchanges

Securities and Exchange Commission (SEC)

Commodity Futures Trading Commission (CFTC)

Questions and Problems

1. Explain carefully the important distinction between real assets and financial assets.

2. Explain what it means to say that financial intermediaries play the "middleman role" in the process of buying and selling dollars. Then explain the way in which different financial intermediaries perform this function.

3. What does it mean to say that financial instruments are the "currency" for buying and selling current dollars?

4. Explain how financial intermediaries, instruments, and markets form an integrated and interdependent system necessary to the healthy functioning of the economy.

5. Explain how you as an individual could create and destroy financial instruments.

6. Explain the difference between the primary and secondary markets for financial instruments.

7. Explain exactly how it is possible to reduce risk by buying or selling a futures contract.

8. Explain the difference between a futures contract and an option contract. Can you think of any reasons for the explosive growth in the number of options contracts on financial instruments? Try to mention some.

9. Explain who is involved in the regulation of the financial markets, what kinds of regulation they impose, and what ultimate results they are trying to achieve.

Suggested Readings

Amnihud, Yakov, Thomas S. Y. Ho and Robert A. Schwartz (eds.). *Market Making and the Changing Structure of the Securities Industry*. Lexington, Mass.: Lexington Books, 1985.

Benston, George J. "Required Disclosure and the Stock Market: An Evaluation of the Securities Exchange Act of 1934." *American Economic Review* 63 (March 1973), 132–55.

Campbell, Tim S. *Money and Capital Markets*. Glenview, Ill.: Scott, Foresman and Co., 1988.

Cook, Tomothy Q. *Instruments of the Money Market*. Federal Reserve Bank of Richmond, 1981.

Cox, John C. and Mark Rubinstein. *Options Markets*. Englewood Cliffs, N.J.: Prentice-Hall, 1985.

Dougall, Herbert E., and Jack E. Guamnitz. *Capital Markets and Institutions*. Englewood Cliffs, NJ: Prentice-Hall, 1980.

First Boston Corporation. *Handbook of Securities of the United States Government and Federal Agencies*. New York, 1984.

Friedman, Benjamin (ed.). *The Changing Role of Debt and Equity*. Chicago: University of Chicago Press for the NBER, 1982.

Gilbert, R. Alton, and A. Steven Holland. "Has the Deregulation of Deposit Interest Rates Raised Mortgage Rates?" *Review*. Federal Reserve Bank of St. Louis (May 1984), 5–15.

Hurley, Evelyn, M., "The Commercial Paper Market Since the Mid-Seventies." *Federal Reserve Bulletin*. (June 1982), 327–44.

Jensen, Frederich, and Patrick M. Parkinson. "Recent Developments in the Bankers Acceptance Market." *Federal Reserve Bulletin*. (January 1986), 1–12.

Kolb, Robert W. *Understanding Futures Markets.* Glenview, Ill.: Scott, Foresman and Company, 1985.

Malkiel, B. G. *A Random Walk Down Wall Street.* New York: Norton, 1965.

Melton, Willian C. "Corporate Equities and the National Market System." *Quarterly Review.* 3, Federal Reserve Bank of New York (Winter 1978–79), 13–25.

Pozdena, Randall J. "Risk in the Repo Market." *Weekly Letter.* Federal Reserve Bank of San Francisco, September 13, 1985.

Rose, Peter S. *Money and Capital Markets.* Plano, TX: Business Publications, 1986.

Silber, William L. "The Process of Financial Innovation." *American Economic Review.* (May 1983), 89–94.

Sobel, Robert. *The Big Board: A History of the New York Stock Market.* New York: The Free Press, 1965.

Stigler, George. "Public Regulation of the Securities Markets." *Journal of Business* 37. (April 1965), 117–142.

Stigum, Marcia. *The Money Market: Myth, Reality, and Practice.* Homewood, Ill: Dow Jones-Irwin, 1984.

CHAPTER 12

Instruments of the Capital Market, the Money Market, and the Role of the Flow of Funds System

Chapter Objectives

This chapter completes the picture of the role of financial intermediaries, instruments, and markets in the flow of funds from SEUs to DEUs. This chapter describes the instruments of the **capital market** and the **money market** and tells briefly how these instruments function. After you study this chapter you will understand and be able to explain:

1. What is meant by the **capital market** and the kinds of instruments traded therein.
2. The characteristics and market behavior of various kinds of
   a. **bonds.**
   b. **corporate stocks.**
   c. **mortgages.**
3. The rapid growth of secondary markets in mortgages and the importance of **securitization**, in making this possible.
4. The **money market** and the characteristics and changing relative importance of the various money market instruments: negotiable CDs, T-bills, commercial paper, repos, acceptances, Fed funds, and Eurodollars.
5. The (sometimes fuzzy) distinction between the **primary** and **secondary** segments of the **capital market** and the **money market**.
6. The vital importance of the interlocked and integrated "spiderweb" international financial system which serves as the **circulatory system** of the U.S. and worldwide economy.

THE CAPITAL MARKET AND THE MONEY MARKET

It's customary to distinguish between the market where longer-term securities—original maturity of more than one year—are traded, and the market for short-term issues—one year or less. The longer-term market is usually called the **capital market** and the short-term market, the **money market**.

The Capital Market: Where Longer-Term Securities Are Traded

In the late 1980s the total value of securities outstanding in the U.S. capital market was approaching $10 trillion. What kinds of securities? The greatest values were in bonds, stocks, and mortgages, with around $3 trillion in each. Most of the balance was made up of longer-term consumer and business loans.

One purpose of this chapter is to give the highlights of the kinds of instruments traded in each of the three major segments of the capital market—bonds, stocks, and mortgages—and to explain how these markets function, and some recent innovations.

The Money Market: Where Short-Term Financial Instruments Are Traded

The market for short-term debt instruments is a very busy market—much busier than the capital market. In the late 1980s the total value of money market (short-term) securities outstanding in the United States was in excess of $1 trillion. When you consider the fact that all of these securities are maturing in less than a year—many in a matter of days—it's obvious that, in addition to its **secondary market** functions, this is a very active **primary market** with billions of dollars of new issues pouring out all the time.

The instruments of the money market include the following: large-denomination ($100,000 and over) negotiable bank CDs, Treasury bills (T-bills), commercial paper, repurchase agreements (RPs, or "repos"), bankers' acceptances (B/As), Federal funds (Fed funds), and Eurodollars. Each of these will be explained in this chapter. But first: The instruments of the capital market.

CHARACTERISTICS OF BONDS, AND THE BOND MARKET

Bonds are **debt instruments** which represent long-term borrowing by the issuer of the bonds. Bonds are issued by corporations, by the federal, state, and local governments, and by government agencies. Bonds are usually issued with face value of $1,000, $5,000, or more. But the U.S. Government issues smaller-denomination "savings bonds" designed for the small saver.

Most bonds pay interest semiannually or annually. The **interest rate** is stated as a percentage of the **face value** (par value) of the bond. Most bonds have a **maturity date** at which time the principal (face value) is paid off. Most bonds are issued with original maturity between ten and thirty years, although some are issued with maturities of less than ten years.

The U.S. Treasury issues debt instruments with original maturity between one and ten years and identifies these as **Treasury notes**. And, as you know, short-term Treasury securities (one year or less to maturity) are called **T-bills**. Sometimes all of these debt instruments—bonds, notes, and bills—are lumped together and referred to by the generic term **bonds**, regardless of their term to maturity. But in this discussion, *think of bonds as all debt instruments with original maturities in excess of one year.*

Zero Coupon Bonds. As you know, the interest rate on a bond is referred to as the coupon rate. But some bonds are **zero coupon bonds** and are sold at a deep discount from face value. At maturity the bond owner receives the face value which in fact represents both "implicit accrued interest," plus the principal. All T-bills are zero-coupon and are sold at a discount from face value.

Municipal Bonds. Bonds issued by state and local governments are called **municipal bonds** or **munis**. Interest on munis is exempt from federal taxes and usually is also exempt from the taxes of the state and locality where the bond was issued.

Munis may be either **general obligation bonds**—meaning that the state or local government is obligated to pay, no matter what—or **revenue bonds**, which are to be paid off from future revenues generated by some public project—perhaps a toll bridge or a power plant. With revenue bonds, if the project doesn't pay off then the bonds don't pay off. So revenue bonds are more risky and therefore must pay higher rates of interest than general obligation bonds.

Callables, Convertibles, and Degree of Risk. There is a great variety of different kinds of bonds trading in the capital markets. Some are **callable** (can be paid off early by the issuer), some are **convertible** (can be exchanged for stock in the corporation), and some are of much **higher risk** than others. Obviously, the greater the risk, the greater the yield required to induce purchasers to buy the bond. Bond quality (degree of risk) is rated by both Moody's and Standard and Poor's (S&P's) bond rating services. Table 12-1 explains these bond ratings.

All Marketable Bond Prices Fluctuate

Each "coupon bond" carries a stated face value (say $1,000) and a rate of interest stated as a percentage of the face value (say 8%). So each bond pays a fixed annual return (say $80). If a bond pays 8% and the present market rate of interest for that kind of bond is 8%, then the bond (*ceteris paribus*) will have a market value equal to its face value. If the market rate rises above 8%, then the market value of the bond will drop below $1,000—enough below to adjust the bond's yield up to the current market rate.

Table 12-1. Bond Ratings by Moody's, and Standard and Poor's

Moody's	S&P's	Descriptions
Aaa	AAA	Highest quality, least risk, strong ability to pay
Aa	AA	High quality but with less financial strength than above
A	A	Strong, upper medium grade, but perhaps vulnerable to changing economic conditions
Baa	BBB	Medium grade, current finances adequate but changes could occur
Ba	BB	Lower medium grade. Capable of making current payments but future somewhat uncertain
B	B	Speculative. Doubt about future payments of interest and principal
Caa	CCC-CC	Poor. High default risk
Ca	C	Highly speculative. May be in or near default
C	D	Lowest grade. S&P uses "D" only for bonds currently in default (not paying interest as scheduled)

As market rates of interest rise and fall, bond prices fall and rise. So it's possible to speculate in the bond market just as in the stock market. Many people do. When market rates of interest are expected to fall, that means that market prices of existing bonds are expected to rise. So you can see that it's possible to make big capital gains (or losses) in the bond market, just as in the stock market.

CHARACTERISTICS OF CORPORATE STOCKS

Stocks are equity securities which represent corporate ownership. Anyone who wants to own a share of a (publicly held) corporation can do so by buying shares of the stock of that corporation.

Common Stock

There are various kinds of stock, the most common of which is **common stock**. The owners of the common stock are the owners of the corporation. They are the ones who vote to elect the corporate directors, so they are the ones who hold ultimate management control over the corporation.

Preferred Stock

In addition to common stock, there are many different kinds of so-called **preferred stock**. Preferred stock is somewhat similar to a perpetual bond. It has no maturity date, and it usually pays a **specified dividend**. Preferred stockholders have first claim on the profits of the corporation—the specified dividends on all preferred stock must be paid before any dividends can be paid to the common stock-holders. You can see why they call it "preferred stock."

There are many different kinds of preferred stock. Usually preferred stock-holders cannot vote for the directors of the corporation, but the holders of partici-pating preferred shares do have the right to vote. Sometimes shares of preferred stock are convertible—can be exchanged (under certain specified circumstances) for shares of common stock.

Common Stockholders Are "Residual Claimants"

The common stockholders are the **residual claimants** to the earnings of the corporation. In disbursing its revenues, the corporation first must pay all of its expenses and pay all due interest and principal to the bond holders. Then (after it pays its taxes) it must pay all specified dividends to the preferred stockholders. Any remaining earnings belong to the common stockholders.

Corporations usually pay out some of their residual earnings as **dividends** to the common stockholders, while holding some earnings to be invested in corpo-rate growth. But there are many exceptions to this general rule. Some "high growth" companies reinvest all of their earnings and pay no dividends. At the opposite extreme, most large and well-established companies will continue to pay dividends even in years when they don't make any profits.

CHARACTERISTICS OF MORTGAGES AND THE MORTGAGE MARKET

Mortgages are financial instruments which are created when money is borrowed and **real estate** (land and buildings) is used as collateral. Usually (but now always) the borrowed money is used to buy the real estate which is used as collateral.

In the late 1980s the value of mortgages outstanding in the United States was approaching $3 trillion and was growing by more than $100 million per year.

Most **residential mortgages** are created by the thrift institutions (S&Ls, mutual savings banks, and the larger credit unions). But in recent years commercial banks have also become important residential mortgage lenders. So the primary market for home mortgages consists of the banks and thrifts all over the country. Mortgages on **commercial real estate** are held mostly by commercial banks and by life insurance companies.

Most Mortgages Are Amortized

Mortgages typically run from 15 to 30 years to maturity. Mortgages are somewhat similar to bonds in that they involve a series of definite periodic payments. But mortgage payments are more frequent—usually monthly—and, unlike bonds, each mortgage payment consists of the interest due, plus a payment on the principal. So the mortgage is paid off a little each month—that is, it is **amortized** over the life of the loan.

Variable-Rate Mortgages. An innovation of the 1980s has been the introduction of **variable rate mortgages** (VRMs)—also called adjustable rate mortgages (ARMs). The interest rate on these mortgages is adjusted periodically to reflect changing interest rates in the nation's financial markets.

Government-Insured Mortgages. Some mortgages are insured by the government, either through the Federal Housing Authority (FHA) or the Veteran's Administration (VA). These **government-guaranteed mortgages** carry lower interest rates than the rates on so-called "conventional" mortgages. (Note, however, that much or all of the advantage of the lower rate is often washed out by an up-front charge to the borrower, called "points.")

The Expanding Secondary Market in Mortgages

In the past, residential mortgages have not been easy to sell in the secondary market, partly because the future of an individual mortgage is not predictable. Mortgages can be (and in fact often are) paid off early instead of being amortized on schedule. But during the 1980s the **secondary market** in residential mortgages has expanded rapidly as a result of the pooling of individual mortgages into investment packages.

Ginnie Mae Pass-Throughs. For example, a savings and loan association can use its available funds to make mortgage loans to individuals. Then it can put together a pool of these mortgages and apply to the Government National Mortgage Association (GNMA, called "Ginnie Mae") for insurance on the mortgages. When the mortgages are insured, the pool of mortgages becomes marketable. The S&L can then sell the package of mortgages, obtain new funds and make more loans.

The investors who buy the pool of mortgages receive all of the interest and principal payments. The payments are collected by the S&L and then "passed through" to the ultimate investors. That's why such packages of mortgages are called **Ginnie Mae Pass-Throughs**. The S&L, in addition to the funds it receives when it sells the package of mortgages, also receives service fees for collecting the payments and "passing them through."

Collateralized Mortgage Obligations (CMOs). Another technique for increasing the marketability of mortgages—the creation of **collateralized mortgage obligations** (CMOs)—was "invented" in 1983. A package of mortgages is put into a trust. Investors can then buy securities (shares in the trust) and receive the future cash flows generated by the mortgages.

A special characteristic of **CMOs** is that investors in the trust will receive their future cash flows and be paid off at different times, depending on which specific shares in the trust they choose to buy. Investors can choose to receive their payouts during the first few years by buying the "A bonds" (or "#1 bonds") which are paid off first. Those who want to receive their payouts later during the life of the CMO trust can buy the B, C, etc. (or #2, #3, etc.) bonds. Banks and thrifts have been primary buyers of the "A" bonds, and life insurance companies and pension funds have been major buyers of the longer maturities.

In addition to providing a convenient and flexible investment vehicle for investors, these CMOs greatly increase the marketability of mortgages in the secondary market through the process which is known as **securitization**. (See box 12-1.)

Real Estate Mortgage Investment Conduits (REMICs). In 1986, one of the many changes in the tax code made it possible and attractive to establish this new instrument. **REMICs** are securitization arrangements similar to CMOs but REMICs offer some tax and accounting advantages and greater flexibility than CMOs. Also, REMICs permit the packaging of commercial mortgages. During 1987–88 the number of REMICs was growing rapidly, adding significantly to the booming mortgage-backed securities market.

Because of the various pooling arrangements, *by the late 1980s mortgages had become a much more liquid asset form than they had been in the early 1980s.* So these days your local thrift institution can make mortgage loans, package and sell these mortgages in the secondary market to replenish its funds, and then make more loans. This rapidly developing secondary market for mortgages increases the availability of funds for residential housing and tends to hold down the interest cost on home mortgages. Exhibits 12-1 and 12-2 show announcements of CMO and REMIC offerings.

Government Agencies Act As Financial Intermediaries in the Mortgage Market

There are three federal government agencies which perform financial intermediary roles in the home mortgage market. These are: The Federal National Mortgage

Question: Exactly What is Meant by Securitization?

The creation of a marketable package of mortgages converts nonmarketable (or not easily marketable) assets into easily marketable, highly liquid assets. This is an example of **securitization**.

Securitization means creating easily marketable debt instruments (securities) that are backed by specifically designated not-so-easily marketable assets. Securitization in both U.S. and international financial markets is growing rapidly. It involves not only mortgages, but several other kinds of financial instruments. Beginning in 1985 **automobile loans** were first packaged and sold as securities. These "certificates of automobile receivables" (**CARs**) are similar to CMOs, but require higher servicing fees because automobile loans are not as dependable as mortgages.

In April of 1986 the first package of **credit card receivables** was securitized. These "certificates of amortizing revolving debts" (**CARDs**) are secured, not only by the credit card debt, but by a reserve fund established by the bank which holds the credit card receivables.

In addition, mobile home loans, small business administration loans, computer leases, and various types of accounts receivable have been securitized during the past few years.

Securitization increases the efficiency of financial markets by increasing the marketability of assets which otherwise would not be easily marketable. For interesting articles on the rapidly increasing practice of securitization, see: Randall J. Pozdena, "Securitization and Banking," *Weekly Letter*, Federal Reserve Bank of San Francisco, July 4, 1986; and Christine Pavel, "Securitization," *FRB Chicago Economic Perspectives*, July/August 1986, pp. 16–31; and Harvey D. Shapiro, "The Securitization of Practically Everything," *Institutional Investor*, May 1985, p. 196.

Association (FNMA: **Fannie Mae**), the Government National Mortgage Association (GNMA: **Ginnie Mae**), and the Federal Home Loan Mortgage Corporation (FHLMC: **Freddie Mac**).

All three of these agencies issue and sell bonds in the financial markets to obtain funds. Then they use the funds to buy mortgages from the S&Ls and other home mortgage lenders, thus providing more funds for home loans. Over the past several years these federal agencies have played the important role of replenishing the funds of mortgage lenders. They have increased the supply of loanable funds in the home mortgage market and thereby have made it possible for a larger number of people to borrow and buy homes, and at lower interest rates than otherwise would have been possible.

Overview of the U.S. Capital Market

In addition to stocks, bonds, and mortgages, the only other important instruments outstanding in the nation's capital market are consumer and business loans. Table 12-2 lists and indicates the approximate value outstanding of each of the kinds of financial instruments of the U.S. capital market.

*This announcement is neither an offer to sell nor a solicitation of an offer to buy any of these Securities.
This offer is made only by the Prospectus and the related Prospectus Supplement.*

New Issue   September 9, 1988

$125,000,000

Suncoast CMO Trust IV

(an affiliate of Suncoast Savings of Florida)

The Bonds will be collateralized by GNMA Certificates.

Certificate Class	Original Principal Amount	Interest Rate	Stated Maturity	Price to Public
Class A	$10,638,000	9.41%	July 1, 2012	99.99653%
Class B	10,303,000	9.36	December 1, 2013	99.99102
Class C	12,100,000	9.44	May 1, 2015	99.72947
Class D	7,838,000	9.44	March 1, 2016	98.53636
Class E	17,709,000	9.44	October 1, 2017	97.24020
Class F	14,500,000	9.44	November 1, 2018	95.75245
Class G	14,063,000	9.44	June 1, 2015	98.56068
Class H	37,849,000	9.44	November 1, 2018	95.15179

An election will be made to treat the arrangement by which the collateral will be held as a REMIC.

*Copies of the Prospectus and the related Prospectus Supplement may be obtained
in any State from the undersigned as may legally offer these Bonds
in compliance with the securities laws of such State.*

UBS Securities Inc.

Source: *The Wall Street Journal*, September 9, 1988, p. 31. Reprinted by permission.

Exhibit 12-2   An Announcement of Mortgage Collateralized Bonds—CMO—which is also a "Real Estate Mortgage Investment Conduit"—A "REMIC"

September 8, 1988

$250,000,000

Kidder, Peabody Mortgage Assets Trust Twenty

Collateralized Mortgage Obligations

	Original Principal Amount	Interest Rate	Stated Maturity
Class 20-A	$ 60,000,000	8.23%	April 1, 2008
Class 20-B	133,750,000	9.20	November 1, 2016
Class 20-C	20,000,000	9.50	October 1, 2018
Class 20-D	33,500,000	9.90	October 1, 2018
Class 20-E	2,500,000	(1)	October 1, 2018
Class 20-R	250,000	(2)	October 1, 2018

(1) The rate at which interest will accrue on the Class 20-E Bonds will be 9.125% per annum with respect to the initial Interest Accrual Period and, with respect to each subsequent Interest Accrual Period, will be a per annum rate of 0.75% in excess of one-month LIBOR, but in no event greater than 20.0% per annum.

(2) The Class 20-R Bonds will bear interest at a per annum rate of 420.40455% during the initial Interest Accrual Period. Thereafter, the rate at which interest will accrue on the Class 20-R Bonds will vary as described in the Prospectus Supplement.

An election will be made to treat the arrangement by which the Bonds are secured as a REMIC.

Copies of the Prospectus and the related Prospectus Supplement may be obtained in any State from the undersigned in compliance with the securities laws of such State.

Kidder, Peabody & Co.
Incorporated

Source: *The Wall Street Journal*, September 8, 1988, p. 44. Reprinted by permission.

Table 12-2.   Financial Instruments of the U.S. Capital Market
             (Billions of dollars. Some figures approximate.)

Type of Instrument	Amount Outstanding beginning of				
	1960	1970	1985	1987	1988
Corporate stocks (at market value)	451	906	2,150	4,005	3,559
Mortgages					
Residential mortgages	160	353	1,505	1,912	2,175
Commercial and farm mortgages	46	115	519	640	750
Bonds					
U.S. government (marketable, long-term)	178	160	873	1,240	1,351
U.S. government agencies	10	51	260	275	303
Corporate	75	167	517	696	789
State and local government	394	144	404	530	562
Loans					
Consumer loans	65	143	594	662	711
Bank business loans	570	314	470	633	681

Source: Board of Governors of the Federal Reserve System, *Banking and Monetary Statistics, 1941–1970, The Federal Reserve Bulletin*, and Federal Reserve Flow of Funds Accounts.

INSTRUMENTS OF THE MONEY MARKET

The money market is a fast-moving, large-volume, high-value market. Funds often flow by wire transfer instantaneously on the basis of a telex or phone call. The minimum denomination of most money market instruments is $100,000, although Treasury bills are issued in denominations as small as $10,000. Clearly, this is not a market for the small individual investor. Money market mutual funds arose to offer small investors access to this large-denomination market.

Large Denomination ($100,000 and Over) Negotiable Bank CDs

Banks issue **large denomination CDs** to "buy current dollars" frequently from corporate treasurers, by offering a little more interest than is paid on Treasury bills. These CDs are easily marketable and therefore, highly liquid. Their prices fluctuate in response to fluctuations in market interest rates. They were first introduced in the early 1960s. By the late 1980s they made up almost 20 percent of the total value of securities outstanding in the U.S. money market.

Treasury Bills (T-Bills)

The U.S. Government issues **T-bills**, typically with maturities of three months, six months, or a year. T-bills have zero default risk and because of their short term, very little capital (market, or interest rate) risk or purchasing power (inflation) risk. Like large negotiable CDs, T-bills are readily marketable and highly liquid.

As mentioned previously T-bills are **zero coupon**. They are sold at a discount from face value and then pay the face value at maturity. Many T-bill buyers sell their bills before maturity in the active secondary market where prices reflect current interest rates.

Before the recent rapid growth of negotiable CDs and corporate commercial paper, T-bills were (by far) the predominant money market instrument. But by the late 1980s, T-bills only accounted for about 20 percent of the total value of short-term securities outstanding in the U.S. money market.

Commercial Paper

Commercial paper consists of short-term debt obligations issued by corporations. The term to maturity is usually 30 days, although maturities ranging from 5 to 45 days are not uncommon. Maximum maturity is 270 days because beyond that the issue would require the time and expense of being registered with the Securities and Exchange Commission (SEC).

Corporations with the highest credit ratings often can reduce their cost of short-term funds by issuing their own commercial paper instead of borrowing from banks. The most common denomination of a commercial paper note is $1 million.

The total value of commercial paper outstanding has grown rapidly over the past two decades. By the late 1980s commercial paper amounted to about 20 percent of the total value of securities outstanding in the U.S. money market.

Repurchase Agreements (RPs, or "Repos")

A **repurchase agreement** is, in effect, a short-term loan (maturity from overnight to two-weeks), with T-bills used as collateral. Repos work like this: Suppose a corporation has $100,000 in its checking account, needed to cover payroll four days from now. The corporation can lend the funds to the bank by "buying T-bills" from the bank (or from any other investor, for that matter) with the agreement that the bank (or other investor) will buy back the securities in four days. So the corporation earns interest on its idle funds for four days, then gets the funds back in its checking account in time to cover the payroll checks.

Banks benefit from repos in either of two ways:

1. When the bank's depositor-corporation takes funds out of its checking account to buy repo securities, that reduces the total amount of checkable deposits held by the bank. So the bank can hold less non-interest-bearing reserves at the Fed.

2. Alternatively, a bank can sell repo securities to the depositors of other banks and then use the funds to increase its reserve deposits at the Fed.

A bank which sells securities (repos) to its own depositor-corporations on Friday afternoon and then buys them back on Monday morning has reduced deposits over the weekend. A bank which sells repos to other banks' depositors over the weekend has increased reserves during that period. Either way, the effect is to reduce the amount of reserves the bank must hold for the remainder of that two-week required-reserve-holding period (explained later).

The widespread use of repurchase agreements is one of the many recent innovations in the financial markets. In 1970 their volume was insignificant. By midyear 1988 the value of repos outstanding had increased to more than $140 billion.

Bankers' Acceptance (B/As)

Bankers' acceptances are short-term debt obligations (notes) which usually arise in financing international trade. The bank advances the funds to pay for imported goods, and the importer owes the bank. Then the bank sells the acceptance to replenish its funds.

A **bankers' acceptance** is really a short-term promissory note indicating that the importer promises to pay in the future. But the note has been stamped "accepted" and therefore *it is guaranteed by the bank*. Since the bank guarantees payment, a bankers' acceptance is as readily marketable as any other debt obligation of the bank (marketable CDs, for example).

In recent years as the volume of international trade has grown, bankers' acceptances have begun to play a significant role. By 1985, acceptances made up almost 10 percent of the total value of securities in the U.S. money market. But later in the 1980s that percentage declined as the volume of other instruments expanded rapidly.

Fed Funds

Banks and other depository institutions have **reserve deposits** in the Federal Reserve banks. These deposits are called "Federal funds" or usually just **Fed funds**. Nobody likes to hold any more Fed funds than legally required because these deposits pay no interest.

Institutions with surplus funds lend (usually overnight) to institutions which need more reserves. Also, banks can borrow from federal agencies and from nonbank securities dealers and classify these borrowings as Fed funds. Overnight Fed funds transactions are made by phone call, the funds are transferred instantaneously via Fed Wire and are secured only by the word and reputation of the borrowing banks.

The Fed funds market is a highly developed and very active segment of the money market. Average daily borrowings amount to $150 billion or more—almost 10 percent of the total value of money market instruments outstanding.

Fed funds play a key role in the money market because the **Fed funds rate** is the basic money market rate to which all other rates tend to adjust. Also, the Fed funds rate has been a key monetary policy instrument, and it is a closely-watched indicator of the future trend of interest rates.

EURODOLLARS AND THE EURODOLLAR MARKET

Eurodollars are "American dollar deposit liabilities" of banks. These dollars are **Eurodollars** *only because the banks which issued the deposit liabilities are located outside the United States*. The bank may be either a foreign bank or an overseas branch of an American bank. It makes no difference, so long as it is located in a foreign country.

Eurodollars are usually defined as "U.S. dollar deposit liabilities of banks located outside the United States." But this definition is no longer precisely true, as explained in box 12-2.

Question: Can Eurodollar Deposits Be Held by Banks Located in the United States? Yes! In IBFs.

Since 1982, U.S. banks have been permitted to establish "overseas branches" which are not overseas. These branches (so-called "offshore" branches) are physically located in the United States—in fact, usually, in the bank's own home-office building. These "home-office offshore branches" are called **International Banking Facilities**—IBFs.

This IBF arrangement has made it possible for many banks to accept Eurodollar deposits and deal in the Eurodollar money market without having to actually establish a physical presence in London, the Bahamas, the Cayman Islands or some other offshore location. But *the IBFs can only accept dollar (Eurodollar) deposits from foreigners and make dollar (Eurodollar) loans to foreigners—not to U.S. residents.*

Initially Eurodollar-deposit-banks were located in Europe. Today U.S. dollar deposits are held by banks in Japan, Australia, Singapore, and all over the world. But we still call these dollar deposits "Eurodollars."

It's important to understand that Eurodollars are the same as any other American dollars. Here's an example which illustrates that fact.

An Example: Creating Eurodollars

Suppose you live in Niagara Falls, New York and you have some surplus funds which you want to deposit, perhaps in a time deposit (CD). You see that the First National Bank of Niagara Falls, New York is offering 7% on CDs.

You also notice that the Niagara Falls, Canada, branch of that bank is offering 7-1/2% on U.S. dollar denominated CDs. So you walk across Rainbow Bridge and deposit your American dollars in the Canadian branch and come back home with your U.S. dollar-denominated CD. You have just created Eurodollars.

Borrowing Eurodollars

Now suppose your sister who operates a local accounting firm wants to borrow funds to buy some new computerized equipment. She finds that she can borrow American dollars from the Niagara Falls, New York bank for 10-1/2%, or from the Canada branch for 10%. So she walks across the bridge and borrows Eurodollars.

How is it possible for the overseas branches of American banks to offer higher deposit rates and lower loan rates? Because some of their costs of operation are lower. They hold no non-interest-bearing required reserves. They pay no deposit insurance premiums. And they are able to avoid some other cost-adding banking regulations and paperwork—red tape. It's no wonder the Eurodollar market has seen explosive growth.

Actually, as you might guess, most overseas branches of American banks are not located in Niagara Falls, Canada, but in London and in other major financial centers throughout the world. But in the modern world of immediate electronic communications, Niagara Falls, New York is just about as close to London and Tokyo and Singapore as it is to Niagara Falls, Canada!

Box 12-3

Different Ways of Defining Eurodollars

There are different ways of defining Eurodollars. An alternative definition is "U.S. dollar deposits in U.S. banks, owned by banks located outside the United States." This definition actually refers to the "Eurodollar reserves" held by the foreign banks so they can pay out U.S. dollars to meet the dollar (Eurodollar) withdrawals of their depositors. It is these Eurodollar reserves which are loaned among banks in the Eurodollar money market.

Figures on the size of the Eurocurrency market, and on the relative importance of Eurodollars as a percent of total Eurocurrencies outstanding, are published by the Federal Reserve bank of St. Louis in their quarterly publication: *International Economic Conditions.*

The Busiest Money Market in the World

The Eurodollar market is the busiest money market in the world. In the late 1980s the total value of Eurodollars in existence—U.S. dollar deposit liabilities of all foreign branches of U.S. banks plus those of all foreign banks—amounted to more than $2.5 trillion. That was almost four times the number of dollars in the U.S. M1 money supply.

But there are other ways of defining Eurodollars as explained in box 12-3. Each definition results in a different total for the number of Eurodollars outstanding. The Eurodollar market is centered in London, and the London branches of American banks play a major role in this market.

Both financial and nonfinancial institutions (both U.S. and foreign) can obtain short-term loans of U.S. dollars in the Eurodollar "money market." When the Fed funds rate rises, banks with reserve deficiencies frequently bypass the high-cost Fed funds market and borrow in the Eurodollar market—often from the London branches of U.S. banks, either their own branches or others.

Innovation and Rapid Changes in Money Market Instruments

Table 12-3 lists the principal money market instruments and indicates the outstanding dollar value of each since 1960. You can see that great changes have

**Table 12-3.   The Changing Mix of Money Market Instruments, 1960–1987
(Billions of dollars. Some figures approximate.)**

Type of Instrument	Amount Outstanding beginning of				
	1960	1970	1985	1987	1988
Large negotiable bank CDs	0	25	325	338	383
U.S. Treasury bills	32	81	374	427	393
Commercial paper	4	33	240	330	381
Bankers' acceptances	2	7	75	65	63
Eurodollar reserves (foreign-bank-owned U.S. dollar deposits in U.S. banks)	1	2	252	310	346
Repos plus Fed funds	1	23	170	220	329

Source: Board of Governors of the Federal Reserve System, *Banking and Monetary Statistics, 1941–1970; The Federal Reserve Bulletin;* Federal Reserve Flow of Funds Accounts; and Federal Reserve Bank of St. Louis, *International Economic Conditions.*

occurred. Several of the most important instruments of the 1980s were either insignificant or did not exist in 1960.

FINANCIAL MARKETS, INTERMEDIATION, AND THE U.S. AND WORLD ECONOMY: AN OVERVIEW

The U.S. and worldwide money-banking-financial system is truly integrated. It is tied together, interlocked, and inseparable—a spiderweb of electronic communications links. Each part influences—and is influenced by—all the others. By now you can appreciate the key role this integrated system plays in the functioning of the U.S. and world economy.

The Circulatory System of the U.S. and World Economy

Money could perform its functions only in a very primitive way without the help of financial intermediaries, instruments and markets. This financial system serves as the **circulatory system** of the economy—the system through which money flows to direct the resource flows of the U.S. and world economy. It's this integrated system on which the health of the U.S. and world economy depends.

Through the financial markets—and more often than not, through financial intermediaries—**current dollars** flow from "oversupply" to "undersupply" economic units, areas, and functions. This **flow of funds** is what causes **real resources** to flow into the desired places and uses. That's how the **microeconomic efficiency** of the economy is achieved and maintained.

The savers in the economy (SEUs) withdraw spending from the circular flow. These savings move through the financial markets—again, mostly through financial intermediaries—to the borrower-spenders (DEUs) so that the withdrawn funds can be reinjected into the spending stream. That's how the **macroeconomic stability** of the economy is achieved and maintained.

Serving the Needs of SEUs, DEUs, and the Economy

When they're working well, financial markets and financial intermediaries serve the needs of the saver-lenders (SEUs) and of the borrow-spenders (DEUs) as well as the efficiency, stability, and growth of the economy. Is it any wonder that so much attention is paid to issues of money and banking? And to financial markets? And monetary policies? The economic fortunes of all of us depend very much on the proper functioning of the financial system—the circulatory system of the U.S. and worldwide economy.

SUMMARY

- Highly developed **financial markets** are essential in the healthy functioning of the U.S. and world economy.
- The **capital market** is the market for long-term equity and debt instruments—original maturities of more than one year. It includes stocks, bonds, mortgages, and some long-term business and consumer loans.

- There are various kinds of **bonds**. All are debts of their issuers and they fluctuate in price in response to interest rate changes.

- **Corporate stocks** represent corporate ownership. Common stockholders are the "residual claimants" and receive dividends only after all other necessary payments have been made.

- **Mortgages** are real estate debts, most of which are amortized over their lifetime. Recently, with the explosive growth of **securitization** (mostly **CMOs** and **REMICS**), an efficient secondary market has developed for mortgages.

- The **money market** is the market for short-term, large-denomination debt instruments. It includes: **negotiable bank CDs, T-bills, commercial paper, repurchase agreements, bankers' acceptances, Fed funds** and **Eurodollars**.

- The outstanding value of money market securities now exceeds $1 trillion. These short-term securities turn over quickly, so the money market is a very active **primary** and **secondary** market.

- It is through the integrated system of financial intermediaries, instruments, and markets that money in the modern world performs its functions and supports the **efficiency, stability**, and **growth** of the U.S. and worldwide economy.

Important Principles, Issues, Concepts, Terms

The importance of financial markets

Characteristics of the capital market

Kinds of and outstanding value of capital market instruments

Characteristics of and different kinds of bonds

Characteristics of and kinds of corporate stocks

Rights of common stockholders

Characteristics and kinds of mortgages

Government mortgage guarantees: FHA, VA

The role of government agencies in the home mortgage market

Fannie Mae, Ginnie Mae, and Freddie Mac

The secondary market in mortgages

Ginnie Mae pass-through securities

Collateralized mortgage obligations (CMOs)

Real estate mortgage investment conduits (REMICs)

Securitization

Characteristics of the money market

Kinds of and outstanding value of money market instruments

Changes in values outstanding of money market instruments

Primary and secondary capital market

Primary and secondary money market

Primary securities

Intermediary securities

Importance of financial intermediation in the U.S. and world economy

Functions of financial intermediaries, instruments, and markets for SEUs, DEUs, and the U.S. and world economy

Questions and Problems

1. Explain as much as you can about bonds: what they are, and characteristics of different kinds of bonds.

2. Describe the characteristics of different kinds of corporate stock.

3. Explain this statement: "Common stockholders are residual claimants."

4. Explain as much as you can about the mortgage market, especially the secondary market for mortgages.

5. Explain what is meant by securitization and some kinds of "securitization instruments" for home mortgages.

6. Give an overview description of the U.S. capital market.

7. List and describe briefly the most important financial instruments of the money market.

8. Describe the Eurodollar market—what it is and how it works.

9. Discuss the importance of the financial system—intermediaries, instruments, and markets—in the functioning of the U.S. and world economy: both the microeconomic and macroeconomic functioning.

Suggested Readings

Belongia, Michael T. "Hedging Interest Rate Risk with Financial Futures: Some Basic Principles." *Review* 66. Federal Reserve Bank of St. Louis (October 1984), 15–25.

Bookstaber, Richard. *The Complete Investment Book.* Glenview, IL: Scott Foresman and Company, 1985.

Brenner, Lynn. "Turning Assets into Securities is Knotty Problem, Panel Says." *American Banker.* May 2, 1986.

Byington, Preston W. *U.S. Treasury Bills: A Working Handbook.* Culver City, CA: Penco Publishing Co., 1978.

Chicago Board of Trade. *Financial Futures: The Delivery Process in Brief.* 1982.

Cook, Timothy Q., and Bruce J. Summers (eds.). *Instruments of the Money Market.* Federal Reserve Bank of Richmond, 1981.

Darst, David. *The Complete bond Book, a Guide to All Types of Fixed-Income Securities.* New York: McGraw-Hill, 1975.

Dufey, Gunter, and Ian H. Giddy. *The International Money Market.* Englewood Cliffs, NJ: Prentice-Hall, 1978.

Fabozzi, Frank J., and Irving M. Pollack (eds.). *The Handbook of Fixed Income Securities.* Homewood, Ill.: Dow Jones-Irwin, 1983.

Federal Reserve Bank of Atlanta. "Repurchase Agreements: Taking a Closer Look at Safety." *Economic Review.* September 1985.

Goodfriend, Marvin, James Parthemos, and Bruce Summers. "Financial Innovations: Causes, Consequences for the Payments System and Implications for Monetary Control." *Economic Review* 66. Federal Reserve Bank of Richmond (March/April 1980), 14–27.

GNMA Mortgage-Backed Securities Dealers Association. *The Ginnie Mae Manual.* Homewood, Ill.: Dow Jones-Irwin, 1978.

Homer, Sidney. *The Great American Bond Market: Selected speeches of Sidney Homer.* Homewood, Ill.: Dow Jones-Irwin, 1978.

Kane, Edward J. "Accelerating Inflation, Technological Innovation, and the Decreasing Effectiveness of Banking Regulations." *Journal of Finance* 36, (May 1981), 355–67.

Lucas, Charles, Marcus Jones, and Thom Thurston. "Federal Funds and Repurchase Agreements." *Quarterly Review.* Federal Reserve Bank of New York, summer 1977.

Summers, Bruce. "Negotiable Certificates of Deposit." *Economic Review.* Federal Reserve Bank of Atlanta, September 1985.

Pavel, Christine. "Securitization." *Economic Perspectives.* Federal Reserve Bank of Chicago, July/August 1986.

Pozdena, Randall Johnston. "Mortgage Securitization and REMICS." *FRBSF Weekly Letter.* Federal Reserve Bank of San Francisco, May 8, 1987.

Stigum, Marcia. *The Money Market.* Homewood, Ill.: Dow Jones-Irwin, 1983.

CHAPTER 13

Financial Markets and Interest Rate Structures: How to Read the Yield Curves

Chapter Objectives

The pattern of different interest yields on different securities is called the interest rate structure. This chapter describes various risk structure and term structure yield curves and explains (1) the factors which influence these curves and (2) the conclusions we can draw by "reading" these curves. After you study this chapter you will understand and be able to explain:

1. The meanings of **term structure** and **risk structure** and how to draw curves to illustrate these.

2. The great variety of different term structure yield curves which have actually existed, and the speed with which these curves can change.

3. Why the term structure yield curve (*ceteris paribus*) tends to slope *upward* and why expectations of falling rates can cause it to be **inverted**—to slope *downward*.

4. The effect of expected future short-term rates on present long-term rates—the **expectations** theory—and the **segmented markets** and preferred habitat theories, and how these various theories, taken together, provide a good explanation of the term structure yield curve.

5. How the **risk structure** of interest rates reflects the degree of perceived default risk and why this default-risk premium increases during an economic downturn.

6. The effects of **liquidity differences** and **tax avoidance** on risk structure yield curves.

7. How the analysis of both term and risk structure helps to understand conditions in and the functioning of financial markets.

INTEREST RATE STRUCTURES: DIFFERENT YIELDS ON DIFFERENT SECURITIES

Different financial instruments yield different amounts of interest income. Why? Several reasons. The differences may be accounted for by differences in

1. risk of default,
2. liquidity,
3. whether or not the income from the financial instrument is taxable, and
4. length of time to maturity.

As you would expect, instruments which carry significant default risk pay more interest than those (such as government securities) which are default free. Also the more easily marketable the instrument, the lower its yield because liquidity is desired. Nontaxable instruments (*ceteris paribus*) offer lower yields than taxable ones. All of these differences influence interest yields in fairly obvious ways. But what about the length of time to maturity?

Suppose you compare the interest yields on two different debt instruments of *equal risk* but *different terms to maturity*—say, a short-term and a long-term government security. Would the yields be identical? Probably not.

Term Structure: Different Yields for Different Terms to Maturity

The yields on long-term instruments usually are not the same as on short-term instruments. Suppose you look in *The Wall Street Journal* and find that yields on 90-day T-bills are 7% and yields on 30-year Treasury bonds are 10%. That tells you that yields on long-term securities are higher than yields on short-term securities.

Or you might find that the yield on the T-bills is 14% while the yield on the long-term bonds is 10%. Or you might want to compare a lot of different securities with different terms to maturity to see how the yields change as term-to-maturity changes.

You might compare securities with 30-day, 60-day, 90-day, 6-month, 1-year, 2-year, 5-year, on up to 30-year maturities to see how yield changes as term-to-maturity changes. As term-to-maturity increases, do yields increase? Or decrease? Or stay the same? These are questions which are answered by the **term structure yield curve**.

On a graph showing interest yields on the vertical axis and time to maturity on the horizontal axis you can plot interest yields on different debt instruments which have identical **risk**, but different **terms to maturity**. When you do that you will produce a **term structure yield curve**. Now look at figure 13-1, panel A, and that's what you'll see.

Risk Structure: Different Yields for Different Degrees of Risk

You may compare two debt instruments of equal term to maturity and find that their interest yields are not identical. Why? Usually because the perceived **degree of risk** for the two instruments is not identical. You would expect a corporate

Figure 13-1.   Term and Risk Interest Rate Structures

Yields are different for different debt instruments, depending on (1) length of time to maturity, and (2) degree of risk.

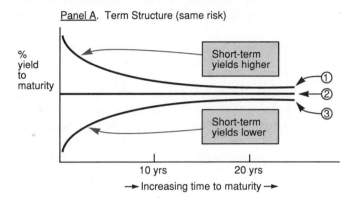

Panel A. Term Structure (same risk)

%
yield
to
maturity

Short-term yields higher

Short-term yields lower

10 yrs   20 yrs

→ Increasing time to maturity →

Panel A

For instruments which all have the same degree of risk (e.g., government securities) the yield curve my be upward sloping, horizontal, or downward sloping.

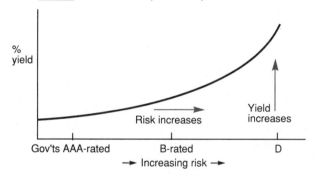

Panel B. Risk Structure (same term)

%
yield

Risk increases

Yield increases

Gov'ts AAA-rated   B-rated   D

→ Increasing risk →

Panel B

For debt instruments with the same term to maturity, as risk increases (*ceteris paribus*), yield increases. The risk-structure curve is upward sloping.

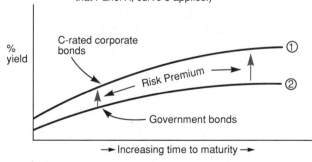

Panel C. Term Structure and Risk Structure Combined. (Assumes that Panel A, curve 3 applies.)

%
yield

C-rated corporate bonds

Risk Premium

Government bonds

→ Increasing time to maturity →

Panel C

The real-world yield curve for any class of security is the term-structure curve, shifted upward to reflect the percieved degree of risk on that class of security.

Note that the risk premium increases as term-to-maturity increases.

bond to pay higher interest than a U.S. Government bond, and the lower the Moody's or S&P's rating of a bond, the higher the yield you would expect it to pay.

On a graph showing interest yields on the vertical axis and degree of risk increasing along the horizontal axis, for securities of identical maturities (say, 10-year bonds) you would expect the curve to slope upward to show that as risk increases, yield also increases. Now if you'll look at panel B in figure 13-1, that's what you'll see.

Panel C in figure 13-1 combines panels A and B. The curves in panel C are term-structure yield curves, with curve 2 shifted upward to reflect a higher risk premium on the C-rated bonds.

In panel C, curves 1 and 2 are not parallel. Why? Because the risk premium on a more-risky security increases as term-to-maturity increases. When term-to-maturity is short, most of the events which might cause a security to default, can be fairly clearly foreseen. So the risk premium doesn't need to be very large.

But as the term gets longer, the "unforeseeables" increase. So the risk is greater and a greater risk premium is required. So, for low-grade securities, as term-to-maturity increases, the risk premium also must increase. That's why the vertical distance between curves 1 and 2 in panel C increases as term-to-maturity increases.

THE TERM STRUCTURE OF INTEREST RATES

In panel A of figure 13-1, which of the curves (curve 1, 2, or 3) would you expect to most closely approximate the empirically observable (real-world) term-structure yield curve? Curve 3 is most likely in "normal times." This chapter will explain why. But the fact is that there have been times in the past when each of these curves would have fit the real-world data. This chapter explains that also.

Figures 13-2, 13-3, and 13-4 show examples of real-world yield curves. When you look at those figures you see that *there has been great variability in the shape and slope of term-structure yield curves.* Why is this true? What are the factors which influence the shape and slope of the term-structure yield curve? These questions will be addressed in the sections coming up. But before you go on, you need to spend a few minutes studying the yield curves in figures 13-2, -3, and -4.

An Explanation of Figure 13-2

Panel A. In panel A of figure 13-2 you see that in 1979 the yield curve was almost flat, but slightly downward sloping. Yields on securities with 1 to 5 years to maturity were about 9-1/2%, while longer-term yields (>15 years) were only about 9%.

By 1980 the yield curve had shifted upward, and the shorter term securities were yielding significantly more than the longer term. Yields on one-year securities were almost 14%, while yields on maturities of 15 years and longer were less than 12.5%.

In 1981 the shape of the yield curve remained approximately the same, but the curve shifted upward so that the shorter-term securities were yielding as much as 14.5%, and the longer maturities were yielding about 13%.

Figure 13-2. The Great Variety of Term-Structure Yield Curves Since 1900

Panel A: Yield curves for high-grade corporate bonds, 1979–1982

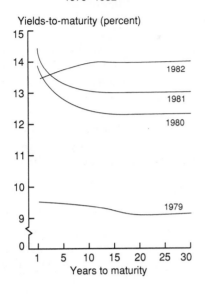

Panel B: Yield curves for high-grade corporate bonds, 1930–1978

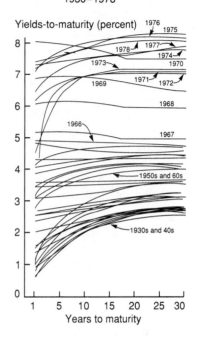

Panel C: Yield curves for high-grade corporate bonds, 1900–1929

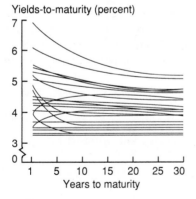

This broad array of term-structure yield curves indicates that, although for many consecutive years the yield curves have sloped upward, there are also many years during which yield curves sloped downward.

You will notice that during years when rates have been relatively low, the yield curve has usually been upward sloping, and downward sloping yield curves have been generally associated with times during which rates have been high. Before you finish your study of this chapter, you will understand why this might be true.

Note that during the 1930s, short-term rates were sometimes less than $\frac{1}{2}$ of 1%, and long-term rates were only a little more than 2%. Compare that with the double digit rates of the early 1980s!

Source: John H. Wood, "Do Yield Curves Normally Slope Up? The Term-Structure of Interest Rates, 1862–1982," *Economic Perspective*, The Federal Reserve Bank of Chicago, May–June, 1985, p. 18.

Then look what happened in 1982. Yields on the shorter-term securities dropped to about 13.5%, while longer-term yields increased to about 14%.

Panel B. Now look at panel B. During the 1930s and 40s, most of the time the yield curve was sharply upward-sloping. Yields on the shorter maturities were usually less than 1%, and sometimes less than 0.5%. Longer term yields generally ranged between 2% and 3%.

During the 1950s and '60s the shape and slope of the yield curves for the most part remained the same as in the 1930s and '40s, but the curves were shifted higher to reflect higher levels of both short-term and long-term rates. This same general shape of the curve existed much of the time during the 1970s, but at increasingly higher rates.

Look carefully at panel B and you will see that from the mid-1960s until 1970 the yield curve was generally flat or downward sloping, indicating higher yields on the shorter-term securities, and each year all rates were higher than the year before. Do rising rates tend to bring a downward sloping yield curve? Yes. This chapter explains why.

Panel C. Now take a look at panel C. With only a few exceptions, prior to 1929 yield curves were usually flat or downward sloping. Why has there been so much difference between yield curves at different times? And what can we conclude from that? Much of this chapter is devoted to answering these questions.

Explanations of Figures 13-3 and 13-4

Figure 13-3 illustrates the rapid changes which can occur in the shape, slope, and level of yield curves during times of high volatility in the financial markets. Then figure 13-4 illustrates the relative stability and gently upward-sloping yield curves which seem to exist in modern times when inflation rates are relatively low and financial markets are stable.

As you look at the yield curves in figures 13-2, -3, and -4, you may wonder if there is any "rhyme or reason" to these curves. Actually, there is. You can see a lot about macroeconomic conditions and about the expectations of the financial community regarding future inflation rates and interest rates by "reading" these curves.

WHAT DETERMINES THE SHAPE AND SLOPE OF THE TERM-STRUCTURE YIELD CURVE?

Which should pay more interest? A short-term security such as a 90-day Treasury bill? Or a long-term security such as as a 15-year government bond?

If you buy a long-term bond and market interest rates rise, the market value of your bond will drop. So you might expect the longer-term security to pay a higher yield because of this market risk.

Market Risk (Capital Risk) Tends to Bring an Upward Sloping Yield Curve

Market risk is the danger that the market prices of your securities will fall. You know that when interest rates rise, bond prices fall. That's the market risk, also called price risk, capital risk, and interest rate risk.

For short-term securities (money market instruments) there is very little market risk. But as the term to maturity gets longer, the market (interest rate) risk gets greater. You would think that the greater market risk on long-term instruments would require that these instruments offer higher yields. So you would expect the yield curve to be positively-sloped—the longer the term, the higher the

Figure 13-3. Volatile Rates and Shifting Yield Curves of the 1980s

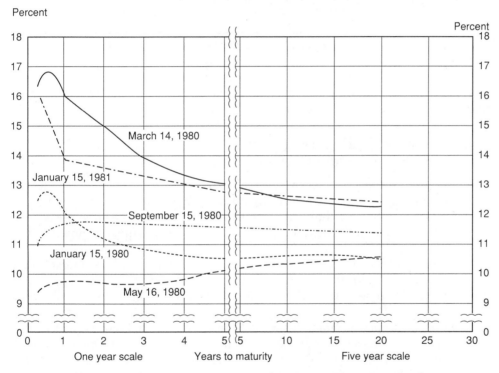

The rapidly changing yields on U.S. government securities between January 1980 and January 1981.

Between mid-January and mid-March of 1980, rates soared and the yield curve became sharply downward sloping. But two months later, by mid-May, short-term rates had dropped by almost 50 percent, while long-term rates dropped only slightly. So the yield curve became slightly upward-sloping. But after May, rates rose again. By mid-January of 1981 some short-term rates were as high as 16%, and the yield curve was again downward sloping.

During the two-month period between mid-march and mid-May of 1980, short-term rates dropped from a high of almost 17% to a low of a little more than 9%.

This graph illustrates a situation which usually holds true in the financial markets: Short-term rates are typically more variable than long-term rates.

Source: Federal Reserve Bank of St. Louis.

Figure 13-4.   Yield Curves for Treasury Securities March 1986 and March 1987

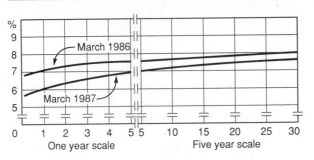

Interest rates in 1986 and '87 (both short and long term) were quite stable and were much lower than in the early 1980s, and as you can see from the graph, the curves were gently upward-sloping.

Source: Data from "Credit Markets" (daily) and "Key Interest Rates" (Tuesdays), *The Wall Street Journal*. Graph prepared by the author.

yield. But in fact, as you saw in figures 13-2 and 13-3, term-structure yield curves frequently have not been positively sloped. Why not?

Expectations of Falling Rates Can Bring a Negatively Sloped Yield Curve

Suppose you are the president of a large corporation and you are considering selling long-term bonds to finance an expansion. And suppose that the lowest rate at which you can borrow the money (sell the bonds) is 14%. And suppose you think that sometime in the next few months interest rates will come down. What will you do?

Will you go into the market and sell long-term bonds and lock yourself into paying this 14% rate for many years to come? Or will you borrow short term and wait for rates to come down before selling your bonds? The answer is obvious.

Lenders Shift Supply of Funds from the Short-Term to the Long-Term Market. The people who are supplying the funds (buyers of debt instruments) would like to "lock in" some of these high long-term rates before they come down. So they are eager to supply long-term funds—i.e., buy long-term instruments. This ample supply of long-term funds (demand for long-term securities) tends to keep long-term security prices up and the yields down.

But in the short term market, funds are in short supply. Short-term rates must be forced up (and long-term rates forced down) to where suppliers of loanable funds are willing to forgo long-term bonds and invest in money market instruments instead.

The bottom line: When interest rates are expected to fall:

● There is increased demand and decreased supply of funds (increased supply and decreased demand for securities) in the short-term market. Short-term securities prices go down and yields go up.

- There is a decreased demand and an increased supply of funds (decreased supply and increased demand for securities) in the long-term market. Long-term securities prices go up and yields go down.

So both from the point of view of the supply and demand for loanable funds, and of the supply and demand for securities it's clear that when the financial community expects rates to fall, an inverted (downward-sloping) yield curve is likely to result.

How Expected Future Short-Term Rates Influence Present Long-Term Rates: The "Expectations" Theory of Term Structure

Assume that you have $1,000 which you would like to invest at maximum interest return, for two years. You could buy a two-year Treasury note and lock in a fixed return for two years. Or you could buy a one-year Treasury bill, then at the end of the year when it matures, buy another one-year T-bill. (Of course you could consider buying a series of 90-day, 6-month, or other maturity bills—but let's not.)

Suppose the yield to maturity on the one-year T-bill is 6% and the yield on the two-year Treasury note is also 6%. Which would you buy? Suppose you think that by next year the short-term rate will be up to 8%. Then you will buy the one-year 6% T-bill and next year (if your expectations materialize!) you will buy a one-year 8% T-bill. Your average yield over the two years will be 7%.

But what if you expect the short-term rate to drop to 4%? Then you will buy the two-year 6% note and be guaranteed a 6% yield. With the 2-year note you avoid the **income risk** of a lower short-term rate in the second year.

Long-Term Rates Tend to Be an Average of Present and Expected Future Short-Term Rates

From the above explanation you can draw the following conclusion: *Present long-term rates depend on—and in fact tend to be an average of—(a) present short-term rates and (b) expected future short-term rates.*

Example: If the short-term rate this year is 6% and the expected short-term rate for next year is 8%, then the yield on the two-year T-note must be 7% to induce you to buy it. The 7% yield is the average of the two short-term yields: 6%, and 8%. And this bring us to the **expectations theory** of the yield curve.

Box 13-1

Question: Which is Preferable: Market Risk? or Income Risk?

Clearly, **market risk** can be avoided by investing only in very short-term securities. But if you do that you incur **income risk**. With a longer-term security *a given yield is guaranteed.* There's no question about how much income you're going to earn in the years to come.

With short-term instruments the income produced is variable and dependent on changing market conditions. So which risk would you choose to bear? market risk? or income risk? That depends on your investment objectives. It's entirely up to you.

This expectations theory leads to the conclusions that:

- *When short-term rates are expected to rise*, present long-term rates will tend to be higher than present short-term rates. The yield curve will tend to *slope upward.*

- *When short-term rates are expected to decrease*, present long-term rates will tend to be lower than present short-term rates. The yield curve will tend to *slope downward.*

Uncertainty and Market Risk Partly Undermine This "Expectations" Theory: A "Risk Premium" Is Required

In the above discussion it was assumed that short-term and long-term securities are perfect substitutes for each other. No mention was made of the increased **market risk** of investing in long-term securities. It was assumed that you were going to purchase securities and hold them to maturity, with no idea of selling those securities in the meanwhile. It also was assumed that you were quite confident of what the short-term rate would be, one year from now. All of these assumptions are somewhat unrealistic. Are long-term securities perfect substitutes for short-term securities? Certainly not.

Market Risk, and Reduced Liquidity. The longer the term to maturity, the greater the market risk—the more the market price of a security will drop if interest rates rise. So there is a greater **loss of liquidity** with the purchase of a long-term security. The portfolio manager who buys a long-term security and then sees market rates rise, cannot then sell that security without experiencing a capital loss.

A Risk Premium to Compensate for Market Risk. Long-term securities are likely to yield more than the average of the present and the future short-term yields. A **risk premium** must be added to induce investors to incur the additional risk (market risk) of going long-term.

If we could know with certainty the future level of short-term rates, this market risk would disappear. But with the lack of certainty which pervades the real world, market risk always must be considered.

The "Segmented Markets" and "Preferred Habitat" Theories

The fact that securities with different maturities are not perfect substitutes for each other has led to the development of the segmented markets and preferred habitat theories.

The basic idea of the segmented markets theory can be stated as follows:

> Short-term securities are a different kind of asset than long-term securities, and the two are not very close substitutes for each other. Demand and supply in the markets for long-term securities will determine long-term securities prices and yields; demand and supply in short-term markets will determine short-term securities prices and yields.

This segmented markets theory assumes the opposite from the expectations theory. The expectations theory assumes that short- and long-term securities are perfect substitutes for each other. The segmented markets theory assumes that each is separate and distinct and that *securities with different maturities are not good substitutes for each other.* Some portfolio managers may have a preference for (have a "preferred habitat" in) securities with some specific term to maturity— maybe short, maybe intermediate, or maybe long.

Contractual Intermediaries May Have a "Preferred Habitat" in Long-Term Securities. Consider the case of life insurance companies and pension funds. Their liabilities are long-term and their future obligations are known with a high degree of certainty.

If they invest in long-term securities which yield a sufficient rate to meet their known liabilities, plus a profit, then they can afford to ignore changing interest rates and market conditions in the meanwhile. With matched maturities between all of their assets and liabilities, their funds managers could relax and spend all their time on the golf course! (But don't you believe it.)

Depository Intermediaries Require a High Degree of Liquidity. For the depository intermediaries the situation is quite different. The liabilities of banks mature over short periods. Many of their liabilities are payable on demand.

This doesn't mean that bank funds managers don't buy long-term securities. But it does mean that when banks "go long" they usually require a significant "risk premium" to induce them to do so. Bank funds managers don't plan to hold long-term securities until maturity. Whenever they invest long term they are betting that interest rates will not rise (and more likely, will fall) while they are holding those securities.

All Funds Managers Try to Maximize Profits at Acceptable Risk. It is true that unforeseeable liquidity demands place a constraint on depository institution portfolio managers which life insurance and pension fund managers escape. But all portfolio managers are looking at the same financial instruments and the same financial markets. *All of them are trying to maximize profits on the portfolio without exceeding acceptable levels of risk.*

No funds manager—at a bank, insurance company, or wherever—would want to hold a large percentage of the portfolio in long-term securities while market rates are rising and long-term securities prices are falling. Conversely, it isn't likely that any funds manager—at a bank or anywhere else—would want to stay entirely invested in short-term securities during a period of falling interest rates and rising prices of long-term securities.

The bottom line: Although commerical bank funds managers are likely to have a strong preference for shorter-term maturities and life insurance and pension fund portfolio managers are likely to be more interested in longer-term maturities, these differences in their preferences aren't likely to greatly affect the shape of the yield curve.

When yields among different maturities diverge very much and potential profits are seen, funds managers will move quite readily out of their preferred segment of the market—their "preferred habitat"—and into other maturities. Why? *To try to increase the overall profitability of the investment portfolio.* Any funds manager who fails to do this, soon will be seeking another job.

The **"Preferred Habitat"**: *Ceteris Paribus, Short-term Maturities Usually Are Preferred.* You can see why some portfolio managers (e.g., at a life insurance company) may actually have a preference to hold some long-term securities. But because of market risk, *for most investors the "preferred habitat" would be in the short-term range of the yield curve.*

To induce portfolio managers to "go long," longer term instruments must pay a premium. But then how can we ever have a downward sloping yield curve? To answer that question we must fall back on the expectations theory, which says: *When interest rates are expected to fall,* supply and demand conditions in the financial markets will push short-term yields up and long-term yields down and bring a downward-sloping yield curve.

Real-World Yield Curves Result from a Combination of Forces

Any observed real-world yield curve results from a combination of—sometimes complementary and sometimes conflicting—forces. The short-term preference will always be exerting some upward pressure on long-term yields, tending to cause the curve to slope upward. Expectations of future rate changes also are constantly exerting their influence—sometimes upward, sometimes downward.

Suppose a yield curve is sloping downward because of an expected decline in future rates. The downward slope will be lessened by the upward-pushing effect of the "preferred-habitat" short-term preference.

The bottom line: The **market risk premium** of going "long" tends to keep long-term yields above short-term yields. So the effect is to decrease the downward slope of an expectations-motivated downward-sloping curve, and to increase the upward slope of an expectations-motivated upward-sloping curve.

When all of the yield-curve theories are integrated, we come to the conclusion that the yield on any long-term debt security will be determined by:

1. The average of *present short-term rates* and *expected future short-term rates* for each year during the life of the security (the expectations theory),

2. *Plus a premium* to compensate for market risk. The size of this premium will be determined by *the strength of the short-term preference.* It will be reduced to the extent that some funds managers have a preference for long-term (instead of short-term) securities.

The Supply of Securities May Have a Short-Run Effect on the Yield Curve

What you've just been reading deals with the *demand for securities* of different maturities. What about the supply side? Suppose for some reason corporations decide to raise a lot of funds by selling 5-year bonds. This will dump a great supply of 5-year bonds into the market and tend to depress their prices and push up their yields. This could result in a "humped" yield curve. The curve would slope upward to the 5-year mark, then downward after that. But how long will this "hump" last?

Asset managers very quickly will see the low prices and high yields of the 5-year securities. So they will readjust their portfolios, buying the 5-year securities and selling something else. Like water flowing to fill up an empty hole, funds tend to flow easily and quickly to the segment of the yield curve where overpriced yields (underpriced securities) are available.

The bottom line: Except for short periods of time, *it is the demand side of the securities market—the flow of funds into different maturities—which controls the shape of the yield curve.* So it is the desire (or reluctance) of funds managers to hold issues of various maturities which ultimately determines the shape of the curve.

How to "Read" the Yield Curve

When you look at a yield curve it indicates quite clearly what the financial markets are expecting regarding future interest rates:

- A **slight upward slope** would indicate that rates are expected to remain the same. The slope reflects only the risk premium.
- A **steeper upward slope** says that short-term rates are expected to rise.
- A **horizontal curve** would indicate that short-term rates are expected to move downward by just enough to offset the risk premium.
- A curve that **slopes downward** says that rates are expected to fall *by more than enough to offset the risk premium.* The greater the downward slope, the greater the expected rate decline.

THE RISK STRUCTURE OF INTEREST RATES

You already know that *riskier debt instruments must pay higher yields.* Figure 13-5 shows a graph of the yields of four different classes of long-term bonds with different degrees of risk. The **risk structure** of the yield is shown by the vertical distances between the curves.

Figure 13-5 shows that the spread between the yields has been much greater at some times than at others. During the early 1930s, Baa bond yields were much farther above Aaa bond yields than at any time before or since. And usually, triple-A corporate bond yields have not been far above government bond yields. But in the 1970s this spread increased.

Also, before the early 1940s municipal bond yields were higher than U.S. Government bond yields. But since then municipal yields have been below U.S. Government bond yields.

The following sections explain the reasons for these yield-structure changes (over time), and explain various *principles and characteristics of* **risk structure** of interest rates.

The Effect of Default Risk

One clear message from the graph in figure 13-5 is that U.S. Government bonds pay a lower yield than corporate bonds. Another is that higher grade (lower risk) corporate bonds pay lower yields than lower grade (higher risk) bonds. The reason for these differences is obvious: differences in **default risk**.

Suppose a corporation is losing market share and S&P's or Moody's decides to downgrade their bonds from Aaa to Baa. What happens? The market prices of the bonds will fall and their yields will go up. Obviously.

Figure 13-5.   The Risk Structure of Long-term Bond Yields, 1926–1987

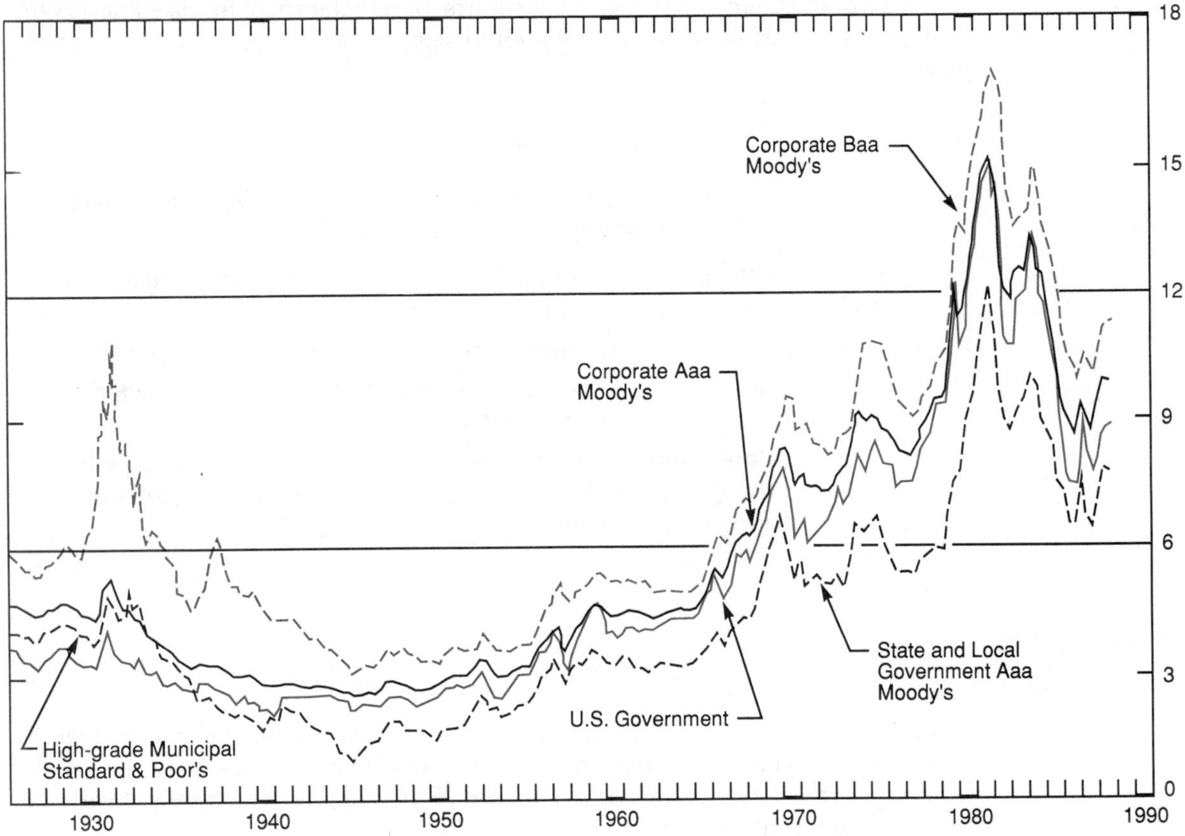

This graph shows that there is a tendency for all rates to rise and fall together, but that the spread between the yield of high grade and low grade securities increases during unsettled times. This pattern might be expected.

  Low-rated bonds are likely to perform well during times of prosperity. But if serious recession is threatening, holders of risky bonds want to sell! So they force prices down and yields up.

  The vertical distance between the yield curves on any date indicates the *risk premium* on the riskier securities, as of that date.

Source: Board of Governors of the Federal Reserve System, *1987 Historical Chart Book*, p. 97. Updated by the author from data in *The Wall Street Journal*.

But here's a different situation. Suppose the economy heads into a recession. The default risk of all corporate securities increases. Alert funds managers will shift out of corporate securities and into default-free Government securities.

  Corporate securities prices will fall and their yields will rise. Government securities prices will rise and their yields will fall. Figure 13-6 uses supply and demand graphs to illustrate this.

Less Liquid Bonds Must Pay a "Liquidity Premium"

All marketable bonds are fairly highly liquid, as compared with, for example, real estate. But some kinds of bonds are more liquid than others. U.S. Government bonds are the most liquid. They are widely traded, with large numbers of buyers

**Figure 13-6.   Increased Default Risk Brings Increased Risk
Premium on Corporate Bonds**

Panel A. The market for corporate
bonds

Panel B. The market for U.S.
government bonds

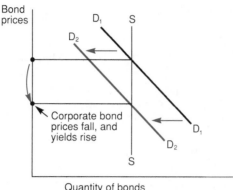

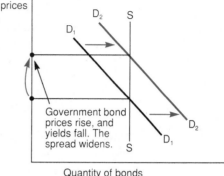

As default risk on corporate bonds
increases, demand for them decreases.
Bond prices fall and interest yields rise.

As portfolio managers shift into
U.S. government bonds, demand for them
increases. Prices rise and interest yields fall.

This graph shows what happens in the bond markets when the economic outlook turns bleak:
Demand for corporate bonds falls, their prices fall, and yields rise. Demand for default-free U.S.
Government bonds increases. Their prices rise and their yields fall.

Now you can look back at figure 13-5 and understand why, in the early 1930s, corporate Baa
bond yields were so far above the yields on U.S. government securities.

The greater the perceived default risk on a class of securities, the lower the demand and the
lower the price (and therefore the higher the yield).

The more threatening the economic outlook, the more desirable it is to find a "safe haven" in
U.S. Government securities. So the demands for Governments (and their prices) go up and their
yields come down. The risk premium between Government securities and corporate securities
widens.

and sellers. But even in the U.S. Government bond market, some of the older
issues trade in a relatively "thin" market. If the holder wanted to sell a block of
these bonds quickly it might be necessary to sell at a (slightly) depressed price.
Funds managers to whom liquidity is highly important are willing to accept
somewhat smaller yields to achieve a higher level of liquidity.

For some corporate bond issues the market is thin. A funds manager who
wanted to sell a block of such bonds quickly might take a significant loss. And
such bonds would trade at prices low enough (yields high enough) to pay a
liquidity premium. So in addition to **default risk**, the risk structure curve for
some securities must also reflect **liquidity risk**.

Effects of Tax Avoidance on Yield Structure

Suppose you could buy "bond A" on which the interest income was fully taxable—federal, state, and local—or "bond B" on which all of the income was tax

exempt. And suppose taxes are now taking more than 30% of your income. No need to ask which bond you would buy! (*Ceteris paribus* that is. But in this case the *ceteris paribus* assumption does not hold.)

Tax-Exempt (Municipal) Bonds ("Munis"). For high-tax-bracket individuals, tax exempt bonds—"munis"—are considerably more valuable than taxable-income bonds. So the prices of tax exempt bonds are bid up to where their yields are lower than yields on comparable taxable bonds.

Tax exempt bond values are significantly influenced by the level of income tax rates (federal, state, and local). The *Tax Reform Act of 1986* which lowered the maximum tax rate has had some disturbing influences on the municipal bond market. But the bond markets during 1986, '87 and '88 have shown that tax exempt bonds still have significant appeal—even when the maximum tax rate for individuals is scheduled to drop to 28%, and for corporations, to 34%. Table 13-1 illustrates the advantage of munis to high-tax-bracket individuals.

"Flower" Bonds. Munis aren't the only bonds which permit some "tax avoidance." Certain specific U.S. Treasury issues are permitted by law *to be used at par value in paying estate taxes.* The investment community refers to these bonds as **flower bonds.** Exhibit 13-1 shows one of these bonds.

Suppose your multimillionaire grandfather is ninety-four years old and would like to shift some investments in order to maximize the after-tax value of his estate and thereby leave you a larger inheritance. He might decide to sell some of his other assets and buy some "flower bonds."

Most of these bonds were issued at interest rates of less than 4% and therefore, in today's market, are selling below par. But not as far below par as if these were not flower bonds!

In the case of flower bonds, yield to maturity depends on when the owner of the bond dies. Those who buy these bonds are betting that the owner will die

Table 13-1. The Higher Your Tax Rate, the More Valuable Tax-Free Income Becomes

TAX-FREE YIELDS vs. TAXABLE EQUIVALENTS
Find your tax bracket below, and see how much your taxable investments would have to earn to keep up with tax-free yields.

	Taxable Equivalent Yield: 1988 Tax Rates		
Tax-Free Yield	28% Bracket ($28,000–39,999)	35% Bracket ($40,000–89,999)	38.5% Bracket ($90,000+)
4%	5.55%	6.15%	6.50%
5%	6.94%	7.69%	8.13%
6%	8.33%	9.23%	9.76%
7%	9.72%	10.77%	11.38%

(Based on joint federal tax brackets. Salary figures represent adjusted gross income).

This table indicates, for example, that a tax-free yield of 7% would be worth 10.77% to a person whose tax rate was 35%. It's obvious why the tax-exempt feature causes the prices of municipal bonds to be bid up, and their yields, down.

Exhibit 13-1   A "Flower Bond" with Three Coupons Attached

This is a U.S. Treasury bond paying a coupon of 3-1/2%. It was issued October 30, 1960 and the due date is November 15, 1998.

DATED OCTOBER 30, 1960   **DUE NOVEMBER 15, 1998**

The fine print says: "This bond, upon the death of the owner will be redeemed—at par (if) the proceeds are to be applied to the payment of federal estate taxes. . . .

Source: Edward J. McCarthy, *Reserve Position: Methods of Adjustment,* Federal Reserve Bank of Boston, 1964, p. 39.

Feature: **An Exaggerated Example of the Tax
Advantage of "Flower Bonds"**

Suppose with the help of his accountant-tax advisor, your uncle buys flower bonds paying a coupon of 3.5% which, because of the low yield, are selling for only $650 per $1,000 of face value. Your uncle buys bonds with face value of $100,000 for a cost of $65,000. Then your uncle dies next week.

The administrator of your uncle's estate uses the flower bonds to pay your uncle's estate taxes, which happen to come to exactly $100,000. So the bonds, which in the market are only worth $65,000, suddenly became worth $100,000 when used to pay estate taxes.

And you, the lucky heir, gained $35,000 by your uncle's timely and thoughtful move!

There are always wealthy elderly people who would like to minimize their estate taxes. So the demand for flower bonds is considerably higher than it would be without this estate-tax-payment feature. That's why the amount of savings shown in this example is exaggerated. The strong demand for the bonds pushes up market prices and pushes down yields to where most of the potential advantage is eliminated.

before the maturity date, and that therefore the yield to maturity will be higher than if the owner had survived until maturity. So the effect of the special estate-tax provision is to raise the prices and lower the current yields on these bonds.

Low-Coupon Bonds. Another tax avoidance opportunity—one which seems to have been eliminated by the *Tax Reform Act of 1986*—has resulted from the lower tax rates on income from capital gains. An investor who buys a low-interest bond at a sharp discount from its face value and then holds the bond until maturity, receives a large capital gain at maturity.

In the past, capital gains income has been taxed at only 40% of the rate charged on ordinary income—e.g., interest income. So bond-buyers looking for maximum after-tax "yield to maturity" have pushed up the prices and pushed down the yields of low-coupon bonds because of this capital gains consideration. The effect has been to raise the prices (lower the yields to maturity) on low-interest-paying bonds.

Summary of Effects of Default Risk, Liquidity Risk, and Tax Avoidance Considerations

The so-called "risk structure" of interest rates involves more than just "default-risk." There are, in fact, three factors involved: The risk of default, the liquidity risk, and the opportunity to avoid taxes. The effect of each of these factors is just as your common sense would tell you.

The greater the default risk, the higher the **risk premium**—that is, the extra yield over the yield of a default-free bond. The less easily marketable (less liquid) a bond, the higher the **liquidity premium**—the extra yield over the yield of a highly liquid bond. And a bond which permits its owner to avoid taxes will pay a lower yield—how much lower will depend on the extent of the tax benefits conveyed by the bond.

SUMMARY

- The yield on each security is always influenced by *perceived degree of risk* and *term to maturity.*

- *The term structure of interest rates* refers to the different yields available on debt instruments of different maturities. A positively sloped curve shows that short-term rates are lower than long-term; a negatively sloped curve shows that short-term rates are higher than long-term.

- Longer term securities require a **market risk premium**. So the yield curve tends to slope upward.

- Expected changes in short-term rates cause long-term rates to move in the same direction. So *expectations of rising rates* will bring a steeply rising yield curve as the *expectations effect* plus the *market risk premium* push upward on long-term yields.

- *Expectations of sharply falling rates* can more than offset the market risk premium, push down long-term yields and push up short-term yields and produce a negatively sloped yield curve.

- The idea of the **segmented markets** theory is that some portfolio managers prefer either short-term or long-term securities and do not consider these to be very close substitutes for each other. The **preferred habitat** theory refers to the "maturity preferences" of portfolio managers.

- Most portfolio managers would prefer to hold short-term securities to avoid market risk.

- Except for short periods of time, it is the demand side of the securities market (the supply side of the loanable funds market) which controls the shape of the yield curve.

- *The risk structure* of interest rates shows the different yields on securities which carry different (perceived) degrees of risk.

- During times of economic downturn, the spread between default-free government bonds and corporate bonds increases, and more for lower grade than for the higher grade bonds.

- In addition to default risk, the "risk structure" is also influenced by *the liquidity* of the security, and by *any tax benefits* conveyed.

- Yield curves convey significant information about economic conditions and about the outlook for inflation and interest rates.

Important Principles, Issues, Concepts Terms

"The structure of interest rates"

Term structure

Risk structure

Historical yield curves in the U.S. financial markets

Unstable yield curves of the early 1980s

Effects of the following on term-structure yield curves:
   -market risk of falling bond prices

   -expectations of rising rates
   -expectations of falling rates

How expected future short-term rates affect present long-term rates

Segmented markets theory

Maturity preferences of different intermediaries

Preferred habitat theory

How to construct a yield curve

How to "read" a yield curve

Causes of a downward-sloping yield curve

Effect of the demand for funds (supply of securities) on the yield curve

Effect of default risk on risk structure

Effect of liquidity on risk structure

Effect of tax considerations on risk structure

Municipal bonds ("munis")

Flower bonds

Low-coupon bonds

Questions

1. State a precise definition for (a) the term structure of interest rates, and (b) the risk structure of interest rates.

2. There has been significant variability in the term structure yield curve in the U.S. financial markets. Describe some of the characteristics of this variability, and then explain some of the reasons why this variability has occurred.

3. If you look in the Tuesday *Wall Street Journal* in the "Key Interest Rates" box you will see that T-bills have a lower yield than any of the other money market instruments of the same maturity. Explain why this is true.

4. Also in the "Key Interest Rates" box in the *Wall Street Journal* you will notice that T-bills have a lower interest rate than any of the T-notes or bonds. Explain why this is true.

5. Suppose the term-structure yield curve for U.S. Government securities indicates that short-term rates are over 10% and long-term rates are less than 8%. Does this downward-sloping yield curve tell you anything? And if so, what? And how reliable is this message?

6. Contractual intermediaries are likely to be more interested than depository intermediaries in holding longer-term maturities. Why? How strong do you thing these term-to-maturity preferences would be? Discuss.

7. Tax rates on both individual and corporate income were significantly reduced by the 1986 Tax Reform Act. What effect do you think this has had (if any) on the prices and yields of: Municipal bonds? Treasury bonds? Zero-coupon bonds? Flower bonds?

8. Explain how the estate of a wealthy elderly person may be able to benefit by investing in "flower bonds."

9. Suppose the economy is now moving into a serious recession. Would you prefer to be holding government bonds? Or corporate bonds? Explain why.

Suggested Readings

Benninga, S. and Protopapadakis, A. "General Equilibrium Properties of the Term Structure of Interest Rates." *Journal of Finance and Economics* 16 (3). (July 1986), 389–410.

Cook, Timothy Q., and Thomas A. Lawler. "The Behavior of the Spread Between Treasury Bill Rates and Private Money Market Rates Since 1978." *Economic Review*. Federal Reserve Bank of Richmond (November/December 1983), 3–15.

Fisher, Irving. *The Theory of Interest Rates*. New York: Augustus M. Kelley, 1965. This is a classic in interest rate theory, originally published in 1930.

Kane, Edward J., and Burton G. Malkiel. "The Term Structure of Interest Rates: An Analysis of a Survey of Interest-Rate Expectations." *Review of Economics and Statistics*. (August 1967), 343–55.

McCafferty, S. "Aggregate Demand and Interest Rates: A Macroeconomic Approach to the Term Structure." *Economic Inquiry* 24 (4). (October 1986), 521–33.

Meek, Paul. *U.S. Monetary Policy and Financial Markets*. Federal Reserve Bank of New York, 1982.

Modigliani, Franco, and Richard Sutch. "The Term Structure of Interest Rates: A Reexamination of the Evidence." *Journal of Money, Credit, and Banking*. (February 1969), 112–120.

Nelson, Charles R. *The Term Structure of Interest Rates*. New York: Basic Books, 1972.

Wood, John H. "Do Yield Curves Normally Slope Up? The Term Structure of Interest Rates, 1862–1982." *Economic Perspectives*. The Federal Reserve Bank of Chicago (May/June, 1985). 18–22.

PART IV

Portfolio Theory and Commercial Banking: The Lending Function, and The Management of Assets, Liabilities and Capital

ONE way to think of a bank is: "a portfolio of assets, owned by (or owed to) the bank's depositors." Banks obtain money from their depositors and then use this money to acquire assets. Part IV goes into some detail on exactly how all of this happens.

In what forms should a bank hold its portfolio of assets? And what are the principles which guide these portfolio choices? You'll be reading a lot about that in this part. Chapter 14 focuses on asset management: **the principles of portfolio choice**.

The most important kind of asset of the typical bank is loans. Successful lending and successful loan portfolio management makes for a successful bank. In fact the key to the success of any bank is: a sound and profitable loan portfolio. So in this part you will be reading a lot about **bank lending**.

After you understand the lending process, then you'll read about how banks manage their **asset portfolios**. After that (in Chapter 17) you'll be reading about how banks manage their **liabilities and capital**. Here you will find out about the different kinds of deposits and other liabilities, and about the nature and importance of the capital account. Then if you read the appendix to Chapter 17 you'll find out about the importance of and techniques banks (and others) use to manage (reduce) **interest rate risk**.

When you finish studying Part IV you will have a good overview understanding of what banks are, what they do, and how they do it.

CHAPTER 14

Asset Management and Intelligent Investing: The Principles of Portfolio Choice

Chapter Objectives

Everyone who has any assets must choose the forms in which to hold those assets. The successful portfolio manager (asset-holder) makes these choices on the basis of **the principles of portfolio choice**. That's what you'll be reading about in this chapter.

When you complete your study of this chapter you will understand and be able to explain:

1. The kinds of **asset choices** people must make, and the importance of the **risk vs. reward** trade-off.

2. The basic idea of and different degrees of **risk aversion**.

3. The meaning and importance of an **efficient portfolio** and its advantages for investors, borrowers, and the economy.

4. How variability of returns creates risk, and how this risk can be reduced by **diversification**.

5. How to calculate
   a. the expected return on a variable-return asset, and
   b. the variance between the returns on two variable-return assets.

6. The importance of choosing assets with **negative covariance**, and the difficulty of finding such assets.

7. How **portfolio management** turns out to be a continuing exercise in **opportunity cost analysis**.

ALLOCATING YOUR WEALTH: WHICH ASSETS TO HOLD?

Everybody has some wealth. Maybe it's just the clothes you wear and the 37 cents in your pocket—not a lot of wealth, to be sure. But it's wealth nevertheless. Most people have a little more wealth than that. So their decisions about what to do with their wealth—about what assets to hold—are a little more complex than yours.

All of a Person's Assets Are "Wealth"

Your personal wealth consists of the sum of all of your *assets*. It includes every-thing from the jug of milk in your refrigerator and the sweaters in your closet to your flashy little sports car (or the old clunker) in the parking lot.

All of us hold some of our wealth in the form of "utility-producing" assets to satisfy our daily needs and wants. Only when we get beyond these **consumer assets** do we have some wealth left over to be "held in inventory"—hopefully to be "stored" in **income-earning assets**.

Many Asset Choices Are Available

When you get some discretionary wealth, what do you do with it? Hold it in cash? Checkable deposits? Savings deposits? Bonds? Stocks? Or what? How do you decide among all of the possibilities? If you decide intelligently you will decide according to **the principles of portfolio choice**. (See box 14-1.)

Your own "portfolio of assets" is the list of everything that you own. It includes all of the items listed on the asset side of **your own personal balance sheet**. Figure 14-1 shows the personal balance sheet of "Typical Student #1" (TS-1). Take a minute to study that balance sheet. Compare your own portfolio of assets (and your liabilities and net worth) with that of TS-1.

Suppose you happen to have exactly the same balance sheet as TS-1. Then you have some choices about how to hold your wealth.

The first six items on the balance sheet are consumer goods. But if you really wanted to there are some things that you could sell. Then you could shift the money into items seven or eight (books, tuition, etc.)—your "long-range capital expenditures"—or you could shift the money into items 9–12 and perhaps earn more income.

Box 14-1

Question: What's the Difference between Portfolio Choice and Asset Demand?

This body of principles relating to portfolio choice is also referred to as **the theory of asset demand**. But when this terminology is used, the word "demand" refers to a *stock*, not a flow. "Asset demand" refers to the quantity of each of various assets which the portfolio manager would prefer to hold "in inventory" in the port-folio.

There is nothing wrong with using the term "demand" to refer to a *stock*. As explained pre-viously, economists use the term "demand" to refer to a stock in the phrase "demand for money." But when this is done, unless the "stocks vs. flows" distinction is made very clear, the results are likely to be confusing. For this reason the terminology chosen for use in this book is **the theory of portfolio choice** —not the theory of **asset demand**. But you should be familiar with both terms and know that both have the same meaning.

Figure 14-1. Personal Balance Sheet of "Typical Student #1" (TS-1)

Assets		Liabilities	
1. car	$4,000	auto loan balance	$ 500
2. clothes	600	credit card balance	350
3. stereo, T.V., etc.	600	student loan balance	1,000
4. other equipment	400		
5. furniture	400		
6. miscellaneous	300		
7. prepaid tuition	600		
8. books, school supplies	200		
9. 20 shares Exxon stock from Aunt Martha	800		
10. savings account	600	Total Liabilities	$1,850
11. checking account	200		
12. cash	50		
Total Assets	$8,750	A − L = Net Worth	$6,900

Items 9–12 are your "portfolio of financial assets." If you are a very frugal person you may be trying to add to your total stock of financial assets. The good thing about having financial assets is that you can earn income on those assets—*income that you don't have to work for.*

Which Financial (Or Other Income-Earning) Assets to Hold?

The principles of portfolio choice are concerned with how to choose the specific income earning assets to hold in your portfolio. Suppose your're TS-1. Right now you're holding Exxon stock, a savings account, a checking account, and cash. Is this the right combination?—the best portfolio of financial assets *for you?* That all depends on your individual circumstances, preferences, philosophy, outlook, etc.

Think big. The possibilities are almost unlimited—stocks, bonds, mutual funds, CDs, etc., etc. And the assets don't have to be financial. You can invest in real estate, paintings, antique cars or any number of things. How do you decide? You follow **the principles of portfolio choice**.

But before we get into that, if your balance sheet really does look like that of TS-1, stop reading this chapter *right now!* Go to the bank and take $350 out of your savings account (on which your're probably earning less than 6% interest) and pay off your credit card balance (on which you're probably paying more than 15%).

PRINCIPLES OF PORTFOLIO CHOICE: COMMON SENSE, PLUS MORE

Every reasonably intelligent and informed member of the general public already knows the most basic principles of portfolio choice. Ask anybody why they do what they do with their assets, and they'll tell you.

Man-on-the-Street Comments: "Common Sense" Principles of Portfolio Choice

First person: "I keep my money in $20 bills in a shoebox in the closet. That way I can look at the money every day. I know it's perfectly safe, and I can spend it anytime I want to. The safety and complete liquidity are more important to me than any earnings I might make by depositing the money, or investing it."

Second person: "I keep my money in a savings account where I can earn some interest, but I don't buy CDs because I want to be able to get my money anytime I want to, with no penalties and no hassles. The extra interest I could earn on the CD would't be worth it to me."

Third person: "I keep my money in government bonds because it pays a pretty good return, and I know that it's safe. And I can sell the bonds whenever I want to if I need the money. I get a reasonable income, plus safety and liquidity."

Fourth person: "I keep my money in the stocks of major corporations that have a record of good growth and earnings. That way I earn some dividends, and I'm pretty sure that the value of the stocks will keep going up as the companies grow. Also, if there's inflation the stock prices ought to go up enough to keep me from losing too much of the purchasing power of my savings. I hold stock in several companies, so that if any one of them gets hit by hard times, I won't get wiped out."

Fifth person: "I put my money in real estate. I keep my eye on the real estate market in my local area, and whenever I see someone trying to sell a piece of land at a bargain I buy it. I know that real estate isn't very liquid—I might not be able to sell it in a hurry without taking a loss—but I don't expect to need the liquidity. The population is growing all the time, but we aren't making any more land. So land prices are going to rise. Also, if we have inflation I'll be protected because the value of my land probably will go up at least as much as the inflation rate."

Sixth person: "I put my money into a carefully selected group of the "penny stocks" of several small, little known corporations. I know that some of these corporations are going to do well. Maybe I will be lucky and hold stock in one of the big winners and strike it rich! I know that I might lose my savings by investing this way. But I have a good job and a good income and in view of the possible rewards, I'm willing to take the risk."

Seventh person: "I have worked hard for my savings, and I don't want to lose this money. But I like to earn a fairly good income, and I don't mind taking a few chances. I hold some stocks—mostly blue chips, but a few risky ones—some government bonds, and some medium grade municipal bonds because they pay a relatively high tax-free income. I also hold some mutual fund shares, a few CDs, a money-market-rate savings account, and an interest-paying checking account. My objective is to earn both income and capital gains. I want a high degree of safety for most of my assets. But I like to hold a few risky ones with chances of big gains, just to keep a little excitement in my life!"

Most People Understand the "Risk vs. Reward" Trade-Off

All of the above hypothetical "man-on-the-street" comments illustrate an understanding of the basic principles of portfolio choice. All of those individuals understand that there is a trade-off between earnings, and safety and liquidity. And most people also seem to understand that as the risk on an asset increases, that asset must pay a higher *expected return*. But, as you'll be finding out soon, there's more to portfolio theory than can be found in the common sense understanding of the general public.

On an Investment, Risk Means Uncertainty (Variability) of Returns

All financial assets offer future returns: income, principal, capital gains, whatever. On any asset, risk is the *lack of certainty* regarding these future returns.

Suppose the amounts and timing of the real returns on an asset are absolutely certain. Then the degree of risk is zero. But as the amounts and timing of the future returns become less certain, the asset becomes more risky. So throughout this discussion, think of **risk** as **lack of certainty** regarding the amounts and timing of future returns.

RISK AVERSION AND THE OBJECTIVES OF PORTFOLIO MANAGEMENT

Most people are **risk averse**—i.e., *ceteris paribus*, would prefer to avoid risk. But some are more risk averse than others. In the quotes you were reading a minute ago you saw examples of different degrees of risk aversion. But *all of those people were risk averse.*

Greater Risk Requires Greater Potential Rewards

You might suggest that the penny-stock investor was not very risk averse. Not *very*, true. But even that investor is investing in the penny stocks of many different companies to reduce the risk of getting wiped out. And, remember, that investor is trying (and hoping) to strike it rich!

Risk aversion doesn't mean that a person is unwilling to incur risk. It only means that *the enticement of expected rewards* must be great enough to overcome the risk aversion. In general, the potential return must be high enough so that in "win or lose" situations, on the average the wins are expected to more than offset the losses.

Portfolio Objectives: More Income at Same Risk, or Same Income at Less Risk

The principles of portfolio choice are concerned with answering one of these questions.
EITHER:

1. Given an investor's willingness to bear a certain amount of risk, what are the most effective techniques of portfolio choice for *maximizing the income of the portfolio given that degree of risk?*

OR:

2. Given an investor's desire to achieve a certain amount of income from the portfolio, what are the most effective techniques of portfolio choice for *minimizing the degree of risk of the portfolio, given that amount of income?"*

Of course, most investors don't really have a set, precise "degree of risk" they are willing to accept, or "size of income" they must achieve. With most investors, both of these objectives are variable.

The Ultimate Objective: An Efficient Portfolio

An **efficient portfolio** is one which produces the greatest possible income for a given level of risk, or conversely, the lowest possible risk for a given amount of income. How do you achieve it? By diversification, with careful selection of the component assets.

Efficient Portfolios Benefit Investors. The most efficient portfolio is one in which the assets are related to each other in such a way that economic circumstances which bring the *worst results* to one group of the assets, simultaneously bring the *best results* to another group of the assets. In such a portfolio, the risks of one group of assets cancel or offset the risks of the other group.

An efficient portfolio would be constructed of assets with significant risk. But the portfolio would be much less risky than any one of its component assets. Such a portfolio would permit the owner to enjoy the higher returns available on more risky assets, and without having to bear the higher risk.

Efficient Portfolios Benefit Borrowers, and the Economy. Also, consider this. Profit-seeking portfolio managers who are building efficient portfolios, demand more higher-risk securities. This bids up the prices and bids down the yields.

The result? Lower financing costs for borrowers. And that holds down production costs and the rate of inflation, and increases productivity and standards of living. The development of efficient portfolios is good for everybody!

A Simple Hypothetical Example of Portfolio Choices by a Risk Averter

Basic fact: On any asset, risk is positively related to *the uncertainty of future returns*. The greater the uncertainty, the greater the risk.

Suppose you were choosing between two investments. On one you would receive a definite and certain return of 9%. On the other you would have an equal chance of earning either 6% or 12%. Which would you choose? Most people (risk averters) would choose the certain return of 9%.

A person who was not very risk averse (someone feeling very lucky!) might choose the variable return. With a 50-50 chance of earning either 6% or 12%, *on the average* an investor would come out with 9%. But on a *one shot deal* the investor who took the variable rate would be taking a chance of coming out with either 6% or 12%.

Any thoughtful risk averter would prefer to have the certain 9% return. Why? Because (on the average) there's no reward for taking on the added risk of the uncertain return. What would it take to get a risk averter to choose the uncertain rate instead of the certain rate? You know the answer: A perceived chance to (on the average) beat the 9% rate. But sometimes risk-averters gamble. Box 14-2 discusses that.

Box 14-2

Question: How Is It Possible That Gamblers Could Be Risk Averters?

Suppose someone throws down a $10 bill and says: "Cover that, and I'll match you for it!" You say, "Right on!" You throw down you $10 and proceed to flip a coin.

In this instance, you and your friend are not risk averters. In fact, you are both *risk seekers*—at least, you are risk seekers up to a total amount of $10. But what if your friend had thrown down a $100 bill? Would you cover it? Ten $100 bills? The title to a car? The deed to a house?

There's a certain amount of excitement involved in taking a risk. Many people seek this excitement, hoping for "the big win." But, except for a few compulsive gamblers, most of us

carefully limit the amount of our assets we are willing to "put on the line" and risk losing.

For almost all of us, when it comes to our annual salary, our personal property, our total savings, etc.—we are risk averters. This doesn't mean that none of these assets will ever be placed at risk. It only means that any risks taken must seem to offer a better than 50-50 chance of reward.

How many of the people in the gambling casinos in Las Vegas or Atlantic City or Nassau or Monte Carlo do you suppose have insurance on their house? And their car? I'd bet almost all of them do. Risk averters? Yes.

Greater Potential Rewards Can Justify Greater Risk

Suppose you had to choose between a security offering a certain return of 9% (Asset A) and one offering an equal chance of a return of either 6% or 14% (Asset B). Now there is some incentive to take the risk. With an even chance of a return of either 6% or 14%, the average return would be 10% (6% + 14% = 20% ÷ 2 = 10%).

The risk-taker in this case would receive, on the average, a 10% return. This higher average return would convince some risk averters to choose the uncertain returns of Asset B. But others would not choose it. It would depend partly on the degree of risk aversion of the individual investor, and *very significantly on the extent of and kinds of diversification within the investor's total portfolio of assets.*

Diversification Can Significantly Reduce Risk

If you could buy a large number of these variable-return (Asset B) securities—and if the 50-50 chance of the 6% or 14% return on each one was *independent* of what was happening with the others— then the "law of averages" (statistical probability) would guarantee you a constant and dependable return of 10% on those securities. Now you can see the advantage of focusing on a **portfolio of assets** as a method of reducing the risks which exist on individual assets.

The risk of any one individual asset in the portfolio isn't the significant consideration. The important question is: "How does the risk (uncertainty of return) of this asset affect the risk (expected certainty or variability of return) of the total portfolio?" The answer to this question, quite obviously, depends on the *kinds of variability of the returns on the various assets in the portfolio.*

When Asset Returns Move Together, Diversification Doesn't Help

Suppose that all of the assets in the portfolio have an equal chance of returning either 6% or 14%. Now assume that these returns tend to move together. In a year when one asset is paying 14%, they will all pay 14%; when one pays 6%, they all pay 6%. Then what good is this kind of diversification? No good. The returns always move together. This is a very risky portfolio.

What about the opposite case? Suppose a portfolio could be selected in which, when one-half of the assets were paying 6%, the other half would be paying 14%. This kind of "offsetting variability" would greatly reduce the riskiness of the portfolio. In fact, if you could be sure that the returns on the assets would always move to exactly offset each other, then all of the risk of the variable returns would be eliminated.

The Objective: Maximum Negative Covariance

Now you have the key to the theory of portfolio choice. Try to choose assets on which the returns move in opposite directions. During times when some assets are weak, that weakness will be offset by strength in other assets.

This approach reduces your chances for either big losses or big gains. You will never be a "big winner." Whenever some of your assets are setting the world on fire, your other (offsetting) assets will be holding down the total return of your portfolio. But neither will you ever be a big loser. When some of your assets are performing very poorly, others will be booming.

A relatively risk-free portfolio is one in which the assets in the portfolio have a high degree of **negative covariance**: The returns on different assets tend to move in opposite directions so that weaknesses in some will be offset by strength in others.

CALCULATING THE EXPECTED RETURN OF AN ASSET

There are some statistical techniques which are helpful in analyzing variability, correlation, and covariance. These techniques can be very helpful in assessing risk, and therefore in making precise decisions regarding portfolio choice.

The "Expected Return" Formula

For each individual asset under consideration, *the average expected return* (R^e) can be calculated by adding up all of *the possible realized returns* (R^r) multiplied by *the probability* (p) that each of those possible realized returns (R^r) will actually occur—i.e., the probability that each of those *possible* realized returns *will actually be realized.* Here's the formula:

$$R^e = p_1 \times R^r_1 + p_2 \times R^r_2 + p_3 \times R^r_3 + \ldots + p_n \times R^r_n$$

Where

R^e = the size of the expected rate of return (the return which, on the average, over the long run, the holder of this security would be expected to receive).

R^r = the size of this "possible realized rate of return." (The size of this realized return which actually will occur some percentage of the time.)

p = the probability that this "possible realized rate of return" will actually occur. (The percentage of the time that this *specific realized return* actually *will be realized*.)

What this formula says is this:
The return which you can *confidently expect* (on the average) will be equal to:

the sum of each of the possible returns which might be realized, where *each of the possible returns is weighted by the statistical probability that it will actually occur.* You can see that the expected return (R^e) is the *weighted* mean of all the "possible realized returns" (R_1^r, R_2^r, ..., R_n^r) which might occur.

An Example Using the Formula

In the case discussed previously there is a security which offers an equal chance of a return of either 6% or 14%. Since there's a 50-50 chance of either return, the probability that each of the possible returns will actually occur, is one-half (0.5).

$$R^e = 0.5 \times 6\% + 0.5 \times 14\%$$

$$R^e = 3\% + 7\% = 10\%$$

This example shows that when the probability of each return is one-half, the result is the simple arithmetic mean (the average) of the two returns which might be realized. For this problem you didn't even need the formula. But for an asset with a broad range of possible returns and a different probability of each, the formula would be very helpful.

Increased Variance Brings Increased Risk

In the above example you know that this security has an expected return of 10%—but that's "on the average." At any particular time the return could be as low as 6% or as high as 14%. And this *variance* in the return from one time to another makes this asset more risky than an asset with a certain return of 10% all the time.

As a general statement you can say that, *ceteris paribus,* the greater the variance, the greater the risk. In fact, *the variance of the return on an asset* is one frequently used *measure of the risk of the asset.* In statistical terminology, variance is calculated as the square of the standard deviations of the returns from the average—from the arithmetic mean.

Since the mean is the "expected return" (R^e in the above formula), it's easy enough to calculate the deviations. Just subtract the mean from each of the returns which might be realized (each R^r). For example:

$$\text{The deviation of } R_1^r = R_1^r - R^e;$$

$$\text{of } R_2^r = R_2^r - R^e$$

$$\text{of } R_n^r = R_n^r - R^e$$

In the case we are talking about, the mean (R^e) is 10%. We are sure that the individual realized return (R^r) is going to be either (R_1^r) 6% or (R_2^r) 14%. So we know that the deviation from the mean in all instances is going to be exactly 4 percentage points—either minus four or plus four—from the mean. ($6 - 10 = -4$;

14 − 10 = 4). So in this case the standard deviation (usual symbol, small sigma: σ) is exactly 4. In real-world analysis the numbers would be more complex. But exactly the same principles would apply.[1]

How to Calculate the Variance (V)

The reason Asset B is more risky than Asset A is because of the greater variance of return on Asset B. For Asset B the variance of the realized returns (R^r) from the average expected return (R^e) is greater. And the greater the variance of returns, the greater the risk. So how do we calculate the variance?

Statistically, variance is defined as *the sum of the squared deviations, where each deviation is weighted by (multiplied by) the probability of its occurrence.* When the numbers are squared the minuses are eliminated, of course. The formula:

$$V = \sigma^2 = p_1 \times (R_1^r - R^e)^2 + p_2 \times (R_2^r - R^e)^2 + \ldots + p_n \times (R_n^r - R^e)^2$$

What this formula says is that the variance (V) is equal to the sum of the squared deviations where each deviation is weighted by (multiplied by) the probability of its occurrence.

In the case of Asset A (on which the return is always a certain 9%), average expected return and actual return would always be the same. So $R^r - R^e$ would always be zero. So there would be no deviation from the mean, and no variance.

For Asset B, for which R^r will be either 6% or 14% with a 50-50 chance (0.5 probability) of each, average expected return (R^e, as calculated previously) would be 10%. The variance would be calculated as follows:

$$V = \sigma^2 = p_1 \times (R_1^r - R^e)^2 + p_2 \times (R_2^r - R^e)^2$$

$$= 0.5 \times (6 - 10)^2 + 0.5 \times (14 - 10)^2$$

$$= .05 \times (-4)^2 + .05 \times (4)^2$$

$$= .05 \times 16 + .05 \times 16$$

$$V = \sigma^2 = 8 + 8 = 16$$

The calculation shows that the income on Asset B has a variance of 16. So it is a more risky asset than Asset A on which the variance is zero.

Suppose you are considering a third asset (Asset C) which will bring a return of 4% half of the time and 16% the other half of the time. For Asset C the average expected return (R^e) is the same as for Asset B: 10%. But the variance of the income is greater. Therefore the degree of risk of Asset C would be greater. For Asset C:

$$V = \sigma^2 = 0.5 \times (4 - 10)^2 + .05 \, (16 - 10)^2$$

$$= 0.5 \times (-6)^2 + 0.5 \times (6)^2$$

$$= 0.5 \times 36 + 0.5 \times 36$$

$$V = \sigma^2 = 18 + 18 = 36$$

---

[1] The usual formula for calculating the standard deviation involves squaring the individual deviations (which eliminates the minus signs), adding them up, and then taking the square root. If you do that, in this case, you'll come out with 4. When the numbers get complex, it would be advisable for you to do it the long way.

The figures show that the variance of the return on Asset C is 36, confirming more precisely the intuitive conclusion that Asset C is more risky than Asset B.

Faced with an opportunity to hold Asset A, B, or C, if average expected returns on all three are identical, Asset A will be chosen. Only when expected returns on B are larger than on A will Asset B be held. And only when expected returns on Asset C are larger than on B, will Asset C be held.

How much more would the expected return need to be on Asset B? Or on Asset C? That depends on considerations mentioned previously:

1. the extent of risk aversion of the portfolio manager, and

2. the size of the total portfolio and the extent of *effective diversification*.

The extent of effective diversification depends on the portfolio manager's ability to find and hold assets on which the returns do not tend to move in the same direction at the same time. The preferred assets are (a) those on which the returns tend to move independently of each other, or even more preferred (b) those on which the returns tend to move in opposite directions—i.e., assets which exhibit **negative covariance**.

Examples of Negative Covariance: Returns Move in Opposite Directions

Portfolio managers are always seeking pairs or groups of assets on which the returns exhibit negative covariance. With such assets they can reduce total portfolio risk. It isn't always easy to find such pairs or groups of assets, but some real-world cases of negative covariance do exist.

Airline Stocks vs. Oil Stocks. In December of 1986 the OPEC members got together and agreed to cut production and to fix the price of oil at about $18 a barrel. The price had been down as low as $10 in the previous months. At the time of the announcement, oil stocks and oil drilling stocks went up. Airline stocks went down.

Higher oil prices mean higher future profits for oil companies and for oil drilling companies. But for airlines higher oil prices mean higher fuel costs and lower profits.

Throughout the first three months of 1987 there were alternating signs regarding the future viability of the December 1986 OPEC accord. Each time the OPEC accord seemed likely to break, oil stocks were weak. Airline stocks were strong. Each time the accord seemed likely to hold, oil stocks were strong. Airline stocks were weak. If you were a risk-averse portfolio manager this information might give you some ideas.

Is it possible to reduce the risk of holding oil stocks by also holding airline stocks? Or the risk of holding airline stocks by also holding oil stocks? To some extent, yes. But there will still be significant risk in your portfolio. If the economy goes into a serious recession, you can guess what will happen to both oil stocks and airline stocks—down they will go. Box 14-3 illustrates the relationship between oil stocks and airline stocks.

What About Airline Stocks vs. Bus Company Stocks?. If you are concerned about the likelihood of recession, you might want to hold some stocks in a bus company,

Box 14-3

Feature: Oil Stocks and Airline Stocks Have Some Negative
Covariance—But It Certainly Isn't Perfect!

Oil, Technology Issues, Lead Rally
As Industrials
Jump 36.36 to High
ABREAST OF THE MARKET

By Beatrice E. Garcia

Oil-related and technology issues led a powerful rally that carried stock prices to records.

The Dow Jones Industrial Average sprinted ahead 36.36 points to close at 2284.80, surpassing its high of 2280.23 established March 6.

...

The strong gains in most oil stocks gave a boost to the industrial average and the S&P 500-stock index, and there was strong demand in the futures market yesterday for contracts based on the S&P index.

Yesterday's rally took many traders and analysts by surprise, since most had expected institutional investors to stay out of the market this week to avoid the wild price gyrations that often accompany the expiration of stock-index futures, index options and individual stock options. March contracts in all three categories will expire Friday afternoon.

Volume on the Big Board rose to 177.3 million shares from 134.9 million Monday as gainers swamped decliners by a 2-to-1 margin.

...

Interest rates declined slightly, despite the continued rise in oil prices. Bond market traders were betting that the oil price rally will be short-lived and they remained somewhat skeptical about the health of the economy. They also took comfort in comments by Treasury Secretary James Baker, who said a recent meeting of big industrialized nations "should foster more stability in exchange rates around their current values."

The oil stock rally that began quietly Monday afternoon exploded yesterday. Among the gainers were Exxon, up $2\frac{1}{4}$ to $84\frac{3}{8}$; Standard Oil,

up $2\frac{1}{2}$ to $64\frac{3}{4}$; Atlantic Richfield, up $3\frac{1}{2}$ to $78\frac{3}{4}$; Chevron up $1\frac{3}{4}$ to $55\frac{1}{2}$; Pennzoil, up 3 to $81\frac{3}{4}$; Texaco, up $\frac{7}{8}$ to 35; British Petroleum, up $1\frac{5}{8}$ to 54; and Royal Dutch Petroleum, up $2\frac{3}{8}$ to $114\frac{7}{8}$.

...

The recent gains in crude oil prices have been fueled by increasing signs that OPEC is holding down oil production. Sanford Margoshes, an oil industry analyst with Shearson Lehman Brothers in New York, added that oil inventories are being drawn down without depressing prices.

Barry Good, who follows the oil industry at Morgan Stanley, said "it looks like we have a buying panic" in the oil stocks. He said that these stocks aren't widely owned by many portfolio managers. So, any money manager who hopes to beat the performance of the S&P 500 and all the portfolios that are patterned on this index will have to buy some of these shares pretty quickly.

...

The stocks of oil service companies moved right along with the oil producers. Halliburton rose 3 to $34\frac{5}{8}$, Dresser International gained $\frac{7}{8}$ to $27\frac{7}{8}$, Schlumberger rose 2 to $39\frac{3}{8}$, Baker International added $1\frac{5}{8}$ to $17\frac{3}{8}$, and Hughes Tool gained $1\frac{1}{2}$ to $13\frac{3}{4}$.

Airline stocks, usually hurt by the higher cost of energy, were spared a beating. Some registered minor gains, while USAir fell 1 to $44\frac{1}{4}$.

The Wall Street Journal Wednesday, March 18, 1987 p. **63**. Reprinted by permission.

thinking that when times are bad people buy bus tickets instead of airline tickets. At times in the past that seemed to be true. But now, with careful planning a person can travel by air about as cheaply—sometimes even more cheaply—than by bus. So that instance of negative covariance doesn't seem to exist anymore.

PERFECT NEGATIVE COVARIANCE COULD ELIMINATE THE RISK OF UNCERTAIN RETURNS

The benefits of *negative covariance* are obvious. A portfolio built with assets on which the returns exhibit negative covariance will have significantly lower risk than the risk of the individual assets included therein. *The degree of risk of a total portfolio decreases as the negative covariance among the asset returns increases.*

If the asset returns in a portfolio could be perfectly negatively correlated, then regardless of the risk of holding any one of the assets, the risk of the total portfolio would be zero. Of course, in the real world it would be impossible to ever achieve perfect negative covariance. That would mean that there would be *a perfect negative correlation* (a correlation of minus one) between the returns on the assets.

But just suppose for a moment that you could find two assets on which the returns were perfectly negatively correlated. When the return on one was at its high point, the return on the other would be its low point. And suppose that each of these assets would return, at its high, 20%, and at its low, zero. If you invested in only one of these assets you would incur great risk. If you invested in both (and if they were *truly* perfectly negatively correlated) then you would bear absolutely no risk at all of variability of your returns.

If you held these two securities you would receive a 10% return at all times. When one was paying 20%, the other would be paying zero. When one was paying 15%, the other would be paying 5%. When one was paying 10% the other would be paying 10%. What a beautiful situation! But remember this: Finding two assets on which the returns are perfectly negatively correlated is not quite as easy as falling off a log! I've been looking for a long time and I haven't found any yet.

Diversification with Independent (Zero Covariance) Assets Significantly Reduces Risk

Portfolio managers are always searching for assets with negative covariance. But such assets aren't easy to find. And even when you find some, the negative covariance may not be very great. So, what to do?

Is there any advantage to be gained from diversifying a portfolio by holding several different *independent* assets? Again, the common sense answer is the right one. Everybody has heard that it isn't wise to "put all your eggs on one basket." That's good common sense. And it's also a good principle of portfolio choice.

Suppose you are considering two equally risky assets (A and B) which are completely independent of each other. And suppose each asset is sure to produce a return of either 20% or zero—and that there is a 50-50 (0.5) chance of each outcome.

The average expected return (R^e) on each of the assets would be 10%. But if you bought one of those assets, the risk would be great.

Here's the calculation:

$$V = \sigma^2 = p_1 \times (R_1^r - R^e)^2 + p_2 \times (R_2^r - R^e)^2$$

$$= 0.5 \times (0 - 10)^2 + 0.5 \times (20 - 10)^2$$

$$= 0.5 \times 100 + .05 \times 100$$

$$V = \sigma^2 = 50 + 50 = 100$$

You can see that the variance of the return *on one of the assets* would be 100. But what if you bought both assets A and B? That would significantly reduce the variance of your returns.

Assuming that the two assets are completely independent, when you hold both (one of each), then you can expect a return of zero (zero on both assets) one-fourth (0.25) of the time and a return of 20% (20% on both assets) one-fourth (0.25) of the time. The other half (0.5) of the time you can expect to earn 10%—20% on A and zero on B one-fourth of the time, and zero on A and 20% on B one-fourth of the time.

In this case, for your realized returns (R^r) you have these possibilities: $R_1^r = 0$; $R_2^r = 20\%$; $R_3^r = 10\%$. So what will be the variance of your returns? Here are the calculations:

$$V = \sigma^2 = p_1 \times (R_1^r - R^e)^2 + p_2 \times (R_2^r - R^e)^2 + p_3 \times (R_3^r - R^e)^2$$

$$= 0.25 \times (0 - 10)^2 + 0.25 \times (20 - 10)^2 + 0.5 \times (10 - 10)^2$$

$$= 0.25 \times 100 + 0.25 \times 100 + 0.5 \times 0$$

$$V = \sigma^2 = 25 + 25 + 0 = 50$$

Now you can see quite clearly the significant reduction in risk which can come from diversification among independent assets. In this case, adding a second asset reduces the variance by 50%—from 100 when only one asset is held, to 50 when two independent assets are held.

The Less the Returns Move Together, the Greater the Benefits of Diversification

The previous examples have illustrated the following fact: *The less the returns on two assets are positively correlated—and the more they are negatively correlated—the greater the potential risk-reduction which will result from building a diversified portfolio of these assets.*

Perfect Negative Covariance. For two assets on which the returns exhibit *perfect negative covariance* (correlation between the two of minus one) the risk of variability of returns can be completely eliminated. And this is true no matter how great the variability risk might be on either one of the assets standing alone.

Complete Independence. If the returns on two different assets are *completely independent*, then holding equal quantities of both assets can reduce the risk of holding one or the other, but *only by one-half as much* as if the two had been perfectly negatively correlated.

Perfect Positive Covariance. The only case in which diversification does not reduce risk at all would be when the returns on the two assets have *perfect positive covariance* (correlation of plus one). But this is not likely to occur between any two different assets. So with but rare exceptions, *diversification can be expected always to result in some degree of risk reduction*.

The Dilemma: Returns on Most Assets
Exhibit Positive Covariance

The difficult task for the portfolio manager is to find assets which do not exhibit very much positive covariance. But that's especially difficult because there are strong tendencies for the returns on many assets to move in the same direction at the same time.

During a severe sell-off, stocks, bonds, real estate, and almost all other assets lose value. One exception (sometimes, but not always) is gold. That's one reason why many portfolio managers maintain a position in gold—either in the metal, or in gold mining stocks or other gold-based securities. The market values of gold and the returns available from holding gold and gold-based securities often have a negative covariance with the returns available from holding most other assets.

Systematic (Market) Risk Cannot Be Diversified Away

By now you know the great wonders of—and the severe limitations on—diversification as a risk-eliminating technique. If you could build a portfolio containing all assets with perfect negative covariance, you could eliminate all risk. But in the real world, you can't do that. You can't even come close! Here's why.

All of those securities and other assets you're using to build your portfolio are out there "in the market." The "market average returns" are going to go up and down in unpredictable ways. And your portfolio is going to feel the effects of that, and there's nothing you can do about it. That's a kind of risk from which you cannot escape via diversification. It's called **systematic risk** or **market risk**. You may sometimes reduce it significantly by insightful and/or lucky shifts among assets. But you cannot diversify it away.

The only kind of risk which can be eliminated via diversification is **unsystematic risk**, also called, unique, specific, residual, and diversifiable risk. That's the kind of risk you've been reading about most of the time in this chapter. It's also called "company risk." With unsystematic risk, you must diversify to keep from putting all of your eggs in one basket. With systematic risk, that's the whole basket—the only basket there is. Shuffeling assets within the basket can't protect you when the basket turns over!

PORTFOLIO CHOICE: AN EXERCISE IN OPPORTUNITY COST

The kinds of decisions required of the portfolio manager are a constant exercise in *opportunity cost*. Each asset in the portfolio is "costing" (i.e., "blocking out") some other asset which otherwise could be there. The opportunity cost of each asset in the portfolio is the "some other asset" which could be in the portfolio in the place of this one.

The Portfolio Manager Is Always Considering Shifting Assets

It is the job of the portfolio manager to compare expected returns and degrees of risk on all assets in the portfolio against alternative assets. Whenever it is possible to replace an asset with another asset which brings the same return and which reduces the total risk of the portfolio—or alternatively, with one which increases the return without increasing the risk—then that switch should be made.

But *note this well: It is not the risk of the individual asset under consideration that is significant. It is the effect of the new asset on total portfolio risk.* Wise asset management—careful portfolio choice—sometimes can succeed in pulling together relatively high risk (and therefore high return) assets into a portfolio which is carefully balanced and diversified so that the degree of risk of the total portfolio is quite low. That's the "efficient portfolio" objective which all portfolio managers are trying to achieve.

The Manager Can Calculate the "Risk Effect" of Each Asset Considered

How does the portfolio manager assess the risk-effect of an additional asset? By estimating the average variance of that specific asset's returns, and calculating the expected covariance between that asset's returns and the returns of the other assets in the portfolio.

As long as returns on the asset to be added are substantially independent of all other returns in the portfolio, even if this is a fairly high-risk asset, the additional risk added to the portfolio will be small. In fact, in a large and well diversified portfolio the added risk will be approximately zero. Much of the unsystematic risk of variable returns on independent securities can be "diversified away" if the number of securities held is sufficiently large. But remember the market crash of October 1987? That illustrates **systematic risk**. We just have to live with some of that.

SUMMARY

- *The principles of portfolio choice* provide guidelines for making decisions among alternative income-earning assets. The most basic principles are mostly common sense, but portfolio managers use sophisticated techniques of analysis to make asset choices much more precisely.

- On an investment, **risk** means the lack of certainty in the amounts and timing of the future returns: interest payments, dividends, principal repayments, capital gains, whatever.

- Most people (portfolio managers) are risk averse—some much more than others. Risk-averse portfolio managers take on additional risk only when justified by larger expected returns.

- An **efficient portfolio** is one which produces the greatest income for a given level of risk, or the lowest risk for a given level of income. Efficient portfolios maximize investor returns, lower borrowing costs, and increase the productivity of the economy.

- The amount of risk-reduction possible via diversification depends upon the kinds of variability of returns among the assets.

- **Variance** is calculated as the sum of the squared deviations of the expected returns from the mean, where each standard deviation is weighted by the probability of its occurrence. The greater the variance of returns the greater the risk of the asset.

- **Negative covariance** means that returns on assets move in opposite directions. With **perfect negative covariance**, risk of variability of returns can be reduced to zero. With **zero covariance**, degree of risk can be reduced by 50%. But with assets with **perfect positive covariance**, diversification does not reduce risk at all.

- **Systematic risk** or **market risk** results from the risk of movements in the total market for all assets. Therefore this risk cannot be eliminated by diversifying among various assets within the market.

- **Portfolio management** is a continuing exercise in **opportunity cost**. Each asset chosen must have the maximum beneficial risk/return effect on the total portfolio.

Important Principles, Issues, Concepts, Terms

Wealth

Principles of portfolio choice

Risk (of an asset)

Risk vs. reward trade-off

An efficient portfolio

Benefits of efficient portfolios

Risk aversion

Diversification

Covariance: negative, zero, positive

The "average expected return" (R^e) formula

Variance and *risk*

The variance ($V = \sigma^2$) formula

Covariance and benefits of diversification

Portfolio choice and opportunity cost

Systematic (market) risk

Unsystematic (diversification) risk

Questions

1. Explain this statement: "The principles of portfolio choice are common sense—and more than that."

2. Explain exactly what is meant by "degree of risk" when referring to an asset.

3. Do you think it is true that when deciding what assets to hold, most people understand the "risk vs. reward" trade-off? Discuss.

4. Explain exactly what is meant by an efficient portfolio.

5. One technique of portfolio management is to try to achieve maximum negative

covariance of returns among assets. Explain exactly what this means, and why it is true.

6. If the returns on the various assets in the portfolio have perfect positive covariance, diversification is of no benefit in reducing the risk in the portfolio. Explain why.

7. Explain why it is impossible to eliminate systematic risk by diversification.

8. In general, do you think a portfolio containing a mixture of stocks and bonds

would be less risky than a portfolio containing either stocks only or bonds only? Explain why. What about including stocks, bonds, gold, and real estate. Would that be less risky? Explain.

Suggested Readings

Amihud, Yakov. "Liquidity and Asset Prices: Financial Management Implications." *Financial Management* 17(1) (spring 1988) 5–15.

———. Thomas S. Y. Ho, and Robert A. Schwartz (eds.). *Market Making and the Changing Structure of the Securities Industry.* Lexington, Mass.: Lexington Books, 1985.

Baker, James. "The Prison of Passive Investment Portfolios." *American Banker.* March 7, 1985.

Benston, George J. "Required Disclosure and the Stock Market: An Evaluation of the Securities Exchange Act of 1934" *American Economic Review* 63. (March 1973), 132–55.

Bradley, Stephen, and Dwight Crane. "Simulation of Bond Portfolio Strategies: Laddered Versus Barbell Maturity Structure." *Journal of Bank Research.* Summer 1975.

Campanella, Frank. *The Measurement of Portfolio Risk Exposure.* Lexington, MA: D.C. Heath Company, 1972.

Campbell, Tim S. *Money and Capital Markets.* Glenview, Ill.: Scott, Foresman and Co., 1988.

Chen, Nai-fu, Richard Roll, and Steven Ross. "Economic Forces and the Stock Market." *Journal of Business.* 1987.

Cohen, K., and J. Pogue. "An Empirical Evaluation of Alternative Portfolio-Selection Models." *Journal of Business.* (April 1967), 166–93.

Copeland, Thomas E., and J. Fred Weston. *Financial Theory and Corporate Policy.* Reading, Mass.: Addison-Wesley Publishing Company, 1983.

Cramer, Robert H., and James A. Seifert. "Measuring the Impact of Maturity on Expected Return and Risk." *Journal of Bank Research.* (autumn 1976), 229–35.

Crum, Roy L., and Keqian Bi. "An Observation on Estimating the Systematic Risk of an Industry Segment." *Financial Management* 17(1) (spring 1988), 60–62.

Fama, Eugene F., and Merton H. Miller. *The Theory of Finance.* New York: Holt, Rinehart and Winston, 1972.

Farrell, James. "Analyzing Covariation of Returns to Determine Homogenous Stock Groupings." *Journal of Business of the University of Chicago* 47. (April 1974), 186–207.

Gultekin, N. Bulent and Richard J. Rogalski. "Government Bond Returns, Measurement of Interest Rate Risk, and the Arbitrage Pricing Theory." *Journal of Finance* 40. (March 1985), 43–61.

Haugen, Robert A., and Dean W. Wichern. "The Elasticity of Financial Assets." *Journal of Finance.* September 1974, pp. 1229–40.

Havrilesky, Thomas M., and John T. Boorman. "Portfolio Theory." in Havrilesky and Boorman, *Current Issues in Monetary Theory and Policy*, 2nd ed. Arlington Heights, Ill.: Harlan Davidson, Inc., 1980.

Hoffland, David. "A Model Bank Investment Policy." *Financial Analysts Journal.* May/June 1978.

Hopewell, Sidney, and Richard L. Johannesen. *The Price of Money, 1946 to 1969*, Rutgers University Press, 1973.

Joaquin, Domingo C. "A Reconsideration of the Focal Outcomes Approach to Portfolio Selection." *Journal of Post Keynesian Economics.* 10(4). (summer 1988), 631–45.

Lintner, John. "The Valuation of Risk Assets and the Selection of Risky Investments in Stock Portfolios and Capital Budgets." *Review of Economics and Statistics.* February 1965, pp. 13–37.

Martin, John, and Arthur Keown. "Interest Rate Sensitivity and Portfolio Risk." *Journal of Financial and Quantitative Analysis.* 12. June 1977, pp. 181–89.

Melton, William C. "Corporate Equities and the National Market System." *Quarterly Review.* 3. Federal Reserve Bank of New York. (Winter 1978–79), 13–25.

Roll, Richard, W. H. Wagner, and S. C. Lau. "The Effect of Diversification on Risk." *Financial Analysts Journal* 26. (November/December 1971), 7–13.

Sharpe, William F. "Capital Asset Prices: A Theory of Market Equilibrium Under Conditions of Risk." *Journal of Finance.* (September 1964), 425–52.

———. "Factors in NYSE Security Returns." *Journal of Portfolio Management.* (summer 1982), 5–19.

———, *Investments*, 3rd ed. Englewood Cliffs, N.J.: Prentice-Hall, 1985.

Value Line Investment Advisory Service, 711 Third Ave., New York. (various periodicals).

Yawitz, J. B., et al. "The Use of Average Maturity as a Risk Proxy in Investment Portfolios." *Journal of Finance.* (May 1975), 235–335.

CHAPTER 15

The Basic Business of Banking: Making Business and Consumer Loans

Chapter Objectives

An understanding of commercial banking requires an understanding of a bank's income and expenses, and of the management of the bank's assets (uses) and liabilities (sources) of funds. That's what you will be reading about in this chapter and the two following ones. After you study this chapter you will understand and be able to explain:

1. The sources of **income**, **expenses**, and **profitability** for the typical bank.
2. The trade-off between **earnings**, and **liquidity and safety**.
3. The changing relative importance of different bank **assets** and the preponderence of **loans**, especially for large banks.
4. The major kinds of **commercial and industrial (C&I) loans**, and the characteristics of each.
5. Different ways of setting (quoting) **interest rates** on loans.
6. Some reasons for the increasing importance of bank **leasing**.
7. The kinds and characteristics of **nonbusiness loans**.
8. Why **loan rescheduling** (when feasible) is usually preferable to default.

BUYING AND SELLING MONEY MEANS ACQUIRING LIABILITIES AND ASSETS

When a bank "buys money" it issues (creates for itself) liabilities—obligations to pay future dollars. Usually (but not always) the liabilities which banks issue are various kinds of *deposit liabilities*.

When a bank "sells money" it acquires assets—financial instruments. These instruments are evidences of debt—evidences of the bank's right to receive future dollars. What the bank's balance sheet shows at any moment is the final result (at that moment) of all of that bank's money-buying and money-selling activities. To say it differently: The balance sheet shows the bank's **sources of funds** (its liabilities) and **uses of funds** (its assets).

The Basic Business of Banking: Asset-Liability Management

The business of buying and selling money is really the business of managing assets and liabilities. So the basic business of banking consists of choosing (and then obtaining) the desired "mix" of both liabilities and assets.

Successful banking requires adjusting the structure (the "mix") of assets and liabilities so as to hold down the cost of funds bought (liabilities), and to hold up the return on funds sold (assets)—and doing so without exposing the bank to an unacceptable level of risk.

You can see that successful banking requires successful management of both assets and liabilities. On the asset side, safety and liquidity must be carefully balanced against asset earnings—i.e., the return on the bank's *uses of funds*. And on the liability side, profitability requires careful control of the cost of the bank's *sources of funds*. So you can see why much of the study of banking focuses on the bank's **balance sheet**. That's where you see the liabilities (sources of funds) and the assets (uses of funds).

BANK INCOME, EXPENSES, AND PROFITABILITY

Most of a bank's costs and most of its earnings result from items you can see on the balance sheet. But there are some other expenses and some other earnings, and to see these you need to look at operating income and operating expenses. If you'll look at table 15-1, that's what you'll see. The table shows the percentage distribution of operating income and operating expenses for the typical large bank and the typical small bank.

Bank Operating Income

Interest on loans is by far the largest income producer for the typical bank. It's 80% of the total for the average large bank, and 50% of the total for the average small bank. For the typical large bank there is no other source of income which even approaches 10% of the total.

For the typical small bank, **interest on securities** is an important item (25% of total income) and interest on **Fed funds sold** is also important (10%). Many small banks keep a pool of Fed funds and sell these funds every day—except on those days when they have some unusual need for liquidity. So instead of buying Fed funds to meet liquidity needs (as a large bank would do), the small bank just sells less Fed funds to accomplish the same purpose.

Bank Operating Expenses

Table 15-1 shows that **salary and wage expenses** are about twice as large as a percentage of total expenses for small banks as for large banks (24% and 12% respectively). Also you see that **interest paid on deposits** makes up 40% of total operating expenses for small banks, but only 25% for large banks. But the biggest "expenses" difference between large banks and small banks is in the **interest paid on borrowed funds**. For small banks this item is only slightly larger than zero, but

Table 15-1. Overview of Approximate Percentage Distribution of Bank Operating Income, Operating Expenses, and Profitability (Late 1980s)

	Large Bank %	Small Bank %
Income		
interest on loans	80	50
interest on securities	8	25
interest on Fed funds sold	2	10
trust dept. income	2	6
service charges, fees, other	8	9
	100	100
Expenses		
salaries and wages	12	24
interest on deposits (all)	25	40
interest on borrowed funds	40	<1
provision for loan losses	5	5
occupancy expenses	4	8
all other expenses (including income taxes)	14	22
	100	100

Profitability
Return on Assets (ROA) = net income/total assets: how much net income per dollar of assets

In recent years ROA has fluctuated between about 0.6% and 0.9%, but with a lot of variability for individual banks.
Return on Equity (ROE) = net income/bank capital, or owners equity. ROE indicates the amount of net income per dollar of "ownership value" in the banking corporation.

In recent years ROE has ranged between 10% and 15%, but with significant variability among individual banks.

Note: Latest figures on bank income, expenses, and profitability can be found in: Federal Deposit Insurance Corporation *Bank Operating Statistics* (annual).

for large banks it makes up 40% of the total. The large banks are borrowing those Fed funds from the small banks? And other funds from others, to meet those big loan demands? Exactly.

Table 15-1 illustrates the fact that (as popularly stated): "Banks make money on other people's money." More precisely: Most of a bank's earnings come from its interest income, from lending and investing deposited (and/or borrowed) funds.

Bank Profitability: Return on Assets (ROA) and Return on Equity (ROE)

A bank's profitability usually is measured in two different ways: return on assets (ROA) and return on equity (ROE).

ROA is net income divided by total assets. It tells how much profit the bank is making per dollar of total assets. Since the bank doesn't use the owners' money to buy the assets, you wouldn't expect the percentage return to the bank on those assets to be very great. And it isn't.

In recent years, ROA for the typical bank has averaged between about 0.6% and 0.9%—but many banks have been significantly above and many significantly below these averages.

ROE is net income divided by bank capital (owners equity, or net worth). It tells how much profit the bank is making per dollar of stockholder value invested in the bank. It tell the stockholders what percentage they are earning on their owners equity.

Since for the typical bank the capital/asset ratio is less than 10%—for some of the large banks, less than 5%—ROE is much greater than ROA. In recent years ROE for the typical bank has been ranging between 10% and 15%. But again, there has been great variability among banks: some with ROE above 15% and others with negative ROE.

Box 15-1 gives a grim reminder of what happens when ROA and ROE drop below zero for very long. After you read that box, most of the remainder of this chapter is concerned with the main source of the bank's earning: business and nonbusiness loans.

THE BANK'S ASSETS: USES OF FUNDS

Figure 15-1 shows a simple "see-saw" diagram which bankers frequently use to illustrate the asset-management balancing task—the task which faces all asset managers every day. The diagram indicates that, at any moment in time, to increase your earnings, some liquidity and/or safety must be given up.

Take a minute to look at figure 15-1 to be sure that you'll never forget about this basic trade-off. Then take a few minutes to study table 15-2 and see the great changes which have occurred over the last three decades on the asset side of the balance sheet of the typical bank.

Table 15-2 shows the percentage distribution of assets of all insured commercial banks at the beginning of 1961, 1971, and 1988. The table shows the sig-

**Figure 15-1.   The Critical Balance in Asset Management:
Earnings, vs. Liquidity and Safety**

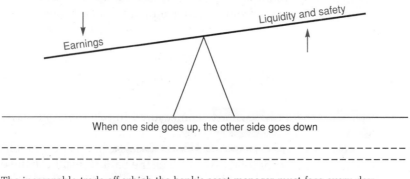

When one side goes up, the other side goes down

The inescapable trade-off which the bank's asset manager must face every day.

Feature: **Negative ROA and ROE Ultimately Result in Insolvency. The Bank Fails.**

Grim Closings Forecast Is Almost Fulfilled
—Reported by Barbara A. Rehm and Jim McTague
Bank Failures Not Quite as Bad As Predicted

It wasn't as bad as predicted, but that's about the only good thing that can be said of bank failures in 1987.

With 184 banks shutting their doors and another 19 kept open only by federal assistance, a post-Depression record was set. The forecast for 1987 had been 200 failures.

The [post 1933] record of bank closings (of 1937) stood unchallenged until 1984, when 79 banks folded. Since then, the Federal Deposit Insurance Corp. has become accustomed to chalking up record bank closings. Annual records were set in 1985, when 120 banks failed, and in 1986, when 138 banks failed.

Nor is the FDIC forecasting less red ink for 1988. Another record may be set this year, according to the federal agency that insures banks.

Only a few months ago, the FDIC was predicting a 25% decrease in the number of bank failures this year. But the stock market tumble on Oct. 19 and the ensuing fears of a recession seem to have forced the agency to reexamine its economic assumptions. No one at the FDIC would be surprised by 200 failures this year.

The FDIC does not expect ever again to see the days of a mere 10 failures a year, as happened as recently as 1981. David C. Cooke, deputy to the FDIC's chairman, said in a speech last October that if closings can be held to 40 annually, the FDIC will be satisfied. ...

The problem bank list expanded in 1987, peaking at 1,635 and ending the year at 1,575. At yearend 1986, the problem bank list was 1,484, or 10% of the approximately 14,800 banks insured by the FDIC. Back in 1982, the FDIC problem list totaled 369 or 2.5% of the insured banks.

FDIC-Insured Bank Failures Around the US

	'87	'86	'85	'84	'83	'82
Alabama	2	1	2	1	1	1
Alaska	2	1				
Arizona						
Arkansas			1	2	1	3
California	8	8	7	6	5	2
Colorado	13	7	6	2	1	
Connecticut						
Delaware						
Dist. of Columbia						
Florida	3	3	2	2		1
Georgia						
Hawaii						
Idaho		1				
Illinois	2	1	2	5	6	5
Indiana	3	1	1	2	0	0
Iowa	6	10	11	3		2
Kansas	8	14	13	7	1	
Kentucky	1	2		1	1	
Louisiana	14	8		1		
Maine						
Maryland						
Massachusetts	2					1
Michigan			1			1
Minnesota	10	5	6	4	1	1
Mississippi	1			1		
Missouri	4	9	9	2	1	2
Montana	3	1			1	
Nebraska	6	6	13	5	1	
Nevada					1	
New Hampshire						
New Jersey			1	1		1
New Mexico		2	3			
New York	1		4		2	4
North Carolina						
North Dakota	2					
Ohio	1					
Oklahoma	31	16	13	5	1	3
Oregon	1	1	3	5	5	
Pennsylvania	1					1
Puerto Rico		1		1	1	1
Rhode Island						
South Carolina						
South Dakota	2	1		1	1	
Tennessee		2	5	11	12	3
Texas	50	26	12	6	3	7
Utah	3	3	1	1		
Vermont						
Virginia						1
Washington						1
West Virginia						1
Wisconsin		1	1			
Wyoming	4	7	5	2	1	
Total	184	138	120	79	84	42

The total of failures for 1987 does not include 19 assistance transactions. The total of failures for 1986 does not include seven assistance transactions.

Sources: American Banker 1988 Yearbook, American Banker Inc., New York, N. Y., pp. 361–62.

Table 15-2. Percentage Distribution of Assets of All Insured Commercial Banks (Beginning of year: 1961, 1971, 1988)

	1961 %	1971 %	1988 %
Cash assets	20	16	10
Total securities	32	26	18
U.S. govt. and agency securities	24	13	10
State and local govt. & other securities	8	13	8
Total loans	46	54	64
Business loans	17	19	20
Mortgage loans	11	13	18
Consumer loans	10	11	11
Other loans	8	11	15
Miscellaneous assets	2	4	8
TOTAL	100%	100%	100%
Total Assets, Dollar Value (Billions)	$256	$576	$2,803

Source: FDIC *Annual Reports,* and *Federal Reserve Bulletin,* Table 1.25, "Assets and Liabilities of Commercial Banking Institutions," p. A18.

nificant percentage decline in cash assets and U.S. Government and agency securities and the significant increase in loans.

Does table 15-2 indicate a decline in the safety and liquidity of the average bank's asset structure? Yes. There's no question about that. But in recent years new sources of liquidity from both assets and liabilities have been developed. So the actual decline in liquidity has not been nearly as great as the figures in table 15-2 seem to indicate.

Reserves, and Other Cash Items

The cash assets listed in table 15-2 include the bank's reserves—deposits in Fed banks, and vault cash—plus deposits in other U.S. banks (correspondant balances) and cash items in the process of collection, plus miscellaneous cash assets.

Cash assets are very safe and very liquid. But generally cash assets do not generate any earnings. The decline in the percentage of total cash assets since the early 1960s is understandable in view of rising interest rates and the increased opportunity cost of holding cash assets. Also the Fed's required reserves which place a limit on how far total cash assets can be decreased, were lowered in the early 1980s.

There are physical limits on how far "cash items in process of collection" can be reduced. But the rapidly increasing use of electronic funds transfers has been speeding the collection process and holding down the size of "cash items in process." Also, as directed by the *Competitive Equality Banking Act of 1987,* the Fed is now in the process of implementing speedier check-clearing procedures.

Secondary Reserves and Other Securities

A part of the bank's securities portfolio is sometimes referred to as "secondary reserves." These are the short-term, highly liquid instruments which the bank can convert to "cash items" (reserves) very quickly. Items usually included in the list of "secondary reserves" are T-bills, short-term securities issued by government agencies, bankers' acceptances, commercial paper, and broker call loans which are repayable on one-day notice.

A large part of the bank's securities portfolio is made up of longer term securities. These usually generate higher earnings, but because of market risk they are not as risk-free (not as safe and liquid) as the very short term securities classed as secondary reserves.

Most of a bank's long-term securities consist of default-free U.S. Government securities—T-notes and T-bonds. But in recent years banks have been holding increasing quantities of state and local government securities on which some or all of the earnings may be exempt from federal income taxes. Also, holdings of mortgage-backed securities (CMOs, REMICs, etc.) have increased greatly during the 1980s. As of midyear 1988 banks still are legally prohibited from holding long-term corporate bonds (as well as corporate stocks) under the *Glass-Steagall Act* (1933).

Bank Loans: Critical Aspect of the Business of Banking

In the balance between safety and liquidity on one side and earnings on the other, bank loans score highest on the earnings side but lowest on safety and liquidity. The degree of safety and liquidity (and the size of possible earnings) varies significantly among various classes of loans, and among individual loans within each class.

More than anything else, *loans are the critical aspect of the business of* banking. Loans are the bottom-line determinant of the success or failure of a bank. When the bank examiners arrive and begin investigating the condition of a bank, what is their major focus? The loan portfolio.

Because of the importance of loans in the business of banking, much of this chapter will be explaining bank loans. But first there's one other item on the balance sheet which deserves a brief explanation: Miscellaneous assets.

Miscellaneous Assets: Mostly "Near Loans"

The last asset item on the bank's balance sheet is "miscellaneous assets." Table 15-2 indicates that this item has grown steadily from only about 2% of total

---

Box 15-2

Question: Do Banks Buy and Sell Stocks? Or Not?

You will notice in table 15-1 that no stocks are included among bank assets. You already know why.

As of midyear 1988, banks still are legally prohibited from holding stocks by the Glass-Steagall Act (1933). But note this: Banks do buy and hold billions of dollars worth of stocks through their trust departments.

The bank's **trust department** is legally separated from the bank itself by what bankers call the **Chinese wall**. The trust department buys, holds, and manages assets for estates, pension funds, and other beneficiaries. But the stocks and other assets are only *held in trust* by the bank. The stocks actually are owned by the beneficiaries of the trust accounts—not by the Bank itself.

assets in 1960 to about 9% in 1986. There are a number of minor assets included in this category, such as buildings, equipment, etc. But the largest part of the miscellaneous assets category is made up of what might be called "near loans" or "almost, but not exactly" loans.

The "Fed funds sold" item (which actually means overnight loans of Fed funds) is included in miscellaneous assets. Another important item is "customers' liabilities on account of acceptances." When the bank stamps a draft "accepted" it creates an "acceptance"—its own liability. But the bank's customer who presented the draft is obligated to pay the draft in the future. From the customer's point of view that's a loan obligation. It's just as if a promissory note had been signed by the customer and then guaranteed by and then sold by the bank in the money market.

Why have miscellaneous assets increased from 2% to 9% of total bank assets since the early 1960s? Mostly because of increases in these "near loans"—Fed funds sold, and bankers' acceptances.

Kinds of Bank Loans

Bank loans can be grouped into four categories: Business loans, real estate loans, consumer loans, and foreign loans. Each of these deserves a brief look. Business loans, because of their relative importance, deserve a more detailed explanation.

KINDS AND CHARACTERISTICS OF BUSINESS LOANS

Why do we call banks "commercial banks?" Because their traditional function is to make **commercial loans**. Historically, the basic financing needs of businesses large and small have been served by the banking system.

For the most part this is still true. But in recent years many large businesses have turned to the commercial paper market and to other alternative sources of financing to meet their needs for short-term funds. And the banks, as you would guess, are cutting their rates and using other techniques to try to entice them back.

Business Loans Are the Largest Category of Bank Loans

Business loans account for about 40% of total bank loans—the largest single loan category. Prior to the 1980s, with few exceptions, only commercial banks were making business loans. But now, as a result of the "revolutionary" banking legislation of the early 1980s, some thrift institutions are also competing in the commercial lending market.

In the highly competitive financial markets of the 1980s, *the most important task of the commercial loan officer* is to maintain contact with businesses in the area, to attract loan applications, to analyze and screen these applications, and then to make all of the loans which pass the credit analysis test.

The business of banking during the 1980s has become a highly competitive attempt to attract borrowers, while simultaneously attracting the deposits needed to fund these loans. Banks which succeed in this task survive, make profits, and grow. Those which do not, do not remain on the scene for very long.

Seasonal Loans and Term Loans

Most commercial and industrial (C&I) loans are either *seasonal loans* or *nonseasonal (usually term) loans*. Seasonal loans are short term and term loans are "fairly short term." Both are supposed to be self liquidating (repayable out of cash flows generated by the borrowed funds, and/or from future profits).

Seasonal loans are important in agriculture, in the tourist industry, and in various manufacturing, wholesale, and retail trade activities. The money is borrowed to prepare for "peak season" and then is repaid from funds generated during peak season. Seasonal loans obviously have a term of one year or less.

Nonseasonal (term) loans are usually made to finance capital expenditures (fixed investments of various kinds). A business which wishes to expand, remodel, or otherwise upgrade its operation would be most likely to apply for a term loan. Term loans usually have maturities ranging from one to five years, with 7- to 10-year maturities becoming fairly common in recent years. In usual practice, term loans are amortized (repaid in installments) from funds generated by the business (the cash flow) over the term of the loan.

Lines of Credit, and Revolving Credit

Banks make most of their business loans under some form of prior authorization—a commitment by the bank that loan funds will be provided on request (up to some previously agreed maximum, and generally subject to the maintenance of sound financial condition by the business). A bank's commitment of "funds on request" permits a business greater certainty in its planning activities. From the bank's point of view it solidifies the relationship with that customer. And, as explained in box 15-3 on **customer relationship banking**, that's important.

The two most frequently used techniques for extending these prior commitments of "funds on request," are (1) a *line of credit*, and (2) a *revolving credit agreement*. Under either of these arrangements the bank commits itself to make the funds available when requested. From the borrower's point of view, an advantage of these loan commitments is that additional funds can be borrowed or repayments can be made at any time—at the option of the borrower.

Compensating Balances: A Charge of "Implicit Interest"

Banks frequently require their business borrowers to keep *a minimum demand deposit balance* as a condition of the loan, or line of credit. Compensating balance requirements historically have been as high as 20% of the amount of the loan commitment. But with the high interest rates and highly competitive financial markets of the 1980s, banks have been negotiating compensating balances in the range of 3% to 7%, or have been eliminating this requirement altogether and charging fees instead.

The effect of a compensating balance requirement is to raise the interest rate on the funds which the borrower actually gets to use. For example, suppose your business borrows $100,000 at an interest rate of 10% and is required to maintain a compensating balance of 20%. You are borrowing $100,000 and must pay the 10% interest charge on $100,000, but you only get to spend $80,000.

Your interest cost is $100,000 × 10% = $10,000. You only get to use $80,000. So what interest rate are you paying on the funds you actually get to use?

Box 15-3

Question: **What Is "Customer Relationship Banking"?**
And Why Is That Important?

During the 1980s as ccompetition among the banks, thrifts, and other financial services institutions has become increasingly intense, one approach in the "bank-marketing game" has been to try to "cross-sell" bank products and services to all customers.

By the late 1980s most of the banks, savings and loan institutions, mutual savings banks, and even the credit unions were suggesting to their customers: "We should be your *only* financial services institution!" All of these institutions now provide a broad range of financial services, including a great number of "deposit products" and "loan products," as well as trust services, brokerage services, investment advice (including in some cases complete financial planning) and in some places insurance, real estate, and other financial services.

By the late 1980s banks were willing to make a significant effort to lock in a long-term relationship with a customer, hoping for multiple sales of their various product lines. In the case of commercial customers, **lines of credit** and **revolving credit agreements** establish long-term relationships. In the case of consumer loans, **home equity loans**—an open line of credit secured by a first or second mortgage on the borrower's home and usually extending for periods as long as 15 years—is ideal for locking in a permanent relationship.

The bottom line on **customer relationship banking** is: "We want to be, not just your only banker, but your only financial services institution."

A $10,000 interest charge on the use of $80,000 works out to a percentage rate of 12.5% ($10,000 ÷ $80,000 = .125; $80,000 × 12.5% = $10,000). In this case the effect of the compensating balance is to raise the "realized" interest cost from 10% to 12.5%.

What about compensating balances from the bank's point of view? Your 20% compensating balance lets them lend to someone else, 20 percent of the funds that they have already lent to you! Banks recognize very well the value of *balances*. That's why many banks often negotiate with businesses regarding the size of balances to compensate the bank for providing "free" services—checking, deposit-taking, payroll preparation, etc.

Collateral: For Security, Not for Repayment

Most C&I loans (and other loans, too) are secured by some kind of collateral—securities, inventories, etc. But good banking practice *absolutely prohibits* the making of loans where it is assumed that the collateral will need to be used to pay off the loan.

Consider this example. Suppose a person offers $10,000 worth of U.S. Government securities to a bank as collateral and applies for a $5,000 loan. Shouldn't the bank be willing to make the loan just on the basis of the $10,000 worth of collateral? Absolutely not! Unless the bank can foresee enough *cash flow* to repay the loan (from income, or from somewhere) then the bank should not—and most reputable banks *would not*—make the loan.

Here's the point: *Reputable banks should not be in the business of seizing assets and selling those assets to cover unpaid loan balances.* What bank would want to get a reputation in the community for seizing and selling people's property?

Suppose you take $10,000 worth of government securities and want to borrow $5,000 but you don't have the projected cash flow to repay the loan. Then your friendly banker probably will advise you to sell your securities to get the money you want. Without the cash flow to repay the loan, *somebody is going to have to sell the securities.* Better you than the bank!

To reemphasize the point: The purpose of collateral is to protect the bank against the possibility of *an unforeseen interruption* in the projected cash flow. *At the time the loan is made, the bank should have no intention of using the collateral as a source of funds for the repayment of the loan.* If the bank expects the loan to default so that the collateral will need to be seized and sold, then the bank should not make the loan.

Interest Rates on C&I Loans

Prior to the mid-1970s, most C&I loans were made at fixed rates. But the high and volatile interest rate environment has since changed that. By the mid-1980s about three-fourths of all C&I loans were being made at floating rates. Because of the perceived interest rate risk, *by the late 1980s most banks had adopted a policy of making very few fixed-rate loans.*

The "Prime" Rate. The so-called *prime rate* is an administered price set by the larger banks and followed by the smaller ones. The prime rate is the quoted rate on short-term loans to "prime" customers: those with the highest credit ratings.

Historically the **prime rate** has been *the lowest rate available to any borrower.* Small business borrowers usually are quoted rates in terms of "prime, plus." For example, a small, not well established firm might be required to pay prime plus two or three percentage points (200 or 300 basis points)—a risk premium, based on the perceived risk of default. The throughout the life of the loan the rate floats upward or downward, based on changes in the prime.

As mentioned previously, prime customers have the alternative of obtaining funds by issuing their own commercial paper—selling it in the commercial paper market. That's one reason why in recent years banks have been willing to negotiate below-prime rates.

Nonprime (Below Prime) Reference Rates. One approach that some banks are taking to hold their prime customers is to lend them Eurodollars at a small margin over the "LIBOR" rate in the London Eurodollar market. (Box 15-4 explains LIBOR.)

For large loans it is not unusual now for a bank to offer the borrower a choice of some reference rate other than the prime rate. For example, the Fed funds rate, the large marketable CD rate, and the Eurodollar rate (LIBOR) all are sometimes used as the reference rate. Since all of these rates are open market rates which reflect the bank's cost of funds, no matter which rate is chosen, the bank is protected. When the cost of funds rises, the rate on the loan rises commensurately.

Floating Rates with a "Cap" or "Ceiling." Prior to the 1980s, banks frequently made "capped-prime" loans—loans at prime, or prime-plus, but with a maximum interest "cap" or "ceiling" included in the loan contract.

When interest rates shot upward in the late 1970s and early '80s, many banks were caught with loans which were capped at rates far below money market rates.

Box 15-4

Questions: Exactly What Is LIBOR?

London is the center of the Eurodollar market—the money market where American dollars are lent among large international banks. The interest rate on borrowed Eurodollars is determined by supply and demand in the London market, and is known as LIBOR (London Interbank Offered Rate).

During the 1970s and '80s there has been explosive growth of the Eurodollar market. By 1988 the value of Eurodollars held by the international banks amounted to about three times the size of the U.S. M1 money supply. So this market is a huge source of American dollars for anyone—including American firms—who may wish to borrow short-term funds.

For some banks the losses on those capped loans were quite heavy. By the late 1980s some capped C&I loans still were being made, but not many. And these days, whenever a business gets a capped loan it is likely to pay for it with a higher rate.

C&I Leasing—An Alternative to Lending

Suppose a business needs capital equipment but would prefer not to borrow—perhaps for tax reasons or because leasing might be less costly or for some other reasons. The business might enter an agreement with a bank whereby the bank would purchase the equipment and lease it to the business. In that way no loan would be made. The business would receive the needed equipment, but the bank would own it.

By the mid-1980s, banks all around the country (and for big-ticket items, groups of banks—so-called "banking syndicates") owned and were leasing ships, airplanes, automobiles, construction equipment, and almost anything else you can think of—even livestock. Many banks now have leasing departments staffed by people whose only function is to conduct leasing operations. In past years the banks have been able to reduce their tax liabilities by using accelerated depreciation deductions for the leased equipment.

Some of the provisions of *The Tax Reform Act of 1986* are resulting in a significant increase in equipment leasing to businesses by banks. Box 15-5 discusses this stimulative effect of *The Tax Reform Act of 1986* on leasing activities.

KINDS AND CHARACTERISTICS OF NONBUSINESS LOANS

As you know, business loans make up about 40% of total bank loans—the largest single category of loans. But the other lending activities are also important. For some of the smaller banks and for all of the thrifts, nonbusiness loans—specifically home mortgage loans and consumer loans—account for the majority of their assets.

Box 15-5

Feature: **The 1986 Tax Act Offers Simulus to Leasing Activities**

Firms Expect Leasing To Save Them Millions Under New Tax Law

Escaping the 'AMT Trap'

By Lee Berton

Staff Reporter of THE WALL STREET JOURNAL

Alaska Air Group Inc. this year will lease as many as 10 commuter aircraft instead of buying them, thereby saving $4 million or more in 1987 taxes.

"If not for the new tax law, we would have purchased at least five of these planes," says J. Ray Vingo, the vice president for finance of the Seattle-based company.

Alaska Air is typical of companies discovering the leasing loophole in the new federal income tax. Collectively, they stand to save billions of dollars in taxes.

Congress expected that one of the law's provisions—a new alternative minimum tax for corporations—would generate at least $22 billion of added revenue over the next five years. But some tax analysts say that *skillful use of leasing could easily cut that in half.*

Surprise, Surprise

Now that the law is on the books, congressional and Treasury tax experts are registering surprise at how sharply leasing may cut into expected tax revenues. They warn that Congress could decide to close the loophole.

"We don't know enough about it right now," a Treasury official concedes. "But based on what we are hearing, we'll watch the trend. If it opens too many tax leaks, we'll have to plug the holes."

Meanwhile, major corporations such as United Technologies Corp., CSX Corp., Goodyear Tire & Rubber Co. and Exxon Corp. are using or planning leasing arrangements to reduce taxes, although they prefer as little publicity as possible about the arrangements. "Such tax information is a private matter," says Oren G. Shaffer, Goodyear's vice president and treasurer. "Our tax attorneys tell us we really shouldn't talk about it."

But leasing brokers are rubbing their hands in glee. The new tax law is "a great marketing tool" for leasing, says Michael J. Fleming, the president of the American Association of Equipment Lessors, a trade group based in

Arlington, Va. He says leasing volume may top $100 billion for the first time this year, up from $97 billion in 1986. Volume was only $15 billion as recently as 1975.

New Vistas

Corporations long have leased such assets as truck fleets and buildings. But because of the new tax law, leasing is spreading to other major assets like fiber-optics telephone lines, container ships, tire-making assembly lines, oil-drilling platforms and petroleum refineries.

Leasing can provide a tax loophole because of the new alternative minimum tax. Corporations have long been keeping two sets of books—one using accounting rules for reporting financial results to shareholders and the other, typically showing much lower profits, to report to the Internal Revenue Service. But alternative-minimum-tax rules now call for a 20% tax on half the difference between income reported to shareholders and income reported to the Treasury. The alternative tax must be paid if its total is more than the regular tax of 34% under the new law.

When a company buys equipment, it uses straight-line depreciation for income reported to shareholders and accelerated depreciation for tax reporting. Accelerated depreciation makes for higher expenses and lower taxable income during the early years of an asset's life. This widens the gap between book and tax income; under the new law, it makes for higher taxes under the alternative minimum tax.

Taxing the Gap

Leasing of equipment helps reduce the tax by preventing a gap between the two types of income. If a company buys $100 million in production equipment, it can deduct $20 million the first year under accelerated depreciation but only $10 million under straight-line depreciation. This creates a $10 million gap between income reported to shareholders and tax income. The bite from the alternative minimum tax, or AMT, on this $10 million gap is $1 million.

But if the company leases the equipment, it applies the same dollar deduction for rent on both sets of books; no gap is created.

"Buying equipment is a sure-fire way to trigger the AMT trap," says Peter K. Nevitt, the chairman of BankAmerilease, a unit of Bank-America Corp. in San Francisco.

"Tax specialists have found ingenious techniques to get around the AMT through complex leasing arrangements," says William Raby, a senior tax partner with Touche Ross & Co., a major accounting firm. "Where there's a will, there's a way."

Because of the new tax law, BankAmeri-lease's Mr. Nevitt expects that *assets leased by his company will rise more than 20% this year from the $15 billion in assets leased in 155 transactions last year.*

. . .

"For every freight car we lease, we can save more than $1,000 in annual AMT taxes," says William H. Sparrow, the treasurer of CSX, which is getting back into leasing arrangements it used in the past.

"Many people thought the new tax act was the death knell of leasing because it kills the investment tax credit and reduces depreciation benefits for the lesssor, providing less benefits to pass along to the lessee," says Mr. Sparrow. "But it hasn't turned out that way. If anything, the AMT will breathe new life into leasing."

CSX's Sea-Land Corp. subsidiary in Menlo Park, N.J., is negotiating the leasing of three huge container ships valued at $170 million from Argent Group Inc., a leasing firm based in New York City.

. . .

Major international oil companies are considering certain leasing arrangements for the first time, to reduce taxes. The plans involve selling and leasing back refineries, pipeline and offshore-drilling rigs. Brokers say Exxon and Texaco Inc. are discussing such tactics with leasing brokers, but the companies won't comment.

Other new tax-law provisions besides the alternative minimum tax are influencing companies' buying and leasing decisions. Many multinational companies formerly bought equipment by borrowing in the U.S., as the interest costs were a fully deductible U.S. expense. The new law requires all subsidiaries filing a consolidated return to prorate interest expense to their U.S. and foreign operations, even if all the interest is paid in the U.S.

Rental expense, on the other hand, now can be allocated to the location of the rented property. Rental expense on equipment located in the U.S., therefore, can be fully deducted.

. . .

"We can only say that we are beginning to look at sale-leasebacks for a wide range of U.S. assets" to reduce U.S. taxes, says Stephen Arbogast, the treasurer of Exxon Capital Corp., a leasing and financing unit of Exxon Corp.

. . .

BankAmerilease is having the busiest first quarter in its history. Says Mr. Nevitt: "We're normally slack this time of the year, but because of leasing volume to avoid the new tax act, six of our leasing specialists have had to cancel ski vacations."

The Wall Street Journal, Wednesday, March 11, 1987 p. 1. Reprinted by permission.

Real Estate Loans

Because of the relative lack of liquidity, commercial banks have traditionally shied away from many kinds of real estate mortgage loans. But in recent years commercial banks have moved more aggresively into this field. Real estate loans now account for about one-third of all bank loans—up from less than one-fourth of the total in the early 1960s.

One reason why banks have increased their mortgage lending is that in today's competitive financial markets, bankers can't afford to leave any potentially lucrative source of earnings untapped. But perhaps more important is the effect of *the rapidly developing secondary markets in mortgages.* As explained in chapter 12, the **securitization** and marketing of mortgages is significantly increasing the liquidity (and therefore the desirability) of this form of asset.

For most of the nonbank depository institutions—the savings and loan companies and mutual savings banks—residential mortgages make up about 60% of total assets. By the mid-1980s the increased marketability (liquidity) of real estate loans, plus the (earlier) introduction of adjustable-rate and variable-rate mortgages (ARMs and VRMs) had significantly reduced the (previously inherent) risk of making mortgage loans. So the market-risk exposure of the thrifts' and of the banks' mortgage portfolios was significantly reduced during the 1980s.

Loans to Consumers

Many purchasers of consumer durables either borrow from banks or buy "on time" from dealers whose loans then are financed by the banks. In addition to loans for consumer durables, credit card loans have become increasingly important. About 20% of total bank loans now consist of various kinds of consumer loans.

A new kind of consumer loan—the "home equity loan"—began gaining widespread popularity during the fall of 1986, stimulated by the *Tax Reform Act of 1986*. Beginning in 1987 the federal income tax deduction for interest paid on consumer loans (credit card balances, automobile loans, installment loans, etc.) is being phased out. But interest on most home loans will continue to be deductable. Enter: the **home equity loan**.

This kind of loan, as previously explained in box 15-4, is an open line of credit granted to a home owner and secured by a first or second mortgage on that person's home equity. In 1987–88, interest rates on these home equity loans were being quoted at considerably below the rates on other kinds of consumer loans. By mid-1987 this new loan "product" had rapidly become an important new addition on the asset side of the balance sheets of many banks and thrifts.

Loans to Foreign Businesses and Governments

Most of the large money center banks and several of the larger so-called "regional" banks have joined together to create "syndicates" to make large loans to foreign firms and governments. Many of these loans rank relatively low on the "safety and liquidity" scale but quite high on the "earnings" scale.

If everything goes well, loans to foreign borrowers, can be quite profitable for the participating banks. The problem (as you well know) is that sometimes everything doesn't go well. During the 1980s several nations with large external debts found themselves unable to meet their loan commitments.

By mid-1988 some of the loans had been written off and many of the still-outstanding loans to Mexico, Brazil, and Argentina were in default on both interest and principal repayments. The banks, the International Monetary Fund (IMF), other international agencies, and the nations involved have worked together to try to "reschedule" the loans. Meanwhile many of the big banks involved have poured much of their recent earnings, not into profits, but into increasing their loans-loss reserves. The result: big losses by Citibank and several others. But now they are ready to absorb additional loan writeoffs if (when?) that becomes necessary.

Rescheduling involves lengthening the term of the loan and reducing the size of current payments. The foreign loan rescheduling agreement frequently includes an injection of additional funds into the debtor country to try to stimulate development and generate more output, exports, income, and repayment potential. Box 15-6 gives an example of foreign loan rescheduling.

Box 15-6

Feature: **An Example of Loan Rescheduling on a Very Large Scale**

Creditor Banks Set Debt Pact With Argentina

Accord Covers $30 Billion; Margin on Most of Debt Is Put as Low as Mexico's

By Peter Truell

Staff Reporter of The Wall Street Journal

NEW YORK—Argentina and its major creditor banks have agreed to a new loan and rescheduling accord totaling about $30 billion, banking sources said.

The agreement gives Argentina an interest margin on most of its bank debt that is as low as that granted Mexico last year, and also will for the first time offer creditor banks a chance to opt out of new lending to the debtor country.

New Loans

Under the terms of the accord, creditor banks will reschedule about $24 billion of debt they lent before 1984 over 19 years, with seven years before principal payments begin, at a margin of 13/16 percentage point over the London interbank offered rate. Libor, which is currently $7\frac{3}{8}$%, is the rate banks pay for funds in the London market.

Argentina's about 360 creditor banks also will reschedule $4.2 billion of credits lent to Argentina since 1984 over 12 years at an interest rate of $\frac{7}{8}$ point above Libor. Debt repayments on this money will begin after five years.

The banks also will lend Argentina about $1.9 billion in new money, although it still isn't clear how much of this may be jointly financed with the World Bank. Terms on this new loan aren't yet completed either, banking sources said late yesterday. The banks and the Argentine negotiators—led by Treasury Secretary Mario Brodersohn—also have agreed that there will be a mechanism to allow banks to opt out of the new loan, although the two sides haven't yet completed details of this plan. Until now, creditor banks have been forced by their peers to join in such loans on a pro rata basis.

Citicorp, which chairs the bank committee negotiating with Argentina, declined to comment on the new loans or other aspects of the accord with Argentina.

Brazil More Isolated

This agreement with Argentina leaves Brazil more isolated. Apart from Brazil, Argentina—which has $50 million for foreign debt, of which about $35 billion is bank debt—was the one remaining large Latin American debtor still to reach a settlement with its creditors. Chile and Venezuela both have recently reached debt settlements with their bankers.

Brazil, meanwhile, is at odds with its bank creditors. It recently suspended interest payments on an estimated $67 billion of bank debt and also has frozen $15 billion of short-term trade credits and money market deposits, lent by foreign banks and companies. Finance Minister Dilson Funaro says Brazil can't continue paying banks the amounts of interest it has in recent years.

But the accord with Argentina also shows that the banks have had to give ground on interest margin. Last year, creditor banks reluctantly agreed to a margin of 13/16 point over Libor in a huge debt rescheduling for Mexico. But they vowed then that Mexico was a special case and that this relatively low interest margin wouldn't be granted to other big debtor countries. Argentina has proved that to be hollow talk.

Loan Rescheduling: Usually Preferable to Default

Sometimes a borrower's economic condition becomes such that there are only two options available: One is default. The other is to reschedule the loan so as to make it "manageable" within the current economic circumstances of the borrower.

This "default, or reschedule" option applies not only to "problem" foreign loans. It applies equally to "problem" domestic loans—loans to businesses, to homeowners, and to consumers. When faced with a "default, or reschedule" choice (assuming that the economic condition of the borrower is not hopeless) it usually is advantageous both for the borrower and the lender to reschedule rather than to default.

Rescheduling Usually Benefits the Borrower. The borrower who defaults loses access to credit. For a foreign country that means no access to foreign exchange. So it becomes very difficult for the country to import the products necessary to keep the economy functioning. And, for example, what do the nation's leaders say to the diabetics to explain that there is no longer any foreign exchange available to buy insulin?

Furthermore, any of the assets of the foreign country which might be located outside that country—bank deposits in other countries, ships in foreign ports, etc.—can be seized by the creditors. Clearly, if there is some reasonable way around it, debtor nations do not wish to default.

With the case of individuals or businesses, however, some find it preferable to declare bankruptcy. When that happens, the bank has no choice but to accept the suspension of payments on those loans. Usually the bank ultimately will have to "charge off" those loans and subtract those amounts from the asset side of its balance sheet. In such cases, *adequate collateral* becomes very important!

Rescheduling Usually Benefits the Lender. Loan rescheduling often is preferable to default from the point of view of the bank also. If the bank forces a borrower into default or bankruptcy then the loan usually must be written down or written off. Unless there is adequate collateral, the bank takes a loss. But rescheduling permits the borrower to survive. So as long as there is a reasonable chance that the loan will be repaid in the future, rescheduling is usually preferable to default.

Rescheduling postpones the balance-sheet effects of writing down or writing off the value of that asset (the loan). So with rescheduling the bank's balance sheet looks better. It shows more assets and more net worth (more capital). But what about rescheduling for the specific purpose of hiding bad loans and making the balance sheet look good? As you might guess, that's quite illegal! Now take a look at box 15-7 and see what the bank regulators have to say about all this.

BANK ASSET MANAGEMENT: ALL ASSETS MUST BE CONSIDERED

The function of *bank lending* (emphasized in this chapter) is of great importance to the success of the bank. Also, in addition to the function of making loans, *the bank's loan portfolio must be managed.* In fact, the management of the loan portfolio is the most important part of bank asset management. But the other two

Box 15-7

Question: What Do the Bank Regulators Have to Say about Loan Rescheduling?

During the 1980s hundreds of banks have failed. The most important cause: poor loan quality. As you would guess, loans which have to be rescheduled are not usually what you would call high quality loans.

When the regulators examine a banks books, they usually carefully scrutinize rescheduled loans which are called "assets," (of course) to see if they really are *valid assets*, or only *fictitous assets*, waiting to be written off and deducted from total assets.

The regulators have the power (and they use it!) to force the bank to charge off poor-

quality loans. According to one banker, by the late 1980s the regulatory agencies were taking an extremely conservative view on this issue. Their position seemed to be: "If there's any real question about whether or not this loan ultimately will default, then *write it off now*. We want the asset side of your balance sheet to show only sound, dependable assets—not fictitous ones."

Source: Norman Potter, Cashier, Avery County Bank, Newland, NC.

major asset categories—*cash assets*, and *securities investments*—both play very important roles. The management of those two asset categories—cash, and securities—plus the overall management of the loan portfolio, are explained in the next chapter.

SUMMARY

- The business of banking is the business of managing assets and liabilities. As the banks "buy money," they issue liabilities. As they "sell money," they acquire assets.

- The major source of income for all banks is **interest on loans. Cost of funds** is the biggest single expense item.

- Return on assets (ROA) for banks is almost always less than 1.0%, and return on equity (ROE) usually ranges between 10% and 15%.

- The critical balance in asset management is the trade-off between earnings on one side and liquidity and safety on the other.

- The major assets of banks are: (1) cash assets, (2) securities, and (3) loans. In the late 1980s cash assets amounted to about 10%, securities about 18%, and loans about 64% of total commercial bank assets.

- Loans include business, consumer, home mortgage, and other kinds of loans. Business loans are the largest category of bank loans.

- Most business (C&I) loans are made under a "line of credit" or "revolving credit" arrangement and frequently compensating balances are required.

- Collateral on a loan is required for security, but should not be expected to be used for repayment.

- Interest rates on C&I loans in the past have generally been based on the "prime" rate, but now the Fed funds rate, the marketable CD rate, and the Eurodollar rate (LIBOR) are also used.

- Banks are now making more real estate mortgage loans, partly as a result of the rapidly developing secondary markets which are greatly increasing the liquidity of mortgages.

- Consumer loans have become increasingly important to banks. In the late 1980s "home equity loans" were being agressively promoted by banks and widely accepted by consumers.

- Foreign loans have been in serious trouble during the 1980s. Several reschedulings of these loans have been worked out, and several banks have increased their loan loss reserves.

- Rescheduling, both for foreign loans and all other loans, when feasible, usually is preferable to default, both for the borrower and the lender.

Important Principles, Issues, Concepts, Terms

The critical balance: earnings, vs. liquidity and safety

Cash assets

Secondary reserves

"Near loans"

C&I loans

Seasonal loans

Term loans

Line of credit

Revolving credit

Compensating balance

Purpose of collateral

The prime rate

London Eurodollar rate

LIBOR

"Capped" floating rates

C&I leasing

Securitization of mortgage loans

ARMs and VRMs

Home equity loans

Consumer loans

Foreign loans

Loan rescheduling

Questions and Problems

1. Describe the typical bank's categories of income and expenses. How do small banks differ from large banks in this regard? Explain.

2. List the major assets of the typical bank, assign an approximate percentage to each asset category, and then explain how these relative percentages have changed significantly over the past few decades.

3. Describe the major kinds of bank loans.

4. Describe some of the different ways of stating the interest rate on a loan.

5. Describe the process of bank leasing, and explain why it has been used increasingly in recent years.

6. Describe some of the kinds of nonbusiness loans and how they work.

7. The textbook says that loan rescheduling, when feasible, is usually preferable to default. Explain why.

Suggested Reading

American Bankers Association. *A Guide to Developing a Written Lending Policy.* Washington, D.C., 1977.

Aspinwall, Richard, and Robert Eisenbeis (eds.). *Handbook for Banking Strategy.* New York: John Wiley & Sons, 1985.

Benbow, Robert F. "Preventing Problem Loans before They Happen: 25 Red Flags." *The Journal of Commercial Bank Lending.* April 1985.

Bennett, Barbara. "Where Are Banks Going?" *Weekly Letter*. Federal Reserve Bank of San Francisco, September 25, 1987.

Benston, George. "Optimal Banking Structure." *Journal of Banking Research* 3. (winter 1973), 220–37.

———. "Scale Economies in Banking: A Restructuring and Reassessment." *Journal of Money, Credit and Banking*. November 1982.

Benston, George, et. al. *Safe and Sound Banking*. Cambridge, Mass.: MIT Press, 1986.

Brady, Thomas F. *The Role of the Prime Rate in the Pricing of Business Loans by Commercial Banks, 1977–84*. Staff Study #146. Washington, D.C.: Board of Governors of the Federal Reserve System, November 1985.

Brick, Jack. "Pricing Commercial Loans." *The Journal of Commercial Bank Lending*. January 1984.

Clark, Daniel. "Banks as Investment Advisors: How Good are They?" *ABA Banking Journal*. January 1986.

Compton, Eric N. *The New World of Commercial Banking*. Lexington, Mass.: Lexington Books/D.C. Heath and Company, 1987.

———. "Credit Analysis is Risk Analysis." *The Bankers Magazine*. March/April 1985.

Conference of State Bank Supervisors. *A Profile of State-Chartered Banking*, 11th ed. Washington, D.C., 1986.

Cramer, Robert, and Peter Struck. "The Present Value Approach to Commercial Loan Pricing." *The Journal of Bank Research*. Winter 1982.

Federal Deposit Insurance Corp. *Bank Operating Statistics*. Washington, D.C.: Division of Accounting and Corporate Services (various years).

Garea, Raymond, and Gail Triner. "What's the Secret of Profitable Retail Banking?" *ABA Banking Journal*. April 1986.

Giardini, Valerie, John Pisa, and Casey Schroff. "A Critical Factor of Bank Profitability Measurement: Parts 1, 2, and 3." *Magazine of Bank Administration*. September/October/November 1984.

Gill, Edward. *Commercial Lending Basics*. Reston, Va.: Reston Publishing Co., 1983.

Havrilesky, Thomas, and John Boorman. *Current Perspectives in Banking*. Arlington Heights, Ill.: AHM Publishing Co., 1976.

Hempel, George, Alan Coleman, and Donald Simonson. *Bank Management: Text and Cases*. New York: John Wiley & Sons, 1986.

Horvitz, Paul. "Now That the Prime Is Back, Should It Stay?" *American Banker*. April 18, 1985.

Johnson, Bradford. "An Analysis of Modern Concepts of Loan Yields." *Magazine of Bank Administration*. August 1977.

Johnson, Frank P., and Richard D. Johnson. *Commercial Bank Management*. Chicago: The Dryden Press, 1985.

Miller, Richard B. "Lawyers Who Cash in on Lender Liability," *Bankers Monthly*. October 1986.

Nadler, Paul S. *Commercial Banking in the Economy*, 3rd ed. New York: Random House, 1979.

Parker, George C. "Now Management Will Make or Break the Bank." *Harvard Business Review*. (November/December 1981), 140–48.

Roosevelt, Joseph. "Product Cost and Profitability: Developing Accurate Information in a Changing Environment." *The Bankers Magazine*. January/February, 1985.

Sinkey, Joseph. *Commercial Bank Financial Management*, 2nd. ed. New York: Macmillan Publishing Company, 1986.

Wetzel, Debra A. "Improving Loan Documentation Demands a Process." *ABA Banking Journal*. May 1986.

CHAPTER 16

Managing Bank Assets: Cash and Reserves, Securities, and the Loan Portfolio

Chapter Objectives

This chapter focuses on the management of the bank's (1) cash assets, (2) securities portfolio, and (3) loan portfolio. After you study this chapter you will understand and be able to explain:

1. The broad range of **asset choices** facing bank managers.
2. The important items in a bank's **cash assets**, and what determines their size.
3. The role of the bank's **money desk manager** in maintaining the bank's **reserve position**, and how "Fed funds sold" can ease the manager's task.
4. The meaning and significance of the shift from lagged reserve accounting (**LRA**) to contemporaneous reserve accounting (**CRA**).
5. The basic principles of managing the bank's investment portfolio, and some factors other than income and risk which influence a bank's securities choices.
6. The basic principles of loan portfolio management and the advantage of "pooling" in reducing loan portfolio risk.
7. Some principles and techniques of **credit analysis** and the importance of **management ability** and projected **cash flow**.
8. Some ways of reducing the risk of "borrowing short and lending long," and of achieving a balanced and diversified loan portfolio.

MANAGING BANK ASSETS: CHOICES BETWEEN AND WITHIN CATEGORIES

The Bank Can Be Viewed as a Portfolio of Assets

Did you ever think of a bank as a **portfolio** of assets? Assets which ultimately are owned mostly by, not the owners of the bank, but the bank's depositors? Sometimes that perspective may be helpful in understanding what a bank is and what it does. The managers of the bank are really "managing this portfolio."

The Questions of Portfolio Management

For every banking institution the ultimate decision makers must decide how much of their assets to hold

a. in non-interest-earning cash assets (including reserve balances),

b. in relatively low-earning but highly liquid short-term securities,

c. in somewhat higher-earning long-term investment securities, and

d. in the highest-earning (and highest risk) form: loans.

Within these overall asset alternatives, the asset managers must decide about the specific forms of the assets to be included in each group. Do they want more of their cash assets in deposits in the Fed banks? Or in correspondent balances? More of their investments in U.S. Government securities? Or state and local securities? And what should be the average term to maturity—or more precisely, the duration (explained later)—of the investment portfolio?

What percentage of their loans would they like to have in commercial and industrial (C&I)? In home mortgages? In consumer loans? And what about the preferred term structure within each of these groups?

In the management of the bank's total assets, all of the principles of portfolio choice come into play. The riskiness of each potential asset needs to be assessed. Existence of (and extent of) covariance (either positive, or negative) between the various assets which are candidates for the portfolio need to be considered.

All forms of risk—default risk, market (interest rate) risk, and liquidity considerations must be assessed. And the tax advantages or disadvantages must be considered. Also, when considering the cash position, the need to maintain legally required reserves is a constant consideration.

MANAGING THE BANK'S "CASH POSITION"

On the "see-saw" balance, cash assets are perfectly safe and liquid. But on the earnings side? *Zero.* All banks hold cash assets, but no bank wants to hold any more cash assets than necessary. So how much is that?

Table 16-1 shows the percentage distribution of cash assets of all insured commercial banks at four different times during the mid-1980s. The major items are reserves, cash items in process of collection, and interbank deposits. Each deserves some explanation.

Table 16-1. Percentage Distribution of Cash Assets of All Insured Commercial Banks, Selected Dates 1985–87

	Dec. 1985 %	Dec. 1986 %	Dec. 1987 %
Total Reserves	23	24	28
Reserve Deposits in Fed Banks	13	15	15
Cash in Vault	10	9	12
Cash Items in Process of Collection	38	41	34
Total Interbank Deposits and Misc.	39	35	38
Correspondent Bank Deposits	17	16	16
Other Deposits, and Miscellaneous	22	19	22
Total	100%	100%	100%
Dollar Value (Billions)	$212	$271	$233

Note: During this period cash assets amounted to about 10 percent of total bank assets.
Source: *Federal Reserve Bulletin*, Table 1.25, p. A18 (various issues).

Cash Items in Process

One of the largest cash asset categories—about 35 to 40% of the total—is "cash items in process of collection." Much of these "cash items in process" are the "deferred availability cash items" which are being held back by the Fed to reduce the level of float—that is, to keep from adding funds to the reserve accounts of receiving banks before those funds are deducted from the reserve accounts of the paying banks. You will be reading all about that in chapter 21 which explains the operations of the Federal Reserve System.

The sooner the bank can get its hands on the funds represented by these cash items in process, the sooner it can convert them into income-earning assets. But "cash items in process" are not easy to reduce. In the future, as electronic funds transfers play an increasing role in the check-clearing process, this cash item will decline.

Balances in Correspondent Banks and Miscellaneous Cash Assets

The total of deposits in correspondent banks, other deposits, and miscellaneous cash assets usually amounts to around 35–40% of total cash assets. These deposits and miscellaneous assets do not earn interest income, but it isn't quite accurate to say that they are not "income-earning." In exchange for the correspondent balances, banks perform a variety of services for each other, including the clearing and collection of checks, securities transactions and safekeeping, information and data processing, and several others.

The banks certainly do not wish to eliminate this cash item. But each bank would like to keep its correspondent and other balances from being any larger than needed to compensate for the services received.

Required Reserves

Table 16-1 shows that total reserves account for about 25% of cash assets, with about 40% of reserves consisting of vault cash and the other 60% in reserve deposits at the Fed banks. This is the one cash item which receives the most attention by the bank's so-called "money desk manager."

The money desk manager has the task of making sure that the bank's reserve requirements are always met, and that none of the bank's assets are "wasted" in unneeded excess reserves. This task is not as easy to perform as you might think, because

1. *the bank's reserve needs are changing* from minute to minute as deposits are made and checks are paid, and

2. *the amount of reserves being held by the bank is changing* from minute to minute, as

   a. clearing checks are adding to and subtracting from the bank's reserve deposits at the district Fed bank, and

   b. customer deposits and withdrawals of cash are adding to and subtracting from vault cash.

With all of this uncertainty from moment to moment, how is it possible to meet the reserve requirement exactly? With no excess, and no deficiency? In truth, it isn't possible to "hit it exactly" all the time. But most bank managers have worked out ways of coming very close to the mark, most of the time.

The amount of excess reserves—reserves held in excess of the amount required—for the American banking system as a whole are reported monthly in the *Federal Reserve Bulletin*. In recent years, total reserves have been running at less than one-quarter of one percentage point above the required percentage. Example: If the average bank is required to hold an amount equal to 12% of its total transactions deposits, the average bank actually winds up holding slightly more than the required 12%, but less than 12.25%. That isn't "hitting it right on." But it's very close!

MANAGING THE BANK'S MONEY POSITION AND MEETING THE RESERVE REQUIREMENT

Most small banks "own" excess reserves, but they don't hold the funds as excess reserves. They sell them in the Fed funds market on a day-to-day basis. Holding more reserves than required means lost income for the bank—forfeited interest earnings. But holding less reserves than required is costly too. A bank with a reserve deficiency must pay the Fed a penalty.

The Two-Week "Required-Reserves Computation Period"

The reserves which a bank must hold on checkable deposits are computed as an average daily amount over a two-week period. The **reserves-computation period** begins with a Tuesday and ends with the Monday which comes two weeks later.

For each day during the two-week period, the total amount of checkable deposits held by the bank at the end of the day is recorded. The bank, in general, tries to hold enough reserves each day to meet the requirement on checkable deposits for that day. But of course it's impossible to do that all of the time. Fortunately, the bank isn't required to do that.

After the two-week "required reserves computation period" ends on Monday, on Tuesday the bank's money desk manager can look back and compute the bank's average daily checkable deposit balances over that two-week period. So on the Tuesday which begins week three, the money desk manager can calculate the exact average daily amount of reserves required during the "week-1 week-2" reserve period.

Example: Suppose this is a small bank with required reserves of 3% on all reservable checkable deposits. And suppose that during the two week period, average daily "reservable checkable deposit balances" came to exactly $30 million. (Not likely, but just suppose.) Then the money desk manager knows that the average amount of daily reserves must be $900,000 ($30 million × 3% = $900,000).

The Two-Week "Required-Reserves Holding Period"

The two-week period during which the "week-1 week-2" required reserves must be held—the "holding period"—is lagged two days from the computation period. So the **holding period** begins with Thursday of week-1 and ends with Wednesday of week-2. That's two days after the computation period ends on Monday of week-2.

So, A-ha! After the **computation period** ends on Monday, the money manager *knows exactly* how much reserves are required for the 2-week period. And there are still two days in the holding period (Tuesday and Wednesday) during which to make adjustments! On Tuesday and Wednesday the money manager can *make up any deficiencies* or *lend and earn income on any surpluses.*

Making the Calculations and Adjustments

Here's an explanation of exactly how it's all worked out. On Tuesday morning the money manager calculates:

1. *The total amount of reserves needed* for this 2-week computation period which just ended on Monday (yesterday).

2. *The total amount of reserves held so far* in this 2-week holding period (which began on Thursday 2 weeks ago and will end on Wednesday of this week—tomorrow).

3. The exact amount of reserves which need to be held on Tuesday (today) and Wednesday (tomorrow) to make the required daily average for the 2-week period (as calculated in #1, above) come out exactly right.

Suppose it turns out that on each day during the computation period exactly the right amount of reserves have been held. Then on the last two days of the reserve holding period (Tuesday and Wednesday) the bank only needs to continue to hold the same amount. Then for the week there will be no deficiency and no surplus.

But what if the bank has been holding more in reserves than required? Then the bank will reduce its reserve holdings on Tuesday and Wednesday, hopefully by enough to offset the surplus. Probably it will sell Fed funds to earn some income on the surplus.

Suppose the bank finds that it has a reserve deficiency. Then it must add reserves. The money desk manager probably will buy Fed funds to bring the bank's average daily reserve holdings up to the required amount.

A Bank Can Carry Forward up to 2% Excess or Deficiency

Suppose on Wednesday (the last day of the holding period) something quite unexpected happens and the bank winds up with either some excess reserves, or some reserve deficiency? The Fed doesn't expect the money desk manager to be a magician! So the Fed permits a bank to run an excess or a deficiency of as much as 2% of required reserves. This excess (or deficiency) can be carried over into and used (or made up) during the next reserve-holding period.

Ways to Adjust the Bank's Reserve Position

The specific action of the money desk manager who wants to adjust the size of reserves will depend on the alternatives (and the prices of the alternatives) in the money market at that moment. The most usual action is to buy Fed funds (surplus reserves) from, or sell Fed funds to, other banks. But there are other alternatives.

To increase the bank's reserves the money manager may also sell T-bills, sell CDs, or perhaps request a discount loan from the Fed bank. Which to do? The least-cost alternative, of course. At a time when the Fed funds rate is unusually high, sell T-bills or CDs, or borrow at the discount window.

If the money manager has surplus reserves, the surplus can be sold in the Fed funds market, or used to buy T-bills, retire CDs, or to repay the Fed bank for prior discount loans. Again, the chosen alternative will be the one which appears most profitable for the bank. Sometimes the money markets are very active on Wednesdays as money-desk managers try to "balance out" their two-week reserve holdings. Box 16-1 tells more about that.

Box 16-1

Feature: "Wild Wednesday" in the Fed Funds Market

Before the close of business on Wednesday of week-2, the bank's money desk must complete all of its "adjustment transactions" to bring its week-1 week-2 reserve holdings into line—no shortage, no surplus.

What if, on Wednesday afternoon:

- most money desks find that their reserve holdings still are deficient. They will be urgently trying to buy Fed funds. But no one wants to sell.
Or what if:

- most banks find themselves with surplus reserves. All of them will be urgently trying to sell Fed funds. But no one wants to buy.

You can see why on Wednesdays, supply and demand in the Fed funds market are subject to large and unpredictable swings.

Fortunately Fed funds are not the only instrument for balancing reserves. When the Fed funds rate begins to get too far out of line, supply and demand shifts to alternative money market instruments: Eurodollars, RPs, and others.

If the Federal Reserve wishes to do so it can initiate defensive open market operations. It can buy or sell T-bills or other securities to inject more or drain off Fed funds and thereby stabilize the market and reduce the "wild swings" in the Fed funds rate.

Money Management the Easy Way: Always Hold and Sell Fed Funds

The "nimble" management of a bank's money position requires the full time attention of some high quality (and high salaried!) people. Wouldn't it perhaps be better to pay somewhat less attention to hitting the target "right on" and thereby reduce this money-management expense? For many small banks, the answer is "yes." And there is an easy way to do it.

Small Banks Don't Have a Full-time Money Desk Manager. Suppose you are running a small bank and you are the money desk manager as well as the chief loan officer, the personnel director, the advertising-marketing-new product development manager, and everything else. How do you handle all of those jobs—including the money desk—without having a nervous breakdown? Put the money desk on "automatic pilot." Here's how.

Carry a sizeable surplus of deposits in your Fed bank account at all times. Each day go to your computer terminal and push the right buttons and in an instant you'll know (1) your checkable deposit figures, (2) how much reserves you are holding, and (3) the amount of your surplus Fed deposits (Fed funds). Still at your computer terminal, push the right buttons (and perhaps make a phone call to your correspondent bank) and sell the surplus Fed funds overnight.

On Tuesday, at the end of the two-week reserve computation period, let your computer calculate for you the exact amount of reserves required for that computation period. Then you can sell more (or less) Fed funds to adjust your average daily reserves to the required amount.

Using this "automatic pilot" approach to money-desk management you may not always hit the reserve requirement "right on the dollar." But almost always you will be within the "plus or minus 2%" carry-forward range.

The bank that uses Fed funds sales to adjust to deposit inflows and outflows and changing loan demands, can do so at very little transactions cost—much lower than with the buying and selling of securities—and there is no interest-rate risk such as with buying and selling securities.

"Fed Funds Sold" Can Serve as Secondary Reserves. Many small banks follow this procedure. They are, in effect, using "Fed funds sold" as *secondary reserves*. When more reserves are needed, less Fed funds are sold.

The amount of Fed funds sold can easily be adjusted in response to deposit inflows and outflows and changes in loan demand. This approach to keeping reserve holdings on target is not exactly "automatic pilot." But it certainly by-passes many of the funds management decisions which must be made by a full-time money desk manager!

Reserves on Nonpersonal Time Deposits— A Different Computation Period

All of the previous discussion about reserves has been concerned with *reserves on checkable deposits*. The only noncheckable deposits which require reserves are nonpersonal time deposits with maturities of 1-1/2 years or less. These are time deposits owned by businesses and other organizations—any entity which is not a natural person—on which the reserve requirement (as of mid-1988) is 3%. A 3% reserve is also required on Eurodollar liabilities.

The **reserve computation period** on nonpersonal time deposits is also a two-week period beginning on a Tuesday and ending on the Monday two weeks later. But in this case the reserves-holding period is lagged, not two days, but three weeks and two days. The holding period is *the two-week period beginning one week and two days after the end of the computation period.*

Here's an example. Suppose the computation period begins on Tuesday the first of March. Then the computation period will be Tuesday, March 1, through Monday, March 14. But the reserves holding period for these time deposits will be the two-week period beginning on Thursday, March 24th, and ending on Wednesday, April 6.

You can see by this example that for time deposits which are held during the first two weeks of the month, reserves need to be held beginning in the fourth week of the month and ending during the first full week of the following month.

More than one week before the time-deposit reserves-holding period begins, the money desk manager already knows exactly how much time-deposit reserves must be held. Money desk managers can be thankful that during the two-week period in which they are trying to estimate how much reserves will be required for checkable deposits, they already know—*with absolute certainty*—the amount of their required time-deposit reserves. Why shouldn't all reserve holding be lagged three weeks? Box 16-2 talks about that.

MANAGING THE BANK'S INVESTMENTS PORTFOLIO

All of the principles of portfolio choice apply in the management of the banks securities portfolio. The "funds management" department must decide how much of the portfolio to hold in U.S. Government securities: T-bills, notes, and bonds—and of what maturities (or, more precisely, duration); how much to hold in tax-exempt bonds, and of which state and local government units—and of what maturities; and how much to hold in other securities such as acceptances, commercial paper, etc.

Prior to the 1960s, banks considered their securities portfolios to be an important source of liquidity. Short-term U.S. Government securities (T-bills) are easily and quickly marketable whenever cash is needed. Also, the securities portfolio was considered as the "holding pool" for surplus funds. During times of weak loan demand, deposited funds were invested in short-term government securities which, later, could be sold to finance increasing loan demands. But since the early 1960s the rapid growth of the market for Fed funds and large CDs has significantly reduced the role of the securities portfolio as a day-to-day source of liquidity.

The choices of which securities to hold in the bank's investments portfolio generally reflect *the principles of portfolio choice.* But the bank's choices are influenced by some objectives other than those of "greater income" and "less risk." For example, pledging requirements and some other considerations also are important.

Box 16-2

Feature: Contemporaneous Reserve Accounting (CRA) and Lagged Reserve Accounting (LRA)

Who decides that reserves on nonpersonal time deposits will be held three weeks later? And that reserves on checkable deposits will be held contemporaneously? (Actually, lagged two days.)

The Contemporaneous Reserve Accounting (CRA) system for checkable deposits which you have been reading about has only been in effect since 1984. Prior to that time the Fed had used a system of Lagged Reserve Accounting (LRA). The LRA system permitted the banks to hold checkable deposit reserves with a lag of two weeks, in the same way that reserves for nonpersonal time deposits now are held with a lag of three weeks.

Obviously it's easier on the bank's money desk manager if the total amount of required reserves is known at the beginning of the holding period. But with CRA the amount of reserves required isn't known with certainty until two days before the end of the two-week reserve-holding period. So why, in 1984, did the Fed change from the LRA to the CRA system?

Some economists calculated that this lag—the time between the holding of deposits and the holding of reserves on these deposits—weakened the Fed's control over the money supply. For example, the money supply could begin to expand rapidly, and this expansion could continue for two weeks before any additional reserves would be required. Under CRA, this possibility no longer exists.

Has the switch from LRA to CRA for checkable deposits, strengthened the Fed's control over the money supply? That is still a matter of controversy among economists. There is no clear evidence one way or the other. The only clear result is that the change to CRA has increased the hectic nature of the life of the money desk manager.

What about the effect of the change on reservable (nonpersonal) time deposits? Before the switch to CRA, reserves on time deposits were lagged two weeks, the same as reserves on checkable deposits. But with the switch to CRA on checkable deposits, reserves on time deposits were lagged one additional week. So for time deposits the lag is now three weeks.

Time deposits are a part of the M2 money supply. Did the 1984 changes in reserve holding periods increase the Fed's control over M1, and reduce its control over M2? Economists disagree about that. These controversial questions are not likely to be resolved soon.

Pledging Requirements: For T&L Accounts and Other Government Deposits

Banks which have U.S. Treasury tax and loan (T&L) accounts (explained in chapter 22) are required to pledge government securities as collateral to secure these accounts. Also, most state and local governments require that their deposits in banks be collateralized by U.S. Government or other specified securities. So banks which wish to hold government deposits (most banks, to be sure!) must hold an adequate quantity of the prescribed securities.

Collateral for Repos, and Discount Borrowing

Repurchase Agreements (RPs or Repos) involve the sale and then repurchase of U.S. Treasury or Federal Agency securities. So a bank which wishes to engage in repos needs to hold a sufficient quantity to be used for this purpose. Also, when a bank borrows reserves at the Fed's "discount window" these borrowings must be collateralized. Usually this is done with marketable U.S. Government securities which are held in book-entry form so that no actual paper needs to be transferred.

"Munis" for Tax Exempt Income

In past years, tax considerations have caused most banks to hold a sizeable portion of their securities portfolio in state and local securities (so-called "municipal bonds," or "munis"). Banking corporations tend to be in high marginal tax brackets. So the after-tax yield on "munis" has been high, relative to other available securities. But the *Tax Reform Act of 1986* significantly lowered the top corporate tax rate, changed the calculation of the tax-exemption deduction, and imposed the alternative minimum tax. So banks now find munis much less attractive than before. Still, some banks may find it to their advantage to continue to hold significant quantities of state and local government securities.

Commercial Banks Are Dealers in Government Securities

Many of the larger commercial banks serve as dealers in government securities. They hold inventories of the securities in which they deal. They earn profits (1) from the spread between the bid and asked prices, and (2) from the transactions fees which they charge.

These government-securities-dealer banks can limit (hedge) their interest rate risk (market risk) exposure for the securities they are holding in inventory by selling futures on those securities. Then even if the market prices of the securities go down, the banks can deliver the securities and receive the previously contracted price. The cost of this hedging reduces the profitability of the bank's securities dealings. But it guarantees the bank against loss.

Banks sometimes are willing to take some market-risk exposure, hoping to profit from guessing right about future interest rate movements. The large banks consider it appropriate under some circumstances to expose themselves to some interest rate risk in the hope of making a profit. But the amount of risk taken is carefully limited. As bankers say: "It's all right to take some risk. But don't bet the bank!"

MANAGING THE BANK'S LOAN PORTFOLIO

More than any other one thing, it is the bank's lending activities and the management of the loan portfolio which determines the degree of success (or the failure) of a bank. This is where *the principles of portfolio choice* play a critical role.

Credit Analysis: Assessing the Default Risk

The process of bank lending—of deciding which loans to approve and which to deny—is mostly the process of credit analysis. And that means *trying to preassess the default risk* of the loan under consideration.

Lending to a Large, Well-Established, Publicly-Traded Corporation. When a bank receives a loan application from a large publicly-traded corporation it really doesn't need to do much "credit analysis." Information about the creditworthiness of such firms is available from Moody's and Standard and Poor's rating services. Also, information on its assets and liabilities, earnings history, outlook, etc., is easily available.

Another indicator of the creditworthiness of a large corporation is movements in the price of its stock on the secondary markets. The efficient markets theory tells us that if the stock has been moving up recently, it is the "average considered opinion" of the financial community that the stock of the firm is worth the higher price. So trends and volatility of the stock price, together with all of the other easily available information, usually provide the loan officer everything needed to assess the default risk.

A large corporation has access to the entire national and international loan market. Such a firm will borrow its money from the least-cost source, and probably at the prime rate or below. But the situation is very different for the small borrower.

Lending to Small Local Borrowers. Small borrowers are not well known outside their local area. So this gives the local banks a comparative advantage in undertaking credit analysis and assessing the degree of default risk.

For the small borrower, credit analysis involves:

1. *For individuals,* consideration of a list of factors such as character and reputation, occupation, how long at present job, income, credit record, home ownership, outstanding obligations, and several others.

    Most banks now have a "credit scoring" system for consumer loan applications. A number is assigned to each of the factors to be considered. When the numbers are added up, if the result falls below a certain level the loan is denied. If it is above a certain (higher) level, the loan is approved. Often there is a "maybe" range between these two levels, where careful scrutiny determines whether or not the loan will be approved.

2. *For a business,* the most important factors are *earnings*—past history and future projections—and character, quality, and reputation of management and their perceived ability to maintain the earnings trend. Also considered are value of assets, outstanding debt, trends in this industry, and a host of other factors.

Regardless of all other factors, the bottom-line requirement is: *Projected cash flow to repay the loan.* The loan will not be made unless the bank can project a flow of funds sufficient to meet the repayment schedule. (See box 16-3)

How Much Risk to Take?

A part of the lending decision Is: How much *risk premium* should be included in the price of (interest rate on) the loan? In general, the higher the perceived risk (as determined by the credit analysis) the higher the rate charged. But sometimes higher-risk applicants, instead of being quoted higher rates, are just turned down. Here's why.

Sometimes banks prefer not to take higher risk loans even though the potential interest earnings might seem high enough to justify the risk. No banker likes to show the bank examiners a portfolio which is made up of many high-risk loans. So the bank may turn down the loan application even though the loan might be profitable—and in view of the bank's total loan portfolio, not excessively risky.

Many of the larger bank holding companies have worked out a way to profit from some of these riskier loans. They have acquired or created subsidiaries

Feature: Don't Make the Term Loan If You Can't See the "Fatsatl"!

Suppose you are a loan officer and the owner of a local business comes in and fills out an application for a 5-year term loan to buy new machinery. How do you decide whether or not to grant the loan?

First you investigate this persons **character, reputation**, and **management ability**. If that assessment is favorable, then you try to identify all of the sources of cash flow which will be coming to the business over the period of the loan. You add up all projected revenues from sales, from accounts receivable, perhaps planned disposal of properties owned by the business, and cash flow from all other sources. This gives you the total **cash inflow**.

Then you add up the outflows: The pro-

jected costs, payments on other debt obligations, insurance, taxes, etc.—all projected **payment obligations.**

When you complete this exercise, you will come up with a balance which tells you: *The amount of future funds (cash flow) available to service additional term loans.*

Don Redding, Senior Vice President and for many years Director of the Commercial Loan Officer Development School (irreverently called the CLOD School) of NCNB National Bank in Charlotte NC, says it this way: "You don't make the loan if you can't see the **FATSATL!**" (*Funds Available to Service Additional Term Loans*).

which specialize in making the kinds of relatively high-risk (so-called "nonbankable") loans which generate high interest income. These include factoring companies which provide working capital secured by accounts receivable, goods in process, etc., consumer loan companies, commercial leasing companies, and others. When a bank receives an "unbankable" loan application, the loan officer may refer the applicant to one of these high-risk-lending subsidiaries.

The Advantage of "Pooling" in Reducing Default Risk

Suppose (to be ridiculous) that a bank only had one large loan in its portfolio. If anything happens to cause that loan to default, there goes the bank! At the opposite extreme, suppose it had one million loans in its portfolio. Then any one of those loans could default and the bank would hardly notice. The point: The more loans in the portfolio, (assuming the loans are in diversified businesses and are independent of each other) the lower the default risk of the total portfolio.

Large banks with large loan portfolios can make larger individual loans without "betting the bank." And they can make some loans which are more risky than would be prudent for a bank with a smaller loan portfolio. Bankers sometimes refer to the **ten-percent rule**: "Never carry a loan which amounts to more than 10 percent of your capital."

The small bank must carefully limit the size of its largest loan, and must be careful to minimize the chances of default on each of its individual loans. As a further precaution, small banks usually share their larger loans with one of their (larger) correspondent banks.

The Risk of Borrowing Short and Lending Long

The maturity of a bank's sources of funds tends to be short-term, while most borrowers prefer to borrow longer-term. The ultimate example of this is the home-buyer who wants a 30-year mortgage from the thrift institution which acquires much of its funds from immediately-withdrawable savings deposits.

How does the bank or thrift reduce exposure to interest rate risk? After the revolutionary upheaval which devastated a significant part of the thrift industry in the 1980s, several ways have been found to lessen or eliminate this interest-rate and liquidity risk.

Repricing (in Effect) Converts Long-Term into Short Term. Most loans these days are floating-rate. Suppose money market rates go up. The bank's cost of funds goes up and the rate on floating-rate loans also goes up. So the bank is protected from the risk of rising interest rates.

By the early 1980s most business loans (for some banks, *all*) were being made at "prime plus" or some other floating rate—perhaps "Fed funds plus" or "LIBOR plus" as explained previously. In the present mortgage market most loans are adjustable rate mortgages (ARMs) or variable rate mortgages (VRMs).

The move to adjustable rate loans accomplishes what the bankers call **repricing** of loans at regular intervals. From the point of view of the interest income from the loan, this practice (in effect) turns long-term instruments into a series of shorter-term instruments, with the effective length-of-term being the period of time between one repricing and the next. The borrower has the commitment of the funds for the entire period, but the cost of the funds to the borrower (and interest income to the bank) is subject to change at regular intervals.

Matching Maturities Reduces Interest Rate Risk. Another technique now widely used is the matching of maturities of assets and liabilities. For example, if a business wants a three-year fixed-rate term loan, then make the loan. But at the same time, sell a three-year fixed-rate CD. And be sure that the fixed rate on the three-year loan is high enough to provide a profitable spread above the rate paid on the three-year CD. Then, on this loan, the bank is *free of interest rate risk* regardless of what happens to market rates.

But matching maturities on very-long-term assets (such as home mortgages) isn't as easy to work out. That's why repricing arrangements (ARMs and VRMs) are being used. Also, by the late 1980s the securitization and marketing of mortgages and other long-term assets (explained previously) was providing new liquidity for long-term assets—another way out of the "borrowing short and lending long" dilemma.

BALANCED DIVERSIFICATION: THE ONLY WAY TO SAFETY AND PROFITS

Suppose this is the last half of the 1970s. Oil drilling and oil production are booming in your area. One day, one of your good customers comes in and wants to borrow a million dollars to buy drilling equipment.

The credit analysis shows that this borower is impeccable. Cash flow to repay the loan is easily projected, and with a wide margin to spare. Should you make the loan?

First, take a look at your total loan portfolio. And remember this: It isn't the amount of risk of this additional asset that matters. It's the additional riskiness of the total portfolio which results from the addition of this asset.

Suppose you find that during this booming period in the oil industry you have managed to get 80 percent of your C&I loans in energy-related businesses. Should you make the loan? Not if you're planning to add this loan to your portfolio. But fortunately, you don't have to do that.

Banks Shouldn't Necessarily Hold All the Loans They Make

You should make the energy-related loan to your good customer. But you should not hold this loan in your portfolio. Nor should you continue to hold all of those other energy-related loans.

A Bank Can Sell Some Loans and Reduce Portfolio Risk. You should either *sell some of your energy-related loans*, or else enter some *participation arrangements* with and through your *correspondent banks* and thereby reduce your exposure to the ups and downs of the energy industry. Through loan sales and participations you can work it out so that other banks will own a significant portion of your energy-related loans. And you can arrange to have a much larger percentage of non-energy-related loans and participations in your portfolio.

The loan resale and participation market has expanded rapidly during the 1980s. This market makes it possible for a bank to originate the kinds of loans for which there is a demand in the local area, and without undue risk exposure. The objectives of portfolio diversification can be achieved by selling and arranging participations for these loans, while simultaneously acquiring ownership of and participations in other loans—ideally, loans which will exhibit a negative covariance with the loans already in your portfolio.

Several Banks Purposely Originate Loans for Sale. During the 1980s many of the larger banks have been actively originating loans for sale, or for participation. Loans which have been sold do not appear as assets on the bank's balance sheet. So the sale of loans reduces the bank's total assets and thereby increases the bank's capital-to-assets ratio. So loan orgination (and sale) can be profitable and desirable for the bank and can serve the credit demands of the bank's local customers as well. Box 16-4 describes the process and some advantages of the securitization and sale of loans.

Banking Syndicates Share Risk and Return. Another technique for achieving diversification of the loan portfolio is to participate in a "syndicate" of several banks which get together for the purpose of jointly making a large loan. Each bank in the syndicate carries a share of the risk and receives some of the return. Several loans to large corporations and to foreign governments are carried in this way, and without undue risk exposure to any individual financial institution.

Trading Loans with Other-Banks Can Reduce Risk for All

The *bottom line* on loan portfolio diversification is this: Regardless of which loans a bank may make, it should *hold in inventory* only those loans which produce a balanced and diversified portfolio.

A bank should sell some loans and buy others to achieve diversity as to industry, geographic area, cyclical nature of the business, and other characteristics. Banks in two different geographic areas, each with loans concentrated in

Box 16-4

Feature: The Securitization and Sale of Loans

More Banks Sell Part of Loan Portfolios
Credits Pooled as Securities, Taken Off Books

By Leonard M. Apcar

Staff Reporter of The Wall Street Journal

More and more banks are offering parts of their loan portfolios to investors in what is becoming one of the most popular bank balance sheet strategies in years.

Until recently, banks grew by making loans and keeping them on their books until borrowers paid them off. Now, some banks are reversing course and getting loans off their books by selling them.

What began with the sale of mortgage loans is spreading to the sale of auto loans, credit-card accounts and, in some cases, even a bank's worst loans.

About $10 billion in loan-backed securities were sold publicly last year, mostly by firms other than banks. But banks, securities firms and bank analysts say that is just the beginning, as an increasing number of banks are deciding whether to shed some loans. The sales aren't without risk to the investors, of course, and regulators are scrutinizing the offerings closely.

The strategy goes like this: Banks package some loans that they use to back a certificate or note. The income from the loans pays interest on the securities and—because the bank receives a higher interest rate on the loans than it pays—allows a profit for the bank, which continues to handle the loan record-keeping for the accounts. The bank wipes the loans off its books and uses the proceeds from the securities sale to make new loans. The loan sale also gives the bank additional room under regulatory capital-to-loan guidelines to make new loans.

"If you can have a stream of income without tying up equity," Scott D. Jackson, *a senior vice president at RepublicBank Corp. of Dallas, asks, "why wouldn't you do that all day?"*

Last week, BankAmerica Corp. began a public offering of $400 million in credit-card-backed certificates, expected to mature in about two years, with 6.95% yield. In January, RepublicBank's Delaware credit-card bank held the first public sale of $200 million in credit-card-backed notes, secured by nearly $240 million in balances outstanding of Visa and MasterCard accounts. The notes were quickly gobbled up by institutional investors that liked its 7.25% yield with an average three-year life. Other banks say they are considering following BankAmerica and RepublicBank.

Asset-Backed Issues

The first public issue of asset-backed securities was about two years ago, when Sperry Corp. offered securities backed by computer leases. Soon after, the finance units of General Motors Corp. and Nissan Motor Co. flooded the market with securities backed by auto loans.

Pawning part of a bank portfolio was unthinkable only a few years ago. For generations, banks grew by booking more assets on their balance sheet; the greater the loan portfolio, the greater the bank's capacity for making loans and profits.

But banks are quickly becoming some of the most innovative players in the sale of asset-backed securities. They have the most diverse loan portfolios of any lenders. And because capital levels are set by government regulators, they are under pressure to invest carefully. "The game has really shifted from asset size to capital management," says James J. McDermott Jr., a bank analyst with Keefe, Bruyette & Woods Inc., New York.

Better Use of Capital

A big reason for selling bank loans is to better use a bank's capital, the financial cushion that banks are required to have to protect deposits. In recent years, some big banks have had to scrape to maintain adequate capital levels. Only a few years ago, lower capital levels were permissible. But now, regulators view capital as a sign of a bank's strength and they require banks to maintain capital levels of at least 5.5% to 6% of a bank's assets.

In simplest terms, the capital rules means that for every $100 in loans, a bank needs about $6 in capital coverage (which consists of a bank's shareholders' equity, loan-loss reserves, retained earnings, and other equity).

"If they want to keep growing, they are going to run into capital constraints," says Saul

Sanders, a Goldman, Sachs & Co. vice president. "If you sell assets rather than hold them, it diminishes your need for capital," he adds.

Capital isn't cheap and raising it in the debt or stock markets may dilute the holdings of existing bank shareholders. Or, banking firms with stocks selling considerably below book value, such as BankAmerica and RepublicBank, may want to avoid issuing new stock now.

Matching Maturities

Asset-backed-securities sales have other advantages, too. They allow banks to match long-term loans with long-term funds. Instead of funding a four-year auto loan with certificates of deposit of a year or less, banks can raise the money to fund the loan with a longer-term note with a fixed interest rate. "Banks with balance sheets under pressure are looking for ways to secure liquidity," says a Patricia Jehle, a Salomon Brothers Inc. director. And if deposits don't grow, the securities offering assures a funding source for the bank's loans, she says

Before the RepublicBank offering, its credit-card receivables were funded with deposits raised mostly by its big Dallas bank, which like all banks, included a mix of time deposits with varying maturities. By raising funds for its credit-card loans with a securities sale, the credit-card operation has a fixed funding base for its credit-card loans and the big Dallas bank has more capacity to deal with the short-term funding needs of the rest of RepublicBank.

Security Pacific Corp. of Los Angeles is moving aggressively into asset-backed-securities sales for other reasons. In the past year, it sold more than $1 billion in mortgage-backed securities and it is weighing the possibility of offering securities tied to credit cards and auto loans.

Lower Cost of Lending

It has been selling off its mortgages so that it can make more mortgage loans and take a larger share of the home lending market. By removing loans from its books and selling them, the bank figures it's lowering its overall cost of lending, thus allowing it to shave a quarter to one-half percentage point off a home loan. "We want more velocity to our capital." says Frederick T. Waldeck, Security Pacific's executive vice president and managing director of the merchant bank group.

Under the old rules of banking, Mr. Waldeck says Security Pacific would have set a limit on how much of its loan portfolio would be set aside for mortgage lending. And when the bank reached that level, "traditionally, we would have turned off our spigot." he says.

. . .

The Next Step

Experts say that the next step is for banks to package home equity loans to back offerings of securities. And Drexel Burnham Lambert Inc. has designed an offering package that would allow a bank to sell its nonperforming loans to investors at a deep discount. Drexel believes that a banker might be willing to accept 50 cents on the dollar for a bad loan today instead of waiting for a higher percentage of the loan over 10 years. With 50 cents on the dollar now, the funds can be reinvested in such a way to allow the bank to recoup the total amount of the loan in fewer years, Drexel says, plus an amount to cover the charge to capital for writing down the bad loans.

Selling off the past-due loans now could help a bank avoid a loan-loss disaster later, Charles W. Peabody, a Drexel analyst, says. But, he adds, "politically, it is very difficult for a bank to accept. For them to do this, they have to admit that they made bad loans, and that is a bad political pill to swallow."

The Wall Street Journal, Wednesday, March 4, 1987 p. 14. Reprinted by permission.

their local industries, can trade some loans with each other and thereby significantly reduce the total risk of both portfolios. But as Steve Salisbury, Senior Vice President of Triangle Bank and Trust, Raleigh, N. C. reminds me, this is sometimes easier said than done.

Successful banking, more than any other one thing, depends on *successful lending practices* and *successful loan portfolio management*. Mostly it's a matter of successful *credit analysis* and successful *application of the principles of portfolio choice*.

SUMMARY

- Bank **asset management** requires considerations of *liquidity, safety, earnings, reserve requirements,* and *pledging requirements.*

- The bank's **money desk manager** must compute average daily required reserves on a two-week period (beginning Tuesday and ending on Monday) and hold average daily reserve balances for a two-week period, lagged two days (Thursday through Wednesday).

- When reserve adjustments are needed the money manager usually buys or sells Fed funds. Some small banks hold excess Fed funds and make reserve adjustments by increasing or decreasing their amounts of Fed funds sold.

- In managing the bank's investments portfolio, the principles of portfolio choice apply. Also pledging requirements, collateral for repos and discount borrowing, and the tax status of "minus" all need to be considered.

- The bank's lending activities and the management of its loan portfolio are critical to the success of the bank. Careful credit analysis is essential.

- Banks frequently sell loans or arrange for participation by other banks. Also, packages of loans are now being "securitized" and the securities sold in the open markets. The greater the number of different kinds of loans (and participations) a bank holds, the greater the "pooling effect" in reducing default risk.

- Market risk (of changing interest rates) can be significantly reduced by variable rates (frequent loan-rate repricing) and by matching the maturities of assets and liabilities.

- The only way to have a highly profitable loan portfolio which is also safe, is to have one which is diversified and balanced as to companies, industry, geographic area, and business cycle fluctuations.

Important Principles, Issues, Concepts, Terms

The bank as a "portfolio of assets"

Cash items in process of collection

Role of the money desk manager

Reserves computation period

Reserves holding period

Wild Wednesday

The 2% excess or deficiency carry-forward

Using "Fed funds sold" to ease the money management task

Contemporaneous Reserve Accounting (CRA)

Lagged Reserve Accounting (LRA)

Pledging requirements

"Munis"

Credit analysis

FATSATL

The bank's comparative advantage in loans to small local borrowers

Pooling

Repricing

Matching maturities

Balanced diversification of the loan portfolio

Loan sales

Loan participations

Questions

1. Describe the broad categories of assets among which bank portfolio managers must decide, then mention some of the specific kinds of assets within each category.

2. List the major kinds of cash assets which banks hold, and briefly describe each.

3. Exactly what does the banks "money desk manager" do? And why is that task sometimes especially difficult? Explain.

4. Explain the difference between LRA and CRA and explain when and why the Fed shifted from the former to the latter.

5. What are some of the factors other than income or risk which influence a bank's investment portfolio choices? Explain.

6. Explain the advantage of "pooling" in reducing the risk of the loan portfolio.

7. Explain as much as you can about *credit analysis*. Mention specific things which should be scrutinized in the credit analysis process, and indicate which of these you think are most important.

8. What is the purpose of collateral?

9. Explain some of the ways that banks use to reduce the inherent risk involved in "borrowing short and lending long."

Suggested Readings

Bender, Roxanne. "Bank Liquidity: Learning to Love It." *Bankers Monthly*. December 1985.

Benston, George, et. al. *Safe and Sound Banking*. Cambridge, Mass.: MIT Press, 1986.

Board of Governors of the Federal Reserve System. *Functional Cost Analysis*. Washington, D.C.: U.S. Government Printing Office, 1984.

Brewer, Elijah. "Bank Funds Management Comes of Age —A Balance Sheet Analysis." *Economic Perspectives* 4. Federal Reserve Bank of Chicago 13–18.

Business Week. "The Home Equity Gold Rush." February 9, 1987.

Cates, David C. "What's an Adequate Loan-Loss Reserve?" *ABA Banking Journal*. March 1985.

Cocheo, Steve. "Anatomy of an Examination." *ABA Banking Journal*. February 1986.

Fielke, Norman. "International Lending on Trial." *New England Economic Review*. Federal Reserve Bank of Boston (May/June 1983), 5–13.

Gendreau, Brian, and Scott Prince. "The Private Costs of Bank Failure." *Business Review*. Federal Reserve Bank of Philadelphia, March/1986.

Gross, Laura. "Tapping Profit in Trust Services." *American Banker*. November 24, 1986.

Havrilesky, Thomas, and John Boorman. *Current Perspectives in Banking*. Arlington Heights, Ill.: AHM Publishing Co., 1976.

Hayes, Douglas. *Bank Funds Management*. Ann Arbor, Mich.: University of Michigan, Graduate School of Business Administration, 1980.

Hempel, George, Alan Coleman, and Donald Simonson. *Bank Management: Test and Cases*. New York: John Wiley & Sons, 1986.

Judd, John P., and Brian Motley. "Ending the lag." *Weekly Letter*. Federal Reserve Bank of San Francisco, March 30, 1984.

Luckett, Dudley G. "Approaches to Bank Liquidity Management." *Economic Review*. Federal Reserve Bank of Kansas City (March 1980), 11–27.

McKinley, John E. III, et. al. *Problem Loan Strategies*. Philadelphia: Robert Morris Associates, 1985.

Pavel, Christine, and Paula Binkley. "Costs and Competition in Bank Credit Cards." *Economic Perspectives*. March/April 1987.

Stigum, Marcia, and Rene Branch, Jr. *Managing Bank Assets and Liabilities*. Homewood, Ill.: Dow Jones-Irwin, 1983.

Tarhan, Vefa. "Individual Bank Reserve Management." *Economic Perspectives*. Federal Reserve Bank of Chicago, July/August 1984.

Toevs, Alden, and Haney, William. *Guide to Asset-Liability Models*. New York: Morgan Stanley, 1984.

Weinstein, Michael. "Credit Card Business Mushrooms at Large Banks." *American Banker*. August 14, 1986.

CHAPTER 17

Managing Bank Liabilities and Capital

Chapter Objectives

This chapter focuses on the other side of the bank's balance sheet: liabilities and capital. From this chapter you'll understand and be able to explain:

1. The major **liabilities** on the bank's balance sheet, and how and why these have been changing, including:
   a. changes in the bank's **deposit structure**,
   b. kinds of and reasons for the increasing use of **borrowings** (managed liabilities), and
   c. the different kinds of **checkable deposits** which have become available during the 1980s.
2. The nature and importance of **bank capital** and how it is defined and accounted for in the bank's balance sheet.
3. The factors influencing a bank's **solvency** and the importance of **capital adequacy** in maintaining solvency.
4. The effect of **deposit insurance** on capital adequacy and on the bank's solvency and liquidity.
5. The relationship between **bank capital** and **return on equity (ROE)**.
6. Alternative techniques bank's can use to meet the **liquidity needs** caused by deposit outflows.
7. Some reasons for and effects of the increasing ratio of **loans** to **deposits**.
8. Basic objectives and techniques of **asset/liability management**.

OVERVIEW OF THE BANK'S LIABILITIES

Table 17-1 presents the percentage distribution of liabilities and capital for all insured commercial banks, with comparative figures from the early 1960s to 1988. You can see that over the past quarter-century several major changes have occurred in the sources of bank funds.

Checkable Deposits: Declining Percentage and Changing Structure

Perhaps the most striking change in bank liabilities has been the sharp decline in non-interest-bearing demand deposits. Demand deposit accounts (DDs, or DDAs)

Table 17-1.   Percentage Distribution of Liabilities and Capital of All Insured Commercial Banks Beginning of year 1961, 1971, 1988

	1961 %	1971 %	1988 %
Transactions (checkable) deposits	61	43	25
Demand deposits	61	43	12
Other checkable deposits	0	0	13
Small nontransactions deposits	29	36	35
Passbook savings	22	17	19
Time deposits	7	19	16
Large negotiable CDs ($100,000 and up)	0	5	12
Borrowings and miscellaneous liabilities	2	9	22
Owners equity (capital)	8	7	6
Total	100%	100%	100%
Dollar Value of Total Liabilities Plus Capital (billions of dollars)	$256	$576	$2,801

Source: Data from FDIC *Annual Reports* (various issues), and *Federal Reserve Bulletin* (various issues), p. A18. Percentages calculated by author.

accounted for more than 60% of bank funds at the beginning of 1961. By the beginning of 1988, DDs had dropped to only 12%. The reason this figure doesn't drop all the way to zero is because businesses are prohibited from having interest-bearing checkable accounts.

Other checkable deposits (OCDs)—which pay interest and which did not exist on a broad scale prior to the 1980s—by 1988 were providing 13% of total bank funds.

Savings and Small Time Deposits

Passbook savings deposits accounted for 22% of bank funds in 1961, but dropped to 17% in 1971. Then in the early 1980s, passbook savings balances decreased to a low of about 5% because of widespread disintermediation.

Savers withdrew their funds because Regulation Q prohibited the banks from raising the 5-1/4% rate on passbook savings accounts, at a time when double digit rates were available from money market mutual funds and other sources. But with the phaseout of Reg Q during the first half of the 1980s, savings deposits again grew. Table 17-1 shows that by 1988 passbook savings deposits were providing 19 percent of total bank funds.

Small time deposits, which provided only 7% of bank funds in 1961, grew rapidly during the 1960s and '70s. Then during the early 1980s, rates on these deposits were deregulated more rapidly than were the rates on passbook savings. So small time deposits grew in relative importance. But in the last half of the 1980s the percentage of small time deposits declined as passbook savings grew, reflecting the final phase-out of Reg Q (March 1, 1986).

Large Marketable Time Deposits

Large negotiable CDs—which did not even exist in 1961—have provided banks an opportunity to obtain funds in the nationwide and worldwide money markets.

These large CDs are money market instruments—instruments of bank **liability management**—and are not really comparable to passbook savings and small time deposits. That's why large time deposits are listed separately in Table 17-1.

Borrowings and Miscellaneous Liabilities

The last liability item shown in the Table 17-1 is "borrowings and miscellaneous liabilities." This item has shown rapid growth, especially since the early 1980s. Most of this increase reflects borrowings, and it includes several sources of funds.

In addition to the "usual and traditional" borrowings—borrowing from other banks in the Fed funds market, and borrowing from the district Federal Reserve bank at the discount rate—two new kinds of borrowings have grown explosively: Banks borrowing from other corporate units within their own holding company structure (from subsidiaries, affiliates, and foreign branches) and (2) banks borrowing through repurchase agreements.

Intercorporate Borrowing. Banks frequently borrow from their parent holding companies. Holding companies purposely acquire funds to lend to their subsidiary banks.

Banks also borrow from their foreign branches. These branches often are established for the purpose of taking Eurodollar deposits and then lending the dollars to the parent bank. Bank holding companies also hold various other subsidiaries and affiliates which sometimes are created for the purpose of acquiring funds and then providing these funds to the parent or affiliate bank within the holding company structure.

Repurchase Agreements (RPs). You have already read about RPs in the section on "money market instruments" in Chapter 12. Banks use these to acquire short-term funds, providing T-bills as collateral. As explained previously, banks frequently use RPs as needed to build their reserve balances at the Fed.

Now that you have an overview of the important sources of bank funds and how these sources have changed since the beginning of the 1960s. The following sections give a more detailed explanation of the major items in Table 17-1. First there's a closer look at the various kinds of **deposits**. Then there's an analysis of **bank capital** (owner's equity).

THE DEPOSIT STRUCTURE OF THE TYPICAL BANK

Back in the early 1960s the deposit structure of "the typical bank" was not very complex. Essentially, the customer's choice was between a non-interest-bearing checking account and a low-interest-paying savings account. But today all banks offer their customers a broad range of accounts—both checkable and non-checkable.

Transactions (Checkable) Deposits

The traditional "checkable deposit" is the "demand deposit." It was not until the 1970s that *other checkable deposits* (OCDs) became available in a few states, and not until 1980 that OCDs became available nationwide. With the nationwide availability of interest-bearing checkable deposits it's understandable that non-interest-bearing demand deposit balances declined, while OCD balances increased.

Checkable deposits now include (in addition to demand deposits) interest-bearing NOW accounts, super-NOW accounts (which require larger minimum balances and pay more interest), and deposit accounts called "money market deposit accounts (MMDAs)" which pay interest based on money market rates. Box 17-1 tells more about NOW accounts.

All OCDs Are Really "Demand" Deposits. All of the differnt kinds of "OCD" accounts—although they go by several different names—are, in practice, *demand deposits*. The bank is obligated to make payments from all of these accounts *on demand*.

Given a choice, your friendly neighborhood banker would prefer that you place your money in a demand deposit (DD) because (as of mid-1988) no interest is paid on these deposits. Other checkable deposits (OCDs) pay interest to the depositor, but usually at lower rates than on non-checkable savings deposits or time deposits.

There are costs involved in maintaining, managing, and servicing checkable accounts. In addition to the interest payments to the OCD depositors, there is the cost of processing checks, sending out statements, providing various banking services (ATMs, tellers, etc.), and responding to the depositors' various other banking needs. These checking-deposit-related costs are a large part of the typical bank's (noninterest) operating costs. So not even non-interest-bearing demand deposit funds are really "cost free" to the bank.

The function of providing services to customers involves employee salaries, cost of physical facilities, etc., and amounts to about 25% of total operating expenses of the average bank.

The Bank's Largest Expense Item: Cost of Funds. The largest single cost item on the typical bank's profit and loss statement is **cost of funds**. And a large part of this cost of funds consists of interest paid on deposits: checkable deposits, plus time deposits. In the late 1980s, for the average bank interest payments on total deposits (including CDs) amounted to more than 50% of total operating expenses.

Box 17-1

Questions: Exactly What Is a NOW Account?

A "NOW" account is an interest-bearing savings account on which "Negotiable Orders of Withdrawal" can be written. A "negotiable order of withdrawal" looks exactly like a check, feels exactly like a check, and works exactly like a check. But it can't be a check because the laws say that checks can be written only on demand deposits. So these "check-like instruments" written on OCD accounts must have another name. Hence: "Negotiable Orders of Withdrawal," and "NOW accounts."

Small Nontransactions Deposits

Table 17-1 indicates that at the beginning of 1988, small nontransactions deposits were the largest single source of bank funds, amounting to 35% of the total. Savings deposits amounted to 19% of the total, while small time deposits made up 16%.

These nontransactions balances are large because banks pay more interest on these than on OCDs. Banks can afford to pay more on nontransactions accounts because they do not provide as many services to the depositor, required reserves are low or zero, and because these deposits do not turn over as rapidly. Competition for funds among banks and between banks and other financial institutions tends to keep these rates relatively high.

Passbook Savings Deposits. Table 17-1 indicates that in 1961 passbook savings deposits were the only major source of funds other than demand deposits. But you know what happened after that.

Reg Q caused funds to flow out of these deposits and into higher interest-paying instruments. Savings deposits never have quite recovered from this experience. Still, passbook savings deposits increased from their low point of about 5% of total sources of funds in the early 1980s, to 19% at the beginning of 1988. Now that banks have been freed from the restrictions of Reg Q they have been able to make these accounts more competitive and attract more deposits.

The holder of a passbook savings account can add or withdraw funds at any time. Deposits, withdrawals, and interest payments are recorded in a "passbook" which is the owner's record of the account. In the last few years many banks are omitting the passbook and issuing computerized monthly statements instead.

Passbook savings deposits technically are not payable on demand. The bank has the legal right to require 30-day notice before withdrawal. But in practice this legally mandated "30-day notice" is ignored.

Small-Denomination Time Deposits (Small CDs). Small-denomination CDs always have a fixed term to maturity, ranging from as little as seven days, up to more than five years. These CDs are withdrawable before maturity, but only with a penalty of lost interest.

Small denomination CDs are not marketable. They are "bought" by depositors who expect to hold them until maturity. These CDs are completely different from the large-denomination marketable CDs, explained previously.

BANK CAPITAL (OWNER'S EQUITY)

Table 17-1 shows that owner's equity, or "bank capital" amounts to about 6% of the total sources of funds for commercial banks. Bank capital is computed as the difference between the value of **total assets** and **total liabilities**. The assets indicate the value of everything the bank **owns**; the liabilities indicate the value of everything the bank **owes**. What's left is the value that belongs to the stockholders—the book value of the bank: **bank capital**.

Capital Value "Floats" on Total Asset Value

The value of a Bank's *capital* depends on the value of the bank's *assets*. With a given amount of total liabilities, if total asset value increases, capital increases. If total asset value decreases, capital decreases.

For example, suppose market conditions for some reason caused the value of the bank's assets to increase (without any corresponding increase in liabilities). Then bank capital would automatically increase. Also, as the bank earns income, that increases total bank assets (cash, or other assets), so bank capital increases. Bank capital initially comes from funds raised by selling stock. After that, most additions come from retained earnings.

What's so important about **bank capital**? Just this: The solvency of the bank depends on it.

The Issue of Bank Solvency

A bank, just as any other corporation, is **solvent** as long as the total value of its assets exceeds the total value of its liabilities. With most (nonfinancial) businesses a fairly large percentage of the assets are bought with funds supplied by the owners of the corporation. But with a bank or other financial intermediary, the very large majority of the assets are bought with funds obtained from depositors and others—not from funds supplied by the owners of the bank. This means that the assets and the liabilities are almost equal in size, and that the owner's equity (capital) is a small percentage of the total.

For the typical bank, for every $100 in assets, there are something like $94 in liabilities. The other $6 is owner's equity.

For one of these "typical banks" let's suppose some sad things happened. Suppose some loans went bad, and suppose the funds management department had made a mistake and bought long-term low-interest-bearing government securities back when interest rates were low and the market values of those securities have dropped about 20%. And suppose all of these events result in a reduction of the value of total assets by 10%. Total assets which were valued at $100, now are valued at $90, but total liabilities continue to be valued at $94. The bank is insolvent. Total amounts owed to depositors and others add up to more than the total value of the bank's assets.

An Insolvent but Liquid Bank Can Survive

The unfortunate bank in the above example will be forced to go out of business only if (a) the banking examiners arrive, discover the insolvent condition, and force it to close, or (b) the bank's depositors find out. If neither of these events occurs, as long as the bank is **liquid**—can immediately meet all demands for withdrawals, and can pay off all CDs and other obligations as they come due—there's no reason why it can't continue to operate even in its insolvent condition.

If nobody finds out, and if it has strong earnings over the coming months, and if it's lucky and market rates of interest come down again so that the value of its securities portfolio goes up, the bank may become solvent again and continue to operate successfully. No one (except a few senior executives with giant beads of perspiration on their foreheads) will be the wiser.

This example illustrates the distinction between solvency and liquidity. An insolvent bank can continue to operate as long as it is liquid, and as long as no one suspects that it is insolvent. An illiquid bank, even though it may be very solvent, will be forced to close.

On the first day a bank finds itself unable to meet a deposit withdrawal or any other obligation requiring immediate funds, it will be faced by a "run" as depositors try to withdraw their funds. The demands of depositors for funds can force a solvent bank to dump assets on the market to obtain funds. If this happens to many banks simultaneously, the prices of all of the assets dumped on the market will plummet. The previously solvent banks will become insolvent as the value of their assets goes down.

Solvency Is Supported by Capital Adequacy

When the size of the capital account (owner's equity) for the average bank is only about 6% of total asset value, you can see that banks are sitting in a somewhat precarious position. Suppose something happens to cause the total value of assets to drop by only a little more than 6%. The bank is insolvent! Bankrupt! And just think how easy it would be for that to happen.

Suppose market rates of interest went up so that securities values went down by 10%. That isn't a very big move. Moves much greater than that have occurred several times during the 1980s.

And/or suppose that because of difficult economic times a number of loans go bad. It wouldn't take very much to reduce total asset value by more than 6%. And then: insolvency.

Throughout the 1980s there have been many depository financial institutions which have survived many months—or years—of "technical insolvency," while continuing to operate. The FDIC and the FSLIC have been very lenient in permitting insolvent banks and thrifts to continue to operate in the hope that future revenues would build asset value and move the institutions back into solvency. The "capital certificates" for S&Ls established in the Garn-St Germain Act (1982) were for the purpose of providing additional assets to thrifts to help to overcome their "technical bankruptcy."

As a bank's assets decrease in value, how soon will the bank be insolvent? Suppose the bank's capital/asset ratio is 12%. Then asset value can drop by 12% before the bank becomes insolvent. But if the ratio is only 4%, any drop in asset value of more than 4% will bankrupt the bank. So a lot depends on the size of the bank's capital in the first place. (See box 17-2.)

The Bank's Capital Account

The bank balance sheet may list several items under the heading "Capital Accounts." One of the headings usually will be either "Capital" or "Owners Equity."

Loan Loss Reserves. Banks also carry an item called "Reserves For Loan Losses." When a bank experiences a loan loss (and all banks do), the loss reduces the total value of the banks assets. So it automatically reduces the total value of the bank's capital. But by the accounting procedure of carrying a part of the capital value under "Reserves For Loan Losses," when these losses occur the account called "capital" or "owners' equity" is not decreased.

Box 17-2

Question: What Would Have Happened in October of 1987 if Banks Were Holding Stocks As an Important Part of Their Assets?

During the week of October 19, 1987, stock values, on the average, decreased by more than 20 percent. Suppose banks had been holding a large part of their assets in stocks. Would this drop in the stock market have caused bankruptcy for many banks? Yes.

When the average bank has total capital of only around 6% of total assets, that means that the bank owes to its depositors and others, 94 percent of the value of its assets. Then suppose the bank's assets decrease in value by 6 percent.

Then *all* of the asset value is owed to the depositors and others. Capital value is zero. Then if asset value drops any more, it means that the bank doesn't have enough in asset value to pay off its depositors and others to whom it has financial obligations.

A more than 20 percent drop in the value of securities in the bank's assets? It would bankrupt a lot of them. And, considering the domino effect in the financial world, there's just no telling what would have happened after that.

The loan loss reserve account says, in effect: "This is that part of the bank's capital which we are not going to call 'capital,' or 'owners equity,' because it may be subject to sudden decreases as a result of unexpected loan losses."

Undivided Profits and/or Surplus. A third item in the bank's capital account is "undivided profits" and/or "surplus." These are the "holding pool" accounts for the bank's earnings. For a profitable bank, the numbers in these acccounts will keep increasing until a decision is made either (1) to transfer these numbers into the "owners equity" or the "loan loss reserve" accounts, or (2) to pay out dividends. A dividend payout will reduce the banks cash assets and reduce undivided profits and/or surplus (and total capital) by the same amount.

To the extent that the stockholders deposit their dividend checks in the bank, a dividend payout will not decrease cash assets. It will increase the bank's deposit liabilities instead. The effect on undivided profits and/or surplus and on total bank capital will be the same, either way.

The Bank's Total Capital Is A Minus L—No Matter What the Accounts Are Called. The point which is important (and which is sometimes missed) is this: Regardless of the names of the different "holding pools" in the bank's capital account, the *total value of the bank's capital is the value of its assets* (A) *minus its liabilities* (L). How this "residual sum" is allocated among the various headings in the capital account has no effect on the total value of the bank's capital.

When asset value falls because of loan losses, that reduces the bank's total capital. The reduction is reflected in the "loan loss reserves" account. When the bank generates earnings, that increases the bank's total capital. But in this case the increase is reflected in the "undivided profits" and/or "surplus" accounts.

The Role of Capital in Protecting Solvency: An Example

Bank capital plays a significant role as a cushion to protect the bank from insolvency in the event of a sharp decrease in the value of the bank's assets. In general, the larger the capital cushion, the greater the degree of safety of the bank. Here's an example. Suppose a community bank, Mt. Airy Fidelity, makes loans to several businesses in its local area. These loans make up a large part of the assets of the bank.

Then suppose the major employer in the area goes bankrupt and closes down. Soon the furniture stores and the appliance stores and automobile repair shops and local restaurants (etc., etc.) cannot make payments on their loans. Some of the local companies go broke. Mt. Airy Fidelity must write off those loans.

When loans are written off, the bank's total asset value decreases. So its total capital decreases. Suppose that all of the loan losses add up to 10% of the value of Mt. Airy Fidelity's assets. And suppose that prior to the losses, the bank's "capital cushion" amounted to only 6% of its total assets. In this case the cushion wasn't thick enough!

The bank's liabilities have remained the same while the value of its assets have dropped by 10%. Before the losses, the computation "assets minus liabilities" $(A - L)$ resulted in a positive figure of 6% of assets. After the loan-loss write-off of 10% the computation $(A - L)$ comes out: minus 4%! Mt. Airy Fidelity is insolvent, meaning: *The value of what it owns is not as great as the value of what it owes.*

In this case, if the bank had held a capital cushion of 12% it would still be solvent. But with a capital cushion of only 6%, with the loss of 10% of the value of its assets it is insolvent (bankrupt). There is no way it can survive without an injection of additional capital from somewhere. Probably the FDIC will work out (and subsidize) the sale of Mt. Airy Fidelity to another financial institution.

The purpose of this illustration is to emphasize the importance of the ratio of bank capital to total bank assets. If that ratio is 6%, then asset value only needs to drop by 6% to put the bank into insolvency. But with a capital-to-assets ratio of 12%, asset value could drop much more before causing a threat to the solvency of the bank.

Deposit Insurance Has Reduced Customers' Concern about Capital Adequacy

In the case of Mt. Airy Fidelity, it isn't likely that any of the local depositors will be hurt. The FDIC will see to that. The FDIC could close the bank, dispose of the assets, then pay off the depositors out of the proceeds, plus FDIC insurance reserve funds. But that is not the usual way.

The FDIC probably would find a bank willing to merge with Mt. Airy Fidelity. Of course the FDIC would need to pay the "rescuing bank" enough to induce them to take on Mt. Airy Fidelity—which has liabilities in excess of assets.

But either way the FDIC decides to proceed, the bank's depositors are not subject to loss—at least not on deposit amounts up to $100,000. So these days the bank's depositors aren't hurt if the bank's capital is inadequate. But back before deposit insurance was established by the *Banking Act of 1933*, a bank's customers were *very concerned* with their bank's **capital adequacy**. In those days, instead of a little sign in the window saying "deposits insured up to $100,000," banks were more likely to have a sign saying "ratio of capital to assets, 15%," or some other indicator of the financial soundness of the bank.

The existence of deposit insurance has made it possible for banks to operate with lower capital/asset ratios, and also to hold somewhat more risky assets. Before the days of deposit insurance, each bank's major customers always kept the bank under scrutiny to make sure that the bank was very safe and very sound.

You can look back at table 17-1 and see that bank capital/asset ratios (total equity capital as a percentage of total assets) have dropped from 8% in 1961 to 6% in 1987. That's a 25% decrease over this 26-year period. By this indicator, banks seem to be getting more risky. But these figures don't tell the whole story.

Ratio of Capital to Risk and Nonrisk Assets

Table 17-1 indicates the increasing riskiness and decreasing liquidity of the average bank's asset structure since the early 1960s: less cash and securities, and more loans. In the late 1980s a much larger percentage of bank assets are *risk assets*.

Point: *The riskiness of bank assets has been increasing at the same time that capital/asset ratios have been decreasing.*

One way to measure the riskiness of a bank's asset structure is to subtract all nonrisk assets—all *cash assets*, and *U.S. Government securities*—from total assets. Suppose we do this for the early 1960s, and for 1988. In the early 1960s, 56% of bank assets were risk assets. By the early 1970s, this 56% had increased to 71%. And by 1988, risk assets had increased to 81% of total assets. So the ratio of bank capital to **risk assets** has declined significantly more than the ratio of capital to **total assets**.

Why don't banks want to carry more capital? Because it's expensive and restricting. Suppose you were operating a bank and you had a capital/asset ratio of 12%. You could increase your profits and return on equity (ROE) by reducing that 12%. Here's how:

First, you could attract enough deposits (and/or "buy" enough funds) to double the size of your liabilities. Then you could acquire assets with those funds. That way you could double the size of your liabilities and assets and double the size of your bank! And then, with good funds management you could double your profits. But if you did all this—and without any increase in your capital—your capital/asset ratio would drop from 12% to 6%. You have a bigger and more profitable bank, but a smaller capital/asset ratio.

Less Capital Means More Return on Equity (ROE)

A basic dilemma of the "capital/asset ratio" is that as a bank becomes more successful—as it takes more deposits and makes more loans—unless its capital grows fairly rapidly, its capital/asset ratio will decline. Also, for a given amount of earnings, the smaller the amount of equity, the larger the percentage return on that equity (ROE) will be.

Here's an example. If a bank's earnings amount to $200,000 and bank capital amounts to $1 million, then ROE is 20%. (A 20% return on $1 million is $200,000.) Not bad! But suppose the bank's capital had amounted to $4 million. Then ROE would only be 5%. (A 5% return on $4 million is $200,000.) Not very good!

At the beginning of 1988, total equity capital of commercial banking institutions amounted to $176 billion. Total assets amounted to $2,801 billion, which works out to an average capital/asset ratio of about 6%. But what about the ratio of *capital-to-risk-assets?*

The Declining Ratio of Capital-to-Risk-Assets

In early 1988, bank holdings of nonrisk assets—U.S. Government securities plus cash assets—amounted to a total of $562 billion. When these nonrisk assets are subtracted from total assets that leaves $2,240 billion in risk assets. The capital-to-risk-assets ratio works out to about 7.9%. Table 17-2 shows the significant decline in the ratio of capital to risk assets between the early 1960s, and 1988: From 15%, to 10%, to 7.9%.

Do these statistics indicate that the U.S. banking system is increasingly unsafe? Perhaps on the road to doom? Not necessarily. Before any conclusions can be drawn on that question we need to take a closer look at the bank's *total asset and liability picture*—and especially at the *bank's sources of liquidity.*

BANK MANAGEMENT AND THE NEED FOR LIQUIDITY

As the bank manager is busy "buying and selling money" (acquiring funds, and making loans and buying securities) what are the objectives? To hold down cost of funds, to hold down risk, to keep earnings on assets high, and to maintain liquidity so as to be able to meet deposit outflows.

How Does a Bank Deal with a Deposit Outflow?

Most banks, most of the time, don't need to be concerned very much about the possibility of unexpected outflows. In a stable and growing economy, most banks will find that both their liabilities (deposits) and their assets (loans) are growing. There seems to be little need for concern about the unlikely event of a significant deposit outflow.

But it is a fact that deposit outflows do occur. And since deposits are payable on demand, the bank must always be ready to meet withdrawal demands as they arise.

A bank can fund a deposit outflow by:

1. Using its excess Fed funds (reducing its "Fed funds sold");
2. Borrowing in the Fed funds market;
3. Selling assets such as T-bills (its secondary reserves);
4. Calling in "call" loans;

Table 17-2.   The Declining Ratio of Equity Capital to Risk Assets (billions of dollars)

	1961	1971	1988
Equity capital (EC)	$ 21	$ 40	$ 176
Risk assets (RA)	$143	$408	$2,240
Ratio (EC ÷ RA)	15%	10%	7.9%

Source: FDIC *Annual Reports*, and *Federal Reserve Bulletin* (various issues).

5. Selling some of its loans to other banks;

6. Borrowing from major corporations or the money market by issuing large ($100,000) negotiable CDs;

7. Borrowing from major corporations, the money market, or from its own major depositors, using repo agreements;

8. Borrowing from the Fed's "discount window."

All of the above alternatives are available to the bank. You will notice that some of the alternatives involve the sale of assets. But several of the alternatives involve borrowing—that is, *actively "buying money" by creating new liabilities.*

Increasing Cost of Funds, and Decreasing Liquidity of Assets

Since the early 1960s the cost of funds for the average bank has increased dramatically. Back when some 60% of bank funds were acquired in the form of non-interest-bearing demand deposits, banks weren't under great pressure to "earn top dollar" on these funds.

In the early 1960s, only about one-fourth of an average bank's operating expenses was accounted for by interest payments on deposits. By the late 1980s, interest on bank deposits and other sources of funds had increased to more than 65% of operating expenses for the average bank.

The dramatic increase in the cost of funds has placed banks under great pressure to maximize earnings on their uses of funds. So banks have reduced their holdings of their more liquid kinds of assets: cash assets, and U.S. Government securities—and have increased their holdings of loans—the least liquid item in the asset structure.

The Increasing Ratio of Loans to Deposits Reduces Bank Liquidity

It's obvious why the banks have been willing to reduce the liquidity of their asset structure: to generate enough earnings to survive in today's highly competitive financial services marketplace!

One measure of a bank's liquidity is the ratio of its loans to its deposits. Since loans are the least liquid of its major kinds of assets, the higher the loan/deposit ratio the lower the liquidity of the bank. The ratio of loans to deposits in the early 1960s was about 50%. By 1970 it had increased to 65%. By 1988 it was up to about 80%.

What about this decline in liquidity? As the asset structure has become much less liquid, how have banks been able to meet their liquidity needs? *Not entirely from liquidity on the asset side* of the balance sheet (which has declined) but also by looking to the other side of the balance sheet: *the liabilities side.*

Obtaining Liquidity by Issuing Liabilities to "Buy Money"

Before the 1960s, bank liquidity management meant: "Hold a sufficient number of highly liquid, easily marketable assets, and a sizeable pool of cash assets as well." During those days, few bankers ever thought of borrowing excess reserves from other banks. And no one was selling $100,000 marketable CDs!

The idea that it is possible to use *liability management* to meet the liquidity needs of a bank first began to catch on in the 1960s. Large negotiable CDs were first introduced by the large money center banks in the early 1960s. Also during the 1960s the Fed funds market grew rapidly. Suddenly it was becoming possible for a bank to reach out into the financial markets and acquire funds on a moment's notice to meet any unexpected need for liquidity. And not only that.

Liability management offers the opportunity for banks to do more than just "take deposits." They can go into the money markets and actively buy as much funds as they wish to buy. And with those funds they can make whatever loans or acquire whatever other assets they wish to hold.

"Growing the Bank" with Managed Liabilities— with "Bought Money"

In the "new modern world of managed liabilities" no longer does the size of the deposit base determine or limit the size of the bank. These days, many major banks make floating-rate loans at "prime plus" and fund these loans by borrowing in the Fed funds market. Since both the Fed funds rate and the prime rate move in response to current market conditions, the bank "locks in a spread" and is protected against market risk.

Now you can understand why, in table 17-1, borrowings and miscellaneous liabilities (now almost entirely *borrowings*) increased from about 2% of total liabilities and capital in the early 1960s to about 22% of the total in early 1988. Without the flexibility provided by *liability management* (including the acquisition of instantly available funds in the money market) it would not have been prudent for banks to shift so heavily into higher-paying assets (loans) and thereby reduce the liquidity of their asset structure.

Asset-Liability Management and Floating-Rate Deposits and Loans

A few years ago it was usually accurate to say that banks were in the business of "borrowing short and lending long." For the banks and other depository institutions, the funds came in as deposits (subject to immediate withdrawal) and were placed in fixed-rate loans with terms of several months or years. During "normal times" this arrangement was profitable for banks. They paid less on their "short-term sources of funds" than they received on their "longer-term uses of funds."

As long as the yield curve slopes upward, borrowing short and lending long pays off. But during the late 1970s and early '80s, banks and thrifts found that this "borrowing short and lending long" exposes them to serious interest rate risk. You read about that in the last chapter. And you read about floating-rate loans and matching maturities to minimize interest-rate risk. But there's another advantage of matching maturities: liquidity.

Matching Maturities Can Provide Liquidity When Needed

When a bank matches the maturities of its assets and its liabilities, in addition to protecting itself from interest rate changes, it also protects itself from facing liquidity problems in the future. As liabilities mature (3-year CDs come due for example) the bank must be ready to pay off. Where does the bank get the funds?

If the bank has 3-year term loans coming due at exactly the same time as the 3-year CDs, then, no problem! The funds from the term loan repayments are exactly sufficient to meet the needs for payoffs on the CDs.

In practice, many of the CDs will be renewed and the funds will not be withdrawn. Also, some of the term loans are likely to be extended. But the fact that both the CDs and the term loans became due simultaneously guarantees that the bank will not face a "liquidity crunch."

These days, most of the bank's assets and liabilities have variable rates. So the cost of funds and returns on funds adjust to reflect financial market conditions. And now the objective of **matching maturities** of assets and liabilities is often justified on the basis of **liquidity** instead of **interest rate** considerations.

Asset-Liability (A/L) Management: A Continuous Process

The experience of recent years has taught the managers of all depository institutions of the absolute necessity of continuous asset-liability (A/L) management. They must be constantly reviewing their assets and liabilities to determine their degree of interest rate risk. Rate-sensitive assets must be compared with rate-sensitive liabilities and (hopefully) balanced. Relative terms to maturity of assets and liabilities must be monitored. Adjustments must be made as needed.

Discretionary Funds Management

At any time, many of the assets and liabilities are "set" for awhile. Once a term loan is made, or a CD sold, there's no need for the A/L managers to be concerned about those items on a daily basis.

But every day, discretionary decisions must be made. Funds are flowing into and out of the bank. Deposits are flowing in and out. Loans are maturing and new loans are being made. Here is where the daily decisions must be made—at the "rolling over edge" of the assets and liabilities. The appendix to this chapter provides much more information on how financial institutions manage interest rate risk.

THE ULTIMATE SOURCE OF SAFETY AND LIQUIDITY: A HEALTHY ECONOMY

With such a large percentage of bank assets (about 65%) now in the form of loans, it's obvious that the health of the banking system depends on the health of the economy. Consumer borrowers expect to continue to be employed. Businesses expect to continue to be profitable and to grow. But a downturn in the economy could change all that.

Clearly, the banking system always is exposed to the potential danger of a serious and prolonged economic downturn. A depression could force sizeable numbers of borrowers to default.

Counterbalancing this potential danger are two very important backup systems. One is the FDIC which guarantees depositors that they will not lose their money if the bank fails. The other is the one source of unlimited liquidity—the central bank—the Federal Reserve System. You'll be reading all about the Fed and its role of "lender of last resort" and its other functions as well in the chapters coming up.

SUMMARY

- The structure of **bank liabilities** has changed significantly over the past 25 years. Checkable deposits (more than half, interest-bearing) now make up 25% of total liabilities. Other (noncheckable) deposits make up 35% of the total.

- Banks issue large negotiable CDs ($100,000 and up) to "buy funds." Also, bank borrowings, including Fed funds purchased, repo borrowings, and intercorporate borrowing among units within a bank holding company have become important sources of funds during the 1980s.

- **Cost of funds**—mostly interest on deposits, plus borrowed funds—is the largest single cost item for the average bank, amounting to more than 60% of total cost.

- Bank capital (owner's equity) is the difference between the value of total assets and total liabilities. The bank's capital account includes the items "capital," or "owners' equity," "reserves for loan losses," and "undivided profits" and/or "surplus." As total asset value rises or falls, (*ceteris paribus*), capital value rises or falls. If capital declines to zero, the bank is insolvent (bankrupt).

- Deposit insurance lets bank customers be less concerned with their bank's capital, or with the soundness of the bank's assets.

- The smaller the capital account (*ceteris paribus*) the greater the **return on equity (ROE)**.

- As the **asset structure** of banks has become less liquid, developments in the money markets—especially the markets for Fed funds, repos, and large marketable CDs—have brought **new sources of liquidity**.

- Asset/liability (A/L) management involves the review of the assets and liabilities and their maturities and interest-sensitivities, and decisions about what changes are needed to maintain the desired A/L balance.

- Ultimately the safety and liquidity of the banking system depends first on *a healthy economy*, and failing that, on *the FDIC and the Fed*.

Important Principles, Issues, Concepts, Terms

Changing structure of bank deposits

Intercorporate borrowing

Repurchase agreements

"DDs" and "OCDs"

Passbook savings accounts

Small-denomination CDs

How capital value floats on asset value

The bank's capital account

Reserves for loan losses

Undivided profits, or surplus

Capital cushion

Insolvency

Effects of deposit insurance (a) on customer attitudes and (b) on bank management policies

Changing ratio of capital to assets

Changing ratio of capital to risk assets

Relationship between capital and ROE

Ways of dealing with a deposit outflow

Why cost of funds has been increasing

Some effects of increasing cost of funds on liquidity of assets

Changes in the loans-to-deposits ratio

The development of "liability management"

Dangers of borrowing short and lending long

How to reduce interest rate risk

The process of asset/liability management

The *ultimate source* of liquidity for the banking system

Questions

1. List the major items on the liabilities side of the typical bank's balance sheet and indicate the approximate percentage of each.

2. Most of a bank's liabilities consist of various kinds of deposits. Describe some of these different kinds of deposits and explain how the relative importance of various ones have changed in recent years.

3. Explain exactly what is meant by "bank capital." If you went to a bank and asked to see their "capital" exactly what would they show you? Explain.

4. Explain the importance of the size of the bank's capital.

5. What has been happening to the ratio of bank capital to assets in recent years, and why?

6. Explain some of the ways that a bank can meet its needs for liquidity, in the case of a deposit outflow.

7. What is meant by discretionary funds management?

8. Explain this statement: "The ultimate source of safety and liquidity is a healthy economy."

Suggested Readings

Apilado, Vince, and Thomas Gies. "Capital Adequacy and Commercial Bank Failure." *The Bankers Magazine.* Summer 1972.

Bennett, Barbara. "Off Balance Sheet Risk in Banking: The Case of Standby Letters of Credit." *Economic Review.* Federal Reserve Bank of San Francisco, Spring 1985.

Bennett, Barbara, and David Pyle. "Risk-Adjusted Deposit Insurance Premiums." *Weekly Letter.* Federal Reserve Bank of San Francisco, August 10, 1984.

Benston, George. "Optimal Banking Structure." *Journal of Banking Research* 3 (winter 1973), 220–37.

Benston, George, et al. *Safe and Sound Banking.* Cambridge, Mass.: MIT Press, 1986.

Binder, Barrett, and Thomas Lindquist. *Asset/Liability Management and Funds Management of Commercial Banks.* Rolling Meadows, Ill.: Bank Administration Institute, 1982.

Brewer, Elijah. "Bank Gap Management and the Use of Financial Futures." *Economic Perspectives.* Federal Reserve Bank of Chicago, March/April 1985.

Brigham, Eugene F. *Financial Management Theory and Practice.* Hinsdale, Ill.: The Dryden Press, 1985.

Chu, Franklin. "Toward a Flexible Capital Structure." *The Bankers Magazine.* May/June 1986.

Dymski, Gary A. "Keynesian Bank Behavior." *Journal of Post Keynesian Economics,* vol. 10, no. 4 (summer 1988), 499–526.

Ehlen, James G. Jr. "A Review of Bank Capital and Its Adequacy." *Economic Review.* Federal Reserve Bank of Atlanta, November 1983.

Flannery, Mark, and Aris Protopapadekis. "Risk-Sensitive Deposit Insurance Premia: Some Practical Issues." *Business Review.* Federal Reserve Bank of Philadelphia, September/October, 1984.

Gilbert, Alton, Courtenay Stone, and Michael Trebing. "The New Bank Capital Standards." *Review.* Federal Reserve Bank of St. Louis, May 1985.

Gilbert, Milton. "Bank Market Structure and Competition: A Survey." *Journal of Money, Credit and Banking* 16 (November 1984), 617–44.

Havrilesky, Thomas, and John Boorman. *Current Perspectives in Banking.* Arlington Heights, Ill.: AHM Publishing Co., 1976.

Hempel, George, Alan Coleman, and Donald Simonson. *Bank Management: Text and Cases.* New York: John Wiley & Sons, 1986.

Hilliard, Jimmy E. *Duration as the Effective Time to Repricing.* Athens, Ga.: The University of Georgia, 1984.

Horvitz, Paul M., "Why Risk-Related Insurance Premiums Are No Answer." *The American Banker.* (May 26, 1983), pp. 4, 6.

James, Christopher. "Off-Balance Sheet Banking." *Economic Review.* Federal Reserve Bank of San Francisco 4 (Fall 1987), 21–36.

Kaufman, George. "Measuring and Managing Interest Rate Risk: A Primer." *Economic Perspectives.* Federal Reserve Bank of Chicago, January/February 1984.

Keeley, Michael C. "Bank Capital Regulation in the 1980s: Effective or Ineffective?" *Economic Review.* Federal Reserve Bank of San Francisco 1 (winter 1988), 3–20.

Maisel, Sherman, ed. *Risk and Capital Adequacy in Commercial Banks.* Chicago: University of Chicago Press, 1981.

McNulty, James. "Interest Rate Risk: How Much is Too Much?" *The Bankers Magazine.* January/February 1987.

Mitchell, Karilyn. "Capital Adequacy at Commercial Banks," *Economic Review.* Federal Reserve Bank of Kansas City (September/October 1984), 17–30.

Moskowitz, Warren E. "Global Asset and Liability Management at Commercial Banks." *Quarterly Review.* Federal Reserve Bank of New York 4 (spring 1979), 42–48.

Nguyen, Chy, and Alan Winger. "The Rudiments of a Duration Model." *Quarterly Review 2.* Federal Home Loan Bank of Cincinnati, 1984.

Reed, Edward, Richard Cotter, Edward Gill, and Richard Smith. *Commercial Banking.* Englewood Cliffs, N.J.: Prentice-Hall, 1984.

Robert Morris Associates. *Asset & Liability Management from the Credit Perspective. Philadelphia:* 1983.

Robichek, Alexander, et. al. *Management of Financial Institutions.* Hinsdale, Ill.: Dryden Press, 1976.

Rose, Sanford. "Beware of Bad Duration Models." *American Banker.* June 1, 1984.

Rosenberg, Joel. "The Joys of Duration." *The Bankers Magazine.* March/April 1986.

Silber, William L. *Commercial Bank Liability Management.* Chicago: Association of Reserve City Bankers, 1978.

Sinkey, Joseph. *Commercial Bank Financial Management.* New York: Macmillan Publishing Company, 1986.

Toevs, Alden. "Gap Management: Managing Interest Rate Risk in Banks and Thrifts." *Economic Review.* Federal Reserve Bank of San Francisco, spring 1983.

Toevs, Alden, and David Jacob. *Interest Rate Futures: A Comparison of Alternative Hedge Ratio Methodologies.* New York: Morgan Stanley, June 1984.

Wall, Larry. "Regulation of Banks' Equity Capital," *Economic Review.* Federal Reserve Bank of Atlanta, November 1985.

Watson, Ronald. "Estimating the Cost of Your Bank's Funds." *Business Review.* Federal Reserve Bank of Philadelphia, May/June 1978.

Weintraub, Robert. *International Debt: Crisis and Challenge.* Fairfax, Va.: Department of Economics, George Mason University, 1983.

PART V

The Money Supply Process: The Banking System, The Fed, The Monetary Base, and Money Multipliers

A nation's money supply is always growing and changing. The growth of the money supply occurs through the lending activities of the banks and other depository institutions: the more lending, the more the money supply increases.

The growth of the money supply is controlled by the central bank—in the United States, the Federal Reserve System. The central bank provides the additional reserves which permit the banks to lend more and cause the money supply to grow. When you finish studying Part V you'll know exactly how all of this happens—how the **money supply process** works.

This part begins (Chapter 18) with an explanation of how money is created by the banking system through bank lending and the **deposit multiplier** process. Then Chapter 19 explains the money supply expansion process in terms of the money multipliers—how much money is created when a given amount of new reserves are released into the banking system.

After you understand how the process works, then Chapters 20, 21, and 22 explain the functions and techniques of the Federal Reserve System in controlling the rate of growth of the money supply. Here you will see how the changes which show up on the Fed's balance sheet have multiple effects on the money supply, via changes in the **monetary base** and **bank reserves**.

From Part V you will gain a thorough understanding of the money supply process. You will know about the role of the banks in expanding the money supply and about the role of the Fed in controlling it. You'll know what the Fed does, and why and how, and the importance of and the effects of the Fed's actions.

CHAPTER 18

Introduction to Money Creation and the Concept of the Deposit Multiplier

Chapter Objectives

Changes in the size of the money supply are very important in the functioning of the economy. But how do money supply changes occur? And how are such changes controlled? That's what you'll be reading about in this chapter and in the following ones.

When you complete your study of this chapter you will understand and be able to explain:

1. The role of borrowers (individuals, businesses, etc.) and of the banking system in the money creation process, and exactly how the process occurs.

2. The importance of **reserve requirements** in limiting money expansion.

3. How the Fed supplies new reserves—new **primary deposits**—to the banking system.

4. The initial and ultimate effects of new loans on the balance sheets and reserve positions of (a) lending banks, and (b) other banks.

5. How to illustrate the money expansion process using balance sheets and T-accounts of typical banks.

MONEY IS CREATED AND DESTROYED THROUGH THE BANKING SYSTEM

Is it possible for an individual—perhaps you, or me—to create money? To actually *increase the size of the nation's money supply?* Yes. We can do that. All we need is a little help from our depository institutions—from the banking system. (As defined in chapter 1, the banking system includes all depository institutions.)

How Individuals Can Increase the Money Supply

Suppose we use the M1 definition of money. Then anything that increases the size of any one of the components of M1 (without some offsetting decrease in some other component) will increase the total size of the nation's money supply. The components of M1, you remember, are:

1. All deposits at depository institutions (banks and thrifts) which are immediately and freely transferable by check;
2. Currency in circulation—that is, paper money and coins in the hands of the public (not in the vaults of the banks); and
3. Travelers checks in the hands of the public.

So if you would like to increase the size of the nation's money supply, it's easy. Take your credit card and go to your bank's nearest automated teller machine (ATM) and draw out $100 in cash and charge it to your credit card account. You'll increase the nation's currency in circulation—and the M1 money supply—by $100. You will *create* an additional $100 of M1 money.

Or you might take $100 out of your savings account (which is not M1 money) and put it into your checking account (which is M1 money). Or suppose everyone who has an American Express card goes to one of those airport "travelers check dispenser" machines and gets $500 in travelers checks and charges them to their credit card accounts. A money supply expansion? Yes. Or suppose you went into your bank and signed a promissory note for $1000 and had the funds deposited into your checking account. Money supply expansion? Of course.

It's easy to see how individuals and businesses can borrow and generate (a) more checking deposits, (b) more currency in circulation, and (c) more travelers checks in the hands of the public—more M1 money. But sometime in the future the borrowed funds must be paid back—either with checkable deposits, currency, or travelers checks. When that happens, we reverse the process and reduce the size of the money supply.

How a Money Expansion Occurs through the Banking System

It's easy to see how money is created, looked at from the *borrower's* side. And it's obvious that unless someone is borrowing—thereby creating new checkable deposits or currency or travelers checks in circulation—there isn't going to be much expansion in the M1 money supply.

But what if there are lots of people clamoring for more money? Do the banks just keep on lending more and more? Adding to their customer's checking accounts? Pushing more currency into circulation? Issuing more travelers checks, on credit? You know the answer. Absolutely not!

> A bank (or thrift) can't lend any more money than it has available (or can get) to lend.

That statement seems so obvious. And yet, paradoxically, the following statement is equally true:

> Banks do in fact create money. Most of the money now in existence in this country (and in the world) has been created by lending activities of the banking system.

When you understand the money creation (and destruction) process from the point of view of the depository institutions, then you will understand how it all works. And you will see that there is no conflict between these two (apparently contradictory) statements.

Required Reserves Limit Money Expansion

Suppose you took about $2,000 worth of stock certificates and went to Ms. Larson, your local banker, and asked to borrow $1,000, pledging the stock certificates as collateral for the loan. What if she told you she couldn't lend you the money because the bank didn't have any excess reserves?—no excess either in its reserve account at its district Federal Reserve bank, or in its vault cash. You might be confused.

Surely you remember from your principles of economics course that banks can actually create money. You ask Ms. Larson about that. She explains that although the banking system, as a system, can create money, no individual bank can lend money unless it has (or can obtain) some excess reserves to lend.

"The problem is this," she explains. "When I lend you $1,000, you're going to spend it. That's the only reason why you would borrow it. Then when you write a check and spend the money, someone else will receive that check and deposit it in some other bank. When that other bank clears the check, that will pull reserve deposits out of our account at our district Fed bank.

"So where does that leave us? Since we have no excess reserves in that account, we can't afford to have $1,000 pulled out! Now do you understand why we can't lend you any money?"

While all this discussion is going on, suppose someone comes in and makes a new checking deposit of $1,000. Then Ms. Larson says, "Now we can lend you some money. We'll put this $1,000 in our Fed account and we will have some excess reserves."

Box 18-1

Question: **Exactly What Are "Required Reserves?" and Why Are They Required?**

Sound banking practices have always required that banks which hold deposits should hold some reserves. Reserves are risk-free, completely liquid assets. So the more reserves a bank holds (*ceteris paribus*) the more safe and liquid it is.

Some reserves are needed to meet withdrawal demands. But during "normal times" only a small amount of "reserves for withdrawals" would be needed, because new deposits coming in will approximately offset withdrawals going out. The only time a bank really needs large reserves to meet withdrawals is when something abnormal happens—a panic. But when the panic comes, any amount of reserves less than 100% of total deposits is likely to prove insufficient!

The purpose of requiring reserves of 3% or 12% of transactions deposits (or whatever amount) is not to meet withdrawal demands. What, then? Two purposes:
(1) to require the bank to keep some risk-free, completely liquid assets, and
(2) to limit the size and the rate of growth of the nation's money supply.

It is through its control over the amount of reserves in the banking system—and the rate of growth of those reserves—that the Fed exercises control over the nation's money supply. The main purpose of the reserve requirement in a modern-day banking system is to provide the central bank a "lever" by which to control the rate of growth of the nation's money supply.

Ms. Larson continues: "The reserve requirement (let's suppose) is 10%. So we must keep 10% of this new deposit on reserve. That's $100. So we will have $900 in excess reserves. You have good credit references and a steady income. So if you would like, we will accept your stock certificates as collateral and lend you the $900. Here. Sign this promissory note and we will open a checking account for you and deposit the $900."

LENDING EXCESS RESERVES CREATES MONEY

After your loan is completed and the money deposited in your new account you ask yourself: "Has any money been created by this transaction?" The answer is: "Yes!"

You now have $900 that didn't exist before. The person who made the $1,000 deposit still has that money. And you have $900. So now there's $1,900, where only $1,000 existed before. Money has been created? Yes. How? By the lending of excess reserves.

Suppose the reserve requirement was 100%. Then the bank would be required to keep $1,000 in reserves to "back up" the $1,000 in new deposits. How much money could have been created? Zero.

It's only because of the **fractional reserve system** (required reserves of less than 100%) that banks have excess reserves which can be lent. It is this lending of excess reserves which permits the creation of money through the banking system.

What you have just seen is the first step in the process—the expansion of $1,000 into $1,900. That's just the beginning.

Excess Reserves Move from Bank to Bank

After you borrow the $900 you will spend it by writing checks, making payments to other people. Those who receive your checks will deposit them in their own bank accounts. So these banks will receive new excess reserves.

When the excess reserves move out of your bank's Fed account and into the Fed accounts of those other banks, then those banks can lend 90% of that amount. Even more money will be created.

Box 18-2

Question: **When Banks Make Loans Do They Really Lend Their Excess Reserves?**

No. They really don't. The only way banks actually lend their excess reserves is when they lend Fed funds to other banks—or they could lend vault cash. But that would be very unusual.

What banks really lend is newly created checkable-deposit money—money which prior to the loan, did not exist!

But when this newly created money is spent, the bank is very likely to lose reserves equal to the size of the loan. So without the excess reserves it could not safely make the loan.

Each time a bank lends its excess reserves, the money is soon spent, received by someone else, and deposited in another bank. Then that bank gets the excess reserves and can make more loans and the money expansion continues.

Banks Sometimes Lend Their Excess Reserves to Other Banks

As long as there are excess reserves anywhere in the banking system, these excess reserves permit the money supply to expand. But what if a bank has excess reserves and doesn't make loans to use them up?

Then the bank might lend the reserves to some other bank which wants funds to meet its loan demands. These excess reserves are borrowed (and lent) between banks in the "Fed funds" market—in fact, billions of dollars worth every day.

Excess reserves anywhere in the banking system are very likely to result in new lending—and that means an expansion in the money supply. This is important. It means that *the size of the money supply* responds quite readily to changes in *the amount of reserves available.*

Now, add this fact: The Fed has the power to push reserves into or pull reserves out of the bank's reserve accounts at a moments notice—whenever it wishes. So clearly, *the Fed has great powers of control over the size of the nation's money supply.* How? By its control over the amount of reserves in the banking system. (See box 18-3.)

An Example of Money Expansion

Suppose you have a $100 government savings bond and you "cash it"—you sell it (through your bank) to the Fed. Then you deposit the $100 in a checkable account. The nation's money supply immediately grows by $100. You have exchanged a $100 government bond—which is not M1 money—for a $100 checkable deposit, which is M1 money. But that isn't all.

New Primary Deposits Create New Excess Reserves. Your deposit is a *primary deposit*—a new injection of reserve funds flowing from the Fed into the banking system. These new reserves will permit a multiple expansion of the money supply.

Suppose the reserve requirement on checkable deposits is 10%. That means your bank is required to hold only $10 in reserves to "back up" your $100 deposit. So the bank now has $90 in excess reserves which it is free to lend.

When the bank lends the $90, that creates $90 of new money. You still have your $100 (no change there) and the borrower has $90 of money which didn't exist before. So $100 has grown into $190.

Money Lent Is Quickly Spent. The borrower will soon spend the $90. Why else would a person borrow money?! The person who receives the $90 check will soon deposit it. The excess reserves ($90) will be transferred from your bank (Bank A) to another bank (Bank B). Now Bank B has new deposits of $90, new reserves of $90, and excess reserves of $81. (New required reserves for Bank B are 10% of $90 = $9, leaving excess reserves of $81.)

Bank B will lend $81 and the money supply will grow by that amount. So now the money supply has grown by $100 + $90 + $81 = $271. And, as you can see, that isn't the end of it either.

Box 18-3

Question: Exactly What Percentage of Transactions Accounts Must Depository Institutions Hold in Reserves?

Prior to March 1980 when the *Depository Institutions Deregulation and Monetary Control Act* (DIDMCA) was passed, there were different reserve requirements and reserve arrangements for Fed member banks, nonmember banks, and thrifts. But the DIDMCA established nationwide reserve requirements for transactions accounts (checkable accounts) at all depository institutions.

The rate established was 3% of the first $25 million of transactions account balances and 12% for deposit balances in excess of $25 million. But the Fed was empowered by that act to make reserve requirement adjustments within a range of 8% to 14% on deposits above $25 million. But as of midyear 1988 it had not done that.

Also the DIDMCA specified that the $25 million figure would be adjusted upward each year by an amount equal to 80% of the rate of increase in total transactions account balances

in the nation. By 1988 the $25 million figure had been adjusted upward to $40.5 million, and was increasing at the rate of more than $3 million per year.

The *Garn-St Germain Depository Institutions Act* of 1982 exempted the first $2 million of "reservable liabilities" (mostly checkable deposits) from all reserve requirements—zero required reserves. Also the act specified that this $2 million figure be adjusted upward each year on the same basis as the upward adjustment of the $25 million—80% of the nationwide rate of increase in transactions account balances. By 1988 the $2 million figure had been adjusted upward to $3.2 million and was increasing at an annual rate of about $300,000.

The DIDMCA (in 1980) abolished reserve requirements on all personal savings and time deposits. Complete figures on reserve requirements (past and present) can be found on page A-7 of the *Federal Reserve Bulletin*.

The Excess Reserves Move to Another Bank. When the Bank B borrower spends the money, the $81 will go into Bank C which then will have excess reserves of $72.90—($81 − $8.10 = $72.90). So Bank C will be able to make additional loans of that amount.

How long can this process go on? Until all of the new deposit ($100) is being held as *required reserves* and *no excess reserves* are remaining in the banking system.

Assume that all of the money created remains in checkable deposits. How much will the money supply expand before the entire $100 is being used as required reserves? If the reserve requirement is 10%, then $100 in new reserves will support checkable deposits of 10 times that amount: $1,000.

The $1,000 includes the original $100 deposit, plus an additional $900 of checkable deposits created by the money expansion process—the process of lending, spending, redepositing, etc.—which continues until there are no longer any excess reserves to lend. And in this case it all happened because you decided to sell your $100 government bond and deposit the money.

Some Simplifying Assumptions in This Example

In this example it is assumed that (1) all of the money created remains in checkable deposits—that none of the money is withdrawn as cash, (2) that none of the $100 in new reserves is used to meet the reserve requirements on "other reservable assets" such as certain time deposits, and (3) that *all* of the new $100 in reserves is entirely used for loans by the banking system so that no excess reserves remain. In actual fact, none of these assumptions would be exactly true in the real world.

The Effect of Cash Drain. Cash withdrawals always occur as a part of the money expansion process. Sizeable sums of currency are pulled out of bank vaults (and therefore out of bank reserves) and this significantly limits the money expansion. In fact this **cash drain** limits the money expansion considerably more than does the reserve requirement.

The "Naive" Deposit Multiplier. The "simple" or "naive" deposit multiplier which considers only the effect of the reserve requirement is the reciprocal of the reserve requirement. With a reserve requirement of 10% the deposit multiplier would be 1/10% or 1/.10 = 10. A reserve requirement of 20% would give a simple deposit multiplier of 1/.20 = 5. So considering only the effect of the reserve requirement, a new injection of reserves when the reserve requirement is 10% would result in a tenfold money expansion; with a reserve requirement of 20% the potential money expansion would be fivefold. With a reserve requirement of 50%, the simple deposit multiplier would be 2.

The more realistic deposit multiplier which takes into account all of the limiting factors on the money expansion will be explained soon. The purpose here is to provide an intuitive (common sense) understanding of how the money supply expands as new reserves enter the banking system.

Box 18-4 shows a simplified example of the money-expansion process. That example assumes a reserve requirement of 20% and an initial primary deposit of $5,000. The ultimate expansion of the money supply is shown to be $25,000. Take a few minutes now to study box 18-4.

NEW RESERVES COME FROM THE FEDERAL RESERVE SYSTEM

It is the Federal Reserve System which creates new reserves to permit the nation's money supply to expand. And it is by limiting the amount of new reserves that the Fed controls the rate of expansion of the money supply.

The Fed Buys Securities

When the Fed wants to expand the money supply, it buys government securities (bonds, T-bills, etc.) "in the open market"—that is, from the public. It buys through brokers, but the ultimate sellers are insurance companies, banks, all kinds of financial institutions, individuals—in fact, anyone who has government securities they want to sell. These open-market securities dealings by the Fed are called **open market operations** (OMOs).

When the Fed buys securities it pays by instantaneously wire-transferring funds for deposit to the sellers' bank accounts and the sellers' banks then transfer the funds into their reserve accounts at their district Fed banks. So when the Fed buys government securities, *it automatically pushes more reserves into the accounts of the depository institutions.*

Box 18-4

Feature: A Simplified Example of the Money Expansion Process
A Summary of the Steps in the
Depositing-Lending-Spending-Redepositing-Relending-Respending Process

This example assumes that Mr. Alber sells government bonds and receives a check from the Federal Reserve for $5,000 and deposits the check in his bank account. This is a new "primary deposit" because it consists of new funds entering the banking system. It comes from the Fed, and not from some other bank.

This example assumes a required reserve of 20%, so Mr. Alber's bank has excess reserves of $4,000 which it lends to Ms. Baker. Ms. Baker spends the money immediately (as borrowers always do) by writing a check to Mr. Culver for $4,000.

Mr. Culver then deposits the $4,000 in his bank, which leaves his bank with excess reserves of $3,200, which it lends to Ms. Dover. Ms. Dover spends the money and pays it to Mr. Elder, who deposits it in his bank, and the process continues, on and on.

Deposited by		Amount of Deposit (money created)		Required Reserve (20%)		Excess Reserve (80%)		Lent to		Paid to
Alber	→	$ 5,000	→	$1,000	→	$4,000	→	Baker	→	Culver
Culver	→	4,000	→	800	→	3,200	→	Dover	→	Elder
Elder	→	3,200	→	640	→	2,560	→	Fuller	→	Garner
Garner	→	2,560	→	512	→	2,048	→	Horner	→	Ilter
Ilter	→	2,048	→	410	→	1,638	→	Joker	→	Keller
Keller	→	1,638	→	328	→	1,310	→	Lester	→	Miller
Miller	→	1,310	→	262	→	1,048	→	Nader	→	Olter
Olter	→	1,048	→	210	→	838	→	Palmer	→	Quaver
Quaver	→	838	→	168	→	670	→	Richter	→	Salter
Salter	→	670	→	Etc., etc., etc.					
		—		—		—				
Ultimate Totals (assuming maximum possible expansion		$25,000 (total demand deposit money)		$5,000 (total required reserves)		—0— (total excess reserves)		No more loans are possible until new reserves come from somewhere.		

This table shows Mr. Alber's original deposit of $5,000 growing into a total of $25,000—that's twenty-five thousand real, spendable dollars of demand deposit money. Mr. Alber has $5,000 of it, Mr. Culver has $4,000 of it, Mr. Elder has $3,200 of it, Mr. Garner has $2,560 of it, and so on.

Only $5,000 existed in the beginning. Where did the extra $20,000 come from? It was created by the banks. The banks created it just by lending their excess reserves.

You can always figure out what the maximum possible expansion is by using the deposit multiplier. Here, with a reserve requirement of 20 percent (1/5) the deposit multiplier is 5. So the maximum possible expansion is $5,000 (amount of new reserves entering the banking system) times 5 (the deposit multiplier)—which equals $25,000.

Note: This table assumes (1) that all excess reserves are borrowed and (2) that no one withdraws any cash. In reality, as the money supply expands, some cash always is withdrawn. This "cash drain" significantly limits the size of the deposit multiplier and therefore reduces the extent of money expansion.

This table also assumes that the $5,000 initial deposit comes from the Fed. If the deposit comes in cash—out of Aunt Martha's mattress, for example—then the money supply can only expand by $20,000. Why? Because the initial $5,000 deposit (in cash) was already a part of the money supply.

Source: This table is reproduced from Elbert V. Bowden, Economics: The Science of Common Sense, Sixth Edition, South-Western Publishing Company, Cincinnati, OH, (1989), p. 129.

Box 18-5

Question: Are All Banks and Thrifts Required to Hold Reserves in Their District Federal Reserve Bank?

Prior to the Depository Institutions Deregulation and Monetary Control Act (DIDMCA) of 1980, only member banks held their reserve deposits in the district Federal Reserve banks. Nonmember banks held their reserves in government securities, in deposits in other banks, and otherwise as specified by the banking regulations of the various states. The Fed had nothing to do with the reserves of nonmember banks.

Then in 1980 the DIDMCA specified that all depository institutions with checkable deposits must either hold reserves in the Fed banks, or hold reserves in correspondent banks which would "pass through" the reserves and deposit them in Fed banks. So now, for all depository institutions which hold checkable deposits (banks, and thrifts), reserves must be held in the form of (a) Fed bank deposits, and/or (b) correspondent bank pass-through balances, and/or (c) currency in the bank's vault.

The Fed Sells Securities

The Fed can drain reserves from the banking system just as easily. It sells securities in the open market. People, businesses, financial institutions, etc. buy the securities and pay with checks. When the Fed deducts the amounts of the checks from the reserve accounts of the banks on which the checks are drawn, what happens? Poof! Some of the banks' reserves are gone.

The Fed can very easily and quickly push reserves into or pull reserves out of the banking system. As it does so, it has an immediate influence on the size of the money supply, both directly, and through the influence on lending activities of the banking system. One good way to see how all this works is to focus on and observe changes in the bank's balance sheet.

FOCUSING ON THE BANK'S BALANCE SHEET

It's possible to observe the money expansion process just by watching the changes in the balance sheets of the banks (or other depository institutions) involved. That's coming up now.

The Initial Balance Sheet

Figure 18-1 shows a condensed balance sheet for *Typical Bank A* (TB-A). This is the bank where the money expansion process is going to be initiated. So take a minute to familiarize yourself with the asset-liability position of Typical Bank A.

Does TB-A Have Excess Reserves?

You can look at figure 18-1 and see something about the reserve position of this bank. But you can't be sure about TB-A's reserve position until you have a few more facts.

Figure 18-1   Typical Bank A: Balance Sheet #1

Assets		Liabilities and Capital	
Loans	$6,500	Checkable deposits	$4,000
Securities (investments)	3,500	Noncheckable deposits	6,000
Cash Items	1,000	Passbook savings 1,000	
Vault Cash 150		CDs 5,000	
FRB deposits 250		Borrowings, and due to banks	1,000
Due from banks 600			
Miscellaneous assets	800	Owners' Equity (Capital)	800
Total Assets	$11,800	Total Liabilities and Capital	$11,800

Reserve Position (assume 10% reserve required on checkable deposits)

Total Reserves: (vault cash + FRB deposits)
$$150 + 250 = \$400$$

Required Reserves: $10\% \times 4{,}000 = \$400$

Excess: −0−

If this is a Fed member bank, the only assets it can count as reserves are (1) vault cash ($150) and (2) Federal Reserve bank (FRB) deposits ($250). But if this is not a Fed member bank it may hold a part of its reserves as deposits in other banks (part of the "due from banks" item) *provided that* the other banks pass the deposits through and deposit them in a Federal Reserve bank.

For Typical Bank A, let's just assume that the deposits in other banks are *not* to be included as part of its reserves. So TB-A has total reserves of $150 + $250 = $400.

What Are the Reserve Requirements?

Next, let's assume that *checkable deposits* are the only deposits on which reserves are required—no reserve requirements on noncheckable savings or time deposits. And assume that the reserve requirement is 10% on all checkable deposits at all depository institutions. This isn't quite true, but it's a useful simplifying assumption.

Based on these assumptions, our typical bank comes out with exactly zero excess reserves. It has $4,000 in checkable deposits and $400 in reserves. That's exactly the required amount—10%. Unless this bank gets additional reserves from somewhere, it cannot make any more loans.

Soon we're going to give Typical Bank A some additional reserves. Then it will make new loans and the nation's money supply will begin to expand. But before that, here are a few more simplifying assumptions.

Deposit Expansion: Some Simplifying Assumptions

1. Assume that all banks desire to maintain zero excess reserves so that all excess reserves are quickly loaned; that the borrowed funds are quickly and totally spent, and that the recipient of the borrower's check quickly deposits it in another bank.

2. Assume that as the money supply expands there are *no currency withdrawals* which would pull currency out of the banks and thereby pull down their "vault cash" reserves. (As you know, this is not a realistic assumption.)

3. Assume that all the money loaned, spent, and redeposited is always redeposited in checkable deposits—never in noncheckable deposits where it would no longer be a part of the M1 money supply.

4. Assume that throughout this process of money expansion, all balance sheet items except those directly involved in the expansion, remain the same.

5. Assume that all of the adjustments to each bank's reserves are made only in its Federal Reserve bank deposits—not in vault cash.

Given these assumptions, as loans are made and the money supply expands, on the balance sheet (figure 18-1) only two assets will change: **total loans**, and **FRB deposits**, and only one liability will change: **checkable deposits**.

A BALANCE SHEET VIEW OF MONETARY EXPANSION

Now that you know the rules of the game, watch what happens when our typical bank gets some new reserves.

"Typical Bank A" Receives New Reserves (Primary Deposits)

Suppose you decide to sell your $100 government bond to the Fed. You receive the Fed's check for $100 and you deposit the check in a checkable account at Typical Bank A.

Typical Bank A adds $100 to your account (a liability for the bank) and sends the Fed's check to the district Fed bank for deposit to its own FRB account (an asset for the bank). Both assets and liabilities of TB-A increases by $100.

The following T-account, and then the new balance sheet in figure 18-2 shows these changes.

Box 18-6

Question: What Is a "T-Account?"

A refresher: A "T-account" is a simplified abstraction of a balance sheet. The only balance sheet items which are included in the T-account are the ones which are being changed: the balance sheet *additions* and *subtractions*.

For example, the T-account for Typical Bank A shows that when you deposited your $100 check in TB-A, that added $100 to TB-A's checkable deposits. That change shows up as a plus item on the liabilities side of the T-account. When Bank A sends the check for deposit to its account in its district Fed bank, that adds $100 to its FRB deposits. That shows up as a plus item on the asset side of the T-account. Balance sheet *changes* are the only items which show up in the T-account.

T-Account #1 For Typical Bank A

New deposits received; check deposited in district Fed bank

Assets		Liabilities and Capital	
FRB Deposits	+$100	Checkable Deposits	+$100

The deposited check adds $100 to checkable deposits. Then TB-A sends the check to its district Fed bank for deposit to its FRB account. TB-A's assets and liabilities both increase by $100. It's now a "$100-bigger bank" than it was before! And, as you see in figure 18-2 it now has $90 of excess reserves.

There is now an additional $100 in checkable deposit money which previously did not exist. The nation's money supply has expanded by $100. But as you know, that's just the beginning.

Figure 18-2   Typical Bank A: Balance Sheet #2.

Assets			Liabilities and Capital		
Loans		$6,500	Checkable deposits (+$100)		$4,100
Securities (investments)		3,500	Noncheckable deposits		6,000
Cash Items		1,100	Passbook savings 1,000		
Vault Cash	150		CDs	5,000	
FRB deposits (+$100)	350		Borrowings, and due to banks		1,000
Due from banks	600				
Miscellaneous assets		800	Owners Equity (capital		800
Total Assets (+$100)		$11,900	Total liabilities and Capital (+$100)		$11,900

New deposits received; check deposited in Fed bank.
(Changes: Checkable deposits + $100, FRB deposits + $100.)
Reserve Position

$$\qquad\qquad\qquad VC + FRB$$
Total Reserves: 150 + 350   = $500.
Required Reserves: 10% × 4,100 = $410.
$$\qquad\qquad Excess:\qquad \$\ 90$$

TB-A now has excess reserves. Checkable deposits have gone up from $4,000 to $4,100. So at 10%, the bank's required reserves have gone up by $10—from $400 to $410. But reserves held by the bank have gone up by $100—from $400 to $500. So the bank now has $90 of **excess reserves** which it probably will try to lend as soon as possible.

Somebody's going to come into TB-A and borrow the $90 of excess reserves and then spend it. Whoever receives the $90 check is going to deposit it in another bank (Typical Bank B). Then TB-B will send the check for deposit to its Fed bank account. The $90 will be taken out of TB-A's account and put into TB-B's account.

The following T-account transactions summarize all of these changes in TB-A's balance sheet #2. Then figure 18-3 shows TB-A's final balance sheet (#3). And after that we'll take a look at what's happening with TB-B.

T-Account #2 for Typical Bank A

	Assets		Liabilities	
TB-A makes a loan of $90	Loans	+$90	checkable deposits	+90
The borrower writes a check and spends the $90 and the check clears	FRB deposits	−$90	checkable deposits	−$90
Final net effect of these two transactions on TB-A's balance sheet	Loans FRB deposits	+$90 −$90		
(The $90 of excess reserves shown in balance sheet #2 have been converted into income-earning loans.)			(No net change in checkable deposits from Balance Sheet #2.)	

Figure 18-3. Typical Bank A: Balance Sheet #3.

Assets		Liabilities and Capital	
Loans (+90)	$ 6,590	Checkable deposits	$ 4,100
Securities (investments)	3,500	Noncheckable deposits	6,000
Cash Items (−90)	1,010	Passbook savings 1,000	
Vault Cash 150		CDs 5,000	
FRB deposits (−90) 260		Borrowings, and due to banks	1,000
Due from banks 600			
Miscellaneous assets	800	Owners Equity (capital)	800
Total Assets	$11,900	Total Liabilities and Capital	$11,900

The $90 of excess reserves in balance sheet #2 have now been converted into loans. *Changes from Balance Sheet #1:* Deposits have increased by $100, loans by $90, and Fed deposits (reserves) by $10.
Reserve position

$$VC + FRB$$

Total Reserves: 150 + 260 = $410
Required Reserves: 10% × 4100 = $410
              Excess: −0−

The New Reserves Move to "Typical Bank B"

Now Typical Bank B has a new $90 deposit. The effect of this new deposit on TB-B is exactly the same as was the initial effect of the $100 deposit on TB-A. The only difference is that TB-B has received only $90 in new checkable deposits and new reserves. Why? Because $10 stayed as required reserves in TB-A's Fed account.

Here are the initial changes as seen by TB-B.

T-Account #1 for Typical Bank B

New deposits received; check deposited in district Fed bank.

Assets		Liabilities and Capital	
FRB Deposits	+$90	Checkable Deposits	+$90

The deposited check adds $90 to checkable deposits. Then TB-B sends the check to its district Fed bank for deposit to its FRB account. TB-B's assets and liabilities both increase by $90, and TB-B now has excess reserves.

Figure 18-4 shows the new balance sheet (#2) for Typical Bank B. (Note: Balance sheet #1 for TB-B was identical to balance sheet #1 for TB-A).

Figure 18-4.   Typical Bank B: Balance Sheet #2.

Assets			Liabilities and Capital	
Loans		$ 6,500	Checkable deposits (+90)	$ 4,090
Securities (investments)		3,500	Noncheckable deposits	6,000
Cash Items (+90)		1,090	Passbook savings 1,000	
Vault Cash	150		CDs 5,000	
FRB deposits (+90)	340		Borrowings, and due to banks	1,000
Due from banks	600			
Miscellaneous assets		800	Owners Equity (capital)	800
Total Assets (+90)		$11,890	Total Liabilities and Capital (+90)	$11,890

New deposits received; check deposited in Fed bank.
(Changes: Checkable deposits +$90, FRB deposits +$90)
Reserve Position

$$VC + FRB$$
Total Reserves: 150 + 340   = $490
Required Reserves: 10% × 4,090 = $409
Excess: $ 81

Money Is Created Each Time Loans Are Made

How much money has been created so far? TB-A has an increase of $100 in checkable deposits. TB-B has an increase of $90 in checkable deposits. So already the money supply has expanded by $190. But that isn't the end of it.

Typical Bank B now has excess reserves because it has received $90 in new checkable deposits and $90 in new reserves. It only needs $9 in new reserves to "back up" its $90 in new checkable deposits. So it has $81 in excess reserves. Soon TB-B will lend the $81, which then will be spent.

First, here are the T-account transactions showing changes from TB-B's balance sheet #2. Then TB-B's final balance sheet is shown in figure 18-5.

When TB-B's borrower spent the $81, TB-B's excess reserves went to another bank: Typical Bank C. Now TB-C has more checkable deposits ($81) and some new excess reserves ($81 minus $8.10 new required reserves equals $72.90 excess). Soon TB-C will lend its excess reserves ($72.90) and keep the money expansion process going.

This pool of "moving excess reserves," will continue to go from bank to bank. At each step along the way the amount of the moving excess will be reduced by 10%. The remaining 90% will be re-lent and passed along, continuing the money expansion process. And each new loan will create a new checkable deposit—a new addition to the money supply.

T-Account #2 for Typical Bank B

	Assets		Liabilites	
TB-B makes a loan of $81	Loans	+$81	checkable deposits	+$81
The borrower writes a check and the check clears	FRB deposits	−$81	checkable deposits	−$81
Final net effect of these two transactions on TB-B's balance sheet	Loans FRB deposits	+$81 −$81		
(The $81 of excess reserves has been converted into loans.)			(No net change in checkable deposits from balance sheet #2.)	

Figure 18-5.   Typical Bank B: Balance Sheet #3.

Assets		Liabilities and Capital	
Loans (+81)	$ 6,581	Checkable deposits	$ 4,090
Securities (investments)	3,500	Non-checkable deposits	6,000
Cash Items (−81)	1,009	Passbook savings 1,000	
Vault Cash 150		CDs 5,000	
FRB deposits (−81) 259		Borrowings, and due to banks	1,000
Due from banks 600			
Miscellaneous assets	800	Owners Equity (capital)	800
Total Assets	$11,890	Total Liabilities and Capital	$11,890

The $81 of excess reserves in balance sheet #2 have been converted into loans.
Changes From Balance Sheet #1: Deposits have increased by $90, loans by $81, and Fed deposits (reserves) by $9.
Reserve Position

$$\begin{array}{lll}
 & \text{VC + FRB} & \\
\text{Total Reserves:} & 150 + 259 & = \$409 \\
\text{Required Reserves:} & 10\% \times 4{,}090 & = \underline{\$409} \\
 & \text{Excess:} & -0-
\end{array}$$

Here you can see that the asset/liability changes for TB-B are exactly the same as for TB-A, only 10% smaller. First, a check for $90 was deposited in a checkable account. The check was sent to the Fed for deposit in the bank's reserve account. This created excess reserves of $81.

Next, the excess reserves were loaned. This transferred the excess reserves (a nonearning asset) into loans (an earning asset). Then the borrower spent the money. When the check cleared, the excess reserves ($81) were transferred out of TB-B's Fed account.

Now you can see that when the Fed releases new reserves—new **high powered money** into the banking system, that permits a multiple expansion of the money supply. How much multiple expansion? That depends on the size of the **money multipliers**. And that's what you'll be reading about in the next chapter.

SUMMARY

- Almost all of the nation's money is created through the banking system as banks lend their excess reserves.

- New reserves enter the banking system as the Fed buys government securities (or anything else). This creates excess reserves and permits the banks to make additional loans, thereby expanding the money supply.

- The money expansion process can be seen by watching the asset and liability changes on the balance sheets of the banks involved.

- When new reserves enter the banking system that creates excess reserves. This excess can be traced as it moves from bank to bank, leaving a trail of newly created checkable deposit money.

- The money expansion can continue until all of the new reserves are being used as required reserves. If the reserve requirement is 10%, then $1 of reserves can support $10 of checkable deposits. So the simple deposit multiplier is 10.

Important Principles, Issues, Concepts, Terms

The role of borrowers in the money expansion process

How individuals can expand the money supply

How a money expansion occurs through the banking system

Why a bank can't lend unless it has excess reserves

How bank lending actually creates money

How the size of the reserve requirement limits money expansion

The significance of the fractional reserve system

The significance of the Fed funds market

The role of new reserves (primarily deposits) in money expansion

Why money lent is quickly spent

How the Fed's open market operations in securities (OMOs) influence bank reserves

How balance sheet changes can illustrate bank activity

How to calculate excess reserves from balance sheet data

How to use T-accounts to illustrate balance sheet changes

How excess reserves move from one bank to another

T-account illustrations of excess reserve movement from bank to bank

Why excess reserves get smaller as they move from bank to bank

The simple (naive) deposit multiplier

Questions

1. Give some examples of ways in which you as an individual might increase the size of the nation's money supply.

2. Describe the process of money creation through the banking system as excess reserves move from bank to bank.

3. In order for the money supply to expand, new reserves must be flowing into the banking system. Where can these new reserves come from? Explain how it happens.

4. What does it mean to say: "Lending excess reserves creates money"? Is this actually what happens? Explain.

5. What does it mean to say: "Only because of the fractional reserve system is it possible for banks to create money"? Explain why this is true.

6. As a rule, if a bank held excess reserves which it did not wish to lend, what would it do with these reserves?

7. Use T-accounts to illustrate the expansion of the money supply through the banking system. Carry the expansion process through at least three banks.

Suggested Readings

Humphrey, Thomas M. "The Theory of Multiple Expansion of Deposits: What it is and Whence it Came." *Economic Review*. Federal Reserve Bank of Richmond (March/April 1987), 3–11.

Rasche, Robert H. "A Review of Empirical Studies of the Money Supply Mechanism." *Review*. Federal Reserve Bank of St. Louis (July 1972), 11–19.

Tobin, James. "Commercial Banks as Creators of 'Money'." in Deane Carson (ed.), *Banking and Monetary Studies*. Homewood, Ill.: Richard D. Irwin, 1963, pp. 408–419.

CHAPTER 19

The Money Supply Expansion Process and the Money Multipliers

Chapter Objectives

In the previous chapter you saw how money expansion occurs through the banking system. Now it's time for a more detailed look at the various "money multipliers." After you study this chapter you will understand and be able to explain:

1. The various formulas for calculating **money expansion multipliers**, and how to interpret each.
2. The importance of **cash drain**, and the effect of non-checkable-deposit reserve requirements.
3. The theoretical relationships between the **monetary base**, the **money multipliers**, and the **money supply**.
4. The empirical data on these theoretical relationships and what the data show for the American economy in the late 1980s.

THE DEPOSIT MULTIPLIER

The *idea* of the **deposit multiplier** is this: When new reserves are released into the banking system, total checkable deposits (and the money supply) will increase by a multiple of the amount of the new reserves. The *process* whereby this occurs is called the "deposit multiplier" process. The *number* by which a new primary deposit can expand total deposits is called the "deposit multiplier."

In the examples you were reading about in the previous chapter (given the simplifying assumptions) the size of the multiplier was determined entirely by the size of the reserve requirement. Here's how to calculate that.

The Simple (Naive) Deposit Multiplier

In the previous examples the reserve requirement was assumed to be 10%, or 1/10. The deposit multiplier was found to be 10. That means that any increase in bank reserves would result in a tenfold increase in checkable deposits, and in the money supply.

The simple deposit multiplier is nothing more than the reciprocal of the reserve requirement (rr). The multiplier can be expressed as 1 ÷ rr) or 1/rr. So if the reserve requirement (rr) is 10%, the multiplier is 1 ÷ 10% = 10. This tells us that when new reserves flow into the banking system, checkable deposits can increase tenfold.

The change in checkable deposits ($\Delta\sqrt{}$D) equals the change in reserves (ΔR) times the deposit multiplier $\left(\dfrac{1}{rr}\right)$:

$$\Delta\sqrt{}D = \Delta R \times \frac{1}{rr}.^1$$

Substituting the figures from our previous example we find:

$$\Delta\sqrt{}D = \$100 \times \frac{1}{.10} = \$100 \times 10 = \$1,000.$$

So according to the simple deposit multiplier, when the reserve requirement is 10% an increase of \$100 in reserves results in an increase of \$1,000 in checkable deposits. But in the real world it doesn't work out exactly that way.

The Reserve Requirement Isn't the Only "Excess-Reserves-Eater"

In reality, the deposit multiplier is somewhat more complicated and isn't nearly as large as the previous example would indicate. Why? Because as the money supply expands, the reserve requirement on checkable deposits isn't the only factor "eating up the excess reserves" as they move from bank to bank. In fact the reserve requirement isn't even the major "excess-reserves-eater." So what is? Cash drain.

---

[1] This equation is a shortcut method for calculating the sum of an infinite geometric series—in this case, the series of steps through Bank A, Bank B, Bank C, etc., in the deposit expansion process. We could write out the formula the long way, as follows:

$$\Delta\sqrt{}D = \Delta R \times [1 + (1 - rr) + (1 - rr)^2 + (1 - rr)^3 + \cdots + (1 - rr)^{n-1} \cdots].$$

Using the figures in the example in the previous chapter where ΔR is \$100 and rr is 10%, the formula says:

$$\Delta\sqrt{}D = 100 \times [1 + .90 + (.90)^2 + (.90)^3 + \cdots + (.90)^{n-1} \cdots].$$
$$\Delta\sqrt{}D = 100 + 90 + 81 + 72.90 \cdots \text{ etc.}$$

The standard formula for the sum of an infinite geometric series (where X is between zero and 1) is:

$$1 + X + X^2 + X^3 + \cdots + X^{n-1} \cdots = \frac{1}{1 - X}.$$

Which in this case becomes:

$$1 + (1 - rr) + (1 - rr)^2 + (1 - rr)^3 + \cdots + (1 - rr)^{n-1} \cdots = \frac{1}{1 - (1 - rr)} = \frac{1}{rr}.$$

So the deposit multiplier is $\dfrac{1}{rr}$, and the formula for calculating the change in checkable deposits ($\sqrt{}$D) becomes:

$$\Delta\sqrt{}D = \Delta R \times \frac{1}{rr}, \text{ which is exactly the formula used in the text.}$$

CASH DRAIN IS THE MAJOR FACTOR LIMITING MONEY EXPANSION

At each step in the money expansion process, *currency withdrawals from the banking system* take a bigger bite out of excess reserves than do reserve requirements. As new reserves flow into the banking system and the deposit multiplier begins to work, the money supply begins to expand. People and businesses find themselves holding larger balances in their checking accounts. Simultaneously, people and businesses begin to demand more cash. So they increase their holdings of cash.

At any given time there seems to be a "desired ratio" between the amount of checking account money and the amount of cash money (currency) that people and businesses want to hold. So as their checking account balances expand, their holdings of currency also expand to maintain this desired ratio.

The Ratio of Currency to Checkable Deposits. In 1986 in the American economy, the total amount of currency held by the public was about $185 billion. The total amount of checking deposit money held was about $520 billion. This gives a currency/checking deposit ratio of 185/520, or (in round numbers) about 35/100, or 35%. This means that for every $1 held in checking deposits, people were holding about $.35 in currency.

Now you can see the importance of cash drain in limiting the deposit expansion. If this ratio of 35% holds for incremental changes, it means that for each additional $1 created in checking account money, the banking system will loose $.35 of its reserves through cash drain—currency being pulled out of vault cash.

Banks can replenish their vault cash by ordering more from their district Federal Reserve bank. But the banks must pay for this new currency out of their FRB reserve accounts. So whether the banks replenish the cash or not, reserves are being lost at the rate of .35 for each new checking account dollar created.

How Cash Drain Limits the Expansion. The effect of this cash drain is exactly like the effect of the reserve requirement, except much larger. The reserve requirement pulls .10 out of excess reserves for each new dollar of checkable deposits created. But cash drain pulls out about .35! So for each $1 created, instead of the banking system having .90 of excess reserves to move on through the system and create more money, the system only has about .55 ($1.00 − .10 − .35 = $.55).

The More Realistic (Much Smaller) Deposit Multiplier

Now you see that the real-world deposit multiplier isn't just the reciprocal of the required reserve ratio. It must be the reciprocal of both (1) the required reserve ratio (rr) and (2) the ratio of currency to checkable deposits (c/$\sqrt{}$D):

$$\text{Deposit Multiplier} = \frac{1}{rr + c/\sqrt{}\text{D}} = \frac{1}{.10 + .35}$$

$$= \frac{1}{.45} = 2.22$$

The total potential expansion of deposits becomes:

$$\Delta\!\sqrt{D} = \Delta R \times \frac{1}{rr + c\!\sqrt{D}}.$$

Using the same figures as previously:

$$\Delta\!\sqrt{D} = \$100 \times 2.22 = \$222$$

These figures clearly illustrate the significance of cash drain in limiting the size of the deposit multiplier. The simple deposit multiplier (1/rr, 1/.10) indicates a potential *tenfold deposit expansion*. A primary deposit of $100 can result in new deposits of $1,000.

What happens when the effect of cash drain is included? The potential tenfold deposit expansion decreases to a 2.22-fold expansion. Now a new primary deposit of $100 can only result in new deposits of $222—quite a drop from the $1,000 calculated previously!

So in this case, how great is the total *money supply expansion*? $222? No. It's greater than $222 becuse the expansion consists of (1) the increase in checkable deposits of $222, plus (2) an increase in currency in circulation of $77.70 ($222 × 35% = $77.70).

Total Money Expansion: Increased Deposits Plus Increased Currency in Circulation

Each dollar of currency withdrawn from the banks (cash drain) has two effects. It is (1) a subtraction from bank reserves. But at the same time it is (2) an addition to currency in circulation. Each dollar of cash drain adds one dollar to the M1 money supply. So in this case the total money supply expansion amounts to $222 (increase in checkable deposits) plus $77.70 (increase in currency in circulation) for a total increase of $299.70.

In this case the *deposit multiplier* is 2.22. But the *total money multiplier* (including new checkable deposits plus new currency in circulation) works out to be 2.997, or, in round numbers, 3. The injection of new reserves ($100), times a multiplier of 3 equals $300, which (in round numbers) is the total money expansion resulting from the $100 injection of new reserves.

RESERVES FOR NONCHECKABLE DEPOSITS LIMIT THE EXPANSION OF CHECKABLE DEPOSITS

Now you know that as the money supply expands, cash drain takes a large bite out of excess reserves. In addition there is another minor factor nibbling away at excess reserves and limiting the expansion of checkable deposits.

When reserves are required for **noncheckable deposits**, that reduces the amount of reserves available to support the expansion of checkable deposits. It's obvious that the more of its reserves the bank must allocate to noncheckable deposits (which are not M1 money), the less reserves it will have available to support the expansion of checkable deposits (which are M1 money).

The bottom line: To the extent that banks are required to hold reserves to back up deposits *other than checkable deposits,* the size of the checkable deposit multiplier—and the size of the M1 money multiplier—will be reduced.

As Checkable Deposits Expand, Noncheckable Deposits Also Expand

Just as people and businesses seem to have a "desired ratio" between checking deposits and cash, they also seem to have a desired ratio between checking deposits and various kinds of noncheckable savings deposits. So as the multiple expansion of checkable deposits proceeds, noncheckable savings deposit balances also increase.

As bank reserves are drained off to support the increasing size of noncheckable deposits, those reserves are no longer available to support the continued expansion of checkable deposits. So the effect of required reserves on noncheckable deposits is the same as the effect of cash drain.

In the American banking system, required reserves on noncheckable savings and time deposits are not very high. In fact, there are no required reserves at all on time and savings deposits owned by individuals.

Since the passage of the Depository Institutions Deregulation and Monetary Control Act (DIDMCA) in 1980, the only reserve requirements on noncheckable deposits have been 3% on Eurodollar deposits and nonpersonal (business) time deposits with original maturities of less than one and one-half years. So today, in the U.S. economy, reserves required for noncheckable deposits have only a very minor effect on the size of the checkable deposit multiplier (and on the M1 money multiplier).

THE CHECKABLE DEPOSIT MULTIPLIER WHEN $r\sqrt{D}$, $c/\sqrt{D}$, AND rnD ARE ALL CONSIDERED

The formula for the deposit multiplier which takes into account (1) the reserve requirement on checkable deposits, (2) cash drain, and (3) the reserve requirement on noncheckable deposits, is as follows:

$$\frac{1}{r\sqrt{D} + c/\sqrt{D} + nD/\sqrt{D(rnD)}}, \text{ where}$$

$r\sqrt{D}$ is the reserve requirement on checkable deposits,

$c/\sqrt{D}$ is the ratio of currency to checkable deposits,

$nD/\sqrt{D}$ is the ratio of noncheckable deposits to checkable deposits, and

rnD is the reserve requirement on noncheckable deposits.

The Effect of Required Reserves on Noncheckable Deposits

From the above formula, you can see that reserves on noncheckable deposits have exactly the same kind of effect on the deposit multiplier as does the reserve requirement or cash drain. The larger it is, the more it limits the size of the multiplier. As the multiplier is operating and total checkable deposits are increasing, the (assumed constant) terms $nD/\surd D$ tells us that noncheckable deposits also will be increasing. This term tells us: "How fast?"

The more the increase in noncheckable deposits (the greater the $nD/\surd D$ ratio) and the larger the reserve requirement on noncheckable deposits (rnD), the more reserves will be drained off into this alternative use. So the less will be available to support the expansion of checkable deposits and the M1 money supply.

An Example of the Checkable Deposit Multiplier When All Reserve Requirements and Cash Drain Are Considered

Now, referring back to the above formula and using the same figures as previously plus new (assumed) figures for the new terms, here are the figures:

$$r\surd D \quad = 10\%$$

$$c/\surd D \quad = 35\%$$

$$nD/\surd D = 2/1 = 2$$

$$rnD \quad = 2.5\%$$

This shows that we're assuming

1. a 10% reserve requirement on checkable deposits,

2. a currency-to-checkable deposits ratio of 35% (an expansion in checkable deposits of $100 would result in an expansion in currency in circulation of $35),

3. that people prefer to hold noncheckable deposit balances twice the size of their in checkable deposits balances, (when checkable deposits increase by $100, noncheckable deposits will increase by $200), and

4. that the reserve requirement on non-checkable deposits is 2.5%. Given all these assumptions, here is the computation of the checkable deposit multiplier:

$$\begin{matrix} \text{Checkable} \\ \text{Deposit} \\ \text{Multiplier} \end{matrix} = \frac{1}{.10 + .35 + 2(.025)} = \frac{1}{.10 + .35 + .05} = \frac{1}{50} = 2.0$$

In this case the inclusion of a 2.5% reserve requirement on noncheckable deposits (and the assumption that the desired $nD/\surd D$ ratio is 2 to 1) reduced the checkable-deposit multiplier from 2.22 as calculated previously, to an even 2.0. Obviously the greater the ratio $nD/\surd D$ and the greater the noncheckable deposit reserve requirement (rnD), the greater will be the non-checkable-deposit reserve drain. So the smaller will be the checkable deposit multiplier, and the M1 money multiplier.

Now you can see the effects of all three of these factors on the size of the checkable deposit (and M1 money supply) multiplier. For each new dollar of M1 money created, required reserves pull out 10 cents, cash drain pulls out 35 cents, and reserves on noncheckable deposits pull out 5 cents. So for each $1 created, instead of the banking system having $.90 of excess reserves as with the simple deposit multiplier, or $.55 of excess reserves when cash drain is also considered, now the system only has $.50 of excess reserves to pass along to support additional expansion of checkable deposits and the M1 money supply.

What About the M2 Multiplier?

What about the effect of all this on the M2 money multiplier? Noncheckable deposits are included as a component of the M2 money supply. Since reserve requirements on noncheckable deposits are much lower than on checkable deposits, a given amount of additional reserves can support *a much greater expansion in noncheckable deposits* than in checkable deposits. So if we take M2 as our chosen measure of the money supply, the greater the flow of funds into noncheckable deposits, the greater the money multiplier will be. So the effect is exactly opposite to the effect when we select M1 as our chosen monetary aggregate.

For example, if the reserve requirement on checkable deposits is 10% (and ignoring all other factors for the moment), an additional $100 in reserves can support an additional $1,000 in new checkable deposits (1/.10 × $100 = $1,000). Suppose the reserve requirement on noncheckable deposits is 2.5%. Then additional reserves of $100 would support additional noncheckable deposits of $4,000 (1/.025 × $100 = $4,000).

In this case the simple deposit multiplier on checkable deposits would be 10. On noncheckable deposits it would be 40. So when thinking about the effect of non-checkable-deposit reserve requirements it's important to be clear about the specific monetary aggregate under consideration. It makes a lot of difference whether you choose M1, or M2. Box 19-1 tells more about this.

What If Banks Don't Lend Their Excess Reserves?

Throughout this discussion we have assumed that banks have always been able and willing to quickly lend their excess reserves. But what if they didn't? If the banks didn't lend their excess reserves, the money supply expansion would be stopped dead in its tracks!

Sometimes, either because of weak loan demand or because of their desire for more safety and liquidity, banks may hold some excess reserves. Or they may decide not to make loans—instead, to use their excess reserves to buy T-bills from the Fed banks.

Box 19-1

Question: **What Are the k-Ratio and the t-Ratio? And How Do They Affect the Money Multipliers?**

The ratio of the public's money holdings between currency and checkable deposits $(c/\sqrt{D})$ is sometimes referred to in monetary analysis as the "k-ratio." The ratio of the public's holdings between noncheckable deposits and checkable deposits $(nD/\sqrt{D})$ is referred to as the "t-ratio." An increase in either the k-ratio or the t-ratio would reduce the amount of reserves available to support checkable deposits, and therefore would reduce the size of the M1 money multiplier. However, an increase in the t-ratio would permit a larger volume of total deposits to be supported by any given volume of reserves. Therefore it would increase the size of the M2 money multiplier.

Note: When you see reference to the "k-ratio" be careful not to confuse it with the "Cambridge k" as used in the Cambridge University version of the equation of exchange: $M = kPQ$. The meanings of "the k-ratio" and "the Cambridge k" are entirely different.

This kind of limitation on money supply expansion usually is not very significant—at least not in "normal times." Usually banks which do not (or cannot) lend their excess reserves will make these reserves available in the Fed funds market where they are borrowed by other banks and then lent.

OUR MONEY SUPPLY IS CREATED BY THE BANKING SYSTEM

The "deposit multiplier" is not so precise or easy to define as we might wish. But even though we don't know what its precise size will be at any moment, we do know that it is there, and that it does work.

Consider this: The M1 money supply in the United States in the late 1980s amounted to over $800 billion. Less than 15 years earlier it only amounted to $200 billion. Where did all that extra money come from? It was created through the deposit multiplier process—through the banking system.

New Primary Deposits Flow into Many Banks

When the Fed buys government securities, the new funds flow simultaneously into the reserve accounts of many banks throughout the banking system. Many banks simultaneously become "Typical Bank A" in our previous example and begin to initiate the expansion process. Then as loans are made and the loan funds spent and redeposited, many banks simultaneously become "Typical Bank B."

The important point: When the Fed releases new reserves into the banking system the money expansion occurs immediately and simultaneously throughout the system. You can see that in its control over bank reserves the Fed has a powerful tool for controlling the nation's money supply.

In the next chapter you'll find out exactly how the Fed exercises its monetary control powers. But first, here's a look at the U.S. monetary base, money multipliers, and the money supply in the late 1980s.

The Fed Supplies New Reserves

New primary deposits (new reserves) are created by the Fed. The Fed buys government securities in the open market and pays with funds which quickly flow into the reserve accounts of the banks. This creates the excess reserves. Then the money expansion (money multiplier) process takes it from there.

THE U.S. MONETARY BASE, MONEY MULTIPLIERS, AND MONEY SUPPLY

The entire money supply of the nation rests on the "monetary base." At any moment, the dollar value of the monetary base, times the money multiplier, equals the size (dollar value) of the nation's money supply.

The Monetary Base

The monetary base consists entirely of reservable assets (assets which can be used by the banking system as reserves) which have been made available to the banking system. A small amount of this pool of reservable assets has been created and issued by the U.S. Treasury (treasury currency). But almost all of the monetary base has been created by the Federal Reserve System.

What assets are included in the monetary base? Only two:

1. total currency in existence, plus
2. bank reserve deposits in the district Fed banks.

In the late 1980s the total amount of currency in existence—that held by the public plus that held by the banks as vault cash—amounted to about $200 billion. About $180 billion consisted of Federal Reserve notes, and the balance (about $20 billion) consisted of Treasury currency (mostly coins). So in the late 1980s, **currency** made up about $200 billion of the monetary base. The balance (about $30 billion) consisted of the banks' **reserve deposits** in the district Fed banks.

The Money Supply/Monetary Base Multiplier

In 1987 the size of the M1 money supply was about $700 billion. The monetary base at that time amounted to about $230 billion ($200 billion currency and $30 billion bank reserve deposits). So the M1 money supply/monetary base multiplier was about 3 ($700 billion money supply divided by $230 billion monetary base equals a money multiplier of 3). Alternatively, the monetary base (about $230) times the M1 money multiplier (about 3) equals the M1 money supply (about $700).

This multiplier (M1 money supply/monetary base) is usually the one economists are referring to when they discuss "the money multiplier." If this multiplier is constant and stable, then each additional dollar added to the monetary base could be expected to result in an additional $3 in the M1 money supply. But in fact, as figure 19-6 illustrates, the M1 multiplier during the 1980s has not been very stable.

The Money Supply/Bank Reserves Multiplier

As you know, cash drain (the $c/\sqrt{}$ D ratio) is by far the largest limiting factor on the size of the money multiplier. Of the total amount of currency available to the public and to the banking system in 1987 (about $200 billion), only about $25 billion was in vault cash where it could be used as bank reserves. So that left about $175 billion which could have been used as bank reserves except that it was being held outside the banking system—by consumers, businesses, coin collectors, illegal drug dealers, etc.

So the total amount of **reserves** held by the banking system in 1987 amounted to about $25 billion in vault cash plus about $30 billion in Fed bank deposits—$55 billion altogether. You can see what a difference it would make if we calculated the money multiplier considering only the reserves held by the banking system—ignoring the currency held by the public.

With banking system reserves of $55 billion and the M1 money supply of $700 billion, this would indicate a multiplier of about 12.7 (700 ÷ 55 = 12.7). Alterna-

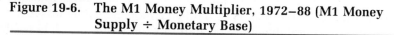

Figure 19-6.   The M1 Money Multiplier, 1972–88 (M1 Money Supply ÷ Monetary Base)

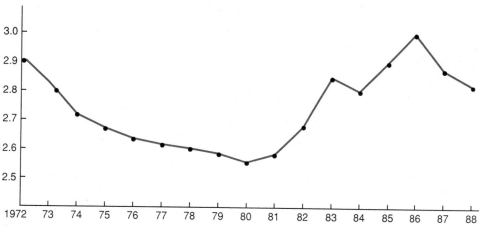

Source: Data from *Federal Reserve Bulletin*, various issues. Chart prepared by author.

Explanation of Money Multipliers

The M1 multiplier as usually defined is the ratio of the M1 money supply to the monetary base. In 1987 this ratio was approximately $700 billion/230 billion, giving a multiplier of about 3.

Of the total monetary base of $230 billion, only $55 billion—less than 25%—was actually serving as bank reserves. The remaining three-fourths of the monetary base was serving as *currency in circulation*.

With actual bank reserves of only $55 billion (FRB deposits $30 billion plus vault cash of $25 billion) the *M1 money multiplier*, if calculated on the basis of bank reserves alone would be $700 billion ÷ $55 billion, or 12.7.

The "total checkable deposits" component of M1 amounted to about $500 billion. So the simple *checkable deposit multiplier*, calculated on the basis of bank reserves alone, was $500 billion divided by $55 billion, or about 9.

tively, reserves ($55 billion) times the multiplier (about 12.7) equals the M1 money supply (about $700 billion).

The Checkable Deposits/Bank Reserves Multiplier

Since about $500 billion of the M1 money supply consisted of checkable deposits—deposits for which bank reserves were required—*the simple checkable deposit multiplier* amounted to about 9 (500 ÷ 55 = 9). Alternatively, total reserves of $55 billion times a multiplier of 9 equals total checkable deposits of about $500 billion.

Money Multipliers Are Significant for Monetary Policy

Why all this concern with money multipliers? Because the sizes of the multipliers determine the effects of monetary policy actions.

We often say that the Fed controls the nation's money supply. But in fact, what it has control over is the monetary base. To the extent that the money supply/monetary base multiplier is stable, the Fed can indeed control the money supply. But if this multiplier changes, the Fed's influences on the monetary base may have unpredicted effects on the size of the money supply.

Any lack of stability (or predictability) of the money multipliers reduces the predictability of the results of the Fed's monetary policies. And in fact that has been a serious problem for the Fed during the 1980s. You'll be reading more about the Fed and monetary policy in the chapters coming up.

SUMMARY

- Both currency in circulation and required reserves for noncheckable deposits limit the expansion of checkable deposits.
- The simple deposit multiplier is *the reciprocal of the reserve requirement*:

$$\frac{1}{rr}, \text{ or } \frac{1}{r\sqrt{D}}.$$

- The deposit multiplier considering the reserve requirement *plus cash drain* is:

$$\frac{1}{r\sqrt{D} + c\sqrt{D}}$$

- The deposit multiplier including consideration of *reserves required for noncheckable deposits*, becomes:

$$\frac{1}{r\sqrt{D} + c\sqrt{D} + nD\sqrt{D}(rnD)}$$

- Money expansion could be limited by the failure of banks to lend their excess reserves. But during normal times this is not an important limitation.
- The monetary base is (1) currency in existence, plus (2) bank reserve deposits. In 1987 there was about $25 billion in vault cash plus about $30 billion in Fed deposits, for total reserves of about $55 billion in the U.S. banking system.
- The M1 money multiplier—the ratio of the M1 money supply to the **monetary base**—in 1987 was about $700/$230, or about 3.
- The simple checkable deposit multiplier, checkable deposits divided by **bank reserves**, in 1987 amounted to about 500/55 = 9.
- The multiplier considering the ratio of the M1 money supply to bank reserves was 700/55 = 12.73.
- Stable money multipliers are necessary for the Fed's monetary control policies to have predictable effects on the money supply.

Important Principles, Issues, Concepts, Terms

The importance of cash drain as a "excess-reserves-eater"

The importance of the $c\sqrt{D}$ ratio

The deposit multiplier formulas

Difference between the deposit multiplier and the total money multiplier

The effects of reserves on noncheckable deposits on the multipliers

The $\sqrt{D/nD}$ ratio

Deposit multiplier formula when required reserves, cash drain, and reserves on noncheckable deposits are all considered

Relative importance of reserves on checkable and noncheckable deposits

Different effects on M1 and M2 of noncheckable deposit reserve requirements

Effects of banks not lending their excess reserves

How our money supply has been created

The present U.S. monetary base

The money supply/monetary base multiplier

The money supply/bank reserves multiplier

The total checkable deposits/bank reserves multiplier

The significance of money multipliers for monetary policy

Questions

1. Explain the importance of cash drain in limiting the expansion of the money supply.

2. Explain the effect of required reserves on noncheckable deposits on the size of the M1 multiplier. What changes would cause the effect to be larger? Or smaller?

3. Write down and then explain each of the terms in the checkable deposit multiplier when all "excess-reserves-eaters" are considered.

4. Explain exactly what would happen (and why) to the money multipliers if banks suddenly decided they would like to hold more excess reserves.

5. Explain the relationship between the M1 and M2 multipliers. An increase in the reserve requirement on noncheckable deposits would have an opposite effect on these two multipliers. Explain why.

6. The chapter explains various different money multipliers. Explain the difference between multipliers related to the monetary base, and multipliers related to bank reserves. Which would be likely to be larger? Which do you think would be more reliable guides to monetary policy? (You are not yet well prepared to answer this question, but it's time for you to begin to think about it.)

7. Explain what is so important about "money multipliers" when we're concerned with the conduct of monetary policy.

Suggested Readings

Boschen, John F. "Should We Reduce the Role of Banks in the Monetary Policy Process?" *Economic Review.* Federal Reserve Bank of Kansas City (February 1988), 18–28.

Pesek, Boris. "Monetary Theory in the Post-Robertsonian 'Alice in Wonderland' Era." *Journal of Economic Literature* 14 (September 1976), 867.

CHAPTER 20

Central Banking: The Fed's Tools of Monetary Control and How They Work

Chapter Objectives

This chapter explains how the **central bank** (in the United States, the Federal Reserve System) controls the nation's money supply. When you finish studying this chapter you will understand and be able to explain:

1. What central banks are, what they do, and their most important function: to control the rate of growth of the nation's money supply.

2. The three monetary control tools: changing **reserve requirements**, changing the **discount rate**, and **open market operations** (OMOs).

3. How to use T-accounts and supply and demand graphs to illustrate the "double whammy" effect of open market operations: (1) on **financial markets** and **interest rates**, and (2) on **bank reserves**.

4. How open market operations are carried out by the system open market account (SOMA) manager at the "trading desk" at the Federal Reserve Bank of New York (FRBNY).

5. How reserve requirement and discount rate changes are used primarily to support (to "back up") the Fed's open market operations.

THE CENTRAL BANK CONTROLS THE NATION'S MONEY SUPPLY

You know that the size of every nation's money supply needs to be controlled. And you also know that most of every modern nation's money supply is created through its banking system. All it takes for the money supply to expand further is for some new reserves to enter the banking system. That's what you were reading about in the last two chapters.

Doesn't this seem to be a dangerous situation? Isn't it possible that our well-meaning central bankers might create too much reserves? And our well-meaning commercial bankers might make too many loans? And thereby increase the money supply too much, leading to inflation? Perhaps even hyperinflation which would result in the ultimate collapse of our money and banking system?

Yes. That could happen. It has happened in several countries during this century. To prevent such a calamity, the size of the **available reserve pool** must be carefully limited and controlled. And who, pray tell, is entrusted with this awesome task? The **central bank**. In the United States, as you know, it's the **Federal Reserve System**.

The Functions of Central Banks

Every modern nation has a central bank. The key function of the central bank is to control the size of (the rate of growth of) the nation's money supply. The central bank exercises this control by limiting the size of (the rate of growth of) the **monetary base**—i.e., the pool of reserves available to the banking system.

Central banks perform several functions, including:

—supplying currency

—aiding in the clearing and collection of checks,

—serving as banker for the government,

—serving as banker for the other banks in the nation,

—supervising and regulating activities of banks,

—performing banking functions for foreign governments and foreign central banks, and

—dealing in and influencing foreign exchange markets.

But *the most important function of the central bank is to exercise control over the nation's money supply by controlling the monetary base*—i.e., by limiting the rate of growth of the "reserve pool" available to the banking system.

Worldwide Importance of the U.S. Federal Reserve System

The most important central bank in the world is the U.S. Federal Reserve System. Because of the importance of the U.S. economy in the world economy, and because of the *premier role* of the U.S. dollar in world financial markets, everything the Fed does is felt instantaneously in financial markets throughout the world.

The central banks of all of the major trading nations can significantly influence international financial markets. For example, the monetary policies and actions of the Deutsch Bundesbank of West Germany or of the Bank of Japan or the Bank of England or the Banque de France can have a significant influence on financial markets worldwide. But none of the other central banks has nearly as much impact on worldwide financial markets as does the U.S. Federal Reserve System.

The policies of the central banks of smaller countries—for example, the Bank of Canada, Bank of Australia, Banco de Mexico, etc.—do not usually have very much influence on financial markets beyond their national borders. But their influence on their domestic economies is of critical importance. Why? Because they control the size of and growth of their nation's money supply.

Throughout this chapter the explanation will focus on the U.S. Federal Reserve System and what it does to control the size of the U.S. money supply. But remember that the central banks of other nations, although not identical to the Fed, have similar responsibilities and similar monetary control tools, and they exercise these tools in similar ways.

The Central Bank Controls the Money Supply by Controlling Bank Reserves

When a central bank wants to alter the rate of growth of the nation's money supply, what can it do? One of two things: (1) it can change the *reserve requirement*—that is, it can change the percentage of deposits which must be held as reserves, or (2) it can *change the amount of* (limit the rate of growth in) *reserves available* to the banking system. The sections coming up will explain how the U.S. Federal Reserve does both of these things, using its "tools of monetary policy."

CHANGING RESERVE REQUIREMENTS

In March of 1980 the U.S. Congress set new required reserve ratios for the U.S. banking system. As explained in a previous chapter, the Depository Institutions Deregulation and Monetary Control Act (DIDMCA) set the reserve requirement on checkable deposits at 3% for small banks and at 12% for large banks. The act gives the Fed the power to adjust the 12% rate for large banks within a range of 8% to 14%. But the act does not authorize the Fed to change the 3% rate for small banks and thrifts.

Increasing the Reserve Requirement

Suppose the money supply is growing faster than the Fed wants it to grow. And suppose the Fed decides that on checkable deposit balances at large banks it will increase the reserve requirement from 12% to 13%. That would mean that banks must immediately begin to reduce their checkable deposits and/or increase their reserves. The money supply expansion could be stopped immediately!

But it isn't likely that the Fed would make a sudden and significant change in the reserve requirement unless drastic measures were considered necessary. Why not? Because the *shock effect* on the economy would be difficult to predict. The growth of the economy could be stopped dead in its tracks. A serious recession might be induced.

If the Fed decided to use a reserve requirement increase as its chosen tool of monetary policy, it would be more likely either to make the change very small—a fraction of a percentage point—or to announce a forthcoming change and phase in the change over a period of time. This would permit the banking system and the rate of money supply growth to adjust smoothly. But, as you will soon see, the Fed has other, more effective ways of bringing about smooth adjustments in the rate of growth of the money supply.

Lowering the Reserve Requirement

If the time ever came when the Fed wanted to create billions of dollars of additional lending power by a stroke of the pen, it could do so by lowering the reserve requirement. But again, the shock effect of such drastic action would be difficult to predict.

If economic conditions were in such a sad state that drastic action appeared necessary, then a major reduction in reserve requirements might be announced. Still, it isn't likely. Other tools of monetary policy can be adjusted much more easily and sensitively, and without such unpredictable effects.

When you read about the other two monetary policy tools (changing the discount rate, and open market operations), you'll understand why these two other tools, used together and to complement each other, are the "usual techniques" of monetary policy. As a monetary policy tool, reserve requirement changes are seldom used. In fact there were no changes in the checkable deposit reserve requirement percentages between March of 1980 and mid-1988 when this book went to press.

The active tools of monetary policy are: (1) changing the discount rate, and (2) open market operations. Both of these tools are designed to control the size of the money supply, not by controlling the amount of reserves required, but by controlling *the amount of reserves available to the banking system.*

CHANGING THE DISCOUNT RATE

From the point of view of an individual bank, when a reserve deficiency occurs it must soon be made up. That means it must (1) get more vault cash, or (2) increase its deposits at the Fed, or perhaps (3) reduce its checkable deposits. So what does it do?

Maybe the bank (1) tries to attract new depositors by using radio and TV commercials. Or maybe it (2) sells some of its government securities or other assets, and then deposits the funds in its Fed bank reserve account. Or maybe (3) as people and businesses pay off their loans the bank just lets its reserve balances build up and doesn't make new loans. Or maybe (most likely) it (4) enters the "Fed funds market" and borrows some of the excess reserves of other banks. All of these are ways individual banks use from time to time to improve their reserve positions. But there's another way.

Banks Can Borrow Reserves from the Fed

Why not just borrow the needed funds from the district Federal Reserve bank? Great idea! The Fed bank will charge interest on this loan, of course. The interest rate the Fed charges is called the **discount rate**.

Depository institutions borrow billions of dollars from the district Fed banks *every week* for the purpose of overcoming or preventing reserve deficiencies. This privilege of borrowing from the so-called "discount window" is available to all depository institutions which have checkable deposits and which therefore are required to meet the Fed's reserve requirements.

Here's a great idea for increasing your bank's earnings! Why not borrow a few million dollars from the Fed bank, pay the "discount rate" of interest, and then lend the money at a higher rate? If there is enough "spread" between the discount rate and the loan rate, you can make a tidy profit. But there's a good reason why you'd better not do this. The Fed frowns upon such practices.

Limitations on "Discount Window" Borrowing

The Fed makes it quite clear that the discount window is to be utilized *only to overcome an occasional reserve deficiency*. In general, it is not to be used for the purpose of borrowing funds to be used for making new loans.

This limitation on discount-window borrowing isn't always easy to interpret. Suppose you're a banker and you lend aggressively. Then suddenly you find that you need to increase your reserves by borrowing at the discount window. Is that any different from borrowing funds from the Fed, and then making new loans?

Sometimes banks *do* overlend and then borrow at the discount window to make up their reserve deficiencies. But if a bank does that week after week the Fed is likely to inform that bank that its discount-window privileges are being curtailed.

Raising the Discount Rate

The Fed can discourage discount-window borrowing by raising the discount rate. The Fed could push the discount rate up so high that it would be unprofitable for banks to lend aggressively and then cover their reserve deficiencies by discount-window borrowing.

When the Fed announces an increase in the discount rate, this usually signals a tightening of monetary policy. Bankers get the signal that perhaps they should follow a somewhat less aggressive lending policy—and that perhaps they should consider increasing the rates on their loans.

Lowering the Discount Rate

When the Fed announces a lowering of the discount rate the effect is exactly opposite. The lower discount rate encourages bankers to make more loans, and at lower rates. With a lower discount rate, bankers can afford to be somewhat less careful about encountering deficit reserve positions and then "covering" by discount-window borrowing.

Adjusting the Discount Rate to Reflect Market Conditions

Suppose the Fed funds rate and the T-bill rate and the large denomination CD rate and other money market rates have been creeping upward or downward over the past several weeks or months. And suppose the Fed's discount rate hasn't been changed. Shouldn't the Fed consider adjusting the discount rate to bring it more in line with money market rates?

Yes it should. And it would. And when the adjustment was made, it would have been already anticipated by the financial markets. It is unlikely that the announcement of the change would have any significant effect. Why? Because the change was *expected*. But for *an unexpected discount-rate change* the results are quite different.

The Announcement Effect of an Unexpected Discount-Rate Change

The **announcement effect** of an unexpected discount-rate change usually has a significant influence on the financial markets. When the Fed announces an increase in the discount rate, this sends a clear signal: The Fed is tightening money!

This message is immediately carried to the banks, securities dealers, investors, and to the entire financial community, both in this country and throughout the world. Interest rates tend to rise immediately, both U.S. and worldwide. Suddenly money is tighter—more expensive to borrow than before.

The Fed does not frequently send clear signals to tip off its intentions. But when it does want to send a clear signal, the announcement of an unexpected and significant change in the discount rate carries this signal immediately and effectively. The impact on the financial markets can be profound. The greater the surprise, the greater the effect is likely to be.

Discount-Window Borrowing: At the Banks' Initiative

Through discount rate adjustments the Fed can make it either more expensive or less expensive for banks to borrow reserves. But the initiative—to borrow or not to borrow—still rests with the banks.

What if the Fed had a monetary policy tool which was so powerful that the Fed could use it to push money into or pull money out of bank reserves *without any initiative on the part of the banks?* And whether the banks liked it or not? That would be a powerful tool of monetary policy!

Would you believe that the Fed has such a tool? They do. It's called "open market operations in government securities," or usually just **open market operations** or **OMOs.**

OPEN MARKET OPERATIONS (OMOs)

Changes of reserve requirements are made very seldom. Discount rates are changed from time to time, but usually not very often. In contrast, open market operations are undertaken daily—hourly, even. In fact, open market operations can be adjusted minute to minute, whenever conditions in the financial markets seem to indicate the need for the Fed's intervention.

The Fed's Daily Balancing Act

Here's how it works.

1. *When the Fed wants to ease money it buys securities.* This increases the demand for securities, pushes securities prices up and pushes interest rates down. At the same time it pushes new reserves into the banks' reserve accounts—whether the banks like it or not.

2. *When the Fed wants to tighten money it sells securities.* That increases the supply of securities, pushes securities prices down and pushes interest rates up. At the same time it pulls reserves out of the banks' reserve accounts—whether the banks like it or not.

The remainder of this chapter explains exactly how it works—how the Fed's open market operations (OMOs) simultaneously alter both (1) interest rates in the financial markets, and (2) the reserves held by the banking system.

The Fed Buys and Sells "Pieces of the Government Debt"

The U.S. government debt—now around $3 trillion and still growing—is made up of government securities. These securities range from short term Treasury bills (T-bills, with maturities quoted in days or months) to long-term government bonds with maturities up to 30 years. Most of these government securities are held by individuals, banks, insurance companies, other corporations, etc., both U.S. and foreign. But the Fed banks hold more than $200 billion of them.

Back in 1980 the Fed's holdings of government securities amounted to less than $125 billion. By 1988 the figure had passed $220 billion. Over this eight-year period the Fed bought about $100 billion of government securities. In the process, it pumped about $100 billion of new reserves into the banking system. Is that what enabled the U.S. M1 money supply to grow from less than $400 billion in 1980 to almost $800 billion in 1988? Exactly!

When the Fed Buys Securities It Adds New Bank Reserves

Suppose the Fed buys a $1,000 government bond. That increases reserves by $1,000. Here's how.

Suppose you're a banker and the Fed buys the bond from your bank. Your bank doesn't even receive a check! Your district Fed bank just adds $1,000 to your bank's account. Your reserves immediately go up by $1,000.

Here are T-accounts to illustrate this transaction:

Your Bank's T-Account		**Fed Bank's T-Account**	
Your bank sells a $1,000 bond to the Fed bank		The Fed bank buys a $1,000 bond from your bank	
Assets	**Liabilities & Capital**	**Assets**	**Liabilities & Capital**
bonds −1,000 Fed Deposits +1,000		bonds +1,000	your bank's reserve deposits +1,000

In this case the money supply has not yet begun to increase. But you can see from the T-accounts that your bank is now poised to initiate the money expansion (deposit multiplier) process. It can now lend $1,000 more than previously.

Now suppose it wasn't a bank that sold the $1,000 bond to the Fed. Suppose it was Travelers Insurance Company or the New York State Employees Retirement System or your Great Uncle Albert who sold it. In the end it would make no difference. Whoever gets the check from the Fed is going to deposit it in some depository institution. And that institution is going to send the check to the Fed for deposit to its reserve account. So some bank is going to get $1,000 of new reserves.

Suppose your Great Uncle Albert sold the $1,000 bond to the Fed. Then here are the T-accounts:

G.U. Albert's T-Account

He sells securities and deposits the check in
his bank account

Assets		Liabilities & Capital
Government securities	−1,000	
Checkable deposits	+1,000	

G.U. Albert's Bank's T-Account

The bank deposits the check in
its Fed account

Assets		Liabilities & Capital	
FRB deposits	+1,000	Customers' checkable deposits	+1,000

The Fed Bank's T-Account

The Fed bank acquires government securities
and adds an equal amount to bank reserve
deposits

Assets		Liabilities & Capital	
Government securities	+1,000	Bank reserve deposits	+1,000

In this case the money expansion (deposit multiplier) process has already begun. Your Great Uncle Albert has $1,000 of M1 money which previously did not exist. If the reserve requirement is 10%, G. U. Albert's bank now has excess reserves of $900 ($1000 minus required reserves of $100 to back up G.U.A.s $1,000 deposit). So the bank now can lend $900. The money supply expansion can continue. If the money multiplier is 3, then an ultimate money supply expansion of $3,000 can be expected.

No matter who sells government securities to the Fed, when the Fed pays, that payment soon becomes additional reserves for the banking system. And if the money multiplier happens to be 3, then we can expect a money supply expansion of three times the dollar value of the securities purchased by the Fed.

But wait! Suppose your Great Uncle Albert turns out to be a miser who hoards currency in his closet. What then? Box 20-1 talks about that.

When a Central Bank Buys Assets, Bank Reserves Are Created

In the above example the Fed has created additional bank reserves "out of thin air." It is because the Fed is the central bank that it has the power to do this. This Fed can, if it wishes, "grow its balance sheet" (add equal amounts of assets and liabilities) *ad infinitum*!

The Fed could buy $1 billion worth of government securities and pay with $1 billion in new bank reserve deposits. This automatically would create a billion dollars of new bank reserves. And if the Fed wished to do so it could do the same thing again and again and again—absolutely without limit! Each transaction would add $1 billion to the Fed's assets (government securities) and also to its

---

Box 20-1

Question: What if the Bond-Seller Doesn't Deposit the Money, but Withdraws Cash Instead?

In the example in the text it is assumed that no cash is withdrawn. But suppose there was a cash withdrawal. What then?

What if your Great Uncle Albert (or any of the others) just cashed the check and withdrew $1,000 in currency? Then the bank wouldn't have any more reserves than before.

When the bank deposits the check in its district Fed bank it will gain $1,000 in its reserve account. But that addition to reserves will

be exactly offset by the subtraction of $1,000 of reserves lost from vault cash.

So did the money supply expand? Yes it did. By a multiplier of one. The M1 money supply is $1,000 larger than before, but no more than that. And in this case that extra money isn't going to have much effect on the economy. Why not? Because Great Uncle Albert has it locked away in his closet!

---

liabilities (bank reserve deposits). The Fed's balance sheet could just keep growing larger and larger and bank reserves and the the monetary base would be growing at the same rate. Dangerous? Yes, it could be. You can see why central banks must be *extremely careful* to limit the growth of their balance sheets! (And bank reserves!)

Since the Fed is the central bank, its purchase of *any asset*—government securities or gold or buildings or even farm land in the midwest—would add reserves to the banking system. Why? Because *checks from the Fed, when they clear, always wind up as additional reserves for the banking system.* That's the special nature of—and the great monetary power of—the central bank.

The Fed Sells Securities to Drain Reserves from the Banking System

When the Fed uses open market operations to tighten money, it sells securities. That pulls reserves out of the banking system. All of the effects are exactly the reverse of what happens when the Fed buys securities.

When Banks Buy the Securities. A few minutes ago you were a banker and you saw what happened when you sold a $1,000 bond to the Fed. You got $1,000 of new reserves. Now you're going to buy securities from the Fed and lose reserves when you pay for the securities out of your Fed bank reserve account.

If you buy $1,000 worth of securities from the Fed, that reduces your reserve account by $1,000. These T-accounts illustrate:

Your Bank's T-Account

Your bank buys securities and pays from its Fed account

Assets		Liabilities & Capital
Government securities	+1,000	
FRB deposits	−1,000	

The Fed Bank's T-Account

The Fed bank sells securities and takes payment from bank reserve deposits

Assets		Liabilities & Capital	
Government securities	−1,000	Bank reserve deposits	−1,000

Your bank has given up one asset (Fed deposits) in exchange for another asset (government securities). But that's a very significant shift of assets. Why? Because *Fed bank deposits serve as reserves.* Government securities do not.

If the Reserve requirement is 10%, a reduction of $1,000 in your bank's Fed deposits reduces your bank's legal checkable deposit limit by $10,000. Suppose your bank had no excess reserves prior to this transaction. Then following the transaction your bank must either acquire $1,000 of new reserves from somewhere, or it must reduce its checkable deposits (and also, *ceteris paribus,* the M1 money supply) by $10,000.

The T-account for the Fed bank indicates that bank reserve deposits have been reduced by $1,000. So the monetary base has been reduced by $1,000. Whenever the Fed sells securities, that's always what happens. The Fed reduces its assets (government securities) and its liabilities (bank reserve deposits). The Fed's balance sheet shrinks. The monetary base contracts.

Why would a bank buy securities and give up $1,000 of its reserve deposits? Usually it wouldn't. But if it had $1,000 of excess reserves which it did not plan to use for making loans—and if it wanted to increase its holdings of default-risk-free assets—then perhaps it would.

When The Securities Are Bought by the Nonbank Public. Suppose your bank didn't have any excess reserves so it didn't choose to buy any securities today. But suppose G.U. Albert buys $1,000 worth of government securities from the Fed bank. He pays the Fed with a check drawn on his account at your bank.

When the Fed bank receives G.U. Albert's check, it will deduct the $1,000 from your bank's reserve account. Then it will send the check back to your bank where it will be deducted from G.U. Albert's account.

See what happened? Your bank lost $1,000 in reserves because your customer (G.U. Albert) decided to buy government securities from the Fed. The following T-accounts show the results:

G.U. Albert's T-Account

He buys bonds

Assets		Liabilities & Capital
Bonds	+1,000	
Bank deposits	−1,000	

Your Bank's T-Account

Your bank loses customer deposits and Fed deposits

Assets		Liabilities & Capital	
Fed deposits	−1,000	GUA's deposits	−1,000

The Fed Bank's T-Account

Bond holdings decreased.
Bank reserve deposits decreased.

Assets		Liabilities & Capital	
Bonds	−1,000	Bank reserve deposits	−1,000

- G.U. Albert has exchanged one kind of asset for another: checkable deposits for government securities.

- Your bank has $1,000 less assets (FRB deposits) and also less liabilities (customers' checkable deposits).
- The Fed bank has $1,000 less assets (government securities) and also less liabilities (bank reserve deposits).

Everything is still in balance, of course. But the banking system's reserve deposits have been reduced by $1,000. So the monetary base is now $1,000 smaller than before.

Here's the important point: If the Fed wants to drain reserves from the banking system it can do so very quickly and effectively *no matter if the banks want to buy the securities or not.* The Fed just sells the securities to anyone who wants to buy. And the money the Fed receives comes right out of bank reserves—no matter who buys the securities, and whether the banks like it or not (which they don't!).

Your bank may have a problem. Assuming that you had no excess reserves to begin with, what's your situation now?

Your customers' checkable deposits have gone down by $1,000, so you need less reserves than before. If the reserve requirement is 10%, you need $100 less reserves.

But you have lost $1,000 in reserves! So you have a reserve deficiency of $900. Unless you do something to make up the deficiency fairly quickly, your bank will be subject to penalties (as explained in chapter 15). And *whatever you do*—borrow Fed funds, sell bonds, reduce your lending, etc.—your actions will have the effect of pushing interest rates up even more and making money even tighter than before.

THE MECHANICS OF OPEN MARKET OPERATIONS

All of the Fed's open market operations—for all 12 of the district banks—are decided on (in general) by the Federal Open Market Committee (FOMC) which includes the seven Fed Board members and five of the presidents of the Fed district banks. Then the FOMC's decisions are carried out by the "system open market account" (SOMA) manager.

The SOMA manager operates the "trading desk"—actually there are many desks and many people involved—at the Federal Reserve Bank of New York (FRBNY). Why at the FRBNY? Because that Fed bank happens to be located in the financial center of the nation and of the world. It is (by far) the largest and most important bank in the system.

The Trading Desk Buys and Sells Through Securities Dealers

Financial experts at the "trading desk" keep a minute-to-minute watch on supply and demand and interest rate conditions in the financial markets. Suppose bond prices have been falling and interest rates rising all morning. By 11 o'clock market conditions seem to indicate the need for more reserves in the banking system. It's time for action!

Several of the "trading desk" securities traders will call several securities dealers. After some comparison price shopping, the Fed's traders will place orders to buy given amounts (usually several million dollars worth) of government securities of various maturities. The dealers will fill these orders partly from their own securities inventories and partly from their customers—perhaps Travelers Insurance Company, or your Great Uncle Albert—who have placed orders to sell.

You can see why the Fed's securities transactions are called "open market operations." When the Fed buys or sells, it deals through securities dealers. The ultimate sellers or buyers are scattered throughout the United States and throughout the world. Truly, these Fed securities transactions are "open market" operations. And their effects on bank reserves are immediate and predictable.

Open market operations provide the Fed a powerful, sensitive, easily adjustable tool of monetary policy. The Fed is poised and ready to undertake open market operations every minute of every hour of every business day—and nighttime and weekends too, as appears necessary. They can do as little or as much buying or selling as they wish, to achieve their desired degree of "ease" or "tightness" in the financial markets.

THE "DOUBLE-WHAMMY" EFFECT OF OPEN MARKET OPERATIONS

Now you know how open market operations exert their powerful effect on bank reserves. When the Fed buys (or sells) securities, funds are automatically pushed into (or pulled out of) bank reserves—and whether the banks like it or not!

But that isn't all. OMOs also have (simultaneously!) a powerful effect on the nation's financial markets.

OMOs Directly Influence Supply and Demand and Interest Rates in the Financial Markets: Whammy #1

When the Fed is selling millions of dollars worth of securities (along with everyone else who is selling securities that day), there is an increased supply of securities in the financial markets. The increased supply pushes securities prices down. Interest yields go up.

Alternatively, when the Fed is buying millions of dollars worth of securities (along with everyone else) there is an increased demand for securities. Securities prices go up. Interest yields go down.

You might call OMOs *the Fed's "double whammy" monetary policy instrument*.[1] The minute the Fed's buy or sell orders hit the financial market, securities prices begin to move up or down and interest yields move in the opposite direction. That's whammy #1.

Then whammy #2 is not far behind. As the Fed pays (or receives payment) for the securities, funds are pushed into (or drained out of) bank reserves. The lending power of the banking system and therefore the supply of loanable funds is increased (or decreased). So money gets easier (or tighter). That's Whammy #2.

---

[1] Should a college level textbook use the terminology "double-whammy" effect? I don't know. What I do know is this: Before I began using this terminology, on the final exam a significant percentage of my students would forget about one or the other of the effects of open market operations. But since I've been using this terminology, no one ever forgets either effect. So the "double-whammy" term is included here, not to be "cute," but for pragmatic reasons. As a pedagogical tool: *It works.* I sincerely hope it doesn't offend anyone.

An Example of Whammy #1. Suppose the Fed is tightening money. It sells government bonds which have face value of $1,000 and which pay 10% interest. Each of these bonds will pay its owner $100 per year.

Suppose (to be slightly ridiculous) that the Fed and other bond sellers are selling so many of these bonds that the open market price is pushed down to $500. The buyer who pays $500 for one of these bonds still will earn $100 per year (a 20% current return on that $500 investment) plus a 100% capital gain at maturity!

The point is this: If the Fed sells bonds and forces the price of bonds down by 50%, it simultaneously forces current yields on those bonds to double and yield-to-maturity (as explained in Chapter 3) goes up even more. And when yields on government bonds are going up, market rates on all debt securities are also going up. Box 20-2 tells more about this.

The Fed's action causes interest rates to rise throughout the economy and throughout the world. Money gets very tight. Borrowing gets very expensive. Many potential borrowers decide it just isn't worth it. So the rate of borrowing (and lending) slows down. So the money supply expansion—and very likely, the economy—slows down.

Effects of OMOs on Financial Markets: A Graphic Illustration

Figures 20-1 and 20-2 illustrate the powerful impact which the "double-whammy" of the Fed's open market operations can have on the nation's financial markets.

Supply and Demand Curves Illustrate the Direct Effects of OMOs: Whammy #1. When the bond traders in the office of the SOMA manager begin calling the government bond dealers and placing sell orders, this immediately increases the supply of government securities for sale in the New York financial markets.

The New York markets are interlinked with other financial markets throughout the United States and the world. So this increased supply immediately begins to push bond prices downward and interest rates upward in financial markets worldwide. This "whammy #1" is illustrated in figure 20-1.

Supply and Demand Curves Illustrate the Indirect Effects of OMOs: Whammy #2. At the same time the Fed is selling securities and increasing the supply

---

Box 20-2

Question: How Do the Fed's Open Market Operations Influence the Markets for *All Securities*?

As the Fed sells government securities and their prices fall, prices of all other debt securities (corporate bonds, municipal bonds, etc.) also begin to fall. You can see why.

People who own nongovernment securities will begin selling them and buying some of the lower-cost, higher yielding government securities. This "market shifting" will continue until it causes relative prices of all debt securities to move into line with government securities. When the Fed performs its open market operations in government securities, prices and yields on all other debt securities adjust very quickly throughout the U.S. and worldwide financial markets.

Figure 20-1. The Direct Effects of the Fed's OMOs on the Markets for Securities and Loanable Funds: Whammy #1

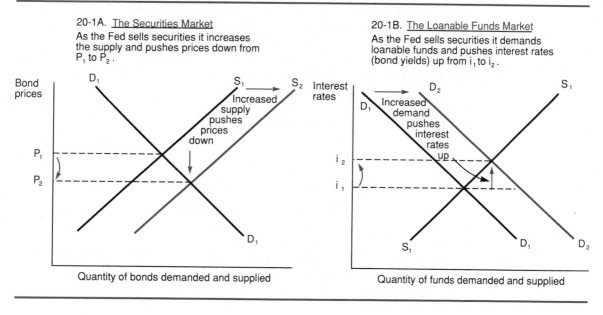

20-1A. The Securities Market
As the Fed sells securities it increases the supply and pushes prices down from P_1 to P_2.

20-1B. The Loanable Funds Market
As the Fed sells securities it demands loanable funds and pushes interest rates (bond yields) up from i_1 to i_2.

Figure 20-2. Effects of OMOs on Financial Markets via Changes in Bank Reserves: Whammy #2

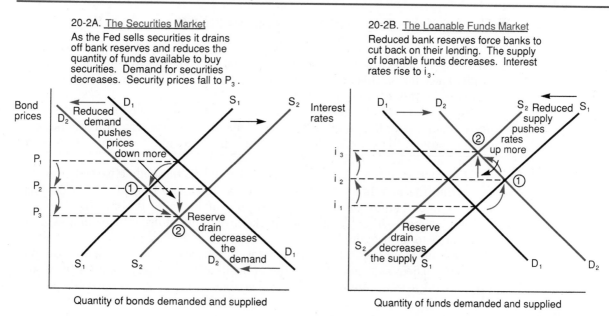

20-2A. The Securities Market
As the Fed sells securities it drains off bank reserves and reduces the quantity of funds available to buy securities. Demand for securities decreases. Security prices fall to P_3.

20-2B. The Loanable Funds Market
Reduced bank reserves force banks to cut back on their lending. The supply of loanable funds decreases. Interest rates rise to i_3.

of securities and increasing the demand for loanable funds, it is draining off bank reserves. As banks lose reserves they are forced to cut back their lending. So this reduces the ability of banks to supply loanable funds.

This *reduced supply of loanable funds* means that there is *a reduced demand for debt instruments* (securities). Banks which find themselves with reserve deficiencies certainly are not interested in demanding securities, or in increasing their loans to securities-buyers! Instead, they are likely to be supplying (selling) securities to acquire funds to make up their reserve deficiencies.

The reduced supply of reserves and of loanable funds in the banking system tends to push up interest rates even more. Money becomes even more expensive and difficult to borrow. Figure 20-2 illustrates the effect of whammy #1, plus the additional effect of "whammy #2."

The Debt Securities Market: Figures 20-1-A and 20-2-A

In figure 20-1-A, initially bond prices are at p1 and the market is in equilibrium. Then when the Fed begins open market bond sales, this increases the supply of bonds from S1 to S2. This pushes the bond price down from p1 to p2.

At the same time, the funds that the bond-buyers spent to buy bonds from the Fed, are draining from bank reserves. This reserve drain reduces the funds available to buy bonds. So there is a decrease in the demand for bonds (figure 20-2-A) from D1 to D2. The decreased demand pushes the bond price on down from p2 to p3.

At the same time that the Fed is *increasing the supply* of bonds by open market sales, it is simultaneously *decreasing the demand* for bonds by draining reserves from the banking system. It is, in effect, "hitting the market from both sides"—the supply side and the demand side. It's this "double whammy effect" which forces bond prices down from p1 to p3 in figure 20-2-A.

The Loanable Funds Market: Figures 20-1-B and 20-2-B

Initially the loanable funds market is in equilibrium with the interest rate at i1. Then the Fed begins to sell securities—that is, it begins to demand loanable funds. The effect of this increased demand for loanable funds (from D1 to D2) is to increase the interest rate from i1 to i2.

At the same time, every dollar paid to the Fed for securities amounts to *a decrease of one dollar in bank reserves*. This drain of reserves from the banking system reduces the supply of loanable funds (from S1 to S2 in figure 20-2-B) and pushes the market rate of interest on up from i2 to i3.

So in terms of the loanable funds market, when the Fed sells securities it is *increasing the demand* for loanable funds at the same time that it is draining reserves and thereby *decreasing the supply* of loanable funds. This "double-whammy effect"—this "hitting the market from both sides" moves interest rates up from i1 to i3 in figure 20-2-B.

As you would guess, open market purchases have the same "double-whammy" effect as sales, only in the opposite direction. Figure 20-3 illustrates this. Spend a few minutes studying that figure and you'll see exactly how it happens.

Figure 20-3.   Integrated View of the "Double-Whammy" Effect of OMOs: The Fed Buys Securities

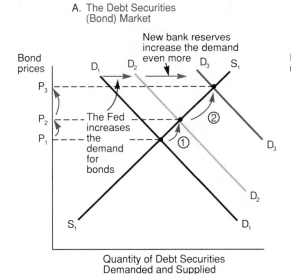

A. The Debt Securities
(Bond) Market

Quantity of Debt Securities
Demanded and Supplied

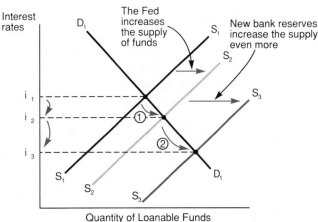

B. The Loanable Funds Market

Quantity of Loanable Funds
Demanded and Supplied

The Debt Securities Market

Initially the debt securities (bond) market was in equilibrium, with bond prices at P_1. Then the Fed initiates its open market purchases and increases the demand from D_1 to D_2. This pushes the price of bonds up to P_2. As the Fed pays for the bonds it's buying, it pours money into the reserve accounts of banks throughout the country (and into the Eurodollar accounts of foreign banks throughout the world).

As new reserves flow into the banking system, the banks begin to use their excess reserves to make loans (to "buy" promissory notes, mortgages, government bonds, etc.) and to lend to other securities buyers. This increases the demand for debt securities from D_2 to D_3 in the graph. The increased demand pushes debt securities prices up to P_3, where the market is once again in equilibrium.

The Loanable Funds Market

Initially the loanable funds market is in equilibrium at interest rate i_1. Then the Fed begins buying bonds, which increases the flow of funds into the loanable funds market. This shift the supply curve to S_2 and lowers the interest rate to i_2.

The new funds which the Fed pours into the market flow into bank reserves and increase the ability and willingness of banks to lend. This shifts the supply of loanable funds to S_3, and brings interest rates down to i_3. You can look at this graph and see that a significant monetary expansion is occurring. The quantity of borrowed funds has increased significantly. A Reminder: Graph A representing the debt securities market and Graph B representing the loanable funds market are both showing the same market from two different perspectives. The increasing bond prices in market "A" are the mirror image of the declining interest rates in market "B." The higher bond prices (P_1, P_2, P_3) result in the lower yields indicated by the falling interest rates (i_1, i_2, i_3).

RESERVE REQUIREMENTS AND DISCOUNT RATES SUPPORT OMOS

With open market operations so powerful and flexible, do we even need the other two "tools" of monetary policy? Yes. In fact the other two tools are very necessary.

It is the *reserve requirement* which gives much of the power to OMOs. Pushing reserves into or pulling reserves out of the banking system might not be very effective if there were no specific reserve requirements. But changes in reserve requirements are seldom used as a tool of monetary policy.

The *discount rate* plays an important role—both psychological and real—in monetary policy. If the Fed is really serious about tightening money, as it begins it's *open market sales of securities*—pushing interest rates up and draining reserves from the banking system—it may simultaneously announce *an increase in the discount rate.*

The *announcement effect* of the discount rate hike will let it be known that the Fed is tightening money—that interest rates soon are likely to be rising. The *real effect* will be to increase the cost of discount window borrowing—to make it more costly for banks to use discount borrowing to offset the reserve deficiencies which are likely to result from the Fed's open market sales.

Discount rate adjustments are used from time to time to supplement and support the Fed's open market operations. But by far the greatest amount of monetary policy adjustment is accomplished through the use of OMOs. Now that you know the power and flexibility of this tool, you can understand why.

SUMMARY

- **Central banks** (e.g., the U.S. Federal Reserve System) perform fiscal functions for the government and regulatory and service functions for the banking system. But by far the most important role is to control the **growth rate** of the nation's **money supply**.

- The Fed's tools of **monetary policy** are: (1) changing **reserve requirements**, (2) changing the **discount rate**, and (3) **open market operations (OMOs)**—buying and selling government securities in the financial markets. The first two tools are used primarily to back up and support the Fed's open market operations.

- Open market operations are used (or poised for use) every day, and have a **"double-whammy" effect**: (1) to influence demand, supply, and interest rate conditions in the financial markets (whammy #1), and (2) to increase or decrease the **reserves** of the banking system (whammy #2).

- When the Fed **sells securities** it (1) pushes down securities prices and pushes up interest rates (whammy #1) and (2) drains reserves from the banking system (whammy #2).

- When the Fed **buys securities** it (1) pushes up securities prices and pushes down interest rates (whammy #1), and (2) pushes new reserves into the banking system (whammy #2).

- Conditions in the nation's and world's financial markets and rates of growth of the U.S. money supply are significantly influenced by these monetary policy actions of the Fed.

Important Principles, Issues, Concepts, Terms

Functions of central banks

Importance of the U.S. Federal Reserve System

How central banks control the money supply

Techniques of monetary control

Questions

1. Describe the functions and the importance of central banks in the modern world.

2. List and briefly explain the different tools of monetary policy.

3. Explain why it is true that when a central bank buys anything, this creates bank reserves.

4. Use T-accounts to illustrate the effect of a purchase of government securities by the Fed, from (a) a bank, and (b) a seller other than a bank.

5. Explain why open market operations are used much more frequently as a tool of monetary policy than are changes in either the discount rate or the reserve requirement.

6. Describe the mechanics of open market operations.

7. Use supply and demand graphs to illustrate the double whammy effect of open market operations on (a) the securities markets, and (b) the loanable funds markets.

8. Explain what is meant by this statement: "Reserve requirements and discount rate changes are used primarily to support open market operations."

9. Explain how it would be possible for a central bank to create excessive quantities of reserves and thereby destroy the nation's monetary system.

Suggested Readings

Anderson, Clay J. "Evolution of the Role and the Functioning of the Discount Mechanism." *Reappraisal of the Federal Reserve Discount Mechanism* 1. Federal Reserve Board of Governors (August 1971), 133–163.

Board of Governors of the Federal Reserve System. *Reappraisal of the Federal Reserve Discount Mechanism.* 1971 and 1972.

Burger, Albert. "Money Stock Control." Federal Reserve Bank of St. Louis, October 1972, pp. 10–18.

Federal Reserve Bank of Boston. *Credit Allocation Techniques of Monetary Policy.* Boston: Federal Reserve Bank of Boston.

Garvy, George. "Reserve Requirements Abroad." *Monthly Review.* Federal Reserve Bank of New York, October 1973.

Gilbert, R. Alton. "Access to the Discount Window for all Commercial Banks: Is it important for Monetary Policy?" *Review* 62. Federal Reserve Bank of St. Louis (February 1980), 15–24.

———. "Benefits of Borrowing from the Federal Reserve when the Discount Rate is Below Market Interest Rates." *Review* 61. Federal Reserve Bank of St. Louis (March 1979), 25–31.

Goodfriend, Marvin. "A Historical Assessment of the Rationales and Functions of Reserve Requirements." *Economic Review* 69. Federal Reserve Bank of Richmond (March/April 1983), 3–21.

Higgons, Bryon, and Gordon H. Sellon Jr. "Should the Discount Rate be a Penalty Rate?" *Economic Review.* Federal Reserve Bank of Kansas City (January 1981), 3–10.

Jones, David. "A Review of Academic Literature on the Discount Mechanism." *Reappraisal of the Federal Reserve Discount Mechanism* 2. Federal Reserve Board of Governors (August 1971), pp. 23–45.

Meek, Paul. *Open Market Operations.* Federal Reserve Bank of New York, 1978.

———. *U.S. Monetary Policy and Financial Markets.* New York: Federal Reserve Bank of New York, 1982.

Melton, William. *Inside the Fed.* Homewood, Ill.: Dow Jones-Irwin, 1985.

Mengle, David L. "The Discount Window." *Economic Review.* Federal Reserve Bank of Richmond (May/June 1986), 2–10.

Motley, Brian. "Should M2 be Redefined?" *Economic Review.* Federal Reserve Bank of San Francisco (Winter 1988), 33–51.

Roosa, Robert V. *Federal Reserve Operations in the Money and Government Securities Markets.* Federal Reserve Bank of New York, 1956.

Roth, Howard L. "Federal Reserve Open Market Techniques." *Economic Review.* Federal Reserve Bank of Kansas City (March 1986), 3–15.

CHAPTER 21

Creating Bank Reserves: The Fed's Balance Sheet, Bank Reserves, and the Monetary Base

Chapter Objectives

This chapter continues from the previous one and explains how changes in the Fed's assets and liabilities alter (1) **bank reserves**, (2) the **monetary base**, and (3) the **money supply**. Afer you study this chapter you'll understand and be able to explain:

1. All of the assets and liabilities on the consolidated balance sheet of the Federal Reserve System.

2. How the Fed's balance sheet shows the **monetary base**: how the Fed's acquisition of **assets** has created the base, and how the Fed's **liabilities** serve as the base.

3. The relationships between Fed liabilities and
   a. bank reserves,
   b. the monetary base, and
   c. the money supply.

4. The relative size of the currency component of the monetary base, and why it is so large.

5. The effect of the Fed's discount loans on
   a. bank reserves,
   b. the monetary base, and
   c. the money supply.

6. How cash items in process of collection create float—interest-free loans of high-powered money—and how deferred availability cash items are used to reduce float.

WHENEVER THE FED BUYS ANYTHING IT CREATES BANK RESERVES

As explained in the previous chapter, since the Fed is the **central bank**, its purchase of *any asset*—government securities or gold or buildings or office supplies or employee services or whatever—adds reserves to the banking system.

When the Fed's checks clear, bank reserves increase. Why? Because:

1. With minor exceptions, *the reserves of the banking system consist entirely of liabilities of the Fed.* And also:

2. With minor exceptions, *all of the Fed's liabilities serve as reserves for the banking system.*

The bottom line: Whenever the Fed acquires assets—whatever those assets might be—it acquires an equal sum of **liabilities**. And with a few minor exceptions, those newly created liabilities serve as new reserves for the banking system. So the way to understand changes in bank reserves is to thoroughly understand changes in the Fed's assets and liabilities—changes in the Fed's balance sheet.

You need to understand each of the various assets which the Fed acquires and holds, and each of its liabilities—both those which serve as bank reserves, and those "few exceptions" which do not. This chapter focuses on the influence of *changes in the Fed's balance sheet* on (1) *the monetary base,* (2) *reserves of the banking system,* and (3) *the nation's money supply.*

THE FED'S MAJOR ASSETS AND LIABILITIES: THE MONETARY BASE

Figure 21-1 shows a very condensed balance sheet for the Federal Reserve System. This is a consolidated balance sheet including the assets and liabilities of all twelve of the district Fed banks. You can see at a glance that the lion's share of the Fed's assets are in government securities, and that more than 90% of its total liabilities (currency, and bank reserve deposits) are components of the monetary base.

The Fed's Purchases of Securities Create Bank Reserve Deposits

As you look at figure 21-1 it's easy to see where the monetary base originates. The Fed, through its open market operations (OMOs) buys government securities. The

Figure 21-1.   Highly Aggregated Balance Sheet of the Federal Reserve System (Percentage breakdown)

Assets		Liabilities and Capital	

Government securities*
    percentage of total assets
	83%	Fed currency issued
		    percentage of total liabilities
			80%

Gold and SDR certificates
    percentage of total
	7%	Bank reserve deposits
		    percentage of total
			14%

All other assets combined
    percentage of total
	10%	All other liabilities & capital
		    percentage of total
			6%

Total	100%	Total	100%

* About 95% of the government securities held by the Fed Banks are U.S. government (Treasury) securities such as T-bills and bonds. The remaining (about 5%) are securities issued by government agencies such as the Social Security Administration, the Commodity Credit Corporation, etc. Also the Fed sometimes buys and holds small amounts of bankers' acceptances.
Source: Computed from the *Federal Reserve Bulletin*, Table 1.11, "Reserves of Depository Institutions and Reserve Bank Credit," p. A4; and Table 1.18, "Federal Reserve Banks: Condition and Federal Reserve Note Statements," p. A10.

money paid for those securities is newly created—previously nonexistent—money. And it is *high-powered money* because it flows immediately into the reserves of banks and thereby permits a multiple expansion of the money supply.

When the Fed is *buying securities*, it is, in effect, *selling high powered money*—high powered money which, prior to the securities purchase, did not exist. This newly created high powered money adds to the monetary base, and to the reserves of the banking system.

As you look at figure 21-1 you see that some 80% of Fed liabilities are in the form of Fed currency, as compared with only 14% in bank reserve deposits. Why so much currency, as compared with reserve deposits? When the Fed buys government securities, its payments add funds to bank reserve deposits. The Fed doesn't usually pay *currency* for securities! So why so much currency? Here's what happens.

The banks which receive new reserve deposits soon lend their new excess reserves. So the money supply expands. As the money supply expands, people demand more currency. As more currency is issued by the Fed and delivered to the banks, the banks pay for this new currency out of their reserve deposits at the Fed. The next section explains exactly how this happens.

As the Money Supply Expands, Currency Replaces Bank Reserve Deposits

When the Fed buys $10,000 worth of securities, it pays the seller with a check. The seller deposits the check in a bank. The receiving bank sends the check to its Federal Reserve bank for deposit to its reserve account.

Now the Fed has an additional $10,000 in assets (securities) and in liabilities (bank reserve deposits). And the banking system has an additional $10,000 in assets (Federal Reserve deposits) and in liabilities (customers' deposits). The following T-accounts illustrate:

A $10,000 Fed Purchase of Securities Initially Adds $10,000 to Bank Reserve Deposits

Federal Reserve System

Banking System

Assets		Liabilities		Assets		Liabilities	
Securities	+$10,000	Bank reserve deposits	+$10,000	Fed reserve deposits	+$10,000	Customers' deposits	+$10,000

Banks Soon Lend Their Excess Reserves. As the banks see their reserve balances increasing, almost immediately they will begin to readjust their assets—out of nonearning excess reserve deposits and into income-earning loans and/or securities. As banks increase their lending, the money supply will expand. As the money supply expands, people will desire to hold more currency.

In the late 1980s the ratio of currency held by the public (Cp) to checkable deposits ($\sqrt{D}$) was fairly stable at about .36. So for every $10,000 increase in $\sqrt{D}$, Cp could be expected to increase by about $3,600.

Currency Is Withdrawn by the Public. As loans are made and the money supply expands, currency drains from the banks into the hands of the public. So the banks find it necessary to order more currency from the Fed banks. This causes a shift of the Fed's liabilities out of *bank reserve deposits* and into *currency issued*.

If we assume for the moment that all the new customers' deposits are in checkable accounts and that the required reserve ratio on checkable deposits is about 11% (and that the $Cp/\sqrt{D}$ ratio is .36), then the ultimate effects of the Fed's open market purchase of $10,000 in securities are illustrated in figure 21-2.

Figure 21-2 shows that the initial $10,000 of Fed-created high-powered money (new reserves) ultimately results in $21,000 in new checkable deposits and $7,600 in new currency in the hands of the public. So the total increase in the money supply amounts to $28,600 ($21,000 + $7,600). In this case the *checkable deposit multiplier* works out to be 2.1 (21,000 ÷ 10,000), and the *money supply multiplier* works out to be 2.86 (28,600 ÷ 10,000).

Notice that in figure 21-2, of the $10,000 initially added to bank reserve deposits, only $2,400 remains there. The balance of $7,600 now consists of newly issued Federal Reserve currency. So now when you look back at Fed liabilities in figure 21-1 you will understand why *currency issued* is much larger than *bank reserve deposits*.

BANKS RESERVES (R), THE MONETARY BASE (B), AND THE MONEY SUPPLY (M)

You know that required reserves—funds banks must hold as a percentage of their deposits—consist of two things: (1) reserve deposits in their Fed bank accounts (R), and (2) currency (including coins) held in their vaults (Cv). The monetary base includes bank reserves (R + Cv), plus currency held by the public (Cp).

The two major items on the liabilities side of the Fed's balance sheet (see figure 21-1) represent almost all (but not quite all) of the monetary base. Only one

Figure 21-2.   A $10,000 Fed Purchase of Securities Ultimately Adds More to Currency Issued Than to Bank Reserve Deposits

Federal Reserve System				Banking System			
Assets		**Liabilities**		**Assets**		**Liabilities**	
Securities	+$10,000	Bank reserve deposits	+$2,400	Fed reserve deposits	+$2,400	Customers' deposits	+$21,000
		Fed currency issued	+$7,600	Loans	+18,600		

As banks make loans, that adds new checkable deposits. For every new $1 in checkable deposits, people want to hold $.36 in currency. So currency is pulled out of the bank vaults and into circulation. The banks then must order more Fed currency, and pay for it out of their reserve deposit accounts. The reserve account balances go down from $10,000 to $2,400 as a result of this "cash drain effect."

Ultimate Money Expansion

$$\sqrt{D} + \$21,000 \quad \text{(deposit multiplier} = \$21,000 \div \$10,000 = 2.1)$$
$$\underline{Cp + \$\ 7,600 \quad (.36 \times \$21,000)}$$
$$Total \quad + \$28,600 \quad \text{(money supply multiplier} = \$28,600 \div \$10,000 = 2.86)$$

Note: This assumes that the banks lend all of their new excess reserves, that all new deposits remain in the form of checkable deposits, that the ratio of required reserves to checkable deposits is about 11%, that the $Cp/\sqrt{D}$ ratio is .36 and that all of the newly issued currency is held by the public (outside the banking system).

monetary base component is missing from the Fed's balance sheet: currency issued by the U.S Treasury.[1]

Figure 21-3 shows a breakdown of bank reserves, the monetary base, and the money supply. Stop now and take time to study that figure thoroughly.

In figure 21-3 you see that in midyear 1986, total currency issued amounted to about $200 billion and consisted of about $183 billion of Federal Reserve notes and about $17 billion of Treasury currency (most of which was coins). With the exception of this small amount of Treasury currency (which has very little variability and for practical purposes can be considered "given"), Federal Reserve credit (Fed liabilities) is the sole source of bank reserves and of the monetary base. So its's clear that the growth of the money supply depends on the growth of

Figure 21-3.   Fed Liabilities, Bank Reserves, the Monetary Base, and the Money Supply (All figures approximate and rounded) (Midyear 1986. Billions of dollars)

Currency Issued:		
Federal reserve notes	183	
Treasury currency (mostly coins)	17	
Total currency	200	
Minus: currency held by the Treasury and Fed banks	−2	
Total currency component of the monetary base		198
Currency Held:		
By the public (Cp)	174	
In bank vaults (Cv)	24	
Total	198	
Bank Reserves (R + Cv):		
Fed reserve deposits (R)	31	
Vault cash (Cv)	24	
Total bank reserves		55
Plus:		
Currency held by the public	174	
Total monetary base (B) = (Cp + Cv + R)		229
The M1 Money Supply ($\sqrt{D}$ + Cp):		
Checkable deposits ($\sqrt{D}$)	484	
Currency held by public (Cp)	174	
Total M1 money supply		658

Significant Ratios:
The Cp/$\sqrt{D}$ ratio = 174/484 = .36, which means that for each dollar in checkable deposits people were holding 36 cents in currency.
The implicit M1 money multiplier = M1 ÷ B = 658/229 = 2.88, which means that for each dollar of the monetary base there was $2.88 in the M1 money supply.
The ratio of $\sqrt{D}$ to bank reserves, 484 ÷ 55 = 8.80, which means that for each dollar of bank reserves there were checkable deposits of $8.80.

Note: The figures in this table are subject to fairly rapid change from year to year—sometimes even from quarter to quarter—and will be quite out of date by the time you are studying the table. Suggestion: Go to the library, find a current issue of the *Federal Reserve Bulletin*, then find the tables cited in the following *source note* and update the figures.
Source: Calculated from figures reported in the *Federal Reserve Bulletin*, Table 1.11, "Reserves of Depository Institutions and Reserve Bank Credit," p. A4; and Table 1.18, "Federal Reserve Banks: Condition and Federal Reserve Note Statements," p. A10.

[1] A large part of Treasury currency—especially the silver coins issued up to 1964— is held by collectors and is no longer a circulating part of the U.S. money supply. Some of these silver coins are still being held in bank vaults where they can be counted as vault cash (legal reserves) at the same time that they can be appreciating in value.

Federal Reserve credit (Fed liabilities). Figure 21-3 clearly illustrates the predominant role which the Fed plays in generating the U.S. money supply.

Now that you have an understanding of the monetary base, bank reserves, and the money supply, it's time to take a step back and study the complete balance sheet of the Federal Reserve System. In the sections coming up you'll be systematically analyzing each of the Fed's assets and liabilities to see how changes in each of these affect bank reserves, the monetary base, and the money supply. But before you go on, be sure you have a thorough understanding of the relationships illustrated in figure 21-3—the relationships between the Fed's liabilities and (1) bank reserves, (2) the monetary base, and (3) the money supply.

THE BALANCE SHEET OF THE FEDERAL RESERVE SYSTEM

Figure 21-4 shows a consolidated balance sheet of all twelve Federal Reserve banks. The only difference between this balance sheet and the highly aggregated balance sheet shown in figure 21-1 is that here (in figure 21-4) there is a more detailed breakdown of the Fed's assets and liabilities.

Figure 21-4.   The Consolidated Balance Sheet of the Federal Reserve System (Midyear 1986. Billions of dollars)

Assets	$	% of Total	Liabilities and Capital	$	% of Total
Securities: U.S. govt. and agency	190.1	83.2	Federal Reserve notes outstanding	181.6	79.5
Gold certificate account	11.1	4.9	Bank reserve deposits	31.3	13.7
SDR certificates account	4.8	2.1	U.S. Treasury deposits	3.1	1.4
Treasury currency (coin)	0.5	0.2	Foreign and other deposits	0.7	0.3
Discount loans to banks	0.9	0.4	Deferred availability cash (credit) items	5.7	2.5
			Other liabilities	2.2	1.0
Cash items in process of collection	5.8	2.5	**Capital**	3.9	1.7
Other Federal Reserve assets	15.3	6.7			
TOTAL	228.5	100.0	TOTAL	228.5	100.0

Note: A small amount of bank deposits at the Fed are "service related" and are not included as a part of bank reserves. These service-related deposits are very minor, are not relevant to the present discussion, and therefore are ignored here.
Source: Dollar figures from the *Federal Reserve Bulletin*, vol. 72, no. 8 (August, 1986), Table 1.11, "Reserves of Depository Institutions and Reserve Bank Credit," p. A4; and Table 1.18, "Federal Reserve Banks: Condition and Federal Reserve Note Statements," p. A10. Percentage figures calculated by the author.

Take a few minutes to study figure 21-4 to familiarize yourself with the various assets and liabilities. Then go on and read the detailed explanations, coming up. Both this chapter and the following one are concerned with explaining how each item on this balance sheet influences *bank reserves, the monetary base,* and *the money supply.*

Additions to Fed Assets Add to the Monetary Base

Whenever the Fed acquires assets of any kind, it adds an equal amount to its liabilities, of course. An addition to its liabilities means an addition to *Federal Reserve credit outstanding.* And an addition to Federal Reserve credit outstanding (with a few minor exceptions) is an addition to bank reserves and to the monetary base.

Most of the Monetary Base Has Been Generated by Fed Purchases of Securities

You have already worked with several T-accounts illustrating the effect of the Fed's open market purchase of securities. So you already understand the effect of changes in *the securities item* on the asset side of the Fed's balance sheet.

All of the securities held by the Fed, as acquired, have added to bank reserves and to the monetary base. It is clear that most of the bank reserves and most of the monetary base of the U.S. economy have been created by these Fed securities purchases.

Discount Loans to Banks Add to R, B, and M

When the Fed makes discount loans to the banking system (banks borrow from the Fed's "discount window") the result is immediate and obvious. The borrowing banks receive the proceeds of those loans in the form of additional reserves in their Fed bank accounts. So there's an immediate and equal increase in bank reserves and in the monetary base. Here's an illustration of a $10,000 increase in discount loans:

The Fed Makes Discount Loans to Banks

Federal Reserve System				Banking System			
Assets		**Liabilities**		**Assets**		**Liabilities**	
Discount loans receivable	+$10,000	Bank reserve deposits	+$10,000	Federal reserve deposits	+$10,000	Discount loans payable	+$10,000

Why do banks borrow from the Fed? To acquire more reserves, of course. So it's obvious that any change in discount loans outstanding will result in an equal change in the same direction in bank reserves—and also in the monetary base.

THE MYSTERIOUS ITEM CALLED "FLOAT"

As checks are cleared through the Federal Reserve System, *this check-clearing process can generate billions of dollars in new reserves.* The newly created reserves are called "Federal Reserve float," or just "float." In the sections coming up you'll read about exactly how float is generated and what the Fed does to minimize it.

Cash Items in Process of Collection Create Float

On the Fed's balance sheet the entry "cash items in process of collection" refers to checks which the Fed banks have in their possession at the moment. These checks are enroute to the banks against which they have been drawn—but they haven't yet arrived there.

As these "checks in process" flow into the Fed banks they are deposited to the accounts of the banks which sent them to the Fed for deposit. Here's an example.

Reserves Are Added to the Receiving Bank. Suppose your Great Uncle Albert in Walla Walla, Washington receives a $10,000 check for a shipment of lumber from a customer in Ypsilanti, Michigan. G.U. Albert deposits the check in his Walla Walla bank. Then that bank sends the check for deposit to its reserve account at the Federal Reserve Bank of San Francisco (actually to the Seattle branch). Here are T-accounts to illustrate:

Walla Walla Bank Deposits $10,000 in the San Francisco Fed Bank: Reserves Are Increased

Federal Reserve Bank of San Francisco

Assets		Liabilities	
Cash items in process of collection	+$10,000	Walla Walla Bank reserve deposits	+$10,000

Walla Walla Bank

Assets		Liabilities	
Federal reserve deposits	+$10,000	Customers' (G.U.A.'s) deposits	+$10,000

This transaction *increases the total volume of reserves* in the banking system (and the monetary base) by $10,000.

Later, Reserves Are Subtracted from the Paying Bank. A day or two later when the check arrives at the Federal Reserve Bank of Chicago (actually, at the Detroit branch of the Chicago bank) the $10,000 is deducted from the reserve deposits of the Ypsilanti bank. Then the check is sent on to the Ypsilanti bank where the $10,000 is deducted from the account of the buyer of G.U. Albert's lumber. Here are the transactions:

Cash Items in Process Are Cleared: Reserves Are Decreased

Federal Reserve Bank of Chicago

Assets		Liabilities	
Cash items in process	-$10,000	Ypsilanti bank reserve deposits	-$10,000

Ypsilanti Bank

Assets		Liabilities	
Federal reserve deposits	−$10,000	Customers' (lumber buyer's) deposits	−$10,000

This transaction reduces the total volume of bank reserves (and the monetary base) by $10,000.

During the time between the addition to the Walla Walla bank's reserve deposits and the subtraction from the Ypsilanti bank's reserve deposits what happened? Total reserves in the banking system were increased by $10,000. This $10,000 of float was created because of the time it takes checks to clear and be charged against the accounts on which they are drawn.

Float Is Interest-Free Borrowed Money. When you write a check on Friday afternoon, you know that the check will not be charged against your account until Monday. Whenever you do that you're enjoying the use of float over the weekend. Float is *interest-free borrowed money*.

In the banking system, Federal Reserve float is *interest-free borrowed high-powered money*. Float adds reserves into the banking system. As you might suppose, the Fed isn't really thrilled about this unplanned addition of interest-free reserves into the banking system. So it has devised a means to eliminate most of the float.

Deferred Availability Cash Items Reduce Float

Suppose the Fed decided not to actually add the $10,000 to the Walla Walla bank's reserve account, until the same time that the $10,000 was also being subtracted from the Yipsilanti bank's reserve account. That way there would be a simultaneous injection into and withdrawal from bank reserve deposits. Presto! No float! Now you can guess what "deferred availability cash items" are. You can see why the availability of these items is "deferred"—to reduce float, of course. Here's an example to show exactly how it works:

The Walla Walla Bank Must Wait for Its New Reserves. When the Fed Bank of San Francisco receives the check from the Walla Walla bank, it does not immediately deposit the amount into the Walla Walla bank's reserve account. Instead it "pays" the Walla Walla bank with a "deferred availability cash item" of $10,000. The Fed promises to deposit $10,000 in the reserve account of the Walla Walla bank within a specified time period—depending on how far away the paying bank is, but never longer than two days. Here are the T-accounts:

The Availability of the W. W. Bank's New $10,000 Reserve Deposit Is "Deferred"

Federal Reserve Bank of San Francisco

Assets		Liabilities	
Cash items in process	+$10,000	Deferred availability cash items	+$10,000

Walla Walla Bank

Assets		Liabilities	
Fed deferred availability cash items	+$10,000	Customers (G.U.A.'s) deposits	+$10,000

The Walla Walla bank has a new asset and the Fed has a new liability: deferred availability cash items. But this Fed liability *does not serve as bank reserves* or as a part of the monetary base. So no reserves are created by this transaction.

The W.W. bank will not get the addition to its reserves until the deferred availability cash items are terminated. At that time the deferred availability funds will be deposited in the W.W. bank's reserve account. But that will not happen *until the end of the deferred availability time period.*

The Deferred Availability Time Period May Result in Either Positive or Negative Float. Suppose the "deferred availability" time period is exactly equal to the time it takes to clear the check and deduct the amount from the reserve deposits of the Ypsilanti bank. Then float on this transaction will be zero.

Or suppose the plane carrying the check from the San Francisco bank to the Chicago bank gets in a fast eastward jet stream and arrives early. Then perhaps the check will be deducted from the reserve account of the Ypsilanti bank even before the deferred availability item is added to the reserve account of the Walla Walla bank. What then?

The Ypsilanti bank would loose reserve deposits before the Walla Walla bank received its deposits. *Total reserves in the banking system would be reduced.* Negative float? Yes. Sometimes this really does happen. But the Fed tries to keep the "deferred availability" time period adjusted so that it will fairly accurately reflect the average time required for the checks to be cleared.

When the "Deferred Availability" Ends, W.W. Bank Gets Its Reserves. At the end of the deferred availability time period the balance sheets of the San Francisco Fed Bank and the Walla Walla bank change as follows:

The Deferred Items Are Added to Bank Reserve Deposits

Federal Reserve Bank of San Francisco

Assets	Liabilities	
	Deferred availability items	−$10,000
	Bank reserve deposits	+$10,000

Walla Walla Bank

Assets		Liabilities
Fed deferred availability items	−$10,000	
Fed reserve deposits	+$10,000	

Note: If the above transaction occurs at the same time that the funds are being withdrawn from the Ypsilanti bank's reserve deposits, then float on this entire transaction will have been zero. If the Walla Walla bank gets its reserve deposits first, float will be positive. If the Ypsilanti bank loses its reserve deposits first, float will be negative.

After the entire transaction is completed the net changes will be as follows:

Reserve Deposits Are Shifted From the Y. Bank to the W. W. Bank

Federal Reserve System

Assets	**Liabilities**	
(no change)	Walla Walla Bank's reserve deposits	+$10,000
	Ypsilanti's Bank's reserve deposits	−$10,000
	(no net change)	

Walla Walla Bank

Assets		**Liabilities**	
Federal reserve deposits	+$10,000	Customers' (G.U.A.'s) deposits	+$10,000

Ypsilanti Bank

Assets		**Liabilities**	
Federal reserve deposits	−$10,000	Customers' (lumber buyer's) deposits	−$10,000

Float: A Summary Statement

Federal Reserve float results from the check-clearing process. It is created whenever checks are added to the reserve account of the receiving bank before the checks are subtracted from the reserve account of the paying bank. Float amounts to an interest-free, unplanned loan of reserves to the banking system.

Each dollar of float is a dollar added to bank reserves, and to the monetary base. The purpose of deferring the availability of funds to the receiving banks is to reduce (or to eliminate) this unplanned addition to bank reserves and to the monetary base.

From the consolidated balance sheet of the Federal Reserve System (figure 21-4) you can see that in midyear 1986, cash items in process of collection amounted to $5.8 billion, while deferred availability cash items amounted to $5.7 billion. So at that time, float—which without the deferred availability items would have amounted to $5.8 billion—only amounted to $0.1 billion.

Float sometimes fluctuates significantly from week to week, day to day. However, in recent times it usually has remained at less than $2 billion. Occasionally it has dropped below zero, becoming negative.

As float increases, bank reserves and the monetary base increase. As float decreases, so do reserves and the monetary base. The Fed's objective regarding float is to keep it steady, and preferably near zero.

Note: The next chapter continues the discussion of the Fed's balance sheet, bank reserves, the monetary base, and the money supply. You will have the *total picture* after you complete your study of the following chapter.

SUMMARY

- Whenever the Fed buys anything it pays with newly-created liabilities which (with minor exceptions) become new reserves for the banking system.

- The Fed's two major liabilities are **currency**, and **bank reserve deposits**. These serve as both the monetary base and bank reserves.

- The currency component of the monetary base is much larger than bank reserve deposits because as the money supply expands, people demand currency and banks must pay their reserve deposits to the Fed to buy currency for their customers.

- The only liability in the monetary base which is not a Fed liability, is **Treasury currenncy** which amounts to less than 10% of total currency.

- Most of the monetary base has been generated by the Fed's purchases of securities.

- **Discount loans** to banks add directly to bank reserve deposits and therefore to bank reserves and the monetary base.

- Federal reserve **float** occurs whenever items are added to the reserve accounts of receiving banks before begin subtracted from the accounts of paying banks. Float increases bank reserves and the monetary base and amounts to an unplanned interest-free loan from the Fed to the banking system.

- To minimize float, the Fed **defers the availability** of funds deposited by receiving banks to allow time for the checks to "clear"—for the funds to be deducted from the reserve accounts of the paying banks.

Important Principles, Issues, Concepts, Terms

How Fed purchases create bank reserves

How the Fed can "grow its balance sheet"

How Fed liabilities serve as bank reserves

The Fed's major assets and the relative importance of each

The Fed's major liabilities and the relative importance of each

Why currency is a much larger Fed liability than reserve deposits

How bank reserve deposits are "transformed" into currency

The role of Treasury currency in the monetary base

Relative size of specific components of bank reserves

Relative size of specific components of the monetary base

The approximate size of the deposit and money multipliers

Why Treasury currency can be taken as "given"

Effect of discount loans on bank reserves and the monetary base

How cash items in process of collection generate float

How deferred availability cash items reduce float

How float could be positive, zero, or negative

Effect of float on bank reserves and the monetary base

Questions

1. List the major items on the Fed's balance sheet and indicate the approximate percentage importance of each.

2. Explain the relationship between the Fed's assets and the monetary base and bank reserves.

3. Explain the relationship between the Fed's liabilities and the monetary base and bank reserves.

4. As the money supply expands, currency replaces bank reserve deposits. Explain why and how this happens.

5. Explain the relationships between changes in bank reserves, the monetary base, and the money supply.

6. Explain the relationship between the deposit multiplier and the money supply multiplier. Which is larger? Explain why.

7. Is it true that most of the present-day U.S. money supply has resulted from Fed purchases of government securities? Explain.

8. Explain this statement: "Float is interest-free borrowed money."

9. Explain how the Fed uses "deferred availability cash items" to reduce the amount of float.

10. When the Fed "defers the availability of cash items," it defers the availability longer for some transactions than for others, ranging from immediate availability, to one-day or two-day deferral. Why do they do that? Explain.

Suggested Readings

Burger, Albert E. The *Money Supply Process*. Belmont, CA: Wadsworth Publishing Co., 1971.

Garcia, Gillian, and Simon Pak. "The Ratio of Currency to Demand Deposits in the United States." *Journal of Finance* 34 (June 1979), 703–715.

Goodfriend, Marvin. "The Promises and Pitfalls of Contemporaneous Reserve Requirements for the Implementation of Monetary Policy." *Economic Review.* Federal Reserve Bank of Richmond, May–June 1984.

Laurent, Robert D. "Lagged Reserve Accounting and the Fed's New Operating Procedure." *Economic Perspectives.* Federal Reserve Bank of Chicago, midyear 1982.

Nichols, Dorothy M. *Modern Money Mechanics: A Workbook on Deposits, Currency and Bank Reserves.* Federal Reserve Bank of Chicago, 1975.

Pierce, J. L. and T. D. Thomson. "Some Issues in Controlling the Stock of Money." *Controlling Monetary Aggregates II: The Implementation.* Federal Reserve Bank of Boston Conference Series No. 9, 1972, pp. 265–288.

Young, John E. "The Rise and Fall of Federal Reserve Float." *Economic Review.* Federal Reserve Bank of Kansas City, February 1986.

CHAPTER 22

The Fed's Treasury and Foreign Transactions and the "Bank Reserves" and "Monetary Base" Equations

Chapter Objectives

This chapter completes the explanation of the Fed's balance sheet and summarizes the factors which influence bank reserves (R), the monetary base (B), and the money supply (M). From this chapter you will understand and be able to explain:

1. The effects of Fed purchases of assets from the U.S. Treasury, or from foreign central banks.

2. The effects of changes in the Fed's gold and SDR certificate accounts, and the modern role of gold in international finance.

3. How Treasury spending and changes in the Fed's holdings of Treasury currency affect B and R.

4. How the Treasury's tax and loan (T & L) accounts are used to minimize the destablizing effects of the Treasury's fiscal actions (taxing, spending, and borrowing).

5. How to compute the size of B and R, focusing first on the Fed's (and some Treasury) liabilities, and then on the Fed's assets.

6. How to construct and explain the equations used for calculating the size of B and R.

FED PURCHASES OF ASSETS FROM THE U.S. TREASURY OR FROM FOREIGN CENTRAL BANKS HAVE NO INITIAL EFFECT ON B, R, OR M

If the Fed buys a new $10,000 bond directly from the U.S. Treasury the initial effect on the monetary base (B) and on bank reserves (R) is zero. The same is true if the Fed buys a security from a foreign central bank. Why? Because in each case the newly created Fed liabilities are held *outside* the U.S. banking system.

A Fed Purchase from the U.S. Treasury

The T-accounts for a Fed purchase of securities directly from the U.S. Treasury are as follows:

The Fed Purchases Securities from the U.S. Treasury

Federal Reserve System				U.S Treasury			
Assets		**Liabilities**		**Assets**		**Liabilities**	
Securities	+$10,000	U.S. Treasury deposits	+$10,000	Fed. deposits	+$10,000	Securities Issued	+$10,000

In this case the newly created Federal Reserve credit (the new Fed liability) belongs to the U.S. Treasury. So it is not available to the U.S. banking system. So it cannot support an expansion of the money supply. So there's no increase in B, R, or M.

A Fed Purchase from a Foreign Central Bank

The effect of a purchase of a security from a foreign central bank is similar, as follows:

The Fed Purchases Securities from a Foreign Central Bank

Federal Reserve System

Assets		**Liabilities**	
Foreign assets (securities)	+$10,000	Deposits in the Fed, owned by foreign banks	+$10,000

Foreign Central Bank

Assets		**Liabilities**	
U.S. dollars on deposit at the Fed	+$10,000	Securities issued	+$10,000

When the Fed acquires foreign assets it creates new liabilities. But these liabilities are not available to the U.S. banking system so they have no effect on B, R, or M. It is only when checks are written against these deposits that these newly created Fed liabilities will flow into the banking system and permit an expansion of the money supply.

The Fed Purchases Gold and SDR Certificates from the Treasury

Now you could guess what happens when the Fed acquires gold certificates or SDR certificates from the Treasury. The Fed acquires new assets (the certificates) and the Treasury acquires new Fed deposits. And what is the initial effect of these transactions on B, R, and M? Zero! It is only when the funds flow out of the Treasury's Fed accounts and into the banks' reserve accounts that B, R, and M begin to expand.

Explanation of Gold and SDR Certificate Accounts. When the U.S. Treasury buys gold it usually "monetizes" the gold by issuing gold certificates equal to the monetary value of the gold. The Treasury then "deposits" the certificates into its accounts in the Fed banks.

SDR certificates work exactly the same way. As the Treasury receives new SDRs from the International Monetary Fund (IMF), it issues SDR certificates and deposits them to its accounts at the Fed banks. In both these cases the Fed is buying assets (certificates issued by the Treasury) and paying by adding deposits to the Treasury's Fed accounts. The following T-accounts illustrate the balance sheet changes:

The Treasury Deposits Gold Certificates or SDR Certificates

Federal Reserve System

Assets		Liabilities	
Gold (or SDR) certificate account	+$10,000	U.S. Treasury deposits	+$10,000

U.S. Treasury

Assets		Liabilities	
Fed deposits	+$10,000	Gold (or SDR) certificates	+$10,000

Following these transactions, the Fed has $10,000 in new assets (gold or SDR certificates) and an additional $10,000 liability (U.S. Treasury deposits). How is this transaction different from one in which the Fed buys newly issued bonds directly from the Treasury? It's no different. The Fed's new asset is called gold (or SDR) certificates instead of government securities. But the initial effect on B, R, and M is identical: zero.

But in all these cases the Treasury now has more funds in its Fed accounts and it's in a position to spend more. And when it does, the new funds will flow into the banks' reserve accounts. Then B, R, and M will begin to expand.

GOVERNMENT SPENDING (ISSUING CHECKS BY THE TREASURY) ADDS TO THE MONETARY BASE

As long as the U.S. Treasury holds its assets in the form of Fed deposits, the monetary base is not affected. But the minute the Treasury begins issuing checks, spending its Fed deposits, the monetary base begins to expand. New reserves begin flowing into the banking system.

Treasury Spending Injects "High-Powered Money" into the Banking System

Whenever the Treasury spends, it transfers funds out of its own Fed deposits and into the Fed deposits of the banking system. The effect on B, R, and M are exactly the same as when the Fed purchases securities in the open market. Why? Because *the Treasury's checks represent high powered money*—new injections of reserves into the banking system—just as do checks issued by the Federal Reserve.

When the Fed writes a check it creates new Federal Reserve credit and pushes it into the reserve deposits of the banking system. When the Treasury writes a check against its Fed deposits, it transfers previously-issued Federal Reserve credit from its own account into the reserve accounts of the banks. Either way the banking system winds up with additional Fed deposits—with more reserves than before.

However, there is a significant difference between the *Treasury's spending* and *the Fed's open market purchases*. When the Fed issues checks to acquire securities, (or other assets), new Federal Reserve credit is created "out of thin air." The Fed's *newly acquired assets* are always equal in value to its *newly issued credit*—i.e., newly acquired liabilities. So the Fed's balance sheet "grows," while remaining in balance. But the Treasury cannot do that.

Treasury Spending Is Limited by the Funds It Has (Or Can Get) in Its Fed Accounts

When the Treasury writes checks it is limited by the amount of funds it has in its Fed accounts. In general, when the Treasury's Fed deposits run low it must replenish those funds by depositing either (1) its receipts of tax (and other) revenues, or (2) receipts from the sale of securities (borrowing). And here's the real difference: *These Treasury receipts pull funds out of the banking system's reserve deposits.*

The bottom line is this: In general, while the Treasury is spending money and pumping reserves into the banking system, it is also collecting and/or borrowing money and *pulling reserves out of the banking system*. But there are some exceptions.

Whenever the Fed buys assets from the Treasury—gold or SDR certificates or Treasury securities—that permits the Treasury to spend and inject additional funds into bank reserve deposits. And with no offsetting (taxing or borrowing) withdrawal from bank reserves.

From this example it is clear that it is the Fed (not the Treasury) which is in control of the rate of expansion of the money supply. If the Fed doesn't buy assets from the Treasury, then the Treasury can't increase B, R, and M! It is *Federal Reserve credit* (Fed liabilities) on which the money supply rests and on which almost all expansions in the money supply depend.

THE ROLE OF GOLD AND SDRS IN INTERNATIONAL FINANCE

For hundreds of years—up until the 1930s—gold played a predominant role in international finance. With gold you could acquire the money of any nation. Then you could buy whatever you wanted from the sellers in that nation.

From the end of World War II until the early 1970s, gold continued to play a significant (but less significant) role in international finance. A nation wishing to acquire the money of some other nation could do so by arranging for a transfer of gold to pay for the desired foreign currency. (Box 22-1 discusses the meanings of "currency.")

In the years following World War II, the volume of international trade expanded rapidly. During the 1960s it became evident that the world's supply of monetary gold was not large enough to adequately serve as the "international medium" for exchanging foreign currencies. Many nations began holding American dollars as their foreign exchange reserves because American dollars had become generally acceptable in exchange for other currencies. But this created problems whenever the international value of the dollar would fluctuate.

The Creation of SDRs—"Paper Gold"

In the late 1960s the members of the International Monetary Fund (IMF) agreed to establish a new kind of international medium of exchange which could be used to buy the currencies of other nations. This new medium of exchange is called "special drawing rights" (SDRs). Newly created SDRs were allocated to all of the IMF member nations, based on the amount of money these members had deposited in the IMF.

All of the major trading nations now hold some of their foreign exchange reserves in the form of SDR deposits at the IMF. A nation can use its SDRs to buy the currencies of other nations, so SDRs are replacing gold as the international medium for exchanging foreign currencies. SDRs are sometimes referred to as "paper gold."

The international monetary fund allocates additional SDRs to its member nations from time to time. When the U.S. Treasury receives an allocation of new SDRs from the IMF, the Treasury issues new SDR certificates and deposits these in its accounts at the Fed banks. So it receives new Fed deposits. See Box 22-2 for a discussion of "electronic certificates."

When the Treasury deposits either gold or SDR certificates in its Fed accounts, as you know, there is no immediate effect on B, R, or M. But what about *the total effect* of a Treasury gold purchase? Here's an example.

The Special Effects of a Treasury Gold Purchase

Suppose your Great Uncle Albert is digging a flower bed in his back yard and uncovers a chunk of gold which he decides to sell to the U.S. Treasury for

---

Box 22-1

Question: Exactly What Is Meant by the Term "Currency?"

Unfortunately the term "currency" has two different meanings. When referring to our domestic money, it means dollar bills and coins. It means "M1 money, excluding checkable deposits." But in international finance it means something quite different.

In international finance a nation's "currency" means "the kind of money used in that nation." For example, British currency is "pounds." The U.S. currency is "the American dollar." When we speak of "buying foreign currency" (or "buying foreign exchange") that means using our "U.S. currency" (American dollars) to buy the kind of "foreign currency" used in a foreign country (example, to buy British pounds, West German marks, etc.). Too bad words must carry double meanings—but sometimes they do.

$10,000. He delivers the gold and receives his check from the Treasury for $10,000. He immediately deposits the check in his account at the local bank and the local bank sends the check to its district Fed bank for deposit to its reserve account. The results of all these transactions are illustrated as follows:

Great Uncle Albert Sells Gold to the Treasury

G.U. Albert

Assets		**Liabilities**
Gold	−$10,000	
Bank deposits	+$10,000	

G.U. Albert's Bank

Assets		**Liabilities**	
Fed. reserve deposits	+$10,000	G.U.A.'s deposits	+$10,000

U.S. Treasury

Assets		**Liabilities**
Gold	+$10,000	
Fed deposits	−$10,000	

Federal Reserve System

Assets	**Liabilities**	
	Treasury deposits	−$10,000
	Bank reserve deposits	+$10,000

These T-accounts show that $10,000 of Federal Reserve credit has been shifted out of Treasury deposits and into bank reserve deposits. The Treasury has

---

Box 22-2

Question: What Does One SDR—Or One SDR Certificate—Or, These Days, A T-Bill—Look Like? Nobody Knows!

In these days of modern electronic banking, no gold or SDR certificates are actually printed. When the Treasury makes its Fed deposit, there is simply an electronic transfer of funds into the Fed's gold or SDR certificate account (a new Fed asset), and an equal amount is added to the Treasury's Fed account (a new Fed liability).

It shouldn't be surprising that gold and SDR certificates aren't actually printed anymore. As a matter of fact, during 1977 and 1978 the U.S. Government phased out the printing of almost all of its securities.

When you buy T-bills now, you never see them, because they do not exist in physical form. You have an account with your name and number, and T-bills are added to your account (a bookkeeping entry) when you buy them. You can transfer them at any time, and if you hold them to maturity you will be paid off. This new system of electronic holding and transferring of government securities is called the "Treasury Direct'" system. It operates through the Federal Reserve banks.

traded one asset (Federal Reserve deposits) for another (gold). In doing this, the Treasury has released $10,000 of new high powered money into the banking system. (Whenever the Treasury issues checks it *always* releases new high powered money into the banking system. Remember?)

So far, this purchase of gold is no different than if the Treasury had purchased a delivery truck or a computer or anything else. When the Treasury's check (drawn on its Federal Reserve account) clears, the funds flow from *Treasury deposits* to *bank reserve deposits*. But what happens next? That is what makes the gold purchase different.

The Treasury now has a $10,000 lump of gold which it ships off for melting, stamping, and safekeeping in its underground vault at Fort Knox, Kentucky. Now the Treasury can issue a $10,000 gold certificate and deposit that certificate in its Fed account—which it does. So the funds in the Treasury's account are replenished. *The Treasury's account balance is as large as it was before the gold purchase.* Here are T-accounts to illustrate:

The Treasury Deposits Gold Certificates in Its Fed Account

U.S. Treasury

Assets		Liabilities	
Fed deposits	+$10,000	Gold certificates	+$10,000

Federal Reserve System

Assets		Liabilities	
Gold certificates	+$10,000	Treasury deposits	+$10,000

As long as the Treasury uses its Fed deposits to buy gold, it can issue gold certificates to replenish those deposits. So it could keep on buying gold *ad infinitum!* If the Treasury buys delivery trucks or computers, unless it gets more money from tax revenues or borrowing (or from somewhere!) sooner or later its money (Fed deposits) will run out. But as long as the Treasury is using its Fed deposits to buy gold, it can issue gold certificates to replenish its Fed deposits. It will never run out of funds!

Summary of the Effects of a Gold Purchase

In this case, after all of the transactions are completed, what has changed?

1. *The Treasury* has a new $10,000 asset (gold in Fort Knox) and a new $10,000 liability (gold certificates issued and deposited in the Fed). It's deposits in its Fed account are the same size as before.

2. *The Fed* has a new $10,000 asset (gold certificates) and a new $10,000 liability (bank reserve deposits). The new bank reserve deposits initially were transferred from the Treasury's Fed deposits. Then the Treasury replenished its Fed deposits by depositing gold certificates. So the increase in Fed liabilities shows up as *new bank reserve deposits*, not as new Treasury deposits.

3. *The banking system* has a new $10,000 asset (Fed reserve deposits) and a new $10,000 liability (G.U. Albert's deposits). The money supply already

has expanded by $10,000 (GUA's deposits). The banking system now has $10,000 in *new reserves*. So the money expansion process can continue.

4. *G.U.Albert* has a new $10,000 asset (checking deposits) and a $10,000 increase in net worth. He is the one who has the $10,000 in new money which was injected into the banking system by this transaction.

The following T-accounts summarize the ultimate effects:

Ultimate Results of the Treasury's Gold Purchase

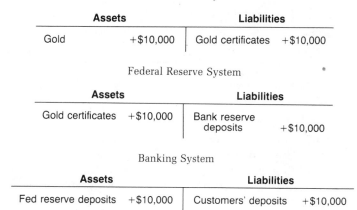

U.S. Treasury

Assets		Liabilities	
Gold	+$10,000	Gold certificates	+$10,000

Federal Reserve System

Assets		Liabilities	
Gold certificates	+$10,000	Bank reserve deposits	+$10,000

Banking System

Assets		Liabilities	
Fed reserve deposits	+$10,000	Customers' deposits	+$10,000

The U.S. Treasury, through gold transactions, can have a considerable influence on the nation's money supply. Back in the days when gold played a much more important monetary role, the Treasury's gold transactions sometimes significantly influenced the nation's money supply. But it has been many years since Treasury gold transactions have had any significant influence.

THE FED'S HOLDINGS OF TREASURY CURRENCY REDUCE THE MONETARY BASE

When the Fed buys *any asset*—unless it is buying that asset from the Treasury or from foreigners—the increase in Fed liabilities (Fed credit outstanding) results in an increase in bank reserves and in the monetary base. You already know that.

But what about when the Fed acquires Treasury currency? Treasury currency outstanding is already a part of the monetary base. So when the Fed holds Treasury currency, that pulls the currency out of—and therefore reduces—the monetary base. To illustrate the net effect, here are some examples.

The Fed Acquires Treasury Currency from the Banking System

Suppose the Fed buys Treasury currency from the banking system. (Banks ship coins for deposit to their accounts at the Fed.) In this case the Fed is simultaneously (1) increasing the monetary base by adding new reserve deposits into the banking system, and (2) reducing the monetary base by pulling Treasury currency out of the banking system. A flow of $10,000 in Treasury currency from the banking system to the Fed would result in the following changes:

The Fed Buys Treasury Currency from the Banking System
(Banks ship coins for deposit to their Fed accounts)

Federal Reserve System

Assets		Liabilities	
Treasury currency	+$10,000	Bank reserve deposits	+$10,000

Banking System

Assets		Liabilities
Treasury currency (vault cash)	−$10,000	
Fed reserve deposits	+$10,000	

You can see that there has been *no change in bank reserves or in the monetary base.* The Fed has absorbed $10,000 of bank reserves (and the monetary base) by pulling in Treasury currency—a subtraction from R, and B. Simultaneously it has created an additional $10,000 in Federal Reserve deposits—an addition to R, and B.

The Fed Acquires Treasury Currency from the Treasury

Suppose there is an increased demand for coins in the economy. As the Fed banks ship coins into the banking system, soon the Fed's supplies of coins run low. So the Fed banks order additional coins from the Treasury.

If the Treasury issues an additional $10,000 in coins and deposits these coins with the Fed, what effect will this have on bank reserves and the monetary base? Initially, none at all.

The issue of $10,000 of additional currency by the Treasury increases the monetary base. But the increase of Treasury currency held by the Fed reduces the monetary base by the same amount. Here are T-accounts to illustrate:

The Fed Buys Newly Issued Treasury Currency from the Treasury

Federal Reserve System

Assets		Liabilities	
Treasury currency (coins)	+$10,000	Treasury deposits	+$10,000

U.S. Treasury

Assets		Liabilities	
Fed deposits	+$10,000	Currency issued	+$10,000

The Treasury now has an additional $10,000 of deposits in its Federal Reserve account. When it spends this money these deposits will be transferred into the banking system. So at that time bank reserves and the monetary base will increase. But until that time, the Fed's purchase of newly issued Treasury currency from the Treasury has no effect on R or B.

The bottom line on all Fed transactions in Treasury currency, is this:

1. When the Fed buys the currency from the banking system, it adds new reserves to the banking system as it pays for the currency, but it pulls reserves out of the banking system as it pulls in the currency. The two results cancel each other, so there is no net change in bank reserves or the monetary base.

2. When the Fed buys newly issued currency from the Treasury, the new currency issue adds to the monetary base. But the fact that the Fed holds the currency subtracts from the base. And since the Fed pays the Treasury in Treasury deposits (which, in that form, are not a part of bank reserves or the monetary base), the transactions cancel each other. So again there is zero change in bank reserves and in the monetary base.

3. Only when the Treasury spends its new deposits will those funds be released into the banking system and added to B, R, and M.

THE TREASURY'S TAX AND LOAN (T & L) ACCOUNTS STABILIZE THE TREASURY'S INFLUENCE ON BANK RESERVES

The U.S. Treasury collects an average of about *$20 billion per week* to finance expenditures. These collections come from the public—individuals, businesses, other organizations, both domestic and foreign—from tax collections and from the sale of government securities. The larger the federal budget deficit, the more funds required from the sale of securities.[1]

So in the average week, the Treasury receives some 20 billion dollars worth of checks written by individuals, businesses, etc., and drawn on banks throughout the U.S. banking system. Suppose the Treasury immediately deposited all these checks in its Fed accounts. That would pull $20 billion out of the reserve accounts of the banks. What a shock!

Ultimately, of course, when the Treasury writes checks and spends the $20 billion, the funds would flow back into the banking system—back into the reserve accounts of the banks. But what would happen meanwhile? Just think of the destabilizing effect of pulling out and then re-injecting $20 billion of bank reserves! So, as you probably already have guessed, the Treasury doesn't do that. It doesn't pull the $20 billion out of the banking system—at least, not immediately.

The Public's Payments to the Treasury Are Deposited in T & L Accounts

The U.S. Treasury has so-called "tax and loan" (T & L) accounts at most of the banks throughout the country. When the Treasury receives a check drawn on the

---

[1] During the 1980s, many billions of dollars worth of U.S. government securities have been bought by foreigners who have chosen to acquire American dollars, and to invest them in "the safety of Uncle Sam"!

account of an individual or a business, it *does not* deposit that check in its Fed account. That would result in a drain of reserves from the banking system.

The Treasury initially deposits the checks in one of its T & L accounts in a commercial bank or other depository institution. In usual practice, the check will be deposited in the very bank on which it is drawn. This way, not only does the Treasury prevent the drain of reserves from the banking system, it also prevents the drain of reserves from the individual banks on which the checks are drawn. (See box 22-3 for an explanation of "pledging requirements.")

Example : Your Great Uncle Albert Buys T-Bills

Suppose your Great Uncle Albert decides to buy $10,000 worth of newly issued Treasury bills. The usual procedure would be for G.U. Albert to write a check to pay for the securities, and for the check to be deposited in the Treasury's T & L account at G.U. Albert's bank. There would be no immediate change in bank reserves, in the monetary base, or even in the reserve position of G.U.A.'s bank. The following T-accounts illustrate:

The Treasury Sells Securities and Deposits the Proceeds in Its T & L Account in the Bank on Which the Check Is Drawn

U.S. Treasury

Assets		Liabilities
T & L account balances	+$10,000	Securities issued +$10,000

Great Uncle Albert's Bank

Assets	Liabilities	
	Customer deposits (G.U.A.'s account)	−$10,000
	U.S. Treasury T & L account	+$10,000

Box 22-3

Question: Exactly What Is Meant by "Pledging Requirements?" and What Is the Effect?

Federal law requires that when the U.S. Treasury deposits money in a privately owned bank (e.g., in a T & L account) the bank must pledge (as collateral) government securities of sufficient value to cover the amount of the Treasury's deposit. That's the **pledging requirement.** If the bank should fail, the Treasury would receive the pledged securities. That way the "public's money" would not be lost.

Because of this T & L account pledging requirement, banks which have these accounts (most banks) are required to hold some of their assets in the form of government securities

Note: Governments have been known to do various kinds of tricky things to increase the demand for their securities—and therefore, their supply of available funds! Remember the government-securities-collateral requirement for national bank notes in the National Banking Acts of 1863 and '64 (Ch. 6)? Another example? Right!

After the above transaction, the U.S. Treasury has an additional $10,000 in its account at G.U. Albert's bank. But the Treasury never writes checks on its T & L accounts. So how will it spend these funds?

Funds Are Transferred from the Treasury's T & L Accounts to Its Fed Accounts: Bank Reserves Are Decreased

When the Treasury is ready to spend the money, it transfers the funds from its T & L account to its Fed account (by electronic transfer, of course). Then it issues checks drawn on its Fed account.

The important point is this: The Treasury doesn't transfer its funds into its account at the Fed—thereby pulling funds out of the banking system—until it is ready to spend those funds—thereby reinjecting the funds into the banking system. The following T-accounts illustrate what happens at the moment the Treasury sends its electronic instructions to shift funds from its T & L accounts into its Fed accounts:

The Treasury Transfers Funds from Its T & L Accounts to Its Fed Accounts

U.S. Treasury

Assets		Liabilities
T & L deposits	−$10,000	
Fed deposits	+$10,000	

Federal Reserve System

Assets	Liabilities	
	Bank reserve deposits	−$10,000
	Treasury deposits	+$10,000

G.U. Albert's Bank

Assets		Liabilities	
Federal reserve deposits	−$10,000	T & L deposits	−$10,000

The above transaction results in a decrease of $10,000 in bank reserves and an increase of the same amount in the Treasury's Fed deposits. But as you already know, the Treasury wouldn't do this until necessary to fund its current rate of spending.

The U.S. government is spending money at the rate of about $20 billion per week. All of that money is coming out of the Treasury's deposits at the Fed. So you can understand that it wouldn't take long after the Treasury shifted it's balances from the T & L accounts to the Fed, for those Fed balances to be reinjected into the banking system.

The Treasury Spends from Its Fed Accounts: Bank Reserves Are Increased

Perhaps the Treasury decides that it will spend this $10,000 on a truckload of paper. (The Federal government uses *lots of paper!*) The Treasury will write a check drawn on its account at the Fed. The paper seller will receive the check and deposit it in a bank. Then you know what happens after that. The bank sends the check to its Fed bank, where funds are withdrawn from the Treasury's Fed deposit and added to the bank's reserve deposit.

The funds which left Great Uncle Albert's bank when the Treasury ordered the electronic transfer from its T & L account into its Fed account—and which therefore were pulled out of the reserves of the banking system—now flow back into the banking system. The only difference is that G. U. Albert's bank has lost reserves of $10,000 while the bank of the paper seller has gained reserves of $10,000.

From the point of view of the banking system as a whole, here are the T-accounts which illustrate the ultimate results:

The Treasury Spends Its New Fed Deposits to Buy Paper

U.S. Treasury			Federal Reserve System		
Assets		**Liabilities**	**Assets**	**Liabilities**	
Fed deposits	−$10,000			Bank reserve deposits	+$10,000
paper	+$10,000			Treasury deposits	−$10,000

Banking System		
Assets	**Liabilities**	
Federal reserve deposits +$10,000	Customers' (paper seller's) deposits +$10,000	

T & L Accounts Serve As a "Holding Pool" for Treasury Collections

The purpose of the Treasury's T & L accounts is to smooth out the monetary effects of the government's tax collections and securities sales. Without the T & L accounts, increased Treasury balances would mean decreased bank reserves; decreased Treasury balances would mean increased bank reserves. But when the T & L account system works well, Treasury fiscal operations have very little effect on R, B, or M.

The T & L accounts serve as a kind of "holding pool" or "reservoir" for Treasury collections. When collections exceed expenditures, the surplus funds flow into T & L accounts. The balances increase. When expenditures exceed collections, T & L account balances are drawn down.

In general, the T & L account system works very well. Funds collected from individuals and businesses are not immediately pulled out of the banking system, but are permitted to remain there until the Treasury plans to spend them—to reinject them into the system. The Fed's monetary control task is tough enough as it is. Without the smoothing effect of the Treasury's T & L accounts, it would be a nightmare!

SUMMARY AND SYNTHESIS OF FACTORS ALTERING BANK RESERVES AND THE MONETARY BASE: THE BANK RESERVES AND MONETARY BASE EQUATIONS

This chapter and the previous one have focused on the way in which changes in the assets and liabilities of the Federal Reserve System alter bank reserves and the monetary base. Now, with this understanding of each of the balance sheet components, it's time for a summary and synthesis of all this. The "monetary base equation" and the "bank reserves equation" provide this summary and synthesis.

The Focus: Liabilities? Or Assets?

One way to look at the monetary base is to focus on the *liabilities* which actually make up (serve as) the monetary base (B). Using this approach, we first add up the total of all monetary-base-type liabilities. Then we subtract those liabilities which are not included as a part of B. The result gives us the size of the monetary base.

The other way to calculate B is to focus on the *assets* which, as acquired, *create the liabilities* which make up (serve as) the monetary base. Then from this total it's only necessary to subtract all of the nonbase liabilities. That leaves only those liabilities which serve as the monetary base.

Which is the better focus? Liabilities? Or Assets? A thorough understanding requires a clear view of both. So in the sections coming up you will see the monetary base (B) and bank reserves (R) computed both ways.

Computing B and R: Focus on the Liabilities

Adding Up the "Base-Type" Liabilities. From the consolidated balance sheet of the Federal Reserve System (Figure 11-5) you can add together Federal Reserve notes issued plus bank reserve deposits—the two main components of B. Then if you add in all U.S. Treasury currency issued, that gives you the total of all "monetary-base-type" liabilities. But then, to compute B you must subtract all currency being held by the Treasury, and Treasury currency (coins) held by the Fed. Why? Because as long as they are holding it, it isn't "in the banking system," so it can't be serving as a part of the monetary base.

Here it is in summary form:

The Monetary Base Equals:

Plus	Minus
Fed currency issued (FC)	Treasury cash holdings (Ctr)
Treasury currency issued (TC)	Fed holdings of Treasury currency (Cfed)
Bank reserve deposits (BRD)	

The Liability-Focus Monetary Base (B) Equation

$$B = FC + TC + BRD - (Ctr + Cfed)$$

From this equation it is clear that increases in Fed notes issued, Treasury currency issued or bank reserve deposits will increase B; increases in currency held by the Treasury or Treasury currency held by the Fed banks will decrease B.

This equation shows the monetary base, computed as the sum of its (liability) components.

With a minor change, this equation becomes the "bank reserves equation." What change? Just subtract currency held by the public—outside the banking system (Cp).

The Liability-Focus Bank Reserves (R) Equation

$$R = FC + TC + BRD - (Ctr + Cfed + Cp)$$

This equation shows that *bank reserves increase* as Fed notes issued (FC), Treasury currency issued (TC), and bank reserve deposits (BRD), increase. *Bank reserves decrease* as Treasury cash holdings (Ctr), Treasury currency held by the Fed (Cfed), and currency held by the public (Cp), increase.

Beginning with Total Liabilities. Here is another way to compute the monetary base and bank reserves, still focusing on the liabilities side of the Fed's balance sheet. You can begin with the Fed's *total liabilities*. Then subtract the non-base-type liabilities (U.S. Treasury deposits, foreign and other deposits, deferred availability items, and other liabilities). Then if you add in Treasury currency issued, what will you get? Exactly the same figure you got when you added FC + TC + BRD in the previous equation.

From then on, the computations are exactly the same as in the previous equations. To get B, just subtract Treasury cash holdings (Ctr) and Treasury currency held by the Fed banks (Cfed). And then to get total bank reserves (R), subtract currency in the hands of the public (Cp).

What's the value of this aapproach to computing B, and R? No special value. It's just that by looking at this in various ways you're likely to gain a better intuitive (common sense) understanding of the interrelationships among these variables.

Computing B and R: Focus on the Fed's Assets

Another interesting and useful way to compute the monetary base and bank reserves is to focus on *the assets which, as acquired by the Fed, create the*

Box 22-4

Question: Why Isn't Fed Bank Holdings of Fed Currency the Same As For Treasury Currency?

The only currency holdings of the Fed which subtract from the monetary base are its holdings of *Treasury* currency. Here's why.

When the Fed is holding its own Federal Reserve notes this is not "an increase in Fed currency holdings." It is a *decrease* in Federal Reserve notes outstanding.

As Fed notes flow from the banking system into the Fed banks, this is not *an increase in assets* of the Fed banks; it is *a decrease in their*

liabilities. Treasury currency is an obligation of the U.S. Treasury and when the Fed banks hold it, that is an asset, for sure. But Federal Reserve notes are an obligation of the Fed bank itself.

If you wrote yourself an I.O.U. for $1 million and stuck it in your pocket, could you call that an asset and go around feeling wealthy? Not likely. That's what the Fed banks would be doing if they increased their holdings of Fed currency and called those holdings "assets."

liabilities which serve as the monetary base. Clearly, it is *the Fed's liabilities* (plus Treasury currency) which serve as B, and R. But what are the sources of these liabilities? Or, stated differently, *what are the sources of B, and R?*

The Fed's liabilities are generated by the Fed's *acquisition of assets.* So, *Eureka!* There's another way to compute B and R!

Suppose the Fed buys $100 million in T-bills (new assets). Unless some offsetting transactions occur to nulify the effect, the monetary base will increase by $100 million.

But what about the offsetting transactions? Before we can be sure about the effects of that $100 million T-bill purchase, we must know about those other changes which might be occurring at the same time and which might significantly influence the outcome. So here's what we need: an equation which includes *all of the items on the Fed's balance sheet*, plus *Treasury currency issued* and *Treasury cash holdings.* Such an equation would include *all of the factors* which influence the monetary base. And here it is:

The Asset-Focus Monetary Base (B) Equation

Plus	Minus
Value of all Fed assets:	Treasury cash holdings
• securities	Treasury currency held by Fed banks
• discount loans	All Fed non-B liabilities:
• gold certificates	• Treasury deposits
• SDR certificates	• foreign and other deposits
• all other Fed assets	• all other non-B liabilities
Federal Reserve float	Fed capital accounts
Treasury currency issued	

Equals: THE MONETARY BASE

From the above equation you can see that any increase in (1) the Fed's assets, (2) float, or (3) Treasury currency issued will tend to increase the monetary base. Increases in (1) Treasury cash holdings, (2) Treasury currency held by the Fed banks, (3) the Fed's non-monetary-base liabilities or (4) the Fed's capital accounts, will *decrease* the monetary base.

Using this equation it is quite a simple matter to compute the size of the monetary base. Figure 22-1 shows the computations.

Figure 22-1 presents a summary of all of the factors which generate bank reserves and the monetary base. Except for the Treasury currency item, all of the monetary base is generated by the acquisition of assets by the Federal Reserve System. As the Fed acquires assets (mostly government securities) it is (in effect) "selling high powered money" which flows into the banking system and becomes a part of bank reserves and the monetary base.

Now you have the complete picture of how the nation's money supply is generated, and how it expands. The Fed acquires assets and thereby supplies new reserves to the banking system. Then the depository institutions begin lending their excess reserves and the money expansion process goes on from there.

Clearly, the central bank plays *the central role* in maintaining the stability and controlling the rate of growth of the nation's money supply. Therefore, it is obvious that *appropriate monetary policies of the central bank* are absolutely essential to the health and growth of the nation's economy.

**Figure 22-1.   The Monetary Base and Bank Reserves Equation
Figures for Midyear 1988 (Billions of dollars)**

Sources of (Factors which Generate and Add to) the Monetary Base

The Fed's assets:	
Securities	251.0
Discount loans	3.0
Gold certificates	11.1
SDR certificates	5.0
Other Fed assets	14.9
Float	0.5
Treasury currency issued	18.5
Total sources	304.0

Factors Which Absorb Potential Base Components (Competing Uses)

Treasury cash holdings	0.5
Treasury currency held by Fed banks	0.5
Treasury deposits at Fed banks	5.5
Foreign and other deposits at Fed banks	0.2
Other Fed (non-base) liabilities	5.1
Fed capital accounts	4.4
Total competing uses	16.2

The Monetary Base (B)

Total sources minus competing uses equals monetary base

$$304.0 - 16.2 = 287.8$$

Bank Reserves (R)

The monetary base minus currency held by the public (Cp) equals bank reserves

$$287.8 - 233.5 = 54.3$$

Source: *Federal Reserve Bulletin*, vol. 74, no. 9 (September 1988), Table 1.11, "Reserves of Depository Institutions and Reserve Bank Credit," p. A4; and Table 1.18, "Federal Reserve Banks: Condition and Federal Reserve Note Statements," p. A10.

SUMMARY

- When the Fed buys an asset from either the U.S. Treasury or from a foreign central bank, *the immediate effect* of this purchase has *no influence on B or R*. But when the Treasury or foreign central bank spends the funds, B and R increase.

- When the U.S. Treasury buys gold, Treasury deposits flow into bank reserve accounts—an addition to B and R. Then the Treasury issues gold certificates and deposits them in its Fed accounts to replenish the funds used to buy gold.

- Special Drawing Rights (SDRs) are issued by the International Monetary Fund (IMF) and used in balancing international payments. When the Treasury receives new SDRs it issues SDR certificates for deposit in its Fed accounts.

- When Treasury currency (mostly coins) is held by Fed banks, it is not a part of the monetary base. So as the Fed acquires Treasury currency, B and R decrease. But as the Fed pays for the currency, B and R increase. So the net change is zero.

- The Treasury initially deposits its received checks in T & L accounts to minimize the effects of the Treasury's fiscal actions on B, R, and M. Only when the Treasury is ready to spend will the funds be transferred to its Fed accounts.

- The "monetary base" and "bank reserves" equations summarize the transactions which influence B and R. With one form of the equation the focus is on the component liabilities. Another form focuses on the Fed's assets. But either way the results are the same.

- From this chapter and the two previous ones you know how the nation's **central bank** plays its key role in the money creation process. And you know that the health and growth of the economy depends heavily on the policies and actions of the central bank.

Important Principles, Issues, Concepts, Terms

Why Fed purchases of assets either from the U.S. Treasury or from foreign central banks have no initial effect on B, R, or M.

Balance sheet effects of a Fed purchase of securities either from the U.S. Treasury or from a foreign central bank

Balance sheet changes when the Treasury deposits gold or SDR certificates

How the initial effect of government spending adds to B, R, and M

The present role of gold and SDRs in international finance

Balance sheet effects of a Treasury purchase of gold from an individual

The special effects (immediate and ultimate) of Treasury gold purchases

Balance sheet effects of a Fed purchase of Treasury currency from the banking system

Balance sheet effects of a Fed purchase of newly issued Treasury currency from the Treasury

Why the Treasury maintains T & L accounts

The Treasury's procedure regarding deposits to and withdrawals from its T & L accounts

How to calculate B and R by adding up the liability components

How to calculate B and R beginning with total liabilities and subtracting nonbase liabilities

How to calculate B and R, focusing on the Fed's assets plus Treasury currency

How to explain the different equations which can be used to calculate B, and R: the liabilities focus and the asset focus.

The approximate relative size of each of the various factors which generate and add to B and R

The approximate relative size of the competing uses for potential base components

How to explain the complete money expansion process

Questions

1. When the Fed purchases assets from either the U.S. Treasury or from foreign central banks, there is no initial effect on B or R. But later these transactions are likely to have a positive effect. Explain what all this means and how it happens.

2. Describe the results of a purchase of gold by the U.S. Treasury: initial transactions, later transactions, and ultimate results.

3. When the Fed obtains Treasury currency from the banking system, this has no effect

on B or R because there are offsetting effects. Explain these offsetting effects.

4. Explain as much as you can about the Treasury's T & L accounts: what they are and why and how they are used.

5. Explain how to calculate B and R focusing on the liability components of the Fed's balance sheet.

6. Explain how to calculate B and R focusing on the Fed's assets plus Treasury currency.

7. What are the competing uses for potential monetary base components? List by order of importance.

Suggested Readings

Balbach, Anatol, and Albert Burger. "Derivation of the Monetary Base." *Review*. Federal Reserve Bank of St. Louis, (November 1976), 2–8.

Dewald, William, and William Gibson. "Sources of a Variation in Member Bank Reserves." *Review of Economics and Statistics*. (May 1976), 143–150.

Federal Reserve Bank of Chicago. *Modern Money Mechanism: Workbook*. Chicago. 1961, pp. 1–14.

Federal Reserve Bank of Cleveland, "The Influence of Government Deposits on the Money Supply." *Economic Commentary*. June 28, 1971.

Johannes, James M., and Robert H. Rasche. "Predicting the Money Multiplier." *Journal of Monetary Economics* 5. 1979, pp. 301–325.

Jordan, Jerry L. "Elements of Money Stock Determination." *Review*. Federal Reserve Bank of St. Louis (October 1969), 10–19.

Lang, Richard W. "TTL Note Accounts and the Money Supply Process." *Review*. Federal Reserve Bank of St. Louis, vol. 61 (October 1979), 3–14.

Modigliani, F., R. Rasche, and J. Cooper. "Central Bank Policy, the Money Supply and the Short-Term Rate of Interest." *Journal of Money, Credit and Banking* 2. May 1979, pp. 166–218.

PART VI

Overview of Monetary Theory and Policy: An Introduction to the Issues, Ideas, and Past Experience

PART VI builds on the theoretical base developed in Part V and looks at how the money supply process operates in the real world. In this part you'll see the difficulty of making precise decisions about central bank policy—about choosing **goals** and **targets**, and then how best to try to achieve those goals and targets.

In Chapter 24 you'll read about the past history of Fed policy. Also you'll read about the controversies concerning the Fed's degree of success (or lack of success) in achieving its monetary policy objectives.

The last two chapters in this part (Chapters 25 and 26) focus on the relationship between changes in the money supply and changes in the macroeconomy, specifically: employment, output, income, and the price level. Here you will read about the controversy regarding the appropriateness of trying to undertake **activist stabilization policies**.

Should the Fed actively adjust the growth rate of the money supply to try to stabilize the economy? Or not? The monetarist and Keynesian theories on this are explained. Also the question of the macroeconomic effects of money supply changes is discussed and illustrated in various ways, including the Phillips Curve framework.

After you finish studying Part VI you will have an appreciation for the difficulty of deciding on and carrying out monetary policy. Also you will understand some of the reasons for the serious disagreement among economists regarding the effects of (and desirability of initiating) activist stabilization policies.

CHAPTER 23

The Conflicting Goals and Targets of Monetary Policy

Chapter Objectives

The purpose of this chapter is to describe and analyze the various **goals** of monetary policy, and the various **strategies** which the Federal Reserve can use for pursuing these goals. After you study this chapter you will understand and be able to explain:

1. The specific goals of monetary policy.
2. The difficulty of defining the **high employment** objective.
3. The meaning, purpose, and method of choosing
   a. an **operating target**, and
   b. an **intermediate target**.
4. Criteria for judging the reliability and usefulness of an intermediate target.
5. Advantages, disadvantages, and dangers of targeting
   a. the **money stock**, and
   b. the **interest rate**.
6. The critical importance of **velocity**.

THE GOALS OF MONETARY POLICY

As the Fed conducts monetary policy, what is it aiming at? Box 23-1 gives a general answer to this, written by a well known Fed monetary advisor, Paul Meek. The three **ultimate goals** of the Fed's monetary policy are:

1. high employment,
2. price stability, and
3. economic growth.

In addition there are three other closely related goals which also are important. The stability of:

4. interest rates.
5. financial markets, and
6. foreign exchange markets.

The Problem of Conflicting Goals

Here's a problem: The policy actions required to achieve some desired goals are exactly opposite from those required to achieve others. Suppose the inflation rate is inching upward, but at the same time, unemployment is high and economic growth is slow. What to do?

To stop inflation the Fed must slow the money supply growth rate. It must sell bonds, push bond prices down and interest rates up, and drain reserves from the banking system. Spending will be discouraged and the inflation will be stopped.

But what about employment? And economic growth? It slows down. So the Fed has a dilemma. The question is: "How much unemployment and growth slowdown will we impose (or tolerate) in the short run, to achieve the desired objective of price stability?"

The "High Employment" Objective Is Difficult to Define

The U.S. government is committed by *The Employment Act of 1946* and *The Full Employment and Balanced Growth Act of 1978* (the Humphrey-Hawkins Act) to

---

Box 23-1

Feature: Functions and Objectives of Monetary Policy: A View from Paul Meek of the New York Fed.

Monetary policy is concerned with money and credit, and their interaction with jobs, production and prices. As the nation's central bank, the Federal Reserve System has a dual responsibility, which Robert Roosa defined years ago as having defensive and dynamic features.[1]

First, there is the responsibility to defend the monetary system against both routine and unpredictable strains, which develop as goods are produced and consumed. The central bank exercises this *defensive* function by insuring that money and credit are readily available to meet the highly variable day-to-day and week-to-week needs of a market economy.

The central bank's *dynamic* responsibility is to see that money and credit grow over longer periods in step with the nation's expanding productive potential. The art of central banking consists of allowing money and credit to flex with society's demands in the short run without compromising the central bank's ability to influence them appropriately over a longer horizon.

Any central bank must operate so that money is available on short notice, so that pro-

ducers and consumers do not lack the cash required for the millions of transactions that bind them together.... The challenge to the Federal Rerserve lies in combining such short-run flexibility with its dynamic responsibility for influencing money and credit growth to foster a healthy economy.

There is little reason to be concerned if money and bank credit rise rapidly for a few weeks or slow down for a month or two. But central bankers and economists discovered long ago that rapid monetary and credit growth, if maintained long enough, leads to inflation while a sustained decline in such growth produces economic recession and deflation.

Monetary policymakers meet regularly to decide whether observed short-run developments in money and credit—and in the economy itself—threaten to undermine balanced economic growth, reasonable price performance, and equilibrium in international transactions. For them, money and credit growth is an intermediate objective, one that lies between the daily business of providing liquidity and their ultimate concern with the economy's performance. ...

---

[1] Robert V. Roosa, *Reserve Operations in the Money and Government Securities Markets*, Federal Reserve Bank of New York, 1956, pp. 2–13.

Source: Paul Meek, *U.S. Monetary Policy and Financial Markets*, Federal Reserve Bank of New York (1982), pp. 2–3.

maintaining a low level of unemployment and a low level of inflation. The difficult question is, "How low is low?"

The Humphrey-Hawkins Act Targets. The Humphrey-Hawkins Act specifies the maximum acceptable **unemployment rate: 4%** of the labor force, and the maximum **inflation rate: 3%**. In 1978 when the act was passed, it placed the responsibility on the President and his administration to achieve these goals by the end of 1983.

The act also puts some of the responsibility on the Fed. The act requires the Fed to report to Congress in February and July of each year to explain their plans for achieving the specified percentages.

After the Humphrey-Hawkins Act was passed, the unemployment rate in the U.S. economy increased each year. And the inflation rate skyrocketed to double digit rates in 1979 and 1980. After 1980 the inflation rate slowed each year, falling to a low of less than 2% in 1986—well below the Humphrey-Hawkins target.

The unemployment rate reached a peak of 10.8% in January of 1983. Then it declined slowly and hesitantly to about 5.5% in 1988. That's significant progress, but still quite a bit above the 4% rate called for by Humphrey-Hawkins.

President Reagan Adjusts the Targets. President Reagan's (and the Council of Economic Advisors') February 1982 *Economic Report* amends both the targets and the timetable, saying (p. 215): "The Federal Government cannot fully anticipate the course of the economy; neither can it direct economic outcomes precisely." The the *Report* goes on to give the 1982 projections: For 1987 the unemployment rate was to be down to 5.3% and the inflation rate, 4.4%. So the inflation target was more than met. But the unemployment target was not.

When the unemployment rate appears "too high" while the inflation rate is low, should the Fed try to stimulate employment?—even at the danger of more inflation?

This question hinges very much on another question: "How low can we expect the unemployment rate to go?" And that depends on the important concept: "the **natural rate** of unemployment."

"Full Employment" Means "A Low Rate of Unemployment"

All economists agree that a realistic definition of **full employment** *must be one which permits some unemployment to exist.* When people change jobs, they don't find new jobs instantaneously. And when people leave high school or college, or when new people decide to enter (or reenter) the labor force, it takes awhile for them to find jobs. This so-called "frictional unemployment" is an essential part of a dynamic economic system.

If we tried to keep frictional unemployment at zero, how would a new business starting up ever find any employees? With zero frictional unemployment it would be impossible for input resources to shift out of inefficient, declining industries and into more efficient, expanding industries. So a realistic definition of "full employment" does not mean zero unemployment. But then, exactly what does it mean?

The framers of the Humphrey-Hawkins Act apparently assumed that full employment meant "not more than 4% unemployment." But we have not seen such a low unemployment rate (4%) at any time since that act was passed (1978).

Some economists now are saying it's time to change that number—that the minimum realistic unemployment rate (the "natural rate") is now somewhere over 5%. Some say betweeen 6% and 7%.

This is still very much an unresolved question—except in the minds of those on each side of the question who are sure that they are right. (On this you may want to re-read Professor Alan Blinder's comments back in chapter 5, box 5-6.) So what is the Fed to do? If it chooses a full-employment objective it must pursue that objective knowing that full employment means "a not too-high level of unemployment"—but without knowing precisely what unemployment percentage to shoot for.

THE FED'S STRATEGY: HOW DOES IT PURSUE ITS GOALS?

Given that the Fed has some difficult-to-define and sometimes conflicting goals—how does it go about achieving them?

The Fed's Tools Do Not Directly Control the Ultimate Goals

The tools of monetary policy, remember, are limited to (1) open market operations, (2) changes in the discount rate and (3) changes in reserve requirements. So the Fed doesn't have a "control lever" to directly affect its three basic goals: (1) full employment, (2) stable prices, and (3) economic growth.

In the case of its other three goals (stability of (4) interest rates, (5) financial markets, and (6) foreign exchange markets) the Fed does have some direct control, through buying and selling securities and foreign currencies. But *on its three most basic goals the Fed's tools work only indirectly.* So to pursue those goals it's essential that the Fed have

1. a **theory** of what factors influence those goals (and how much), and
2. an **operating strategy** for influencing the factors which do (ultimately) influence those goals.

The Purpose of Operating Targets

Since the Fed can't exercise direct control over its ultimate goals, it must focus on, or "target" something over which it can exercise direct control: an **operating target**. An operating target must be something

1. that the Fed knows (from monetary theory) will **influence** the ultimate goals,
2. that the Fed can **monitor** closely, and
3. that the Fed can **control**.

For example, the Fed might decide to use as an operating target, **total reserves** (R) in the banking system. Or it might target the **monetary base** (B). Either B or R could be used as operating targets. Why? Because:

1. Monetary theory tells us that R and B bring changes in the money supply (ΔM), and ΔM brings changes in total spending (ΔE), and ΔE brings changes

in the ultimate goals: employment, prices, and GNP growth. So the first requirement is met.

2. The Fed can closely monitor B and R.

3. Through its open market operations the Fed has fairly close control over B and R.

Let's assume that the Fed has chosen to target, monitor, and carefully control the growth rate of bank reserves (R). Now suppose the Fed decides unemployment is too high and the GNP growth rate is too low. So the Fed buys T-bills and pushes more funds into bank reserves. The operating target (R) responds immediately. Great!

But it's quite a long way from a given increase in R to the resulting increase in GNP growth. Here's an example to illustrate the need for something to monitor *in addition to an operating target.*

Suppose the latest figures indicate that real GNP has been growing at about 2%, but the Fed has chosen a real GNP growth goal of 4%. So the Fed buys securities. Bank reserves (R) increase.

Did the Fed take the right action? Not too much and not too little? The results won't show up in the GNP statistics for quite awhile. Meanwhile, how do we know? We watch an "intermediate target"—one with a somewhat closer relationship to the ultimate "real GNP growth rate" goal.

The Purpose of an Intermediate Target

An **intermediate target** is something to watch to see if the assumed "theoretical linkages" between the operating target and the ultimate goals are on track—to see if the $\Delta R \rightarrow \Delta M \rightarrow \Delta E \rightarrow \Delta GNP$ sequence is going the way the theory says it should. As the Fed is controlling and adjusting its operating target, it would like to be watching one or more *intermediate targets* to see what effects its *operating target* changes seem to be having.

The two important intermediate targets which the Fed has used are: (1) rate of growth in the **money supply**, and (2) the level of and changes in **interest rates**. Either of these could serve as an intermediate target because both have a definite relationship to the real GNP growth rate—and also to the rate of employment and the price level.

To put it all together: Suppose the Fed decides to use total bank reserves as its operating target and the M2 money supply as its intermediate target. Then the Fed can (1) make adjustments in bank reserves and (2) watch the effect on M2.

Assuming that there is a predictable relationship between bank reserves and M2 changes and between M2 changes and GNP changes, the Fed can **increase bank reserves** just enough to **increase M2** just enough to **increase GNP growth** to the desired 4% rate.

The Chosen Policy Depends on the Chosen Theory

You can see that as it decides on its monetary policy, the Fed must have a theory about the relationship (1) between the operating target and the intermediate target, and (2) between the intermediate target and the ultimate goal. The effectiveness of monetary policy can only be as good as the accuracy of the theory interlinking these variables.

Example: What will happen to the size of M2 if bank reserves are increased by 5%? It depends on the size of the M2 multiplier.

Next question: What effect will that much increase in M2 have on the real GNP growth rate? That depends on the relationship between M2 and total spending, and between total spending and GNP growth. Is M2 velocity stable so that a given increase in M2 will result in a predictable increase in spending? Or is velocity likely to change?

You can see that the Fed's choice of targets must depend on an understanding of the cause and effect relationships (the multipliers) which link the targets and the goals. Disagreements in theory (and among economists, there are many!) lead to disagreements as to the appropriate operating and intermediate targets for monetary policy. So how does the Fed choose?

How Does the Fed Choose Its Operating Targets?

It makes sense for the Fed to choose, as operating targets, variables over which it has some direct control. There are two kinds of these:

1. *Money-supply-growth variables* such as bank reserves and the monetary base which the Fed can control through its open market operations, and

2. *Money-market-related variables* such as interest rates on T-bills or Fed funds which in the short run the Fed can influence, also using open market operations.

The basic (very important!) question is this: Which of these two kinds of operating targets should the Fed choose? A money-stock-related target? Or a money-market-related target? Much of the remainder of this chapter will be concerned with answering this question. First you need to know more about these two alternative kinds of targets.

Alternative Money-Stock-Related Operating Targets: R, B, etc.

There are several different operating target options which relate to changes in the size of the money supply. One is total bank reserves (R). That's something the Fed can both (a) watch closely and (b) control fairly directly. So one option is **total bank reserves**.

But banks, on their own initiative, can borrow from the Fed's "discount window." Or they can repay previous discount loans. Either way they can directly influence total bank reserves. So perhaps only **nonborrowed reserves** should be targeted. That's another option.

Also, currency inflows and outflows alter the size of the **vault cash** component of bank reserves. So perhaps the **monetary base** (total bank reserve deposits at the Fed, plus total currency outstanding) should be chosen as the operating target. Or perhaps only the **nonborrowed** part of the base?

Alternatively, an indication of the "tightness" of bank reserve positions might be the extent of **discount-window borrowing**. Perhaps that should be considered as an operating target. When discount borrowing increases, perhaps that's a sign that money is getting too tight and that the Fed should add more reserves into the banking system.

You'll be reading more about money-stock-related targets soon. But first, what about a money-market-related target?

Money-Market-Related Operating Targets: Interest Rates

Perhaps the Fed should decide to focus, not on money-stock-related variables, but on financial market conditions and interest rates. For example, the Fed could target the Fed funds rate, pushing it down to expand the economy and pushing it up to slow the economy.

The Fed can change the Fed funds rate by buying or selling T-bills. Should the Fed use this variable as an operating target? Maybe. But first there are some other things to think about.

The **operating target** needs to be related in a predictable way to the chosen **intermediate target**, and to the **ultimate goals**. So before making choices about operating targets, we need to make some choices about intermediate targets.

WHICH INTERMEDIATE VARIABLE TO TARGET? MONEY SUPPLY? OR INTEREST RATES

In practice, for intermediate targets there are only two alternatives: (1) the general level of and changes in **interest rates**, and (2) changes in the size of the **money supply**. Which to choose?

A good intermediate target must meet three requirements. It must be something that

1. the Fed can accurately monitor,
2. the Fed can control by adjusting its operating target, and that
3. has a *predictable effect* on the ultimate goals.

Both the Money Supply and Interest Rates Can Be Monitored—But Not Precisely

The Fed obtains data on changes in the monetary aggregates (M1, M2, etc.) with about a two-week delay. The general level of nominal interest rates can be observed daily. Still, neither of these intermediate targets is precisely monitorable.

The problem with money-supply-monitoring is that the preliminary (two-week-old) monetary aggregate figures are frequently more *timely* than *accurate*. The figures often turn out to be wrong and require adjustment.

The problem with interest-rate-monitoring is that nominal interest rates don't tell the whole story about the real cost of borrowing. *Real rates* can change while *nominal rates* are constant. A change in inflationary expectations brings a perceived change in real rates.

For example, suppose nominal rates are rising. If inflationary expectations are also rising then the nominal rate increase may not represent any increase at all in the perceived real cost of borrowing. Since the Fed has no good way to monitor changes in expected inflation it can't very accurately monitor changes in real rates.

Money supply changes and interest rate changes aren't perfect intermediate targets. But they're best available. And as the "ultimate goal" figures—GNP, employment, and price level changes—come out then the Fed can check on the reliability of its intermediate target. If it isn't predicting accurately then adjustments can be made.

A Good Intermediate Target Must Be Controllable

The Fed does not exercise *complete control* over changes in either the size of the money supply or the level of interest rates. But if it decides it wants to do so, in the short-run it certainly can have a very quick and significant influence on either one.

By contrast, suppose the Fed decided it would directly target "nominal GNP." If the nominal GNP figure comes out "too low," there's no quick and direct way that the Fed can change it. Clearly, in terms of the "controllability" criterion, both the monetary aggregates and interest rates are better intermediate targets than any next-best alternative.

A Good Intermediate Target Must Have a Predictable Relationship With the Ultimate Goals

How predictable is the relationship between a money supply change and future GNP? Or an interest rate change and GNP? This question about the relative predictability of the effects of money supply or interest rate changes is both important and controversial.

In the chapters coming up you will be going deeply into this. For now you only need to know that it depends a lot on the stability of (or predictability of changes in) the *velocity* of the targeted monetary aggregate. And it depends a lot on the responsiveness of total spending to changes in interest rates. The following sections explain more about this.

THE MONEY-STOCK TARGET: FOCUSING ON THE GROWTH-RATE OF THE MONEY SUPPLY

Suppose the Fed decides to use money supply changes as the intermediate target. Then it must choose a money-supply-related operating target, such as bank reserves, or the monetary base. And how (and how well) does it work?

Suppose the Multipliers Are Known, and Constant

Suppose we assume (step one) that the "money multiplier"—the relationship between either bank reserves or the monetary base, and the money supply—is constant. Then by controlling the growth of either reserves or the base we can definitely (predictably!) control the growth of the money supply.

Example: Suppose we know that the ratio of the monetary base (B) to the money supply (M) is one-to-three. Then we can be sure that *one additional dollar* added to the monetary base will result in *three additional dollars* in the money supply.

Suppose Velocity Is Constant

Now suppose we know (step two) that for every additional dollar in the money supply, total spending in the economy will increase by $6. (The velocity of circulation of the average dollar is 6.) Then we know for sure that for each additional $1 released by the Fed into the monetary base, the money supply will increase by $3, and total spending in the economy will increase by $18 ($1 × 3 × 6 = $18).

In this case there is precise linkage between the Fed's control variables and their *ultimate goals*. What a beautiful situation! A given change in the monetary base (ΔB) will result in a predictable change in spending (ΔE).

Then, suppose our theory can tell us exactly how much total spending there should be to support the desired level of employment, output, and income, and without any inflationary pressures. If we want all of these macroeconomic variables to increase at an annual rate of 4%, we know *exactly* how many additional dollars to release into the monetary base to bring about the desired 4% increase in total spending. A stable 4% growth rate of B will keep the economy stable at full employment, with a 4% growth rate and no inflation. Ideal!

With such a beautiful opportunity available to the Fed, why should it ever target anything except the monetary base and the money supply? If everything was as precise and predictable as in this example, it shouldn't. And it wouldn't. But in the real world it doesn't turn out to be quite that simple.

The Relationships (Multipliers) Are Not Perfectly Stable

In the first place, the multipliers linking the monetary base with the size of the money supply, and the size of the money supply with total spending, have proven to be somewhat less than perfectly stable and/or predictable, especially during the 1980s. In the second place, when the Fed looks only at money-stock-variables (bank reserves, the monetary base, and monetary aggregates) this leaves no room to accommodate unexpected changes in the demand for money or other supply or demand shocks in the financial markets.

Shocks sometimes can bring violent swings in interest rates and be very disruptive to both the financial markets and the economy. And there's another factor reducing the precision of the money control process: The Fed, from week to week or even month to month, cannot precisely control the growth rate of the money supply.

Short-Run Money-Growth Rates Cannot Be Precisely Controlled

Suppose the Federal Open Market Committee (FOMC) really wants to precisely control the money supply growth rate. From week to week. Can it do that? No. There will be some errors because of the nature of the system.

In the first place, the Fed can't precisely control total reserves from day to day. Banks at their own initiative can borrow from the Fed's discount window. The Fed can always raise the discount rate to discourage this, but in the meanwhile precise control of reserves is lost.

Another problem is that the multiplier relationship between existing reserves and the money supply is not fixed. The level of excess reserves fluctuates from day to day. Also, small banks are required to hold checkable deposit reserves of only 3%. Large banks must hold 12%. Suppose much of the new reserves going into the system flow into small banks. Then the multiplier will be larger than if those same reserves had flowed into the larger banks.

Another factor is the relationship between time deposits and checkable deposits, and the question of whether or not we are dealing with M1, M2, or perhaps M3 as our "targeted" money supply. Also, for every dollar of currency withdrawn from the banking system, reserves drop by one dollar. Neither the banks nor the Fed have any control over that.

Some economists have suggested that one way to tighten up the slack and give the Fed somewhat greater control would be to make the discount rate a *penalty rate*—perhaps floating one percentage point or more above the Fed funds rate. The way it is now, when the Fed begins to tighten and the Fed funds rate goes up, banks can dash to the (low cost) discount window to make up their reserve deficiencies. So they wind up *expanding the total quantity of reserves* in the banking system at exactly the time when the Fed is trying to tighten money.

The bottom line: Everybody agrees that the Fed doesn't have the power to *precisely* control the rate of growth of the money supply from day to day, week to week, or even month to month. But they can come fairly close. Many economists argue that if they really tried they could do a better job of it than they have done in the past.

Clearly, the money supply intermediate target is not "the perfect target." The only available alternative is the general level of interest rates. The next section evaluates that alternative.

TARGETING THE GENERAL LEVEL OF INTEREST RATES

If the Fed's *intermediate target* is to be the general level of interest rates, then the *operating target* will need to be one which is closely related to and can have a predictable influence on this target. The Fed could use as an operating target the T-bill rate, the repo rate, or some other short-term rate. In practice the *Fed funds rate*—the most sensitive money market rate—has been the Fed's choice.

Interest-rate targeting is based on the ideas that (1) stable financial markets are conducive to economic health and growth, and (2) the level of interest rates plays a significant role in influencing total spending (E)—and therefore employment, output, income, growth, and the price level. This is based on the idea that (*ceteris paribus*) there will be more borrowing and spending when people can borrow at low interest cost than when the interest cost is higher.

Inflationary Expectations Can Reduce the Fed's Control over Interest Rates

Suppose the Fed eases money to bring down interest rates. But then suppose *expectations of increased inflation* are triggered by the Fed's easy money policies. An expected increase in the rate of inflation would cause nominal interest rates to go up, not down. And this consideration means that during times when inflationary expectations are likely to play an important role, the Fed's control over interest rates is nowhere near as great as some economists once believed.

Is Interest Rate Targeting an Invitation to Inflation?

Many economists (especially monetarists) have charged that interest-rate-targeting is biased in the direction of inflation. Suppose, for example, economic indicators seem to be pointing upward, the stock market moves up to new highs, future profit projections are high and a wave of optimism is sweeping through the business community.

All businesses are borrowing money, issuing new bonds and commercial paper, planning to double their plant capacity and build up their inventories. Heavy loan demands deplete bank reserves and banks enter the Fed funds market to borrow more reserves.

Every bank wants to borrow Fed funds. No bank wants to lend. The Fed funds rate rises rapidly. The rising Fed funds rate spills over into other markets. The T-bill rate, the commercial paper rate and other short term rates—as well as the cost of long-term borrowing—all move up. Higher interest rates dampen some of the enthusiasm to borrow and buy and build.

Interest Rates Rise to Curb an Inflationary Boom. The dampening effect of rising interest rates is what is supposed to prevent this surge of investment demand from triggering serious inflation. But suppose the Fed is targeting the Fed funds rate and doesn't recognize the extent of the excess demand which is building up in the economy. Then the Fed will ease money to hold down the Fed funds rate. That will add to the inflationary pressures in the economy.

The argument goes like this: By the time the Fed realizes that this is not just a "temporary disequilibrium" between the supply and demand for funds, it is already too late. Already billions of dollars of new reserves have been pumped into the banking system—and at exactly the time when the Fed should have been carefully restricting money growth.

An Interest Rate Target Doesn't Automatically Protect Against an Unexpected Demand Shock. One clear advantage of using a money aggregate target and trying to hold the line on increases in the money supply is that this approach automatically protects the economy from the shock of a sudden major increase in business or consumer spending. But when interest rates are targeted and not permitted to rise very much, this automatic inflation-preventing effect doesn't occur. That's one of the strong arguments for targeting the money supply and not interest rates.

An Interest Rate Target Must Be an Adjustable Target

The argument in favor of interest targeting goes like this: The members of the Federal Open Market Committee who decide monetary policy are neither blind nor stupid. If excessive investment demand is developing in the economy, there are several economic indicators which will show this. Therefore the Fed, to head off inflationary spending increases, will adjust its interest rate target upward. So instead of feeding additional reserves into the system, the Fed will initiate increases in interest rates to dampen the spending boom before serious inflationary pressures can develop.

The argument is that when the Fed targets interest rates it doesn't "freeze on a rate, then put blinders on"! When targeting interest rates the Fed must follow other economic indicators to see what is happening in the economy. Then it must adjust its interest rate target in response to the broad variety of indicators.

An interest rate target obviously requires discretionary action on the part of the Fed. And this is what the monetarist economists strongly object to. When the money supply is targeted and a "fixed rate of growth" established, no discretionary decisions are required. The only action required is to try to keep money growth on target.

What If There Is a Shift in the Demand for Money?

What if there is a shift in the desire of the public to hold money balances? Suppose the desired size of money balances increases from say 1/6 to 1/5 of the national income—that is, suppose k increases from 1/6 to 1/5—which means that velocity slows from 6 to 5?

If this increase in the quantity of money demanded occurs while the Fed is targeting the money supply and following a "fixed money growth" rule, then the Fed will not permit the money supply to expand. So the money supply will not be large enough to satisfy people's desires to hold money balances. Money will be very tight.

Since the money supply is not permitted to expand, people's desired money balances (Mqd) must be forced to decrease. Mqd can be decreased either by (1) increasing interest rates which will raise the opportunity cost of holding money or (2) decreasing national income which will lower the transactions demand for money balances. The actual outcome probably would be both (1) higher interest rates and (2) an economic slowdown—a tight-money-induced recession.

When Velocity Is Unstable, Targeting the Money Supply Is Destabilizing

If the money demand function (the velocity of circulation) is unstable, a "fixed money growth" rule becomes *destabilizing*. Until the mid-1970s, most of the time the money demand function was quite stable and changed only in fairly steady and predictable ways. But since the mid-1970s this stability and predictability (at least with respect to the M1 money supply) has not held. In fact, during the 1980s the velocity of M1 decreased so much (the "Cambridge k" ratio of M1 to national income increased so much) that by mid-year 1986 the Fed decided to abandon M1 as a target variable. Looking at the statistics, it's a good thing they did!

At the July 1986 FOMC meeting the M1 money supply was targeted to grow at the annual rate of somewhere between 3% and 8%. But the actual M1 growth rate from August through December 1986 turned out to be more than 20%! Suppose the Fed had been trying to hold M1 growth to its 3% to 8% target. That would have amounted to a *seriously restrictive* policy which surely would have pushed the economy into a recession. It was at the July FOMC meeting that the Fed (as it turns out, *wisely*) decided that under the circumstances it would ignore its M1 targets for the remainder of the year.

When Velocity Is Constant, Steady Money Growth Is Stabilizing. When the money demand function is stable (when V is constant), a monetary aggregate target and a "steady-money-growth rule" insulates the economy from destabilizing shifts in total spending. A too-big spending boom chokes itself off because of tight money and high interest rates. A slack economy stimulates itself through

Box 23-2

Feature: **Monetarist Economists Have Been Highly Critical of (But Never in Control of) The Fed**

Monetarist economists have always held that interest rate targeting and discretionary monetary policy are destabilizing and should never be done. But the Fed has never been under the control of "strict monetarist" economists.

In one case when a member of the monetarist school of thought was appointed Chairman of the Fed Board, he soon changed his strict monetarist "money-growth-rule" convictions.

The case in point is that of Professor Arthur F. Burns, Ph.D., who was appointed by President Nixon to the Fed Board chairmanship in 1970. Some time after his appointment, in a public meeting Burns was asked how he could harmonize his current views with those expressed in an article he had written when he was an academic economist in 1965. His reply: "I was wrong in 1965."[1]

Sherman Maisel who was a member of the Fed Board from 1965 to 1972 made the following comment about Fed Chairman Arthur Burns:

> In 1965, as an academic economist, he (Burns) was willing to base his arguments primarily on pure theory. When he became responsible for policymaking, he became more pragmatic, examining the situation as it actually existed, using his vast economic knowledge and analytical ability to arrive at a practical solution which differed greatly from that of pure theory.[2]

[1] Sherman J. Maisel, *Managing The Dollar: An Inside View By A Recent Governor Of The Federal Reserve Board,* W. W. Norton and Company, Inc., New York, 1973, p. 281.

[2] Ibid.

easy money and low interest rates. No "intelligent discretionary" policies or actions are required.

When Velocity Is Not Constant, Steady Money Growth Is Destabilizing. When the money demand function is unstable and unpredictable (as with M1 during the 1980s) a fixed-rule money growth target leads to money-supply-induced instability in the economy. In these circumstances, interest rate targets—adjusted in view of changing economic indicators—may play an important role in the formation and implementation of monetary policy.

At different times in the past the Fed has used different operating and intermediate targets. You'll be reading about the Fed's monetary targets and policies (past and present) in the next chapter.

SUMMARY

- The basic goals of monetary policy are high employment, price stability, and economic growth. Additional (sometimes conflicting) goals are stability of interest rates, financial markets, and foreign exchange markets.

- The high employment objective means less than 100% employment, but economists disagree about "how much less?"

- The Fed's tools cannot directly control the ultimate goals. So the Fed needs **operating targets**—either money-supply-related or money-market-related—which it can monitor and control.

- Intermediate targets are focused on either the money supply (M) or interest rates (r). But neither is precisely monitorable and neither has an always precisely predictable relationship with the ultimate goals.

- If the relationships between the **monetary base**, the **money supply**, and **economic conditions** were known and constant, then the money supply would be the perfect intermediate target. But these relationships are neither always known, nor always stable. And short-run money-growth rates cannot be precisely controlled.

- Interest rate targeting assumes (1) a predictable relationship between interest rates and economic conditions, and (2) that the Fed can control interest rates. But neither condition is precisely true.

- **Money-supply targeting** in the case of an unexpected demand shock, automatically protects against inflation. But interest rate targeting does not.

- **Interest rate targeting** reduces the destabilizing effects of money demand (velocity) shifts. Unstable money demand requires that targets other than the money supply be used.

Important Principles, Issues, Concepts, Terms

Goals of monetary policy

Conflict among goals

Difficulty of defining "full employment"

Employment Act of 1946

Humphrey-Hawkins Act

Operating target—meaning, and alternatives

Intermediate target—meaning, and alternatives

Purposes of operating and intermediate targets

Money-stock-related targets

Money-market-related targets

Importance of relationships between targets and goals

Importance of velocity in determining appropriate targets

Effects of a shift in money demand

Limitations on interest rate monitoring

Limitations on money supply monitoring

The importance of "the multipliers" in monetary policy

Questions and Problems

1. List the different goals of monetary policy and explain why these goals are conflicting.

2. Explain what the Humphrey-Hawkins Act tried to do. Did it succeed? Explain.

3. Explain this statement: "Full employment really means a low-enough rate of unemployment."

4. Explain the relationship between the Fed's operating targets, intermediate targets, and ultimate goals.

5. Explain why the chosen monetary policy depends on the chosen monetary theory.

6. Explain the characteristics of a good intermediate target. In view of these characteristics, does the Fed have a really good intermediate target? Discuss.

7. Under what circumstances would a money-stock target be destabilizing? And under what circumstances would an interest rate target be destabilizing?

8. Explain the important role of *velocity* in determining the effectiveness of an intermediate target variable.

Suggested Readings

Barth, James R., and Robert E. Keleher. "'Financial Crises' and the Role of the Lender of Last Resort." *Economic Review*. Federal Reserve Bank of Atlanta (January 1984), 58–67.

Beck, Nathaniel. "Politics and Monetary Policy." in Thomas Willet (ed.), *The Political Economy of Stagflation*. San Francisco: Pacific Institute, forthcoming.

Brunner, Karl, and Allen H. Meltzer. "Strategies and Tactics for Monetary Control." *Carnegie-Rochester Conference Series on Public Policy* 18. (Spring 1983), 59–116.

Black, Robert. "The Fed's Mandate: Help or Hindrance?" *Economic Review* 70. Federal Reserve Bank of Richmond (July/August 1984), 3–7.

Bronfenbrenner, Martin. "Monetary Rules: A New Look." *Journal of Law & Economics* 8 (October 1965), 173–94.

DeLeeuw, F., and E. Gramlich. "The Channels of Monetary Policy." *Journal of Finance* 24 (May 1969), 265–90.

Federal Reserve Bank of Boston. *Controlling the Monetary Aggregates III*. Conference Series no. 23. Boston: Federal Reserve Bank of Boston, 1980.

Friedman, Benjamin M. "Using a Credit Aggregate Target to Implement Monetary Policy in the Financial Environment of the Future." *Monetary Policy Issues in the 1980s*. a symposium sponsored by the Federal Reserve Bank of Kansas City, at Jackson Hole, Wyoming, August 9–10, 1982, pp. 19–247.

Friedman, Milton. "A Case for Overhauling the Federal Reserve." *Challenge*. (July/August 1985), 4–12.

———. "Monetary Variability in the United States and Japan." *Journal of Money, Credit and Banking*. (August 1983), 339–43.

———. *A Program for Monetary Stability*. New York: Fordham University Press, 1960.

Kane, Edward. "External Pressures and the Operations of the Fed." in Raymond Lombra and Willard Witte (eds.). *The Political Economy of Domestic and International Monetary Relations*. Iowa City, Iowa: University of Iowa Press, 1982.

Latane, Henry A. "Income Velocity and Interest Rates: A Pragmatic Approach." *Review of Economics and Statistics* 42. (November 1960), 445–49.

Maisel, Sherman. *Managing the Dollar*. New York: W. W. Norton, 1973.

Meek, Paul. *U.S. Monetary Policy and Financial Markets*. Federal Reserve Bank of New York, 1982.

Mehra, Yash. "Inflationary Expectations, Money Growth and the Vanishing Liquidity Effect of Money on Interest: A Further Investigation." *Economic Review* 71,2. Federal Reserve Bank of Richmond, (March /April 1985), 23–35.

Meltzer, Allan H. "Discussion." *Monetary Policy Issues in the 1980s*. a symposium sponsored by the Federal Reserve Bank of Kansas City, at Jackson Hole, Wyoming, August 9–10, 1982, pp. 249–55.

Motley, Brian, and Robert H. Rasche. "Predicting the Money Stock: A Comparison of Alternative Approaches." *Economic Review*. Federal Reserve Bank of San Francisco (Spring 1986), p. 51.

Motley, Brian. "Should Money be Redefined?" *Weekly Letter*. Federal Reserve Bank of San Francisco (September 5, 1986), 1–3.

Poole, William, and Charles Lieberman. "Improving Monetary Control." *Brookings Papers on Economic Activity*, no. 2. 1972.

Radecki, Lawrence J., and John Wenninger. "Recent Instability in M1's Velocity." *Quarterly Review*. Federal Reserve Bank of New York (Autumn 1985), 16–22.

Sargent, Thomas J., and Neil Wallace. "Some Unpleasant Monetarist Arithmetic." *Quarterly Review* 9. Federal Reserve Bank of Minneapolis (Winter 1985), 15–31.

Simons, Henry C. "Rules Versus Authorities in Monetary Policy." *Journal of Political Economy* 44. 1936. Reprinted in *Readings in Monetary Theory*. Homewood, Ill.: Richard D. Irwin, 1951, pp. 337–68.

Taylor, Herb. "What has Happened to M1?" *Business Review*. Federal Reserve Bank of Philadelphis (September/October 1986), 3–14.

Tobin, James. "Monetary Policy: Rules, Targets and Shocks." *Journal of Money, Credit and Banking* 15. (November 1983), 506–18.

Trehan, Bharat, and Carl Walsh, "Examining the Recent Surge in M1." *Weekly Letter*. Federal Reserve Bank of San Francisco (October 24, 1986), 1–3.

Wallich, Henry, and Peter Kier. "The Role of Operating Guidelines in U.S. Monetary Policy." *Federal Reserve Bulletin* 65. September 1979, pp. 679–91.

Wojnilower, Albert. "The Central Role of Credit Crunches in Recent Financial History." *Brookings Papers on Economic Activity* 2. 1980, pp. 277–326.

CHAPTER 24

The Fed's Monetary Targets and Policies, Past and Present

Chapter Objectives

This chapter goes more deeply into the question of money supply or interest rate targeting. Then it gives the highlights of the Fed's targets and policies from the time of World War II to the present. After you have studied this chapter you will understand and be able to explain:

1. Why it is not possible to strictly control the **money supply** and **interest rates** at the same time, and how to use supply and demand graphs to illustrate this.
2. Why the **fixed money growth rule** is the only policy which does not require discretionary decisions by the Fed.
3. The reasons for and effects of the Fed's **bond price pegging** from 1941 to 1951, and the Fed-Treasury **Accord** of 1951 which ended this episode.
4. The logic of and problems with targeting **free reserves** in the banking system.
5. Fed policy during the 1970s with increased emphasis on the **money supply**, culminating with the so-called **monetarist experiment**, October 1979–October 1982.
6. The sharp and unexpected **decrease in M1 velocity** during the 1980s, leading to (a) a shift of emphasis toward M2, and to (b) more flexible Fed policies, including the use of **ultimate goals** as targets.

A STABLE MONEY SUPPLY AND STABLE INTEREST RATES: BOTH DESIRABLE OBJECTIVES

In the previous chapter you were reading about the choice between intermediate monetary policy objectives. Which to seek: stable money growth? Or stable interest rates? We would like to have both. In a "long-run natural full employment equilibrium economy" with no disruptive influences—no "shocks" upsetting the equilibrium—we would expect to have both.

Monetarist theory tells us that the best monetary policy to help us to get to and maintain this desirable long-run equilibrium condition is a "hands off" monetary policy. Let the money supply grow at a steady rate approximating the real growth rate of the economy. Then let the natural market forces work the economic system into and thereafter maintain the long-run equilibrium.

But suppose some really significant shock, or "departure from equilibrium" occurs in the economy. Or suppose there are a series of short-run shocks which cause conditions in the financial markets and interest rates to be highly unstable. Then shouldn't the Fed, in addition to its "stable money growth" objective, add in the additional objective of stabilizing the financial markets? Of keeping interest rates steady?

Simultaneous Control of Both Money Supply Growth and Interest Rates? Impossible!

Why shouldn't the Fed (a) control the monetary base and let the money supply expand at just the right rate, while (b) keeping an eye on the Fed funds rate and taking action as necessary to keep it stable? During several past years that's what it seemed that the Fed was trying to do. The problem is: You just can't do that— and especially not when economic conditions are changing, with shifting supply and demand conditions in the financial markets. Why not? Figures 24-1, 24-2 and 24-3 explain why not.

Figure 24-1 shows supply and demand in the loanable funds market. That figure illustrates the dilemma of trying to target the money supply and interest rates at the same time.

In the dynamic financial markets of the real world, demand for funds is shifting constantly. When these shifts occur, if the money supply is not permitted to adjust, then interest rates will move up or down in response to the changing demand for funds.

How could the Fed prevent the interest rate increase shown in figure 24-1? Only by permitting the money supply to increase (M_0 to shift to the right) in response to the increase in demand. But to do that would mean abandoning the money supply target. See the problem?

Here's the point: The *only way* the Fed can hold its interest rate target, is to abandon its money supply target and permit the money supply to change. That's

---

Box 24-1

Question: **What's the Appropriate Symbol for the Interest Rate?** *i or r?*

In figures 24-1, 24-2, and 24-3 the letter i is used as the symbol for the interest rate. At other places in this book you will see the letter r used. Why?

It has become conventional (more or less) among economists to use "*i*" for the market rate of interest—the nominal rate—and to use "*r*" for the real rate. Whenever prices are assumed to be fixed and unchanging, the nominal rate

and the real rate are the same. So the letter r will be used. Also, when the interest rate under consideration is the market rate minus the inflation rate, "r" will be used.

At other times, "*i*" will be used to indicate that the interest rate is the nominal rate—the market rate. It may be the real rate or not, depending on whether or not prices are stable.

Figure 24-1.   To Strictly Control Money Supply Changes, Interest Rates Must Be Ignored

Why the Fed cannot strictly limit the growth of the money supply without abandoning the interest rate as a target.

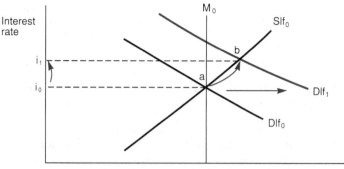

Quantity of money (stock) and quantities
of loanable funds (flow)

If the money supply is not permitted to change, as the demand for loanable funds shifts from $D1f_0$ to $D1f_1$, the interest rate will rise from i_0 to i_1.

As long as the money supply remains at M_0, the supply of loanable funds will remain at $S1f_0$. So when the demand for loanable funds increases, since the supply does not shift, there will be a shortage of loanable funds. To eliminate the shortage the price (interest rate) must rise to where the quantity supplied equals the quantity demanded. That occurs at interst i_1 (point b).

The only way the Fed could prevent this increase in i would be to abandon its fixed money supply target and permit M to increase. Figure 24-2 shows that.

what you see in figure 24-2. The money supply is permitted to increase (M shifts from M_0 to M_1) and more funds flow into the loanable funds market. So Slf shifts rightward from Slf_0 to Slf_1. The increased supply of funds equals the increased demand so there's no shortage of funds at interest rate i_0. So the stable interest rate objective is achieved. But to achieve this objective the money supply had to expand from M_0 to M_1.

To maintain a stable interest rate the Fed must permit the **money supply** to change enough to adjust the supply of loanable funds enough to accommodate all changes in the **demand for loanable funds**. Some economists would say that the Fed shouldn't do that. When the demand for loanable funds increases, that's when inflationary pressures are likely to exist. And if that's true, then that's exactly when the money supply should not be permitted to expand.

From looking at figures 24-1 and 24-2 it is obvious that to freeze the interest rate, money supply changes must become completely flexible and uncontrolled. Alternatively, to freeze the size (or growth rate) of the money supply, the level of interest rates must become completely flexible and uncontrolled. But suppose the Fed doesn't really like either one of these options?

The Fed cannot do anything to stabilize or control interest rates
without abandoning its specific-money-growth-rate target.

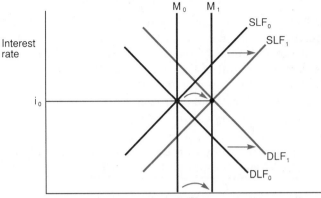

Quantity of money (stock) and quantities of
loanable funds supplied and demanded (flow)

When interest rates are targeted, the money supply must be permitted to shift to achieve the interest rate target. When the demand
for loanable funds shifts from $D1f_0$ to $D1f_1$, in order to prevent the
interest rate from rising, the money supply must be increased sufficiently to shift the supply of loanable funds to $S1f_1$. So the money
supply must be permitted (or induced) to increase from M_0 to M_1.

Box 24-2

Question: What's the Relationship Between the Money Supply (M) and the Supply of Loanable Funds (Slf)? Stocks vs. Flows Again? Right!

This box tells more about figures 24-1, 2, and 3.
In each figure the size of the money supply
is the **money stock** assumed to be fixed by
the Fed. It is represented by the vertical line
"M"—a fixed quantity of money—a stock.

The supply of loanable funds (Slf) curve, as
explained in chapter 10, represents a flow of
funds. It shows the various quantities of funds
that would be flowing from surplus economic
units (SEUs) to deficit economic units (DEUs) at
the various different interest rates which might
exist. At higher rates of interest, greater quantities of loanable funds would flow into the market. That's what the upward slope of the Slf
curve indicates.

The demand for loanable funds (Dlf) curve
represents the flow of funds out of the financial
markets—pulled out by the DEUs. The higher
the interest rate, the smaller the quantity of
funds demanded so the smaller the flow of
funds pulled out of the financial markets.

Equilibrium in the financial markets occurs
at the interest rate where the supplied inflow of

loanable funds is exactly equal to the demanded outflow.

An increase in the money supply (a rightward shift of the vertical M curve from M_0 to M_1
in figure 24-2) makes more money available in
the economy. So that increases the supply of
loanable funds (shifts the curve to the right).
With the new Slf curve (Slf_2), at each interest
rate there is a greater quantity of loanable funds
supplied.

The bottom line: An increase in the money
supply—a larger **money stock**—results in an
increase in the supply of loanable funds—a
larger **funds flow supplied** at each interest rate.
So a rightward shift in the "M stock" curve
(*ceteris paribus*) results in a rightward shift in
the "Slf flow" curve. So by inducing changes in
the money stock the Fed can (*ceteris paribus*)
induce changes in *the supply of loanable funds*
and thereby can influence the level of and
changes in interest rates.

THE FED CAN "MONITOR" BOTH M AND *i*, STRICTLY TARGETING NEITHER

Can the Fed "sort of" target both M and *i* at the same time?—monitoring both and then focusing more on one or the other, depending on the circumstances? The monetarists say the Fed should never try to do that. But the fact is that the Fed has spent a considerable amount of time doing exactly that.

Figure 24-3 illustrates how the Fed can monitor both money supply changes and interest rate changes without a "frozen target" for either one, and with policy

**Figure 24-3.   Monetary Policy Can Be "Aimed At" Controlling Both
The Money Supply and Interest Rates**

The Fed can *monitor* changes in both the money supply and interest rates without strictly targeting either one. Then it can take policy actions to stabilize either one or the other (or some of both), as the specific conditions (in their judgment) seem to warrant.

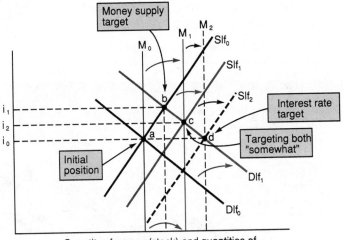

Quantity of money (stock) and quantities of loanable funds (flow)

Here the Fed is monitoring changes in both the money supply and interest rates, but without following a "rule" of strictly limiting either money supply growth or interest rate fluctuations.

The increase in the demand for loanable funds from Dlf_0 to Dlf_1 with no increase in M would push the interest rate up from i_0 to i_1 and move the economy to Point b. If the Fed wants to maintain the interest rate at i_0, it must increase the money supply from M_0 to M_2, increase the supply of loanable funds to Slf_2, and move the economy to Point d.

But suppose the Fed decides to limit both the increase in M and the decrease in *i*. So it expands the money supply only from M_0 to M_1. The supply of loanable funds increases from Slf_0 to Slf_1 and the interest rate rises only to i_2. The economy moves to Point c. In this case the Fed permits both M and *i* to increase somewhat. It has not been unusual for the Fed to take this approach.

reflecting the FOMC's judgment about which of these two targets should be given priority (and how much) at different times. Now study figure 24-3 and the explanation and all this should be very clear.

THE FED'S WORLD WAR II AND POST-WAR POLICIES

Throughout the period from World War II to the present the Fed has gone through some "mind changing" about what to use as operating targets and what to focus on as intermediate targets. But observers haven't always been able to tell exactly what the Fed was targeting.

It wasn't until the 1970s that Congress amended the Federal Reserve Act to require that the Fed establish monetary aggregate targets and report these targets to Congress in February and July of each year. But looking back it's usually possible to see what the Fed was targeting from one period to another.

"Pegging" the Bond Market: 1941 to 1951

During World War II the Fed followed a policy of buying unlimited quantities of government securities, either directly from the Treasury or in the open markets. The Fed was maintaining (pegging) the prices of all government securities at par so that their market values could not fall. So their yields could not rise. This means that market rates of interest on government securities—and therefore on securities in general—could not rise.

Anyone who wanted to sell a government security at par could do so because the Fed was the guaranteed buyer. The ceiling interest rate was pegged at 3/8 of 1% on 90-day T-bills, 7/8 of 1% on one-year Treasury certificates, and 2.5% on 10-year or longer government bonds. During the period December 1941–June 1946 the Fed's holdings of Treasury securities increased from $2.3 billion to $23.4 billion. What a flood of high-powered money (new reserves) flowing into the banking system!

After the war was over, the Fed (in 1947) stopped pegging short-term securities (T-bills and certificates) so that these rates were free to move. But market prices and interest yields on longer-term government securities continued to be pegged? Why? Consider this.

If interest rates had been permitted to rise in the longer-term markets, bond prices would have fallen and holders of government securities throughout the economy would have suffered capital losses. At that time the asset structures of many financial institutions were heavy with government bonds. No one wanted to see these institutions hit with the capital losses which would result from rapidly falling bond prices.

The U.S. Treasury was strongly in favor of continued bond-price pegging because it did not want to see a sharp increase in the cost of financing its (at that time considered *massive*) government debt. So the Fed continued its pegging policy on long-term government securities. The result: During this period the Fed abdicated its role of "controller and protector of the money supply." Instead, it permitted the money supply to expand willy-nilly.

The Fed-Treasury "Accord": 1951

Soon after the United States entered the Korean War in 1950, the inflation rate began to pick up. Many holders of government bonds began selling their bonds. Since the Fed was pegging bond prices, it found itself required to purchase increasing quantities of bonds, thereby feeding a flow of new reserves into the banking system.

In 1950 the consumer price index began rising sharply. In fact it rose by 11% between June 1950 and December 1951. In the fall of 1950 the Fed announced its intensions to depart from its pegging policy and let bond prices fall and interest rates rise. President Truman and Treasury officials strongly opposed this move.

After several months of wrangling on this issue, finally, in March of 1951 the Fed reached an agreement with the President and the Treasury. In this so-called **Accord** the Fed agreed that it would continue to peg government securities prices, but their prices would be permitted to fall somewhat below par. Then, soon after its inauguration, the new Eisenhower administration (in 1953) restored the freedom of the Fed to make its own decisions regarding monetary policy.

CHANGING POLICIES AND TARGETS—1950s–1970s

During the years following "the Accord" the principal operating target of the Fed became *the amount of free reserves in the banking system*. Free reserves are nonborrowed excess reserves—total excess reserves minus discount borrowing. Free reserves were targeted because it was assumed that "the existing lending power" of the banking system is indicated by the volume of nonborrowed excess reserves.

Targeting "Free Reserves" (1953–1966)— Is That a Good Idea?

On the surface, the "free reserves" target seems to make sense because as free reserves in the banking system are increasing, the lending power of the banking system would seem to be increasing. But this conclusion ignores the fact that *there may be times when banks actually wish to hold excess reserves*— especially during times when heavy reserve drains are expected, such as, for example, during a recession. (This would be less true today because of the now highly developed Fed funds and repo markets which can provide instant liquidity—instant new borrowed reserves. In the 1950s and '60s these markets were not so well developed.)

Here's an example: Suppose a recession is in progress and banks are building excess reserves for defensive reasons. If the Fed is targeting free reserves, it may decide that there is too much liquidity in the system. So it begins tightening up, (draining off reserves by open market sales of securities) when in fact exactly the opposite policy is what the economy needs to recover from the recession.

During the 1960s the "free reserves" operating target came under severe criticism by the monetarists. In 1966 the Fed abandoned this target and shifted to the Fed funds rate as its operating target.[1]

Targeting Fed Funds and (With Increasing Emphasis) the Money Supply: The 1970s

During the 1970s the Fed seemed to be aiming at two targets: The Fed funds rate, and the rate of growth of the money supply. As the decade wore on, greater emphasis was placed on money supply growth.

In 1975 the Congress passed a resolution requiring the Fed to establish and to announce its targets for money supply growth. The resolution required the Fed Board Chairman to appear before the House and Senate banking committees to explain and justify the chosen targets. The provisions of this resolution were later incorporated into *The Federal Reserve Reform Act of 1977* and also in *The Full Employment and Balanced Growth Act of 1978* (the Humphrey-Hawkins Act).

These restrictions on the Fed were not really as great as they might appear, for three reasons:

1. *Target ranges.* The Fed could choose a broad range for its "money supply growth target," so as not to restrict itself very much. For example suppose the Fed set a growth-rate for M1 of "between zero and 20%." The Congress would surely complain about that—but they seem to have no problem with ranges such as "3% to 6%" or "4% to 8%." So the announced "target" really isn't a specific target, but a fairly broad range instead.

2. *Base drift.* Every quarter the Fed could choose the present size of the money supply as the "new base" and apply its growth targets from there—even though the new base was outside the previously projected growth range. (Under current rules the Fed can only readjust the base once a year, not quarterly.)

3. *Several aggregates are targeted.* The Fed sets target ranges for several different measures of the money supply: M1, M2, etc., and if even one of them happens to fall within its target range, they can claim to be "on target."

THE SO-CALLED "MONETARIST EXPERIMENT": OCTOBER 1979–OCTOBER 1982

On October 6, 1979 there was an emergency meeting of the Fed Board at the White House. At this meeting, decisions were made to take dramatic action (1) to support the international value of the U.S. dollar and (2) to bring down the U.S. inflation rate.

---

[1] Important articles by monetarist economists criticizing the use of free reserves as an operating target include: William G. DeWald, "Free Reserves, Total Reserves, and Monetary Control," *Journal of Political Economy*, vol. 71, April 1963, pp. 141–153; and K. Bruner and A.H. Meltzer, "The Federal Reserve's Attachment to The Free Reserve Concept." Subcommittee print, U.S. Congress, *House Committee on Banking and Currency, Subcommittee on Domestic Finance*, 88th Congress, 2nd Session, 1964.

Following the meeting the Board increased the discount rate, increased selected reserve requirements, and announced a new operating procedure— *targeting only the money supply*. Money supply growth was to be tightly restricted.

The Fed funds rate was set free to fluctuate in a broad range. Interest rate stabilization was abandoned because it would have interfered with the Fed's newly stated objective of *tightly restricting the growth of the (M1) money supply*.

Following the Fed's announcement the dollar strengthened in the foreign exchange markets and money growth slowed. Nominal interest rates increased sharply and thereafter fluctuated widely.

How well did the Fed succeed in achieving its announced objective of strictly controlling the growth rate of the M1 money supply? It didn't do very well at all. Some observers say it really didn't try. Others have concluded that it just isn't possible to prevent sizeable short-run deviations of actual money-supply growth from a predetermined growth-target path.

The graph in figure 24-4 shows what happened. It would be difficult to look at that figure and conclude that the Fed had succeeded in exercising "precise control" over the M1 money supply.

Until October of 1982 the Fed continued to permit nominal interest rates to remain high and volatile. As inflation rates fell sharply, nominal interest rates also declined, but not nearly enough to prevent *real rates* from rising sharply—in fact, to the highest levels in modern times.

Figure 24-4.   The Fed's Announced Growth Targets for M1 Compared with Actual Growth Rates of M1, September 1979–December 1982

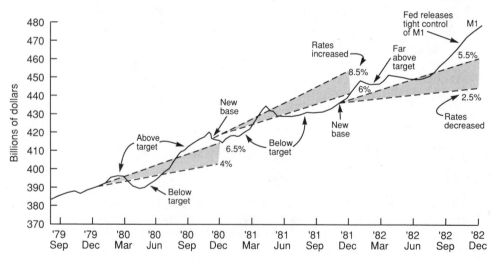

This figure covers the period from October 1979 through October 1982—the period during which the Fed's "operating procedure" called for close control of the growth rate of the M1 money supply. The figure indicates that most of the time the money-growth rate was either above or below target. Some observers say that the Fed didn't really try to keep money growth "on target." Others conclude that close control over money growth from month to month is not possible.

Source: The Brookings Review (Spring 1983).

The Unexpected Decrease in M1 Velocity

During the early 1980s, while the Fed was trying to hold tight on the money supply, there was a sharp and unexpected decrease in velocity. Throughout the 1960s and '70s the trend in velocity had been for a 3% per year increase. But between 1981 and 1982, velocity dropped by 4%—the first significant drop in about thirty years.

The Fed had expected velocity to continue to rise, according to the past trend. But with this drop in velocity, it turned out that money was significantly tighter than the Fed had intended. Remember the previous explanation of what happens when the money supply is targeted and the demand for money increases? That's what began happening in 1981. And from then on M1 velocity continued to decline right up to 1988.

The End of the Fed's So-Called "Monetarist Experiment"

In 1982 there was widespread dissatisfaction with what the Fed was doing. The economy was in the worst recession since the Great Depression of the 1930s. The money supply was tight and real interest rates were higher than at any time in recent decades.

Dissatisfaction with the Fed's tight money policy and high interest rates led to the introduction of bills in both houses of Congress which would require the Fed to specify *interest rate targets*, and to report these targets to Congress. But before Congress acted, the Fed acted.

During the second half of 1982 the Fed decided that its hold on M1 money growth should be relaxed. This policy shift was announced in October and thereafter the M1 growth rate accelerated rapidly (see figure 24-4). Milton Friedman and several other monetarist economists warned that a sharp rise in inflation soon would result.[2] But that isn't what happened. The demand for money balances continued to increase (velocity continued to decrease) instead.

By 1983 the decrease in velocity (increase in the demand for money balances) was clearly observable. So what about the idea of targeting the M1 money supply? It was becoming, at best, questionable. The availability of interest-bearing checking accounts and other financial innovations obviously had significantly shifted (increased) the demand of the public to hold M1 money balances.

FLEXIBLE POLICIES FOR UNCERTAIN TIMES: THE LATE 1980s

In 1982 the Fed moved away from its money supply target. It has been taking a more pragmatic and eclectic approach ever since. The Fed members now seem to try to watch all of the available indicators all of the time and to use as targets the one or ones which appear to be giving the most reliable signals.

---

[2] Milton Friedman, "Why a Surge of Inflation is Likely Next Year," *The Wall Street Journal*, Thursday September 1, 1983.

The Fed has continued to watch money supply figures, of course. But by the mid-1980s it was clear that M1 was no longer reliable as an intermediate target. M1 was growing at double digit rates much of the time in the mid-1980s, while the inflation rate remained below 4% and the rate of GNP growth remained below 3%. What was happening to all of that new M1 money? It was puddling up in people's money balances—responding to the public's desire to hold larger money balances.

Present Fed Policy: Targeting the Ultimate Goals

What can the Fed do when there appears to be a breakdown in some of its "honored indicators?" The Fed now appears to be paying more attention to its *ultimate goal figures* and using those in deciding on monetary policy.

What's happening to the inflation rate, right now? At what rate has GNP been growing lately? What's the employment (and unemployment) picture in the economy? What's happening to the international value of the dollar? Are the financial markets and interest rates performing appropriately? Are there any other visible indicators which should be considered as we decide on appropriate monetary policy?

A Comment by Minneapolis Fed Bank President Gary Stern. In the 1985 *Annual Report* of the Federal Reserve Bank of Minneapolis, the bank's president, Gary Stern, says (on pp. 3–5):

> "The Fed ... uses all the information available ... to move as closely as possible to its broad goals. This means not targeting anything except those goals. ... the Fed's money measures are not targeted. They are instead among the many variables the Fed uses to determine how next to aim at its goals by adjusting its instruments."[3]

Clearly, President Stern of the Minneapolis Fed is telling us that the Fed does not, in a strict sense, target the money supply variables. Instead, it makes its policy decisions on the basis of *all available information*.

A Comment By St. Louis Fed Bank Economist Philip A. Nuetzel. An article in the February, 1987 *Review* of the Federal Reserve Bank of St. Louis confirms Stern's conclusions. The article, "The FOMC in 1986: Flexible Policy for Uncertain Times," By St. Louis Fed Bank economist Philip A. Nuetzel, says (p. 15):

> "As the year (1986) progressed, the (Federal Open Market) Committee deemphasized M1 as a guide to policy while focusing on the broader monetary aggregates, M2 and M3, and several indicators of economic and financial conditions. In the uncertain economic environment that prevailed in 1986, the Committee was flexible in its approach to monetary policy."

Box 24-3 gives more of what Neutzel said about the FOMC and its activities (flexible policies) during 1986.

---

[3] Gary Stern, "The Fed's Money Supply Ranges: Still Useful After All These Years," Federal Reserve Bank of Minneapolis, 1985 *Annual Report*, pp. 3–5.

Box 24-3

Feature: Philip A. Neutzel's Report on the FOMC in 1986

The Federal Open Market Committee (FOMC) consists of 12 members: the seven members of the Federal Reserve Board of Governors and five of the 12 Federal Reserve Bank presidents. The chairman of the Board of Governors is, by tradition, also chairman of the Committee. The president of the New York Federal Reserve Bank is, also by tradition, its vice chairman. All Federal Reserve Bank presidents attend Committee meetings and present their views, but only those who are members of the Committee may vote. Four memberships rotate among Bank presidents and are held for one-year terms beginning on March 1 of each year. The president of the New York Federal Reserve Bank is a permanent voting member of the Committee.

The Committee met eight times at regularly scheduled meetings during 1986 to discuss economic trends and to decide upon the future course of open-market operations.[1] As in previous years, telephone or telegram consultations were held occasionally between scheduled meetings. During each regularly scheduled meeting, a directive was issued to the Federal Reserve Bank of New York. Each directive contained a short review of economic developments, the general economic goals sought by the Committee, the Committee's long-run monetary growth objectives and instructions to the Manager of the System Open Market Account at the New York Bank for conduct of open-market operations. These instructions typically were stated in terms of the degree of pressure on reserve positions. The latter were associated with expected short-term growth rates for M1, M2 and M3 that were in turn considered to be consistent with desired longer-run growth rates of the monetary aggregates.[2] The Committee also specified intermeeting ranges for the federal funds rate. These ranges provide a mechanism for initiating consultations between meetings whenever it appears that the constraint of the federal funds rate is proving inconsistent with the objectives for the behavior of the monetary aggregates.

The account manager has the major responsibility for formulating plans regarding the timing, types and amount of daily buying and selling of securities in fulfilling the Committee's directive. Each morning the manager and his staff plan the open-market operations for that day. This plan is developed on the basis of the Committee's directive and the latest developments affecting money and credit market conditions, the growth of the monetary aggregates and bank reserve conditions. The manager also consults with the Board of Governors' staff. Present market conditions and open-market operations that the manager proposes to execute are discussed each morning in a telephone conference call involving the staff at the New York Bank, the Board and one voting president and his staff. Other members of the Committee may participate and are informed of the daily plan by internal memo or wire.

The directives issued by the Committee and a summary of the reasons for Committee actions are published in the "Record of Policy Actions of the Federal Open Market Committee." The "Record" for each meeting is released a few days after the Committee meeting. Soon after its release, it appears in the *Federal Reserve Bulletin*. In addition, "Records" for the entire year are published in the annual report of the Board of Governors.

Source: Philip A. Nuetzel, "Organization of the Committee in 1986," Federal Reserve Bank of St. Louis, February 1987, pp. 20–21.

---

[1] No formal meetings were held in January, March, June and October.

[2] In July, the FOMC agreed that M1 growth in excess of its annual target range would be acceptable and discontinued statements regarding the Committee's expectations for short-run growth in M1.

SUMMARY

- It is impossible for the central bank to follow a fixed-money growth rule and at the same time to stabilize interest rates. Strict adherence to either objective requires that the other be abandoned.

- It is possible for the Fed to *monitor* both money supply and interest rate changes and to "trade off" some stability in one to try to achieve more stability in the other.

- From 1941 to 1951 the Fed followed a policy of "pegging" bond prices and interest rates. The Fed bought billions of dollars worth of bonds and poured these new reserves into the banking system.

- In March of 1951 an **Accord** was reached between the Fed and the Administration in which the Fed agreed to continue to peg long-term bond prices, but at somewhat less than par.

- From the early 1950s to the mid-'60s the Fed used "free reserves" as an operating target. This approach was severely criticized by the monetarists, and the Fed abandoned free-reserves targeting in 1966 and shifted to a Fed funds rate target.

- During the 1970s the Fed was monitoring both interest rates and the money supply, trying to keep both within "target ranges." Since 1975 the Fed has been required by Congress to choose money-growth targets.

- During the period from October 1979 to October 1982 the Fed largely abandoned the interest rate target and followed an announced "operating procedure" of targeting only the money supply. Interest rates were high and volatile, and the economy experienced a serious recession. During this period M1 growth was erratic and money was tighter than intended because of an unexpected drop in M1 velocity.

- During the 1980s M1 velocity slowed and became so unstable that the Fed abandoned this aggregate as a policy target.

- By the late 1980s the Fed was following a flexible, pragmatic approach, monitoring all available indicators but strictly targeting none. Increasingly it has been considering **ultimate goals** in making its monetary policy decisions.

Important Principles, Issues, Concepts, Terms

The conflict between money supply and interest rate targeting

The difference between the money stock and the supply of loanable funds

Effect of an increase in the demand for loanable funds

Interest rate response to an increase of Dlf

Effect of money stock changes on supply of loanable funds

Why a "money-growth rule" policy requires no discretionary decisions

How it's possible to "sort of" target both M and i

The Fed's World War II bond prices and interest rate pegging episode

The Fed-Treasury "Accord"

The logic of and problems with targeting "free reserves"

Targeting Fed funds

Targeting Fed funds and the money supply

The 1975 Congressional resolution requiring money supply targeting

The *Federal Reserve Reform Act of 1977*

Why Congressional requirements for monetary targeting are not strict

The so-called "monetarist experiment" (Oct. 1979–Oct. 1982)

M1 growth during the "monetarist experiment"

The behavior of M1 velocity during the 1980s

Pragmatic, eclectic monetary policy

"Ultimate goals" targeting

Questions

1. Explain why the Fed cannot target both interest rates and the money supply at the same time. Use supply and demand graphs to illustrate.

2. Explain this statement: "Perhaps the Fed can monitor both the money supply and interest rates without strictly targeting either one."

3. Describe the Fed's "bond market pegging" episode (1941–1951) and the 1951 "accord."

4. Describe the changing policies and targets of the 1950s through the 1970s.

5. Describe the so-called "monetarist experiment" of 1979 through October 1982.

6. What happened to M1 velocity during the 1980s, and why was this significant for monetary policy?

7. In the late 1980s, what was the Fed targeting? Do you agree or disagree with Fed policy during the 1980s? Discuss.

Suggested Readings

Acheson, Keith, and John Chant. "Bureaucratic Theory and the Choice of Central Bank Goals: The Case of Canada." *Journal of Money, Credit and Banking* 5. (May 1973), 637–56.

Antonvic, Madelyn. "High and Volatile Real Interest Rates: Where Does the Fed Fit In?" *Journal of Money, Credit and Banking* 18. (February 1986), 18–27.

Berkman, Neil G., and Richard W. Kopeke. "The Money Stock: Out of Control or What?" *New England Economic Review.* Federal Reserve Bank of Boston (January/February 1979), 5–19.

Blinder, Alan S. "Tight Money and Loose Fiscal Policy." *Society.* July/August 1987.

Bluestein, Paul. "Monetary Zeal: How Federal Reserve Under Volcker Finally Slowed Down Inflation." *The Wall Street Journal.* December 7, 1984.

Board of Governors of the Federal Reserve System. *New Monetary Control Procedures.* Board of Governors: Washington, D.C., 1981.

Brunner, Karl. "The Case Against Monetary Activism." *Lloyds Bank Review* 139. (January 1981), 20–30.

Burns, Arthur. *The Anguish of Central Banking.* Washington, D.C.: American Enterprise Institute, 1980.

Cagan, Phillip. *Determinants and Effects of Changes in the Stock of Money, 1875–1960.* New York: Columbia University Press, 1965.

Cukierman, Alex. "Central Bank Behavior and Credibility: Some Recent Theoretical Developments." *Review.* Federal Reserve Bank of St. Louis (May 1986), 5–17.

D'Arista, Jane. "Federal Reserve Structure and the Development of Monetary Policy: 1915–1935." Staff Report of the Subcommittee on Domestic finance. Committee on Banking and Currency, House of Representatives, December 1971.

Friedman, Milton. "Lessons from the 1979–1982 Monetary Policy Experiment." *American Economic Review* 74. (May 1984), 397–400.

———. *A Program for Monetary Stability.* New York: Fordham University Press, 1959.

Goodfriend, Marvin. "Discount Window Borrowing, Monetary Policy, and the Post-October 6, 1979 Federal Reserve Operating Procedure." *Journal of Monetary Economics,* vol. 12, 1983.

Greenfield, Robert, and Leland Yeager. "A Laissez-Faire Approach to Monetary Stability." *Journal of Money, Credit and Banking* 15. (August 1983), 302–15.

Holmes, Alan. "Operational Constraints on Stabilization of Money Supply Growth." *Controlling the Monetary Aggregates.* Federal Reserve Bank of Boston (June 1979), 65–77.

Humphrey, Thomas M. "The Classical Concept of the Lender of Last Resort." *Economic Review.* Federal Reserve Bank of Richmond, January/February 1975.

Kane, Edward. "Good Intentions and Unintended Evil: The Case Against Selective Credit Allocation." *Journal of Money, Credit and Banking.* February 1977.

Kopcke, Richard W. "How Erratic is Money Growth?" *New England Economic Review.* (May/June 1986), 3–20.

Lombra, Raymone E. "Reflections on Burn's Reflections." *Journal of Money, Credit and Banking.* February 1980, pp. 94–105.

Meigs, A. James. *Free Reserves and the Money Supply.* Chicago: University of Chicago Press, 1962.

Melton, William. *Inside the Fed.* Homewood, Ill.: Dow Jones-Irwin, 1985.

Meltzer, Allan H., Alfred S. Eichner, Marc A. Miles, and James K. Galbraith. "Symposium: Reagan's Economic Policies." *Journal of Post Keynesian Economics.* vol. x, no. 4. (Summer 1988), 527–71.

Morris, Frank E. "Rules plus Discretion in Monetary Policy—An Appraisal of our Experience Since October 1979." *New England Economic Review.* Federal Reserve Bank of Boston (September/October 1985), p. 6.

Pierce, James. "The Political Economy of Arthur Burns." *Journal of Finance* 24. (May 1979), 485–96.

Poole, William. "Burnsian Monetary Policy: Eight Years of Progress?" *Journal of Finance* 24. (May 1979), 473–84.

———. "Monetary Policy During the Recession." *Brookings Papers on Economic Activity* 1. 1975, pp. 123–29.

Rowan, Hobart. "It Is Time to Relegate Monetarism to a Museum?" *The Washington Post.* March 28, 1982, p. G5.

Wicker, Elmus. *Federal Reserve Monetary Policy 1917–1933.* New York: Random House, 1966.

CHAPTER 25

Money Supply, Output and Prices: Monetarist and Keynesian Theories, and Real-World Experience

Chapter Objectives

This chapter and the next give a nontechnical overview of the role of money in influencing the economy, and of some agreements and disagreements among economists on this issue. After you study this chapter you will understand and be able to explain:

1. More about the relationships between money, national output and income, and the price level.

2. Areas of agreement and disagreement between Monetarists and Keynesians concerning these relationships.

3. The equation of exchange: $MV = PQ$, and its relationship to the circular flow of the economy.

4. The meanings of and important differences between demand-pull and cost-push inflation.

5. The different analysis required and conclusions reached when the macroeconomic focus is short run instead of long run.

6. Some of the causes, effects, and conclusions to be reached from the 1980–82 recession.

EVERYBODY KNOWS THAT "MONEY MATTERS," BUT HOW MUCH? AND WHY?

Far back into history, people have been theorizing about cause and effect relationships in economics. All this time some economic philosophers have been developing theories to explain the relationships between *money* and *the output level* and *the price level*. Would you believe that ideas about money and inflation can be traced all the way back to Confucius, some five centuries before Christ? It's true.[1]

---

[1] For example, see: Hugo Hegeland, *The Quantity Theory of Money*, New York: Augustus M. Kelly, 1969.

Early Economic Philosophers Dealt with This Issue

Economic philosophers during the medieval period and later during the Renaissance were developing theories to try to explain the relationship between money, and output and prices. Beginning in the 1500s, several well-known British philosopher-economists—including John Hale in the mid-1500s, John Locke in the late 1600s, and David Hume in the mid-1700s—focused on this issue. And of course Adam Smith analyzed this issue in his famous book, *An Inquiry into the Nature and Causes of the Wealth of Nations* (1776).

Since Adam Smith's time, the analysis of the relationship between the supply of money and the output level and the price level has been a major issue of economic investigation, analysis, and controversy. And even today (in the late-1980s) economists are still investigating and analyzing this issue and there are still some important areas of disagreement.[2]

Most Economists Agree That Money Plays an Important Macroeconomic Role

Almost all economists now agree that there is a positive relationship between the size of the money supply and (1) the level of output in the short run and (2) the level of prices in the long run. That is, an increase in the money supply tends to bring *more output in the short run* and *higher prices in the long run*. But *how close* is this positive relationship? Will a 10% increase in the money supply result in a 10% increase in output in the short run? And then a 10% increase in prices in the long run? Or perhaps more (or less) than 10%?

And how does this "cause and effect mechanism" work? What are the factors that would cause the relationship to be close? Or not so close? These are issues you'll be investigating in this chapter.

AN INTRODUCTION TO THE KEYNESIAN-MONETARIST CONTROVERSY

Whenever economists are discussing questions about how money influences the economy and the price level, the Keynesian-monetarist controversy is sure to surface. So right up front, you need to know what this controversy is all about.

What Is Meant by Monetarist? And Keynesian?

The term "monetarist" has been applied to theories (and to economists who espouse the theories) which focus on the importance of the quantity of money (and changes in the quantity of money) in influencing the price level (the inflation rate). Traditional monetarist theory concludes that money supply changes result in price level changes, not in changes in the real quantity of output or income in

---

[2] For a good explanation of the historical development of theory regarding the quantity of money and its relationship to output and the price level, see: Edmund Whittaker, *Schools and Streams of Economic Thought*, Chicago: Rand McNally and Co., 1960.

the economy. Professor Milton Friedman is, and has been for many years, the recognized leader of the modern monetarist school of thought.

The word "Keynesian" (KAYN-zian) refers to the theories (and to the economists who espouse the theories) introduced by John Maynard Keynes (KAYns) during the 1930s, especially the theories explained in his book *The General Theory of Employment, Interest and Money* (1936). Keynesian theory disagrees with the monetarist conclusions regarding the predictable relationship between changes in the **money supply** and changes in the **price level**. It focuses on factors other than money and attributes to them a causal role in influencing the macroeconomy. Keynesian theory sees *real output* (real income) as variable, and responsive, both to changes in the size of the money supply, and to other factors as well.

The "Long-Run" View of Monetarist Theory

The root cause of the disagreement between traditional monetarist theory and Keynesian theory lies in the *conflicting assumptions* about the economy. Traditional monetarist theory is based on the assumptions of neoclassical economics. It assumes that the economy is basically stable and self-correcting. It focuses on the long run and assumes that any short-run "ups and downs" in the economy (a recession, for example) is a temporary condition which natural market forces will work out, in due time.

Monetarist theory assumes that "full employment and stable prices" is the natural condition of the economy. This "natural condition" assumes that the money supply growth rate is exactly equal to the output growth rate. Economic conditions will deviate from this equilibrium only temporarily, and any such deviations are entirely self-correcting. Any economic policies which might be introduced to try to stabilize the economy—to reduce unemployment and increase real output—not only would fail, but ultimately would worsen conditions in the economy. So if the economy is temporarily depressed, there's nothing we can effectively do to improve the situation. We must wait for the automatic adjustments which, in the long run, will bring full employment.

The "Short-Run" View of Keynesian Theory

Keynesian theory accepts the idea that natural market forces are powerful. But Keynesian theory concludes that sometimes these forces are not sufficiently powerful to guarantee a healthy full-employment economy. Keynesian theory focuses, not on the *long-run equilibrium* condition, but on the *short-run deviations* from the long-run full-employment equilibrium.

Keynesian theory does not accept the monetarist theoretical description of the long-run equilibrium as an accurate approximation of the real world, or as the appropriate guide for economic policy. About waiting for the arrival of "long-run equilibrium," you know what Keynes said: "In the long run, we are all dead!"

Long-Run Focus? Short-Run Focus? What Difference Does It Make?

The question we are investigating here concerns the relationship between changes in the size of the money supply and changes in the level of output and prices. So what difference does it make? Suppose you take the monetarist long-run view, that the economy (because of the natural forces of the market) can be assumed to be fully employed. Or suppose you take the Keynesian short-run view and assume that at this moment the economy may not be fully employed—may, in fact, be in a serious recession or depression. It makes a world of difference which theoretical model of the economy you choose!

Suppose you assume that the economy is at full employment. Then suppose, in that theoretical model, that the money supply increases by 10% and total spending increases by 10%. Where do the goods and services come from to increase aggregate supply (Q) by 10% to meet that 10% increase in aggregate demand (MV)? Nowhere![3] So what happens? Prices must go up by 10%. In the equation of exchange (MV = PQ), with MV increasing and Q fixed, what happens? Prices (P) must go up. Inflation.

The Nominal Value of the "Real Flow" Always Equals the Nominal Value of the "Money Flow"

You already know that in our simplified model of the circular flow of the economy the nominal value of the *real flow* (goods and services) will always be exactly equal to the nominal value of the money flow. In this simplified model, all spending is for *output* and generates *income*. Transactions in used goods and spending for financial instruments are ignored.

In this model, if the dollar value of the money flow increases by 10%, then the dollar value of the real flow (inputs and outputs) will also increase by 10%. If the quantity of real goods and services cannot increase, then the prices of the goods and services must go up by 10%.

The Monetarist Conclusions. If we are willing to accept the monetarist assumptions (1) that the value of goods and services being produced can't increase very much because the economy tends to operate near full employment, and (2) that a 10% increase in the size of the money supply will result in a 10% increase in total spending, then the resulting conclusions are obvious. A 10% increase in the size of the money supply will result in a 10% increase in the level of prices.

The monetarists do not say that as soon as the money supply increases, total spending will increase by the same proportion and that prices will immediately adjust by the same proportion. The disequilibrating influence of the money supply increase will take some time to work itself out. There will be a lag between the time that the money supply increases and the time that total spending increases.

As total spending increases, in the short run, output will increase. There will be a period during which the economy will operate at a rate *greater than* its "natural full employment rate." The monetarist position is that ultimately—after all of the intermediate conditions have worked themselves out—the price level in the economy will be higher by the amount of the increase in the money supply, minus any growth in the size of the real flow of goods and services which may

---

[3] If surplus resources or products existed in foreign countries perhaps it would be possible to buy goods and services from foreigners to meet the 10% increase in demand. But let's ignore that possibility, for now.

have occurred because of increased productive capacity during the adjustment period.

The Keynesian Conclusions.   Suppose we accept the Keynesian view of the economy and visualize an underemployed situation in which the economy is operating substantially below its full-employment rate. Now there are opportunities throughout the economy to expand production—to produce more goods and services—to generate more output, and income. This is a totally different ball game!

Now if the money supply is increased by 10% and if that results in a 10% increase in total spending, the speed of the economy will increase by 10%. The 10% increase in spending will represent *increased aggregate demand* for goods and services. Businesses soon will begin to hire more workers and buy more material inputs, to step up production and produce more outputs. The "real flow" of goods and services in the economy soon will increase by 10% in response to the 10% increase in the size of the money flow.

In this "Keynesian" case, when the money supply increases, prices remain the same while the size of the *real flow* increases. In terms of the equation of exchange, a 10% increase in MV results in a 10% increase in Q while P remains constant. This is the Keynesian scenario of an economic recovery. The economy moves from an underemployed to a more fully employed position.

The Policy Implications of the Keynesian-Monetarist Controversy

The monetary policy implications of the Keynesian-monetarist controversy are obvious. Keynesians would say: "Let the money supply expand whenever necessary to permit economic expansion and overcome unemployment." Monetarists would say: "Don't do that! The economy will be brought to full employment by the stimulus of its own natural forces. If the money supply is permitted to expand, that will add an additional and unwarranted stimulus—an overdose—and the ultimate effect (the *only* ultimate effect) will be to push up prices."

In the monetarist model of the macroeconomy, monetary policy changes certainly affect the economy, but often with *long and variable lags*. So the effect of a policy change is never anywhere near immediate, and we can't accurately predict when the effect will begin to hit the economy. The conclusion: Attempts to stabilize by adjusting monetary policy are likely to turn out to be destabilizing.

You can see that decisions regarding "appropriate" economic policy could depend greatly on whether the policymakers are looking at the world from a "monetarist" or "Keynesian" perspective. Now look at figure 25-1 and you'll see the difference between the monetarist and Keynesian conclusions regarding the use of easy money to try to prevent or overcome a recession.

THE EQUATION OF EXCHANGE (MV = PQ) AND THE KEYNESIAN-MONETARIST DEBATE

The equation of exchange is actually an analysis (a breakdown) of the "output loop" of the circular flow diagram.

**Figure 25-1.   Keynesian vs. Monetarist Views on the Results of
Stimulative Stabilization Policies**

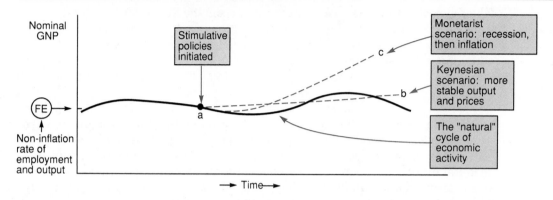

At point a, Keynesians recommend easy money and other stimulative policies to try to abort the recession—to keep unemployment from increasing, to keep real output and income from declining, and to keep the economy growing along path a——b.

The monetarists conclude that stimulative policies added to the natural recovery forces would overshoot full employment and take the economy into inflation along path a——c.

An Analysis of the Output Side of the Circular Flow: MV = PQ

You know that the money supply (M) times the velocity of circulation (V—the number of times the "average dollar" is spent for output in one year) equals total spending for output (and total income) in the economy. That's the spending flow (from households to businesses) illustrated in the circular flow diagram.

The "flow of outputs" (goods and services) can be represented by "P" times "Q," where P is *the average price* for a unit of output and Q is *the number of units of output* being produced and sold during the year.

Here's an example. Suppose there are one billion units flowing in the output flow and the average price per unit is $10. Then the total value of the output flow (PQ) will be $10 billion. So the size of the total spending flow required to pay for this output flow must also be $10 billion. And total income received (national income) must also be $10 billion.

Since total spending for output (by definition) must always be equal to the total value of goods and services bought, MV must always equal PQ. Now take a look at figure 25-2 and you'll see an illustration of *the equation of exchange* in terms of *the output half of the circular flow diagram.*

Is this equation of exchange—this identity—of any help in understanding the relationship between *the size of the money supply* and *the level of output and prices in the economy?* For example, can it help us to see what would happen if the money supply would increase by 10%? Yes it can.

What if V and Q Are Constant?

Suppose we assume that the economy is operating at its "natural full-employment rate." That means that the real flow of goods and services can't expand—at least, not very much—so we can assume that Q in the equation is constant.

Figure 25-2. A Circular Flow Illustration of the Equation of Exchange

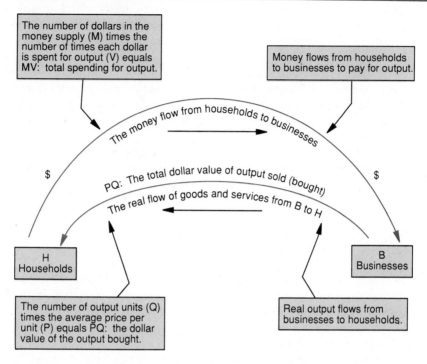

The number of dollars in the money supply (M) times the number of times each dollar is spent for output (V) equals MV: total spending for output.

Money flows from households to businesses to pay for output.

The money flow from households to businesses

PQ: The total dollar value of output sold (bought)

The real flow of goods and services from B to H

$

$

H
Households

B
Businesses

The number of output units (Q) times the average price per unit (P) equals PQ: the dollar value of the output bought.

Real output flows from businesses to households.

In this view, MV = PQ means: "The total amount spent to buy output (MV) equals the total dollar value of the output bought (PQ)."

Box 25-1

Question: **What Are the Different Ways the Equation of Exchange Might Be Expressed? and How Might That Be Helpful?**

It's obvious that the equation of exchange (MV = PQ) can be expressed in various ways so as to define individually each of the terms in the equation:

$$MV = PQ; M = \frac{PQ}{V}; V = \frac{PQ}{M};$$

$$P = \frac{MV}{Q}; Q = \frac{MV}{P}.$$

One useful form of the equation is: $M = \frac{1}{V}PQ$.

You will recognize that the fraction $\frac{1}{V}$ is really k. So this equation can also be expressed:

$$M = kPQ.$$

This M = kPQ form of the equation shows the quantity of money (the money supply) on the left and the quantity of money demanded (expressed as a fraction of national income) on the right. This latter form of the equation of exchange is referred to as the "Cambridge equation" because it uses the "Cambridge k" which was developed and used by Alfred Marshall, A. C. Pigou and other economists at Cambridge University in England.

The MV = PQ form of the equation is associated with the early twentieth century American economist, Irving Fisher.

Suppose we also assume that in these "normal and stable" times, nothing has happened to abnormally influence the velocity of turnover of money—no new definitions of the money supply, no shocking news which might cause people's expectations regarding inflation or economic conditions to change—then there would be no reason to expect any change in velocity. So we could assume velocity to be constant.

If both Q and V are constant, it's obvious what happens when M increases by 10%. Since V is constant, a 10% increase in M will (must!) translate into a 10% increase in the size of the money flow (spending flow). And since Q is constant the *real* size of the output flow can't increase. So prices must increase. How much? By 10%.

With Q and V constant, there is a direct link between M (the size of the money supply) and P (the price level). Any percentage increase in the money supply will result in the same percentage increase in the level of prices.

The Long-Run View: V and Q Can Be Assumed to Be Constant

But who believes that V and Q (in the real world of the 1980s) are really constant? In the short run, nobody. But the monetarist position is that in the long run there is a strong tendency toward constancy for both V and Q.

The monetarist position is that the relationship between M and P is very strong—in fact, strong enough to be used as *the most important guide* for directing the nation's monetary policy. The bottom line of monetarist theory is this: All money supply increases in excess of the rate of output growth will (in the long run) translate into price increases—inflation.

The Keynesian Short-Run View: V and Q Are Variable

You can already guess what Keynesians would have to say about this. They wouldn't accept the constancy of either V or Q. They would say that:

1. *Increased M may not cause increased spending.* In any short-run period, velocity is neither stable nor predictable. Therefore a change in the size of the money supply will not have a predictable influence on the size of total spending. Suppose the money supply is increasing during a time when people want to build up their money balances. Then the increase in M may be entirely offset by a decrease in V, in which case there would be no change at all in total spending. The increase in M would be entirely offset by the decrease in V.

2. *Increased spending may not cause increased P.* Even when increased M does cause total spending to increase, this will not necessarily cause prices to rise. Output might increase by an amount equal to the increase in spending. That is, Q might increase enough to absorb all of the spending increase, leaving P unchanged.

Box 25-2

Question: What's the Difference Between the Transactions Velocity and the Income Velocity of Money?

There are two (basically different) definitions of the term "velocity of circulation": (1) "total transactions" velocity and (2) "income" or "output" velocity.

Many exchange transactions do not generate income or output. If you buy my shares of IBM stock or my old house or my old car, we're just exchanging assets between ourselves. All such transactions are outside the circular flow because no new income or output is generated. (Minor exception: If there's a stock broker or real estate broker involved in the deal, some "commission income" will be generated.)

If you want to include all of these non-income- and non-output-generating transac-

tions in your equation of exchange, then you must use the form: MV = PT where "T" means *total transactions.* In this equation, "V" means the *transactions velocity*—the "total turnover velocity" of money.

The volume of income- and output-generating spending is considerably smaller than the volume of total exchange transactions. So "income" or "output" velocity is much smaller than "total turnover" velocity. In the equation MV = PQ, the "V" represents only "income" (or "output") velocity. That's the definition of velocity that will be used throughout this book except where otherwise noted.

The Monetarists Cite the Historical Statistics

How do the monetarists respond? They say that the Keynesians are looking at and emphasizing the wrong things. The monetarists agree that during short-run periods of time the claims of the Keynesians sometimes appear to be true. But the monetarists point out that throughout recorded history there has never been a time when inflation was not associated with an increasing money supply. And there has never been a time when the money supply has increased very fast and over an extended period of time when the level of prices did not also increase.[7]

In the United States in the late-1980s, consumer prices are about eight times as high as they were in the late 1930s, and more than three times as high as in the early 1960s. Have increases in the size of the U.S. money supply paralleled these increases in prices? Not exactly. But as you look at figure 25-3 you can see that—at least up until the beginning of the 1980s—there appears to have been a definite relationship.

The 1980s: An Apparent Break in the Link Between M1 and the Economy

Figure 25-3 seems to indicate that now, in the 1980s, something is different in the relationship between money supply changes and price level changes. And to be sure *there have been* some significant changes during the 1980s, not only in the relationship between money supply changes and price level changes, but between money supply changes and real output (and income) as well. By the mid-1980s

---

[7] For historical evidence of this P = *f*(M) relationship, see the monumental study by Milton Friedman and Anna Schwartz: *A Monetary History of the United States, 1867–1960,* Princeton, N.J.: Princeton University Press, 1963.

Figure 25-3.   M1 Growth and Inflation M1 Growth Lagged Eight Quarters

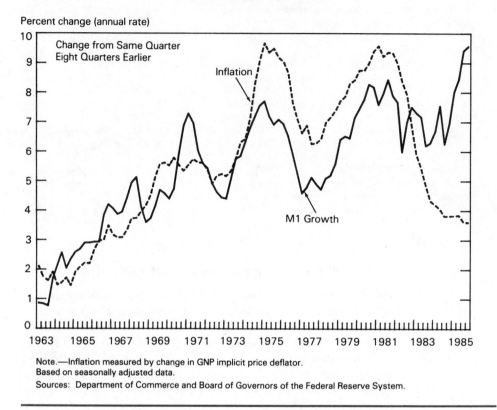

M1 Growth and Inflation
M1 Growth Lagged Eight Quarters

Percent change (annual rate)

Note.—Inflation measured by change in GNP implicit price deflator.
Based on seasonally adjusted data.
Sources: Department of Commerce and Board of Governors of the Federal Reserve System.

Source: The Economic Report of the President, February, 1986, Washington D.C., U.S. Government Printing Office, p. 28.

many economists were referring to the "breakdown" of the relationship between money, and prices, output and income. To quote a recent study:

> For years M1 has been regarded as the single most reliable tool for the information and execution of monetary policy. Serving as both compass and rudder, it forecast future rates of economic growth and inflation, while providing the Federal Reserve with a powerful mechanism to affect those rates.... But after 1980, the M1 models suddenly lost their forecasting ability and they have not recovered it since.[8]

The article goes on to explain various recommendations for changing the measures of the monetary aggregates, or changing the measures of income, to try to improve the strength of the relationship between money supply changes and price, output, and income changes. But none of these redefinitions have been able

---

[8] Diane F. Siegal and Steven Strongin, "Can the Monetary Models Be Fixed?," *FRB Chicago Economic Perspectives,* November/December 1986, p. 3.

to re-establish a close relationship between these variables. The article concludes that:

> These findings have several implications for monetary policymakers. First, increases in the rate of money growth should not be entirely ignored as an indicator of possible future increases in inflation. Second, the money/real income model needs significant revision before it can be relied on for policy purposes. Pure monetary models cannot adequately explain the path real economic growth has taken in the 1980s.[9]

Questions regarding the "new relationships" between money and the economy are receiving much serious effort by economists during the 1980s. But at the time this book goes to press, there are no clear answers in sight. During the last half of the 1980s there is considerably less certainty about the relationship between the M1 money supply and the economy than there was at the beginning of the decade.

MONEY AND INFLATION: TOO MUCH MONEY CHASING TOO FEW GOODS? COST PUSH? OR WHAT?

There has been much investigation (and controversy) regarding the causes of inflation. This section goes into that issue.

Excess Money Can Cause Demand-Pull Inflation

The classic explanation of inflation—the one which economic philosophers have been using for hundreds of years—is that there is too much money chasing too few goods. As more and more money is created, it is owned by people and businesses who proceed to spend it. As they spend it they are trying to buy more goods than are being produced—more than are available to be bought. As the money supply continues to increase, people keep bidding against each other for the increasingly scarce goods. Prices just keep going up.

The obvious thing to do is to stop creating money. So whenever inflation begins, why don't we just do that? Because sometimes stopping inflation isn't quite so simple.

In a modern-day economic system, perhaps money isn't the only culprit in the inflation process. Perhaps there are factors other than the size of the money supply—or the size of the total spending flow as compared with the size of the output flow—which may be partly responsible for pushing prices up and causing inflation.

What About Cost-Push Inflation?

Do you suppose any sellers have every raised their prices even when there wasn't too much money chasing after what they were selling? Do you suppose labor unions have ever pushed for wage increases which were then passed forward as

---

[9] Ibid. pp. 12–13.

price increases? Even in the absence of too much money chasing those output goods?

The OPEC cartel provides a prime example. OPEC pushed up the international price of oil by about 1400 percent between the early 1970s and the early 1980s. The oil price was so inflated over this period that the relative value of the oil-buying dollar dropped to about 7 cents—that is, in the early 1980s, one dollar would only buy as much oil as you could have bought with 7 cents back in the early 1970s.

In the U.S. and world economy there are many sellers of goods and services who have enough power in the market to push their prices up. That's true of businesses, labor unions, governments, professional people, and others. And there's no question that these people often try to exercise their economic power to push up their prices. The point is that in the case of cost-push inflation, sometimes the money supply may be the *follower* (not the leader) in the inflation process. But note this: Unless the money supply is permitted to expand, the inflation cannot continue. The following sections explain.

Higher Prices Require either (1) More Spending, or (2) Less Output

Consider cost-push inflation in terms of the equation of exchange: $MV = PQ$. Assume for the moment that V is constant. Then if P is increasing because sellers are raising their prices, either M must be increasing or Q must be decreasing. Suppose M is not permitted to increase. Then Q will be forced to decrease. Production will be cut back. The economy will slow down and unemployment will increase.

It's obvious that at higher prices, more dollars of total spending are required to buy all of the output. Suppose sellers push output prices up by 10%. Then to buy all of this output, total spending must also increase by 10%. But suppose the money supply is not permitted to increase. Then, with V assumed to be constant, *total spending cannot increase.* So 10% of the output will not be bought.

As businesses see their unsold output inventories piling up, they have a choice. Either they can cut back their prices (thus solving the inflation problem) or they can cut back their production (thus creating an unemployment problem). Which will they do?

A business cannot survive if it cuts prices while costs are rising. So usually, businesses with unsold outputs will initially cut production. They will hold the line on prices for as long as they can. Unemployment will increase. Surpluses will develop in the labor and other input markets.

Feeding the Fires of Cost-Push Inflation

Monetary policymakers are faced with a dilemma. If they let the money supply expand to stimulate more spending and try to reduce the unemployment, that will feed the fires of cost-push inflation. In this case, it wasn't a money supply increase which caused prices to start going up. But if we let the money supply keep expanding to try to hold down unemployment, *the increasing money supply will permit the cost-push inflation to continue.*

Restricting Money Growth May Cause Serious Recession

So what should we do? Let the money supply expand to reduce unemployment? And feed the fires of continuing cost-push inflation? Or should we do the opposite?—hold tight on the money supply, let unemployment stay large and grow larger, and let businesses go broke because they can't sell enough of their high-cost, high-priced products?

Should we let the economy go into a serious recession?—bad enough so that the high-cost workers will be willing to work for lower wages? And the high-priced producers will be willing to sell their products for lower prices, even if it means selling below cost?

Eventually a tight money policy would cure the inflation. But how much unemployment and recession would the economy have to experience before the inflation process would be stopped? Different theories give different answers to this question and each real-world case would be unique and not likely to behave exactly like any other case. But the experience of the American economy during the recession of 1980–82 provides an interesting example of one such case.

THE "TIGHT MONEY" RECESSION OF 1980–82

In the early 1960s, the annual inflation rate in the U.S. economy was less than 2%. By the end of the 1960s it was about 5%. In the first half of the 1970s it was about 7%. During the last half of the 1970s it was about 9%. During 1979 the inflation rate moved over 10%. Alarming!

In early October of 1979 Fed Board Chairman Paul Volcker and other Board members participated in a secret weekend meeting with President Carter and his advisers at the White House. Following the meeting on Saturday, October 6, 1979, Volcker announced strong money-tightening measures. He said that, effective immediately, the money supply would no longer be permitted to expand, no matter how "tight" it might become—and no matter how high interest rates might go. Following that announcement, interest rates soared and the stock and bond markets tumbled.

The Highest U.S. Interest Rates in Modern Times

By April of 1980 the "prime rate"—the interest rate banks charge their most credit-worthy short-term borrowers—had risen from the more normal levels of less than 10%, to 21.5%. High quality corporate bonds were paying interest rates of more than 15%.

These rates seemed exceedingly high. But in *real* terms they weren't high at all. In fact, part of the time they were *negative*.

Real Rates and Nominal Rates

The nominal rate of interest is the rate actually quoted. The real rate is the nominal rate minus the inflation rate. Why subtract the inflation rate from the nominal rate? Here's why.

The nominal rate is "the nominal rate of increase in the value of your money assets, over time." The inflation rate is "the actual rate of decrease in the value of your money assets over time." For example, if you're earning a 10% nominal rate and the inflation rate turns out to be 15%, that's *a negative real rate* of 5%. Your money assets are decreasing in value at the rate of 5% per year.

For a brief time in early 1980 the U.S. inflation rate reached a peak of 20%. So at that time, a nominal prime rate of 20%, in real terms, wasn't high at all. In fact it was zero! But regardless of the real rates, it appears that the high nominal rates did discourage business investment. By mid-1980 the economy was moving rapidly into recession. Unemployment increased from the less than 6% rate in 1979 to about 8% by mid 1980.

The Serious Recession

During the period 1980–1982 the American economy experienced the most serious recession since World War II. The unemployment rate increased from 7.4% in January 1981 to 8.6% in January 1982 and to 10.8% in January 1983—the highest rate in more than 40 years.

In January of 1983 more than 12 million people were unemployed. In 1982, total output of the economy—real GNP—experienced the worst year-to-year decline in 36 years. Average percentage utilization of industrial capacity in December of 1982 was at a post-war low of 67.3%.

The high nominal interest rates of the early 1980s had a devastating effect on the housing construction industry, on real estate firms, and on new home purchases. Many savings and loan associations and several banks were forced into near bankruptcy and had to be bailed out by the Federal Deposit Insurance Corporation (FDIC) and the Federal Savings and Loan Insurance Corporation (FSLIC).

In early 1982 some people were talking about the possibility of a serious depression brought about by the very high interest rates. Several utility companies cancelled plans to build new power plants and some airlines cancelled orders for new aircraft because of the prohibitively high interest cost.

By the summer of 1982 there was much strong opposition to the Fed's tight money policies. Several members of Congress were working on legislation to amend the Federal Reserve Act and force a change in Fed policy. But before the Congress acted, the Fed acted.

The Inflation Rate Slowed

As the economy slowed, the inflation rate dropped from the high of 20% in early 1980, down to an average for the year (1980) of 12.4%. For 1981 the inflation rate averaged 8.9%. But it was much lower near the end of the year than at the beginning of the year.

By the first quarter of 1982 the inflation rate was down to less than 5%, and it kept decreasing throughout the year. The average inflation rate for the entire year (1982) was only 3.9%—the lowest since the price-controlled year of 1972.

Both *the tight money policy of the Fed* and *the declining prices* of energy were given credit for slowing the inflation. But 1982 was a year of serious recession. Many economists expected inflation to accelerate as the economy began to recover in 1983. But that didn't happen.

The Fed Abandons Its Tight Money Policy

During the first half of 1982 the U.S. money supply increased only very slightly. But in October of 1982 the Fed announced that it was permitting the money supply to increase more rapidly. From mid-year 1982 to mid-year 1983 the money supply increased at the annual rate of about 15%.

In 1983 the economy experienced the most rapid recovery since World War II, yet the inflation rate did not accelerate. And from 1983 until this book went to press in mid-1988, the Fed continued to follow a flexible and fairly permissive monetary policy. Monetary expansion was permitted as appeared necessary to keep interest rates from rising much and to prevent the economy from slipping into recession. The money supply was growing fairly rapidly during this period—much more rapidly at some times than at others—yet inflation remained low. Figure 25-4 indicates that the inflation rate remained at less than 4% until 1987, and that for 1986 it was less than 2%.

Conclusions from the "Tight Money Recession" of 1980–82

The recession of the early 1980s was a special case, and we can't conclude that any other tight-money-induced recession would behave in the same way. But in that special case we can draw some definite conclusions:

* When prices are rising rapidly and the money supply is not permitted to expand very much, the *economy can be forced into a serious recession.*

Figure 25-4.

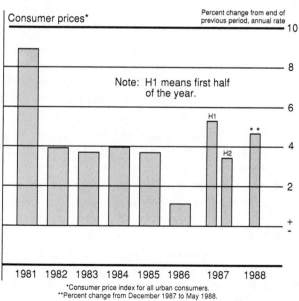

*Consumer price index for all urban consumers.
**Percent change from December 1987 to May 1988.

Source: Board of Governors of the Federal Reserve System, *Monetary Objectives for* 1986, and for 1988, mid-year review of the Federal Reserve Board, Washington D.C., July 1986, p. 6, and July 1988, p. 10.

- After some considerable period of time, *the inflation rate can be expected to come down.*

- Once the inflation rate comes down, an expanding money supply can result in *economic recovery and significant increases in output (Q) without bringing any immediate increase in prices (P).*

In the 1980–82 experience, the "tight-money" method of stopping the inflation proved to be very painful for many people. But, looking back, most people seem to think that, under the circumstances, the painful recession was necessary to break the inflationary spiral—and that therefore the painfulness was justified.

SUMMARY

- The specific relationship between money, output, and prices has long been a subject of controversy—in recent decades, controversy between monetarists, Keynesians, and some others.

- Monetarists assume a "full employment and stable prices" economy, while Keynesians focus on economic instability and assume unemployment exists.

- Keynesians recommend activist policies for economic stabilization, while monetarists conclude that such policies result in increased instability.

- In monetarist theory, changes in the money supply exert their entire influence on the price level, but Keynesian theory assumes that money supply (and total spending) changes can influence employment, output, and real income.

- In terms of the equation of exchange, if both V and Q are constant, a change in M will influence only P. This is the monetarist assumption.

- If both V and Q are variable, increased M might be offset by decreased V, or it might result in increased Q. P remains the same. This is the Keynesian assumption.

- Until the beginning of the 1980s, the M1 growth rate and the inflation rate were closely related. But during the 1980s this relationship has no longer held.

- Demand-pull inflation results from "too much money chasing too few goods." But cost-push inflation results from monopoly power on the sellers' side of the market.

- When prices rise, unless nominal spending also increases, some of the output will not be bought, production will be cut, and unemployment will increase. But increased money supply and increased spending can permit inflation to continue.

- During 1980–82 the U.S. economy experienced the most serious recession since World War II, induced by the Fed's tight money policy. The unemployment rate peaked in January, 1983 at 10.7%—the highest since the Great Depression of the 1930s.

- Throughout the remainder of the 1980s the inflation rate remained low, and the unemployment rate moved slowly down to less than 6%.

- The experience of the 1980–82 recession seems to indicate that tight money can stop inflation, that a serious recession may follow, and that the economy can recover with increased money supply and total spending, without reigniting inflation.

Important Principles, Issues, Concepts, Terms

How the money supply affects output

How the money supply affects prices

Effects of money supply changes in the short run

Effects of money supply changes in the long run

Highlights in the Keynesian-monetarist controversy

Basic assumptions of monetarist theory

Basic assumptions of Keynesian theory

The important differences between long-run focus and short-run focus

The value of the real flow equals the value of the money flow

The real flow can increase in real units or in money value

Policy implications of the Keynesian-monetarist controversy

Different views regarding the effects of government stabilization policies

The equation of exchange (MV = PQ)

The constancy (or variability) of V and Q

Historical relationship between M and P

The 1980s breakdown in the relationship between M1, economic growth, and inflation

Demand-pull inflation

Cost-push inflation

Cost-push inflation requires more M, or less Q

Effects of using tight money to stop cost-push inflation

The Fed's tight money policy of October 6, 1979

Inflation rates and interest rates in the U.S. economy 1979–86

Real and nominal rates of interest

The recession and recovery of 1979–83

Federal Reserve policy 1979–88

Conclusions from the "tight money recession" of 1980–82

Questions

1. Explain the highlights of the Keynesian-monetarist controversy.

2. Explain the policy implications of this controversy.

3. Use the equation of exchange to illustrate the opposite positions of the Keynesian short-run view and the monetarist long-run view.

4. During the 1980s something happened to the relationship between M1, total spend-ing, and the economy. Explain what happened.

5. Describe the monetary policy and economic conditions in the United States during 1980–82. What can we conclude from this experience? Discuss.

6. Explain the role of foreign competition in helping to limit domestic inflation in the United States.

Suggested Readings

Auerbach, Robert D., and Jack L. Ruther. "Money and Income, Is there a Simple Relationship?" *Monthly Review.* Federal Reserve Bank of Kansas City (May 1975), 13–19.

Barro, Robert. "Interest Rate Smoothing." unpublished manuscript, University of Rochester, February 1987.

Berman, Peter I. "The Basic Cause of Inflation, I." *Across the Board* 14 (November 1977), 23–27.

———. "The Basic Cause of Inflation, II." *Across the Board* 15. (May 1978), 67–70.

Breckling, Frank, and Kathleen Classen Utgoff. "Taxes and Inflation." *Policies for Employment, Prices, and Exchange Rates.* A supplement to the *Journal of Monetary Economics* 11. Amsterdam: North Holland, 1979, pp. 223–46.

Clower, Robert. *Monetary Theory: Selected Readings.* New York: Penguin, 1970.

Fieldstein, Martin. "Inflation, Income Taxes, and the Rate of Interest: A Theoretical Analysis." *American Economic Review.* (December 1976), 809–20.

Gibson, Williams. "Interest Rates and Inflationary Expectations: New Evidence." *American Economic Review.* (December 1972), 854–65.

Goodfriend, Marvin. "Interest Rate Smoothing and Price Level Trend-Stationarity." *Journal of Monetary Economics.* May 1987.

Hafer, R. W. "Inflation: Assessing its Recent Behavior and Future Prospects." *Review* 65, no. 7. Federal Reserve Bank of St. Louis (August/September 1983), 36–41.

Kopcke, Richard W. "Financial Assets, Interest Rates, and Money Growth." *New England Economic Review.* (March/April 1987), 17–30.

McCulloch, J. Huston. *Money and Inflation: A Monetarist Approach.* New York: Academic Press, 1975.

Okun, Arthur M. "The Invisible Handshake and the Inflation Process." *Challenge* 22. (January/February 1980), 5–12.

Samuelson, Paul A., and Robert M. Solow. "Analytic Aspects of Anti-Inflation Theory." *American Economic Review* 50, no. 2. (May 1960), 179–94.

Sargent, Thomas J. *Rational Expectations and Inflation.* New York: Harper & Row, 1986.

Tatom, John A. "Does the Stage of the Business Cycle Affect the Inflation Rate?" *Review* 60. Federal Reserve Bank of St. Louis (September 1978), pp. 7–15.

Thornton, Daniel. "Why Does Velocity Matter?" *Review.* Federal Reserve Bank of St. Louis, (December 1983), 5–13.

CHAPTER 26

Money and Inflation: Keynesian and Monetarist Theories Viewed in the Phillips Curve Framework

Chapter Objectives

This chapter goes more deeply into the relationship between money and inflation, and it explains the **Phillips Curve** framework for analyzing this issue. From studying this chapter you will understand and be able to explain:

1. More about the relationships between money and spending, and between the unemployment rate and the inflation rate, and how the Phillips Curve illustrates this.

2. Exactly what a Phillips Curve is, why it is shaped as it is and located where it is, and what factors might cause it to shift.

3. Conditions in the economy which may result in
   a. an unemployment bias, and
   b. an inflation bias.

4. More about the idea of the **natural rate** of unemployment, and how this leads to the **accelerationist** hypothesis.

5. Different conclusions which result from monetarist theory and Keynesian theory on the "unemployment-inflation trade-off."

6. The movement toward some synthesis in the Keynesian-monetarist debate.

THE CONCEPT OF THE PHILLIPS CURVE

In the previous chapter you read about the "tight-money recession" of 1980–82. During that period, unemployment increased significantly while inflation decreased significantly.

The Fed's tight-money policy forced a spending slowdown and this helped to bring down the inflation rate. But the slowdown brought a large increase in unemployment. This experience—inflation down sharply; unemployment up sharply—illustrates the basic idea of what is called the **Phillips Curve**.

The Phillips Curve illustrates the short-run trade-off between unemployment and inflation. The idea is that lower rates of inflation are associated with higher rates of unemployment.

The Trade-Off Between Unemployment and Inflation

The Phillips Curve illustrates this concept: We can have a smaller unemployment rate only if we are willing to accept a larger inflation rate. If we are willing to trade off some price stability (accept a higher inflation rate), then we can have a lower unemployment rate; if we're willing to trade off some employment (to accept a higher unemployment rate), then we can have a lower inflation rate. The Phillips Curve is named for Professor A. W. Phillips who developed the "Curve" in the 1950s.[1]

The Phillips Curve in Terms of MV = PQ

The Phillips curve can be viewed in terms of the equation of exchange (MV = PQ). The Phillips Curve indicates that if we let M increase at a faster rate so that total spending (E) will speed up and result in increased employment and output (Q), we can succeed in doing that. But at the same time (like it or not) prices (P) also will go up.

Also the Phillips Curve tells us that if we restrict the growth of the money supply (M) to slow down total spending (E) to hold down the inflation rate (P), again, we can succeed in doing that. But, like it or not, we'll also see some decrease in Q and therefore, some increase in unemployment.

THE HYPOTHETICAL SHORT-RUN PHILLIPS CURVE

On the Phillips Curve, each point indicates an unemployment rate and the corresponding inflation rate. The inflation rate is measured on the vertical axis and the unemployment rate on the horizontal axis.

The Curve is negatively sloped to indicate that as we get less of one we get more of the other: less inflation means more unemployment; less unemployment means more inflation. Figure 26-1 shows and explains the hypothetical Phillips Curve.

How Stable Is the Phillips Curve?

How stable is the Phillips Curve, from year-to-year, or decade-to-decade? Is it plausible that the Phillips Curve might shift from one short-run period to another? Yes, it is.

In the short run, this "Phillips Curve phenomenon"—the trade-off between unemployment and inflation—is empirically observable. The 1980–82 recession

---

[1] A.W. Phillips, "The relationship between unemployment and the rate of change in money wage rates in the United Kingdom, 1861–1957," *Economica*, New Series 75, November 1958, pp. 283–99.

Figure 26-1.   The Hypothetical Short-Run Phillips Curve

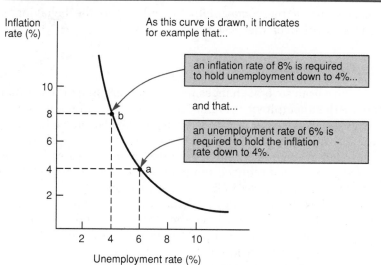

A graphic illustration of the short-run trade-off between inflation and unemployment. In this figure, assume that the inflation rate in the economy is 4% and the unemployment rate is 6% (point a). The curve tells us that an increase in the money supply which would stimulate spending and reduce unemployment to 4%, would simultaneously push the inflation rate up to 8% (point b.)

provides a good example. But for the future, no one can predict what the specific numbers might be.

How much unemployment will correspond to how much inflation? We just don't know. The numbers is one instance might be quite different from the numbers in another instance. What this means is that the Phillips Curve (if we are willing to accept the hypothesis that such a curve exists) is not stable. It shifts.

The only thing we can say with certainty is this: In the short run it is possible to reduce unemployment by easing money to stimulate spending to speed up the economy. But when that is done, the inflation rate is likely to accelerate. Or conversely, inflation can be slowed by tightening money. But when this is done, the economy is likely to slow down. Unemployment is likely to increase.

WHAT MIGHT CAUSE THE CURVE TO SHIFT?

It is obvious that any exogenous influence (outside force) which would push the unemployment rate upward, would shift the Phillips Curve to the right. More unemployment would be associated with each inflation rate.

It is also obvious that any exogenous influence which would push the inflation rate higher would cause the curve to shift upward. For each unemployment rate, the rate of inflation would be higher.

During the last two decades there have been some significant exogenous influences operating on both the unemployment rate and the inflation rate. A brief look at some of these may help to understand the behavior of the short-run Phillips Curve over the past several years.

The Unemployment Bias

There have been several changes in the economy since 1964 which have tended to increase the unemployment rate. The composition of the labor force has changed. Women, teenagers, and part-time workers have become a larger percentage of the labor force. These workers tend to change jobs more often and to experience higher than average unemployment rates. Also, increases in unemployment benefits have somewhat reduced the pain of being unemployed. So now people can afford to remain between jobs for a longer time.[2]

There has been a change in the kinds of labor demanded. Many of the unemployed people do not have the abilities or skills required for the kinds of jobs which are now opening up. Also, minimum wage laws give employers more incentive to replace unskilled labor with machines. Higher wages, pushed by aggressive unions, have also provided businesses increased incentives to reduce the size of the workforce by automating production operations and by all other available means.

All these changes in the labor markets would tend to shift the Phillips Curve to the right, indicating a higher unemployment rate associated with each inflation rate.

The Inflation Bias

What about the inflation rate? Have there been changes which may have biased the economy toward more inflation? There certainly have been some.

As unions push for higher wages they not only stimulate employers to try to reduce the number of employees. They also raise production costs. These higher costs tend to be passed alsong as higher output prices. The substantial amount of market power of some businesses has made it fairly easy for them to pass along cost increases. (Cost-push inflation, remember?)

Sometimes producers with substantial market power can succeed in raising product prices even when cost increases are not involved. OPEC's 1400 percent increase in the price of oil between the early 1970s and the early 1980s provides a clear example of this.

Another important inflationary bias in recent years has come from *inflationary expectations*. From the late 1960s to the early 1980s, labor, businesses, consumers—all of us—were thinking in terms of continuing inflation. We wanted to "buy now before prices go higher." And all of us tried to build some protection against inflation into our employment contracts and into all other kinds of contracts. These built-in contractual price increases pushed the inflation rate up even more.

---

[2] Milton Friedman develops the argument that in recent years there has been an increase in the "natural rate of unemployment" because of such changes. For a thorough analysis, see Milton Friedman, "Nobel Lecture; Inflation and Unemployment," reprinted in the *Journal of Political Economy*, vol. 85, no. 3, 1977, pp. 451–71.

The Biases Eased in the 1980s

By the mid-1980s, neither the unemployment bias nor the inflation bias was as strong as before. During the 1980–82 recession, many labor organizations lost some of their power to push up wages. So employers are not now under such great pressure to reduce their work force and/or to raise prices.

The inflation bias has been greatly reduced by increased competition in product markets—to a significant extent, increased foreign competition—and by the lessening of inflationary expectations.

By the late 1980s, the majority opinion in the business and financial community seemed to be that serious inflation was not an immediate threat to the American economy. The weakening of the OPEC cartel and the collapse of world oil prices is an example of the power of markets to generate competition and to collapse artificially high "cost-push" prices.

Looking back, it appears that there may be some good reasons to assume that the short-run Phillips Curve would have been shifting upward during the 1960s, '70s, and early '80s, and downward since 1982. But is that really what happened? What do the data reveal?

A PHILLIPS CURVE? THE EMPIRICAL EVIDENCE

Figure 26-2 shows the real data for the U.S. economy—the inflation rate and the associated unemployment rate—for each year, 1964 through 1987. What does this graph tell us?

What Do the Inflation-Unemployment Data Points Reveal?

The lesson to be learned from the data points depends on how you choose to view them. If you want to you can connect the points in chronological order (as in figure 26-2) and it's difficult to see any pattern.

Or you might try drawing a series of negatively sloped curves through the data points. If you do that, you'll be drawing Phillips Curves and assuming that the curves are shifting from one time period to another. That's what you'll see in figure 26-3.

Take a few minutes now to study, compare, and read the explanations accompanying figures 26-2 and 26-3.

The Shifting Phillips Curve? A Plausable Explanation

Between the 1960s and the early 1980s, clearly there were increases in both the unemployment bias and the inflation bias in the American economy. You were reading about that a few minutes ago. Then what happened after that?

Effects of the Tight-Money Recession. The tight-money recession of 1980–1982 took its toll on employment. The unemployment rate increased throughout 1980–82, while the inflation rate declined. In January of 1983 the unemployment rate peaked at 10.7%—up from about 6% in 1979—while the inflation rate came down from 12.8% in 1980, to less than 4% in 1983.

**Figure 26-2.   Unemployment Rates and Inflation Rates, 1964–1988:
The "No Phillips Curve" Graph**

When connected in chronological sequence these
data points appear to be randomly distributed.

Inflation Rate (annual percentage increase in consumer prices)

Unemployment Rate
(percentage of civilian labor force
unemployed and seeking jobs)

When you look at the data points indicating
unemployment rates and inflation rates in the
U.S. economy 1964–1988, what you see depends
on how you choose to look at it. Here, the points
are connected in chronological sequence and
there is no obvious pattern. But there are other
ways to look at the data points as you will see in
figure 26-3 on the next page.

Note: The sharp drop in the inflation rate in 1986 reflects the collapse of world oil prices during that year. Excluding
energy prices. The CPI inflation rate in 1986 was 3.8%. The same as in 1985.

Lessening of Unemployment and Inflation Biases. In each of the years after 1982
there was some lessening of both the unemployment bias and the inflation bias in
the American economy. Each year the effects of inflationary expectations lessened. Foreign competition continued to exert its downward pressure on domestic prices. Opportunities for cost-push inflation, both by workers and producers,
significantly decreased. And during the 1980s, world agricultural and raw material prices dropped, while oil prices plummeted—from more than $30 a barrel in
1980 to less than $12 a barrel in early 1986.

So it is not unreasonable to assume that from the end of 1982, as the unemployment and inflation biases weakened, the short-run Phillips Curve shifted to
the left and then stabilized. The data points for 1983 through 1988 could be
interpreted as indicating that result.

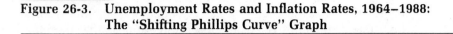

**Figure 26-3.   Unemployment Rates and Inflation Rates, 1964–1988:
The "Shifting Phillips Curve" Graph**

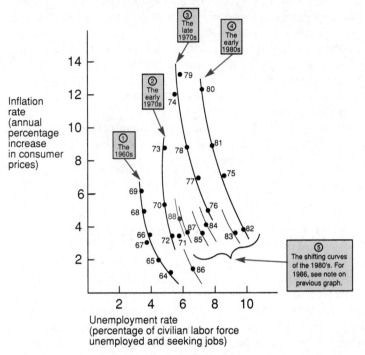

Unemployment rate
(percentage of civilian labor force
unemployed and seeking jobs)

The data points for the 1960s seem to fall into a short-run Phillips Curve
pattern. And the data points for the early 1970s also seem to fall into the
Phillips Curve pattern, but at higher rates of both unemployment and
inflation. Then the data points for the late 1970s seem to fall into a
Phillips Curve pattern at an even higher level—and the points for the
early 1980s, even more so.

Is it possible that the data points 1964–1982 illustrate an upward-
shifting Phillips Curve? And that the points since 1982 illustrate a
downward-shifting and then stabilizing curve? Some economists thinks
so, and, as explained in the text, there is some logical support for their
position.

Is There Really a Phillips Curve?

Some economists deny the existence of any meaningful Phillips Curve. Why?
Because they begin their analysis from a different perspective—with a different
set of assumptions.

For example, suppose it is assumed that the economy will come to its natural
full employment position (Q) by itself, and that velocity (V) is stable. Then the
obvious conclusion is that since the natural employment rate will occur automatically, any increase in M (the money supply) can only (in the long run) exert its
influence on P (the price level). Unemployment will not be affected at all. Therefore no unemployment-inflation trade-off—and that means **no Phillips Curve!**

The opposite set of assumptions leads to the opposite conclusion. Suppose it is assumed that the economy has a tendency (sometimes) for an unnecessarily high rate of unemployment to exist. And suppose that the inflation rate is low. Any increase in the money supply (M) which results in increased total spending (increased aggregate demand) will stimulate production, increase total output (Q) and decrease unemployment.

But then as unemployment declines and output increases, continued increases in the money supply and in total spending soon will begin to exert inflationary pressures. Prices will begin to rise. Further decreases in unemployment can be "bought" only at the cost of an increasing inflation rate. So now we have a Phillips Curve.

This "now you see it, now you don't" problem results from the set of assumptions you adopt at the outset. It depends significantly on the concept of "the natural rate of unemployment."

THE NATURAL RATE OF UNEMPLOYMENT

As you know, some unemployment is a necessary condition in a modern economic system. This fact gives rise to the idea of the "natural rate of unemployment."

There are several factors which influence the size of the natural rate of unemployment. In a dynamic, rapidly changing economy, many jobs (and many workers) are always becoming obsolete. So the more rapidly the economy is changing, the larger the natural rate of unemployment is likely to be. On the other hand, the better the level of education, training, and job placement, the smaller the natural rate is likely to be.

Other factors which influence the size of the natural rate of unemployment were discussed under the heading "the unemployment bias" which you were reading about a few minutes ago. Economists generally agree that there is some most appropriate, welfare-maximizing rate of employment (and unemployment). But there is considerable disagreement about how large it is, and about the factors which might cause it to change.

The Long-Run (Vertical) Phillips Curve

If there is a "natural rate" of unemployment, then is there really an inflation-unemployment trade-off? In the long-run, no. But in the short run, yes.

Anytime spending slows down, there will be a tendency for (1) unemployment to increase and (2) the inflation rate to decrease. Anytime spending speeds up, there will be a tendency for (1) unemployment to decrease and (2) the inflation rate to increase. That's what the Phillips Curve shows. Empirical evidence conclusively establishes the fact that these relationships hold true. They are clearly observable in the short-run.

But many economists believe that *in the long-run* there is a tendency for the natural rate of employment to exist—regardless of the dollar volume of total spending. For example, suppose total spending doubles. The theory says that in the long run the unemployment rate will be the same as if spending had not changed. Unemployment will be at the "natural rate"—no less and no more. So what doubles? Only prices.

Figure 26-4 shows a graph which is based on these assumptions. This graph doesn't show any inflation-unemployment trade-off at all! What the figure says is: "There's no inflation-unemployment trade-off (a vertical Phillips Curve—meaning no Phillips Curve) in the long-run."

The vertical curve in figure 26-4 denies the existence of any trade-off between the inflation rate and the unemployment rate. This curve offers the following advice to monetary policymakers:

> Do not permit the money supply to expand to try to stimulate the economy and reduce unemployment. The ultimate result of such a policy—the only result in the long-run—would be inflation. The unemployment rate would not be affected at all because it will remain at its natural level.

What if monetary policymakers do not heed this advice? Suppose they are concerned about the level of unemployment. They have seen the empirical evidence which shows that easier money which brings increased spending can bring increased production and decreased unemployment. Keynesian theory explains how it happens, and the data prove that it's true—at least in the short-run.

Suppose the policymakers opt for easier money to try to stimulate the economy. What happens? The "accelerationist" hypothesis tries to answer that question.

Figure 26-4.   The Hypothetical Long-Run Phillips Curve: No Phillips Curve

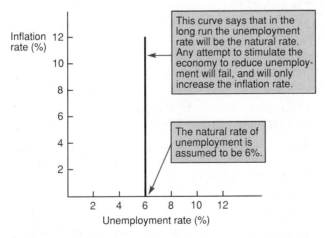

The long run Phillips curve is a vertical line located at the natural rate of unemployment. What it says is: "There is no inflation-unemployment trade-off—and therefore no Phillips Curve—in the long-run."

THE ACCELERATIONIST HYPOTHESIS

Let's assume that there really is a natural rate of unemployment and that the rate happens to be 6%. And suppose unemployment in the economy is, at this moment, 6%. What would happen if we would permit the money supply to expand to try to increase total spending and thereby reduce this unemployment rate to less than 6%?

If we assume a natural rate of unemployment of 6%, then the answer is obvious. In the long run we're going to (a) fail in our unemployment objective, and (b) cause the inflation rate to increase. This leads us to what is sometimes called the "accelerationist" hypothesis. This hypothesis concludes that the U.S. inflation rate has been accelerated by monetary policies which have not given adequate consideration to the natural rate of unemployment. Here's one of the arguments.[3]

An Accelerationist Scenario

1. Suppose the economy has a 6% unemployment rate, and 6% happens to be the "natural rate." But policymakers would like to reduce the rate of unemployment to less than 6%. So they initiate expansionary monetary policies to stimulate increased spending.

    The increased spending brings increased demand for goods and services. Wages and prices begin to rise. The frictionally unemployed people (people "between jobs") hurry to get new jobs at the higher wages. Frictional unemployment (and therefore total unemployment) declines. So we have more inflation and less unemployment—a short-run Phillips Curve! But then . . .

2. Workers begin to realize that at the higher inflation rate, because of cost-of-living increases their *real wages* are no higher than before. So there's no longer any higher wage inducement to hold it down, so frictional unemployment again increases until it returns to its original natural level.

3. So in the short run, money expansion policies can succeed in reducing unemployment somewhat below the "natural rate." But this will push up costs and prices and increase the inflation rate.

4. In the long run, unemployment will return to the natural rate. The only difference will be that the rate of inflation will be higher than before.

5. If the government keeps on expanding the money supply, trying to reduce unemployment below its natural rate, inflation will continue to accelerate. That's the conclusion of the accelerationist hypothesis.

    Figure 26-5 shows short-run Phillips Curves and a long-run "natural rate of unemployment" Phillips Curve to illustrate the inflationary "ratchet effect" described by the accelerationist hypothesis. The graph indicates the effects of "misguided" easy-money policy.

---

[3] The ideas presented here are thoroughly developed by Milton Friedman and E. S. Phelps. See Milton Friedman, "The Role of Monetary Policy," *American Economic Review*, vol. 58, March 1968, pp. 1–17; and E. S. Phelps, "Money Wage Dynamics and Labor Market Equilibrium," *Journal of Political Economy*, vol. 76, 1968, pp. 678–11.

The accelerationist hypothesis says that money expansion, by increasing spending, can reduce the unemployment rate and increase the inflation rate in the short-run. Each short-run Phillips Curve in figure 26-5 illustrates this effect. But then as time passes, unemployment again increases. The short-run Phillips curve shifts to the right. Unemployment returns to the natural rate. Now study figure 26-5 and the accompanying explanation and you'll understand the graphic illustration of all this.

Figure 26-5.   The Accelerationist Hypothesis: The "Ratchet Effect"

Whenever the unemployment rate drops below the "natural rate" (assumed to be 6%), the short-run Phillips Curve begins to shift to the right to move unemployment back to the natural rate.

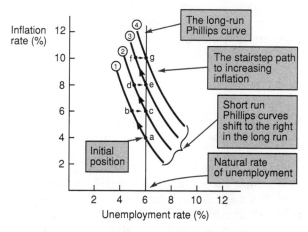

The initial unemployment rate is 6% (assumed natural rate) and the inflation rate is 4% (point a). Then easy money policies are introduced in an attempt to reduce the unemployment. Businesses offer higher wages and attract more employees. In the short-run, unemployment decreases to about 5% and the inflation rate rises to 6% (point b). At the higher inflation rate (6%), workers soon realize that their real wages are no higher than before, so they begin to go back to their "natural pattern." The short-run Phillips Curve shifts from position 1 to position 2. The inflation rate now is 6% and the unemployment rate is again 6% (point c).

Then expansive monetary policies again are introduced. Unemployment again declines to about 5%. The inflation rate moves up to 8% (point d). But the same thing happens again. The short run Phillips Curve shifts to position 3 and unemployment again moves to its natural rate of 6% (point e).

The accelerationist hypothesis says that this "ratchet effect" will continue to push up the inflation rate for as long as the misguided monetary policymakers continue their expansionary policies to try to reduce unemployment below its natural rate.

The Accelerationist Conclusion: Monetary Expansion and Other Stimulative Policies Cannot Succeed in the Long-Run

For those who believe the accelerationist hypothesis the obvious policy conclusion is: Never try to stimulate the economy to try to reduce the unemployment rate. In the short run such a policy will seem to work. But in the long run the only result will be a higher rate of inflation.

The appropriate policy is to keep the money supply growing slowly and steadily. That will hold inflation down and permit growth. Do nothing about unemployment. The economy will find its own rate of employment (and unemployment)—the natural rate.

Not All Economists Agree with the Accelerationist Conclusion

Not all economists agree with these conclusions. And not all economists would agree that "the long run" is the only useful analytical framework for macroeconomic analysis and policy. To some economists it is the short run—the time during which monetary policy *can* influence output and employment—that is sometimes the more appropriate focus for macroeconomic analysis and policy.

MOVEMENT TOWARD SYNTHESIS IN MACRO-MONETARY THEORY

Fortunately, the disagreements among economists on this "short run vs long run" issue—as well as on other issues in the Keynesian-monetarist debate—are not now as great as in the past. Many economists now accept the validity and usefulness of both the short run (loosely, "Keynesian") and the long run (loosely, "monetarist") focus in macroeconomic analysis and policy. About the controversy between Keynesian theory and monetarist theory, many economists now are taking the position that *they are both right.*

More than twenty years ago, in *Dollars and Deficits* (Prentice-Hall, 1968) Milton Friedman had this to say: "In one sense, we are all Keynesians now; in another, no one is Keynesian any longer." That statement is much more true today than it was in 1968. And today it is also true that in one sense we are all monetarists now; in another, no one is a monetarist any longer.

The Extreme Positions Have Been Tempered

The extreme positions of the early Keynesian and monetarist theories have been tempered by further analysis, and each body of theory has been modifiied by empirical evidence. Many of the basic principles of monetarist theory and of Keynesian theory are now generally accepted by most economists.

Empirical evidence shows us quite clearly that if we look at macroeconomic conditions over a period of several years, the relationships explained in monetarist theory really do hold. But if we wish to analyze macroeconomic fluctuations in the economy from month to month or quarter to quarter, Keynesian theory usually provides a more useful framework.

Many Economists Now Take an Eclectic Approach

Keynesian economics gives us tools which usually are more helpful in understanding shorter-run macroeconomic fluctuations. Monetarist theory gives us the cause and effect relationships needed to understand longer-term changes and trends. Both of these "kits of tools" are essential to anyone who wishes to understand what's happening and why in the real world of macroeconomics.

Many economists now take an eclectic approach. They choose the appropriate theory, depending on the specific situation they wish to investigate.

SUMMARY

- In the short run, lower inflation rates are associated with higher unemployment rates. This trade-off is illustrated by the **Phillips Curve**. Increased spending to generate more employment brings higher inflation; decreased spending to hold down inflation brings more unemployment.

- Data on the American economy over the past 20 years show a wide scatter of relationships between the inflation rate and the unemployment rate. A graphic array of these data points can be looked at as a random scattering, or as a series of shifting short-run Phillips Curves.

- For those who wish to read the data that way, it appears that between the early 1960s and the early 1980s, the short-run Phillips Curve shifted upward and to the right, and that since that time it has shifted back downward and to the left.

- The idea of the "natural rate of unemployment," and the accelerationist hypothesis, is that stimulative monetary policy can reduce the unemployment rate while increasing the inflation rate in the short run. But that in the long run the economy will return to its "natural rate" and the only remaining effect will be **inflation**.

- Disagreements among economists regarding the appropriateness and accuracy of Keynesian theory and monetarist theory are not now as great as they once were. Almost all economists now accept the validity and usefulness of both the short-run and long-run focus in macroeconomic analysis and policy, and many find something useful in both monetarist and Keynesian theory.

Important Principles, Issues, Concepts, Terms

The idea of the Phillips Curve

The 1980–82 recession, and the Phillips Curve

Professor A.W. Phillips

The Phillips Curve in terms of the equation of exchange

A graph of the hypothetical short-run Phillips Curve

Factors which would cause the short-run Phillips Curve to shift

The unemployment bias

Changing composition of the labor force

Increasing labor costs

The inflation bias

Monopoly power and cost-push inflation

Inflationary expectations

Easing unemployment and inflation biases in the 1980s

The empirical evidence on unemployment and inflation, 1964–87

Different interpretations of the data

Plausible explanation for a shifting Phillips Curve, 1964–87

The natural rate or unemployment

The long-run (vertical) Phillips Curve

The accelerationist hypothesis

The ratchet effect

The accelerationist conclusion

Movement toward synthesis in macroeconomic theory

The eclectic approach to macroeconomic theory

Questions

1. Explain why there might be, in the short run, a trade-off between the unemployment rate and the inflation rate.

2. Draw and explain the hypothetical short-run Phillips Curve. Why is it shaped as it is? What might cause it to shift, either rightward or leftward, or upward or downward?

3. Looking at the data on the U.S. macroeconomy since the early 1960s, what can we conclude about the short-run Phillips Curve? Does it exist? Does it shift?

4. Explain the concept of the natural rate of unemployment, and what this has to do with the shape of the Phillips Curve in the long run.

5. Explain the accelerationist hypothesis of monetarist theory, and illustrate with a graph the "ratchet effect."

6. Explain some of the movement toward synthesis in macroeconomic theory which has occurred over the past two or three decades.

Suggested Readings

Blinder, Alan S. "The Policy Mix: Lessons from the Recent Past." *Economic Outlook USA.* (Fall 1986), 3–8.

———. "Supply-Shock Inflation: Money, Expectations, and Accommodation." in M. June Flanders and Assaf Razin (eds.) *Development in an Inflationary World.* New York: Academic Press, 1981.

Bosworth, Barry P. "Conflicts in Economic Policy." *Economic Outlook U.S.A.* 7. (Spring 1980) 27–29.

The Conference on Inflation (proceedings of a conference held at the request of President Gerald R. Ford and the Congress of the United States, September 27–28, 1974), Washington, D.C.: U.S. Government Printing Office, 1974.

Federal Reserve Bank of Boston. *After the Phillips Curve: Persistence of High Inflation and High Unemployment.* Boston, 1978.

Friedman, Milton. "A Monetary and Fiscal Framework for Economic Stability." in *Essays in Positive Economics.* Chicago: University of Chicago Press, 1966.

———. "Nobel Lecture: Inflation and Unemployment." *Journal of Political Economy.* (June 1977), 451–72.

Gibson, William, "Interest Rates and Monetary Policy." *Journal of Political Economy.* (May/June 1970), 431–55.

Goodfriend, Marvin. *Monetary Policy in Practice.* Federal Reserve Bank of Richmond, 1987.

Gordon, Robert J. "Inflation, Exchange Rates, and the Natural Rate of Unemployment." in Martin N. Baily (ed.) *Workers, Jobs and Inflation.* Washington: Brookings Institution, 1982.

Griffiths, Brian. *Inflation: The Price of Prosperity.* New York: Holmes and Meier Publishers, 1976.

Higgins, Bryon. "Monetary Growth and Business Cycles." Part II, "The Relationship Between Monetary Decelerations and Recessions." *Economic Review.* Federal Reserve Bank of Kansas City, April 1979.

Humphrey, Thomas M. "The Evolution and Policy Implications of Phillips Curve Analysis." *Essays on Inflation*, 5th ed. Richmond, Va.: Federal Reserve Bank of Richmond, 1986, pp. 99–118.

Keyserling, Leon. "Will It Be Progress or Poverty?" *Challenge.* (May/June 1987), 30–36.

Laidler, David. "Expectations and the Phillips Trade Off: A Commentary." *Scottish Journal of Political Economy.* February 1976.

Levinson, Marc. "Economic Policy: The Old Tools Won't Work." *Dun's Business Month.* (January 1987), 136–39.

Lipsay, R. G. "The Relation Between Unemployment and the Rate of Change of Money Wage Rates in the United Kingdom, 1862–1957: A Further Analysis." *Economica.* (February 1960), 1–31.

Lucas, Robert E. "Some Evidence on Output-Inflation

Tradeoffs." *American Economic Review* 63. (June 1973), 326–34.

Marshal, Ray. "The Inflation Battle: Winning Labor's Support." *Challenge* 21. (January/February 1979), 18–25.

McCallum, Benrett. "Some Issues Concerning Interest Rate Pegging, Price Level Determinancy, and the Real Bills Doctrine." *Journal of Monetary Economics.* (January 1986), 135–60.

McNees, Stephen K. "The Phillips Curve: Forward or Backward Looking?" *New England Economic Review.* Federal Reserve Bank of Boston (July/August 1979), 46–54.

Morley, Samual A. *Inflation and Unemployment,* 2nd ed. Hinsdale, Ill.: The Dryden Press, 1979.

Mortensen, Dale T. "Job Search, the Duration of Unemployment, and the Phillips Curve." *American Economic Review* 60. (December 1970), 847–62.

Phelps, Edmund S. *Inflation Policy and Unemployment Theory.* New York: W. W. Norton, 1972.

———. "Money Wage Dynamics and Labor Market Equilibrium." *Microeconomic Foundations of Employment and Inflation Theory.* New York: W. W. Norton, 1970, pp. 124–66.

———. "Phillips Curves, Expectations of Inflation and Optimal Unemployment over Time." *Economica.* (August 1967), 254–81.

Phillips, A. W. "The Relation between Unemployment and the Rate of Change of Money Wages in the United Kingdom. 1861–1957." *Economica* 25. (November 1958), 283–99.

Rappoport, Peter. "Inflation in the Service Sector." *Quarterly Review.* Federal Reserve Bank of New York, (Winter 1987), 35–45.

Routh, Guy. "The Relation between Unemployment and the Rate of Change of Money Wage Rates: A Comment." *Economica.* (November 1959), 299–315.

Sargent, Thomas. "A Note on the 'Acclerationist' Controversy." *Journal of Money, Credit and Banking.* (August 1971), 721–24.

Spechler, Martin C. "Big Inflations Need Potent Cures." *Challenge.* (November/December 1986), 26–32.

Stein, Herbert. "Price-Fixing as Seen by a Price-Fixer." *Across the Board* 15. (December 1978), 32–43.

Tobin, James. "Inflation and Unemployment." *American Economic Review* 62. (March 1972), 1–18.

Trebing, Michael E. "The Economic Consequences of Wage-Price Guidelines." *Review* 60. Federal Reserve Bank of St. Louis (December 1978), 2–7.

PART VII

Monetary Theory I: The Basic Models and the IS-LM Framework

There are various frameworks and theoretical models which economists have developed for viewing and analyzing the macroeconomy. In this part, first you will see an explanation of the self-regulating macroeconomy—a body of theory which is basic to the classical, neoclassical, and monetarist models. Then you will see an explanation of the Keynesian theory which challenges the conclusions of this "self-regulating" model.

Then Chapter 29 explains the IS curve—a curve which shows combinations of national income (output), and interest rates which bring equilibrium in the nation's input and output (product) markets. Then, after some further explanation and analysis of the demand for money and the role of money in the macroeconomy (in Chapter 30), you will see (in Chapter 31) the development of the LM curve which shows combinations of national income and interest rates which bring equilibrium in the nation's financial markets.

Finally, the IS and LM curves are put together in the same graph to show simultaneous equilibrium in both the product and money markets—the unique national income and interest rate combination which brings equilibrium in the macroeconomy.

After studying Part VII you will have a thorough understanding of the theory of the self-regulating macroeconomy, and you will understand the IS and LM curves. Also you will know that simultaneous equilibrium in both the product and money markets is necessary for macroequilibrium to exist.

In this part you will read about the various kinds of influences which can cause stable macroequilibrium to be upset, and the process whereby equilibrium is reattained. All of this is explained in the ISLM framework which also is used to illustrate both monetarist and Keynesian theories of the macroeconomy.

CHAPTER 27

The Theory of the Self-Regulating Macroeconomy: Foundation of the Classical and Monetarist Models

Chapter Objectives

This chapter explains the theory of how the macroeconomy tends to automatically adjust to full-employment equilibrium. After you study this chapter you will understand and be able to explain:

1. The **internal adjustment mechanisms** of the self-regulating macroeconomy which tend to maintain full employment.

2. Why, given **Say's Law** and the **quantity theory of money,** changes in the size of the money supply have no effect on the real economic variables: employment, output, income.

3. Why and how the real value of the **money supply** tends to automatically adjust itself so that the dollar value of the **spending flow** is exactly equal to the real value of the **output-income flow.**

4. The important role of the **demand for money** in influencing the price level and (therefore) the real value of the money supply.

5. How the **marginal productivity of labor** determines the wage rate, and how adjustments in **real wage rates** tend to move the economy to full employment.

6. How the **marginal productivity of capital** determines the demand for loanable funds and how the **supply and demand for loanable funds** determines interest rates.

7. How the **loanable funds market** operates as an **automatic recycling mechanism** to channel savings into investment (where S = I) via **interest rate adjustments**.

BASIC THEORIES OF THE SELF-REGULATING MACROECONOMY: SAY'S LAW, AND THE QUANTITY THEORY OF MONEY

The "bedrock foundation" of the theory of the self-regulating macroeconomy is **classical monetary theory**. There are two basic propositions: **Say's Law** and the **quantity theory of money**.

Say's Law says that "supply creates its own demand." This means that as more output is produced, more income is generated. The added income generates added demand. The added demand is sufficient to buy up the added output. From Say's Law we can conclude that the economy's rate of output is determined by **supply**. And supply is determined by the economy's productivity: by the quantity and quality of the available inputs.

The quantity theory of money concludes (1) that **total spending** (E) depends on the **quantity of money** (M) in the economy, and (2) that changes in total spending (ΔE) influence only the **price level** (ΔP)—not **real output** (Q). These two basic propositions require some explanation.

SAY'S LAW: SUPPLY CREATES ITS OWN DEMAND

Suppose you look back over a period of years to see what has happened to aggregate output (Q). You'll find that the rate of increase has been determined (more or less) by the rate of growth in the quantity and productivity of available inputs: natural resources, capital, labor, entreneurship.

Sometimes there are recessions or depressions when output falls below its potential. But if you focus only on the long-run trend, these temporary slowdowns can be ignored.

Say's Law Is True—In the Long-Run View

When the focus is on **long-run equilibrium**, output growth is determined by productivity growth. So in the long run the limiting factor on the economy's output is **supply**—not **demand**.

In the long run, **increased productivity** means increased output, increased income, and increased demand for output. A given increase in supply creates an equal increase in demand. In the long-run view, Say's Law is really true!

Here's an example. What do you think will determine the size of U.S. GNP in the year 2000? Will that be a recession year? Or a boom year? We don't have any way to predict that. But we *can* predict that in the year 2000 *the productive capacity of the U.S. economy* will be an important determinant of real output.

Suppose productive capacity grows at an annual rate of 4% throughout the 1990s. Then we can confidently predict that in the year 2000 real output (and real income and aggregate demand) will be much larger than if the average growth rate during the 1990s turns out to be only 1.5%.

Conclusion: Money Supply Changes Can't Affect Real Output

The conclusions of Say's Law strictly limit the influence which money supply changes (ΔM) can have on the economy. If output-size is determined entirely by productive capacity, then what effect can ΔM (and ΔE) have on output? None.

THE QUANTITY THEORY: INCREASED M CAUSES ONLY INCREASED P

In its simplest form, the quantity theory says:

1. Say's Law holds true: The economy's output rate is determined by **productive capacity**—by (a) how much labor and management skills and capital and other inputs are available and (b) how productive they are. It is assumed that the economy operates at full employment, so for any given level of productive capacity *the size of the output flow* (Q) *can be taken as given*.

2. The size of the **money supply** (M) determines the size of the **total spending flow** (E) so that money supply changes (ΔM) result in *proportionate changes in total spending* (ΔE). To say it differently, velocity of circulation (V) is fixed so that ΔM translates directly and proportionally into ΔE. But

---

Box 27-1

Question: Exactly What Is Meant by the Term "Classical" As in the Phrase "Classical Economics," or "Classical Monetary Theory?"

In general, the term *classical* means something that is **standard, generally accepted, authoritative**—for example, the art works, music, or writings of the "ancient masters" which have been passed down from earlier times. What classical *does not* mean is new, different, challenging to the established truths, or experimental.

Classical economics began to develop early in the mid-eighteenth century, and major contributions were made by Adam Smith, David Ricardo, T.R. Malthus, J-B Say, J.S. Mill, and several others.

Then in the late nineteenth century and on into the early part of this century further developments in economic thought—the introduction of demand and supply curves, and other significant developments—brought in "neoclassical economics," with many significant developments in macro-monetary theory.

Today, both the old classical and neoclassical theories are appropriately referred to as "classical," in the sense that these are the traditional theories which explain how the market economy operates. Much of classical microeconomics—how the basic resource-allocation questions are worked out via the price mechanism—is generally accepted by a large majority of economists.

Classical macroeconomics—the primary subject of this chapter—explains how the economy automatically adjusts itself to full-employment macroequilibrium. Prior to the depression of the 1930s, classical/neoclassical economics (both micro and macro) reigned supreme among economists. But in the case of classical macroeconomics, that isn't true anymore. In the next chapter you'll be reading about the Keynesian attack on classical macroeconomics. Then in the chapters that follow you'll see that there are various other ways of viewing the macroeconomy.

since *output* (Q) is already predetermined, money-supply-induced changes in spending can only bring changes in *prices* (ΔP).

In terms of the equation of exchange (MV = PQ, explained previously), V and Q are fixed so that the equation becomes

$$M\bar{V} = P\bar{Q}.$$

The only variables are M and P, where M is the independent and P the dependent variable. Changes in M cause changes in E which cause changes in P. Here's an example.

Suppose M doubles. Suddenly there are twice as many dollars in existence, so E doubles. When E doubles with Q fixed, P doubles.

When P doubles, the purchasing power of each dollar is cut in half. There are now twice as many dollars in existence but each dollar has lost half of its purchasing power. The result? The total purchasing power of the money supply is exactly the same as before M doubled. It is always true that the purchasing power of the money supply is the reciprocal of the price level: $\frac{1}{P} \times M = \frac{M}{P} =$ the real value (purchasing power) of the money supply.

A Nominal Increase in M Will "Self-Destruct": Real M (M/P) Remains the Same

According to the quantity theory, the purchasing power of the total money supply automatically adjusts (through price changes) to equal the real value of the goods to be bought—that is, to equal *the real value of the full-employment output of the economy* (Q). Changes in M only result in changes (in the opposite direction) in the value of the monetary unit (P). The "real effect"—effect on real output, production, employment, income, interest rates, investment, etc.—is zero.

Real conditions in the economy are determined by *supply-side factors* (the available inputs and their productivity). So the economy's real output and income are not influenced at all by the demand side—by changes in M and E. Here's the point: *Money is completely neutral as a factor influencing real conditions in the macroeconomy.*

Money Demanded Is Only for Transactions—Expected, Plus Unexpected

The accuracy of the quantity theory rests on the assumption of a stable demand for money. The theory assumes that the quantity of money demanded (Mqd) is determined entirely by the size of nominal national income (Y). It is not influenced by interest rates or by anything else—so in the quantity theory, Mqd can be stated as follows:

$$Mqd = kPQ; \text{ or}$$

$$Mqd = kY.$$

These two equations say exactly the same thing. Both express Mqd as a fraction of nominal national income. If you need to, read box 27-2 to refresh your memory on the relationships among Mqd, k, V, PQ, Y, and M.

Box 27-2

Question: What Exactly Are the Relationships Between V and k? And Y and PQ?

This was explained previously, but as a refresher, here's an example:

Assume that national income and output (Y, or PQ) is $600 per year and k is 1/6. Then the quantity of money demanded (Mqd) = 1/6 × $600 = $100. And since M = $100 and Y = $600, each dollar is being spent 6 times during the year. So V = 6.

Then suppose Y and PQ increase to $1200. Mqd will increase to 200 (1/6 × $1200 = $200).

Again, V = 6. The "Cambridge k" relates the size of desired money balances (Mqd) to the size of national income. It expresses Mqd as a fraction of Y, or of PQ.

Note that Y and PQ are two different ways of expressing the same magnitude. Y is the nominal national income and PQ is the nominal value of the national output—exactly the same thing expressed in two different ways.

In the classical model money plays but one role: To serve as the medium of exchange. So the only reason for wanting to hold money balances is for transactions purposes.

Precautionary Balances Are Included with Transactions Balances

Classical economics recognizes that people want to hold somewhat more money than they expect to spend for planned transactions. Some **precautionary balances** are held for *unexpected transactions*. In the classical model, money held for both planned transactions and unforeseen transactions are considered to be *transactions balances*. Is this logical?

When the only purpose for holding money balances is to *make planned transactions*, then the relationship between Mqd and Y is obvious. If Y doubles, transactions double. So desired money balances double. It makes sense to say "Mqd = kY," which is just another way of saying "when Y changes, Mqd changes in the same direction and by the same percentage."

But would precautionary balances also tend to double if Y doubles? Yes. Here's an example.

Suppose the national income doubles because of inflation. The purchasing power of the monetary unit is cut in half. To hold the same real precautionary balance as previously, the *nominal balance* must double. Since both respond in the same degree to the same variable (ΔY) it is appropriate to lump together the transactions and precautionary demands for money balances.

Figure 27-1 shows a graphic illustration of this relationship between the size of **nominal national income** (Y) and the size of the public's **desired money balances** (Mqd).

In the Classical Model Mqd Is Unresponsive to Interest Rate Changes (Δr)

The quantity theory assumes that the interest rate elasticity of Md is zero—i.e., *that Mqd and Md are always equal regardless of the level of or changes in interest rates* (Δr). So in the Md graph, with the interest rate on the vertical axis and Mqd

**Figure 27-1.   In the Theory of the Self-Regulating Macroeconomy,
Mqd Depends on (Is a Stable Function of)
Nominal National Income (Y)**

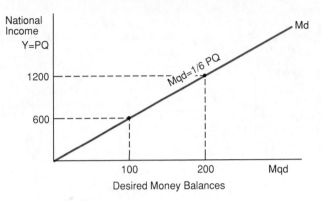

As nominal national income increases, the desire for money balances increases proportionally.

In this graph the ratio is assumed to be 1 to 6, meaning that $k = 1/6$ and $V = 6$.

$Mqd = kY$. When k is $1/6$ and $Y = 600$, $kY = 1/6 \times 600 = 100$.

Mqd: quantity of money demanded: Size of money balances desired by the public. It's the total amount of money which the public wishes to hold, given the current circumstances. In the classical model the only reason for wanting to hold money balances is for transactions (planned, and unforseen). So Mqd increases as national income increases.

Y: size of the nominal national income—i.e., the national income *in dollar terms*. The nominal national income can increase or decrease with no change in *real national income*, where nominal changes reflect only price changes (inflation or deflation).

PQ: real output (Q) in physical units, multiplied by the prices (P) of those physical units. PQ always amounts to the nominal value of the national output, which is identical to the nominal value of the national income. PQ can increase as a result of either an increase in real output or an increase in prices—or some of both. But in the classical model, since Q is fixed at the full-employment rate, all changes in PQ result from changes in P (and/or from changes in productive capacity).

on the horizontal axis, the Md curve is vertical—perfectly inelastic. The public will want to hold the amount of money necessary to support their foreseen and unforeseen transactions—no more, and no less—and the level of interest rates has nothing to do with it.

Suppose people find themselves holding more money than their desired amount. They will spend it right away. Prices will rise, which is to say: The value of the monetary unit will go down. The extra money (surplus purchasing power) will automatically "self-destruct." The total quantity of "real M" (M/P) will be decreased by inflation ($\uparrow$P) until all of the surplus (undemanded) money is eliminated. Neat! And it goes the other way too.

Whenever people find themselves with less than their desired money balances they will cut back spending and try to hold more money. But then with the spending slowdown, surpluses will begin to show up in the product markets. Soon prices will begin to fall ($\downarrow$P). So the value of the monetary unit will increase. This price level decrease ["real M" (M/P) increase] will continue to equilibrium. That's where there's exactly enough purchasing power so that everyone is holding as much money as they'd like to. That's where M = Mqd.

These examples show how, in the classical model, the **real money supply** (M/P) automatically adjusts to where there's just enough purchasing power to buy the full-employment output of the economy—where total spending is exactly equal to the real value of the economy's output. Figure 27-2 illustrates this.

**Figure 27-2.   The Passive Role of Money in the Classical Macro Model.
All Changes in M Translate into Changes in P.**

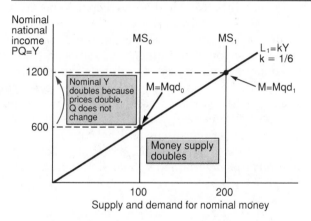

As nominal national income (Y) doubles, the transactions demand for money (L_1 = Mqd) also doubles. So in this example Mqd increases from $100 to $200 where the economy is again in equilibrium: $M = L_1 = Mqd$. The only difference is that prices have doubled. Real employment, production, output, income, and standards of living have not changed.

M: The nominal size of (actual number of dollars in) the money supply.

L_1: The same as Md in the Classical model. L_1 means desired money balances—the amount of money which the public would like to hold—*for transactions* (planned, and unforseen). (The reason it is L_1, and not just L is that later a nontransactions demand for money [L_2] will be integrated into this analysis.)

kY: The quantity of money demanded (Mqd) defined as a fraction of nominal national income. For example, if k is 1/6 and Y is $600, then the quantity of money demanded is 1/6 × $600 = $100.

According to the quantity theory, when M doubles, total spending doubles. Since the economy is already operating at its full-employment rate, real output cannot increase. For twice as many dollars to be spent for a given quantity of output, prices must double.

With Inflation or Deflation, Relative Prices Remain the Same

Suppose the money supply doubles in the Classical model. The general level of prices will double. As the money supply increases and prices rise, what guarantees that the prices of some things will not rise more than the prices of others? For example, how can we be sure that wage rates will rise by exactly the same amount as product prices?

If you have the proper "mental set" and you're "thinking in the classical model," then it's intuitively obvious why (in the long run, which admittedly may take awhile) relative prices cannot be altered by either inflation or deflation. Relative prices throughout the economy always are determined by real supply and demand conditions in all of the markets throughout the economy.

For example, the real wage rate is determined by the real marginal productivity of labor. And labor's real productivity is determined by the real production functions in the economy: the "input mix" of labor, together with capital, resources, and entrepreneurship. None of these *real conditions* are affected at all by changes in the size of the money supply or by the resulting changes in the general level of prices. So here again you can see that in the classical model money is **completely neutral** when it comes to influencing real economic conditions.

The classical economists recognized that during the adjustment period—as the economy moves to a higher or lower general level of prices—some distortions among relative prices are likely. But in each market in which price distortions occur, market forces will automatically bring readjustments to equilibrium.

A market with nonequilibrium prices will not "clear." There will be either surpluses or shortages until relative prices are forced back into their proper relationships—relationships determined by real supply and demand conditions.

THE THEORY OF WAGES AND EMPLOYMENT

In the theory of the self-regulating macroeconomy, **productive capacity**—the availability and productivity of various inputs—determines the size of total real output (Q). But will the economy's labor supply be fully employed? In this model, yes. Wage rates will move to adjust the economy to full employment. This section explains how that happens through the interaction of the supply of and demand for labor.

The Supply of Labor

The classical theory of wages assumes pure or perfect competition in all labor and product markets—i.e., large numbers of buyers and sellers and no monopoly power or artificial supply restrictions in any markets. With perfect competition, the supply of labor is determined by the population, the skills and abilities of the labor force, and the desire of people to work. Leisure is considered to be more desirable than working. Therefore at lower wages less labor hours will be "offered for sale" than at higher wages.

The worker (rational seller of labor) compares the **marginal disutility** of work against the **marginal utility** of the wages offered. The worker's equilibrium comes where the marginal disutility incurred by the last unit of work is exactly offset by the marginal utility of the income received.

The individual's labor supply curve slopes upward to indicate that at higher wages, more units of labor are offered. The aggregate supply of labor in the entire economy is the (horizontal) sum of the supply curves of the individual workers. So the aggregate supply curve also slopes upward. (For a possible exception, see box 27-3.)

The Demand for Labor

The demand for labor (as for any factor of production) reflects its **productivity**. And the productivity of any one factor depends largely on the availability of other factors—other inputs to work with. As the firm hires more and more units of labor, the **law of diminishing returns** tells us that labor's marginal physical product (additional output per unit of additional labor) eventually will decline.

In competitive markets the profit-maximizing firm continues to employ additional units of labor as long as the **value of the marginal product** of the additional unit of labor is greater than the **marginal input cost** of hiring the additional unit. The value of the marginal product (VMP) of each additional unit of labor is the marginal physical product (MPP) times the market price of the product (P):

$$VMP = MPP \times P.$$

For example, if an additional worker adds ten units of physical product and the price per unit is $10 then the value of that worker's marginal product is $100. Figure 27-3 illustrates and further explains this.

The **marginal input cost**—the cost of employing an additional unit of labor—is the wage rate (W). The equilibrium employment rate for a firm is where

---

Box 27-3

Question: What about the Idea of a Backward-Bending Supply Curve for Labor?

There may be an exception to the upward-sloping labor supply curve. There may (sometimes) be a "backward-bending" supply curve for labor, indicating that above some (high) level of wages, even higher wages will result in less labor supplied (not more). Here's why.

As wages get increasingly higher, incomes get increasingly larger. So the value of leisure time (now that people have so much money to spend) increases. Here's an example.

Suppose the nominal wage rate rises from $5 to $10 per hour. Suddenly people can work *fewer hours* than before and earn *more income!* It's likely that some people would decide to do

that. So for them, the higher wage would result in less labor offered for sale—not more. So their labor supply curves in this wage range would be negatively sloped.

The idea is that as wages rise from a low level, more labor is offered. But above some level, additional wage increases result in less labor supplied—thus, a backward-bending labor supply curve. However, it's much more likely that this backward-bending labor supply curve would apply to certain individuals than to the aggregate labor supply for the economy as a whole.

Figure 27-3.   The Labor Production Function and the Demand for Labor: Illustrations of the Law of Diminishing Returns

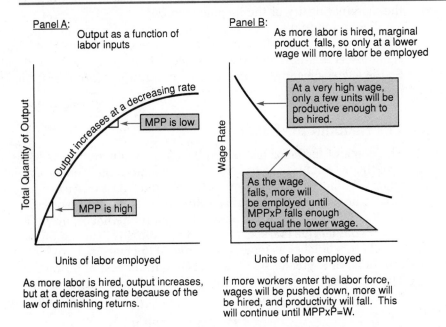

Panel A:
Output as a function of labor inputs

Output increases at a decreasing rate

MPP is low

MPP is high

Total Quantity of Output

Units of labor employed

As more labor is hired, output increases, but at a decreasing rate because of the law of diminishing returns.

Panel B:
As more labor is hired, marginal product falls, so only at a lower wage will more labor be employed

At a very high wage, only a few units will be productive enough to be hired.

As the wage falls, more will be employed until MPPxP falls enough to equal the lower wage.

Wage Rate

Units of labor employed

If more workers enter the labor force, wages will be pushed down, more will be hired, and productivity will fall. This will continue until MPPxP=W.

The law of diminishing returns says that if all other productive inputs are held constant while one input (in this case labor) is added in increasing quantities in the "input mix," at some point the additional output generated by the additional unit of this variable input will begin to decline. This situation is illustrated in the above panels.

As more people enter the labor force and the wage rate falls and more people are hired, it is the diminishing MPP which ultimately brings the labor market into equilibrium. You can look at Panel B and see that if the labor supply is very small, the wage rate would be high and MPP would also be high. If the labor supply happened to be great, the wage rate would be low and the MPP of labor would be low.

You can see the same result in Panel A. If only a small number of units of labor are employed, the MPP is high. So the equilibrium wage rate will be high. If a large number of units of labor are employed, the MPP is low and the equilibrium wage rate will be low.

Conclusion: ceteris paribus, the more labor available in an economic system the lower will be the MPP of labor and the lower will be general level of wages.

---

the value of the marginal product produced by the last-hired unit of labor is exactly equal to the marginal input cost of that unit of labor (i.e., the wage rate). So for a competitive firm, equilibrium occurs where MPP × P = W. Box 27-4 explains more about this equation.

In the above example where MPP × P = $100, suppose W > $100. Then the labor will not be hired. But if W < $100, additional labor will be hired until the *law of diminishing* returns pushes MPP down to where VMP equals the wage rate.

For the total economy the demand for labor is the sum of all of the individual-firm demands. The aggregate labor demand curve slopes downward reflecting the law of diminishing returns and showing that at lower wage rates (*ceteris paribus*) more labor will be demanded.

Box 27-4

Question: Does the Equation MPP × P = W Express
          Nominal Values? Or Real Values?

The equation (1) MPP × P = W can also be written (2) MPP = W/P. The two are algebraically identical. To convert equation (1) to (2), just divide both sides of (1) by P.

In equation (1), everything is in nominal (money) terms. The marginal physical product is multiplied by the price to express it in nominal terms, and the wage rate is also expressed in nominal terms.

The second form of the equation (2) translates everything into real terms. MPP now is *real physical product* and W/P divides the wage rate by the price index to also translate wages into real terms.

If equation (1) gave us $100 worth of product on the left and a wage rate of $100 on the right, this would be equilibrium. The other equation (2) would give us the number of units of product produced on the left and on the right, the number of units of product paid to labor as the wage rate. The former equation compares dollars' worth produced by labor with dollar costs of labor; the second equation compares units of product produced by labor with units of product paid to labor.

Wages Adjust to Guarantee Full Employment

With positively sloping aggregate supply and negatively sloping aggregate demand for labor, the equilibrium wage occurs where the quantity supplied equals the quantity demanded. At that equilibrium rate, all who wish to work can find jobs and all who wish to hire can find workers. But at the equilibrium wage, many units of labor may not be employed. The classical model calls this **voluntary unemployment**. Those who choose not to accept employment at "the going wage" are voluntarily choosing leisure instead of employment.

Figure 27-4 shows aggregate demand and supply in the labor market and it shows the **equilibrium wage** where all involuntary unemployment is eliminated.

This graph explains why in the classical model in the long run—after all adjustments have been made—if wages are free to move downward, *involuntary unemployment* cannot exist.

In the Classical Model, All Unemployment Is "Voluntary Unemployment"

In figure 27-4, the supply curve is drawn to indicate that many workers are unwilling to take jobs at wage rate W_e or below. In the Classical model, jobs are always available at some wage. So if unemployment exists it's because workers have voluntarily decided not to take those low-wage jobs. In figure 27-4, all of those workers represented by the segment of the labor supply curve above W_e (to the right of q_e) are voluntarily unemployed.

According to the classical paradigm, all of those workers to the right of q_e are "voluntarily unemployed." The supply curve shows that they would prefer to remain unemployed than to sell their labor at wage rate W_e or below. Figure 27-5 gives another labor market illustration of this "voluntary unemployment."

At W_e, labor-use is at "full employment" and the output of the economy is at the "natural full-employment rate."

Figure 27-4.   The Classical Model of the Labor Market

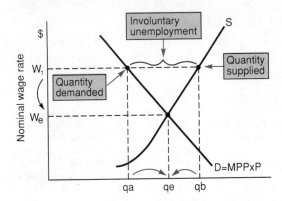

This graph shows that the equilibrium wage is W_e, and that q_e is the "full employment quantity of labor supplied and demanded."

Suppose the wage rate was higher—say, at W_1. There the quantity supplied is q_b, but the quantity demanded is only q_a. Many workers would like to work at W_1 who cannot find jobs. These people are "involuntarily unemployed."

These unemployed workers will seek jobs at lower wages. So the wage rate will fall, ultimately to W_e. At W_e everyone who wants to hire labor at that rate can do so, and everyone who wants a job can find one.

Figure 27-5.   The Labor Market in Equilibrium

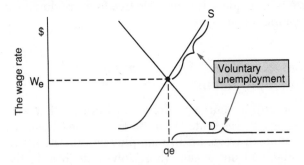

The wage rate tends to move to equilibrium where the quantity of labor demanded and supplied are equal. At that rate, all workers who are unemployed are "voluntarily" unemployed. The classical model says that unemployment results from the decisions of workers not to accept lower wages. Therefore any unemployment which exists is voluntary and is not a problem of "inadequate aggregate demand" (total spending).

THE CLASSICAL THEORY OF INTEREST: HOW S = I IS AUTOMATICALLY ACHIEVED

According to classical theory, changes in the quantity of money have *zero effect* on interest rates. People hold money balances for transactions purposes, and that's all. So this gives us a vertical money demand function. Also, the money supply function is vertical with respect to interest rates because the quantity of money is determined by the amount of monetary gold in existence, or actions by the monetary authorities, or whatever.

The point: Mqd and M are both totally unresponsive to changes in the interest rate (both would be represented by vertical curves in a "price-quantity" graph). So how, pray tell, are interest rates determined? And what possible role could they play in the functioning of the macroeconomy?

That's what you'll be finding out in this section. But for a quick answer: Interest rates are determined by the demand for and the supply of **loanable funds**. And the role they play? You'll be surprised how critical it is in rounding out and completing the classical model of the macroeconomy. First, here's a look at the loanable funds market.

The Demand for Funds: Marginal Productivity of Capital

The demand for borrowed funds reflects the expected profitability of investment. So the demand depends on the marginal productivity of the capital in which the borrowers plan to invest. At lower rates, more investments are profitable. So the quantity of funds demanded increases. The demand curve slopes downward.

The Supply of Funds: The Rate of Savings

Classical theory recognizes different motives for saving. One is to save for future needs—to buy a house, or for retirement. Another motive is to earn interest income on savings.

The **time preference** or **abstinence** theory of interest says that people would rather spend their current incomes now, but higher rates will induce them to abstain from current consumption and save more. This theory concludes that as interest rates rise, the rate of savings—and therefore the quantity of loanable funds supplied—increases.

Equilibrium in the Funds Market Brings S = I

Figure 27-6 illustrates the loanable funds market in the classical model.

The supply and demand curves show the equilibrium interest rate where the quantity of funds supplied by savers is exactly equal to the quantity demanded by borrowers. And this equilibrium interest rate is also the rate which brings into equality the rate of savings and investment (S = I) in the economy. Here's how:

1. Suppose there's an increase in the savings rate so that S > I. That will increase the supply of loanable funds, create a surplus in the loanable funds market, and the surplus will push down interest rates. The lower

rates will cause (a) more borrowing and investing and (b) less saving. This adjustment will continue until S = I.

2. Suppose investors begin demanding more funds and I > S. There will be a shortage of funds in the loanable funds market and interest rates will rise. The higher rates will cause (a) less borrowing and investing and (b) more saving. Again this adjustment will continue until S = I.

Figure 27-6.   Supply and demand for Loanable Funds: The Classical Theory of Interest Explains Why S = I

Equilibrium in the macroeconomy occurs at the interest rate which equates the supply and demand for loanable funds. At that equilibrium r, all current **savings** will be offset by current **investment spending**. Therefore total **current spending** is exactly equal to total **current income** and Say's Law holds true.

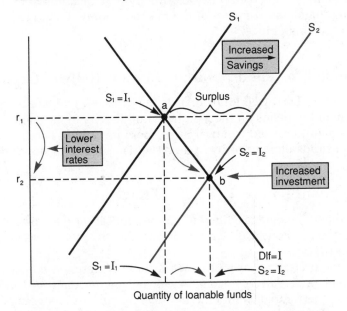

D = demand for loanable funds. It is determined by the marginal productivity of capital. At lower rates of interest more investments become profitable. So as interest rates fall, more funds are demanded.

S_1 = Supply of funds offered by savers. This curve assumes that at higher rates of interest, income-earners will be induced to abstain from current consumption—to save more. So they will offer more funds to borrowers.

The shift to curve S_2 indicates that people have decided to be more thrifty—to save a larger portion of their incomes. The increased supply of funds creates a surplus and pushes the interest rate down to r_2. The lower rate induces (a) increased borrowing and investing, and (b) a decreased rate of saving. When the interest rate moves down to r_2, the loanable funds market is again in equilibrium. Also S = I and macroequilibrium is reestablished.

The bottom line: In classical theory, the loanable funds market is the **recycling mechanism** whereby all savings leakages from the macroeconomy are pumped back into the spending flow as investment. The S = I equilibrium is brought about via adjustments in interest rates.

Interest rates adjust to equate the quantities of loanable funds demanded and supplied. And this equilibrium automatically brings S and I into equality— where the **planned savings outflow** *from the income-spending stream is exactly equal to and offset by the* **planned investment inflow** *into the stream. So by interest rate adjustments the equilibrium of the macroeconomy is assured.*

SUMMARY

- The theory of the **self-regulating macroeconomy** is the basic foundation of the classical, modern monetarist, and several other models of the economy. It operates via supply and demand in the **product markets, labor markets**, and **funds markets**, and it assumes that prices are free to move in response to changing supply and demand conditions so that all surpluses and shortages soon are eliminated and all markets are cleared.

- The Classical model of the macroeconomy is based on **Say's Law** and the **quantity theory of money**.

- **Say's Law** tells us that increased output generates increased income which results in the increased demand necessary to buy the increased output. **Supply creates its own demand**.

- The **quantity theory of money** says that changes in the money supply (ΔM) bring proportionate changes in the rate of spending (ΔE), and that all of   E is absorbed by changes in the price level (ΔP). So ΔM has no effect on employment or on real output or income.

- The quantity theory can be illustrated by the **equation of exchange**, where both V and Q are fixed. This shows the purely nominal (nonreal) role of money:

$$M\bar{V} = P\bar{Q}$$

- The classical theory of **wages and employment** concludes that in long-run equilibrium any unemployment which exists is **voluntary**. All who are willing to work for the equilibrium wage can get jobs and all employers who wish to hire workers at this wage can find workers.

- The **loanable funds market** moves into equilibrium at an interest rate where (a) the quantity of funds supplied equals the quantity demanded, and (b) the public's desired level of savings is exactly equal to and offset by business firms' desired level of investment: **where S = I**.

- The workings of **supply and demand and price movements** in the product, labor, and funds markets bring the macroeconomy to a **stable, full-employment equilibrium**. This is the system that Keynes challenged during the 1930s. You'll be reading about that in the next chapter.

Important Principles, Issues, Concepts, Terms

Classical monetary theory

Say's Law

Quantity theory of money

Equation of exchange

$M\bar{V} = P\bar{Q}$

Nominal M vs. real M

Role of M in the classical model

$Mqd = kPQ$; $Mqd = kY$

Transactions balances

Precautionary balances

Effect of interest rate changes (Δr) on Mqd

Stability of relative prices

Supply of labor

Demand for labor

Law of diminishing returns

Value of the marginal product

Marginal input costs

Labor production function

Voluntary unemployment

Involuntary unemployment

Demand for loanable funds

Marginal productivity of capital

Supply of loanable funds

Time preference or abstinence theory of interest

How r moves to where S = I

Questions

1. Explain the basic idea of Say's Law, and why it tends to be true in the long run.

2. Explain the quantity theory of money, and how this theory concludes that in the long run, changes in the money supply (ΔM) have *zero effect* on the real economic variables: employment, output, income.

3. According to the quantity theory of money, a change in the money supply exerts its entire impact on the size of the total spending flow. Why so? And with this change in spending (ΔE), how can it be that the real economic variables are unaffected? Explain.

4. What does it mean to say that an increase in "nominal M" will automatically "self-destruct"? Is this conclusion significant for the accuracy of the theory of the self-regulating macroeconomy? Explain.

5. Explain what is meant by transactions balances, and why it is logical to also include precautionary balances in this category.

6. How does the classical model justify the assumption that the demand for money is absolutely inelastic with respect to interest rate changes (Mqd completely unresponsive to Δr)?

7. Explain what determines the demand for labor in the classical model, and illustrate with a production function and a demand curve for labor.

8. How does the classical model conclude that in long-run equilibrium, all unemployment is *voluntary unemployment*? Illustrate with a supply and demand graph.

9. Explain what determines the demand for and supply of loanable funds in the classical model. Use a supply and demand graph to illustrate.

10. Explain why, in the classical model, when the macroeconomy is in equilibrium because S = I, this is certain to be a full-employment equilibrium.

Suggested Readings

Dean, Edwin, ed. *The Controversy Over the Quantity Theory of Money.* Lexington, Mass.: D.C. Heath, 1965.

Eagly, Robert V. *The Structure of Classical Economic Theory.* London: Oxford University Press, 1974.

Fisher, Irving. *The Theory of Interest*. New York: Macmillan, 1930.

———. *The Purchasing Power of Money*. New York: Macmillan, 1911.

Friedman, Milton. "Money—The Quantity Theory." *International Encyclopedia of the Social Sciences* 10. New York: Macmillan and the Free Press, 1968, pp. 432–47.

———. *Studies in the Quantity Theory of Money*. Chicago: University of Chicago Press, 1956.

Hegeland, Hugo. *The Quantity Theory of Money*. New York: Augustus M. Kelly, 1969.

Pigou, A.C. "The Value of Money." *Quarterly Journal of Economics*. (November 1917), 38–65.

Sowell, Thomas. *Say's Law: An Historical Analysis*. Princeton: Princeton University Press, 1972.

Whittaker, Edmund. *Schools and Streams of Economic Thought*. Chicago: Rand McNally, 1960.

CHAPTER 28

An Introduction to Keynes and His Model of the Macroeconomy

Chapter Objectives

During the 1930s John Maynard Keynes developed a **depression economy** model which rejected Say's Law—"Supply creates its own demand"—and replaced it with that is now sometimes called Keynes' Law: "Demand creates its own supply." This chapter gives an overview of Keynes and his macroeconomic model of the economy.

From this chapter you will understand and be able to explain:

1. The specific differences between the assumptions of classical theory and Keynesian theory, especially
   a. on the question of flexible vs. inflexible wages and prices, and
   b. on the short run vs. long run issue.

2. How the Keynesian model focuses on and breaks down and analyzes the income-spending flow.

3. The Keynesian income (or investment or expenditure) multiplier and how and why it works in the Keynesian model.

4. The basis on which Keynes challenged the automatic "S = I equilibrium condition" described in the classical model.

5. The Keynesian idea of the depression-inducing "savings gap," and the pragmatic Keynesian prescription for overcoming depression.

6. Why macroequilibrium in the Keynesian model doesn't necessarily occur at full employment, but occurs where planned saving equals planned investment—and how this condition can be illustrated in
   a. the circular flow diagram and
   b. the Keynesian Cross diagram.

7. How to use the Keynesian Cross diagram to illustrate the "consumption function" and effects of changes in spending flows on macroeconomic conditions.

KEYNESIAN ECONOMICS FOCUSES ON DEPRESSION: CAUSES, AND CURES

During the 1930s John Maynard Keynes offered the world a new way of explaining the depression problem. His book *The General Theory of Employment, Interest, and Money* (1936) explains why the economy might go into depression and what the government might do to overcome it.[1]

Keynes didn't suggest (as the classical economists did) that we should just wait for the natural market forces to work things out. He offered suggestions for *positive actions* by the government.

Keynes Rejected the Conclusions of the Classical Macroeconomic Model

The first chapter of Keynes' *General Theory* consisted of a single paragraph in which Keynes said that the classical economic model didn't fit the real world of the 1930s—that the model was "misleading and disastrous" as a guide to public policy. He rejected the idea of *waiting for the long* run to bring full employment. In his previous writings he had made the statement: *"In the long run we are all dead."*

The most respected economists of the day (all classical/neoclassical economists) denounced Keynes' *General Theory* and worked vigorously to defend the classical position. But as time went on, many economists and policymakers came to accept **Keynesian economics** as helpful in understanding how the macroeconomy works and what can be done to overcome depression.

It was not that Keynesian economics invalidated all of the classical theories. Of course not. The most basic principles of economics are explained in the classical model. That model explains the functioning of the price mechanism and how the market economy works. But that model requires *flexible prices*.

What Keynes said was that there are times—because of price inflexibilities and other conditions in the economy—when the classical macroeconomic model is more misleading than helpful. And Keynes charged that when the real world doesn't behave according to the assumptions of the model, then the classical model will tend to lead to exactly the wrong conclusions.

The Keynesian Focus: The Short-Run, with Inflexible Wages and Prices

Keynes did not deny the classical idea that prices, wages, and interest rates *in the long-run* would tend to move in response to market forces. His argument was that this "long run" was much too long a period of time to just wait and suffer through. To Keynes there was a way to make things better. He counseled that during depression we should forget about "the long-run" and focus on the existing short-run problems and take positive action to deal with them.

---

[1] John Maynard Keynes, *The General Theory of Employment, Interest, and Money* (New York: Harcourt, Brace and World, 1936).

Box 28-1

Feature: The Writings of Keynes before the General Theory

Keynes was about fifty years old when *The General Theory* appeared in 1936. But much earlier, before he reached thirty-five, he had been dealing with the economic realities of the world. In 1919 he wrote a book called the *Economic Consequences of the Peace*. In this book he explained why the World War I peace agreement was unworkable. The book severely criticized the agreement. It said that the agreement would break down and that serious economic disruptions would result. The book cost Keynes some friends. But as it turned out, he was right.

During the 1920s, Keynes was the editor of the *Economic Journal* (one of Britain's most honored economic publications). He continued to write articles criticizing the government. In the mid-1920s he attacked Britain's decision to return to the gold standard. He predicted that this move would be harmful to the nation and that it would fail. But no one seemed to be listening. Again, as it turned out, he was right.

In 1930, Keynes published his two-volume *Treatise on Money*. This *Treatise* explained many of the concepts which later were integrated into his *General Theory* in 1936. But in 1930, no one was ready for a "new look" in economics. Everyone expected the depression to be short. Soon everything would be rolling along again. Keynes disagreed. He saw some serious fundamental problems. Some of these are explained in his *Treatise on Money*. But at that time no one was listening very well.

As the years passed and the depression deepened, Keynes continued to give advice to government leaders. He wrote an open letter to President Roosevelt (published in the *New York Times* in 1933) and he served as occasional adviser to Roosevelt in the 1930s. Then in 1936 *The General Theory* was published. It presented the Keynesian model of the macroeconomy and the Keynesian prescription for overcoming the depression. And it initiated what was to become the **Keynesian Revolution** in macroeconomics.

Recurrent depressions were considered by economists to be "the natural troughs of the business cycle." But Keynes argued that we should not just passively accept these "troughs" and wait for the "natural forces" to return the economy to full employment. Instead, we should take positive action to "fill in the troughs." By lessening these times of wasted manpower and resources we could significantly improve economic welfare.

To Keynes, when there exists a surplus of labor and other inputs, an increase in total spending (aggregate demand) can generate increased employment and output—and with no increase in prices. In terms of the equation of exchange, an increase in total spending (MV) will result in an increase in Q with no increase in P, so the equation of exchange becomes

$$MV = \overline{P}Q.$$

In this situation, P is assumed fixed so that all of an increase in spending ($\uparrow MV$) translates into an increase in real output ($\uparrow Q$). There are no shortages in the labor or other input or output markets and therefore there's no reason for prices to rise.

THE BASIC FOCUS OF KEYNESIAN ECONOMICS

Keynesian economics looks *directly* at the questions: What determines the economy's "operating rate"?—how fast it will run?—*how much* (in total) will be produced? Will all of the labor, capital, land (factors of production) be employed as fully as their owners (and the society) want them to be employed? And, from day-to-day, week-to-week, month-to-month, what would cause the economy to speed up? or slow down?

During the depression there was no denying the fact that total spending for output was not great enough to buy up all of the output. Businesses slowed or stopped production. Unemployment went from bad to worse. Many businesses collapsed. When businesses collapsed, workers lost their jobs and their incomes. So consumer spending dropped.

Many farmers couldn't sell their products. So they couldn't buy tractors, gasoline, fertilizer. The tractor, gasoline, and fertilizer companies had to cut back. Banks—which had made loans to all of these distressed businesses and people—couldn't collect on their loans. Many failed. The moving finger of economic ruin touched more and more units in the economy—more households, farms, businesses. The statistics in box 28-2 tell the sad story.

Keynesian Economics Focuses on the Spending Sectors

Keynes focused directly on what he saw as the problem: *Not enough total spending!* If people and businesses and governments are spending enough to buy up all of the output of the economy, then the economy will keep producing: Full speed ahead! But during the 1930s the total amount that people and businesses were buying decreased and total output and employment slowed down.

Keynes focused on the observed fact that when businesses can't sell all of their output, they don't quickly cut prices. They cut back production and lay off workers. And workers don't quickly accept lower wages either. That's what Keynes saw happening during the Depression.

Keynes took the total spending stream apart and looked at who was doing the spending, and why. He split the basic spending stream into two sectors—spending for consumer goods, and spending for capital goods. Then he tried to get at the *motives* underlying each kind of spending—to try to see what determines

---

Box 28-2

Question: How Bad Was the So-Called "Great Depression" of the 1930s? Very Bad!

In 1929 the size of the real U.S. GNP measured in 1972 dollars amounted to about $300 billion. The unemployment rate amounted to 3.2% of the civilian labor force. Then came the Depression.

Real GNP declined each year, 1930–1933. Then it bottomed out at about $200 billion, with the unemployment rate up to 25%. And when did GNP regain its 1929 level? Not until 1939—ten years later! The unemployment rate did not drop to its 1929 level until the middle of World War II in 1943.

Between 1929 and 1933, investment spending collapsed—down from $55.8 billion to $8.4 billion (in 1972 dollars). This more than 80% drop in investment spending was the largest ever recorded.

In March of 1933 when the government declared a "banking holiday" and closed all the banks, some 24,000 banks were closed. Only about half of them—some 12,000—ever reopened. And the people and businesses who had deposits in the failed banks found that their money was gone.

It's quite understandable why, in 1936 when Keynes' *General Theory* appeared, many people were ready for some alternative to "waiting for the long-run."

how much each sector will spend. The Keynesian idea: If we can understand the *causes* of spending increases or decreases by each sector, then we can understand why the economy speeds up and slows down. And then perhaps we can induce total spending to adjust and move the economy to the desired (full employment) level.

The Keynesian Spending and Income Equation

The basic Keynesian spending and income equation (assuming a closed economy and no government involvement) says that consumer spending (C) plus investment spending (I) equals total spending (E). In the Keynesian model, E is what determines the size of total output—and therefore, total income (Y). All of this can be expressed this way:

$$C + I = E \qquad E = Y \qquad C + I = Y.$$

Suppose C is low because the rate of savings (S) is high. Then unless the rate of investment (I) is equally high, national income (Y) will decrease. Recession. What can be done? This is when the government enters the model.

Keynes said the government can initiate an expansionary monetary policy and cut taxes and thereby (perhaps) stimulate increases in either C or I (or both). But during the Depression Keynes did not expect easy money policies to be of much help.

In the Keynesian model, easy money could stimulate the economy only by **lowering interest rates** enough to stimulate more investment. But with nominal rates already very low and with widespread pessimism in the business community, Keynes didn't think easy money policies could help much. So the Keynesian model emphasizes **fiscal policy**—specifically **increased government spending** (G)—as the most effective technique for overcoming depression.

Keynes recommended that, in addition to cutting taxes, the government should increase its own spending (G) to make up for the deficiencies in C and I. So the spending-income equation becomes:

$$C + I + G = Y$$

Box 28-3

Feature: Keynes at Bretton Woods

From the time *The General Theory* appeared in 1936 until his death ten years later, Keynes continued to play an active role as an adviser to governments on national and international policy. One of his last major involvements was in the Bretton Woods conference (at Bretton Woods, New Hampshire) in 1945. There the postwar system of international exchange was worked out.

At Bretton Woods, Keynes suggested that some alternative to gold should be used in international finance. He suggested using some kind of "paper credits" instead of gold. But at that time the idea of using paper credits was just too far out. He predicted that the time would come when the world would have no choice but to move to some such system.

Almost twenty-five years later the major nations agreed to establish paper credits as an alternative to gold in balancing international financial accounts. A system of "special drawing rights" (SDRs) was initiated in the late 1960s and is now being used in international finance.

The Income (or Investment or Expenditure) Multiplier

In the Keynesian model, when the government increases its spending (↑ G), this generates more income (↑ Y) and that induces consumers to spend more (↑ C). This generates more income for others who then spend more. This is the Keynesian "income multiplier" concept *An increase in either I or G will have a multiple effect on Y because of induced increases in C.*

The multiplier could also be triggered by lowering taxes and leaving both consumers and businesses with more of their incomes to spend. Or easy money and lower interest rate policies might sometimes stimulate increases in both I and C, both of which would have multiple effects on Y. But, as previously explained, Keynes did not expect the easy-money approach (acting alone) to be very effective during serious depression.

In the Keynesian model the only sure way to overcome serious depression is to *increase government spending* (↑ G). Increased G will trigger the income multiplier and get the economy on the road to recovery.

Keynes Challenged the Automatic "S = I at Full Employment" Conclusion of the Classical Model

In the classical model, *interest rate adjustments* ensure that investment spending is exactly great enough to buy up all of the surplus products left in the market by savers. And because all product and labor markets are automatically cleared by price adjustments, this S = I equilibrium is a **full-employment equilibrium**.

Keynes disagreed. Keynes emphasized the importance of *business expectations* (not just interest rates) in influencing investment decisions. And Keynes said that during a severe and lengthy depression, business expectations regarding future profits were likely to be very pessimistic. During the Depression of the 1930s, when nominal interest rates were already very low (short-term rates were less than 1%) Keynes asked: "In these circumstances, how could further reductions in interest rates stimulate investment spending?"

The Keynesian "Savings Gap"

Keynes said that sometimes there is a tendency for savings withdrawals ("leakages") from the spending stream to exceed investment injections. This "savings gap" results in unbought products in the markets. When businesses can't sell all of their output they cut production and lay off workers. Given these conditions, the Keynesian prescription was this.

If the I injection is not great enough to offset the S withdrawal from the income-spending flow, then taxes (T) should be cut to stimulate C + I spending, and government spending (G) should be increased. As government spending adds to the income flow, soon C and I spending will be stimulated. So ultimately the government spending injections can be eliminated. Box 28-4 explains more about this **pragmatic Keynesian prescription**, and why it was quickly and widely accepted by President Roosevelt and many other political leaders during the 1930s.

Feature: The Pragmatic Keynesian Prescription for
Overcoming Depression

The great popular appeal of early Keynesian economics was that it told how to overcome the depression. The prescription was simple: *Take positive actions to stimulate spending!*

When the focus is on the **spending flow**, then the most direct government policy becomes obvious: *Increased government spending!* Also, do whatever possible to induce businesses and consumers to spend more. In a nutshell, this was Keynes' prescription.

Much of what was done during Roosevelt's New Deal went along (more or less) with the Keynesian prescription—not because the actions were theoretically inspired, but because they were **pragmatic**. When people are unemployed it's pragmatic for the government to create money and spend it to hire the unemployed

people. So Keynes gave Roosevelt and the Congress a theory to justify what they were already doing.

Did the Keynesian prescription work? To some extent, maybe. Many unemployed people got government jobs. But the prescription wasn't really tried. There were many anti-Keynesians in the 1930s advising against activist fiscal policies.

The depression lingered on until the government began its massive military spending program for World War II. When the wartime spending began, the depression came to a rapid end. Almost immediately the government had to start working on the opposite problem: too much aggregate demand. Shortages, and inflation.

KEYNESIAN MACROEQUILIBRIUM: WHERE PLANNED SAVING EQUALS PLANNED INVESTMENT

In the Keynesian model, saving is a withdrawal (a leakage) from the income stream. Whenever saving occurs, that means that some of the income earned in the production of the output is not being spent to buy output. So whenever people save, Say's Law wouldn't work unless investment injects enough spending to make up for and offset the saving withdrawals.

When S > I The Economy Slows Down

Whenever the amount of output left in the market by the savers is not all bought up by the investors (by planned investment spending), that means producers are left holding products which they had produced and hoped to sell. This unplanned inventory accumulation means that businesses have money tied up in unsold inventories (unplanned investment). In the Keynesian model, this triggers an economic slowdown.

Looking back at this example, notice that the amount of actual investment by businesses automatically increased enough to equal the amount of saving by consumers. The savers succeeded in saving as much as they wanted to save, but the investors wound up investing more than they had planned to. (The unsold output inventories are unplanned investment.)

Will the businesses cut back production in an attempt to reduce the size of their output inventory accumulation? Of course they will. And this is the Keynesian explanation for an economic slowdown—for a "downturn" which leads to a "trough" in the business cycle.

Macroequilibrium Results from Output (Not Price) Adjustments

In the Keynesian model, the rates of saving and investment are brought into equality *by adjustments in real output and income.* As long as people are trying to save more than businesses want to invest, unplanned investment will occur. When businesses see their unplanned inventories piling up, they cut back production. The economy slows down.

As the economy slows, employment, output, and income will decrease. So the "savings leakage" will decrease. The economic slowdown will continue until the savings leakage from the spending stream is reduced to exactly the size of the planned investment spending injection. And notice that this equilibrium (where S = I) can occur even when there is **widespread unemployment**. How different this is from the classical model!

In the Classical Model, No Slowdown Is Required

In the classical model, remember, a business slowdown was not necessary to bring saving into equality with planned investment. Increased saving would mean increased funds in the loanable funds market. Interest rates would fall and cause investment to increase to where S = I.

Also, in the classical model producers would cut their prices to get rid of those unsold inventories. Workers would work for lower wages so that there would be no involuntary unemployment. All these factors working together would bring savings and investment into equality and all markets would be cleared **at full employment**. No slowdown in the economy would occur.

During Past Recessions Prices Haven't Adjusted Downward Quickly

Keynes looked at the real world and saw that during recessions neither prices nor wages have moved down quickly. Nor have interest rates proven capable, in the short run, or bringing saving and investment into equality. The Keynesian model tries to explain these observable short-run real-world conditions.

MACROEQUILIBRIUM IN THE CIRCULAR FLOW DIAGRAM: THE KEYNESIAN TWO-SPENDING-SECTOR (C + I) MODEL

In the private domestic economy—in the two-spending-sector (C + I) model—macroequilibrium occurs where the rate of planned saving (the only withdrawal from the spending flow) is exactly equal to and offset by the rate of planned investment (the only injection into the spending flow).

Figure 28-1 shows a simplified version of the circular flow diagram. This figure illustrates the fact that for the spending flow to remain the same size, the planned investment injections must be exactly equal to the planned saving withdrawals. When planned investment injections are smaller than saving withdrawals the size of the spending flow will decrease.

Figure 28-1.   The Circular Flow Diagram: The Spending Flow from Households to Businesses Increases or Decreases Depending on the Savings-Investment Relationship.

Panel A. When $S < I$ the spending flow (Y) increases from Period 0 to Period 1.

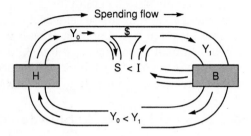

Panel B. When $S > I$ the spending flow (Y) decreases from Period 0 to Period 1.

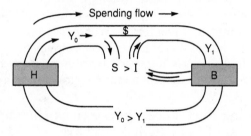

Panel C. Only When $S = I$ does the size of the spending flow remain the same from Period 0 to Period 1. Y is in equilibrium.

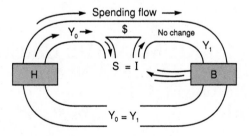

When planned investment injections are larger than planned savings withdrawals the spending flow will increase. Only when S = I will the size of the spending flow remain the same. And since the Keynesian model assumes that prices are fixed, changes in the size of the spending flow are entirely reflected in the real flows—numbers of units of real employment, real output, and real income.

Is S = I a Desirable Condition? Or not?

So in the Keynesian paradigm, which is preferable? S = I? or S > I? or I > S? That depends entirely on the condition of the economy at the moment. Suppose aggregate demand is so great that shortages are showing up in most markets and inflationary pressures are strong. The S > I alternative would decrease aggregate demand and relieve the inflationary pressures.

But what if the economy is in a depression? Then the I > S alternative would increase total spending (aggregate demand) and bring increased employment, output, and income. Whenever excessive unemployment exists, the I > S condition would be preferred. Only when aggregate demand is just great enough to bring full employment—and no greater than that—would the S = I condition be most desirable.

IN THE KEYNESIAN MODEL, TOTAL SPENDING (E) HOLDS THE KEY

In the Keynesian model total spending is the driving force which keeps the economy going and growing. Much of Keynesian economics is concerned with the question: "What determines the level (rate) of total spending?" That's the key question which the Keynesian model is designed to answer.

The Propensity to Consume

In the Keynesian model, the amount the public will want to spend for consumer goods (C) is determined by the size of their disposable income (DI). Assuming no taxes, DI is equal to the national income (Y). As Y changes, consumer spending changes in the same direction. C is a positive function of Y: $C = f(\overset{+}{Y})$. This is what Keynes called "the propensity to consume."

For any given level of national income, there will be an **average propensity to consume** (APC). *The APC is the fraction of national income which the public will want to spend for consumer goods.* APC = C/Y.

For example, suppose national income is $100 billion and the total amount that the public would like to spend for consumer goods is $90 billion. Then the APC (C/Y) is 90/100 = 9/10 = 90% = 0.9.

The Propensity to Save

If you know that the APC is 9/10 or 0.9 then you know that the **average propensity to save** (APS) must be 1/10 or 0.1 because *savings is defined as income earned but not spent for consumer goods.* If 0.9 of the earned income would be spent for consumer goods, then the remaining 0.1 would be "not spent for consumer goods," and therefore (by our definition) "saved." APS = 1 − APC; 1 − 0.9 = 0.1. Suppose Y = 100 and S = 10. Then APS = S/Y = 10/100 = 1/10 = 0.1.

MACROEQUILIBRIUM IN THE KEYNESIAN CROSS DIAGRAM

Now spend a few minutes studying figure 28-2 which shows and explains the Keynesian national spending-national income diagram, often referred to as the "Keynesian Cross" diagram.

The consumption function (straight-line curve) in figure 28-2 indicates that the larger the Y, the smaller the APC. For example, when Y is $50, C is $50. APC is 100% and APS is zero.

Suppose Y is $100, C will be $90. That's *a larger total amount* of C but it's *a smaller fraction of Y*.

At Y = $100, APC is 90/100, or 0.9. APS is 10/100 or 0.1. The more Y increases, the more APC decreases and APS increases. This consumption function curve indicates that as incomes rise people tend to save a larger percentage. It also indicates that national income could never drop below $50.

At Y = $50, C would support the total Y, with no spending injections required from investors or anyone else. But the curve also indicates that the only way that Y could ever be greater than $50 is for spending from some other source—other than spending for consumer goods—to be injected into the spending flow.

Given this consumption function.

1. if the only spending source is consumer spending, and

2. if all income received is already being spent for consumer goods, then

3. there's no way for C to increase, and therefore

4. Y cannot increase unless a non-C spending injection comes in from somewhere.

The Marginal Propensity to Consume, and to Save

The consumption function curve in figure 28-2 slopes upward, indicating that as income rises, people will want to spend more for consumer goods. The steepness of the curve answers the question: How much more?—i.e., the slope indicates the **marginal propensity to consume** (MPC). *The MPC is defined as that fraction of an increase in income which consumers would want to spend for consumer goods:* MPC = $\Delta C/\Delta Y$.

Suppose national income increases by $10 billion and consumer spending increases by $8 billion. Then MPC is 8/10, or 0.8. And when MPC = 0.8 it's quite obvious that the **marginal propensity to save** (MPS) is 0.2. MPS = 1 − MPC. 1 − 0.8 = 0.2. MPS = $\Delta S/\Delta Y$ = 2/10 = 0.2.

The Consumption Function: The Rate of C (and of S) Is Determined by—Is a Function of—Y

The consumption function curve shows the size of consumer spending (C) at each size of national income (Y). The curve shows how much C changes in response to

Figure 28-2.   The Keynesian Cross Diagram: The Consumption and Savings Functions

When consumer spending is the only spending source, equilibrium Y is at Ye, far below full employment at Yf. The only way to move toward Yf is to have spending injections added into the basic consumer spending flow. An investment injection is called for!

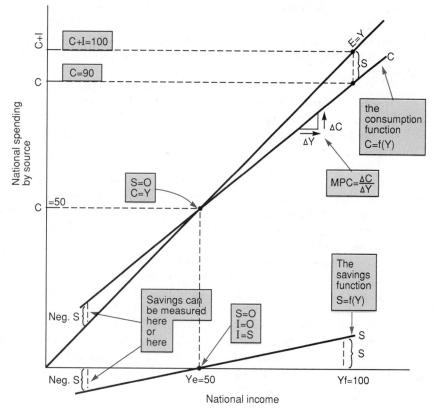

The vertical axis measures expenditures, by source. In the two-sector model the spending sources are only C and I. The horizontal axis measures the total size of the national income (Y). Total spending for output bought (C + I) must always be equal to total received for output sold (Y). So if total expenditures on the vertical axis amount to $50 billion, then national income on the horizontal axis must also equal $50 billion. The 45-degree line shows that.

The 45-degree line is the "national expenditure (E) equals national income (Y)" line—i.e., the E = Y line. For any expenditure level (E) on the vertical axis, the E = Y line indicates the corresponding level of Y on the horizontal axis.

any given change in Y. If all of an increase in income was spent for consumer goods, then the C line would rise as rapidly as the E = Y line. But it doesn't because of the marginal propensity to save (MPS).

The C curve indicates that MPC is less than 100% (less than 1), because MPS is positive—greater than zero. The upward slope of the saving curve shows the same thing.

Equilibrium Occurs Where S = I

In figure 28-2, suppose the only spending source is consumer spending. Then the equilibrium level of Y is at Ye = 50. That's where the savings withdrawal is zero. Since I is zero, equilibrium Y must be where S is also zero.

At all levels of Y greater than Ye, saving withdrawals would be positive and the spending flow would be shrinking since I = 0 and S > I. The spending flow would keep decreasing to where S = 0 (where S = I), at Ye = 50.

At any level of Y less than Ye there would be *negative savings*. This means that on the average, people would be spending amounts *greater than* their incomes—spending past savings, or going into debt to try to maintain their standards of living (or to keep from starving to death!).

Negative saving—also called "dissaving"—is an injection into the income stream. In terms of the circular flow diagram (figure 28-1), negative saving would mean a net inflow (rather than the usual outflow) through the "savings withdrawal pipe." As long as negative saving continues, the size of the spending flow will increase. This will push national income up to Ye in figure 28-2.

At Ye, national income is in equilibrium. In the Keynesian short-run, fixed-prices model this is the level of spending-output-income which will continue to exist. There is nothing in the Keynesian model which would tend to change it.

But what if Ye is a seriously depressed level of Y? Suppose full employment rate of Y is at Yf. It would be desirable for spending and income to increase to Yf. But how could that happen?

You already know that if the level of investment spending—injections into the income stream—happened to increase above zero, then the size of the spending flow would increase, and real employment, output, and income would increase. Suppose investment spending increased above zero. Then the size of the total spending flow would keep increasing for as long as the size of the investment inflow continued to be greater than the size of the saving outflow. For the common sense logic of this, look back at the circular flow diagram in figure 28-1. *As long as the injection inflows are larger than the withdrawal outflows, the total spending flow will continue to increase.*

A Given Investment Injection Will Result in a Multiple Expansion of Spending, Real Output, and Income

Figure 28-3 shows the same diagram as the previous figure except that here there is an investment injection. The C + I curve lies $10 billion higher than the C curve, indicating that in this basic "initial view" of the Keynesian model, the size of the investment injection is assumed to be unaffected by changes in the size of national income. Here, I is considered to be autonomous—i.e., independent of changes in Y.

Figure 28-3 indicates that a constant rate of investment of $10 billion in this economy results in an increase in Y of $50 billion. Equilibrium Y moves up from $50 billion to $100 billion as a result of ↑I of only $10 billion.

When the national income is $100 billion, national spending must also be $100 billion. C is $90 billion and the remainder is I = $10 billion. In terms of the circular flow diagram (figure 28-1), the investment inflow of $10 billion is now being exactly offset by a savings outflow of $10 billion. So the size of the circular spending flow is constant at $100 billion.

**Figure 28-3.   The Keynesian Cross Diagram: The Effect of an
Inflow of Investment Spending**

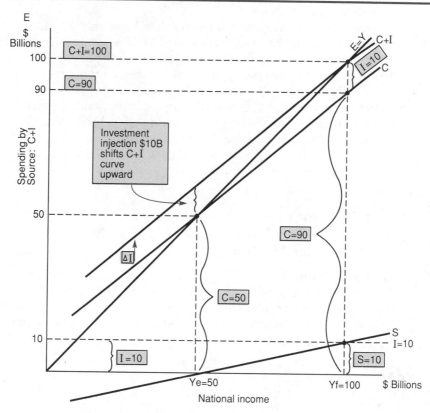

An investment injection of $10 billion increases Y by $50 billion—from $50 billion to
$100 billion. Induced consumer spending—the multiplier effect—generates $40 billion
(80%) of the increase. Only $10 billion (20%) of the increase represents the investment
injection. The new equilibrium is at the level of Y where S = $10 billion, where S = I.

Box 28-5

Question: What About a Shift of the Consumption Function?

In the Keynesian model the consumption function is usually considered to be stable. However, a significant change in consumer optimism or pessimism—perhaps a big runup in the stock market or some other influence—might shift the consumption function curve upward. The effect of this would be the same as if a new investment injection (I) or a government expenditure injection (G) had been added into the income stream.

An *upward shift* of the consumption function means a *downward shift* of the savings function. Following the shift, national income would need to increase enough to bring the savings withdrawal back up to the previous level of equality with investment. So the multiplier effect would be the same as with an investment injection.

In figure 28-3, the $10 billion investment injection forced national income to increase from Ye ($50 billion) to Yf ($100 billion). Why? Because of the income multiplier. Only at Yf will the saving outflow be $10 billion—exactly equal to the investment injection inflow.

Suppose the investment injection had been only $5 billion. Then Y would have increased only half as much—to $75 billion, where S = $5 billion and S = I. (These numbers can be read from the graph in figure 28-3, or can be calculated using simple algebra, as explained in the appendix to this chapter.)

The bottom line: The size of the saving outflow is a function of the size of national income: S = f(Y). An increase of investment spending of any size will force an increase in the size of the spending flow. *The spending flow will (must!) continue to increase in size until the saving outflow is induced to increase enough to exactly equal and offset the investment inflow.* The economy will stop expanding and will be in macroequilibrium only at the level of Y where S = I.

Equilibrium National Income Depends on (1) The Size of the Spending Injections, and (2) The Size of the Income Multiplier

The equilibrium level of Y in the Keynesian model depends on two important factors: (1) the size of the investment inflow, and (2) the extent of the "income multiplier effect." So it is necessary to understand the determinants of these key variables. That's what you'll be reading about in the next chapter.

SUMMARY

- Keynes' revolutionary book, *The General Theory of Employment, Interest, and Money* (1936) focused on causes of the depression and offered a new way of explaining what was happening.

- The *General Theory* builds a model which focuses on the short run, with inflexible wages and prices. The model emphasizes **total spending** (aggregate demand) as the driving force which generates the economy's output and income.

- The basic two-sector Keynesian "spending and income equation" is C + I = Y, but the government (G) could spend and increase the level of Y: C + I + G = Y. Keynes recommended ↑ G to compensate for ↓ I and keep the economy running at full employment.

- The Keynesian **income multiplier** says that increases in spending from any source will have a multiple effect on Y because of the MPC—the **consumer-responding effect**. As Y increases, C increases (by the MPC) and induces further increases in Y which induce further increases in C, etc.

- In the Keynesian model, when I > S, injections into the income stream are greater than withdrawals so the stream gets larger. When S > I, withdrawals are greater than injections so the stream gets smaller. Only **where S = I** does macroequilibrium exist.

- In the **Keynesian Cross diagram** the consumption function curve indicates the amount of consumer spending at each level of income. The height of the curve indicates the **average propensity to consume** (APC). APC = C/Y.

- The upward slope of the C curve shows how much consumer spending increases for each unit of increase in Y. So it tells the **marginal propensity to consume** (MPC). MPC = ΔC/ΔY.

- In the simple Keynesian model presented in this chapter, the level of investment spending and the size of the income multiplier determine the equilibrium level of Y. The next chapter explains all this in more detail.

Important Principles, Issues, Concepts, Terms

John Maynard Keynes

Keynesian economics

The General Theory of Employment, Interest, and Money (1936)

The short-run view

Wage and price inflexibility

"Troughs of the business cycle"

The Keynesian view: MV = $\bar{P}$Q

The "Spending sectors" breakdown

C + I = Y

C + I + G = Y

The income (investment, expenditure) multiplier

The "savings gap"

The pragmatic Keynesian prescription

Why S = I is macroequilibrium

How S = I is achieved in the Keynesian model

Macroequilibrium in the circular flow diagram

Macroequilibrium in the Keynesian Cross diagram

Propensity to consume: APC and MPC

Propensity to save: APS and MPS

Negative saving (dissaving)

Questions

1. Explain some of the reasons Keynes used for rejecting the classical model during times of depression.

2. Keynes placed much emphasis on the existence of *inflexible prices*. Explain why this issue is so important in the Keynesian macroeconomic model.

3. What was the *pragmatic Keynesian prescription* for overcoming the depression? What does it mean to say that the prescription was "pragmatic?"

4. When Keynes said: "In the long run we are all dead," what was the point he was trying to make? And why did he consider this point to be so important?

5. It is sometimes said that Keynes turned around Say's Law and came up with what might be called Keynes Law: "Demand creates its own supply." Can you explain what all this means? Try.

6. Explain the equation C + I + G = Y. Exactly what does this say? Would it always be true? Explain.

7. In the classical model, the S = I equilibrium condition is brought about by interest rate adjustments in the funds markets. But in the Keynesian model the S = I equilibrium is brought about by changes in the size of Y. Explain what all this means, and how the adjustment works in each case.

8. Why did Keynes reject the idea that interest rate adjustments could play an important role in overcoming the depression?

9. In the classical model, macroequilibrium always occurs at full employment. In the Keynesian model it does not. Explain (in each case) why this is true.

10. Keynes talked about a "savings gap" which, in the Keynesian model, tends to get larger as Y increases. Explain the idea of the "savings gap" and why it might tend to get larger.

11. In the Keynesian Cross diagram, Y could never drop below the level at which the C curve crosses the E = Y curve. Explain why.

Suggested Readings

Chick, Victoria. *Macroeconomics After Keynes: A Reconsideration of the General Theory.* Cambridge, Mass: MIT Press, 1984.

Clower, Robert W. "The Keynesian Counter-Revolution: A Theoretical Appraisal." in Robert w. Clower, ed. *Monetary Theory, Selected Readings.* Baltimore: Penguin Books, 1969, pp. 270–297.

Friedman, Milton. *A Theory of the Consumption Function.* Princeton: Princeton University Press, 1957.

Hansen, Alvin H. *A Guide to Keynes.* New York: McGraw-Hill, 1953.

Kaldor, N. "Keynesian Economics After 50 Years." in *Keynes and the Modern World.* edited by Worstwick and Trevithick, Cambridge: Cambridge University Press, 1983.

Keynes, J. M. *The General Theory of Employment, Interest and Money.* London: Macmillan, 1936.

Klein, Lawrence Robert. *The Keynesian Revolution,* 2nd ed. New York: Macmillan, 1966.

Leijonhufvud, Axel. *On Keynesian Economics and the Economics of Keynes: A Study in Monetary Theory.* New York: Oxford University Press, 1968.

Meltzer, Allan H. "Keynes General Theory: A Different Perspective." *Journal of Economic Literature* (March 1981), 34–64.

Niman, Neal B. "Keynes and the Invisible Hand Theorem." *Journal of Post Keynesian Economics* 10(1), Fall 1987, pp. 105–115.

Patinkin, D. *Keynes' Monetary Thought.* Durham, N.C.: Duke University Press, 1976.

Shapiro, Robert J. "Look Who's Making a Comeback." *U.S. News and World Report.* (Feb. 1, 1988), 43–45.

CHAPTER 29

Points of Income-Spending Equilibrium: The "IS" Curve

Chapter Objectives

This chapter continues the analysis of the total spending flow. It emphasizes the relationship between **investment injections** and **savings withdrawals** and it explains *why and how the savings withdrawals automatically adjust to equal the investment injections*, and how this is illustrated by **the IS curve**.

After you study this chapter you will understand and be able to explain:

1. The **income multiplier** and how it works, and the influence of the **marginal propensity to consume** on the size of the multiplier.

2. How to use the Keynesian Cross diagram to illustrate (a) the multiplier and (b) the **macroequilibrium level** of national income, where $S = I$.

3. The relationship between **interest rates** and the rate of **investment spending** and how to use the **marginal efficiency of investment** (MEI) curve to illustrate this.

4. How changes in real interest rates (r) and national income (Y) cause changes in the rate of investment spending (I) and the rate of savings withdrawals (S), and how to use the IS curve to illustrate these changes.

5. The various factors which influence the location and the slope of the IS curve.

6. Why each point on the IS curve indicates equilibrium in the spending flows and product markets, and why macroequilibrium of the economy can only occur at some point on this curve.

THE INCOME (OR INVESTMENT, OR EXPENDITURE) MULTIPLIER

The previous chapter introduced you to the Keynesian income multiplier. This chapter explains it more thoroughly.

Suppose that for some reason there is an increase in national income (Y). The marginal propensity to consume (MPC) indicates that as Y increases, people are induced to spend more for consumer goods. So whenever Y increases (by whatever amount and for whatever reason) the increased Y will induce consumer spending (C) to increase. Then the increased C will cause Y to increase even more. That's the multiplier at work.

The Multiplier Results from the MPC

In the Keynesian Cross diagram, the upward slope of the consumption function (C) illustrates this relationship: Greater Y brings greater C. The steeper the C curve the greater the MPC and therefore the greater this "induced consumer respending effect."

This effect is variously called: "the investment multiplier" or "the income multiplier" or "the expenditure multiplier." Whichever term is used, it means the same thing: *Any increase in expenditures—any upward shift of the expenditure (C + I) curve—will cause national income (Y) to increase. The increase will induce consumer spending (C) to increase and that will cause Y to increase more, causing C to increase more, etc., etc.*

The Multiplier Is Limited by the MPS

It is the MPC—induced consumer spending as income increases—which generates this **income multiplier effect**. It is the MPS—induced savings as income increases—which **limits the size** of the multiplier.

In terms of the circular flow diagram, suppose the rate of investment spending increases. Now the flow of investment spending into the income stream will be larger than the savings withdrawals. The income stream must increase until the savings outflow is large enough to equal and offset the (now larger) investment inflow.

As income increases, the rate of savings withdrawals increases (because of MPS). National income will continue to increase until S is induced to increase to where S = I.

Suppose MPC happened to be 100% = 1. Then MPS would be zero. People with increased incomes would spend all of the increase to buy consumer goods and there would be no increased saving. Therefore there would be no limit to the size of the multiplier. It would be infinite!

With increased investment injections (nominal I) and no increase in savings withdrawals (nominal S), the size of I would remain perpetually greater than the size of S. So any increase in the rate of investment spending would cause Y to go on increasing forever! The MPS is what prevents this from happening.

What about the opposite case? Suppose MPS happened to be one. Then MPC would be zero. An increase in the rate of investment spending (and in national income) would induce an immediate and equal increase in savings withdrawals. National income would increase by the amount of the investment injection, but by no more than that. There wouldn't be any "multiplying effect" at all! The multiplier would be one, meaning that Y would increase one time—by the amount of the increased rate of investment spending, and that's all.

National Income Will Continue to Increase Until S = I

For how long will an increased rate of investment injections cause national income to continue to increase? Until national income increases to where *the savings outflow* from the income stream will be exactly equal to (and will exactly offset) *the investment inflow* into the stream. The larger the marginal propensity to consume (MPC) the smaller the marginal propensity to save (MPS) and the more national income must expand to induce the savings outflow to increase enough to equal the investment inflow.

Example: If MPS is 0.2, then for each $10 billion increase in national income, savings withdrawals will be induced to increase by $2 billion. So to induce the savings withdrawal to increase by $10 billion, Y must increase by $50 billion. But if MPS was 0.5, Y would only need to increase by $20 billion to induce a savings-rate increase of $10 billion.

The Income Multiplier Formula

The income multiplier can be thought of as *a number*, which answers the question: "By what multiple of ↑I must Y increase to induce S to increase to where $\Delta S = \Delta I$?" For example, if I increases by 10, how many times ten must Y increase to induce S to increase by 10? That's exactly what the income multiplier number tells you.

The formula for the income multiplier is nothing more than the reciprocal of the marginal propensity to save:

$$\text{Income multiplier} = \frac{1}{1 - \text{MPC}}, \text{ or } \frac{1}{\text{MPS}}.$$

When MPC = 0.8 then 1-MPC (=MPS) = 0.2 and the multiplier is 1/0.2 = 5. This says that when the rate of investment spending increases by ∆I, Y must increased by five times I. Why? Because that's how much Y must increase to induce S to increase to where $\Delta S = \Delta I$ and S = I.

Example: With a multiplier of 5, each $1 increase in the rate of investment will cause a $5 increase in Y. That's how much Y must increase to induce S to increase by $1. Until S increases by $1, I > S. So Y will continue to increase. Only when S = $1 will $\Delta S = \Delta I$ to reestablish macroequilibrium where S = I.[1]

Once you know how to calculate the multiplier, the step-by-step period analysis you read through a moment ago is unnecessary. When you know that the multiplier is five, you know that a $10 billion increase in the rate of investment spending is going to result in a five-fold ($50 billion) increase in Y. National income *must* increase by $50 billion to induce the savings rate to increase by $10 billion where S = I.

Figure 29-1 illustrates all of this in the Keynesian Cross diagram. There you can see the key role of the MPC, the MPS, and the income multiplier in the Keynesian model of the macroeconomy. The figure shows the investment injection added to the consumption function at each level of Y, so that the C curve becomes the C + I curve.

THE KEYNESIAN FOUR-SPENDING-SECTOR MODEL

So far you have been reading about the Keynesian two-spending-sector (C + I) model. In this model the only injection is investment spending and the only withdrawal is savings. But in fact there are other injectons into and withdrawals from the spending stream, and all of the injections have multiplying effects. Here's a brief look at the expanded Keynesian model.

---

[1] The appendixes to this chapter explain how to use algebra to calculate and work with the income multiplier.

Figure 29-1.   The Income Multiplier in the Keynesian Cross Diagram

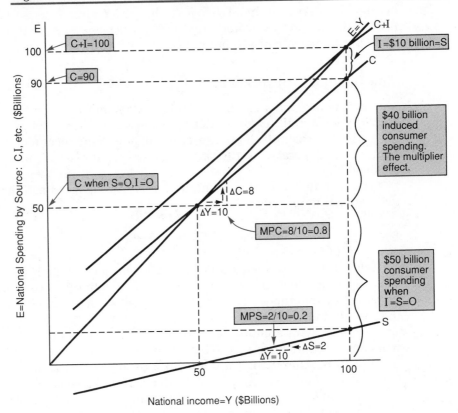

With a $10 billion investment injection, the C curve becomes the C + I curve and ultimately results in a $50 billion increase in Y. MPC = 0.8, so MPS = 0.2 and the multiplier is 1/0.2 = 5. A $10 billion increase in the rate of I, times 5, equals a $50 billion increase in Y.

Note: This graph assumes that the rate of I does not change as Y increases from $50b to $100b. In the following chapters in the IS-LM diagram you'll see that this assumption isn't realistic, and you'll find out how to define a more realistic macroequilibrium, where I is variable.

The Four Spending Sources: C + I + G + EX

The total spending flow is made up of spending by the public for consumer goods (C), spending by businesses (I), government spending (G), and foreign spending for our goods—our exports (EX).

In the Keynesian model the basic size of the spending flow is determined by C. All of the other sources of spending are looked at as injections which tend to increase the size of the spending flow above the basic level determined by C. But there are withdrawals which tend to offset these injections.

The Three Withdrawals: S + T + IM

Withdrawals from the spending flow include savings (S), taxes, (T) and our spending for foreign goods—our imports (IM).

Macroequilibrium in the Keynesian model occurs where total injections into the spending flow are exactly equal to and offset by total withdrawals from the flow—where I + G + EX = S + T + IM. You should be aware that there are these other spending injections (other than I) and these other withdrawals (other than S). But for understanding the Keynesian model and how it works, the two sector (C + I) model is quite sufficient and less likely to be confusing. So that's the model which you will be reading about and working with most of the time.

NATIONAL INCOME (CETERIS PARIBUS) IS A FUNCTION OF THE RATE OF INVESTMENT SPENDING

Figure 29-2 shows the savings function from figure 29-1 and indicates different equilibrium levels of national income. The figure shows that each time the investment inflow increases, national income increases to where the savings outflow equals the (larger) investment inflow.

Figure 29-2.   Macroequilibrium: The level of Y Where S = I

Increased I brings increased Y. Increased Y brings increased S. Y increases until S = I. Equilibrium Y occurs where the rate of investment inflow is exactly equal to and offset by the rate of savings outflow.

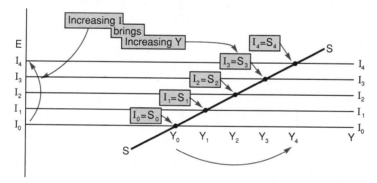

- When I > S, Y will increase and force S to increase to where S = I.
- When I < S, Y will decrease and force S to decrease to where S = I.

With a given **consumption function**, since Y − C = S, the **savings function** is also given. So equilibrium Y depends on the rate of I. As I increases from I_0 to I_1, I_2, etc., the equilibrium level of Y increases from Y_0 to Y_1, Y_2, etc.

This result must be true, because as the size of I increases from I_0 to I_1, then national income will begin to increase. It must continue to increase until the rate of the savings outflow is exactly equal to the rate of the investment inflow.

The Model Works Because C and S Are Functions of Y

The Keynesian consumption function illustrates the assumption of the Keynesian model that consumer spending is mostly *induced spending*—it depends on (is a function of) the size of national income: $C = f(Y)$.

Since C is a function of Y, S is also a function of Y. In fact, the automatic adjustment mechanism in the Keynesian model depends on $S = f(Y)$. Given this functional relationship, Y can change (increase or decrease) and thereby force S to increase or decrease to where $S = I$. That's what you saw in figure 29-2.

Given C, the Ultimate Outcome Depends on I

With any given consumption function, the ultimate size of Y depends on the size of the injections into the spending flow. The key injection is **investment spending** (I). So in this model, with the C function given, the key to the size of equilibrium Y is the *level of investment spending*.

Figure 29-2 shows that because of the multiplying effect of changes in investment spending, relatively small changes in I can bring relatively large changes in Y. The figure shows several possible equilibrium positions (Y_0, Y_1, Y_2, etc.). Each equilibrium position is determined by the size of the investment spending inflow.

Note that each equilibrium position is located by the equality between savings and investment ($S = I$). And note also that there is no reference to a "natural rate" of output, employment, or income. In this short-run model, equilibrium can occur just as easily with high unemployment as with full employment. It all depends on the rate of investment spending. That's why the Keynesian model places great emphasis on analyzing the factors which influence investment spending.

THE INVESTMENT SPENDING DECISION: EXPECTED RETURNS AND INTEREST COSTS

A business firm will only make an investment when the returns on the investment are expected to cover all costs and yield an adequate profit. The cost of making an investment is the cost of tying up those funds over the life of the investment. Either it is the cost of the borrowed funds, or, if the business uses its own funds, it is the opportunity cost—the alternative income opportunities foregone.

No investment would be made unless it was expected to be profitable—to return the amount of the original investment, plus something more. How much more? That depends on the **interest rate**. Why? Because the investment decision depends crucially on the relationship between the *interest cost* and the *expected rate of return* on the investment.

There Are Always a Variety of Investment Opportunities

In the Keynesian model it is assumed that there will be, at any moment, (1) a limited number of opportunities to make investments promising a very high return, (2) additional opportunities to make investments in projects offering somewhat lower returns, and (3) even more opportunities to make investments in even lower-return projects. This leads to the idea of a downward sloping **investment opportunities** curve as shown in figure 29-3.

From figure 29-3 you can conclude that if interest rates are very high, only the few very-high-expected-return projects will be undertaken. But at lower interest rates a greater number of investment opportunities would be feasible. So, *ceteris paribus*, falling interest rates would lead to increased investment spending, greater injections into the spending flow, and rising national income.

The Marginal Efficiency of Investment (MEI)

The link between *the real rate of interest* and *the rate of investment spending* plays a key role in the Keynesian model. Keynes focused on the **marginal efficiency of investment** (MEI), which is *the expected additional return from an*

Figure 29-3.   The "Investment Opportunities" Curve

As the number of projects undertaken increases, the expected rate of return on the marginal projects decreases.

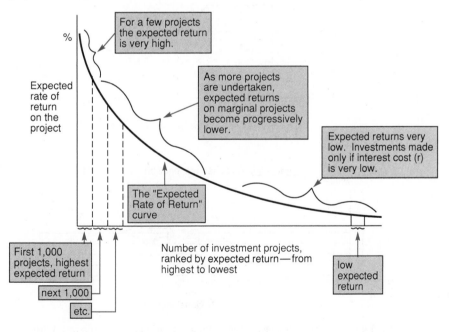

From this curve you can intuitively conclude that *ceteris paribus*, the lower the interest rate:

1. the greater the number of investment projects which will be profitable and (therefore) undertaken and

2. the greater the total amount of investment spending (I) injected into the income stream, and therefore

3. the greater national income (Y) will be.

additional investment. It's the **expected marginal productivity** of an additional unit of capital. Keynes related the MEI to the real cost of making the investments—i.e., to the real interest rate. Figure 29-4 shows the MEI curve. It shows
the increase in investment spending which would result from a drop in the real
interest rate (r).

You will notice that the MEI curve in figure 29-4 looks quite similar to the
"investment opportunities" curve in figure 29-3. Actually both are showing the
same situation, but the focus is different. The "investment opportunities" curve
focuses on the *falling expected returns* on marginal investments. The MEI curve

Figure 29-4.   The MEI Curve and Equilibrium Y Where S = I

Panel A. The investment function. Given the MEI curve, I = f(r).
The number of projects undertaken depends on the real interest cost
(r), so lower r induces higher I.

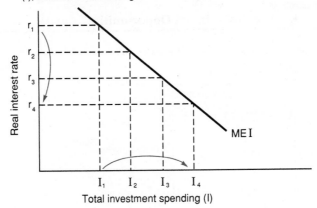

Panel B. The Savings Function. As I changes, equilibrium Y moves to
where S = I.

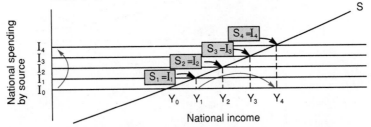

The MEI curve shows the level of investment at various rates of interest. With
this information you can insert I in Panel B, and immediately see the equilibrium level of national income: Where S = I.

In Panel A, interest rate r_1 leads to an investment rate of I_1. In Panel B you
see that an investment rate of I_1 leads to national income Y_1, where savings
(S_1) is equal to investment (I_1).

At the opposite extreme, interest rate r_4 leads to investment rate I_4, which
brings national income rate Y_4 where again in the savings rate is equal to the
investment rate ($S4 = I_4$).

focuses on the *falling interest rates* required to induce businesses to invest in those marginal projects. You can see that both curves are showing exactly the same thing:

1. As more projects are undertaken, the marginal projects become progressively less profitable, and
2. Only at lower interest cost will the less profitable investments be made.

From figure 29-4, Panels A and B, you can draw an interesting conclusion: If this model really works, all we need to do to increase employment in the economy is to bring down interest rates! Lower interest rates will stimulate more investment and bring more employment, output, and income. Also, as long as these curves in figure 29-4 stay in place (do not shift) *the only way* we can get an increase in employment, output, and income is through a decrease in interest rates.

You can see that *in the Keynesian model the level of real interest rates plays a very important role.* That conclusion will become even more obvious as you read the next section which develops the "IS" curve.

THE IS CURVE: COMBINATIONS OF *r* AND Y AT WHICH S = I

In figure 29-4 you saw a two-step process for finding equilibrium Y, where S = I. First, r determines I (Panel A), then I determines Y (Panel B). Wouldn't it be possible (and useful) to combine both of these effects (Panels A and B) into a single curve? Yes!

You can leave out the intermediate step—the effect of r on I—and say it this way: As interest rates fall from r_1 to r_4, equilibrium national income increases from Y_1 to Y_4. And if you plot this relationship, what you get is an "I equals S" curve which is called "the IS curve."

The **IS curve** shows combinations of r and Y which bring I and S into equality. At each point on the IS curve, I = S and the spending flow is in equilibrium. Since injections into and withdrawals from the flow are equal, that means that the amount being spent to buy the output of the economy is exactly equal to the amount of income being received. So the product markets are cleared—no surpluses, no shortages.

The IS curve shows all combinations of r and Y at which S = I, meaning that the spending flows and the product markets are in equilibrium.

Figure 29-5 shows the IS curve. You can see that when the interest rate is high (r_1), the equilibrium level of national income is low (Y_1). Why? Because the high interest rate keeps investment low; the low investment keeps national income low; the low national income keeps savings low: High r brings low I which brings low Y which brings low S. Low S = low I. Macroequilibrium.

When the interest rate is low (r_4), the equilibrium level of national income is high (Y_4). The low interest rate brings high investment which brings high national income which brings a high rate of saving: Low r brings high I which brings high Y which brings high S. High S = high I. Macroequilibrium.

Figure 29-5.   The IS Curve: Macroequilibrium Combinations of
_r_ and Y, Where I = S
As interest rates fall, national income increases.

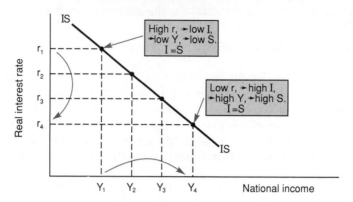

Lower interest rates (↓ _r_) induce greater investment spending (↑ I). The
↑ I causes national income to increase (↑ Y). National income continues to increase as long as I > S. Increasing Y induces increasing S.
Eventually S will increase enough to equal I. At that level of Y the
economy is in macroequilibrium.

The IS Curve Does Not Identify a Specific Equilibrium Level of Y

As you look at the IS curve you may ask: "What good is it?" It certainly doesn't tell
you what the equilibrium level of national income will be.

The IS curve tells you that it is possible to have an equilibrium with a high
level of employment, output, and income, at Y_4—but only if the interest rate
happens to be at r_4. And it also tells you that you could have a very low level of
employment, output, and income (at Y_1) if the interest rate happened to be at r_1.

Box 29-1

Feature: A Real-World-Type Hypothetical Example of the IS Curve:
The Effects of _r_ on I, I on Y, and Y on S

Suppose the economy is depressed, and suppose many corporations would like to sell
bonds and build new plants. But suppose all
these decision makers think interest rates are
too high. So they don't borrow and spend.

Then suppose interest rates fall. Suddenly
all this money is borrowed and spent, people
are hired, incomes rise and the people with the
higher income increase their spending for consumer goods. National income continues to
rise. Incomes must continue to rise until people

are induced to save enough to drain off this
high rate of investment spending.

How much must Y increase to bring the
economy into equilibrium? That depends on
the slope of the IS curve. It depends on (1) how
responsive investment spending is to interest
rate changes, and (2) the size of the marginal
propensity to save. The size of MPS determines
how much Y must increase to induce S to increase enough to equal the new rate of I.

But from the IS curve you have no way to figure what the equilibrium level of national income will be.

The IS Curve Illustrates the Effect of *r* on Y

The IS curve indicates that when interest rates are high, the spending flow will be small. The investment injection will be small and the savings withdrawal will be small. The economy will be depressed.

Conversely, at low interest rates the size of the spending flow will be large. The investment injection will be large and the savings withdrawal will be large. The economy will be booming.

Which of these possible outcomes will occur? It depends on the interest rate. So before we can go any farther we must know *what determines the interest rate in this model.* You'll find out about that in the next chapter.

Box 29-2

Feature: **Summary of Factors Influencing the Slope and Location of the IS Curve**

THE SLOPE OF THE CURVE

A steeper IS curve would indicate:

1. I less responsive to Δr—i.e., lower interest rate elasticity of I. A given Δr brings less ΔI and therefore less ΔY

    and/or

2. MPC smaller, MPS larger. A given ΔY brings more ΔS. So a given ΔI requires smaller ΔY to bring ΔS into equality with ΔI.

    Stated differently:

    The smaller MPC (the larger MPS) the smaller the income multiplier. So the smaller ΔY in response to a given ΔI.

Conversely, a flatter IS curve would indicate:

I more responsive to Δr—i.e., greater interest rate elasticity of I.

MPC higher; MPS lower, meaning a larger income multiplier.

THE LOCATION OF THE CURVE

The IS curve would **shift rightward** to reflect (1) any increase in I or other spending injections, or (2) any decrease in S or other withdrawals:

$\uparrow$ C $(= \downarrow$ S) (an upward shift of the consumption function)

$\uparrow$ I (an upward shift of MEI)

$\uparrow$ G

$\uparrow$ EX

$\downarrow$ T

$\downarrow$ IM

Conversely, the IS curve would **shift leftward** to reflect (1) any decrease in I or other spending injections, or (2) any increase in S or other withdrawals.

Note: In the Keynesian model, C is assumed to be generally stable, while I is assumed to be unstable—easily variable in response to changing conditions and profit expectations. Keynes said that G should be purposely adjusted to offset undesired shifts of I (e.g., $\downarrow$ I, $\uparrow$ G) thereby stabilizing IS at the desired level of Y.

SUMMARY

- The focus of Keynesian economics is total spending. An important part of the Keynesian model is the income (expenditure) multiplier, which results from the marginal propensity to consume (MPC).

- In the Keynesian two-sector model, consumer spending (C) is the "basic flow." An increased rate of injections into the income stream ($\uparrow$ I) will cause income to continue to increase ($\uparrow$ Y) until the rate of withdrawals increases ($\uparrow$ S) to equal the new rate of injections. Macroequilibrium occurs at the rate of Y where S = I.

- The four spending sources in the complete Keynesian model are C, I, G, and EX. The three withdrawals are S, T, and IM. When the injections (I + G + EX) are equal to the withdrawals (S + T + IM), the economy is in macroequilibrium.

- In the Keynesian Cross diagram, any increase in injections will cause an upward shift in the C + I curve and trigger a multiple increase in national income (Y).

- The rate of investment spending (given the marginal efficiency of investment) is determined by the interest rate. Lower rates bring more investment.

- The IS curve shows combinations of interest rates (r) and national income (Y) at which savings and investment would be equal (S = I). So it shows points of equilibrium in the **spending flows** and in the **product markets**.

- The IS curve indicates that, for any given level of r (and I) Y must adjust to move S into equality with I. The IS curve must have negative slope (lower r associated with higher Y) because at lower r, since I is greater, for I and S to be equal, S must be greater—which means Y must be greater.

- Macroequilibrium in the economy must occur at some point on the IS curve. But until you know the interest rate you can't tell where.

Important Principles, Issues, Concepts, Terms

Income (or investment or expenditure) multiplier

Marginal propensity to consume (MPC)

Marginal propensity to save (MPS)

Keynesian Cross diagram

Consumption function

Multiplier formula

Keynesian two-spending-sector model

Four-spending-sector model

Marginal efficienty of investment (MEI)

"Investment opportunities" curve

IS curve

Factors influencing the IS curve

Effect of Δr on I, of ΔI on Y, and of ΔY on S

Questions

1. Explain this statement: "The multiplier results from the MPC and is limited by the MPS."

2. Following an increase in the size of the spending injections, national income will continue to increase until savings increase enough to equal the size of the new (larger) spending injection. Explain why this must be true.

3. Explain the Keynesian four-spending-sector model.

4. In the Keynesian model, the ultimate size of national income depends on the size of autonomous injections. Explain what this means and why it is true.

5. Draw a graph showing the MEI curve, and then explain why it is shaped as it is.

6. Draw a graph illustrating the IS curve, and explain exactly why the curve is shaped as it is.

7. Explain what changes would cause the slope of the IS curve to change.

8. Explain what changes would cause the IS curve to shift.

9. Explain the meaning of this statement: "The entire Keynesian model of the macroeconomy is based on the assumption that C (and S) is a function of Y."

10. In the Keynesian model, the size of national income (*ceteris paribus*) is determined by the rate of investment spending. Explain why this is true.

11. The IS curve combines the results of the investment function (the MEI curve) and the savings function into one curve. Can you explain how this is done, and use curves to illustrate? Try.

12. What does it mean to say that at each point on the IS curve, both the spending flows in the economy and the product markets are in equilibrium? How can we be so sure of that? Explain.

Suggested Readings

Bailey, Martin. "Saving and the Rate of Interest." *Journal of Political Economy* 65, 1975, pp. 102–18.

Bogan, Elizabeth C. and Joseph J. Kiernan. *Macroeconomics: Theories and Applications*. St. Paul: West Publishing Co., 1987.

Carlino, Gerald A. "Interest Rate Effects and Intertemporal Consumption." *Journal of Monetary Economics*. (March 1982), 223–34.

Gordon, Robert J. *Macroeconomics*, 4th ed. Boston: Little Brown, 1987.

Hageland, H. *The Multiplier Theory*. New York: Augustus M. Kelley, 1966.

Hall, Robert E. "Investment, Interest Rates, and the Effects of Stabilization Policies." *Brookings Papers on Economic Activity*. Washington, D.C.: Brookings Institution, 1977, 1, pp. 61–103.

Hicks, John. "IS-LM: An Explanation." *Journal of Post Keynesian Economics* 3 (2). (Winter 1980–81), 139–54.

Hicks, John. "Mr. Keynes and the 'Classics': A Suggested Interpretation." *Econometrica* 5. 1937, pp. 147–59.

Jorgenson, Dale W. "Anticipations and Investment Behavior." in James Duesenberry et al., *The Brookings Quarterly Econometric Model of the U.S.*. Skokie, Ill.: Rand McNally, 1965.

———. "Econometric Studies of Investment Behavior." *Journal of Economic Literature*. (December 1971), 1111–1147.

Kopcke, Richard W. "Investment Spending and the Federal Taxation of Business Income." Federal Reserve Bank of Boston *New England Economic Review*. (September/October 1985), 9–33.

Rubin, Laura S. "Aggregate Inventory Behavior: It's Response to Uncertainty and Interest Rates." *Journal of Post-Keynesian Economics*. (Winter 1979–80), 201–11.

Smith, Warren L. "A Graphical Exposition of the Complete Keynesian System." *Southern Economic Journal*. (October 1956), 115–25.

Wright, A. L. "The Genesis of the Multiplier Theory." *Oxford Economic Papers*. (June, 1956), 183–84.

CHAPTER 30

A Closer Look at the Demand for Money and the Role of Money in the Macroeconomy

Chapter Objectives

This chapter focuses on the **demand for money** and *the role money plays in influencing the rate of flow of the macroeconomy.* After you study this chapter you will understand and be able to explain:

1. The **role of money** in the classical model and in the Keynesian model, and the **money demand function** in both models.

2. The meaning and significance of the idea of the **speculative demand** for money.

3. The idea of the **liquidity trap** and the role it played in the early (serious depression) Keynesian model.

4. How the demand for money can be viewed as consisting of two distinctly different segments: the L1 (transactions plus precautionary) demand, plus the L2 (speculative) demand.

5. The interrelationships between money demand, money supply, and interest rates, and the important role of interest rates in the Keynesian model.

MONEY DEMAND IN THE CLASSICAL AND KEYNESIAN MODELS

Previous chapters have explained several of the distinctions between basic Keynesian monetary theory and the basic classical "quantity theory." This section goes more deeply into that. But first, a word of caution.

Modern Monetary Theories Are Different from the Early Classical and Early Keynesian Theories

Modern monetary theory—both modern monetarist theory and modern Keynesian theory—have evolved from and in several respects are significantly different from these earlier (sometimes called "näive") models. But a thorough understanding of modern monetary theory requires an understanding of these basic classical and Keynesian models because in these earlier models the distinctions come into sharpest focus.

Much development in monetary theory has occurred during the half-century since Keynes' *General Theory* appeared. We have seen the development of "modern monetarist" theory spearheaded by Milton Friedman, and the development of "modern Keynesian" (or neo-Keynesian or post-Keynesian) theory as well. These new theories have developed partly as a result of the dialectic between "the Keynesians and the monetarists." The distinctions between these modern theories are not nearly as great as between the earlier theories. But significant distinctions still exist.

The word of warning is this: As you are reading about these early classical (long-run full-employment equilibrium) and Keynesian (short-run serious depression) models, don't think you're getting the latest word on modern monetary theory. You aren't. Not yet. But by learning about the sharp differences between these earlier models you are taking *an essential step toward a thorough understanding of the evolution of modern monetary theory.*

Money in the Classical Model

You will recall that in the classical model, the demand for money (desire to hold money balances) is perfectly inelastic—the quantity demanded is completely unresponsive to changes in interest rates. In the classical model, money is held only for the purpose of undertaking planned transactions, and for precautionary purposes (for unforeseen transactions). To hold larger money balances than required by the transactions and precautionary motives would be "hoarding money." And that would be irrational, given the opportunity to invest the money in income-earning assets.

In the classical model, all households and businesses hold **minimum money balances**. Each dollar is held for the shortest possible period of time. And since everyone has already adjusted to this "absolute minimum money-balance" position, changes in interest rates can have no effect on the size of money balances.

Desired money balances would be determined by the size of national income, rising or falling as nominal national income goes up or down. The ratio of desired money balances (Mqd) to Y (the k ratio) would always be the same. So the velocity of circulation (V) would be constant.

In the classical model an increase or decrease in the size of the money supply would result directly and proportionately in increased or decreased prices. The price level would adjust so that the real money supply (purchasing power = M/P) *after* the change in the nominal money supply would be exactly the same as before the change in nominal M.

In the classical model, money plays no role in influencing employment, output, incomes, or interest rates. The only role of money is to move the price level up or down so as to keep the real value of the money supply proportional to the nominal value of the economy's real output—where $(M/P)V = Q$. In the classical model the effect of money on the real macroeconomic variables (employment, output, etc.) is zero.

Money in the Keynesian Model

In the Keynesian model money plays no *direct* role at all in moving the macroeconomy to equilibrium. *Equilibrium occurs where the spending flows and output-income flows* are in equilibrium—where injections (I) equal withdrawals (S) and the size of the total spending flow is stable. Although money plays *no direct role* in that spending flow model, it plays a very important *indirect role*.

In the Keynesian model the role of money is to influence the **interest rate**. Then the interest rate influences investment spending. And (given the society's consumption-savings function) the rate of investment determines the equilibrium level of national income—and therefore real employment, output, and income. You found out all about that in the IS curve explanation in the last chapter.

In the Keynesian model it is via the interest rate that money plays its key role in influencing the macroeconomy. The Keynesian chain of monetary influence is: Money influences interest rates which influence investment which (with a multiplying effect) influences national income. In symbols: $\Delta M \to \Delta r \to \Delta I \to \Delta Y$.

Transactions Demand Plus Precautionary Demand = L1 Demand = f(Y)

Keynes agreed with the classical model that the basic demand for money results from the desire to hold transactions and precautionary balances. In the Keynesian model this demand reflects the size of the national income and is not very responsive to changes in interest rates. Keynes did not disagree with the classical practice of lumping together the transactions (T) and precautionary (P) motives to come up with the basic demand for money (L1), which is a function of the size of national income:

$$Mqd\ T + Mqd\ P = L1 = f(Y),$$

which says that the quantity of money demanded for transactions purposes (Mqd T) plus the quantity demanded for precautionary balances (Mqd P) is equal to L1 which is determined by the size of national income (Y).

In the classical model the quantity of money demanded was completely unresponsive to interest rates (or anything else other than the size of national income). So with respect to interest rate changes the money demand curve would be perfectly inelastic (vertical) at the desired quantity, as determined by the level of national income (Y). Figure 30-1 illustrates this classical demand for money.

As you look at figure 30-1 you can see why, in the classical model, there is no need to distinguish between "demand for money" (the entire curve) and "quantity of money demanded" (a point on the curve). The quantity demanded is identical at all points on the curve. But in the Keynesian model, as you'll see in a moment, the distinction between Md and Mqd becomes critical.

KEYNES EMPHASIZED THE SPECULATIVE DEMAND FOR MONEY

During the 1930s, interest rates were very low. Velocity of circulation of money was low—meaning that people were holding larger money balances than they were using for transactions. In the classical model this would be "irrational behavior."

Figure 30-1.   Money Demand in the Classical Model

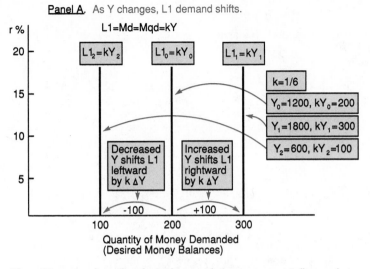

Panel A. As Y changes, L1 demand shifts.

$L1 = Md = Mqd = kY$

$L1_2 = kY_2$ $L1_0 = kY_0$ $L1_1 = kY_1$

$k = 1/6$

$Y_0 = 1200, kY_0 = 200$

$Y_1 = 1800, kY_1 = 300$

$Y_2 = 600, kY_2 = 100$

Decreased Y shifts L1 leftward by $k\Delta Y$

Increased Y shifts L1 rightward by $k\Delta Y$

-100 $+100$

Quantity of Money Demanded
(Desired Money Balances)

These L1 curves show that desired money balances are not influenced at all by interest rates. $L1 = Mqd$ is the same whether r is 5% or 20%. Why? Because *people have already reduced their money balances to the bare minimum required to meet their L1 needs.* And once that condition is reached, no further reduction in money balances is possible no matter how high interest rates may rise!

Panel B. As Y increases, Mqd increases by kY.

$Mqd = kY. \ k = 1/6$
$Mqd = 1/6Y$

This graph shows the same picture as Panel A, only here the focus is on the positive relationship between Y and Mqd.

In the classical model the demand for money is based entirely on the desire to hold money balances for transactions, foreseen and unforeseen. The size of the desired balances will be exactly kY, where k is a constant—the ratio of desired money balances to the size of national income. Whenever Y changes, desired money balances will change by k times that amount.

Example: Suppose k is 1/6. Then if Y increases by $600, desired money balances will increase by $100. The L1 curve shifts to the right $100 as measured on the horizontal axis.

Box 30-1

Question: Is L1 (Mqd T + Mqd P) Responsive at All to Interest Rate Changes?

In the classical model L1 was perfectly inelastic with respect to interest rates. Rational people reduced their L1 balances to the minimum required, given the level of nominal national income. Since the balances are already at the minimum, interest rate changes can have no effect.

During the 1950s, in separate studies, both Baumol and Tobin found that the transactions demand for money is indeed sensitive to interest rates.[1] A few moments of careful thought will convince you that this conclusion, in the modern world of immediate funds transfers, instant repos, etc., *it must be true*.

Here's an example. Suppose you are holding $3000 to cover your expenditures over the next 30 days. That's $100 a day. You're a big spender! And suppose interest rates on short-term alternative investments (perhaps overnight repos on T-bills) go up as high as 20%. Will you put any of your $3,000 in nonmoney (perhaps overnight) interest-earning assets? I would bet on it!

These days, a wise asset-holder probably could arrange to shift the entire $3,000 into interest-earning assets, with $100 maturing each day. There is some cost involved in shifting from money into other (income earning) financial assets (OFAs) and then back into money. But when the interest rate is 20%, it's worth it!

Now suppose the interest rate had been only 3%. Would you go to the trouble and expense of investing in daily-maturing repos? Probably not. But even at an interest rate of 3% you might consider holding some of the $3,000 in OFAs, at least for a part of the 30-day period.

---

[1] The original articles explaining the interest rate sensitivity of the transactions demand for money are:

   William J. Baumol, "The Transactions Demand For Cash: An Inventory Theoretic Approach," *Quarterly Journal of Economics*, vol. 66 (November, 1952), pp. 545–56; and James Tobin, "The Interest-Elasticity Of The Transactions Demand For Cash," *Review of Economics And Statistics*, vol. 38 (August, 1956), pp. 241–47. These articles outline the model (now called the Baumol-Tobin model) in which the transactions demand for money is somewhat elastic with respect to interest rate changes so that L1 becomes a function of both national income and interest rates: L1 = f(Y, r).

Was it irrational for people to hold large money balances during the depressed, very-low-interest-rate conditions of the 1930s? Keynes said "No, because of the **speculative demand** for money." To really understand what this means you need a clear picture of the distinction between *money* and *OFAs*.

The Key Difference Between Money Balances and OFAs

Here's the key difference between holding money and holding most other financial assets: For assets held in the form of money the *nominal value* is fixed—absolutely and completely nonvariable—while for most other financial assets (OFAs) nominal value can increase or decrease. Nominal capital gains or losses can result when you hold OFAs. But not when you hold money.

But what about *real* capital gains or losses? Those can occur just as easily when you hold money as when you hold OFAs! When prices of things (including OFAs) fall, money-holders enjoy *real gains*. But when prices rise, money-holders lose.

To Keynes it was perfectly rational to hold assets in the form of money whenever OFA prices are expected to fall. And this explains Keynes' **speculative demand** for money, which says: Asset managers will hold their assets (money, vs. OFAs) in the form which is expected to increase in value, relative to the other. Whenever OFA prices are expected to rise, rational asset managers will shift out of money and into OFAs. But when OFA prices are expected to fall, they will hold money—i.e., they will have a "speculative demand" for money. (See box 30-2 for an explanation of the meaning of the **speculative motive**.)

Suppose long-term bond prices are expected to increase in the future. Then assets should be shifted out of money and into long-term bonds. An increase in the value of long-term bonds means a decrease in the value of money, relative to long-term bonds. To shift assets out of money and into long-term bonds in anticipation of an increase in the price of long-term bonds is an example of "speculation."

Conversely (and to Keynes, this was the situation during the 1930s) suppose interest rates are as low as (and long-term bond prices are as high as) they are expected to get. Then the most likely interest rate move appears to be *upward* and the most likely move in bond values *downward*. Then the speculative motive says: If you hold OFAs you are going to experience *capital losses* as interest rates rise and OFA values come down. So hold your assets in the form of money!

The bottom line on the speculative motive: When the value of money (relative to OFAs) is expected to rise, *hold money*. When the value of OFAs (relative to money) is expected to rise, *hold OFAs*.

Are There Times When Interest Rates Are Perceived to Be "Too High?" or "Too Low?"

At any given time, does the financial community and the general public have a perception of what the market rate of interest "ought to be?" And therefore of which direction it's most likely to move? Keynes thought so.

Suppose present rates are significantly higher than in the past. Then people may expect future rates to fall. Or if present rates are significantly lower than in the past people may expect rates to rise. According to Keynes, this latter condition existed during the 1930s.

If you think interest rates are abnormally low and are likely to rise, you certainly would not invest in long-term OFAs. When rates rise, prices of those long-term OFAs will fall and you'll lose. You might try to invest in very-short-term OFAs where the risk of capital loss would not be significant. But suppose (as

---

Box 30-2

Question: The Speculative motive: Exactly What Does It Mean? And Why Does It Matter?

Everyone knows that speculation means taking a chance. Doing something risky. Gambling, perhaps. But an understanding of the speculative demand for money requires a more precise meaning of "speculation." It means: "Choosing and holding assets on the basis of *expected gains from future price movements*."

The word "speculative" in the Keynesian "speculative demand for money" means that asset owners (portfolio managers) are trying to adjust their asset portfolios so as to gain (and not lose!) from future price changes. For example, when the prices of OFAs are expected to fall, portfolio managers will hold money balances. Lower prices for OFAs means higher

relative value for money balances. Alternatively, portfolio managers will not want to hold money balances when the prices of OFAs are expected to rise. Higher OFA prices means lower value of money relative to OFAs.

In the Keynesian model the speculative motive causes people to hold money balances whenever they expect interest rates to rise and OFA prices to fall. The idea of "speculative demand" brings in an entirely new reason for wanting to hold money—a reason totally unrelated to the desire to make transactions, and therefore unrelated to the size of—or changes in the size of—national income. So if speculative demand exists, Mqd cannot be stated as kY.

Box 30-3

Question: Exactly What Are OFAs?

At the time of Keynes, and until the 1970s with the introduction of interest-bearing checking accounts (NOW accounts, etc.), money (M1) was a non-income-earning asset. A portfolio manager had to decide how much asset value to hold in money (non-income-earning) and how much in other (income-earning) financial assets. OFAs are income-earning **other financial assets**—financial assets other than money.

Now there is widespread use of interest-bearing checking accounts by individuals. So there's somewhat less incentive to shift assets from money to OFAs. However, earnings available from OFAs usually are higher than on checking accounts—and currency pays no return at all. Also, as of 1988 banks still were prohibited from providing interest-bearing checking accounts to businesses. Therefore, although somewhat lessened, there still is considerable incentive to shift assets from money into OFAs.

In Keynesian monetary theory the shifting of portfolio holdings between money and OFAs plays a critical role. In explaining this portfolio shifting between money and other assets,

Keynes grouped all of the other financial assets (OFAs) and referred to them as "bonds." So in Keynesian analysis the term "bonds" really doesn't mean only bonds. It means all non-money income earning financial assets (OFAs).

This use of the word "bonds" as a generic term poses no problem for economists and financial professionals. But for some students, it does. That's why in this book the term "OFAs" (not "bonds") is used to refer to these non-money "other" financial assets. But remember that in the writings of Keynes and in most other writings on this subject the term "bonds" will be used to refer to what here are called "OFAs."

It isn't surprising that Keynes would use the word "bonds" instead of something like "OFAs." Keynes never went far out of his way to make things perfectly clear to the general public—or even, for that matter, to the economics profession. He left that to his many interpreters and analysts including Sir John Hicks, Alvin Hansen, Franco Modigliani, Don Patinkin, Paul Samuleson, Axel Leijonhufvud (Lay-own-hu-fud) and so many others.

in the 1930s) many people were trying to place their surplus money in very-short-term OFAs. The supply of loanable funds (i.e., demand for securities) in the very-short-term market would be great and short-term rates would be pushed down very low.

In the 1930s when short-term rates were down to a fraction of one percentage point, Keynes asked: "Why would people bother trade their money balances for short-term OFAs? Considering the trouble and costs involved—decisions about what to invest in, and transactions costs—why wouldn't asset managers just hold money balances? And wait for interest rates to rise (the prices of OFAs to fall)? And then shift their money balances into OFAs?

According to Keynes, during the 1930s many people were doing exactly that. They were holding money balances and *speculating that the value of money relative to OFAs would rise by more than enough to offset any lost interest income in the meanwhile.*

Speculative Demand (L2) Is a "Portfolio Choice" Demand for Money Balances

The speculative demand for money (L2) is completely different from the L1 demand. It has absolutely nothing to do with "holding money because you want to use it as money." Speculative (L2) demand is concerned only with holding money *as an asset in your portfolio*—because money is the most desired form in

---

Box 30-4

Question: Is There Any Empirical Evidence That People Sometimes Feel That Interest Rates Are "Too High?" or "Too Low?"

Does the financial community have a general feeling about how high interest rates "ought to be?"—a feeling based on past experience, present conditions, future outlook and who knows what else? This question is important when we're considering the idea of a **speculative demand** for money (vs. OFAs).

If you'd like some empirical evidence that some such subjective feeling exists, look back in chapter 13 which explains yield curves and you can find that evidence.

During years in which interest rates have been significantly lower than in the preceding years, yield curves have sloped upward steeply, indicating that yields on long-term securities were much higher than on short-term securities. This indicates that most of the loanable funds were pouring into the short-term (low-interest-rate) market. It says that asset managers were reluctant to invest long-term at such low rates. The yield curves illustrate the fact that when asset managers consider current rates to be abnormally low they will tend to invest short-term.

During times when nominal interest rates have been "abnormally high"—for example during the late 1970s and early 1980s when short-term rates sometimes exceeded 20%—yield curves have been "inverted"—down-

ward sloping. In 1979–80, short-term yields were much higher than long-term yields. Yet portfolio managers continued to buy long-term OFAs. They were locking in high rates for long periods of time, and looking for capital gains from falling future rates. (As it turned out, market rates did fall. Investors who bought long-term securities during the early 1980s made significant capital gains during the following years.)

The bottom Line: An analysis of past yield curves provides some support for the idea that a "subjective, natural rate of interest" exists in the minds of the financial community, and that this idea has a significant influence on asset choices. Portfolio managers give up potential interest earnings in order to stay short-term when they expect interest rates to rise. Also, they give up high potential short-term earnings in order to lock in somewhat lower long-term earnings whenever they expect interest rates to fall.

Note: The shifting between short- and long-term OFAs is not quite the same as shifting between OFAs and money balances. So the analysis of yield curves cannot definitely prove the existence of a speculative demand for money.

---

which to hold these assets (this wealth) at this time. The speculative-balance-holders are trying to protect their wealth and (with luck) gain from future increases in the value of money relative to OFAs.

The Speculative Demand for Money: A Major Break with Classical Monetary Theory

What was the big deal about having a speculative demand for money?—an *asset demand* in addition to the transactions and precautionary demand? Just this: With the speculative demand (L2) in the picture, the conclusions of the classical macroeconomic model, based on the equation of exchange ($MV = PQ$ or $M = kPQ$) and the money demand function ($Md = kY$) no longer hold.

With a speculative demand it's possible for a change in the quantity of money to result in *zero change* in spending. Suppose M increases by 10% and all of the increase flows into speculative balances. The 10% increase in M is offset by a 10% decrease in V and a 10% increase in k. Spending doesn't change. So the relationship between ΔM and ΔE is not stable.

Also, with speculative demand, interest rates—current rates as compared with expected future rates—become very important. The money demand function is no longer tied only to the level of national income. Suddenly the quantity of money demanded becomes quite responsive to *current levels and expected future levels of interest rates.*

SPECULATIVE DEMAND AND THE "LIQUIDITY TRAP"

In normal times an increase in the money supply results in increased spending. If unemployed resources exist, the increased spending can result in increased employment, output and income. But suppose the economy is seriously depressed and the outlook is bleak. Interest rates will be very low and generally expected to rise (someday). In the Keynesian model, in these circumstances if the money supply increases, all of the new money may pour into speculative balances.

The "Liquidity Trap": L2 Demand for Money Balances

According to Keynes, if the economy is seriously depressed and interest rates are thought to be "abnormally" low, any newly created money would flow into speculative balances. The increased supply of money would have no downward influence on the (already very low) interest rates, so it would not stimulate investment spending. There would be no change in the spending flow, employment, output, or anything else. Keynes call this the **liquidity trap**. This is what he was talking about when he said that trying to cure the depression by increasing the money supply, was like "trying to push with a string."

Figure 30-2 shows a graph of the speculative demand for money. The curve illustrates that above some (fairly high) rate of interest, the speculative demand for money would be zero. Everyone would want to shift their assets out of money and into high-interest-paying OFAs. The curve also indicates that below some (very low) rate of interest, additional increases in the money supply would have no effect on interest rates. All of the new money would be held as speculative balances pending higher interest rates and lower OFA prices.

The Significance of the Speculative Demand for Money

As you study Figure 30-2, think of the significant effect of the *speculative demand for money.* During any short-run (disequilibrium) period it challenges the basic assumptions and expected results of *the quantity theory of money.*

1. It brings *interest rates* into the picture as a very important determinant of the quantity of money demanded (Mqd), and therefore of velocity (V).

2. It makes *changes in the size of the money supply* play a key role in interest-rate determination.

3. And because in the Keynesian model interest rates play a key role in influencing investment spending—and therefore national output and income—the money supply now enters the picture *as a key player in influencing the macroeconomy.*

Figure 30-2.   The Speculative Demand for Money in the Keynesian Model

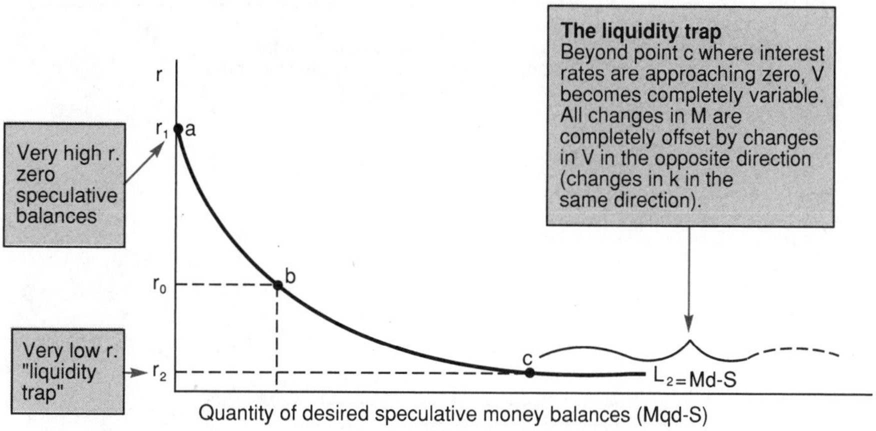

Very high r. zero speculative balances

The liquidity trap
Beyond point c where interest rates are approaching zero, V becomes completely variable. All changes in M are completely offset by changes in V in the opposite direction (changes in k in the same direction).

Very low r. "liquidity trap"

Quantity of desired speculative money balances (Mqd-S)

The idea of the Keynesian "liquidity trap" is that interest returns are too low to justify the cost and risk of shifting assets out of money balances and into OFAs. So if more money becomes available it will go into idle balances and have no effect on r, spending, or the macroeconomy.

Note: The actual existence of a "liquidity trap" condition during the 1930s has never been established, and no data since the '30s have suggested the existence of a "liquidity trap." But it's an interesting concept, and it's the "ultimate extreme"—the *reductio ad absurdum* of the Keynesian speculative demand for money.

THE TOTAL DEMAND FOR MONEY: L1 + L2 = L

In the Keynesian model, to construct a curve showing the total demand for money it is only necessary to add together the L1 and L2 demand curves from figures 30-1 and 30-2. That's what is shown in figure 30-3.

The Speculative Demand for Money (L2), and Interest Rates

In the classical model a change in the supply of money influences only the price level. Not so in the Keynesian model. Because of the speculative demand for money a change in the supply of money brings a change in interest rates. Why? Because the interest rate must adjust to induce the public to adjust their desired asset-holdings between money balances and OFAs. The next section explains.

When M Increases, Mqd Must Also Increase

When the money supply increases, that means the public is now holding larger money balances than before. The entire money supply is being held by the public at all times, remember? And that's true whether they want to hold it all or not. So *as M increases (ceteris paribus), r must fall to induce the public to want to hold the larger money balances which they find themselves holding.* The interest rate must continue to go down—causing the size of desired speculative balances to go up—until Mqd = M.

Figure 30-3.   The Total Demand for Money Combines L1 (Panel A) and L2 (Panel B) into L = Md (Panel C)

Panel A. L1 Demand. Desire to hold money balances for planned transactions plus precautionary (unplanned) transactions

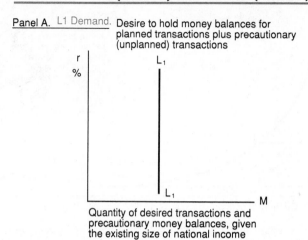

Quantity of desired transactions and precautionary money balances, given the existing size of national income

The L1 (transactions + precautionary) demand for money curve here is drawn as a vertical line indicating perfectly inelastic demand for L1 balances—i.e., zero responsiveness of L1 to changes in r. This was the original classical assumption. Economists now know that desired transactions balances do in fact exhibit some interest rate sensitivity. But the curve as drawn here does not reflect that.

Panel B. L2 Demand. Speculative demand. Desire to hold money balances, (instead of OFAs) as portfolio assets.

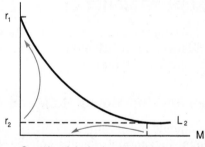

Quantity of desired speculative (portfolio) money balances, given the current outlook regarding future interest rates.

This L2 curve illustrates Keynes' idea that at lower interest rates people hold more money as a *preferred asset* in their "total wealth portfolio." The rationale: At low rates (high OFA prices) there is significant market risk (interest rate risk) in holding OFAs. Said differently: At low rates (high OFA prices) the value of money relative to OFAs is expected to increase.

At interest rates above r_1, all speculative balances would have been exchanged for high-interest-earning (low-priced) OFAs. The quantity of desired speculative balances would be zero and only L1 would apply. At interest rate r_2 you see the liquidity trap. Here, any increase in the money supply would be absorbed in speculative balances and would have no effect on interest rates or on total spending, employment, output, income, or prices.

continued

Figure 30-3.   *continued*

Panel C. L1 + L2 Demand. **The Keynesian Money Demand**
Curve. At interest rates above
r_1, only L1 demand applies.
Below r_1 the curve becomes
more interest-rate elastic
because of L2 (speculative)
demand.

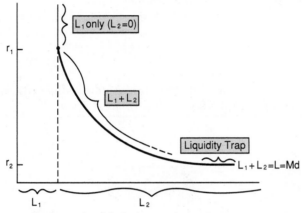

This curve illustrates the demand for money in the Keynesian
model. The demand curve shows very little interest rate elasticity when rates are high. At lower rates the elasticity is
greater. In the liquidity trap range the curve becomes perfectly
interest-rate elastic.

Note: This money demand curve is basic to the Keynesian theory of interest, and to the entire Keynesian macroeconomic model. It is impossible to understand the Keynesian macroeconomic model without a thorough understanding of
this curve: what it says, what it means, and why.

Here's an example. Suppose the central bank decides to permit the money
supply to expand by 10%. According to Keynesian interest theory, the effect of
this 10% increase in the money supply (*ceteris paribus*) would be to push interest
rates downward.

In the Keynesian model it would work this way: When the Fed adds reserves
and lets the money supply expand, people find themselves holding more of their
assets in money balances than they want to hold as money. People know that
when the money supply is expanding, that's probably a good time to hold OFAs
because interest rates are likely to fall. If so, OFA prices will rise. So people begin
reducing their money balances by buying OFAs. As demand for OFAs increases,
their prices rise and yields fall.

Notice that in the Keynesian model the *initial effect* of the increased money
supply is to push the public's holdings of money above the level of their desired
holdings (M > Mqd). The next step is when people begin trying to get rid of their
surplus money balances by buying OFAs. The increased demand for OFAs pushes
up OFA prices and pushes down yields. So interest rates fall. Rates continue to

fall until speculative Mqd increases to where people are satisfied to hold the larger money balances which they find themslves holding. Figures 30-4 and 30-5 illustrate all this.

Falling r Brings Increasing I and Y

You just saw how falling interest rates brought Mqd into equality with M. Now here's how the lower interest rates have their effect on employment, output, and income—on the spending flows and product markets. As interest rates fall, more investment projects become profitable. The rate of investment spending increases.

Figure 30-4.   The Keynesian Interest Rate Model: Money Demand and Money Supply Determine Interest Rates

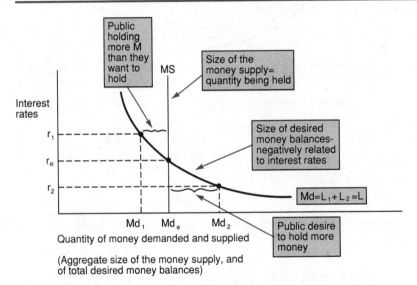

The equilibrium interest rate equates Mqd (=L) with M. The vertical money supply curve assumes that the quantity of money is fixed by the central bank and is not responsive to changes in r.

At the equilibrium interest rate (r_e), aggregate *desired* money balances are exactly equal to *existing* (realized) money balances—i.e., desired balances are exactly equal to the size of the money supply.

At any interest rate above r_e (e.g., r_1) people will find themselves holding larger money balances than they desire. So they will begin to decrease their money balances by buying OFAs. With the increased demand, OFA prices will rise, so interest rates will fall—ultimately to the equilibrium rate, r_e.

At all interest rates below r_e (e.g., r_2) people will want to hold larger money balances than they are holding. So they sell OFAs to increase their money balances. The increased supply of OFAs will cause their prices to fall and yields—and interest rates in general—to rise, ultimately to the equilibrium rate r_e.

As this graph illustrates, in the Keynesian model it is the asset-shifting between money and OFAs that causes r to change to r_e, which brings Mqd (=L) into equality with M. Any change in M (or in Md) would trigger this asset-shifting process and cause r to move to the new equilibrium rate (new r_e) where Mqd (=L) is equal to M.

Figure 30-5. In the Keynesian Model a Money Supply Increase Pushes Interest Rates Down

---

The effect of M on r depends on how high (or low) current interest rates happen to be. Here it is assumed that the central bank releases new reserves into the banking system and lets the money supply expand from MS_1 to MS_2, etc.

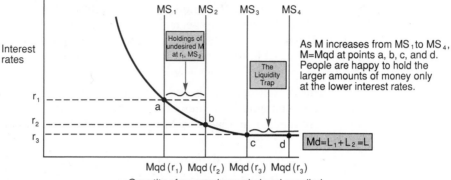

Quantity of money demanded and supplied

Money supply increases push interest rates down. But at lower rates the effect is smaller. At very low rates, because of the liquidity trap, the effect is zero.

At the equilibrium interest rate, aggregate *desired* money balances are exactly equal to existing (realized) money balances—which means that desired balances are exactly equal to the money supply.

Increased money supply pushes money balances above desired levels, so portfolio managers exchange money for OFAs. OFA prices are pushed up and interest rates go down until $Mqd = M$.

If the money supply is increased all the way to MS_3, interest rates will be as low as they can go.

So increases beyond MS_3—to MS_4, for example—will have no effect on the interest rate or on the rate of spending, employment, output, income, or anything else. It's the Keynesian "liquidity trap." That's where increases in the money supply would be completely offset by decreases in velocity.

Because this is assumed to be a depressed, surplus-laden economy, the increase in investment spending brings real increases in employment, output, and income.

Keynesian interest rate theory concludes that during "normal times" monetary policy can have a powerful effect on real macroeconomic conditions. If the Fed wishes to stimulate the economy it can buy bonds. As it does so it will push up bond prices and push down interest rates. That's the initial effect.

Then, payments for the bonds flow into the banking system and become excess reserves. Banks will lend, and the money supply will expand by a multiple amount. With the increased money supply, portfolio managers will find their money balances larger than desired. So they too will enter the markets for bonds and other OFAs and begin pushing up prices and pushing down interest rates.

Between the Fed's effects and the portfolio managers' effects, OFA prices are pushed up significantly. Interest rates fall, stimulating more investment spending. The economy speeds up. So the Keynesian money demand function indicates that (given certain circumstances—explained later) monetary policy can be quite effective.

SUMMARY

- The **money demand function** is much more elastic with respect to interest rates in the Keynesian model than in the classical model because the Keynesian model includes a non-transactions-related motive for holding money: the **speculative motive.**

- The idea of the **speculative motive** is that rational asset-owners will hold money when its value is expected to rise relative to other financial assets (OFAs). When interest rates seem abnormally low (OFA prices abnormally high) people will hold money and wait for interest rates to rise (OFA prices to fall).

- The ultimate extreme—the *reductio ad absurdum*—of the Keynesian speculative demand for money is the **liquidity trap**, where interest rates are so low that all increases in M will flow into zero-velocity speculative balances.

- In Keynesian theory the demand for money consists of L1 (for transactions and precaution) plus L2 (speculative demand) $L1 = f(\overset{+}{Y})$ and $L2 = f(\overset{-}{r})$, so that L (=Mqd) is positively related to national income (Y) and negatively related to the interest rate (r).

- In the Keynesian model, interest rates are determined by the demand for and supply of money. When people are holding more money than they desire to hold (M > Mqd), they exchange money for OFAs. OFA prices rise and interest rates (r) fall. At lower r, Mqd is larger because of the desire for larger speculative balances. This brings Mqd into equality with M, and *this is how interest rates are determined in the Keynesian model.*

- Interest rates play a key role in the Keynesian model because r influences I, and thereby significantly influences the spending flows and the operating rate of the economy.

Important Principles, Issues, Concepts, Terms

Money demand in the classical model

Role of money in the classical model

Money demand in the Keynesian model

Role of money in the Keynesian model

Why Md always equals Mqd in the classical model

Transactions and precautionary demand for money

Speculative demand for money

L1 + L2 = L

Difference between money and OFAs

Money as a "portfolio asset"

Liquidity trap

Keynesian interest-rate theory

How interest rates move to where Mqd = M

How interest rate movements affect the macro-economy

Questions

1. Explain and illustrate graphically the difference between the money demand function in the early classical and early Keynesian models.

2. Explain the Keynesian "speculative mo-tive" for holding money balances, and explain why this is so important in the Keynesian model of the macroeconomy—especially during depression.

3. Explain why it is true that when the

money supply increases, the quantity of money demanded must also increase for the economy to be in macroequilibrium.

4. In the classical model money supply changes have no effect on real output or income. In the Keynesian model it has no *direct* effect, but it has a very significant *indirect* effect. Carefully explain what all this means.

5. The chapter explains that in the classical model the distinction between Md and Mqd is not at all necessary, while in the Keynesian model it is very important. Explain why.

6. Explain the key difference between *money balances* and *other financial assets* (OFAs).

7. Do you think the financial community usually has some idea about whether cur-rent interest rates are "too high" or "too low?" And in which direction interest rates are most likely to move in the future? And why is this question important in the context of "the speculative demand for money"? Explain.

8. If there is in fact a speculative demand for money, then Mqd cannot be stated as kY. Explain what this means, and why it is true.

9. Explain what is meant by the "liquidity trap." Do you think there is one? Ever was one? Ever will be one? Discuss.

10. When M is not exactly equal to Mqd, interest rates will move to bring this equality. Explain exactly how this adjustment process occurs in the Keynesian model.

Suggested Readings

Brunner, Karl, and Allan Meltzer. "Liquidity Traps for Money, Bank Credit, and Interest Rates." *Journal of Political Economy.* (January/February 1968), 1–37.

———. "Money, Debt, and Economic Activity." *Journal of Political Economy.* (September/October 1972), 951–77.

Fisher, Douglas. *Monetary Theory and the Demand for Money.* New York: Halsted Press, 1978.

Friedman, Milton. *The Optimum Quantity of Money and Other Essays.* Chicago: Aldine, 1969.

Friedman, Milton, and Anna Schwartz. *Monetary Trends in the United States and the United Kingdom.* Chicago: University of Chicago Press, 1982.

———. "Money and Business Cycles." *Review of Economics and Statistics* 45. February 1963, supplement pp. 32–64.

Judd, John P. and John L. Scadding, "The Search for a Stable Money Demand Function." *The Journal of Economic Literature* 20 (3). (September 1982), 993–1024.

Laidler, David. "Money and Money Income: An Essay on the Transmission Mechanism." *Journal of Monetary Economics* 4. (April 1978), 151–92.

Modigliani, Franco. "Liquidity Preference and the Theory of Interest and Money." *Econometrica*, 1944, 12, pp. 45–88.

Patinkin, Don. *Money: Interest, and Prices: An Integration of Monetary and Value Theory.* New York: Harper & Row, 1965.

Tobin, James. "Liquidity Preference as a Behavior Toward Risk." *Review of Economic Studies.* (February 1958) 65–86.

CHAPTER 31

Points of Money Supply-Money Demand Equilibrium: The LM Curve, and IS-LM Equilibrium

Chapter Objectives

This chapter develops the LM curve and then puts the IS and LM curves together to show a simultaneous equilibrium (a) in the spending flows and product markets where I = S and (b) in the relationship between the money supply and money demand where L (=Mqd) = M.

From this chapter you will understand and be able to explain

1. **The LM curve**: combinations of Y and r at which L (**liquidity preference**, or Mqd) equals M.

2. Why equilibrium requires that the economy be at a point on the LM curve, and how the economy automatically moves to there, where L = M.

3. The role of **financial asset shifting**—from money to OFAs and vice versa—in automatically adjusting the economy to where L = M.

4. How, given the assumption of **fixed prices**, each specific pair of IS and LM curves identifies a **unique simultaneous equilibrium** for the macroeconomy.

5. The important role of **interest rate adjustments** in bringing equilibrium conditions: both I = S, and L = M.

6. How **movement to equilibrium** occurs from each point of disequilibrium in the IS-LM diagram.

DEVELOPING THE LM CURVE: COMBINATIONS OF Y AND r AT WHICH L (=Mqd) EQUALS M

In the Keynesian model the two major factors which influence the desire of the public to hold money balances are:

1. the size of the national income (Y), and

2. the current rate of interest on financial assets (OFAs).

As national income increases, people want to hold larger money balances for transactions purposes. But as interest rates increase, people desire to hold smaller money balances because (1) the opportunity cost of holding money balances increases, and (2) the perceived market risk of holding OFAs decreases.

Figure 31-1 illustrates this positive relationship between Y and Mqd, and the negative relationship between r and Mqd. Take a look at that figure and ask: "Is it possible that simultaneous increases in both Y and r could be just the right size to be exactly offsetting—the 'increasing Y effect' exactly offset by the 'increasing r effect' so that Mqd (=L) would remain exactly the same size?" Answer: Yes it is!

An Example of the Offsetting Effects of Y and r on Mqd

Suppose the money supply in an economy is absolutely fixed at $100 billion. (*Absolutely fixed!* Don't forget.) Also in this model it is assumed that the price level is fixed so that all changes in national income (Y) represent changes in real units of output (Q)—not price level changes (P).

The national income is $300 billion and the interest rate is 5%. And suppose that at this moment, Mqd in this little economy amounts to exactly $100 billion. People are holding the entire money supply (which is always true) and that happens to be exactly the amount of money they would like to hold—no more and no less. That's money demand-money supply equilibrium. L (=Mqd) = M.

Now suppose something happens to push the national income up from $300 billion to $450 billion. People want to hold larger money balances. But M is fixed at $100 billion so they can't hold but $100 billion. *They absolutely can't!* So what happens? Since M cannot change, to regain the Mqd = M equilibrium, Mqd (=L) must change. Take a look at the curves in figure 31-2 and you'll be able to see how it happens.

**Figure 31-1.   Graphic Illustration of the Response of
            Mqd to Changes in Y and r**

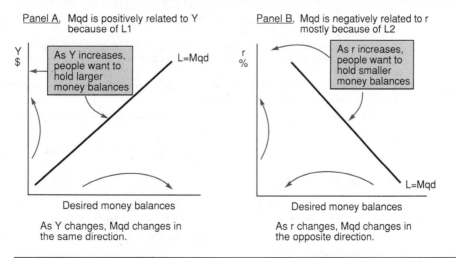

Panel A. Mqd is positively related to Y
          because of L1

As Y increases, people want to hold larger money balances

L=Mqd

Desired money balances

As Y changes, Mqd changes in the same direction.

Panel B. Mqd is negatively related to r
          mostly because of L2

As r increases, people want to hold smaller money balances

L=Mqd

Desired money balances

As r changes, Mqd changes in the opposite direction.

Figure 31-2.   A Graphic Illustration of the Offsetting Influences of Y and r on Mqd (= L)

As Y increases, Mqd increases. But as r increases, Mqd decreases. The effects of increasing Y can be offset by the effects of increasing r, so that Mqd can remain the same.

Panel A. The L_1 demand for M balances

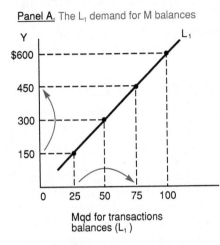

Panel B. The L_2 demand for M balances

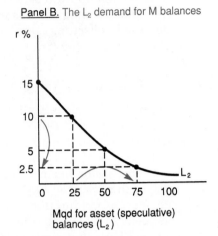

Mqd for transactions balances (L_1)

Mqd for asset (speculative) balances (L_2)

Panel A shows that with national income of $300 billion, the L1 demand for money would amount to $50 billion. So the only way that Mqd in this little economy could equal M (which is fixed at $100 billion) would be for L2 balances to amount to $50 billion. Panel B shows that desired L2 balances of $50 billion would occur at an interest rate of 5%. Now you can see how the "Mqd = M" (or "L = M") equality came about: Y = 300 so L1 = 50; r = 5% so L2 = 50. L1 + L2 = 50 + 50 = 100 = M.

As national income increases (in Panel A) from 300 to 450, the size of desired L1 money balances increases from 50 to 75. But since the money supply is fixed, the only place the additional desired money can come from is out of the speculative asset balances (Panel B). And the only way to squeeze the money out of the asset balances is for the interest rate to rise to 10% where L2 is 25. L1 + L2 = 75 + 25 = 100 = M.

What causes the interest rate to rise to accommodate the increased demand for transactions balances? It happens automatically, as people find themselves desiring larger money balances.

When larger money balances are desired, people begin selling their OFAs to try to build up their money balances. OFA prices fall and interest rates rise. (See figure 31-3.) As long as people are trying to build their money balances, this adjustment will continue and interest rates will continue to rise.

When desired speculative balances (L2) have decreased by exactly as much as desired transactions balances (L1) have increased, equilibrium will again exist between money demand and the (fixed) money supply.

Both Y and r are higher than before. So L1 balances are larger and L2 balances are smaller than before. But still L (= Mqd) = M.

Increased Y Can Be Supported by Decreased L2 Balances

In figure 31-2 you can see that there are various combinations of Y and r which would result in total desired money balances (Mqd) of exactly $100 billion. As Y increases, r must increase to maintain equilibrium. Table 31-1 lists some of the combinations.

Table 31-1.   Various Combinations of _Y_ and _r_ at which Desired Money Balances (_Mqd_ = L) Equal $100 Billion.

Y ($ bil)	r %	L1 ($ bil)	L2 ($ bil)	L = Total _Mqd_ ($ bil)
600	15	100	–0–	100
450	10	75	25	100
300	5	50	50	100
150	2.5	25	75	100

When these offsetting combinations of Y and r are plotted in a graph they produce "the LM curve." You'll be reading about that in the following section.

Table 31-1 shows exactly the same picture as the graphs in figure 31-2, only in tabular form. At any one of the Y and r combinations shown in the table, people would be holding exactly as much of their assets in money as they wanted to hold. There would be no desire to shift from money balances into OFAs, or vice versa. So there would be no upward or downward pressures on OFA prices or interest rates.

You could look at table 31-1 and say: "When M = $100b, these are the combinations of Y and r at which L (=Mqd) = M." Or you could say: "It shows for each level of Y, what r must be to bring equilibrium between L and M and equilibrium in the financial markets." Both statements mean the same thing.

THE LM CURVE JOINS POINTS OF Y AND r WHERE L (=Mqd) = M

The **LM curve** indicates combinations of national income (Y) and interest rates (r) which bring total desired money balances (Mqd = L) into equality with the money supply (M). The LM curve assumes a fixed (say $100 billion) money supply. Then it answers the question: "For each level of Y, at what rate of r would the public want to hold exactly $100b?"

Box 31-1

Question: What Are the Effects of a Shift of Desired Money Balances from L2 to L1?

A shift from desired L2 to L1 balances brings increased V, and it has the same effect as an increase in the money supply.

The velocity of the dollars in L2 balances is zero. Those dollars are being held as assets—for speculative reasons—and aren't being spent at all. So as dollars are shifted from L2 to L1 balances, V increases and total spending (MV) can increase without any increase in M.

The L1 balances might be thought of as "money that's turning over—to support aggregate demand, total employment, output, income, and prices." So the effect on total spending of _an increase in L1 balances_ is similar to the effect of _an increase in the money supply._ Total spending is permitted to increase. In both cases there is an increase in the number of "spendable dollars"—dollars immediately available to support the spending flow.

The LM Curve Represents "Stocks," Not "Flows"

The LM curve indicates **stocks**. It shows combinations of Y and r where the **existing stock** of money is exactly equal to the **desired stock**. That's all. It tells you nothing about the spending flows in the economy. It tells you nothing about the demand for or supply of output, or about levels of employment or income or any other real macroeconomic variables. All the LM curve deals with is the size of money balances at this moment.

Adjustments to Where L = M in the Classical Model

If people are holding more money than they want to hold, they will be trying to do something about that. In the classical model they will go out and spend the extra money for goods and services. But since the economy is already at full employment, output cannot increase. So prices will be driven upward. Inflation will push down the real value of the average dollar. People's "real money balances" will shrink to the point where their shrunken real balances are exactly the size balances they desire to hold.

Example: Suppose people find that they are holding twice as much money as they want to hold. They will go out and spend this money and force prices to double. After prices double they will want to hold twice as much nominal money as before. So Mqd = M. People are holding twice as many dollars as before, but each dollar has only half the purchasing power.

Adjustments to Where L = M in the Keynesian Model

In the Keynesian model, if people find themselves holding more money than they wish, they may spend some of it for goods and services just as in the classical model. But in the Keynesian model, assuming a depressed economy, the increased spending will result in increased employment, output and income—not increased prices. But this adjustment process—increased spending for goods and services—is not the focus of the Keynesian model. The Keynesian focus is on asset shifting—portfolio readjustments—*shifting between money and OFAs.*

When people find that they are holding too much of their assets in the form of money, they buy OFAs. Prices of OFAs rise and interest rates fall. At the lower interest rates, people desire larger money balances. Conversely, when people find their money balances smaller than they desire, they sell OFAs to get more money. OFA prices go down and interest rates go up. At the higher rates people want more in OFAs and less in money balances.

Constructing the LM Curve

Whenever people are shifting their assets between money balances and OFAs, L ≠ M and the financial markets are not in equilibrium.

- When most people are trying to increase their money balances (Mqd > M) they will be selling OFAs to get more money. OFA prices will be falling and r will be rising.

- When most people are trying to reduce their money balances they will be buying OFAs. OFA prices will be rising and r will be falling.

The disequilibrium in the financial markets will be corrected as Mqd responds to changes in r. At the level of r where Mqd = M, the financial markets will be in equilibrium. That's where Mqd (=L) = M. And that's a point on the LM curve. Now look at figure 31-3 and you'll see a graphic (supply and demand) illustration of this adjustment process.

The LM curve joins points of equilibrium between the **demand for money** and the **supply of money**—all combinations of Y and r where Mqd = M. The LM curve shows that as Y increases, r must also increase to maintain the Mqd = M (the L = M) equilibrium.

The graphs in figure 31-2 or the numbers in Table 31-1 give all the information needed to draw an LM curve. Figure 31-4 shows the LM curve plotted from Table 31-1. Then figure 31-5 gives more information about the LM curve. Stop now and study, and practice drawing LM curves.

Money Supply Changes Shift the LM Curve

Suppose the money supply increases. In terms of the LM curve, that would mean that people can have their desired transactions balances (L1) and there's more money available to go into their speculative (L2) balances. People who see their L2 balances building up will begin trading some of that money for OFAs. OFA prices will rise and interest rates will fall until people are willing to hold the larger L2 balances.

Or you could say it the other way. When people find themselves holding more money, they can spend more and generate a higher level of national income without having to deplete their speculative (L2) balances. Either way, an increase in the money supply amounts to a rightward shift in the LM curve—which means lower r or higher Y or some combination of the two. A decrease in the money supply would shift the curve leftward and have the opposite effects.

Figure 31-5 illustrates the shifting LM curve, responding to changes in the money supply. In that figure you see that when LM shifts there must be a change

---

**Figure 31-3. Shifting Between Money and OFAs Moves
the Interest Rate to Equilibrium**

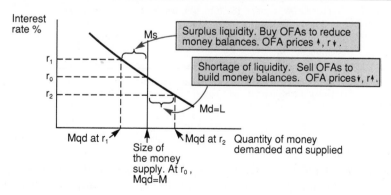

Whenever L ≠ M, people will be shifting assets in their portfolios. This shifting (between OFAs and money) will continue until r moves to r_0 and L = M.

Figure 31-4. Plotting the LM Curve: Points of Equilibrium r at Different Levels of Y

Points along the LM curve indicate all of the unique combinations of Y and r which will push L (= Mqd) into equality with the (fixed) money supply (M). (This curve is plotted from table 31-1).

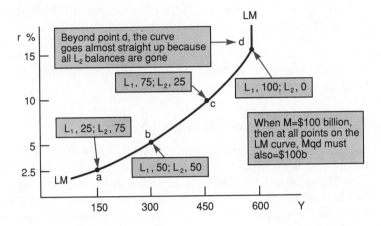

The Keynesian model, with its shifting of desired money balances out of speculative and into transactions balances (from L2 to L1), permits considerable variability of velocity, and produces the upward-sloping LM curve.

As Y increases, people want to increase the size of their transactions balances (L1). But with a fixed money supply, the only way they can do this is to reduce the size of their speculative (L2) balances. The only way to get people to desire smaller speculative balances is for the interest rate to rise. So with a given money supply, as Y increases, r must increase to maintain the L = M equilibrium.

In the Keynesian model, r will increase as the public sells bonds and other OFAs to try to build up their money balances. As OFAs are sold, their prices are forced down and interest rates are forced up. *This process continues until the public desires to hold exactly the quantities of money which they are holding*—i.e., until L = M—until a point on the LM curve is reached.

With a fixed money supply ($100b) the graph shows Y increasing from $150b to $600b. So V quite obviously is increasing. V = Y/M. So if Y = $100b then Y/M = V would be 1. When Y gets up to $300b, V = 3, and at Y = $600b, V = 6.

Note: Throughout this discussion, to simplify it is assumed that L1 is entirely a function of Y and that L2 is entirely a function of r. As explained in a previous chapter, this is not exactly true. But this assumption makes it easier to understand all this.

in either Y or r, or some of both. But from that figure you can't say which will happen. It all depends on where we are at the moment.

At what point are we on the LM curve? And also, at what point on the IS curve? We can't go any further with this analysis until we bring the two curves together to find a *simultaneous solution*—a simultaneous equilibrium of both IS and LM—where I = S and L = M. That's what we'll be doing in the remainder of this chapter.

**Figure 31-5.   The Generalized LM Curve: With M Fixed, Higher Y
              Requires Higher V and (Therefore) Higher r**

The LM curve illustrates increasing V (decreasing L2 balances) as interest rates rise, because (a) the opportunity cost of holding speculative balances increases and (b) the expectation that interest rates will rise in the future, decreases.

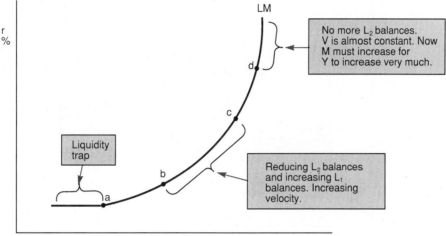

This curve indicates that when interest rates are very low, the velocity of circulation is low because much of the money supply is being held as speculative balances—as "portfolio assets" instead of "spending money." The near-horizontal slope of the curve between points a and b indicates that only small increases in interest rates are required to squeeze considerable sums of money out of desired speculative (L2) balances to satisfy the desire for larger transactions (L1) balances.

By the time interest rates rise to the level indicated by point C, the remaining part of the money supply still being held in desired speculative (L2) balances is not very great. The steepness of the curve between c and d indicates that interest rates must rise significantly to make people want to give up these small remaining L2 balances.

Beyond point d, all of the speculative balances are gone so only very small increases in V can occur. For Y to increase very much beyond this point the money supply must increase.

MEANWHILE, WHAT'S HAPPENING IN THE MACROECONOMY?

So far the discussion in this chapter has been focused on Mqd (= L)—the size of the money balances which people would like to hold. The discussion has been concerned entirely with *stocks of money at rest*—not flows of employment, output, and income.

Why be concerned with stocks? Because in the Keynesian model, money stocks (quantities demanded and supplied) determine interest rates. And interest rates play an important role in influencing investment spending. And investment spending is a *key player* in determining the level of employment, output, and income—the real macroeconomic variables.

Figure 31-6.   Changes in M Shift the LM Curve

When M decreases, LM shifts leftward (upward) indicating less liquidity and therefore higher r at each level of Y. When M increases, LM shifts rightward (downward): indicating more liquidity and lower r at each Y.

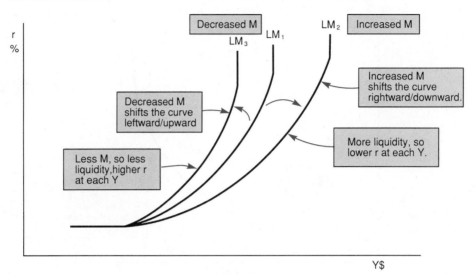

When the money supply increases, at each level of Y there is suddenly a surplus of liquidity. The curve shifts to the right to indicate that either Y must increase or r must fall (or some of both). That *must happen* to induce the public to want to hold the increased money balances which they suddenly find themselves holding.

Will Y increase? Or will r fall? Or how much of each? That depends on the prior condition of the economy and the financial markets. From this figure you can't say whether ΔM will affect mostly Y or mostly r. You'll find out about that in the sections coming up.

In the Keynesian model of the macroeconomy the interest rate is the essential link between the "stocks of money at rest" (quantities demanded, and supplied) and the spending flows and the real input, output and income flows in the economy.

In order to understand how it all ties together you need to look at both the spending-output-income flows (which respond to interest rates) and the desired holdings of money balances (which influence interest rates). That's what you'll be doing in the next section. There the IS curve and the LM curve are used together to obtain a unique, simultaneous equilibrium, both (1) between Mqd and M and in the financial markets, and (2) in the spending flows and product markets.

You know that equilibrium in the financial markets must occur at a combination of Y and r indicated by some point on the LM curve—where L = M. But you don't know which of those combinations will be compatible with equilibrium in the spending flows and product markets where I = S. Equilibrium in the macroeconomy can exist only when L = M and *simultaneously*, I = S. When either the *money stocks* or the *spending and real flows* are out of balance, both Y and r

Box 31-2

Feature: Summary of Factors Influencing the LM Curve

THE SLOPE OF THE CURVE

A steeper LM curve would indicate:

1. Mqd = L less responsive to Δr. A given Δr would have less effect on people's desires to hold money balances and/or

2. Mqd = L more responsive to ΔY. A given ΔY would have more effect on people's desires to hold money balances.

Note: a steep LM curve indicates that the desire for money balances is closely related to the *transactions motive* and that the Keynesian speculative motive is not playing an important role. It means that *velocity* doesn't change much.

Conversely, a flatter LM curve would indicate:

1. Mqd = L more responsive to Δr, and/or

2. Mqd = L less responsive to ΔY.

A flat LM curve indicates that speculative balances are playing an important role and that money shifts freely between L1 and L2 balances. It indicates that velocity is highly variable.

THE LOCATION OF THE CURVE

The LM curve would shift rightward to reflect (1) an increase in the money supply, or (2) an autonomous decrease in people's desires to hold money balances. Either way, people will find themselves holding larger money balances than they wish. Demand for OFAs will increase, OFA prices will rise, and r will fall.

Conversely, the LM curve would shift leftward to reflect (1) a decrease in the money supply, or (2) an autonomous increase in people's desires to hold money balances. In either case, people will find themselves with smaller money balances than they wish. They will sell OFAs, pushing OFA prices down and r up.

What might cause an **autonomous change** in people's desires to hold money balances— i.e., a shift in liquidity preference =Mqd = L? A shift in expectations—in the perceived outlook for inflation, for interest rates, or for the economy and/or the financial markets. Events such as the stock market "crash" of October 1987 can have a significant impact. So can the appearance of best-selling books predicting a forthcoming depression. Any shift in the demand for money (Md) has the same effect as a change in the money supply, only in the opposite direction: $\downarrow$ Md is approximately equivalent to $\uparrow$ M.

will be changing. The economy will be speeding up or slowing down. So we must have a solution that brings both the stocks (L = M) and the flows (I = S) into equilibrium at the same time. For that we need the IS-LM graph, coming up soon.

For Macroequilibrium, Planned Spending Must Equal Current Income

Whenever planned spending from all sources is exactly equal to the size of current income, the spending flows and product markets are in equilibrium. This equilibrium is referred to as "equilibrium in the product markets."

When total withdrawals from the income stream are exactly offset by planned spending injections, then planned spending is exactly equal to current income. So the value of output produced equals the value of output bought and the markets are "cleared"—no surpluses, no shortages.

In the Keynesian model this product-markets equilibrium does not occur at any one specific rate of output and income (Y). It can occur at full employment, or with unemployment. The IS curve shows the various possibilities and indicates that (*ceteris paribus*) the lower the rate of interest the higher equilibrium Y will be.

The Interest Rate Holds the Key to Macroequilibrium

Why is r so important in the Keynesian model? Because the rate of interest (*ceteris paribus*) determines the rate of planned investment spending. Macroequilibrium occurs where savings withdrawals are exactly equal to investment injections.

When r falls, I increases. So S must also increase. To induce S to increase, Y must increase. That's exactly what the IS curve shows. And you can see that *with any given IS curve, r determines the exact size of Y.*

In the Keynesian model, the interest rate is determined by the interaction between (1) the desire to hold money balances (Mqd = L), and (2) the size of money balances currently being held (M). Whenever Mqd ≠ M, r will be increasing or decreasing.

When r increases or decreases to bring Mqd into balance with M, each of these interest rate changes will cause a change in investment spending. The economy will speed up or slow down as indicated by the IS curve. But here's a problem.

Changing r Causes Changing Y Which Causes Changing r, etc.

After some initial change in r, as Y moves toward equilibrium, r doesn't stay put and let the economy move to the new equilibrium. In fact, each time Y moves toward its new equilibrium, that change in Y brings a change in Mqd. (The transactions demand for money—L1—is positively related to Y, remember.) So as each change in r causes Y to move, the moving Y causes r to change again.

To say it differently: An equilibrium between Mqd and M and in the financial markets (a point on the LM curve) produces an interest rate which, given the IS curve, identifies a specific equilibrium in the spending flows and product markets where I = S (a point on the IS curve). But as the economy moves toward that equilibrium point on the IS curve, that movement upsets the LM equilibrium. So r moves again and that upsets the IS equilibrium. So around and around we go.

In this situation a *simultaneous solution* is needed. We must simultaneously find (1) an equilibrium between Mqd and M in the financial markets where r is determined, and (2) an equilibrium in the spending flows and product markets where Y is determined. How do we get a simultaneous solution? Quite easily. Just put the IS and LM curves (or equations) together and the simultaneous solution appears.[1]

Figure 31-7 brings the IS and LM curves together. In that graph you can see the simultaneous equilibrium where both I = S and L = M. You can see that there is one (and only one) combination of r and Y which permits this simultaneous equilibrium. It occurs at point e, where r = r_e, and Y = Y_e, and I = S and L = M.

At no other point in the graph (other than e) would equilibrium exist simultaneously in both the product markets and the financial markets. At all points other than e, disequilibrium exists in at least one of the two markets.

---

[1] The equations are explained in appendix A31-1, located at the back of this book.

Figure 31-7.   The IS-LM Diagram; Simultaneous Determination of Y and r

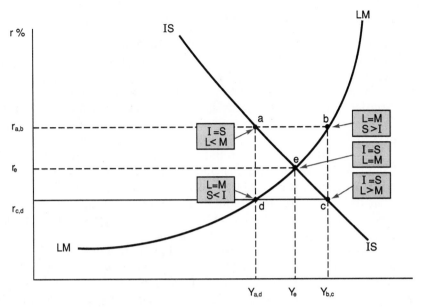

This graph illustrates the unique macroequilibrium at point e, with interest rate r_e and national income Y_e.

At all interest rates either above or below r_e, "corrective forces" will automatically push the interest rate toward r_e.

At all levels of national income other than Y_e, corrective forces will automatically push national income toward Y_e.

In the diagram, changes in r are related to the LM curve. Changes in Y are related to the IS curve. But changes in r (because of LM relationships) upset the IS equilibrium; changes in Y (because of IS relationships) upset the LM equilibrium. So the two (r, and Y) must move simultaneously to bring the economy to equilibrium at point e where both I = S and L = M at the same time.

Box 31-3

Question: Is the Ultimate Objective of IS-LM Analysis to Find r? or Y?

The IS-LM diagram shows a simultaneous solution for Y and r. A simultaneous solution is necessary because changes in Y affect r and changes in r affect Y. You can't identify the equilibrium value of either variable until you know where the other variable will be at that time.

But the purpose of all this analysis really isn't to determine r. Determining r is an essential step in the process—just "a means to an end." What we are trying to find out is the equilibrium level of Y. We want to know what is happening with the flows in the macroeconomy—employment, output, income, and all that—and whether there is unemployment or full employment—or pressures for inflation.

The point: The objective of all this is to find

the size of Y. But finding the simultaneous value of r is an essential part of the process. Why? Because r (*ceteris paribus*) determines I, and I (*ceteris paribus*) determines Y.

In a previous chapter when working with the Keynesian Cross diagram, to find equilibrium Y (where S = I) we "assumed" a constant rate of investment of $10 billion. Remember? But with the IS-LM analysis we can drop that unrealistic assumption. Now, I = f(r). So I changes to reflect conditions in the financial markets, which change to reflect changing conditions in the economy. And that's exactly what you see in the IS-LM framework. So now you can see why, to find equilibrium Y, finding equilibrium r is an essential part of the process.

Excess Liquidity Forces r Down

In Figure 31-7, suppose r happened to be higher than r_e and Y·smaller than Y_e, as indicated by point a in the graph. What would cause the economy to move to point e?

At point a, the interest rate is up to r_a and national income is down to Y_a. The circular flow of the economy is in equilibrium because I = S. But the financial markets certainly are not in equilibrium. Interest rate r_a is too high for this level of Y.

Y_a is a low level of national income, so the transactions demand for money balances (L1) is low. Interest rate r_a is high, so the desire to hold speculative balances (L2) is small. So total desired money balances (L1 + L2 = L) is smaller than the money supply (Mqd < M). People are holding more money than they wish to hold, so they begin buying OFAs. The increased demand pushes up OFA prices and pushes down interest rates.

Interest rates fall toward point d, which would bring equilibrium in the financial markets. But as r begins to fall, the lower r stimulates more investment spending. That breaks the equilibrium in the circular flow of the economy. Now I is greater than S. The spending flow begins to expand. Y increases.

See what's happening? As r moves downward, Y moves rightward. The decreasing r brings increasing I. The increasing I brings increasing Y. Figure 31-8 gives a schematic illustration of this process.

With Each Drop in r, I Increases so Y Increases

You might think of the economy as moving from point a to equilibrium (point e) by a series of zig-zag steps as shown in figure 31-8. Beginning at point a, as people try to reduce their money balances they push down interest rates toward point d. But before the economy reaches point f in figure 31-8, the decreasing interest rates trigger increased investment spending. So national income increases toward point g.

But at the same time, portfolio managers are continuing to rid themselves of their surplus money balances. They are buying more OFAs, pushing interest rates down even more and further stimulating investment spending. As interest rates are being pushed ever lower, the rate of investment spending is constantly increasing. So Y continues to increase. Ultimately the economy will arrive at point e where the interest rate is r_e and the national income is Y_e.

Clearly, the economy would not actually follow the series of zig-zag steps shown for schematic illustration in figure 31-8. Since r is falling and I (and Y) are increasing continuously, if this happened to be a frictionless economy and if the adjustment began from a point on the IS curve (e.g., point a), the economy would never depart from the IS curve. As r began to fall, I and Y would simultaneously increase and the economy would move down along the IS curve to point e.

Excess I (I > S) Forces Y to Increase

Suppose the economy happened to be at point d in figure 31-8. Both Y and r are quite low. The financial markets are in equilibrium. Desired transactions (L1) balances are low because of the low level of Y. But because of the low interest rates, desired speculative (L2) balances are large enough to offset the low level of

Figure 31-8.   A Schematic View of Movement to Equilibrium in the IS-LM Diagram

Each change in r brings a change in Y. Each change in Y brings a change in r. The changes continue to the levels of r and Y where both I = S and L = M.

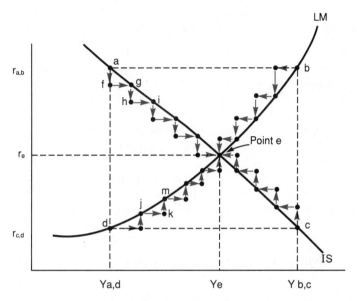

In this graph, movements in r results from departures from the LM curve. At any point above and to the left of the LM curve (e.g., point a) people are holding greater money balances than desired. To reduce their balances they buy OFAs, push up OFA prices and push down interest rates toward point d on the LM curve.

At any point below and to the right of the LM curve (e.g., pt. c) people will desire larger money balances than they are holding. So to build their money balances they will sell OFAs, push down OFA prices, and push up interest rates toward point b on the LM curve. The only place where the interest rate can remain stable is where L = M—a point on the LM curve.

Changes in the level of Y are induced by the lack of equality between I and S—i.e., by departures from the IS curve. At any point below and to the left of the IS curve (e.g., pt. d) investment injections into the spending stream will be greater than savings withdrawals from the stream. So the size of the spending stream (Y) will be increasing toward point c on the IS curve. It will continue to increase until I = S.

At any point above and to the right of the IS curve (e.g., pt. b) the savings withdrawal from the spending flow will be greater than the investment injection. So the size of the spending flow (Y) will be decreasing toward point a on the IS curve. It will continue to decrease until I = S—a point on the IS curve.

desired L1 balances. So at point d, L = M. But the graph indicates that the relationship between I and S is far from equal.

At such a low level of Y the savings rate is very low, while at such a low level of r the investment rate is high. Planned investment spending is gushing into the spending flow, but only a small trickle of savings is leaking out. Y is going to be rapidly expanding toward point c.

Increasing Y Causes L (=Mqd) to Increase, so L > M

As Y increases and the economy moves toward point c, that upsets the equilibrium in the financial markets. People want to hold larger money balances because of the increased rate of transactions. So the LM equilibrium is broken. People begin selling OFAs to increase their money balances. OFA prices go down and r goes up.

As r increases the money markets move toward equilibrium at point j. But surplus investment spending is still pouring into the income stream. Y is continuing to increase, pushing the economy toward point k in the diagram.

As the economy moves toward point k, the L1 desire for money balances increases even more. So people sell more OFAs, interest rates go up more and the economy moves toward point M. This process continues with Y and r increasing until the simultaneous equilibrium is reached at point e.

From All Points to the Right of IS the Economy Will Slow Down

The situation at point b is exactly opposite from that at point d, so from point b an exactly opposite set of steps would move the economy to equilibrium. At point b the financial markets are in equilibrium. But because of the high Y, savings are gushing out of the income flow and because of the high r the investment spending inflow is only a trickle. Total planned spending is much smaller than current income. So the spending flow is shrinking fast. The economy moves toward point a.

As Y decreases, people desire smaller L1 money balances, so they begin buying OFAs with their surplus balances. OFA prices rise, and r falls. The lower r increases the L2 demand for money balances, so money shifts out of L1 balances and into L2 balances.

The lower r stimulates investment some, but still S > I so Y continues to decrease. That frees up more L1 balances, increases the demand for OFAs, and pushes r down more. The economy is moving down along the LM curve toward point e.

As long as S > I, Y will continues to decrease. So L1 will continue to decrease, OFA demand will continue to increase and r will continue to fall. Both Y and r will continue to decrease all the way to point e. In this case it is the falling Y that causes the falling L (=Mqd) which causes the falling r.

From All Points to the Right of LM, r Will Rise

At point c, S = I, but people want to hold much larger money balances than they are holding. The high level of Y means that L1 is large. The low level of r means that L2 is large. I don't know how we ever got into this situation, but one thing is sure: We won't stay here long!

Everybody wants larger money balances. Nobody wants more OFAs! Everybody is selling OFAs and nobody is particularly interested in buying. OFA prices plummet and interest rates rise sharply. The economy moves from point c toward point b.

The rising interest rates break the spending flow equilibrium. The higher rates discourage investment spending. Suddenly I is smaller, so S is greater than I. Surplus products are left in the market. Unplanned investment exists throughout the economy. Producers cut back and Y decreases. The economy is moving toward point e.

As long as people continue to be dissatisfied with their too-small money balances, they will continue to sell OFAs, push OFA prices down and push interest rates up. And as long as this continues, planned investment will be discouraged even more. So S will continue be greater than I and Y will continue to fall. This process will continue until the economy arrives at point e.

Where IS-LM: A Simultaneous and Unique Equilibrium

In summary, whenever the financial (LM) markets are in equilibrium, but the income-spending flow and product markets are not, changes in the product markets and spending flows will occur to move the economy toward equilibrium. But as this happens, it will upset the LM equilibrium.

Whenever the income-spending flow and product markets (IS) are in equilibrium but the financial markets are not, changes in the financial markets will occur to move those markets toward equilibrium. But that will upset the IS equilibrium. Movements toward equilibrium in either the spending flow and product markets or the financial markets will bring disequilibrium in the other markets. So the markets must adjust simultaneously to move the economy to its unique macroequilibrium.[2]

The IS-LM Equilibrium Ignores the Effects of Price Changes

Does the unique simultaneous equilibrium identified in the IS-LM diagram identify true macroequilibrium for the economy? Actually, no. This section explains.

The IS-LM framework gives us a powerful tool for macroeconomic analysis. You might call it the "crowning achievement" of the Keynesian model. But as such, it is still limited by a most basic assumption of the Keynesian model: **fixed prices**.

Everyone knows that in the real world as the economy is speeding up or slowing down, and as demand and supply for OFAs in the financial markets are waxing and waning, prices of inputs and outputs throughout the economy do not remain fixed. And the longer the time period under consideration, the more flexible prices become.

If price rigidities are strong and the time period under consideration is short, it may be that little price flexibility is possible. In that case the simultaneous IS-LM equilibrium may be approximately accurate. But the greater the degree of

---

[2] The IS-LM curves were not actually drawn and presented by Keynes in *The General Theory*. In fact there was only one diagram in that entire book. The IS and LM curves were developed by Sir John Hicks and presented in his famous paper, "Mr. Keynes and the Classics: A Suggested Interpretation," *Econometrica*, (April 1937). All of this IS-LM graphical analysis was first developed by Hicks.

price flexibility and the longer the time period under consideration, the less accurate the results of the IS-LM analysis will be.

The IS-LM framework gives us simultaneous equilibrium of the macroeconomy considering two important variables: Y and r. But it leaves out the other important variable: price changes (ΔP).

So what can we do about this problem? We can develop an analytical framework which takes into consideration price level changes. What framework? The aggregate demand-aggregate supply (AD-AS) diagram, introduced in the next chapter.

SUMMARY

- The LM curve indicates combinations of Y and r at which the desired quantity of money balances (Mqd = L) is exactly equal to the quantity of money in the money supply (M).

- As Y increases, Mqd for L1 balances increases. So r must increase to decrease Mqd for L2 balances so that total Mqd (=L) = M. That's why the LM curve slopes upward, showing that, given M, higher rates of Y require higher r

- Whenever people are holding more of their assets in the form of money than they desire (Mqd < M), they will buy OFAs. Prices of OFAs will rise and interest rates will fall until people are willing to hold larger money balances and Mqd (=L) = M.

- An increase in the money supply ($\uparrow$ M) or a decrease in money demand ($\downarrow$ Md) would shift the LM curve to the right, resulting in greater Y and/or lower r. A decrease in the money supply ($\downarrow$ M) or an increase in money demand ($\uparrow$ Md) would have the opposite effect.

- The IS-LM diagram identifies a unique simultaneous equilibrium for the economy where (1) total planned spending is exactly equal to *total current income*—which means that S = I, and (2) *the quantity of money demanded* (Mqd = L) is exactly equal to *the size of the money supply* (M)—which means that L = M. The economy will move, via adjustments in both the product markets and the financial markets, to the levels of r and Y where this simultaneous equilibrium exists.

- The simultaneous IS-LM equilibrium holds only to the extent that prices are fixed—which is what the Keynesian model assumes.

Important Principles, Issues, Concepts, Terms

Relationship between Mqd and Y

Relationship between Mqd and r

Effects of Δr on L2 balances

Effect of L2 balances on velocity

Stocks vs. flows in the IS-LM diagram

Adjustments to where L = M

Definition of the LM curve

Construction of the LM curve

Shifting the LM curve

Factors influencing LM slope

Factors influencing LM location

Effects of a change in Md

Need for a simultaneous I = S and L = M solution

Movement to equilibrium in the IS-LM diagram

Questions

1. Draw a graph showing the LM curve. Then explain why the curve is shaped as it is. The curve shows that as Y increases, r also must increase. Explain why this is true.

2. Explain this statement: "The IS curve represents flows while the LM curve represents stocks."

3. Explain the variables which might cause the LM curve to become more steep, or less steep.

4. Explain the variables which might cause the LM curve to shift to the right, or left.

5. Explain why it is impossible to define a unique equilibrium in the economy without considering both the IS and the LM curves.

6. Explain this statement: "The ultimate objective is IS-LM analysis is to determine Y, but determining r is an essential step in the process."

7. In the Keynesian model, even though the money supply is fixed, it is possible for national income (and total spending) to increase significantly. Explain why, and illustrate with graphs, and/or a numerical example.

8. When most people are trying to sell financial assets to build up their money balances, that means that the economy is not located at a point on the LM curve. What will happen to cause the economy to move to a point on the curve?

9. Draw an IS-LM diagram and illustrate the movement of the economy to equilibrium from four different disequilibrium points, one in each quadrant of the graph.

10. Explain exactly what it means to say: "Assuming prices are fixed, where IS = LM, that is a simultaneous and unique equilibrium of the macroeconomy."

Suggested Readings

Akerlof, George A., and Janet L. Yellen, Alan S. Blinder, and Bennett T. McCallum. Symposium of papers on "The Contribution of Keynes After 50 Years." *The American Economic Review, Papers and Proceedings* 77 (2). (May 1987) , 125–42. The titles of the papers are:
Akerlof and Yellen: "Rational Models of Irrational Behavior."
Blinder: "Keynes, Lucas, and Scientific Progress."
McCallum: "The Development of Keynesian Macroeconomics."

Brothwell, John F. "*The General Theory* After 50 Years: Why are we not all Keynesians now?" *Journal of Post Keynesian Economics* 8 (4), (Summer 1986), pp. 531–47.

Pekkarinen, J. "Early Hicks and Keynesian Monetary Theory: Different Views on Liquidity Preference." *History of Political Economy* 18 (2). (Summer 1986), 335–49.

Rotemberg, Julie. "The New Keynesian Microfoundations." *NBER Macroeconomics Annual 1987.* (National Bureau of Economic Research), Cambridge, Mass.: The MIT Press, 1987.

Samuels, Warren J. "What Aspects of Keynes' Economic Theories Merit Continued or Renewed Interest?" *Journal of Post Keynesian Economics* 9 (1). (Fall 1986), 3–16.

Samuelson, P. A. "The Simple Mathematics of Income Determination." *Income, Employment, and Public Policy: Essays in Honor of Alvin H. Hansen.* New York: W. W. Norton, 1964.

PART VIII

Monetary Theory II: Developing and Using the AD-AS Framework to Analyze the Macroeconomy in the Modern Monetarist, Modern Keynesian and Other Recent Models

In Part VIII you will learn some different ways of viewing and analyzing the macroeconomy. First (in Chapters 32 and 33) the aggregate demand-aggregate supply (AD-AS) framework is developed and explained. Then in Chapter 34 this framework is used to analyze the modern monetarist and modern Keynesian theories, and to illustrate the different results which these different theories produce. Here you will find that when analyzing cause and effect relationships in the macroeconomy it makes a world of difference which initial assumptions you choose!

Then in Chapter 35 you will read about the "new classical" model of the macroeconomy in which the assumption of "rational expectations" plays a key role. And finally (in Chapter 36) you will see various supply side theories illustrated in the AD-AS diagram, and you will learn about the development during the 1980s of "real" business cycle theory—a new emphasis which focuses on the role of supply-side disturbances in initiating macroeconomic speedups and slowdowns.

After you study Part VIII you will have a good understanding of the modern theories and the current agreements and disagreements in macroeconomics. And you will understand the AD-AS framework and how to use it to analyze the results of the various theories: classical, modern monetarist, modern Keynesian, new classical, and supply side.

CHAPTER 32

Understanding Aggregate Demand and Developing the AD Curve

Chapter Objectives

The aggregate demand-aggregate supply (AD-AS) framework is another way of viewing and analyzing the macroeconomy. This chapter explains aggregate demand. The next chapter explains aggregate supply and then shows how to use the AD-AS framework to analyze the macroeconomy. After you study this chapter you will understand and be able to explain:

1. The purpose of the AD-AS framework.

2. The AD curve: what it means, reasons for its negative slope, and factors which would cause it to shift.

3. Some different assumptions and theories concerning the position and slope of the AD curve.

4. How to derive the AD curve by shifting the curves in the IS-LM diagram, and how different AD curves result from different assumptions regarding the slopes of the IS and LM curves.

5. The important distinction between a change of AD—a shift of the AD curve—and a change in aggregate quantity demanded (AQD) in response to ΔP—a movement along the AD curve.

THE AD-AS FRAMEWORK—ANOTHER WAY TO ANALYZE THE CIRCULAR FLOW

Each macroeconomic framework—each way of visualizing and analyzing the macroeconomy—has its own special focus. Each reveals a different set of cause and effect relationships.

The simplest way to view the macroeconomy is in the circular flow diagram. All of the other (more complex) ways of analyzing the macroeconomy can be viewed in terms of "how various influences affect the circular flow."

Aggregate Demand Is What Supports the Spending Flow

In the circular flow diagram, in the output loop the money flow is actually the aggregate quantity of output demanded (AQD). It's equal to the aggregate quantity

569

of output supplied (AQS). In the AD-AS diagram we can look more closely at the factors which influence the level of and changes in the money flows and the real flows. And we can see causes of and effects of changes in the price level.

Why is the macroeconomy (the circular flow) as it is today? Why *this* level of employment, output, and income? And why *this* price level? And what does *money* have to do with it? These are questions which AD-AS analysis can help to answer. And both Keynesian and monetarist theories can be viewed in the AD-AS framework. (See box 32-1.)[1]

Overview of the AD-AS Framework

The AD-AS diagram relates total quantities of goods and services demanded and supplied to *the general level of prices*. In the short run, the lower the general level of prices, the greater the total quantity demanded and the smaller the quantity supplied. Equilibrium in the macroeconomy—as you could guess—occurs where total quantity demanded equals total quantity supplied.

From this brief description it's obvious that the AD-AS graph will appear quite similar to a demand and supply graph for an individual product. The AD curve will be sloped negatively indicating greater quantities demanded at lower prices, and the AS curve (in the short run) will be positively sloped indicating greater quantities supplied at higher prices. But the slope of the AS curve—as with the supply curve for an individual product—depends very much on *the length of time allowed for supply adjustments to occur*.

So you won't be surprised to find that the AD and AS curves look just like the "regular" demand and supply curves which you have seen so many times. But note this well: The reason for the shapes and slopes of the AD and AS curves are *quite different* from the reasons why supply and demand curves for individual products are shaped and sloped as they are. All this will be explained in the

---

Box 32-1

Feature: **Keynesian Theory and Monetarist Theory: Often More Complementary Than Competing**

A word of caution: Throughout this chapter you will continue to see distinctions between different theories: Keynesian, classical, and modern monetarist. As these distinctions are explained, remember that the purpose is not to "see which theory is right." That depends on the assumptions, and on the existing circumstances.

Modern Keynesian theory and modern monetarist theory are often more complementary than competing. It is in fact impossible to have a thorough understanding of the functioning of the real-world macroeconomy—and of the role of money in the economy—without an understanding of classical-neoclassical-modern monetarist theory, and early and modern Keynesian theory as well.

In a chapter coming up soon you will be reading much more about "modern monetarist" and "modern Keynesian" theory. Both of these have developed significantly beyond the early theories. Extreme positions have been modified so that now many of the sharp differences between the models no longer exist.

---

[1] This AD-AS analysis is frequently called AS-AD analysis. You'll see it referred to both ways. Either way it means exactly the same thing.

sections coming up. But first, read box 32-2 which tells about the relationships among the different frameworks for analyzing the macroeconomy.

Several Views of the Macroeconomy Identify "Aggregate Quantity Demanded" (AQD)

There are various ways of viewing the macroeconomy which focus on *aggregate* (*total*) *spending* (for output) as the "driving force" in the macroeconomy. In these views, aggregate quantity demanded (AQD) controls the rate of flow of the macroeconomy—i.e., the size of the output flow is determined by **demand** (the spending flow), not by **supply** (the productive capacity of the economy).

In the circular flow view of the economy, AQD is indicated by the size of the spending flow. In the Keynesian spending and income equation, AQD is $C + I + G + Ex$. In the Keynesian Cross diagram, AQD at each level of national income is shown by the height of the consumption function curve, as that curve is shifted upward to reflect not only C, but also all spending injections: $I + G + Ex$. In the equation of exchange ($MV = PQ$), AQD is indicated by MV: the number of dollars in the money supply times the velocity of circulation of the average dollar.

In all of these views the focus is on AQD: What determines AQD? And what causes it to change? But none of these views deal with the effect of **price changes** on AQD. It's time to address that question now.

AD-AS Diagram Reflects Price Level Changes

After you understand the relationship between *price level changes* and AQD, then you'll be ready to look at the effect of price level changes on *the aggregate quantity of output supplied* (AQS). And then you'll be able to use another useful framework for analyzing the macroeconomy: **the AD-AS diagram**.

Box 32-2

Question: Is the AD-AS Framework Related to the IS-LM Framework? Of Course It Is!

Since the AD-AS framework is another way of visualizing and analyzing the macroeconomy, you would expect it to be related somehow to the IS-LM framework—and to be sure, it is. All of our tools of macroeconomic analysis are related.

So what's the difference between one analytical framework and another? Mostly this: Variables which are **explicit** in one analytical framework often are **implicit** in another. The "given and fixed" parameters in one framework can become the variables in another. For example for any given pair of IS-LM curves, the **price** **level** is given and fixed. But in the AD-AS framework the price level becomes the key variable.

Also it's important to emphasize that the IS-LM framework relates entirely to the **demand side** of the macroeconomy, while AD-AS obviously relates to both the demand and supply sides.

Soon you will see how to use IS-LM curves to derive the AD curve. That exercise will illustrate all of this, and it will increase your understanding of both of these important theoretical frameworks.

HOW PRICE LEVEL CHANGES AFFECT AQD: THE AD CURVE

Figure 32-1 shows a graph of the aggregate demand (AD) curve. The vertical axis shows the price level. More precisely, the vertical axis is the *price index* axis. It indicates price level movements above or below an initial position. The horizontal axis shows quantities of output—numbers of units of real goods and services. The negative slope of the AD curve shows that as the price level decreases, the aggregate quantity of goods and services demanded (AQD) increases. Why so?

The most important reason for the downward slope of the AD curve is this: As prices fall, the average person can buy more. Suppose you have a given amount of money to spend. Then the lower the price level, the greater your purchasing power. So the more goods and services you are able to (and are likely to) buy. So decreasing prices result in increasing AQD.

In both the monetarist and Keynesian models of the macroeconomy the AD curve slopes downward. But the exact explanation of why this happens is somewhat different in the Keynesian model than in the monetarist model.

Given MV (=E), the AD Curve Illustrates "PQ"

The AD curve can be explained in terms of the equation of exchange. Assume that both M and V are constant. That means that the dollar amount of total spending (E) is *absolutely fixed*. Then suppose prices go down ($\downarrow$ P). With E fixed, the total quantity of output bought must go up ($\uparrow$ Q). Or suppose prices (P) increase. Then given E, the number of units of output bought (Q) must go down. *Any ΔP must be exactly offset by an opposite ΔQ; any ΔQ must be exactly offset by an opposite ΔP.*

Figure 32-1.   Understanding the AD Curve

Aggregate Quantity Demanded (AQD) Changes as the Price Level Changes

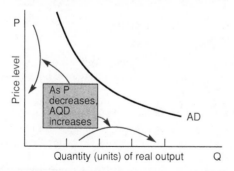

As the price level falls, more output is bought. With a given level of total spending (MV), lower prices ($\downarrow$ P) means a greater quantity of output is being demanded ($\uparrow$ Q) so that PQ remains constant.

Example: Suppose M = $10 billion and V equals 5. Total spending will be $50 billion. The aggregate quantity of goods and services demanded will be "$50 billion worth." So how much is that? It depends on how high prices are.

Suppose the average price of the average unit bought (P) is $1. Then the aggregate quantity demanded (AQD) will be 50 billion units. Now suppose the price level drops to where the average price per unit is only 50 cents. The $50 billion of spending now will buy 100 billion units! You can see that this purchasing power effect tends to result in an inverse relationship between ΔP and ΔQ.

The AD curve tends to be *a graphic illustration of the PQ side of the equation of exchange.* The P is on the vertical axis and the Q is on the horizontal axis. Since MV = PQ, if MV (total spending) is assumed to be constant, then PQ must also be constant. And with PQ constant, any change in P must be exactly offset by an opposite change in Q; any change in Q must be exactly offset by an opposite change in P.

The Purchasing Power Effect: Lower P Means More "Real Money"

What you've just been reading is no great surprise. If prices fall by one half and people still have as many dollars as they had before, *they now have twice as much real purchasing power* and they're likely to buy a lot more goods than previously. This effect says that as prices decrease, the real value of people's money increases. So people can (and will) buy more. So decreasing prices ($\downarrow P$) bring increasing aggregate quantities demanded ($\uparrow AQD$). The shape and slope of the AD curve reflects this. Box 32-3 tells more about price level changes and the size of the **real money supply**.

The Money Market (Interest Rate) Effect of More "Real Money"

Here's another possible effect of ΔP. As prices fall and real purchasing power increases, some of the increased "real money" may flow into the financial markets. In the Keynesian model this increased supply of funds means an increased demand for bonds and other financial assets. So bond prices are pushed up.

As bond prices rise, interest rates (yields) are pushed down. Lower interest rates stimulate investment spending. So *as the price level falls, interest rates tend to fall. Investment spending tends to be stimulated, causing AQD to increase by more than the amount of the simple "purchasing power" effect.*

The Wealth Effect of ΔP

The wealth effect is similar to the purchasing power (real balances, or Pigou) effect, except that *all dollar-denominated assets* (not just money) are included. Here's how it works.

Most people hold some of their assets (their wealth) in the form of money, and also some in CDs, bonds, and other kinds of dollar-denominated assets. Suppose the price level falls. The real value (purchasing power) of these dollar-denominated assets (both money and other financial assets) increases. Or if prices rise the real value of these other financial assets decreases.

Suppose prices are rising. People who hold dollar-denominated assets will see their real wealth dwindling. So they may cut back their spending to try to

Box 32-3

Question: In AD-AS Analysis, Why Use "M/P" As the Measure of the Size of the Money Supply?

Changes in real purchasing power—and in the size of the "real money supply"—are indicated, not by "M," but by "M/P."

The *real money supply* of an economy is the *existing purchasing power* in the hands of all of the spending units in the economy. If everyone has $100 and if the average price of a unit of goods is $1.00, then everyone has the power to purchase 100 units. Everyone has "100-units-worth" or purchasing power—of *real money.* (M/P = $100/1.00 = 100.)

When Prices Fall by One-Half, Purchasing Power Doubles

Suppose the price level falls to where the average price of a unit of goods is now 50 cents. Then, if everyone still has the same number of *nominal dollars* ($100), their *real purchasing power* is doubled. They now have "200-units-worth" of purchasing power—of real money. (M/P = $100/.50 = 200.)

In this example, has the nation's money supply increased? In *nominal* terms, no. But in real terms, yes. It has doubled.

When M/P is used to measure the size of the money supply, the effect of inflation on the value of money is clearly illustrated. It shows that on the other side of the *rising prices* coin, is the shrinking real money supply—the *decreasing quantity of real money.* The M/P indicator shows inflation, not as rising prices, but as a shrinking real money supply—decreasing purchasing power of the spending units in the economy.

Real M Can Change With No Change In Nominal M

Viewed in this perspective it's clear that the aggregate size of *real M* (M/P) can change, without any change in *nominal M.* If the price level falls while nominal M is constant, real M increases. The effects of such an increase in real M tend to be similar to the effects of an increase in nominal M with constant prices. The result: Increased aggregate quantities demanded.

In the Keynesian model the increased purchasing power would cause macroeconomic speedup because of the increased supply of loanable funds (demand for OFAs) bringing lower interest rates to stimulate additional spending.

Conversely, when P is rising, unless nominal M is also increasing, the aggregate size of real M is decreasing. As M/P decreases, total spending is retarded. Also the supply of real money (loanable funds) in the financial markets (the demand for OFAs) decreases. Interest rates rise. Aggregate real spending tends to be depressed even more.

You can see why it's essential to use the "M/P" measure of the money supply in AD-AS analysis. Clearly, *it is the real purchasing power in the hands of the public*—not the number of nominal monetary units—*which translates into the AQD of real goods and services.*

rebuild their wealth. You can see that *the wealth effect* works in the same direction as the purchasing power effect: As prices rise, the wealth effect tends to cause AQD to decrease; as prices fall the wealth effect tends to cause AQD to increase. (Box 32-4 gives an alternative view on the idea of a "wealth effect.")

Substitutions Between Foreign and Domestic Goods. Another possible effect of ΔP on AQD results from changing *relative prices* between domestic and foreign goods. Suppose domestic prices rise. If foreign prices don't rise as much, then foreigners tend to buy fewer of our goods while we tend to buy more of the lower-priced foreign goods. So AQD for domestic goods tends to decrease. This is another factor tending to work in the same direction as all of the others—making the AD curve more price elastic—making real AQD more responsive to changes in the price level.

Box 32-4

Question: Is AQD Really Influenced by a "Wealth Effect?"

Some economists dispute this "wealth effect" theory on the ground that for every saver who owns bonds and other wealth, there is a debtor who owes money. When prices rise, the real value (purchasing power) of bonds falls. So savers (bond holders) have less purchasing power—**less real wealth**. So AQD tends to decrease.

But what about the borrowers? They are better off! As prices rise, their real debt burdens (the real purchasing power they owe) decrease. So they have **more real wealth**. That tends to increase AQD.

If you assume that the borrowers' real wealth is increased by exactly the same amount as the lenders' real wealth is decreased, then you could assume that AQD would remain constant and the "wealth effect" would be zero.

WHAT CAUSES AD TO SHIFT? MONETARIST AND KEYNESIAN EXPLANATIONS

The reasons for a shift of the AD curve are somewhat different in the monetarist model of the macroeconomy than in the Keynesian model.

The Monetarist Model Emphasizes Changes in the Money Supply

In the monetarist model a shift in the aggregate demand curve can be explained in terms of the equation of exchange and the quantity theory of money. The quantity theory assumes that velocity is stable. So any increase in the money supply translates into an increase in total spending. And that means an increase in aggregate demand (↑ AD). So whatever the level of prices, AQD will be greater than before.

After the increase in AD—the rightward shift of the curve—what are the alternatives?

a. if prices stay the same, real output must be greater;

b. if real output remains the same, prices must be higher; or

c. some combination of a and b must occur.

Now take a minute to study figure 32-2 where these possibilities are illustrated by points a, b, and c. Which result would actually occur? That depends on the shape of the aggregate supply (AS) curve, coming up later. But first what causes AD to shift in the Keynesian model?

In the monetarist model a shift of the AD curve is easy to explain: Money supply changes are directly and entirely responsible. In the Keynesian model it is more complex.

The Keynesian Model Emphasizes Changes in Expectations

Keynesian theory agrees that money supply changes can shift the AD curve. But in the Keynesian model it doesn't happen directly, or automatically—not just by "increased M" as in the monetarist model. In the Keynesian model,

Figure 32-2.   Aggregate Demand Increases

The AD Curve Shifts to the Right to Show That Total Spending for Output Is Greater at Each Price Level

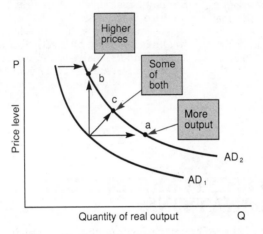

After the AD curve shifts from AD1 to AD2, either output increases to point a, or the price level increases to point b, or some of both, to a point between a and b—e.g., point c. The actual result will depend on the slope of the aggregate supply (AS) curve.

Soon you'll find out that the slope of the AS curve depends greatly on your chosen model of the macroeconomy—monetarist, Keynesian, or other—and that it makes a world of difference whether you're thinking of the short run or the long run.

money supply changes influence AD *by influencing financial markets and interest rates*—by shifting the LM curve, upsetting the equilibrium between Mqd and M, thus causing r to change, then I to change. And ΔI causes ΔAD.

But Keynesian theory does not focus on the money supply as the only (or even the most important) factor in shifting the AD curve. In Keynesian theory, money supply changes often are seen as *more responsive and permissive* than *causal*—i.e., *money supply changes let things happen*—but *do not necessarily cause them to happen.* For example, a change in the expected profitability of investments (ΔMEI) may *cause* AD to shift and M may change as a response—to *permit* the AD shift to occur.

Keynesian theory emphasizes the importance of *changing expectations* in influencing aggregate demand—especially demand for capital goods (investment spending). Also, the role of *government spending* in increasing AD (and of *taxes* in decreasing it) is emphasized.

Consumer spending in the Keynesian model is seen as responsive to changes in the level of income (ΔY). Suppose an increase in investment spending ($\uparrow$I) brings an initial increase (shift to the right) of the AD curve ($\uparrow$AD), and increased national income ($\uparrow$Y). The $\uparrow$Y, via the multiplier effect, will generate more **consumer spending**, which means more $\uparrow$AD—more rightward shifting of the AD curve.

Aggregate Demand: A Summary Statement

Both the monetarist and Keynesian models agree on *the negative slope* of the AD curve. In both theories the purchasing power effect of price level changes forms the basic shape and slope of the curve. But Keynesian theory depicts the curve as somewhat more elastic (less steep) because of the inclusion of interest rate, wealth, and foreign-good-substitution effects. In recent years these additional effects are also being included in some of the modern monetarist models.

In the traditional monetarist model, shifts of the AD curve result almost entirely from changes in the size of the **money supply**. With V assumed fixed, ΔM translates into ΔE which means ΔAD—and for any given level of P, it translates into ΔAQD.

In the Keynesian model the major cause of AD shifts is changes in **expectations** which brings changes in **spending decisions**—i.e., shifts of the IS curve. Money supply changes are seen as "causal" only to the extent that ΔM brings a shift of the LM curve which causes *interest rates* to change and thereby causes the rate of *investment spending* to change.

RELATIONSHIPS BETWEEN THE IS-LM DIAGRAM AND THE AD CURVE

You will better understand the AD curve when you know the precise relationship between AD and the IS-LM diagram. In the IS-LM diagram, national income is also national output and national spending. All of these are represented by Y, measured on the horizontal axis. So at any point, Y shows both aggregate demand and aggregate supply—total spending, real output, and real income.

In the IS-LM diagram, neither aggregate demand nor aggregate supply is related to *price changes*. For any given pair of IS-LM curves, prices are fixed, remember? And so is the money supply. So in terms of the equation of exchange, any given pair of IS-LM curves assumes:

$$\overline{M}V = \overline{P}Q.$$

which says that, given these curves, both M and P are fixed. The only variables are V and Q.

The Variability of V. The LM curve shows that V varies in response to changes in r; as indicated by the slope of the curve. The variability of V could range from infinite if the LM curve was horizontal (the liquidity trap), to zero if the curve was vertical (the classical fixed-velocity case).

The Variability of Q. Since prices are fixed, all changes in national income (Y) are *real* changes—changes in real output. So Y = Q, and ΔY = ΔQ. The slope of the IS curve indicates how Y (=Q) changes in response to changes in r: Δr $\rightarrow$ ΔI $\rightarrow$ ΔY = ΔQ.

In IS-LM analysis, the "givens" (fixed parameters), in addition to both M and P, include all of the other relationships reflected in the locations and slopes of any specific pair of IS-LM curves. The following section explains this more specifically.

The Fixed Parameters in IS-LM Analysis

For any pair of IS-LM curves, all of the following are assumed to be constant and given (fixed parameters):

1. the size of the money supply (M).
2. the price level (P).
3. the "MEI" investment function which determines the responsiveness of I to Δr.
4. the consumption function, which determines the responsiveness of C and S to ΔY.
   (Items 3 and 4 determine the location and slope of the specific IS curve.)
5. the demand function for money with respect to interest rates—the responsiveness of Mqd (=L) to Δr.
6. the demand function for money with respect to national income—the responsiveness of Mqd (=L) to ΔY.
   (Items 5 and 6 determine the location and slope of the specific LM curve.)

As you look through the above list of fixed parameters, you can see that once a specific pair of IS-LM curves has been chosen, most of the variables which exist in the real world macroeconomy have become "givens" within the diagram. The only remaining variables are, r, I, and Y (=Q).

Now you can understand why IS-LM analysis is most valuable in analyzing the effects of **shifting parameters** which would shift the curves and cause the economy to move to a new equilibrium. In the case coming up we'll introduce an exogenous shock—a change in the nominal money supply—and see how the economy moves to a new equilibrium.

When Nominal M Changes, LM Shifts

An increase in the money supply will shift the LM curve to the right. Why? Because at each level of r, there's more liquidity—more nominal money in existence (and being held by the public) than before. Only at a lower level of r (less opportunity cost for holding money balances), or at a higher level of Y (more transactions, creating a higher transactions demand for money balances) would people be willing to hold the additional money. So what happens?

In the classical model, since V is constant, all of the M will be spent. Since output cannot increase, prices will rise. The new nominal money will "self-destruct." You read all about how this happens back in Chapter 27. But in the Keynesian model it's a little more complicated.

In the Keynesian model, people who were holding exactly their desired money balances before the increase, begin buying OFAs to reduce their excessively large money balances. OFA prices rise. Interest rates fall. As r falls, I will increase, causing Y to increase. The macroeconomy speeds up.

Now we have lower r, and greater Y, both of which cause Mqd to increase: lower r means less **opportunity cost** for holding money balances; higher Y means greater **transactions demand** for money balances. The adjustment process will continue until the lower r increases desired L2 (speculative) balances and the larger Y increases desired L1 (transactions plus precautionary) balances to the point where L1 + L2 = L = Mqd increases enough to be exactly equal to the (now larger) nominal money supply.

When Prices Change, Real M Changes, So LM Shifts

What about the effect of a change in the price level? *A change in the price level amounts to a change (in the opposite direction) in the real money supply.*

Suppose prices decrease by 10%. If there's no change in nominal M, then real M increases by 10%. So in the IS-LM diagram (with nominal M fixed) decreasing prices means increasing real M. The LM curve is shifting rightward just as in the above example where nominal M increased. And the effects on r, I, and Y are exactly the same as in the above example.

As the Price Level Changes, AQD Changes: Presto! The AD Curve!

In the IS-LM diagram any change in the fixed-price-level parameter brings a change in real M. So it shifts the LM curve and brings a new equilibrium level of Y—and therefore of total spending (AQD), and of total real output (Q). So each shift in the price level brings a new level of Y, of AQD, and of Q.

Idea: In the IS-LM diagram we could shift the price level parameter (P) a few times and find out what AQD is associated with each price level. This would give us a series of "P and AQD" relationships. Then we could graph these relationships and would have the aggregate demand curve! Specifically, to derive the AD curve from the IS-LM diagram, here are the steps:

1. In the IS-LM diagram, draw a series of LM curves, each representing a different price level.

2. Identify the equilibrium level of Y (AQD) at each price level.

These relationships between P and AQD give us the points on the AD curve. Figure 32-3 illustrates all this.

In figure 32-3, the IS-LM diagram in Panel A shows the price level falling from P_0 to P_3, causing the LM curve to shift rightward from LM_0 to LM_3. Why? Because lower prices mean greater purchasing power (more real M) for any given size of the nominal money supply.

As M/P (real M) increases, this increased liquidity gives people larger money balances than they wish to hold (M > Mqd). The demand for OFAs increases, their prices rise, and interest rates fall. That's what you see in Panel A of figure 32-3.

Also in Panel A you see real output and real income increasing from Y_0 to Y_3. This *real increase* in output and income results from the *real increase* in the size of the money supply. This conclusion assumes that the economy has sufficient unemployment so that an increase in real M can result in this increase in employment, real output, and real income.

Figure 32-3.   Deriving the AD Curve from IS-LM

Panel A: Detailed Explanation: As prices fall, real M increases. So
            LM shifts, r decreases, I increases. So Y increases–
            meaning that total spending (=AQD) increases.

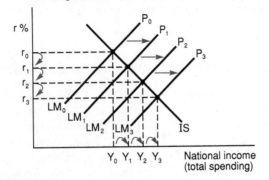

Panel B: Shortcut: As prices fall the purchasing power of money
            increases, so AQD increases.

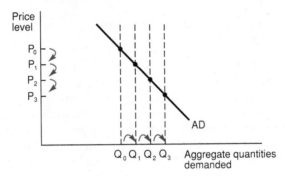

In Panel A, as prices fall from P_0 to P_3, real M increases. The
LM curve shifts to the right and Y increases from Y_0 to Y_3.

Panel B shows the Panel A results in the form of an AD
curve: the lower P, the greater AQD. As P moves down from
P_0 to P_3, AQD increases from Q_0 to Q_3.

Constructing the AD Curve

Panel B in figure 32-3 translates the information from Panel A into the aggregate
demand framework. The AD curve in Panel B shows exactly the same situation as
is shown by the IS and LM curves in Panel A. In both Panels the actual number of
dollars in the money supply is assumed fixed. But as P falls from P_0 to P_3, real
purchasing power increases and therefore AQD increases from Y_0 to Y_3.

Figure 32-3 illustrates the fact that *all points on the AD curve indicate P, Q*
combinations

a.   where *the spending flows and product markets are in equilibrium (I = S)*,
     and

b.   where *M = Mqd and therefore the financial markets are also in equilib-*
     rium (L = M).

RELATIONSHIPS BETWEEN THE IS CURVE AND THE AD CURVE

Here the IS Curve Is Assumed to Be Unaffected by ΔP

In figure 32-3 you saw the price level move down from P_0 to P_3 and equilibrium Y increased from Y_0 to Y_3. This increase in Y is caused by a drop in the interest rate from r_0 to r_3 and the resulting increase in I, and C. But note that as the price level falls the IS curve remains in the same position. This stable position of IS illustrates the fact that here we are assuming that a falling price level amounts to an increase in the size of the real money supply, and *that's all*.[2]

Spending, Output, and Income All Equal AQD (=Y)

The IS curve indicates levels of spending for real units of input and output. As explained previously, Y measures the flows of (1) real spending for output, (2) real units of output, and (3) real income earned by those who produced the real output. Since all three flows are equal (Y refers to all three), the income earned (purchasing power received by producer-sellers) is always exactly large enough to buy all of the output produced. And what difference does the price level make? No difference.

If prices of the output units are doubled, then what happens to the income received by the owners of the input factors—the ones who produced those doubled-price units? Their incomes are also doubled. The doubled nominal factor incomes produce exactly enough purchasing power to buy all of the doubled-price outputs. Right back to square one? Exactly.

In real terms, all is the same as before. The only difference is that the value of the monetary unit—the "money-unit measuring stick"—is only one-half as large as before. All *nominal values* are doubled but *real values* are unchanged. So for any given level of Y, the real consumption and savings rates are the same as before.

Lower Prices ($\downarrow P$) Bring More Real $M(\uparrow M/P)$, $\downarrow r$, $\uparrow I$, $\uparrow Y$

The rate of *real investment spending at each interest rate* is not affected by price level changes. If the price level doubles, *nominal I* doubles so that *real I* remains the same. But note this important difference: At lower price levels, *r is lower*. So *I is greater*.

As the price level falls, I increases. But the increased I does not result from a shift of the IS curve. It results from a downward movement along the IS curve, caused by falling interest rates. The falling r results from the "easy money" conditions in the financial markets caused by the increase in real M.

How Stable Is the IS Curve?

How stable are the "givens"—the parameters and functional relationships—which determine the position and slope of the IS curve? Does the IS curve

---

[2] In this case we are ignoring all direct effects of price level changes on either consumer or investment spending. For example, as P changes, the "wealth effect" (explained previously) could influence either C or I or both and thereby shift the IS curve. But that effect is ignored here.

illustrate stable and dependable relationships, well insulated from exogenous (external) shocks? No. Quite the opposite. Keynes emphasized the importance of **exogenous influences**—especially the effects of **changing expectations**—on the rate of investment spending.

In the Keynesian model, investment spending reflects expected profitability—**marginal efficiency of investment** (MEI), remember? Profit expectations can be highly volatile—can change from minute to minute. Each change in expected MEI brings a shift of the IS curve. Greater expected MEI shifts the curve to the right. Smaller expected MEI shifts it to the left.

To Keynes, human emotions—Keynes used the term **animal spirits**—sometimes have more to do with expected profitability of investments than changes in fundamental market conditions. (Everyone remembers what happened to the stock market on October 19, 1987. Do you suppose that crash reflected a sudden change in fundamentals? Or perhaps a shift in some "animal spirits?")

What Might Cause the IS Curve to Shift?

In the Keynesian model, a wave a pessimism in the business community can bring a leftward shift in the IS curve. Aggregate demand will decrease. (In the AD-AS diagram the AD curve will shift leftward.) The economy will go into depression. If this happens, what can be done?

In the Keynesian model, all that is needed to speed up the economy is to get the IS curve (and AD curve) shifted back to the right. Keynes recommended an increase in government spending—a new injection (G) into the spending flow to compensate for the low rate of investment spending: ↑G to offset the ↓I. To Keynes, because of the depressed conditions and widespread pessimism, ↑G was the only feasible way to move the economy back to full employment.

In the modern Keynesian models, government spending is still seen as an effective means to stimulate a depressed economy. But most modern Keynesian economists agree that using fiscal policy to adjust the macroeconomy is not as easy as it appeared in the earlier Keynesian models.

A Rightward Shift of IS Means More Spending Coming from Somewhere

When the IS curve shifts to the right, that means more spending is flowing into the income stream. Perhaps a wave of optimism has captured the investment community and they're spending more (↑I). Or perhaps the government is spending more (↑G). Or perhaps we're selling more exports (↑Ex). And there'a a fourth possible explanation for a rightward shift in the IS curve.

What if the consumption function (C) has shifted so that consumers are spending more (saving less) at each income level? Increased consumer spending (reduced saving) could shift the IS curve to the right just as effectively as an increase in investment spending. But in Keynes' model, C was assumed to be a stable function of Y. That's why it's called "the consumption function." The level of consumer spending depends on (is a function of) the level of national income: $C = f(Y)$. So in Keynes' model, shifts of IS were attributed to changes in I or G, not C.

When IS Shifts, AD Shifts—But Not As Much

When IS shifts rightward, AD increases (shifts rightward) and that increases equilibrium Y. By how much? That depends on the slopes of the IS and LM curves. In figure 32-4, the total extent of the rightward shift in the IS curve (if that were the only influence) would increase national income from Y_0 to Y_2. But because of simultaneous effects in the financial markets, the actual increase is only from Y_0 to Y_1—not to Y_2. And the rightward shift of the AD curve is only from Q_0 to Q_1—not to Q_2. That's significantly less than the rightward shift of the IS curve. Why? Because of rising interest rates and the **crowding-out effect**.

Figure 32-4.   A Shift of the IS Curve Brings a Shift of the AD Curve

The Extent of the Rightward Shift of the AD Curve Is Limited by the "Crowding Out" Effect of Higher Interest Rates.

<u>Panel A</u>: The IS curve shifts to the right: more spending injections.

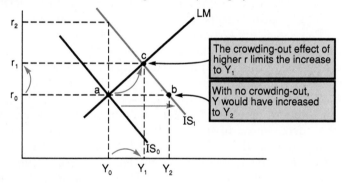

<u>Panel B</u>: The AD curve shifts to the right--but not as far.

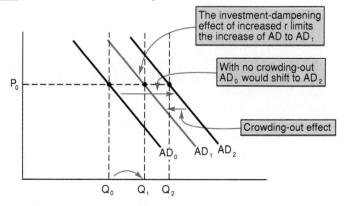

As Y increases, increasing demand for L1 balances pushes r up from r_0 to r_1 and discourages (crowds out) some of the planned I. So Y only increases to Y_1—not to Y_2. And also because of crowding out the AD curve shifts only from Ad_0 to AD_1—not to AD_2. So at P_0, AQD increases only from Q_0 to Q_1.

INCREASING Y BRINGS ↑ r WHICH LIMITS ↑ I: THE CROWDING-OUT EFFECT

When Y increases, that generates more demand for transactions (L_1) balances. So people sell OFAs to get more money. OFA prices fall, interest rates rise, and I is discouraged. In Panel A of figure 32-4, you might say that investment spending "backs up" from point b, along the IS curve to the point of intersection with LM at point c.

With any IS curve shift the extent of the shift of the AD curve depends on the slope of LM. Suppose the LM curve had been horizontal as in the hypothetical "liquidity trap" case. Then there would have been no crowding out. The interest rate would have remained at r_0 and Y would have increased all the way from Y_0 to Y_2. The AD curve would have shifted all the way from AD_0 to AD_2 and AQD would have shifted from Q_0 to Q_2. That's what Keynes said would happen when the economy was seriously depressed. But that didn't happen here because of the upward slope of the LM curve.

Suppose the LM curve had been completely vertical, as in the classical model. Then the AD curve would not have shifted at all! With a vertical LM curve, all of the effect of a shift of IS is on r, and Y doesn't change at all.

In Panel A if the LM curve had been vertical at Y_0, r would have increased from r_0 to r_2 and Y would have remained at Y_0. This would be an example of the "pure classical" case: *complete crowding out*. This example shows you the classical model's verdict on the effectiveness of Keynesian fiscal policy in trying to increase employment and output: *Zero effectiveness*. Only inflation would result.

The modern monetarist models no longer take such an extreme view regarding the effectiveness of fiscal policy—except in the long run. In the modern monetarist models the economy in the long run will operate at "the natural rate." Any attempt to stimulate the economy either by fiscal or monetary means will, in the long run, result only in inflation. That's "complete crowding out." But in the short run, crowding out is not complete. The extent of it depends on the slopes of the short run AD and AS (and IS and LM) curves.

THE EFFECTS OF A SHIFTING LM CURVE

Figure 32-5 shows a shift of the LM curve bringing a shift of the AD curve in the same direction. Assuming that the price level is fixed, a shift of LM from LM_0 to LM_1 means either (1) that the money supply (M) has increased, or (2) that money demand (Md) has decreased.

The rightward shift of the LM curve brings a rightward shift of the AD curve. But the shift of the AD curve is limited by the effect of falling interest rates. As r falls, people begin building up their L_2 balances. That absorbs some of the surplus liquidity. We might call this the **reverse crowding-out** effect.

As you can see from the graph, the extent of the AD shift depends on the slopes of the IS and LM curves. In the earlier "naive" classical and Keynesian models there were extreme differences regarding the slopes of these curves. But in the modern monetarist and modern Keynesian models no one assumes either vertical or horizontal IS or LM curves anymore. Still, modern monetarist models

Figure 32-5.   A Shift of the LM Curve Brings a Shift of the AD Curve

The Extent of the Shift of the AD Curve Is Limited by the Increase in Mqd (greater desired L_2 balances) Which Results from the Drop in Interest Rates.

Panel A. The LM curve shifts to the right

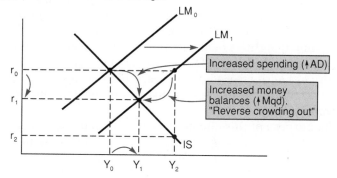

Panel B: The AD curve shifts to the right

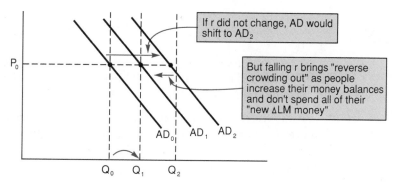

In Panel A, the LM curve shifts to the right either as a result of (a) an increase in the real money supply, or (b) a decrease in the public's demand for money balances. After the shift, people begin buying OFAs. OFA prices rise and r falls from r_0 to r_1, stimulating I and increasing Y from Y_0 to Y_1.

In Panel B, the extent of the shift of the AD curve depends on the slopes of the IS and LM curves. The flatter IS and the steeper LM, the smaller Δr and the greater the AD shift.

generally assume that IS is somewhat flatter and LM is somewhat steeper than is assumed in most modern Keynesian models. This is another case where empirical evidence (and common sense) have significantly modified the earlier, more extreme positions—but the differences still remain.

Why Does LM Shift? Lower Prices? Or Increased M (or decreased Md)?

What's the difference between the rightward-shifting LM curve in figure 32-5, and the rightward shifting LM curve you saw back in figure 32-3? Both are illustrating the same thing—a rightward shift of LM. But there's a very significant difference.

Look back at figure 32-3. There you see increased AQD resulting from **falling prices**. *That's a movement along the AD curve.*

Figure 32-5 shows a different picture. Now prices are fixed. With these fixed prices, the increase in LM results in an increase in total spending—an increase in AQD. But since the price level is fixed, this cannot be a movement along the AD curve. So this increase in spending *indicates a shift of the AD curve.*

In figure 32-3 we are dealing with the negative relationship between price changes and quantities demanded, which means *movements along the AD curve.* At any given price level, AQD doesn't change. In figure 32-5 we are dealing with fixed prices and increased quantities, which means *a shifting AD curve*—greater AQD at each price level. Be sure that you understand this very important distinction before you go on.

The purpose of this chapter has been to explain aggregate demand (AD). The next chapter explains aggregate supply (AS), and how to use the AD-AS framework to analyze the macroeconomy.

SUMMARY

- The aggregate demand (AD) curve illustrates the fact that when the price level (P) changes, real output (Q) changes in the opposite direction. Why? Four possible reasons:

  1. With a given amount of nominal money (M) lower prices ($\downarrow$ P) mean more real money ($\uparrow$ M/P), so as prices fall, people can—and do—buy more.

  2. More real M ($\uparrow$ M/P) tends to push down interest rates ($\downarrow$ r) and stimulate more investment spending ($\uparrow$ I).

  3. Holders of money and of all other dollar-denominated assets (OFAs) have more wealth when prices fall and less when prices rise. They may adjust their spending to offset these changes.

  4. When prices in this economy change (relative to world prices), AQD for domestic goods tends to change in the opposite direction as buyers (both domestic and foreign) substitute the lower priced for the higher priced goods.

- In the classical model, AD increases result from money supply increases. The Keynesian model adds three more factors: increased government spending ($\uparrow$ G), decreased taxes ($\downarrow$ T), and most important, more optimistic profit expectations ($\uparrow$ MEI).

- The AD curve can be derived by assuming different price levels (P) in the IS-LM diagram and then shifting the LM curve to reflect the changing "real M." Each specific P will be associated with a specific rate of Y (= Q = AQD), and that relationship, when graphed, is the AD curve.

- As prices fall, LM shifts rightward, increasing Y, Q, and AQD. The price elasticity of the AD curve is determined by the slope of the IS curve. The flatter the IS curve, the more price-level-elastic the AD curve.

- When IS shifts, AD also shifts in the same direction, but not as much because of the **crowding out effect** of changing interest rates. The extent of crowding out depends on the slopes of the IS and LM curves.

- When LM shifts, AD also shifts but not as much because of induced changes in r: the "reverse crowding out effect." Again the extent of the effect depends on the slopes of the curves.

- If LM shifts because of ΔP, that's an example of the $\Delta P \rightarrow \Delta Q$ relationship depicted by the AD curve. So it's a movement along the AD curve. But if LM shifts because of ΔM or ΔMd (with no ΔP), that's an example of a shift of the entire AD curve.

Important Principles, Issues, Concepts, Terms

Aggregate demand (AD)

Aggregate quantity demanded (AQD)

How the AD curve illustrates "PQ"

Purchasing power effect

Real money equals M/P

Interest rate effect of ΔP

Wealth effect of ΔP

Foreign trade effect of ΔP

Causes of a shift of AD

How price changes shift LM

How shifting LM can describe the AD curve

Causes and effects of IS curve shifts

The crowding out effect

Causes and effects of shifting LM

"Reverse crowding out effect"

Change in AD vs. change in AQD

Questions

1. Explain as much as you can about the aggregate demand curve: exactly what it means, what determines its location and its slope, what are some of the things that would cause it to be more (or less) price elastic, and what would cause it to shift.

2. Explain how to derive the AD curve by shifting the curves in the IS-LM diagram, and illustrate with a graph.

3. Explain what it means to say that: "Given MV (=E), the AD curve illustrates "PQ."

4. Explain the meaning of each of the following, and how each influences the AD curve:
   a. the purchasing power effect
   b. the wealth effect
   c. the money market (interest rate) effect
   d. the foreign goods substitution effect

5. Explain exactly why the expression "M/P" is referred to as the *real* money supply.

6. A shift in the AD curve is explained somewhat differently in the monetarist model than in the Keynesian model. Explain some of these differences.

7. In the IS-LM diagram, a shift of either IS or LM results in a shift of the AD curve in the same direction, but the AD shift is less than the shift of either IS or LM, because of the *offsetting effects* of changes in r. Explain what all this means, and illustrate with IS-LM and AD curves.

8. Explain what Keynes had to say about the question of the stability (or instability) of the IS curve.

9. Explain this statement: "As long as prices are fixed, changes in IS or LM which cause changes in AQD represent shifts in AD—in the aggregate demand curve. But

when prices are permitted to change, this causes shifts in the LM curve and changes in AQD, but these changes do not represent changes in AD—shifts in the AD curve. They represent only movements along the curve."

Suggested Readings

Barro, Robert J. *Macroeconomics*, 2nd ed. New York: John Wiley & Sons, 1987.

DeLorme, Charles D. Jr., and Robert B. Ekelund, Jr. *Macroeconomics*, 2nd ed. Plano, TX; Business Publications, Inc., 1987.

See also suggested readings at the end of the following chapter.

CHAPTER 33

Understanding Aggregate Supply, and Analyzing the Macroeconomy in the AD-AS Framework

Chapter Objectives

The previous chapter explained aggregate demand. This chapter explains aggregate supply, then puts the two together and uses this AD-AS framework to analyze the macroeconomy. When you complete your study of this chapter you will understand and be able to explain:

1. The distinction between **long run** and **short run assumptions** when analyzing **aggregate supply** (AS), and how to draw and explain the long-run and short-run aggregate supply (ASlr and ASsr) curves.

2. Why the ASsr curve slopes upward, and what determines the steepness of the slope.

3. What causes the ASsr curve to shift in the long run, and why it tends to shift so as to move the economy toward the ASlr curve.

4. The effect of the modern monetarist **natural rate hypothesis** on the shape and location of the ASlr curve.

5. Some causes and effects of unexpected AD and AS shifts, called **exogenous shocks.**

6. Why, according to the **modern monetarist model** and the **natural rate hypothesis**, a short-run supply shock (ASsr shift) has short-run effects on both P and Y, but no long-run effects on either P or Y.

7. How to use the AD-AS framework and the natural rate hypothesis to explain the **accelerationist hypothesis.**

UNDERSTANDING AGGREGATE SUPPLY

You previously saw that a shift of the AD curve will have its effect either (a) on aggregate output, or (b) on the price level—or (c) to some extent on both. What will actually happen? That depends on the slope of the aggregate supply (AS) curve.

The Extreme Classical and Extreme Keynesian AS Curves

In the circular flow diagram, aggregate supply is the flow of real outputs in the output loop of the circle. In the equation of exchange (MV = PQ), aggregate supply is represented by "Q."

In the classical model the aggregate output of the economy will be determined by the availability and productivity of the economy's inputs—the factors of production. This isn't something which can change quickly. So *in the classical model, aggregate supply is a fixed quantity of output.*

It's a **long-run equilibrium** concept. It is not responsive to changes in demand or prices—or to anything else except changes in the productive capacity of the economy. This means that in the classical model *the aggregate supply (AS) curve is vertical at the full-employment rate of output.*

In contrast, the Keynesian AS curve is a **short-run disequilibrium** concept. The model assumes an economy with *high unemployment.* With slack in the labor and other input markets, producers can hire more and increase output. And costs will not go up, so there's no reason for prices to rise. More output can be produced at the existing price level! *So the AS curve is horizontal: Aggregate quantity supplied (AQS) is completely responsive to AD changes.*

These two extreme positions are shown in figure 33-1. In Panel A (the extreme classical case) a change in aggregate demand has no influence on output. The entire effect is on the price level. In Panel B (the extreme Keynesian case) a change in AD has no effect on the price level. All of the effect is on the quantity of real output. Take a few minutes to study figure 33-1 and I think you will understand this extreme "classical-Keynesian distinction" very well.

The Less Extreme AS Curves of the More "Modern" Models

Few modern economists would agree with either of the two extreme views shown in figure 33-1—at least, not in the short run. In most modern models, the short run AS curve is upward sloping, showing that *a shift in AD brings a short-run change in the same direction in both output and prices.*

The short-run aggregate supply (ASsr) curve slopes upward indicating that as prices rise, more output will be supplied. But the closer the economy is to full employment, the smaller the output increase will be. That's why the ASsr curve gets steeper as output increases. Now look at figure 33-2 and that's what you'll see.

Why, as prices rise, does the aggregate quantity of output supplied (AQS) increase? One reason is because, when prices begin to rise, *output prices tend to go up faster than input costs.*

In the short run many production costs are fixed. Inputs—labor and others—frequently are bought under long-term contracts. And most of the "fixed costs" of a firm (rent, interest on indebtness, and others) are set for long periods—sometimes several years.

As prices rise, firms can increase their production and sell their outputs at the higher prices. And since input costs don't go up as fast as output prices, profits go up. So firms are induced to produce more. That's what the ASsr curve in figure 33-2 shows: that *in the short run, rising prices bring more real output* (↑ AQS).

Figure 33-1.   The AD-AS Diagram: An Illustration of the Extreme Classical vs. Extreme Keynesian Theories

Panels A and B both show an equal decrease in aggregate demand. The effect on the economy depends on the shape of the AS curve.

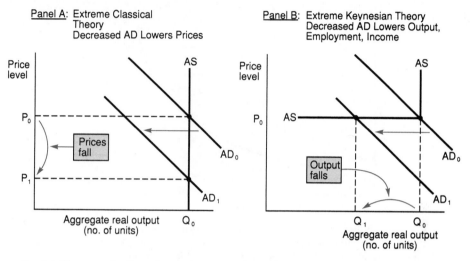

Panel A: Extreme Classical Theory
Decreased AD Lowers Prices

Panel B: Extreme Keynesian Theory
Decreased AD Lowers Output, Employment, Income

Panel A illustrates the "supply creates its own demand" result in classical theory: prices will fall, the real purchasing power of money will increase, and the quantity of output (as determined by the productive capacity of the economy) will (after an adjustment period) be exactly the same as before the AD decrease. This conclusion obviously rests on the assumption of downward flexibility of wages and prices.

Panel B illustrates the "demand creates its own supply" assumption of Keynesian theory. The reduction in aggregate demand from AD_0 to AD_1 results in a reduction in real output (and real income) from Q_0 to Q_1. Serious depression! But wages and prices do not fall to stimulate output and employment. *The initial thrust of Keynesian theory was on how to get AD_1 to move back to AD_0 and bring the economy back to full employment.*

Aggregate Supply is Different from the Supply for an Individual Product

Suppose the demand for and price of an individual product goes up. The suppliers of that product will enjoy increased profits, and the output of that product will be increased in the short run, largely by **substitution**. Resources will flow out of the production of other products and into the production of this product. But in the case of aggregate supply, that can't happen!

When the demand for and prices of *everything* go up at the same time, how can we employ more? And produce more? Unless there's some slack in the economic system, we can't. But here's the important point: *There's always some slack in the economic system.*

Suppose you are a producer and the price of your product just went up so high that it would be profitable for you to pay high overtime rates to produce more. Suppose you offer $50 an hour to get your workers to work overtime. Do you think you'll get any takers? I'd bet on it!

Figure 33-2.   The Short-Run Aggregate Supply (ASsr) Curve

An Increasing Price Level Brings More Real Output. But
How Much More Depends on the Present Condition of the
Economy: Unemployment? or Full Employment?

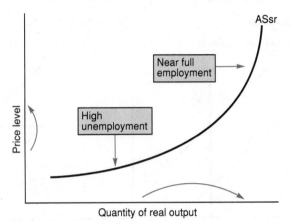

When output is low (the economy is depressed) the
ASsr curve is nearly horizontal indicating that large increases in output can occur with very little increase in
prices. So in a depressed economy, increased AD can bring
a lot more output (and employment and income), without
causing much inflation.

As the economy approaches full employment, ASsr
becomes very steep indicating that not much more output
can be produced. So when output is already high, any
increase in AD will have most of its effect on prices—not
on output.

I think you see the point. If output prices go up enough, producers will find
ways to expand their output to "over-full employment" levels. So when output
prices rise, output quantities also are likely to increase. But (don't forget) production costs are going up, too. And the longer this goes on, the more production
costs are likely to rise. And when production cost goes up, supply decreases. The
supply curve shifts upward and to the left.

You can see that (at least in the short run) higher prices bring more output. So
the short-run aggregate supply (ASsr) curve slopes upward. That's what you saw
in figure 33-2. Now you understand a little more about why.

As Input Prices Rise, ASsr Shifts Leftward

When output prices are going up and the economy is operating "too fast," there
will be shortages in some labor and other input markets. Input prices will begin
going up. It's just a matter of time before cost of production goes up and those big
profits begin to shrink.

When costs rise and profits shrink, producers begin cutting back their unsus-
tainably high rates of production. When that happens, quantities produced at the

existing (now higher) price level will begin to decrease. That means that the ASsr curve is shifting leftward. That's what you see in figure 33-3.

As costs continue to increase and profits fall and producers keep cutting back production, the ASsr curve continues to shift leftward (from ASsr1 to ASsr2). As ASsr shifts leftward, either output must decrease or prices must rise—or there must be some of both. What will actually happen in the short run will depend on *the slope of the AD curve.* So first, take a minute to study figure 33-3. Then go on into the next section and see how to put these two curves together.

Figure 33-3.   A Cost Increase Shifts ASsr Leftward

At Each Price Level the Quantity of Real Output is Smaller

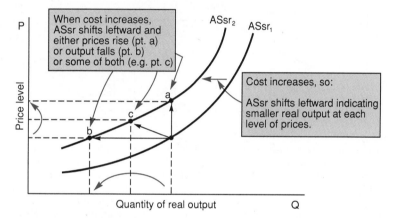

The ASsr curve reflects the cost of labor and other inputs. Any input cost increase will shift the curve upward and leftward. Any cost decrease will shift the ASsr curve downward and rightward.

THE AD-ASsr DIAGRAM AND SHORT-RUN MACROEQUILIBRIUM

Figure 33-4 combines the AD annd ASsr curves and shows the short-run equilibrium position of the macroeconomy. Take time now to study that figure—and the explanation with it—or else the next section won't make much sense.

How Much Change in Output? And How Much in Prices?

Suppose there's a shift in AD (a "demand shock"). As the economy adjusts to equilibrium (to point e in figure 33-4), how much of the adjustment will represent output changes? And how much price changes? That depends on the **responsiveness of supply** to price changes—i.e., on the steepness of the AS curve.

You can see from figure 33-4 that the steeper the ASsr curve (the less responsive to price changes), the more adjustment there will be in the price level and the

Figure 33-4.   Short-Run Macroequilibrium in the AD-ASsr Graph

The price level will move up or down to where AQD and AQS are equal.

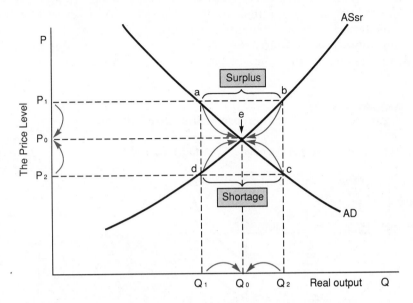

Only at point e could equilibrium exist. At any price level above P_0 the aggregate quantity supplied and flowing into the market (AQS) would exceed the aggregate quantity demanded (AQD). Surpluses would exist. Sellers would begin cutting prices to clear out their unsold products.

For example, suppose the price level was at P_1. Suppliers would be supplying Q_2 of real output, but demanders would only be buying quantity Q_1. A massive supply of unsold products! The price level would be forced down.

As the price level moves down from P_1 toward P_0, producer-sellers cut back production. They reduce overtime and lay off their least productive workers. Output moves down along the ASsr curve. Also, as the price level moves down, AQD increases—moves down along the AD curve. This decreasing AQS and increasing AQD ·continues until output moves down from Q_2 to Q_0 and AQD increases from Q_1 to Q_0 and the output markets are cleared.

At any price level below P_0 there would be shortages. For example, at P_2 buyers are trying to buy output Q_2. But output is only Q_1—a serious shortage—an inflationary situation. Dissatisfied buyers will be bidding against each other for the very scarce products. Prices will rise.

As prices go up (inflation), producers will increase output. So AQS increases, moving up along the ASsr curve. At the same time, AQD decreases, moving up along the AD curve. Inflation will continue until short-run macroequilibrium is attained at P_0, Q_0.

less in the output rate. The more nearly horizontal the ASsr curve (the more responsive supply is to price changes), the more adjustment there will be in real output and the less in prices.

And what determines if ASsr will be steep? Or flat? A lot depends on the condition of the economy at the moment. Suppose there's widespread unemployment. Then the ASsr curve is likely to be more horizontal. So the output change will be greater. Conversely, the less unemployment, the more nearly vertical the ASsr curve, the smaller the output change and the greater the price change.

In models of the economy which assume "full employment" (the classical, modern monetarist and other long-run full-employment equilibrium models) a change in AD has most of its effect on prices. In models which assume unemployment (Keynesian short-run models), most of the effect is on output.

WHAT HAPPENS TO ASsr IN THE LONG RUN DEPENDS ON THE ECONOMIC CONDITION IN THE SHORT RUN

In figure 33-3 you saw the ASsr curve shift leftward as a result of an increase in input costs. What might cause input costs to go up?

A Stable "Natural Rate" Economy

Suppose prices in this economy had been stable for the past several years. Then there would have been no reason for the economy to "overheat," cause tight input markets, and push input costs upward. So there would be no cause for costs to rise and shift the ASsr curve leftward.

Conclusion: If price level "P_0" in figure 33-4 is a stable price level—one which has existed for awhile—then there is reason to believe that (barring unforeseeable exogenous shocks!) point e (P_0, Q_0) in figure 33-4 shows an equilibrium which will endure in the long run. But what if not?

What If the Economy Is Booming?

Suppose we are in a booming economy and output prices have been creeping upward. Profit margins have expanded, so businesses have increased production. Real output is high. Labor and other input markets are tight.

In this case it's just a matter of time before shortages in the labor and other input markets will begin to push up wages and other input prices. So costs will begin to rise. As that happens, ASsr will begin shifting leftward as you saw in figure 33-3.

What If the Economy Is in a Recession?

Suppose, instead of a booming economy and excess demand, the opposite condition exists—a recession. Now there are surplus inputs. In this case input costs are likely to go down and cause the ASsr curve to shift rightward.

Conclusion: The short-run equilibrium shown at point e in figure 33-4 will continue to exist in the long run *only if at point e the economy is operating at a normal rate.* The economy must be operating at a rate at which there are no abnormal shortages or surpluses in the input or output markets—a rate at which there is no reason to expect a change in the cost of production, and therefore no reason to expect a shift of the ASsr curve. And what do we call this "normal rate of operation" for the macroeconomy? You could guess. Most economists now call it the "natural rate" of employment, output, and income. But, as explained elsewhere, there is considerable disagreement about exactly what it means.[1]

Long-Run Adjustments Reflect Cost Changes— Mostly the Cost of Labor

In the U.S. economy, labor cost amounts to about 70% of total production cost—by far the largest single component. So changes in total production costs mostly reflect changes in the cost of labor. And this interesting fact brings us back to a concept developed previously: *the natural rate of unemployment.*

Suppose unemployment is very low—lower than the natural rate. What that means is that the current rate of employment is too high to be sustained. Labor markets are tight. Employers are bidding against each other for workers. Soon wage costs will begin to rise. As that happens the ASsr curve will shift leftward.

Or suppose the current unemployment rate is high—higher than the natural rate. Then there will be surplus labor. Labor costs (and production costs) will tend to fall and shift the ASsr curve to the right.

The bottom line: Only when employment (and unemployment) is at the natural rate will the short-run equilibrium shown at point e in figure 33-4 continue to exist in the long run.

Natural Rates of Output, Employment, and Unemployment: The ASlr Curve

According to the "natural rate" theory, *in the long run, the aggregate quantity supplied is not a variable quantity* which responds to changes in either aggregate demand or the price level. Long run aggregate supply (ASlr) is a fixed quantity of output. It is determined by "the natural rate of flow of the economy"—by the economy's productive capacity.

The Vertical ASlr Curve Depends on a Shifting ASsr Curve. The natural rate theory says that in the short run, actual output (as indicated by the ASsr curve) can be either larger or smaller than ASlr. But whenever it is smaller, economic forces (mostly input price adjustments) will automatically cause output to increase—to move toward ASlr. Whenever it is larger, those same forces working in the opposite direction will cause output to decrease—again, to move toward ASlr.

The Shifting ASsr Curve Depends on Flexible Input Prices. How is the adjustment to the "long-run natural rate" supposed to happen? It all depends on *input cost adjustments.* So it assumes *flexible input prices.*

The theory says that whenever current output is *above the natural rate,* tightness in the input markets will *push up production costs.* As production costs increase, ASsr will decrease—*the curve will shift leftward* indicating that at each existing price level, employment and output are being cut back toward the natural rate.

---

[1] See for example, in the papers and proceedings of the American Economic Association, May 1988, the session: "The Natural Rate Theory Reconsidered," and also the article in that session by Richard S. Krashevski, "What Is So Natural about High Unemployment?"

Suppose the current level of output is *less than the natural rate.* Then slack in the labor and other input markets will *push down wages and other input prices.* Production costs will go down. Profit margins will increase so businesses will increase their outputs. *The ASsr curve will shift to the right* indicating greater output at each existing price level. This adjustment will continue until output increases to the natural rate. Now look at figure 33-5 and you'll see the "natural rate" ASlr curve, and the shifting ASsr curves which move the economy to this long-run equilibrium.

Figure 33-5. Cost Changes Cause the ASsr Curve to Shift and Move the Economy to Long-Run Equilibrium on the ASlr Curve

Panel A. Production Cost Increases and ASsr Shifts Leftward. When real output is above the natural rate, input costs rise. ASsr shifts leftward, bringing less output, higher prices.

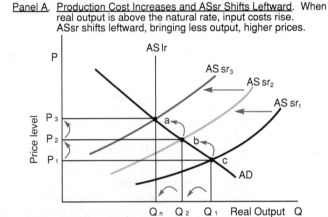

Panel B. Production Cost Decreases and ASsr Shifts Rightward. When real output is below the natural rate, input costs fall. ASsr shifts to the right, bringing more output, lower prices.

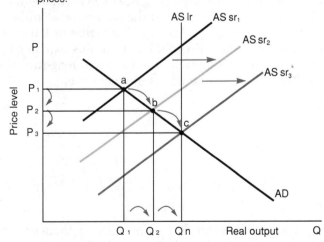

In Panel A the economy is at point c, with output Q_1, far above the natural rate. Tightness is the input markets will push up costs and ASsr will begin shifting leftward from $ASsr_1$ and $ASsr_2$. The economy will move to point d, and the quantity of output will decrease to Q_2.

The price level rises from P_1 to P_2, reducing aggregate quantity demanded so that it is equal to

(continued)

Figure 33-5. *Continued*

aggregate quantity supplied at point b. But the economy is still operating at a rate too high to be sustained. Production costs continue to rise and ASsr continues to shift leftward to $ASsr_3$, where the economy is at point a, prices are up to P_3, and the output has decreased to Q_n—the natural rate.

Panel B shows the opposite situation. The economy begins at point a with output quantity at Q_1—far below the natural rate. Slack in the input markets will push down the prices of inputs. Costs of production fall and ASsr will shift rightward from $ASsr_1$ to $ASsr_2$, carrying the economy to point b. Now output has increased from Q_1 to Q_2 and prices have fallen from P_1 to P_2.

The decrease in prices increases aggregate quantity demanded so that at point b AQS equals AQD. But at point b, the economy still is depressed. Input prices will continue to fall, costs of production will come down more, ASsr will shift to $ASsr_3$, and the economy will move to point c. Now prices are down to P_3, and the output quantity is up to Q_n—the natural rate.

EFFECTS OF CHANGES IN AGGREGATE DEMAND IN THE MONETARIST MODEL

The AD-AS diagram can be used to illustrate the effects of automatic forces which tend to move the economy to long-run equilibrium. But what about a shift in aggregate demand (AD)—called a **demand shock**?

In the monetarist model a demand shock would most likely result from a change in the growth rate of the money supply. But whatever the cause, a shift in AD will cause *in the short run, both the price level and the level of real output to change in the same direction.*

Then, according to the "natural rate" hypothesis, as time passes, the initial *output effect* will continually diminish. ASsr soon will begin to shift. As it does, output will begin to drift back toward the natural rate. *In the long run the only remaining effect of a change in AD will be a higher or lower level of prices.*

Now study figure 33-6 and you'll see all of this explained and illustrated in AD-AS diagrams. Panel A shows the short-run and long-run effects of an increase in AD. Then Panel B shows the effects of a decrease.

SHORT-RUN AND LONG-RUN EFFECTS OF A SHIFT IN AS (A "SUPPLY SHOCK")

You already know that when cost of production increases, supply decreases. When production cost increases, ASsr shifts leftward. Up goes the price level. Inflation.

Suppose the economy is operating at a high rate of output—above the "natural rate." Demand pressures and shortages in the labor and other input markets will force input prices (and production costs) to go up. So the ASsr curve will shift to the left. But "naturally tight input markets" aren't the only possible cause of such ASsr shifts.

Monopoly Power, Expected Inflation and Other Supply Shocks Can Shift ASsr (and also ASlr) Leftward

Expected inflation may cause labor and other input suppliers to push harder for higher prices. Also, increased monopoly power of labor or other input suppliers could result in higher input prices, increased production costs, and leftward shifting ASsr and ASlr curves.

In recent years ASsr and ASlr have been shifted by various kinds of **supply shocks**. The impact of the OPEC cartel on world energy costs during the 1970s and early '80s was a powerful example of a negative supply shock, shifting both ASsr and ASlr leftward.

Figure 33-6. Short-Run and Long-Run Effects of a Change in AD in the Modern Monetarist (Natural Rate) Model

---

The initial effect of a shift of the AD curve is to move both prices and output in the same direction. But in the long run, the rate of output moves back to the "natural rate." The only lasting effect of the AD shift is a higher or lower price level.

A reminder: This model assumes free competitive markets with flexible prices and mobile resources.

Panel A. A Demand Shock: AD Increases.

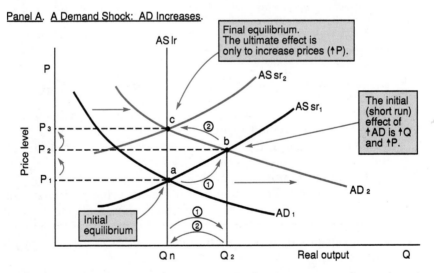

As aggregate demand increases from AD_1 to AD_2 the economy moves from point a to point b. Prices increase to P_2 and stimulate increased output (as shown by $ASsr_1$) to quantity Q_2. But as time passes, the cost of production begins to catch up with price level P_2. Rising costs cause ASsr to shift leftward from $ASsr_1$ to $ASsr_2$.

As ASsr shifts leftward, AQS decreases, pushing prices up. The higher prices cause AQD to decrease. This adjustment process continues until output is back at Q_n (where it was in the first place) and prices are up to P_3. The long-run effect of the demand shock (the AD increase)? Only higher prices.

continued

Figure 33-6. *Continued*

Panel B. The Opposite Demand Shock: AD Decreases.

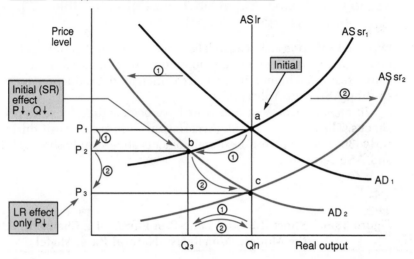

Aggregate demand decreases from AD1 to AD2. The economy moves from point a to point b. The price level decreases to P_2. That causes output to move downward along the ASsr curve to quantity Q_3. But with the slack employment and the lower price level, cost of production creeps downward. The decreasing cost increases ASsr —shifts the curve to the right. That means that output increases, pushing prices down.

This adjustment process continues until the economy moves to point c with price level P_3 and output back at the natural rate (Q_n). All of the effect of the demand shock (the decrease in AD) has been absorbed by the decrease in prices from P_1 to P_3.

Increasing Productivity Can Shift Both ASsr and ASlr Rightward

On the positive side, new and better technology, increasing worker productivity, a more favorable tax and regulatory climate for businesses, and in fact *anything which reduces per-unit production cost brings a rightward shift in the ASsr curve.* But what about the long-run (ASlr) curve?

Technology improvements bring greater productivity. That means lower cost per unit of output. Permanent improvements bring permanent rightward shifts in the long-run aggregate supply curve. Such shifts indicate *a higher natural rate of output for the economy.* In fact, as the economy grows from year to year and its output capacity increases, each year ASlr shifts to the right by the amount of the increase.

Graphic Illustrations of ASsr Shifts (Supply Shocks)

Figure 33-7 illustrates the effects of shifts in aggregate supply. Panel A illustrates both the short-run and long-run effects of an increase in production cost. In the short run the price level rises from P_1 to P_2 and output decreases from Q_n to Q_2. At this position there is unemployment and recession—much slack in the input markets—and at the same time, a higher price level.

Figure 33-7.   The Short-Run and Long-Run Effects of Aggregate Supply Shifts

Panel A.   Oil Price Increase Supply Shock

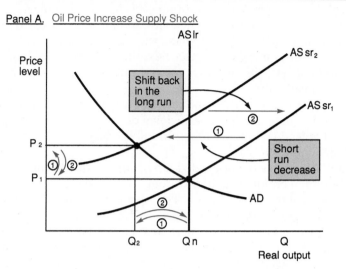

Increased input cost shifts the ASsr curve leftward. The economy slows and prices rise. In the long run, economic slack brings down input costs and the curve (and the economy) moves back to the original position.

Panel B.   A New Technological Breakthrough

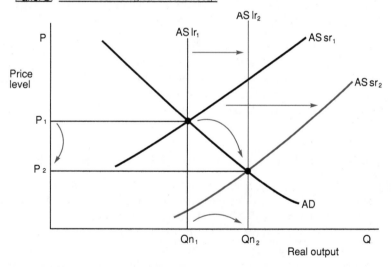

Decreased production cost shifts both the ASsr and ASlr curves to the right. More output and lower prices too!

This illustrates the "stagflation" condition which existed in the U.S. economy in the late 1970s—high unemployment and rising prices at the same time. Is this sort of condition self-correcting? The modern monetarist model says "yes." This conclusion results from the price-flexibility and resource-mobility assumptions of the monetarist "natural rate" model.

With flexible prices and mobile resources, the aggregate supply-aggregate demand theory tells us that widespread unemployment (surplus labor and other inputs) will force wages and other input costs to come down. As costs come down the ASsr curve will shift to the right. This adjustment process will continue until ASsr is back in its original position and the economy is back in macroequilibrium at Q_n and P_1. So assuming wage-price flexibility and resource mobility, in the long run the original level of employment and output (the natural rate) will be reattained—automatically.

And—assuming that the supply shock was not sufficiently strong to cause a leftward shift of the ASlr curve—the level of prices in the economy will return to the original level, leaving *zero long-run inflationary effect!* That's what you see in Panel A of figure 33-7.

Panel B illustrates the opposite kind of supply shock. Here you see the effects of an important technological breakthrough which significantly decreases production costs throughout the economy. The ASsr curve shifts far to the right, bringing a significant increase in output and decrease in prices.

In this case, since this is *a permanent increase in the productivity of the economy*, the ASlr curve also shifts to the right. Now the natural output rate of the economy is significantly larger than before. More output, at lower prices. Standards of living just took a great leap forward!

THE MONETARIST "ACCELERATIONIST HYPOTHESIS" IN THE AD-AS MODEL

Back in chapter 26 you read about the "accelerationist hypothesis," the natural rate of unemployment, and the long-run (vertical) Phillips Curve. That explanation showed that according to the "natural rate" hypothesis, repeated attempts to reduce unemployment below its natural rate would only result (in the long run) in continuing inflation. All of this can be analyzed more precisely in the AD-AS framework.

Greater AD Increases Output Only in the Short Run

Suppose the economy is operating at its natural rate but policymakers aren't satisfied with that. So they use stimulative policies to try to increase aggregate demand—to try to shift the AD curve to the right and increase employment, output, and income above its natural rate. In the modern monetarist model, this objective can be achieved for short periods of time. But in the long run the economy will return to its natural rate and the only lasting effect will be **increased prices**. This situation is depicted in figure 33-8.

The Long-Run Effect of Increased AD: Only Higher Prices

In figure 33-8 the economy is in long-run equilibrium at Point a, with price level P_1 and the natural rate of output, Q_n. But policymakers desire to increase output above Q_n. So they use monetary and/or fiscal stimulus to increase aggregate demand from AD_1 to AD_2. In the short run, both output and prices increase, indicated by Point b with output at Q_2 and prices at P_2. But in the long run the

**Figure 33-8.   The Accelerationist Hypothesis: Attempts to Continue
                 Stimulating Output above Its Natural Rate Only Cause Inflation**

Each time money growth is increased, causing the AD curve to shift to the
right, at first both output and prices increase. Then the inflationary pressures cause labor and other input costs to increase and the ASsr curve
shifts leftward. Output moves back to Q_n. Only the higher price level
remains.

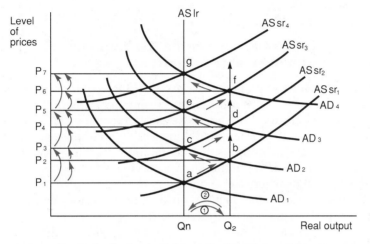

According to the "natural rate" hypothesis, policies which attempt to
stimulate the economy above its natural rate—e.g., from Q_n to Q_2—can
only result in inflation.

higher prices result in increased production costs. So the ASsr curve shifts
leftward from $ASsr_1$ to $ASsr_2$. The economy moves to Point c, where output is
back to Q_n. The only difference is that the price level is now up to P_3—much
higher than when the stimulative policies were initiated.

Continuing Stimulative Policies Bring Only Inflation

The misguided policymakers again decide that the economy is moving too slug-
gishly. So they again undertake policies to stimulate aggregate demand. The curve
shifts rightward from AD_2 to AD_3. The economy moves to point d, with output
again at Q_2 and prices up to P_4. So again, the initial effect is to increase both
output and prices. But again, as time passes, increasing costs shift ASsr to the left
from $ASsr_2$ to $ASsr_3$. The economy moves to Point e where output is back at the
natural rate, (Q_n) and the price level now is up to P_5.

The ultimate effect of all this (assuming that the "natural rate" hypothesis is
true) is obvious. Attempts to stimulate the economy by activist monetary and/or
fiscal policies can, in the short run, succeed in increasing output. But even in the
short run, prices will rise. Then in the long run the output rate will drift back to
the natural rate. The only remaining effect of the stimulative policies will be
higher prices. As long as the stimulative policies continue, the price level will
continue to rise. But there will be no sustained increase in the level of output.

The accelerationist hypothesis makes a powerful argument against the use of activist policies to try to stimulate the economy. According to the "natural rate" hypothesis, natural market forces will ensure that the economy is operating at or near its natural rate, even though government statistics may show unemployment at a fairly high rate. But, according to this hypothesis, policymakers should not be deceived into undertaking activist policies to try to stimulate the economy. Policymakers should follow a "hands off" policy, confident that *the natural market forces will result in more desirable conditions than discretionary policies could achieve.*

The Conclusions Depend on the Assumptions: Where Was the Economy Initially?

The accelerationist hypothesis assumes that the economy initially was operating at its natural rate. Prices are flexible, resources are mobile, and the "long-run equilibrium condition" is here. Keynesian economics doesn't accept these assumptions. The Keynesian model focuses on an underemployed economy, and on the price inflexibility and resource immobility which do exist in the short run. So a key difference between the Keynesian view and the accelerationist view is in the assumption of where the economy is in the first place.

Keynesian economics focuses on unemployment—why it exists, and what policies might be undertaken to reduce it.

To the accelerationists, the unemployment which exists is likely to be "the natural rate," and therefore impossible to reduce on a permanent basis. The Keynesian position is that there are times when unemployment rises significantly above any assumed "natural rate" and that at times when this occurs, activist policies can succeed in improving macroeconomic conditions.

You'll be reading more about similarities and differences between modern monetarist and modern Keynesian theories in the next chapter.

SUMMARY

- The **short-run aggregate supply (ASsr) curve** slopes upward to indicate that as prices rise, **more real output** is produced. But the **long run (ASlr) curve** is vertical, indicating the economy's **natural rate** of employment, output, and income.

- **Short-run equilibrium** in the AD-ASsr graph occurs where the curves cross. At any other combination of output and prices there would be either an **output surplus** to force prices down, or an **output shortage** to force prices up.

- **The long run result** depends partly on your **assumptions** about the macroeconomy. In the **modern monetarist model**, in the long run, output will move to the natural rate—to ASlr. In the **Keynesian models** there's less certainty about if, and how quickly the economy, left alone, will get there.

- In the **modern monetarist model**, in the short run an aggregate demand shift results in changes in the same direction **in both output and prices**. But according to the "natural rate" theory, in the long run the only effect is to change **the price level**. The output level will automatically readjust to the natural rate (Q_n = ASlr).

- ASsr reflects **input costs**. Input costs will rise and ASsr will shift leftward if (a) the economy is trying to operate **above its natural rate**, (b) **inflationary expectations** are strong, or (c) suppliers of labor or other inputs gain **monopoly power**.

- **Supply shocks** sometimes play an important role in pushing production costs upward—or, in the case of new technological breakthroughs, downward. A **negative supply shock** shifts ASsr to the left, reduces output, and raise prices: **stagflation**. A **positive supply shock** brings more real output and lower prices: more goods for less money!

- The AD-AS framework can be used to illustrate the modern monetarist **accelerationist hypothesis**, which concludes that activist policies which try to push employment and output above the natural rate can succeed (somewhat) in the short run, but in the long run the only result will be **inflation**.

- The **Keynesian disagreement** with the accelerationist hypothesis concerns the question of the initial condition of the economy. In modern Keynesian models, wage-price inflexibilities and resource immobility permit unemployment to persist, calling for **activist policies** to stimulate the economy. The next chapter goes more deeply into this question.

Important Principles, Issues, Concepts, Terms

Relationship between the AD-AS model and the circular flow

Definition of aggregate demand (AD)

Definition of aggregate supply short-run (ASsr)

Definition of aggregate supply long-run (ASlr)

AD-AS graph: short-run and long-run

Some relationships between Keynesian theory and monetarist theory

Why the AD curve slopes downward: Monetarist and Keynesian explanations

What causes the AD curve to shift: Monetarist and Keynesian explanations

The purchasing power effect

The money market (interest rate) effect

Why M/P is the definition of the "real" money supply

The wealth effect

The effect of substitution of foreign goods

The role of expectations

Why the ASsr curve is shaped as it is, and why it shifts

How the economy adjusts to short-run and long-run equilibrium in the AD-AS model

Natural rates of unemployment, employment, and output

Effects of shifting AD curve, long-run and short-run

Effects of shifting AS curve, long-run and short-run

The accelerationist hypothesis in the AD-AS model

How Keynesian theory draws different conclusions than monetarist theory in the AD-AS model

Questions

1. The aggregate supply curve in the extreme classical model is exactly opposite to that in the extreme Keynesian model. Explain why.

2. How is it possible that the long run aggregate supply curve could be vertical, when the short run curve slopes upward? Explain this as thoroughly as you can.

3. The short run aggregate supply curve indicates that as prices begin to rise, output increases. Since this is not possible through substitution of one product for another, how does it actually happen? Is it possible that the idea of the "natural rate" of the economy includes some slack?

4. Explain the difference between the short run supply for an individual product and the short run aggregate supply.

5. In the monetarist "natural rate" model, ASsr always tends to shift toward the ASlr curve whenever actual output is greater than the natural rate. Explain exactly what this means, why it is true, and illustrate with a graph.

6. Explain exactly what it is that causes the ASsr curve to shift (a) when the economy is operating at faster than the natural rate, and (b) when the economy is operating slower than the natural rate. Illustrate with graphs.

7. Explain as much as you can about supply shocks. What are they? What are some of the ways in which they might be caused? What are some of the different ways that a supply shock can affect the macroeconomy? Give some examples of supply shocks which have occurred in the real world. Can you illustrate any of these graphically? Try.

8. Explain exactly what is meant by the accelerationist hypothesis and how it is supposed to work. What conditions are necessary to make this hypothesis hold true? Explain why.

9. The accelerationist hypothesis doesn't fit very well within the Keynesian model. Yet it works very well in the monetarist model. Explain why this is true.

Suggested Readings

Feldstein, Martin S. "The Economics of the New Unemployment." *Public Interest.* (Fall 1973), 3–42.

Friedman, Milton. "Inflation: Causes and Consequences." *Dollars and Deficits.* Englewood Cliffs, N.J.: Prentice-Hall, 1968.

Gallaway, Lowell E., and Richard K. Vedder. *"The "Natural" Rate of Unemployment.* Staff Study for Subcommittee on Monetary and Fiscal Policy of the Joint Economic Committee, Congress of the United States, Washington, D.C.: U.S. Government Printing Office, 1982.

Modigliani, Franco. "The Monetarist Controversy, or Should We Forsake Stabilization Policies?" *American Economic Review* 67 (March 1977) 1–19.

Phelps, Edmund. *Microeconomic Foundations of Employment and Inflation Theory.* New York: W. W. Norton, 1970.

Stockton, David J. "Relative Price Dispersion, Aggregate Price Movement, and the Natural Rate of Unemployment." *Economic Inquiry* 26 (1). (January 1988), 1–22.

Tobin, James. "Inflation and Unemployment." *American Economic Review* 62. (March 1972), 1–18.

Weiner, Stuart. "The Natural Rate of Unemployment: Concepts and Issues." *Economic Review* 71 (4). Federal Reserve Bank of Kansas City, April 1986.

CHAPTER 34

Modern Monetarist and Modern Keynesian Theories Viewed in the AD-AS Framework

Chapter Objectives

Previous chapters have explained how the **modern monetarist** and **modern Keynesian** theories have departed from the extreme positions of the earlier models. This chapter focuses directly on these **modern models**.

From this chapter you will understand and be able to explain:

1. The importance of **real world evidence** in influencing the development of the modern monetarist and modern Keynesian theories.

2. The specific factors which influence the quantity of money demanded (Mqd) in **Milton Friedman's modern quantity theory**, and important differences between Friedman's theory and the **classical quantity theory**.

3. The meaning and importance of Friedman's **permanent income hypothesis (PIH)**.

4. How **Friedman's money demand model** is, on the surface, very similar to the Keynesian theory, but how, when interpreted, it turns out to be quite different.

5. Why **interest rate changes** (Δr) are much less important in the Friedman model than in the Keynesian model.

6. The important difference between the monetarist long-run **market-clearing models** and the Keynesian short-run **non-market-clearing models**, and how the "natural rate hypothesis" depends on the existence of **automatic market-clearing** as assumed in the monetarist models.

7. The **modern Keynesian models** which explain non-market-clearing on the basis of **fixed wages and prices** in the short run, but which (eventually) are **market clearing**—in the long run.

8. That the modern monetarist and Keynesian models are much more similar than the earlier models, but that the **policy conclusions** are about as far apart as ever.

THE GREAT DEPRESSION AND THE KEYNESIAN ATTACK

Following Keynes' attack on the classical model—and almost a decade of continuous depression from the end of 1929 until the beginning of World War II—what happened? By the end of World War II it was generally accepted by economists that the classical model did not accurately explain everything about—did not tell "the whole truth"—about the functioning of the macroeconomy. Keynes' outspoken comment in *The General Theory* was:

> "The extraordinary achievement of the classical theory was to overcome the beliefs of the 'natural man' and, at the same time, to be wrong."

Not all economists were ready to subscribe to such a brash statement. But everyone was aware that short-run conditions which deviate from the full employment assumptions of the classical model *do sometimes exist*, and (sometimes) persist.

Keynes Ignored the Long Run

The Keynesian explanation focused directly on the short run and completely ignored the long-run conclusions of the classical model. It denied even the tendency for the economy to adjust to full employment, except perhaps in some very long-run period—to Keynes, a period too long to be significant when trying to understand what's happening in the macroeconomy. So Keynes threw out the classical paradigm and built his theories based entirely on **short-run conditions**—on factors which cause the economy to speed up or slow down from month to month, quarter to quarter, year to year.

Classical Macrotheory Ignored the Short Run

By the end of the 1940s it was generally accepted among economists that most of the assumptions of the classical theory did not hold true in the short run. It was clear that the demand for money (and velocity) does not remain constant as the economy speeds up and slows down. During the 1930s everyone could see that the quantity of output (Q) did not automatically adjust and remain stable at the full employment level.

After the 1930s it was not easy for economists to accept the idea that a decrease in the money supply (and AD) would result in an immediate downward adjustment of prices—and with no decrease in employment or output. So it seemed to be time for classical economists to do some "model rebuilding." And so they did.

THE DEVELOPMENT OF THE MODERN MONETARIST MODEL

When the real-world facts of the 1930s were too obvious to be ignored, what were the classical quantity theorists to do? Desert all of their previous theories and join Keynes in focusing only on the short run? Or try to develop a model which still contains the classical assumptions of a "self regulating economy," but which also can explain short-run departures from the long-run full-employment condition?

If any parts of the classical macroeconomic model and the quantity theory were to survive, economists had to develop *a reconstructed theory in which the fixed long-run relationships were allowed to become variable in the short run*. And that's exactly what was done by the "modern monetarist" school.

The Counterattack, Spearheaded by Professor Milton Friedman

The modern monetarist school was centered for many years at the University of Chicago, and headed by Professor **Milton Friedman**. Friedman did not do it all by himself. But it's a safe bet that without his incisive intellect, diligent tenacity and powers of persuasion, the modern monetarist model would not have been as precisely developed or as widely accepted as it has been.

It was in 1956 that Milton Friedman launched his powerful and continuing counterattack on the Keynesian model. In his now-famous article. "The Quantity Theory of Money: A Restatement," Friedman set the stage and laid the groundwork for what was to develop into the **modern monetarist school of thought**.[1]

In the Short Run, Both Q and P Respond to Changes in MV (Aggregate Demand)

The modern monetarist model *in the short run* leads to conclusions which are surprisingly similar to those of the Keynesian model. For example, both models conclude that changes in aggregate demand will influence both real output and the price level in the short run. That's what you saw in the previous chapter in the upward-sloping short-run aggregate supply (ASsr) curve.

In terms of the equation of exchange the upward-sloping ASsr curve says that an increase in MV (in the short run) brings an increase in both P and Q—not just in P as in the classical model and not just in Q as in some early Keynesian models. Both modern monetarist and most modern Keynesian models now include the upward-sloping ASsr curve. Also, in both models, the more unemployment there is in the economy, the more an increase in aggregate demand will be reflected in increased output and the less in increased prices—i.e., the more the economy is depressed, the flatter (more nearly horizontal) the ASsr curve will be.

Velocity (V) Is Not Absolutely Fixed

In the modern quantity theory it is possible for a change in M to result in some change in V. So it isn't certain that a change in M will result in a proportionate change in aggregate quantity demanded (AQD = total spending = E). But in the modern monetarist models *most* of ∆M results in ∆E, with ∆V relatively minor.

The most significant distinction between modern monetarist models and modern Keynesian models is in the dependability of the relationship between ∆M and ∆E. Modern monetarist theory concludes that the **demand for money** (and

[1] Milton Friedman, "The Quantity Theory of Money: A Restatement," in Milton Friedman, Ed., *Studies in the Quantity Theory of Money*, (Chicago: University of Chicago Press, 1956).

therefore V) exhibits a strong tendency to *stability and predictability* and that *Mqd is largely independent of changes in the money supply.*

This position leads monetarists to conclude that changes in expenditures (ΔE) reflect prior changes in M. In general the monetarist models conclude that money supply changes (ΔM) are *the single cause* of changes in the level of spending (ΔE) and therefore (in the short run) in the condition of the macroeconomy—employment, output, and prices.

A key element in modern monetarist theory is *Friedman's theory of the demand for money* (explained in the next section). His theory explains that (and why) the demand for money tends to be quite stable and predictable. So that means that (the other side of the coin) *velocity* tends to be quite stable and predictable. Stable and predictable V means that changes in the money supply (ΔM) cause stable and predictable changes in total spending (ΔE = ΔAQD).

The conclusion of the modern monetarist model is: If the money supply is kept stable, total spending and the macroeconomy will be stable. If M is allowed to fluctuate, instability will result.

How do the modern monetarist models arrive at the conclusion that V,—and therefore the effect of ΔM on ΔE—is stable and predictable? When you learn the specifics of Friedman's "modern quantity theory," you'll see.

FRIEDMAN'S "MODERN QUANTITY THEORY"

Friedman's modern quantity theory focuses on the **demand for money**. The conclusions of all of the modern monetarist models depend on the **stability** of the demand for money. That's what Friedman's quantity theory explains.

Why do people want to hold some of their assets in the form of money balances? In the Keynesian model, remember, it's based on these motives: transactions, precaution, and speculation.

The Friedman model doesn't focus on "motives." It focuses on relationships between the size of desired money balances (Mqd) and (1) the size of income, (2) the opportunity costs of holding money balances, and (3) the utility (satisfaction) derived from holding money balances.

How much does the Friedman money demand function differ from that of the Keynesian model? Up to this point, not very much. In fact, it looks quite similar. But let's take a closer look.

Friedman's "Permanent Income Hypothesis" (PIH)

The first major break of the Friedman model from the Keynesian model is in the definition of "income." In the Keynesian model, it is the **current level of income** which influences the desire to hold transactions and precautionary (L1) balances. So the desired size of these balances increase or decrease as current income rises or falls. Not so in the Friedman model.

Friedman introduces much greater stability in his money demand function by defining income as *permanent income* (not current income). According to Friedman's **permanent income hypothesis** (PIH), spending is mostly influenced by permanent income and is not very responsive to changes in *current income*. Therefore as current income rises and falls, in the Friedman model desired money balances (Mqd) remain much more stable than in the Keynesian model.

The logic of Friedman's PIH is this: People tend to make their spending decisions mostly on the basis of their perceived permanent incomes. Their perceptions are based on their past incomes and their expected future incomes. People who expect rising incomes will spend more than the average of their past incomes, while those who expect falling incomes will spend less.

Permanent Income Is More Stable Than Current Income

Permanent income is *long-run income* instead of *short-run income*. Therefore, over the ups and downs of the business cycle it's much more stable than current income. And because of this, Friedman's PIH deals a devasting blow to the Keynesian model. Just think what the PIH does to the Keynesian consumption function!

In the Keynesian model, as national income (Y) increases, consumer spending (C) increases. That's the consumption function [C = f(Y)]. The consumption function is what causes the **income multiplier effect** which plays such an important role in moving the economy to macroequilibrium in the Keynesian model.

The slope of the IS curve is influenced by the size of the income multiplier. Suppose consumer spending does not increase in response to an increase in current income. That means that all of an increase in current income will flow immediately into savings. Following a given increase in Y, there would be no increase in C to bring further increases in Y. The income multiplier would be one—meaning: No "multiplying effect" at all!

In the Friedman model the multiplying effect of MPC isn't completely destroyed—just almost. The PIH doesn't say that the present level of spending and the present demand for money does not respond *at all* to current income. As current income changes, permanent income also tends to change in the same direction—but not nearly as much. So in the Friedman model, the Keynesian income multiplier effect, although not completely eliminated, is very weak.

The idea of the PIH is easy to understand, and it is conceptually attractive because it introduces greater stability into the macroeconomic picture. It seems reasonable to assume that—at least for many individuals—expenditures for goods and services—and therefore the quantity of money demanded for transactions balances—might be more responsive to "permanent income" than to the level of income which may exist this week or this month. So Friedman's PIH has been accepted—more or less, and in varying degrees—by many modern-day economists.

The Opportunity Cost of Holding Assets in the Form of Money

The Friedman money demand model recognizes the (now empirically established) idea that the size of money balances (Mqd) is negatively related to changing interest rates. In the Keynesian model this interest rate effect on Mqd plays a key role. In fact the LM curve *illustrates the negative relationship between r and Mqd*. But in the Friedman money demand model this interest rate effect is not very important. Here's why:

The Friedman model assumes that people can earn income on their money balances. So the opportunity cost of holding money is less than the amount of interest income forfeited by holding money—by not holding OFAs. In the Friedman model the opportunity cost of holding money balances is calculated as the returns available on OFAs, minus the returns available on money balances. For example, if OFAs are paying 8% and NOW account deposits are earning 5%, the opportunity cost of holding "NOW account money" is only 3%.

Many individuals now hold a good bit of their money in the form of interest-paying checkable deposits. But interest on deposits isn't the only return available from assets held in the form of money. Banks provide a great range of "free" services to their customers. Usually the larger the balances, the more services provided.

The Friedman model also recognizes that as market rates of interest rise (a) returns on interest-bearing checking accounts also rise, and (b) banks are willing to provide more "free" services in exchange for deposit balances.

In the Friedman Model the Opportunity Cost of Holding Money Is Not Very Significant

The conclusions in the Friedman model are that:

1. The opportunity costs of holding money are not very great because of the returns available on money balances, and

2. When market rates of interest change, returns on money balances also change. For example, when returns on OFAs go up, returns on NOW accounts and "free" banking services also go up. Therefore:

3. The size of desired money balances (Mqd) is not influenced very much by either the level of or changes in interest rates.

Here you see another important distinction between the Friedman model and the Keynesian model. In the Keynesian model, as market interest rates rise, people shift out of money balances and into OFAs to capture the higher returns. This shifting between money and OFAs occurs because of the Keynesian speculative demand for money. The slope of the Keynesian LM curve depends on this relationship. The Friedman model disagrees.

But even in the Friedman model the LM curve isn't completely vertical. As returns rise on OFAs, returns on checkable deposits also rise, but not as much. And some forms of money—e.g., currency and travelers checks—pay no returns at all. So even in the Friedman model, as interest rates rise the opportunity cost of holding money does increase to some extent. So some shifting out of money and into OFAs would be expected to occur. That's why the LM curve in the Friedman model is not vertical. But it's much steeper than in the Keynesian model.

The Effect of Expected Inflation

The inflation rate is the rate at which money balances are losing value. So expected inflation is a cost of holding money. If the annual inflation rate is 10%, money balances are losing value at the rate of 10% per year. So the **inflation cost** of holding money is 10%.

The inflation rate ($\Delta P/P$) can be viewed either as the rate of decrease in the value of money (relative to goods), or as the rate of increase in the value of goods, relative to money. So the expected inflation rate is really *the expected return from holding goods instead of money.*

As prices rise, goods-holders receive capital gains equal to the inflation rate. Money-holders forfeit these gains. At higher inflation rates the penalty for holding money is greater. So as the **expected inflation rate** $(\Delta P/P)e$ increases, asset managers will shift out of money and into goods. An increase in $(\Delta P/P)e$ causes shifting from money to goods in the same way than an increase in r causes shifting from money to OFAs.

Not all of the expected inflation rate $(\Delta P/P)e$ represents opportunity cost of holding money balances. The returns available on money balances must be subtracted from $(\Delta P/P)e$ to find the opportunity cost of holding money. So $(\Delta P/P)e$ minus the returns on money balances (rm) equals the opportunity cost.

Two Other Variables: h, and u

Friedman included in his demand for money equation the term "h" to represent the fraction of total wealth held in the form of *human capital*. Why? Because wealth held in the form of human capital is much less liquid than wealth held in the form of financial assets. Here's an example.

Suppose you are highly skilled professional receiving an income of $100,000 per year, while I happen to own stocks and bonds which bring me a return of $100,000 per year. Would I want to hold a large money balance? No. I can cash out financial assets whenever I wish. But you can't do that. So your desired money balance probably will be larger than mine.

Friedman also included a final term, u, as a catch-all, reflecting subjective tastes and preferences—all other reasons for wanting to hold money balances. For example, for some people it may be important to keep enough money in their checking accounts so that they never have to worry about carefully balancing their checkbooks. Some people may not want to be bothered having to decide which OFAs to buy, when to switch, or other worrisome investment decisions. And some people may sleep better when they know that their assets are in the form of immediately spendable money.

The Equation for Friedman's Money Demand Function

The equation for Friedman's general demand function for real money balances is as follows:

$$\frac{Md}{P} = f\left(\underset{+}{Yp}, \underset{-}{\underbrace{rb - rm}}, \underset{-}{\underbrace{re - rm}}, \underset{-}{\underbrace{\left(\frac{\Delta P}{P}\right)e - rm}}, \underset{-}{h}, \underset{\substack{+ \\ or \\ -}}{u}\right)$$

Note: The sign underneath each term indicates whether this term has a positive $(+)$ or negative $(-)$ effect on the size of desired money balances.

This equation illustrates what you have just been reading. It summarizes all of the factors which influence desired money balances in Friedman's "modern quantity theory."

The symbols in the equation mean:

Md/P =   The demand for real money balances. Md is the demand for nominal money. P is an index which reflects changes in the general price level.

Dividing by P eliminates the effect of inflation and converts nominal M into real M.

Yp =   Friedman's "permanent income"—average long-run (past, and expected future) income.

rm =   The expected return available on money balances.

rb =   The expected return on bonds—actually defined as all nonequity financial assets.

re =   The expected return on equity securities (common stocks), including both dividend payments and capital gains.

$(\Delta P/P)e$ =   The expected rate of inflation.

h =   The ratio of human capital to total wealth—i.e., the fraction of total wealth held in the form of "human income-earning abilities."

u =   All other factors which would influence people's desires to hold money balances—e.g., subjective tastes and preferences, risk aversion, convenience, whatever.

How Does Friedman's Quantity Theory Differ from Keynesian Theories?

Friedman's money demand equation doesn't appear to be greatly different from the Keynesian view. The replacement of current income (Y) with permanent income (Yp) is very significant. But aside from that, the theories appear to be quite compatible. Both recognize inflation, and returns on financial assets other than money (OFAs). The Friedman equation contains six variables covering everything that Keynesians would want to include. But that overview doesn't tell the true story.

The disagreement comes when Friedman in fact dismisses all but two of the variables: Permanent income (Yp) and inflationary expectations ($\Delta P/P)e$, and then goes on to dismiss ($\Delta P/P)e$ as well, leaving only Yp.

Friedman dismisses the significance of interest rate changes by postulating that as returns on OFAs increase, returns on money balances also increase. So the net effect is not very significant. In the Friedman model there is no speculative demand for money, and the interest rate sensitivity of Mqd is very low.

By replacing current income with permanent income and then washing out most of the effect of interest rate changes, the Friedman model strikes at the heart of Keynesian theory. Friedman goes on to assume that the inflation rate will be zero by assuming that the money supply will not be permitted to expand beyond the growth rate of the economy. So in the Friedman model the demand for money becomes a function of permanent income:

$$Md/P = f(Yp).$$

Since Yp is stable and predictable, the demand for money is stable and predictable. Therefore V is stable and predictable. So changes in the quantity of money will produce predictable changes in total spending: $\Delta M \rightarrow \Delta E$. Changes in the money supply bring proportional changes in total spending.

THE MODERN KEYNESIAN VIEW OF FRIEDMAN'S QUANTITY THEORY

If Friedman's modern quantity theory is an accurate representation of what happens in an economy, then much of Keynesian theory is erroneous and misleading. So how do modern Keynesians respond?

They say that the PIH does not hold true in a seriously unemployed economy. And they insist that as the economy goes through a business cycle Mqd is significantly responsive to interest rate changes.

When Does the PIH Hold True?

The Keynesian response to the PIH is that it depends on the condition in the economy at the moment. If we assume a prosperous full employment economy then the PIH makes sense. People whose basic wants are taken care of and who have achieved a satisfactory standard of living have no need to rush out and spend some "temporary increment" in their income flow. So with full employment, during any short period of time the marginal propensity to consume from a temporary addition to income might be low. But what about a depressed economy?

When there is widespread unemployment and millions of people are going hungry, is the PIH relevant? When unemployed and hungry people receive new income, do they save it? The Keynesians say: Not likely! In the Keynesian "unemployment" model, MPC is high, the PIH is irrelevant, the income multiplier works just fine, and the L1 money demand is responsive to changes in current income: $Mqd = f(Y)$.

What About the Responsiveness of Mqd to Changes in r?

Is there truly a "speculative demand for money" which causes people to hold larger money balances when interest rates are unusually low? And to hold smaller balances at higher rates? Keynesians have always said "Yes." But no one has been able to absolutely establish the existence of this speculative motive.

The **monetarist position** is that there are always some highly liquid and risk-free assets which could be held instead of money and which offer some return—short-term T-bills, for example. The **Keynesian response** is that when interest rates are very low, the transactions costs—brokerage, time and trouble involved in deciding which investments to hold, etc.—just aren't worth it. So people hold money waiting for OFA prices to fall and interest rates to rise.

What do the **empirical studies** show? Studies by Baumol and Tobin (cited previously) and others have established that there is a negative relationship between interest rate movements and Mqd. What that means is that as interest rates fall, people increase the size of their money balances. So velocity decreases. This breaks the proportional relationship between ΔM and ΔE.

The Existence of "The Speculative Motive" Cannot Be Empirically Established

Does the observed relationships between Δr and ΔMqd establish the existence of a **speculative motive** for wanting to hold money balances? No. The empirical studies can only show that a relationship exists—not *what motives* produce this result. But to the modern Keynesians, why argue about motives? So long as the negative relationship exists, the Keynesian model works.

Here's another problem with the early Keynesian models which Tobin and other modern Keynesians have dealt with. Keynes' speculative demand as initially explained would seem to require asset holders to make "all or none" decisions between holding money and OFAs. Obviously this would not make sense. Portfolio managers try to achieve diversity according to the principles of portfolio choice (the theory of asset demand) as explained previously.

Modern Keynesians recognize that it isn't a question of all money or all OFAs. It's a question of *the appropriate balance* between the two. And it isn't only *relative returns* which must be considered. *Relative riskiness* between money and various OFAs is also a factor. Modern Keynesian models have been designed to accommodate these considerations.

MORE DEVELOPMENTS IN MODERN KEYNESIAN THEORY

The continuing dialectic between economists on the issue of **Keynesianism versus monetarism** during the 1950s, '60s, and '70s produced significant new developments and refinements in both models. And this ongoing dialectic contributed to the development of new theories based on the classical heritage: rational expectations, "new classical" economics, and others. You'll be reading about some of these in the next chapter. The remainder of this chapter deals with the developments in the modern Keynesian and modern monetarist models.

Keynesian Models Are "Non-Market-Clearing"

All students of basic economics know that it is through *price adjustments* that markets are "cleared." Whenever the quantity demanded (QD) is not equal to the quantity supplied (QS), the market is uncleared—either a shortage or a surplus exists.

If there is a shortage, dissatisfied buyers will bid against each other and force the price up. As the price rises, QS will increase and QD will decrease. The price will continue to rise until QS = QD and the market is cleared.

In the case of a surplus, sellers will cut prices, QS will decrease and QD will increase until QS = QD and the market is cleared. Market clearing results from (and depends on) price adjustments. There is no argument about that.

Were the Labor Markets Cleared During the Depression?

During the 1930s there was widespread unemployment. It certainly appeared to most observers that surpluses existed in the labor markets and in the markets for many other goods—both inputs and outputs. It appeared that there were uncleared markets throughout the economy. But were there?

Nature Abhores Uncleared Markets. In classical theory, an uncleared market is a very temporary condition—one which will be automatically self-corrected very soon. Just as the early physicists discovered that "nature abhores a vacuum," classical economists discovered that "nature abhores uncleared markets."

The classical theory of the "automatically adjusting economy" depends entirely on the supposition that markets will clear through the automatic operation of the price mechanism. In classical economics and in modern monetarist economics as well, any economic theory which would permit uncleared markets to persist would challenge a basic law of economics: "Nature abhores uncleared markets."

But what about the easily observable unemployment which existed during the Depression? Wasn't that a surplus in the labor markets? The classical models said "no." The models go on to explain that markets which appear to be uncleared are actually cleared. The workers who are unemployed are actually *voluntarily unemployed* because they are unwilling to work for a market-clearing wage rate—a wage rate which would clear the labor markets. So all of those unemployed people are not a surplus in the labor market. The fact is that they have withdrawn from the market voluntarily, because they are unwilling to work for the (admittedly very low) market-clearing wage.

The Keynesian Model Permits and Tries to Explain Uncleared Markets. Keynes disagreed. Keynes saw the widespread unemployment as surplus labor, and he saw unsold products as surpluses in product markets. To Keynes there were clearly observable uncleared markets throughout the economy. One basic purpose of the Keynesian model was to explain the persistent existence of these uncleared markets.

The Keynesian model was focused on the special conditions which exist during depression—conditions which in the Keynesian model tend to perpetuate uncleared markets. In the early Keynesian models, the conclusion was that *these markets would not clear automatically*—at least, not until after "we are all dead." So in the Keynesian model, **activist government policy** was essential to bring economic recovery and clear these uncleared labor and product markets.

The Keynesian Non-Market-Clearing Model Depends on Inflexible Prices

Keynes had studied classical economics. He knew very well that "nature abhores uncleared markets." But Keynes was certain that markets were not clearing automatically during the Depression and he set out to build a theory to explain why.

The key to the "non-market-clearing" aspect of the Keynesian model is this: As aggregate demand falls and surpluses begin to appear in the labor, other input, and product markets, prices do not fall to eliminate those surpluses. Producers cut back production, while holding the line on prices. This brings increasing unemployment of labor and other inputs. But the prices of labor and other inputs do not fall to eliminate the surpluses. So the surpluses persist.

To Keynes, markets throughout the economy remained uncleared because wage rates and product prices did not move down easily. He saw **wage-price inflexibility** as an observable fact and he did not try to explain why. But new Keynesian models go more deeply into this question. They ask: Why are wages and prices inflexible in the short run?

The Modern Keynesian Explanation for Non-Market-Clearing

New Keynesian models go to some length to establish the existence of and the reasons for the inflexibility of wages and prices.

Long-Term Contracts. One focus is on the fact that businesses enter into long-term contracts (1) in the employment of labor, (2) for the purchase of material inputs, and (3) for the sale of future outputs. Recent Keynesian analyses conclude that the prevalence of such contracts—some of which extend for periods of three years and longer—plays a significant role in fixing wages and prices. This price-fixing affects the contracted markets and, via inter-market competition, the non-contracted markets as well.

Markup Pricing. Another thrust of the investigation focuses on the fairly widespread practice of "markup pricing." Many business set the prices they charge to their buyers on the basis of "cost plus markup." The investigations conclude that in the short run, businesses which follow such practices will not quickly depart from their established markups. So prices during any short-run period can be taken as fixed and unresponsive to short-run changes in supply and demand conditions.

In the New Keynesian Models, Wage-Price Flexibility Exists in the Long Run

Just as the modern monetarist models depart from classical theory and include a short-run focus, modern Keynesian models depart from the early Keynesian theory and recognize the significance of "the long run." In modern Keynesian models, long-term wage and price contracts do not last forever. And markup pricing is not impervious to market conditions in the long run.

A Graphic Illustration of a Modern Keynesian Model in the AD-AS Framework

A modern Keynesian fixed-price model is illustrated in figure 34-1. In that figure you can see the effects of fixed wage and price contracts and fixed markups. Here it is assumed that all prices and wages are fixed over some very short period of time, and that only with the passage of time will those prices and wages adjust downward.

Based on the assumption of temporarily fixed prices, the very-short-run aggregate supply (ASvsr) curve can be viewed as horizontal. What that means is that quantities of inputs and outputs can adjust, with no change in the price level. The key point is that if AD decreases (shifts leftward), in the very short run, employment and output will decrease but prices will not change.

Note this interesting fact: What you see in figure 34-1 is an example of the fixed-prices assumption which underlies each pair of IS-LM curves, only now expressed in the analytical framework of the AD-AS diagram.

Panel A in figure 34-1 shows equilibrium at full employment. Panel B shows a significant decrease in aggregate demand. The immediate effect is to reduce real output and income. There is no immediate effect on prices.

Figure 34-1.   A Modern Keynesian Model in the AD-AS Framework

Panel A. Equilibrium at Full Employment

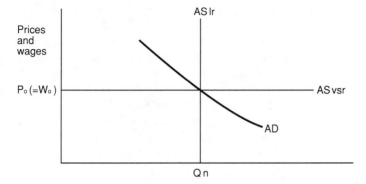

Panel B. Aggregate Demand Decreases. Employment, Output, and Income
Decrease. Prices do not decrease.

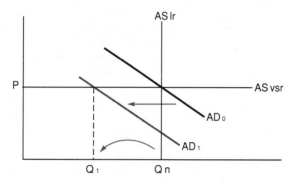

Panel C. As Time Passes, Wages and Prices Fall. ASvsr Shifts
Downward. Employment, Output, and Income increase.

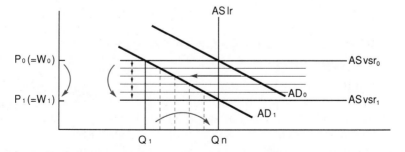

Eventually, wages and other input prices begin to fall and ASvsr shifts
downward. (This shifting was explained in terms of the ASsr curve in the
previous chapter.) The downward movement of wages and prices continues
until all labor and product markets are cleared. That occurs when the economy is back at full employment at Q_n.

In panel B, for some reason there is a sharp decrease in aggregate demand from AD_0 to AD_1. When AD decreases, there is unplanned investment. Firms cut back employment and production because they can't sell their full employment output. The laid-off workers can't find jobs. Involuntary unemployment exists because wages and prices don't move down quickly. National output (and income) falls from Q_n to Q_1. The price level does not change. (Not yet.)

Panel C shows what happens as time passes and wages and prices adjust downward. As production costs decrease, the ASvsr curve shifts downward. As that begins to occur, Q begins to increase. Ultimately $ASvsr_0$ will shift downward to $ASvsr_1$ and the economy will again be in full employment equilibrium at Q_n.

This adjustment process can also be explained in terms of the IS-LM diagram. As prices fall, lower prices mean more real M ($\uparrow M/P$). So LM shifts rightward. Also lower costs tend to increase MEI, increase I, and shift IS rightward. As both curves shift rightward, Y ($= Q = AQD$) increases.

The Modern Keynesian and Modern Monetarist Models Are Quite Similar

In reviewing what happens in Figure 34-1 you may see that this doesn't look significantly different from what the modern monetarist model shows in the AD-AS diagram. The only difference is that here the ASvsr curve is horizontal. If we had chosen to let it slope upward somewhat, that would not have materially affected the results.

Do the modern monetarist and modern Keynesian models come to the same conclusions? Ultimately (in the long run), yes. But in the short run, no. The difference is in how long it takes for the wage and price adjustments to occur and for the full-employment to be reattained.

In the modern monetarist model the adjustment process is fairly smooth and quick and relatively painless. In the modern Keynesian model the process may take a year or two or longer. What Panel C illustrates is a prolonged recession—serious unemployment—a long, deep trough in the business cycle.

Opposite Conclusions Regarding Activist Macroeconomic Policy

According to the modern monetarist model there is no need for activist government policies to return the economy to full employment. But in the modern Keynesian model, activist policies are called for.

To modern Keynesians, a period of prolonged recession and unemployment represents unnecessary waste of resources and human suffering. Keynesians recommend activist policies to increase AD and move the economy back to its natural rate and prevent the painful process illustrated in Panel C of figure 34-1.

Figure 34-2 shows the modern Keynesian recommendation. Suppose some shock occurs and causes AD to shift to the left from AD_0 to AD_1. Then monetary and fiscal actions should be taken to stimulate AD and shift it back from AD_1 to

Figure 34-2. The Keynesian (Activist) Conclusion: Following a Negative AD Shock (Movement Leftward from AD_0 to AD_1) Initiate Policy Actions to Shift AD Rightward from AD_1 to AD_0.

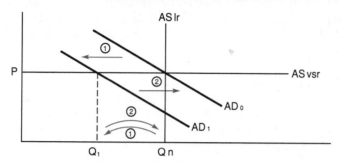

Because of the painfully slow adjustment process shown in Panel C, modern Keynesians conclude that it would be socially desirable for the government to take action to shift AD back from AD_1 to AD_0 and bypass a long, painful depression.

AD_0. That will move the economy back to full employment (Q_n) and avoid the pain and waste of a long deep trough in the business cycle.

Modern Keynesian models recognize the classical tendency of the economy to move toward a full-employment equilibrium. But because of wage-price-inflexibility, the movement is considered to be too slow. So the policy recommendations which emerge from these modern models are the same as in the earlier Keynesian models: Activist policies are called for to prevent or overcome prolonged recession—to "fill up the troughs in the business cycle."

Since full-employment eventually would come back by itself, in these modern Keynesian models, in the long run we aren't "all dead." But we have passed up the opportunity for more economic growth and for higher levels of economic welfare—and many unemployed people have suffered unnecessarily.

THE SIGNIFICANCE OF THE MODERN MONETARIST AND MODERN KEYNESIAN MODELS

The early classical and early Keynesian models were much farther apart than are the modern models. In the early classical model there was no short-run focus. In the early Keynesian model there was no long-run focus. In the modern monetarist model there is a short-run focus which, at first glance, appears very "Keynesian." And some modern Keynesian models accept the long-run equilibrium conditions defined in the modern monetarist model.

The Modern Models Arrive at the Same Conclusions as the Earlier Models

The modern developments in both monetarist and Keynesian theory have eliminated most of the distance that existed between the early models. *But the remaining distance is very significant.* Why? Because that difference is sufficient to permit each modern model to support the same ultimate conclusions as the earlier models.

Modern Monetarist Models. The modern monetarist models (just as the classical models) conclude that there are direct links between ΔM and total spending (ΔAD), and between ΔAD and the price level. In the modern monetarist model the economy has powerful self-adjusting mechanisms. So a **nonactivist policy** is called for. *Maintaining the stability of money growth is all that is necessary as an economic policy.* To do otherwise would not bring stability, but instability. So Hands Off! The economy will take care of itself.

Modern Keynesian Models. Modern Keynesian models, while accepting the long-run full-employment tendencies, conclude that the automatic adjustments are very slow. So they call for **activist policies** to improve economic conditions. But in the modern Keynesian models the earlier emphasis on **fiscal policy** has been greatly reduced, and activist **monetary policies** now are emphasized. So modern Keynesian theory arrives at the same ultimate conclusion as earlier Keynesian theory: *Discretionary stabilization policies can be and should be used as needed to improve conditions in the macroeconomy.*

Why Activist Policy Won't Work: The Modern Monetarist Argument

The **nonactivist stance** of the modern monetarist school is supported by the findings of the modern monetarist models: The models conclude that real-world prices are flexible enough so that *the automatic adjustment forces can bring us the best available macroeconomic conditions.* The modern monetarists don't promise perfect stability for the macroeconomy. But they promise results better than could be achieved by trying to use activist stabilization policies.

The Problem of Time Lags. To the modern monetarist, activist policies cannot work well because of the **time lags** involved. First, it takes a while to know there is a problem. Then it takes a while to take the actions. After the actions are initiated it takes a while for the effect to begin.

While all of this time is passing, the automatic corrective forces in the economy are at work. By the time the activist policies begin to have an impact, it's too late. Those policies are no longer appropriate. So the attempt to stabilize turns out to be destabilizing.

The Problem of Political Considerations. Another consideration is that, like it or not, the Fed (just as every other central bank) operates in a political environment. Regardless of its so-called "independence" no central bank can be completely insulated from politics. The only way to ensure that monetary policy will be insulated from political considerations is to follow a **constant-money-growth-rate rule**. *Let the money supply grow at the same rate that real output is growing and never deviate from that.* Back in chapter 5 you read Milton Friedman's recommendation that the Fed's monetary policy functions be turned over to a computer. Remember? That's the modern monetarist position.

The Modern Keynesian Position

Modern Keynesians, although at complete odds with the monetarist nonactivist position, have backed off a long way from the earlier Keynesian position. Modern Keynesians no longer talk about using activist policy to "fine tune" the macroeconomy. Modern Keynesians understand that activist macroeconomic adjustments are not as easy to achieve as early Keynesians seemed to think.

Modern Keynesians are satisfied to permit the economy to experience some fluctuations without initiating activist counter-cyclical policies. But they hold strongly to the position that *when the economy moves into a period of serious recession and widespread unemployment, activist policies can and should be undertaken to reduce the amount of resource waste and human suffering*—to move the economy more quickly to higher rates of employment, output, and income and keep the economy on an upward-growth path.

SUMMARY

- By the end of the 1930s it was generally recognized that a theory explaining short-run macroeconomic fluctuations was essential. **Keynesian economics** offered such a theory.

- In the 1950s and '60s Friedman and his colleagues developed the **modern monetarist model**, which has both a long-run and a short-run focus, and is based on Friedman's "modern quantity theory." In this theory Mqd is not very sensitive to interest rate changes and depends mostly on "permanent income." Therefore Mqd is stable and predictable.

- Friedman's **permanent income hypothesis** (PIH) insulates consumer spending from changes in current income so that MPC would be very low and the Keynesian income multiplier would be small. But the Keynesians reply that in a depressed economy, the PIH doesn't hold—that more *current income* would result in more *consumer spending* (MPC).

- Modern Keynesian models are non-market-clearing because they permit surpluses to persist in the labor and product markets. The explanation: Price inflexibility. The fixed prices result from long-term contracts and from markup pricing. **Activist policies** are called for.

- Modern monetarist models depict a fairly quickly and smoothly self-regulating macroeconomy in which activist policies can only be destabilizing.

- The modern monetarist and modern Keynesian models look much more alike than different. Still, the monetarists say: "Follow the fixed money-growth-rate rule!" And the Keynesians say: "Adjust money growth and other monetary policy targets as required to achieve desired macroeconomic objectives." So the policy recommendations are as far apart as ever.

Important Principles, Issues, Concepts, Terms

Keynes' view of the classical theory

Focus of Keynesian macrotheory

Focus of classical theory

Milton Friedman

Modern monetarist model

Modern monetarist vs. earlier classical models

Modern Keynesian vs. earlier Keynesian models

Friedman's modern quantity theory

Friedman's permanent income hypothesis

Effect of PIH on MPC and the income multiplier

Effect of r on Mqd in Friedman's money demand model

Effect of expected inflation on Mqd

The equation for Friedman's money demand function

Differences between Friedman's and Keynesian money demand theories

Keynesian view of Friedman's PIH

Empirical evidence regarding the speculative motive

Market-clearing models

Non-market-clearing models

Voluntary vs. involuntary unemployment

Role of long-term contracts and markup pricing

The very-short-run aggregate supply (ASvsr) curve

Activist vs. nonactivist policy

Time lags

Political considerations

The "constant-money-growth-rate" rule

The Keynesian position on the activist-nonactivist issue

Questions

1. In the *General Theory*, Keynes argued that the self-adjusting mechanism of the classical model was not working, and was not going to work within any reasonable period of time and that therefore activist policies should be initiated to overcome the depression. How did he justify this position? Explain in as much detail as you can.

2. What does it mean to say that the classical model ignored the short run, and the Keynesian model ignored the long run? Are these two time periods so different? This is an important issue in macroeconomics. Spend some time thinking and talking about it.

3. Explain some of the ways that the modern monetarist model disagrees with the classical model. Then explain why these distinctions could be significant.

4. Describe Milton Friedman's permanent income hypothesis (PIH), and explain why it challenges some of the basic tenets of the Keynesian model.

5. Explain what the Keynesians have to say about Friedman's PIH, and why.

6. In the Friedman money demand model the opportunity costs of holding money are not very great. Explain why.

7. Write the general demand function for real money balances according to the Friedman model, then explain what each of the terms means. Then explain how Friedman dismisses all of the terms in the equation except permanent income.

8. Empirical studies have been unable to definitely establish the existence of a speculative motive for holding money balances. What conclusion do modern Keynesians draw from this, regarding the reliability of the Keynesian model?

9. Explain what is meant by the phrase "nature abhores uncleared markets" and then explain why Keynesian models permit uncleared markets to exist.

10. The modern Keynesian models, just as the earlier models, depend on the exist-

ence of *price inflexibility*. How do the modern models explain price inflexibility? Discuss.

11. Explain how the monetarists use the existence of *monetary lags* to criticize Keynesian conclusions regarding activist stabilization policy.

12. The Keynesian and monetarist theories, although much closer together now than in earlier decades, still come to the same *opposite* conclusions regarding *activist policies*. Explain as thoroughly as you can the positions of each side in this debate— what each side concludes, and why.

Suggested Readings

Barro, Robert J. "Long-Term Contracts, Sticky Prices and Monetary Policy." *Journal of Monetary Economics.* July 1977.

Buchanan, James, and Richard Wagner. *Democracy in Deficit: The Political Legacy of Lord Keynes.* New York: Academic Press, 1977.

Chick, Victoria, J. A. Kregel, and Paul Davidson. "Symposium on Lessons from Keynes' *General Theory.*" *Journal of Post Keynesian Economics* 10 (1). (Fall 1987), 123–52.

Friedman, Milton. *A Theory of the Consumption Function.* Princeton: National Bureau of Economic Research, 1957.

Gordon, Donald. "A Neo-Classical Theory of Keynesian Unemployment." *Economic Inquiry.* December 1974.

Gordon, Robert J., (ed.) *Friedman's Monetary Theory.* Chicago: Aldine Publishing Co., 1974.

Gordon, Robert J., Arthur M. Okun, and Herbert Stein. "Postwar Macroeconomics: The Evolution of Events and Ideas." Martin Feldstein, ed. *The American Eco-*nomy in Transition. University of Chicago Press, 1980, pp. 101–82.

Lucas, Robert E. Jr., and Thomas J. Sargent. "After Keynesian Macroeconomics." Federal Reserve Bank of Minneapolis *Quarterly Review* 3, (Spring 1979), 1–15.

Mayer, Thomas, ed. *Permanent Income, Wealth, and Consumption.* Berkeley: University of California Press, 1972.

Mayer, Thomas et. al. *The Structure of Monetarism.* New York: W. W. Norton, 1978.

Salant, Walter S. "Keynes and the Modern World: A Review Article." *The Journal of Economic Literature* 23 (3). (September 1985), pp. 1176–85.

Selden, Richard. "Monetarism." in Sidney Weintraub (ed.), *Modern Economic Thought.* Philadelphia: University of Pennsylvania Press, 1976, pp. 253–74.

Tobin, James. "The Monetary and Fiscal Policy Mix." *Economic Review.* The Federal Reserve Bank of Atlanta, August/September 1986, pp. 4–17.

CHAPTER 35

The New Theory of Rational Expectations and "New Classical" Economics

Chapter Objectives

During the 1970s and '80s there has been a significant shake-up in macroeconomic theory. The theories of **rational expectations** and **new classical economics** have had significant influence. This chapter explains these new theories.

After you study this chapter you will understand and be able to explain:

1. The difference between **adaptive expectations** and **rational expectations** and the significance of this difference.

2. The logic of the **Lucas Critique** and how it argues against **activist policies**.

3. The macroeconomic theories of the **new classical economics** and the key role of rational expectations in the "new classical" models.

4. The meaning and signifiance of the **policy ineffectiveness proposition**.

5. How the new classical models conclude that activist stabilization policies will produce **unpredictable results**.

6. How the rational expectations theory can be integrated into models other than the new classical model.

7. How rational expectations in the new classical model shorten the time required for the economy to adjust to its "long-run natural-rate equilibrium."

THE MEANING AND IMPORTANCE OF "RATIONAL EXPECTATIONS"

Economists have long recognized the important role of expectations in influencing economic decisions. But the new theories based on the concept of **rational expectations** have brought a new emphasis both on the nature of expectations and on the role of expectations in influencing the economic process.

The Role of Expectations in Economic Decisions

It would be difficult to think of any economic decision or action which isn't influenced in some way by expectations. Before you go into debt to buy a new car, you expect your income in the future to continue. Before investors spend money for new plant and equipment, expected profitability of the investment is a matter of careful concern.

The expected rate of inflation has a significant influence on the decisions of economic units—individuals and businesses—often called "economic actors." From previous chapters you know the importance of expectations in influencing both the risk structure and the term structure of interest rates. Expected default risk determines the risk structure; expected future declines in rates bring higher short-term rates than long-term rates—an inverted yield curve. The importance of all this on future interest rate movements and the building of "an efficient portfolio" is obvious. Even faith in the future viability of our monetary and banking system is based on optimistic expectations! And the whole idea of economic policy hinges on our ability to forsee future conditions in the economy.

Expectations play a significant role—either explicitly or implicitly—in every macroeconomic model. But in the new theories based on *rational expectations* the specific focus is on expectations: how they are formed, and how they influence economic behavior, and the economy.[1]

Adaptive Expectations? Or Rational Expectations?

According to the concept of rational expectations, how do "economic actors" form their expectations? Is the future expected to be some repetition of the average of what has happened in the past? Or will economic actors look for indications that the future is going to be different, somehow?

Expectations based entirely on the average of what has happened in the past are called **adaptive expectations**. Expectations which take into consideration *new circumstances* which seem likely to alter some basic conditions so that the future *will not* (on the average) reflect the past, are called **rational expectations**.

An Example of "Rational Expectations"

Here's a very simple example. Suppose you are thinking about establishing a small farm in a remote area of your state. You have investigated and found that the average rainfall, temperture, and humidity in that area over the past twenty years have all been ideal. So you assume those conditions will continue to exist in the future. That's "adaptive expectations."

Then, suppose you hear that there is a plan to divert the river from that area, and to cut all the trees within a fifty-mile radius. And suppose you have reason to believe that these changes will significantly alter future temperatures, humidity, and rainfall in that area. So now (if you're rational) you will make new estimates which depart from the past averages. That's rational expectations.

---

[1] The ideas of "rational expectations" have been having a significant and growing impact on economic theory throughout the 1960s, '70s and '80s. By the end of the 1980s there were many different economic models which incorporated the concept of rational expectations. The existence and effects of rational expectations can be incorporated into modern Keynesian models and modern monetarist models as well as in the models of the "new classical economics." In each model the conclusions would be different because the initial assumptions are different.

Even in the various models of the new classical school where the rational expectations concept plays the key role, the models and predicted results are not always identical. So please be forewarned that in the discussion of rational expectations in this chapter, not all of the statements and conclusions would be precisely true for all models which incorporate the rational expectations concept.

The idea is that a person who would cling to a future forecast based entirely on what had happened in the past when there is good reason to believe that the future will be different, would not be forming expectations rationally. More precisely: *A rational person when forming expectations will consider all available information which has a bearing on the future.* Not to do so would not be rational.

The Basic Idea of Rational Expectations Is Common Sense

The basic idea underlying rational expectations is really common sense. If you have every reason to believe that a variable will move in the future, on the average, more or less in the same way that it has moved in the past, then *adaptive expectations* and *rational expectations* come out in the same place. But if there are indications that movements of a variable in the future are going to be different than in the past—something has happened to alter the way in which this variable moves—then to stick with adaptive expectations would be irrational. It would mean closing your eyes to things which in the future can be rationally expected to cause results to be different from the past.

No intelligent person would disagree with these common sense conclusions. But the theory of rational expectations goes much deeper than that. In 1961, a path-breaking article by John Muth developed the rational expectations hypothesis. The question: How do rational decision-makers arrive at the probable future value of a variable? The answer: They consider *all available information.*[2]

When using rational expectations the probable future value of a variable depends partly on past experience. But it includes all other relevant information, including (very importantly) any systematic errors—repeated under- or overestimates—which have been showing up in past predictions.

For example, suppose someone has been consistently (systematically) underestimating the rate of future inflation. Their rational expectations will tell them that there's something wrong with the system they're using to forecast inflation. So they know that they should adjust their future inflation forecasts upward.

Rational Expectations Produce "Unbiased" Predictions

Economic actors who would continue to make predictions based only on adaptive expectations could keep making systematic forecasting errors over and over. But that wouldn't be a rational thing to do! With rationally formed expectations it is possible to avoid repeating systematic errors.

Rationally formed expectations are not necessarily accurate. Nobody has perfect information or perfect foresight! So some forecasts will be too high and some, too low. But when a person uses rational expectations the forecasts will not be biased in any one direction. So "on the average" rationally expected values would turn out to be correct.

What does the idea of rational expectations have to do with macroeconomic theory? Quite a lot. All macroeconomic "econometric forecasting models" are built on assumptions about the propensities to consume and save, the responsive-

---

[2] John F. Muth, "Rational Expectations and the Theory of Price Movements," *Econometrica*, July 1961. For a review of the theories of rational expectations, including an extensive bibliography, see: Steven M. Shefrin, *Rational Expectations* (Cambridge, England: Cambridge University Press, 1983).

ness of investment to interest rate changes, and many other variables. These models reflect *past behavior patterns*.

What would happen if people changed their behavior patterns when they saw that the government was undertaking stabilization policies? Then the model could no longer accurately predict what the results of the stabilization policies would be. This insightful conclusion is called *the Lucas Critique*.

The "Rational Expectations Revolution"

During the 1970s and '80s this new thrust in macroeconomic theory—sometimes referred to as **the rational expectations revolution—**has been spearheaded by Robert Lucas of the University of Chicago.[3] Several other economists have been involved, including Thomas Sargent of the University of Minnesota, Robert Barro, formerly of the University of Rochester and now of Harvard University, and Edward Prescott and Neil Wallace of the University of Minnesota.

These (and other) leaders of the rational expectations revolution have a strong conviction—an abiding faith—in the basic conclusions of the classical model—in the automatically self-regulating macroeconomy. These models provide strong support for this position and argue strongly that "macroeconomic *laissez faire*" is the only sensible alternative.

The "Lucas Critique"

The Lucas Critique adds more support for macroeconomic *laissez-faire*. It says: Macroeconomic models cannot accurately forecast the effects of activist macroeconomic policies. Here's why.

When the government initiates policy changes to try to influence the macroeconomy, that causes people's expectations to change. The changed expectations will cause people's behavior to change. Therefore the "givens" (the parameters) in the model will change. Therefore the ultimate results of the policies will be different from the results predicted by the (now inaccurate) model.

So *with rational expectations the effects of stabilization policies become unpredictable*. The result? It becomes impossible to design and carry out effective stabilization policies!

If the results of activist monetary and fiscal policies are unpredictable, then should such policies be undertaken? The new classical theorists conclude: "Absolutely not!" The Lucas Critique doesn't try to say what results will occur. It only says that the outcome is unpredictable and too dangerous to risk.

THE EFFECT OF THE LUCAS CRITIQUE IN THE IS-LM MODEL

Suppose government stabilization policies cause people's economic behavior to change in unpredictable ways. Then the outcomes of the policies are unpredictable. So it's impossible to design and carry out effective stabilization policies. Here's an example.

---

[3] Robert Lucas, Jr., "Econometric Policy Evaluation: A Critique," in Karl Brunner and Allan H. Meltzer (Eds.), *The Phillips Curve and Labor Markets*, Carnegie-Rochester Conference on Public Policy 1 (1976), pp. 19–46.

Suppose the economy is in a recession. Unemployment is high; output and income are low. In figure 35-1 this condition is indicated by the intersection of the IS and LM curves at Point a. In the figure, according to the Keynesian model if the policymakers would increase the money supply enough to shift the LM curve to LM_1 and increase government spending (or cut taxes) enough to shift the IS curve to IS_1, then: Presto! The economy would move to full employment at Yfe.

Altered Expectations Will Cause the Curves to Shift

The Lucas Critique says it won't happen this way—that as soon as people figure out what the government is doing, the IS and LM curves will shift. So the results shown in figure 35-1 won't happen at all. According to the Lucas Critique, inflation would be the more likely result. Here's how it might happen.

**Figure 35-1.   IS-LM Curves Illustrate Expansionary
                 Monetary and Fiscal Policy**

Monetary expansion and increased government spending (or reduced taxes) shift both LM and IS rightward. The economy moves to full employment at Yfe.

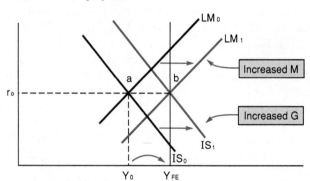

Keynesian econometric forecasting models are built on the assumption that both the LM and IS functions are stable relationships. The model also assumes that the responses from increasing the money supply and from increasing government spending (or cutting taxes) are predictable. So these models provide guidance as to how much the money supply needs to increase and how much fiscal stimulus is required to shift the curves from IS_0 to IS_1 and from LM_0 to LM_1 as shown in the figure. And the models tell us that these shifts to IS_1 and LM_1 will move the economy from Point a to Point b where full employment will be achieved at Yfe.

But the "Lucas Critique" says it won't happen that way. It says that when the monetary and fiscal policies are initiated, people will alter their behavior. So the IS and LM curves will shift and the outcome will be unpredictable. Perhaps economic conditions will be made worse instead of better. The conclusion: *The effects of stabilization policies are unpredictable and therefore such policies should never be initiated.*

As the money supply begins increasing this triggers inflationary expectations. Inflationary expectations influence the quantity of money people desire to hold (Mqd). Also inflationary expectations influence financial markets, pushing interest rates up. *The expected inflationary loss of purchasing power* can cause a reduction in Mqd—a rightward shift of the LM curve.

The IS curve is also likely to shift, and the extent of the shift is not predictable. If consumers expect rapidly rising prices their "propensity to spend for consumer goods" may increase significantly. This means that their *propensity to save* decreases. So the IS curve shifts to the right to reflect the smaller savings withdrawal at each level of national income.

Investment spending can also be expected to change unpredictably. Inflationary expectations may trigger an inventory buildup—"borrow now before interest rates go up any more, and buy now before prices rise any more." Such an investment spending boom could shift the IS curve far to the right. But how far? We don't know. Figure 35-2 illustrates one possible outcome.

Figure 35-2.   Illustration of the Effects of Rational Expectations—
The "Lucas Critique"—in the IS-LM Framework

As people observe the government's stabilization policy, their expectations change regarding the rate of inflation, future nominal interest rates, and other variables. So both their money-holding desires and their spending patterns change. Both the IS and LM curves shift.

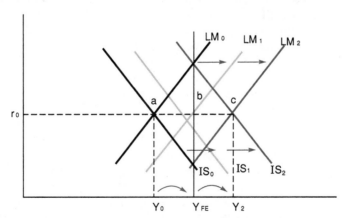

Changed rational expectations shift the LM curve to LM_2 and the IS curve to IS_2. This carries the economy to Point c, at Y_2— a level of national income much larger than Yfe.

The condition at point c would be highly inflationary. So antiinflationary policies probably would be initiated, throwing the economy into recession—perhaps reducing national income to less than Y_0.

The new classical conclusion is obvious. It would have been better not to initiate the stimulative policies in the first place. Since the results are unpredictable, *stabilization policies should never be undertaken.*

The Outcome of Activist Policy Is Indeterminate

Suppose these kinds of changes occur in both the LM and IS curves. Then the economy could wind up in the position illustrated by Point c in figure 35-2. That's far beyond the full employment level and indicates a highly inflationary condition. And if that's a likely result of the expansionary policy, should the policy be initiated? The new classical theorists conclude: "Absolutely not!"

The Lucas Critique doesn't attempt to foretell what will happen as a result of different stabilization policies. The Critique only says that the outcome is indeterminate—unpredictable.

THE MACROECONOMIC MODEL OF NEW CLASSICAL ECONOMICS

You already understand the macroeconomic model of classical economics. Wages, prices, and interest rates all adjust as necessary to maintain a full-employment economy. However, *there are short-run lags (delays) in the adjustment to long-run equilibrium.* But in the "new classical" model? Not so!

Rationally Expected Price Adjustments Occur Very Quickly

The "new classical" model is even more "classical" than the original classical model or the modern monetarist models. In the modern monetarist model there are lags which permit short-run deviations from the "natural rates." In the new classical model these lags are shortened or eliminated. How? By the "anticipation effect" in the theory of rational expectations.

The new classical model assumes that expectations are rational and wages and prices are flexible—not only in response to *realized changes,* but also (and very importantly!) in response to *rationally expected changes* in supply, demand, and price conditions.

For example, suppose the general price level is expected to rise. Then this expectation will tend to cause *immediate wage and price increases.* It happens because of immediate demand and supply adjustments.

In all markets throughout the economy, demand will increase. Buyers will want to buy now before prices rise. And supply will decrease. Why? Because expected cost of production is higher. So less output will be supplied at each price.

These same demand and supply changes will occur in the labor markets. So wages will go up. But the increasing output prices will cover the increased input costs.

You can see why the economy will very quickly experience an upward shift of the price level. The public's rational expectations will very quickly bring increased AD and decreased AS. And that means: Shortages and higher prices! The upward moving prices and wages soon will take the economy to a new long-run macroequilibrium at a higher wage/price level.

In the New Classical Model the Long Run Comes Quickly

Think for a moment about the implications of this model. Suppose something happens to cause the economy to slow down (or speed up) too much. How long will it take for long-run equilibrium to return? Not very long! People and businesses, guided by their rational expectations, will change their behavior and cause the economy to move very quickly to the new long-run equilibrium.

Here's an example in terms of the AD-AS diagram. Suppose the money supply is expanding rapidly. People "rationally expect" the price level to rise. So they alter their behavior. The result: There will be *an immediate increase (rightward shift) in AD and an immediate decrease (leftward shift) in ASsr.*

The general level of prices and wages will go up. But because of the price level increase, the purchasing power of each dollar goes down, so that *real prices and wages are unchanged.* Perhaps people are receiving 10% more dollars. But because of the 10% increase in prices they have no more purchasing power than before. So aggregate quantity demanded—and output—remains the same as before—at the natural rate. Figure 35-3 illustrates this.

Figure 35-3.   The New Classical Model: Effects of a Rationally Expected Increase in the Price Level

The move to a new long-run macroequilibrium occurs very quickly. Q doesn't change. Only P goes up.

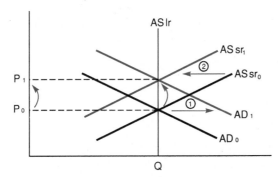

The expected price increase causes buyers of outputs to try to buy now before prices rise. So AD increases. The curve shifts rightward from AD_0 to AD_1.

The expected price increase causes labor to insist on higher wages and other input sellers to insist on higher prices. The supply of labor and other inputs decreases. The cost of production goes up, causing ASsr to decrease. The curve shifts leftward from $ASsr_0$ to $ASsr_1$.

The price level goes up from P_0 to P_1. But real employment, output, and income are unchanged. Economic activity remains stable at the natural rate.

The new classical model deposits a very stable and automatically adjusting economy. So, in this model, when should activist macroeconomic policies be initiated to try to improve conditions? Never!

Thinking back to the classical model of the macroeconomy you can understand why this new rational-expectations-based model is referred to as **new
classical economics**. We get the same results as in the classical model, only more
quickly. People know it's going to happen eventually, so they take actions which
cause it to happen immediately. *Self-fulfilling prophecy?* Yes. And you can see
the devastating effect of this model's conclusions on "the Keynesian prescription"
for activist stabilization policies.

Rational Expectations Block the Intended Effects of Activist Policies

Suppose the policymakers initiate "easy money" policies to try to speed up the
economy. And suppose economic actors "rationally expect" these easy money
policies to cause inflation. What happens? The *expectation of price increases*
quickly results in *realized price increases*. The economy does not speed up at all.
Only prices go up.

The new classical model concludes: *If expansionary monetary and/or fiscal
policy is rationally expected to push prices and wages up eventually, then the
only effect of this policy will be to push up prices and wages immediately.* There
will be no real macroeconomic effect—no changes in employment, output, or
income.

But suppose the economic actors didn't know what the policymakers were
doing. Suppose nobody expected any price increases. Then *in the short-run* the
new classical model produces quite different results. If you have no reason to
expect a price level change, then there's no way you can alter your economic
behavior in expectation of it!

Only Unexpected Expansionary Policies Have Any Real Effects

Figure 35-4 illustrates the effects of an unexpected expansionary policy—either
monetary, or fiscal—in the new classical model. In this case an increase in
aggregate demand in the short run will increase both output and prices. But in
the long run, because the economy is operating above its natural rate, input costs
will rise. So the ASsr curve will shift leftward. Then real output (and employment
and income) will move back to the natural rate. The only remaining effect will be
the higher price level. That's exactly the same scenario you saw in the previous
chapter in the modern monetarist model.

But suppose all of the economic actors had been able to forsee the ultimate
result shown in figure 35-4. *If that's what they thought was going to happen in the
long run, then the short-run increase in employment and output wouldn't happen
at all!* That's the point of the new classical theory.

According to the theory, if the government's expansionary policy is completely and accurately anticipated, point b in figure 35-4 is bypassed. The economy moves quickly from point a to point c. The expansionary policy is a
complete failure. All it does is to produce inflation. Now study figure 35-5 which
illustrates this result (the same result as in figure 35-3) and tells more about it.

Figure 35-4. The New Classical Model: Effects of an Unexpected Expansionary Policy Shown in the AD-AS Diagram

Increased AD brings both increased output and prices in the short run, but only increased prices in the long run.

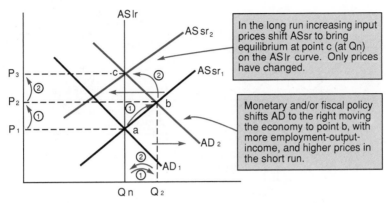

In the long run increasing input prices shift ASsr to bring equilibrium at point c (at Qn) on the ASlr curve. Only prices have changed.

Monetary and/or fiscal policy shifts AD to the right moving the economy to point b, with more employment-output-income, and higher prices in the short run.

Stimulative government policies shift the AD curve to the right. In the short-run this moves the economy to point b. The quantity of output increases from Q_n to Q_2 and prices move up from P_1 to P_2. The result: Increased output and employment as well as higher prices. No price increase was "rationally ex-pected," so ASsr does not decrease (shift to the left) in the short run.

In the long run, tightness in the input markets pushes up the prices of labor and other inputs and shifts ASsr from $ASsr_1$ to $ASsr_2$.

As ASsr shifts to the left, output decreases and prices rise even more. The long-run equilibrium occurs where the rate of output and income is back at the natural rate and the price level is up to P_3.

The Policy Ineffectiveness Proposition

Figure 35-5 illustrates what new classical economists call the **policy ineffective-ness proposition**. The proposition says: Stabilization policy which is accurately anticipated has no real effect on the economy—on employment, output, or in-come. According to this proposition, only when a policy is unexpected—comes as a surprise—can it have any real effects.[4]

Suppose the public underestimates the inflationary effect of an expansionary policy so that actual inflation turns out to be greater than expected inflation. Then there's an element of surprise. In Figure 35-5 the ASsr curve will not shift all the way to $ASsr_2$ and prices will not rise all the way to P_3. So there will be some increase in employment and output in the short run.

Conversely, suppose the public expects inflationary effects to be greater than they really are so that actual inflation turns out to be less than expected inflation. Then $ASsr_2$ will shift *farther* to the left than indicated by $ASsr_2$ in figure 35-5. The intersection of the new ASsr curve with AD_2 will be to the left of Q_n. Real

[4] On the implications of the policy ineffectiveness proposition, see: Thomas Sargeant and Neil Wallace, "'Rational' Expectations, the Optimal Monetary Instrument, and the Optimal Money Supply Rule," *Journal of Political Economy*, vol. 83 (April 1975), pp. 241–54.

**Figure 35-5.   The New Classical Model: The Policy Ineffectiveness
Proposition Shown in the AD-AS Diagram**

Increased AD brings no increase in Q—only increased P. The long run arrives
very quickly.

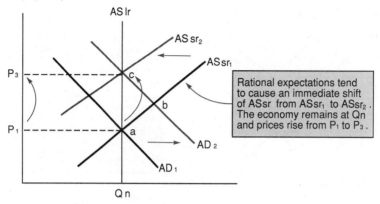

When the price level is rationally expected to move from P_1 to P_3, ASsr
shifts very quickly from $ASsr_1$ to $ASsr_2$. The intermediate position at point b is
bypassed because of the rationally expected inflationary effects of the expansionary policy.

According to the new classical model's **policy ineffectiveness proposition**,
when the effects of activist fiscal or monetary policies are *completely expected*,
these policies have *absolutely no real effect on the economy's employment,
output, or income*—not even in the short run.

When aggregate demand is increased the economic actors know what is
happening and they immediately take defensive action. Supply and demand
conditions in the input markets immediately adjust and force up production
costs. The ASsr curve immediately shifts leftward from $ASsr_1$ to $ASsr_2$.

Simultaneously the sellers and buyers in the output markets—who are also
aware of what's happening—adjust their behavior and cause supply and demand conditions in these product markets to adjust to "the new rationally
expected reality." Supply decreases and demand increases. Prices quickly go
up from P_1 to P_3. So the economy moves quickly from point a to point c. No real
variables are changed. Real output remains at Q_n—the natural rate.

---

employment, output, and income will decrease in the short run and prices will go
higher than P_3. Stagflation again!

Policy Implications of the New Classical Model

The policy implications of the new classical model are quite clear:

1. It is impossible for policymakers to know what the effects of their actions
   will be *unless they know the public's expectations* regarding macroeconomic policy.

2. It is impossible to know (a) exactly what the public is expecting at any
   moment, and (b) exactly how the public will revise their expectations as
   policies begin to unfold.

3. Therefore any effect which stabilization policies may have on real employment, output, and income will be unpredictable.

4. And therefore discretionary stabilization policy will not work as planned, and may do more harm than good.

5. *The obvious conclusion:* No discretionary stabilization policy should be initiated—not ever!

The new classical model concludes that constancy and stability of both monetary and fiscal policy should be maintained at all times. Why? Because the only thing that activist policy can do is to influence the price level. And only stable policies will result in stable prices. This brings the new classical economists to support the classical and modern monetarist conclusion that *the only appropriate monetary policy is: slow and steady growth of the money supply.*

WHAT ABOUT RATIONAL EXPECTATIONS WITHOUT FREE-MOVING WAGES AND PRICES?

Many economists look at the real world and see that wages and prices do not in fact move with total freedom and flexibility. So they question the relevance of a model which starts out with this assumption. Does that mean that the whole idea of rational expectations has no meaning except in the new classical model? No, it doesn't mean that at all.

The Non-Classical Rational Expectations Model

Several economists—including Stanley Fischer of MIT, Edmund Phelps of Columbia University, and John Taylor of Stanford University—have developed what is called "the non-classical rational expectations model." This model assumes that expectations are formed rationally. It also assumes that the expected effects of government policies are considered by economic actors and do influence their decisions and actions. But this model does not assume complete wage-price flexibility.

The Policy Ineffectiveness Proposition Doesn't Hold

What difference does it make when so-called "sticky" prices and wages are included in the model? The policy ineffectiveness proposition no longer holds. That shouldn't be surprising, when you think about it.

The policy ineffectiveness proposition results from (1) the fact that the effects of government policy are *completely and accurately expected,* and (2) wages and prices adjust completely to negate the effectiveness of the policy. So anything which prevented the expectations from being precisely accurate, or anything which prevented the adjustment of all wages and prices, would negate the proposition.

The non-classical rational expectations model still holds, however, that *anticipated stabilization policy will have a smaller effect on real employment, output, and income than if the policy is unanticipated.* But because of the assumed inflexibility of wages and prices, expectations in the non-classical model do not make as much difference as in the new classical model.

Inflexible Prices Reduce the Effect of Rational Expectations

When prices are not free to adjust in response to the rational expectations of economic actors, then the speedy automatic adjustment to a new price level as shown in figure 35-5 obviously can't occur. Suppose all wages and prices were absolutely frozen. Then rational expectations could make people very frustrated. But (in figure 35-5) in terms of shifting the ASsr curve and moving prices from P_1 to P_3, it couldn't happen.

Figure 35-6 shows the same basic graph as figure 35-5, and it shows different results, depending on the assumptions. When government policies cause AD to shift from AD_1 to AD_2 if this move is completely unexpected then the economy

---

**Figure 35-6.   Short-Run effects of a Rationally Expected
                Expansionary Policy: Three Models Compared**

When expansionary policy shifts the aggregate demand to AD2, in the new classical model rational expectations cause ASsr$_1$ to shift to ASsr$_2$. In the non-classical model the curve only shifts to ASsr$_3$ because of wage-price inflexibilities. In the modern monetarist model ASsr doesn't shift in the short run.

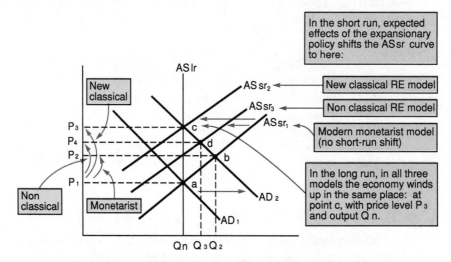

Initially the economy is in equilibrium at Point a, with price level P_1 and output Q_n. Then the government's expansionary policy shifts aggregate demand to AD_2. If this shift was completely unanticipated, then the effect will be the same in all three models.

When expansionary policies are unexpected, rational expectations can have no effect on outcomes. When the expansionary policy is expected, then it makes significant difference which model you choose—but only in the short run.

From this example you can see that the greater the accuracy of the expectations and the greater the degree of price flexibility built into the model, the less employment and output will increase in the short run and the closer the economy will come to the "policy ineffectiveness proposition"—where the policy has zero effect on real macroeconomic conditions.

will move from point a to point b. The price level will move up to P_2 and output will increase to Q_2. This is what would happen (a) in the modern monetarist model which does not attempt to take into account rational expectations, (b) in the new classical model in cases in which the expansionary policy is completely unexpected, and (c) also in the non-classical rational expectations model when the expansionary policy is unexpected.

In all three models, in the long run the price level is going to move to P_3, and output and income will be at Q_n (the natural rate). *But if the expansionary policy is anticipated, then what happens in the short run depends on which model you choose.*

1. In the traditional monetarist model which does not consider rational expectations, the economy would move to point b and employment, output, and income would increase to Q_2.

2. If you choose the new classical model with complete and immediate flexibility of all wages and prices, the economy moves immediately to point c, with price level P_3. There is no increase in output at all, even in the short run. The policy ineffectiveness proposition holds.

3. If you choose the non-classical rational expectations model in which wages and prices are not completely flexible, then in the short run the economy moves to point d, with price level P_4 and output Q_3. In this model, rational expectations *reduce* the extent of output expansion in the short run, but the policy ineffectiveness proposition does not hold. Output and income temporarily increase from Q_n to Q_3.

RATIONAL EXPECTATIONS IN THE "COMPLETELY NON-CLASSICAL" CASE: THE KEYNESIAN MODEL

The non-classical rational expectations model with price inflexibility built in is really only "semi-non-classical." That model still includes the classical idea of the tendency of the economy to move to the "natural rate" of employment, output, and income—the idea that all deviations from this position are temporary and automatically self-correcting.

The Keynesian Model Does Not Assume Full Employment

In all of the graphs presented so far in this chapter the initial point was the "natural rate" of output. Suppose we begin from a position of serious unemployment and widespread excess capacity in the economy. Then would expansionary monetary and fiscal policies be rationally expected to bring inflation? With an immediate increase in all wages and prices? Would the "policy ineffectiveness proposition" hold during a depression? The Keynesians say: "Not likely!"

In figure 35-7 the AD-AS framework is used to illustrate the Keynesian model. Now the initial assumptions are Keynesian—and you can see what a difference that makes! In figure 35-7 *none of the conclusions of the new classical model would hold.*

You will notice that there is no vertical long-run aggregate supply curve in this graph. The vertical ASlr curve is based on the assumption that there is a

Figure 35-7.   In the Keynesian Model, Expansionary Policies Can Increase Output and Income—With No Price Increase

When widespread unemployment and excess capacity are the assumed beginning point, the results of an expansionary policy appear quite different than when the "natural rate" of output and employment is the assumed point of departure.

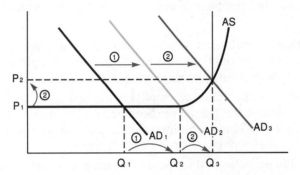

1. As expansionary policy shifts AD from AD_1 to AD_2, Q increases from Q_1 to Q_2. Employment, output, and income increase and there is no increase in the price level.

2. If expansionary policy continues beyond AD_2—for example, to AD_3—output and employment will continue to increase. But this will bring tightness in some labor and other markets and prices will be pushed up to P_2.

"natural rate" of output to which the economy automatically will move. Some Keynesian models do not accept that proposition.

Even if there is a natural rate of output, the economy at the moment may be operating far below this level. In figure 35-7 at output level Q_1 the economy has much excess capacity. That's depression. When the economy is depressed there is no reason for an increase in aggregate demand to trigger inflationary expectations. So there's no reason for the ASsr curve to shift upward and leftward. An increase in spending can rationally be expected to result in increased employment, output, and income—not increased prices.

In this Keynesian model the relevant aggregate supply curve is the one that exists *right now*. And this model concludes that policymakers should target this ASsr curve as they design policies to stimulate employment, output, and income and try to overcome the depression.

As you can see, the basic difference in the "mental set" (the initial assumptions) of the Keynesians and the modern monetarists carries on into the basic difference between Keynesian theory and new classical theory.

The Keynesian Model Explains Dynamic Short-Run Changes

Keynesian economics is concerned with understanding and explaining the **dynamic short-run changes** which occur in the economy—the process by which it gets itself into recession or inflation and the process by which it gets itself out. The new classical theory, as did the old, concentrates on **long-run equilibrium** and doesn't focus on the dynamic process of causes and effects which move the economy to (or away from) this long-run position.

THE PUBLIC'S RATIONAL EXPECTATIONS CAN HELP IN FIGHTING INFLATION

Suppose the government decides to use monetary and fiscal policies to bring down the rate of inflation. Aggregate demand must be held down. In the modern monetarist model, in the short run the decreased demand can result in production cutbacks and a serious drop in employment, output, and income. In this model the social cost of fighting inflation is high. But not so in the **new classical model**.

Suppose economic actors accurately and completely anticipate the effects of the anti-inflation policy. Suppose everyone is sure that the policy will be undertaken and steadfastly implemented and that it will succeed. Then the inflation can be stopped dead in its tracks—without any loss of jobs, output, or income.

When the inflation rate is high, that means that (1) the short-run aggregate supply curve keeps shifting leftward as cost of production increases, and (2) the aggregate demand curve keeps shifting rightward (in nominal terms) as total spending increases reflecting the ever-higher price levels. Now assume that money growth is restricted so that aggregate demand cannot continue to increase.

Holding Down Aggregate Demand Brings Recession

With ASsr decreasing more and more—the curve shifting leftward reflecting higher costs—and the price level going up commensurately, what happens if aggregate demand is not permitted *to increase*? There's unsold output. Production cutbacks. Recession.

Figure 35-8 shows this on a graph. There you see ASsr shifting from $ASsr_1$ to $ASsr_2$ and the price level moving up from P_1 to P_2. With ASsr located at $ASsr_2$, for Q to remain at Q_n, AD must increase to AD_2. If that happens, the increase in prices from P_1 to P_2 will be confirmed by the AD shift.

Modern monetarist theory predicts that if the money supply is not permitted to increase then aggregate demand will not shift to AD_2. So the economy, instead of moving to Point b with full employment and high inflation, will move to point c with high unemployment and less inflation in the short-run. Then in the long-run, surpluses in the labor and product markets will push prices down, surplus funds in the money markets will push interest rates down, and (ultimately) decreasing costs will shift $ASsr_2$ back to $ASsr_1$ and the economy will return to point a: full employment (Q_n) at the original price level P_1. But before that happens, considerable output, income, and growth will be lost. This is where rational expectations theory and the new classical model come to the rescue.

The New Classical Model: Stopping Inflation without Recession

When the anti-inflation policy is completely anticipated and completely credible, then inflation will be stopped automatically, and without any decrease in output.

Figure 35-8.   In the New Classical Model, If Policy Is Credible, Inflation Can Be Stopped with No Recession!

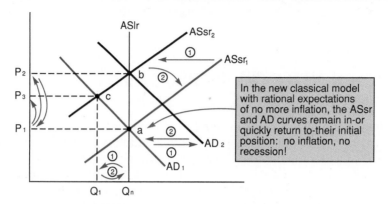

In the new classical model with rational expectations of no more inflation, the ASsr and AD curves remain in-or quickly return to-their initial position: no inflation, no recession!

As costs are pushed up by inflation, ASsr shifts leftward to $ASsr_2$. If AD_1 shifts to AD_2, Q_n is maintained and prices rise to P_2. If AD *does not* increase, point c applies and output decreases to Q1. But if the anti-inflation policy is anticipated and credible, ASsr will remain at (or shift back to) $ASsr_1$: no more inflation, and no recession!

The new classical model says that no period of unemployment will occur if the anti-inflation policy is anticipated and credible. If everyone knows the inflation soon will be over, then wages and prices will stabilize. There will be no need for the economy to go through a period of unemployment and reduced output and income.

Why? Because labor and other sellers of inputs, knowing that the price level is not going to rise, will not push up input prices. Costs will stop rising so $ASsr_1$ will remain where it is—or if it has begun to shift toward $ASsr_2$, will quickly shift back.

As a practical matter, it isn't always easy for the monetary authorities to convince the public that anti-inflation policies will be followed and will be successful. People remember that the Fed has conflicting goals, and that stopping inflation is not always its top priority.

The rational expectations conclusions regarding stopping inflation with no pain—as explained in figure 35-8—are very appealing. But so far nothing like this has ever happened. The end of the U.S. inflation of the late 1970s and early 80s was bought at the cost of the worst recession since the 1930s.

The rational expectations theorists explain that a lack of credibility resulted in this high cost—that if people had believed that the Fed was going to succeed in stopping the inflation then the inflation would have been stopped much more quickly and at much less economic cost.

SUMMARY

- **Rational expectations** differ from **adaptive expectations** in that adaptive expectations are based on an average of what has happened in the past, while rational expectations are based on this information plus **all other available information**—including inaccuracies of past expectations.

- The **Lucas Critique** says that people, following their rational expectations, adjust their behavior in response to activist macroeconomic policies. Because of this **behavior adjustment** it is impossible to accurately predict the effects of activist policies.

- In the **new classical model**, wages, prices, and interest rates are completely flexible. External influences on the economy are quickly absorbed as the economy moves rapidly to a new long-run position.

- The **policy ineffectiveness proposition** says that accurately anticipated stabilization policies do not effect the economy. Only unforeseen policies have any real effect.

- In models which assume **wage-price inflexibility**, rational expectations somewhat reduce (but do not eliminate) the effectiveness of stabilization policies.

- In a **Keynesian model**, rational expectations do not alter the results at all. Unemployment brings a **horizontal short-run aggregate supply curve** and permits the economy to respond in real terms to changes in aggregate demand.

- In the new classical model, the effect of rational expectations is to **bypass the short-run conditions** specified in the modern monetarist model, and to move quickly to the long run position at the natural rate of employment, output, and income.

Important Principles, Issues, Concepts, Terms

Rational expectations

Adaptive expectations

The Lucas Critique

New classical economics

The policy ineffectiveness proposition

Effects of rationally expected price adjustments

Effects of rational expectations in the IS-LM diagram

Effects of rationally expected changes in the AD-AS diagram

Rational expectations in the new classical model

Rational expectations in the non-classical model

Rational expectations in the Keynesian model

Rational expectations and inflation

Expected vs. unexpected activist policy

Questions

1. Explain as much as you can about the meaning of rational expectations, and how this differs from adaptive expectations.

2. Explain as thoroughly as you can what is meant by the "Lucas Critique."

3. Explain the important difference in the new classical model between expected and unexpected activist macroeconomic policies. Can you illustrate this graphically? Try.

4. Explain the policy ineffectiveness proposition, how it is supported by the new classical school, and what the Keynesians have to say about it.

5. Rational expectations eliminate the repeated occurrence of systematic errors. Explain what this means and why it is true.

6. In the new classical model, the long run comes more quickly than in the modern monetarist or traditional classical models.

Explain what this means, why it is true, and illustrate with a graph.

7. Explain why the policy ineffectiveness proposition doesn't hold in any of the models other than the new classical model.

8. Explain how the existence of inflexible prices would affect the conclusions of the new classical model.

9. Compare and contrast the modern monetarist and "new classical" models. In what ways are these models similar? In what ways are they different?

10. The modern monetarists and new clas-

sical economists have some very strong arguments against the use of activist stabilization policies. They emphasize the danger of creating more instability, the danger of "overkill." And the new classical economists emphasize the Lucas Critique and the policy ineffectiveness proposition. In view of all this, suppose you were a member of the Federal Reserve Board and had to vote on a proposed activist policy to increase AD and bring down the unemployment rate. Suppose the unemployment rate was up to 10% of the labor force. Which way do you think you would vote? Explain why.

Suggested Readings

Barro, Robert J. "Unanticipated Money Growth and Unemployment in the United States." *American Economic Review* 67, 1977, pp. 101–15.

Fischer, Stanley, ed. *Rational Expectations and Economic Policy.* University of Chicago Press, 1980.

Garrison, Roger W. "'Rational Expectations' Offers Nothing That's Both New and True." *The Austrian Economics Newsletter.* (Fall 1985), 5–6.

Hoehen, James G. *Designing Monetary Policy Under Rational Expectations: Analysis and Practical Implications.* Federal Reserve Bank of Cleveland Working Paper 8612, December 1986.

Hoover, Kevin D. "Two Types of Monetarists." *The Journal of Economic Literature* 22 (1). (March 1984), 58–76.

Lovell, Michael C. "Tests of the Rational Expectations Hypothesis." *American Economic Review* 76 (March 1986), 110–24.

Lucas, Robert E. Jr. "Econometric Policy Evaluation: A Critique." in Karl Brunner and Allan H. Meltzer (eds.), *The Phillips Curve and Labor Markets.* Carnegie-Rochester Conference on Public Policy 1, 1976, pp. 19–46.

———. "Methods and Problems in Business Cycle

Theory." *Journal of Money, Credit and Banking.* (November 1980), 696–715.

McAuliffe, R. E. "The Rational Expectations Hypothesis and Economic Analysis." *Eastern Economic Journal* 11 (4). (October/December 1985), 331–41.

McCallum, Bennett. "The Significance of Rational Expectations Theory." *Challenge* 22. (January/February 1980), 37–43.

Sargent, Thomas. "The Ends of Four Big Inflations." in Robert E. Hall, ed., *Inflation: Causes and Consequences.* Chicago: University of Chicago Press for the NBER, 1982, pp. 41–98.

Sargent, Thomas and Neil Wallace. "Rational Expectations, The Optimal Monetary Instrument, and the Optimal Money Supply Rule." *Journal of Political Economy* 83. (April 1975), 241–54.

Solow, Robert M. "What to Do (Macroeconomically) when OPEC Comes." in Stanley Fischer, ed., *Rational Expectations and Economic Policy.* National Bureau of Economic Research, Chicago: University of Chicago Press, 1980, pp. 249–64.

Taylor, John. "The Role of Expectations in the Choice of Monetary Policy." *Monetary Policy Issues in the 1980s.* Federal Reserve Bank of Kansas City, 1982, pp. 47–76.

CHAPTER 36

Supply-Side Theories: Supply Shocks and "Real" Business Cycles

Chapter Objectives

This chapter deals with **aggregate supply**: what influences it, and how it influences the economy. When you finish studying this chapter you will understand and be able to explain:

1. What is meant by **supply-side macroeconomics** and the important role of **increasing productivity**.

2. How **supply-side policies** can be used to try to combat inflation, and how to illustrate this in the AD-AS diagram.

3. The meaning of a **negative supply shock** and how its effects depend on whether or not the money supply expands to accommodate the shock.

4. The meaning of a **positive supply shock** and how it brings lower prices and more output.

5. What is meant by **real business cycles**: macroeconomic fluctuations induced from the supply side.

A DIFFERENT VIEW: FOCUS ON THE "SUPPLY SIDE"

A significant development in economic theory during the 1970s and '80s was the shift in emphasis toward **"supply-side" economics**. The basic idea of supply-side economics is that the focus of theoretical macroeconomics on **aggregate demand** (total spending in the economy) may be insufficient. Perhaps attention also should be focused on *factors which directly influence the flow of real goods and services—the "real output" flow.*

In terms of the **circular flow diagram**, what supply-side economics says is this: "Don't focus so much attention on the spending flow—on investment injection inflows and savings withdrawal outflows and all that. Focus on *the volume of real output, and on what factors have a direct influence on that.*"

In terms of the equation of exchange (MV = PQ) the supply side emphasis says that perhaps we should focus on factors which influence the output (Q) directly, rather than focusing on what is happening on the MV side of the equation.

In terms of the **AD-AS framework**, it says that we should focus on factors which have a direct influence on the AS curve. *Perhaps aggregate supply could sometimes be the independent (causal) variable instead of the dependent variable.*

Attacking Inflation from the Supply Side

Suppose there is a problem of rapid inflation. Instead of *holding down the increase in aggregate demand* (the increase in the size of the spending flow) we could try to *increase aggregate supply.* If the productivity of the average worker in the economy could be increased by 10%, this would increase the aggregate quantity of output supplied by 10%. In terms of its inflation-fighting effect, this would have about the same effect as a 10% decrease in aggregate quantity demanded. But there's an important difference.

With a supply increase, the economy prospers and grows while the inflation problem is being solved. Demand-restricting policies tend to cause *reduced output, increased unemployment, and recession* during the time that the inflation rate is being brought down. The supply-side approach promises a much happier solution.

As you may have guessed, however, nobody has figured out how to get productivity to increase by 10% in a short period of time. But now you can see why "suppy-side" economics focuses its attention on *increasing worker productivity* and on ways to achieve that.

Supply-Side Conditions in the U.S. Economy

In the U.S. economy in the 1970s and early '80s, productivity growth was slow. In some years the growth rate dropped to about zero. When there's no increase in output per worker, and when wages are going up, inflation is the sure result.

When people are being paid more while their output is not increasing, that means that the cost of production (per unit of output) is going up. So either prices must be going up, or else businesses will suffer losses and cut back production. Output (and incomes) will fall. So as per-unit costs increase, we must have either (a) inflation, or (b) recession, or (c) some of both—called **stagflation**—and that's what we had in the late 1970s and early '80s. So there was good reason to want to do something to stimulate the growth of productivity.

"Supply-Side" Economics and "Demand-Side" Economics

The supply-side economists of the 1970s and '80s focused on the economic conditions of the time—completely different conditions than existed during the Great Depression when Keynes was offering his policy recommendations. During the 1930s the economy was glutted with supply. The demand was missing. During the late 1970s there was adequate demand, but **productivity** was not increasing. The supply to satisfy the demand, was missing. Clearly, this was a different kind of problem.

During the depression years, it made sense, both pragmatically and in Keynesian theory, to concentrate on the demand-side problem. The question then was: "How do we increase the spending flow enough to get all these products bought up and all these unemployed workers hired and get the economy back into production again?" **Supply-side** economics look at the other side of the question.

In the American economy of the 1970s and early 1980s the slow rate of productivity growth, together with increasing nominal incomes of the people, had led to a serious "supply-side" problem. The obvious way to solve this problem would be to increase productivity—produce more output—more supply.

Supply-Side Fiscal Policy and Reduced Government Regulations

The Reagan administration's approach to increasing productivity was (1) to **cut taxes** to stimulate productivity, and (2) to **reduce government regulations** to free up businesses to be more productive.

Taxes can retard productivity and economic growth. Taxes on a person's income are a "disincentive" to be productive. Taxes on businesses reduce the expected returns on investments. An investment which would return 20% before taxes would be much less attractive if taxes reduced the return to 10%. Many kinds of productivity-increasing investments would be feasible with low taxes or no taxes, which would not be feasible at higher tax rates.

And what about high-wage and high-salary and professional people? If taxes are taking a large portion of their marginal incomes, they have very little incentive to work more. For such people, taxes on income are a real incentive to cut back on their working hours, and to retire early. How much more would these highly productive people work if there were no taxes on their incomes? Nobody knows, of course.

Now you can see why a tax cut might stimulate productivity. But what about the *revenue loss*? Would you believe that there might not be any? Suppose the tax cut causes a big increase in productivity, output, and income. Then the higher income will generate more tax revenues. Is it possible that the higher income would generate more tax revenues than were lost by the rate cut? Some economists say "Yes"!

Suppose tax rates were cut by 10% and that caused incomes to increase by 20%. Then tax revenues would be higher than before the rate cut! That's what some supply-side theorists were saying in the early 1980s. One such theorist, Arthur Laffer, developed the hypothetical **Laffer Curve** to illustrate this idea.

The Hypothetical "Laffer Curve". The Laffer Curve illustrates the basic idea that as tax rates go up, productivity is discouraged. So (beyond some point) a *tax rate increase* will reduce output and incomes so much that it will cause a *decrease in tax revenues*. Under such circumstances a rate cut could stimulate the economy enough to generate increased revenue.

Figure 36-1 illustrates the hypothetical Laffer Curve. That figure indicates that as tax rates increase, government revenues increase to points a, b, and c. But after point c has been reached a rate increase will result in reduced revenues, as indicated by points d and e.

The hypothetical Laffer Curve is an interesting construction. The problem is that nobody has any real idea what the shape of this curve is, or whether we are located at point b or point d. Suppose I think we're at point d and you think we're at point b. Then if we want more revenues to try to balance the budget, I will be

---

**Figure 36-1. The Hypothetical "Laffer Curve": Tax Rate Cuts May
Bring either Increased or Decreased Revenue**

As tax rates are increased, beyond some point a rate
increase will slow the economy and dampen productivity growth so much that it will result in a total
revenue decrease.

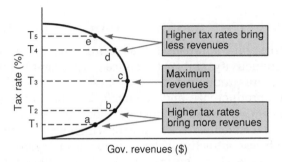

Gov. revenues ($)

If the economy is at point a or b (tax rate T_1 or T_2), a
rate increase will result in increased government revenues. But if the economy is at point c, d, or e (tax rate
T_3, T_4, or T_5), a rate increase will result in reduced
government revenues.

At rates above T_3, higher tax rates will depress
economic activity, productivity growth, and national
income so much that total tax revenues will decrease.
For example, if a rate increase of 10% results in a
reduction in income of 15%, tax revenues will be
smaller after the rate increase than before.

The Laffer Curve is an interesting and plausible
concept. But no clear "Laffer Curve effect" has been
identifiable from recent empirical evidence.

---

arguing for a rate cut and you will be arguing for a rate increase. Who would be
right? We don't know.

The Reagan Administration's "Supply-Side" Program. Presidential Candidate
Ronald Reagan campaigned on a platform which promised: reduced taxes, increased spending for national defence reduced federal spending for domestic
programs, lower federal deficits, and reduced government regulations on business. After his election, the phrase **supply-side economics** was popularized in the
press as "the new economics" of the Reagan administration.

The *Economic Recovery Tax Act of 1981* reduced tax rates on individual and
corporate incomes. This act was supposed to stimulate both savings and investment and increase the rate of growth of productivity. But the program didn't
produce the hoped-for results.

During 1981–82—the first two years of the Reagan three-year **supply-side tax
cuts**—the economy was in serious recession. Investment spending declined to the
lowest level since the depression years of the 1930s. The already large federal
budget deficit tripled in size. President Reagan and his supply-side advisers said

that the Fed's very tight and inflexible **monetary policy**—which brought very high and volatile interest rates, less investment and consumer spending and serious recession—had offset and cancelled the desired effects of their supply-side program.

By the late 1980s, productivity in the American economy was increasing more rapidly than in the 1978–1981 period. Average output per worker was increasing at the average annual rate of a little more than 2%. But that's low as compared with the years before 1978. The Reagan administration's attempted supply-side program probably helped some. But as of the late 1980s it had not produced the hoped-for results.

AD-AS ANALYSIS OF A SUPPLY-SIDE ANTI-INFLATION PROGRAM

Figure 36-2 uses AD-AS graphs to illustrate the kind of results the Reagan Administration was trying to achieve.

A successful supply-side anti-inflationary program requires (1) that ASlr be increased (shifted to the right) sufficiently to eliminate the inflationary pressures, and (2) that the supply-side policies do not stimulate aggregate demand and thereby exacerbate the inflationary problem which existed in the first place. Not easy objectives to achieve! Figure 36-2 illustrates the alternatives.

No Supply-Side Changes: Inflation

In figure 36-2, Panel A is an AD-AS graph showing the short-run and long-run effects of an increase in aggregate demand. Here there are no offsetting changes on the supply side. In the short run, both output and prices increase. But according to the **modern monetarist** model and the **natural rate** hypothesis, in the long run *the only effect of the increased AD is inflation.*

Complete Success: More Output, No Inflation

Panel B shows the effects of *a completely successful supply-side program.* Aggregate supply is increased (shifted to the right) far enough to completely eliminate the **inflationary gap**. Now *at the existing price level the aggregate quantity of output supplied at the "natural output rate" is exactly equal to the aggregate quantity of output demanded.* Increased output has come forth to equal the increased spending for output. There are no shortages—no "tight markets"—no reason for prices to rise.

The result shown in Panel B is a happy one. Inflation has been stopped, and real output and incomes (and standards of living) are higher than before. But unfortunately, the results shown in Panel B are very difficult—perhaps impossible—to achieve. One reason is because of likely **demand-side effects** of intended supply-side programs.

Suppose taxes are cut to try to stimulate productivity. The tax cut is sure to result in some increase in total spending—in aggregate demand. Even new spending for plant and equipment—which will increase aggregate supply in the long

Figure 36-2. Possible Effects of an Anti-Inflation Supply-Side Program

Panel A: Effects of an AD increase with no induced changes on the supply side.

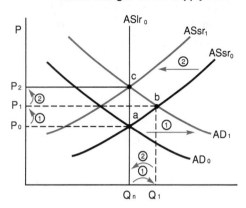

1. Initially, AD shifts from AD_0 to AD_1—perhaps because of an increase in the money supply, or inflationary expectations, or an increased government deficit, or for some other reason. In the short run the economy moves to point b. Prices increase from P_0 to P_1 and the quantity of output increases from Q_n to Q_1. But the output increase is only temporary.

2. In the long run, since the economy is operating above its natural rate, tightness in the labor and other input markets will push up wages and prices. So production costs will increase. That will cause ASsr to shift leftward from $ASsr_0$ to $ASsr_1$. As that happens, prices will rise from P_1 to P_2 and output will decrease from Q_1 back to Q_n—the natural rate. So in the long run the only effect of the AD increase is: inflation.

Panel B: Effects of an AD increase with a *completely successful* supply-side program.

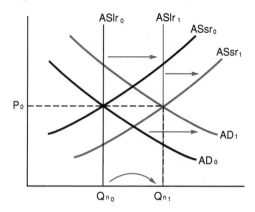

As AD is increasing, AS is also increasing. The economy is growing. Because AS is increasing as much as AD, there are no shortages and no inflationary pressures.

In this case, the supply-side policies succeed. Productivity and output increase. As AD is shifting rightward from AD_0 to AD_1, both ASsr and ASlr are shifting rightward—from $ASsr_0$ to $ASsr_1$ and from $ASlr_0$ to $ASlr_1$.

The natural rate of output increases from Q_{n0} to Q_{n1}. The price level remains at P_0. Here more output is demanded and more is supplied. There is no market tightness, no inflationary gap, and no inflation!

Panel C: Effects of a completely unsuccessful supply-side program.

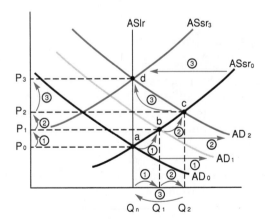

Here AS does not increase at all. The inflation is worsened by demand-side effects of the (intended) supply-side program.

1. AD_0 increases to AD_1 creating inflationary pressures and shifting the economy from point a to point b (to P_1, Q_1), bringing more output and higher prices. That's the same move as shown in Panel A.

2. Intended supply-side programs only succeed in further stimulating aggregate demand. AD shifts rightward from AD_1 to AD_2. In the short run the economy moves to point c (P_2, Q_2). Both output and prices increase more. Now the economy is operating far above its natural rate.

3. In the long run, as the overheated economy forces production costs to rise, $ASsr_0$ will shift leftward to $ASsr_3$. The economy will move to point d where prices are up to P_3 and output is back at Q_n—right where it was in the beginning.

This is a "worst case scenario." The programs intended to combat inflation by increasing AS, only succeeded in worsening inflation by further increasing AD.

Note: These graphs all assume that in the beginning the economy is operating at its natural rate (on ASlr), that wages and prices are flexible, and that AD is increasing, bringing inflationary pressures.

run—shows up in the short run as *an increase in aggregate demand*. So the happy results shown in Panel B could not be expected to occur in the short run. But in the long run? It might be possible.

Complete Failure: More Demand, No More Output—More Inflation!

Panel C in figure 36-2 shows the opposite results from Panel B. Panel C shows the worst possible outcome from a supply-side program. In this case, aggregate supply has not been increased. The only effect has been *to increase aggregate demand and force prices higher*—some in the short run and more in the long run.

In the real world, which results should we expect? Panel B? Or Panel C? Most likely, somewhere between the two, with short-run effects being more like Panel C and long-run effects (if the program is well designed) more like Panel B.

EFFECTS OF A NEGATIVE SUPPLY SHOCK: MONETARY ACCOMMODATION? OR NOT?

Most of the macroeconomic theory you have been reading about so far has been focused on *aggregate demand*. Even in the sections you just read—about using supply-side policies to try to combat inflation—the initial inflationary thrust came from the demand side—from the shift of the AD curve from AD_1 to AD_2 in figure 36-2. But inflation can also be caused by a supply-side disturbance: a **supply shock**.

Suppose the economy is operating at the "natural rate." What if some exogenous (from outside) change forces up production costs and causes the ASsr curve to shift to the left? No matter what caused it, this would be called a "supply shock." After the shock, at the existing price level *the aggregate quantity supplied (AQS) would be less than the aggregate quantity demanded (AQD)*. Shortages would exist and prices would begin to rise.

The Oil and Agricultural Supply Shocks of the 1970s

From previous chapters you already know about **cost-push inflation**. Wages and other input costs are pushed upward (for whatever reason) and **ASsr shifts leftward**. After the ASsr shift, quantity supplied is less than quantity demanded. So prices go up. The most outstanding example in modern times of a cost-push-type supply shock is what happened to the price of oil between the early 1970s and the early 1980s.

In the early 1970s the world price of crude oil was pushed up by some 400%. Then it was increased several times during the 1970s, finally doubling again in 1979. The total increase in the price of oil between the early '70s and early '80s amounted to about 1400%.

At the same time, during several of these years there were disappointing harvests of various agricultural products so that the prices of these inputs moved up sharply. The question: Were these supply shocks responsible for the double-digit inflation rates which existed in the late 1970s and early '80s? Or was monetary expansion during this period the culprit?

The Inflationary Effect Depends on Monetary Accommodation

A negative supply shock shifts the ASsr curve leftward. Suddenly at the existing price level AQS is less than AQD. Shortages! So prices go up. The economy moves to a new short-run equilibrium with (a) less output and (b) higher prices. Recession with inflation? Yes. You know the name: **stagflation**.

Now if you'll take a look at figure 36-3, in Panel A you'll see the stagflation picture—not a very pleasant one. However, if a high degree of wage and price flexibility exists so that the the short run is a very short period of time—perhaps a few months—then all we need to do is wait for the ASsr curve to shift back to its original position and return the economy to its natural employment and output rate. Then all will be well. But suppose wages and prices don't move down very quickly. Then what?

In the Keynesian model of the macroeconomy, wages and prices do not move downward quickly. So the economy might go on with high unemployment and low output and income, quarter after quarter—perhaps even year after year. Keynesian economists would say that the Federal Reserve should permit the money supply to expand. That would tend to stimulate aggregate demand and bring the economy back to full employment. In figure 36-3 Panel 8 illustrates the effect of this **monetary accommodation** within the assumptions of the modern monetarist model.

Figure 36-3.   The Effect of a Negative Supply Shock Depends on Whether or Not the Money Supply Expands

<u>Panel A</u>: <u>No Monetary Accommodation</u>. Increased production cost shifts the ASsr curve leftward. But with no monetary accommodation, in the long run, slack in the economy will bring down production costs and shift it back.

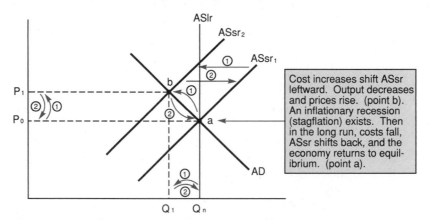

Cost increases shift ASsr leftward. Output decreases and prices rise. (point b). An inflationary recession (stagflation) exists. Then in the long run, costs fall, ASsr shifts back, and the economy returns to equilibrium. (point a).

When ASsr shifts leftward from $ASsr_1$ to $ASsr_2$, the economy moves from point a to point b. Output decreases from Q_n to Q_1 and prices rise from P_0 to P_1. Serious recession, high unemployment, and also inflation. **Stagflation**. Bad scene!

The modern monetarist model and the "natural rate" hypothesis conclude that in the long run, because of the depressed conditions, wages and prices will fall and bring down the cost of production. So ASsr will increase (shift back to the right to $ASsr_1$) and return the economy to point a, with full employment (Q_n) and at the original price level (P_0).

continued

Figure 36-3. *Continued*

Panel B: The Supply Shock Is Accommodated: **Monetarist Model**
After the supply shock (leftward shift of ASsr), the Fed buys
bonds and pushes new reserves into the banking system. So
the money supply expands, AD shifts to the right and returns
the economy to full employment with higher prices.

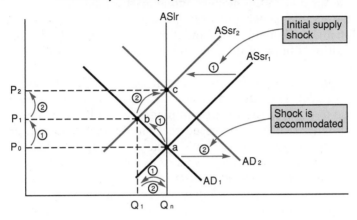

The supply shock shifts ASsr from $ASsr_1$ to $ASsr_2$ and moves the economy to point b. Stagflation. Then the money supply increases and shifts
aggregate demand to AD_2 and moves the economy to point c. Prices go up
to P_2 and output goes up to Q_n. The economy returns to long-run equilibrium, but with a higher price level than before—partly because of the
supply shock and partly because of the monetary accommodation.

Panel C: The Supply Shock is accommodated: **Keynesian Model.** With
Keynesian-shaped ASsr curves the monetary accommodation
and rightward shift of the AD curve returns the economy to full
employment and brings little or no additional inflation.

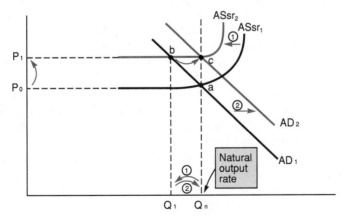

Here the monetary expansion accommodates the shock and validates
the increased price level—from P_0 to P_1. Following the supply shock
this new price level (P_1) would be accepted as the new existing
condition. There would be no attempt to keep the economy depressed
to force prices back to P_0.

In the Keynesian model, the shift of AD from AD_1 to AD_2 would
not cause prices to go up any more because there is plenty of slack in
the labor and product markets. You can see that from the horizontal
segment of the ASsr curve.

The Effect of Monetary Accommodation Depends on the Slope of the ASsr Curve

Panel B shows that in the **modern monetarist model** the monetary accommodation of the supply shock not only validated the new price level (P_1). It also resulted in an additional burst of inflation, from P_1 to P_2. In this model, the extent of this additional burst of inflation depends on the assumed upward slope of the ASsr curve.

But suppose the curves were drawn according to the assumptions of the Keynesian model. Then this additional increase in the price level would be slight, if it occurred at all. In the **Keynesian model**, when there is high unemployment, an increase in AD brings increased real employment, output, and income and little or no increase in prices. That's what you see in Panel C of figure 36-3.

Clearly, in the case of negative supply shocks, as in the case of just about everything else, the expected results of a given change—as well as the most desirable policy alternative—depends very much on your "assumed model" of the economy. Assumptions regarding the flexibility of wages and prices are especially critical.

A POSITIVE SUPPLY SHOCK: INCREASING PRODUCTIVITY SHIFTS BOTH ASsr AND ASlr TO THE RIGHT

On the positive side, new and better technology, increasing worker productivity, and anything else which *reduces input cost per unit of output* brings a rightward shift in both the ASsr and ASlr curves.

New technology can bring increased productivity and lower per-unit cost. Such developments bring *permanent increases in aggregate supply*—rightward shifts in the ASsr and ASlr curves. Such shifts indicate *a higher natural rate of output* for the economy. And in fact, each year as the economy grows and its output capacity increases, the ASsr and ASlr curves shift to the right.

Figure 36-4 illustrates the result of an important **technological breakthrough** which lowers the cost of production. The ASsr and ASlr curves shift far to the right so that *the economy's natural rate of output and income is much larger than before*. We now have more output and lower prices too! Our standards of living just took a great leap forward.

SUPPLY-INDUCED FLUCTUATIONS: "REAL BUSINESS CYCLES

The graphs you were just looking at in figure 36-3 and 36-4 give extreme examples of **real business cycles.** The term "business cycle" refers to the recurrent speed-ups and slow downs of the macroeconomy. In the speed up, or expansion phase of the cycle, the economy operates for some period of time above its long-range growth trend. In the slowdown or recession phase, it operates below its trend.

Figure 36-4. The Effects of a New Technology Breakthrough Illustrated in the AD-AS Diagram

In this case, new kinds of computer assisted production and robots brought lower production costs. Both the ASsr and ASlr curves shift to the right. The result? More output and lower prices too!

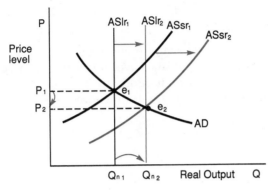

Improved technology reduces the cost of production. It's now profitable for firms to produce more, so that's just what they do. The rightward shift of the ASsr curve from $ASsr_1$ to $ASsr_2$ shows this. As the increased quantities flow into the product markets, surpluses develop and prices are pushed down.

As the quantity of real output increases from Q_{n1} to Q_{n2}, that forces the price level down from P_1 to P_2. The lower prices induce AQD to increase to Q_{n2}. That eliminates the surpluses and "clears the markets."

The new technology enables the economy to produce more output, and with no shortages in the labor and other input markets. The natural rate of output of the economy now is larger than before. That's what is show by the shift of ASlr from $ASlr_1$ to ASl_2. In the long run the economy is in a new equilibrium at point e_2, with lower prices (P_2) and greater output (Q_{n2}).

In a business cycle, many different industries speed up and slow down at the same time. The question: What causes this to happen? Several things can. Up to this point, most of the investigation of causes has been focused on changes in **aggregate demand**. Real business cycle theory focuses on the supply side.

In figure 36-3, Panel A shows a serious recession, together with inflation, which resulted not from monetary or spending influences, but *from a real, supply-side change in the economy.* Real business cycle theory is concerned with explaining the effects of various kinds of **supply-side causes** of economic fluctuations.

In real business cycle theory it is not necessary to have a massive OPEC-type shock to generate a cycle. There are all kinds of relatively minor, diffuse shocks resulting from technological change, labor supply changes, etc. which are constantly occuring in a dynamic real-world economy. A basic idea underlying real business cycle theory is that these dynamic supply-side changes, especially when they occur in several industries at once, can trigger an acceleration or a deceleration of the macroeconomy.

And what about *money* in the real business cycle models? It doesn't play any causal role at all. All it can do is to accommodate—or not accommodate—the effects of the real supply-side influences.

Real Business Cycle Theory: A New Development in Theoretical Macroeconomics

The development of real business cycle theory has been very recent—almost entirely in the 1980s. Some economists have not been satisfied with the past theories and have aimed their research efforts in this new direction. This new focus is on causal influences occuring within the *real flow*—not the *spending flow*.

Real-Flow Changes Can Cause Spending-Flow Changes

It has long been recognized that changes in the *real flow*—units of goods and services being produced—can bring changes in the size of the money flow. Remember Say's Law? "Supply creates its own demand." What that means is: *The size of the real flow determines the size of the spending flow*: as output increases, incomes increase—so spending increases. So you can see that this supply-side focus certainly is not new.

How important are *supply shocks, innovations, allocative disturbances* (e.g., sharp demand increases in some industries with sharp decreases in others), and other *real changes* in the economy in generating macroeconomic ups and downs? Most of the real business cycle models conclude that these supply-side, real-flow fluctuations are of significant importance.

Until recently these influences have been largely overlooked in the predominantly *demand-side spending-flow-focused macroeconomic models. As we come to the end of the 1980s, real business cycle models have not yet had a very significant impact on the overall body of macroeconomic theory. But it is receiving increasing attention.*[1]

SUMMARY

- During the past decade there's been some shift in emphasis in macroeconomic theory toward focusing on the supply side. **Supply side economics** became the "new economics" of the Reagan administration.

---

[1] For some recent ideas on the development of real business cycle theory, read the three papers by Davis, Long and Plosser, and Christiano, in the American Economic Association Symposium: "Real Business Cycle Theory: What Does It Explain," *The American Economic Review*, vol. 77, no. 2 (May, 1987), pp. 326–41; and also J. B. Long and C. I. Plosser, "Real Business Cycles," *Journal of Political Economy*, vol. 91 (February, 1983), pp. 39–69; also Katherine Abraham and Lawrence F. Katz, "Cyclical Unemployment: Sectoral Shifts or Aggregate Disturbances?," *Journal of Political Economy*, vol. 94 (June, 1986), pp. 507–22; and Steve J. Davis, "Allocative Disturbances and Temporal Asymmetry in Labor Market Fluctuations," University of Chicago Working Paper Series No. 86–38, 1986.

- A supply side **anti-inflation program** attempts to shift both the short-run and long-run aggregate supply curves to the right to eliminate the inflationary gap. The danger is that the policies will increase aggregate demand and worsen the inflationary gap.

- A decrease in short-run aggregate supply would be called a **negative supply shock** and would cause **stagflation**: increased unemployment with increased prices.

- If the negative supply shock is accommodated by increased M and increased AD, full employment will return but prices will be higher.

- A positive supply shock would result from a significant increase in productivity—e.g., a new technological breakthrough.

- The likely effects of anti-inflation supply-side programs, and of accommodating negative supply shocks as well, depend significantly on which model of the macroeconomy you choose: monetarist, new classical, nonclassical, Keynesian, or what.

- **Real business cycle theories** focus on supply-side influences as an important cause of macroeconomic fluctuations. This has become an area of new emphasis in macroeconomic theory during the 1980s.

Important Principles, Issues, Concepts, Terms

Demand side economics

Supply side economics

Supply-side fiscal policies

Supply-side anti-inflation program

Economic Recovery Tax Act of 1981

Reagan administration's supply-side program

Demand-side effects of supply-side policies

Cost-push inflation in the AD-AS diagram

Negative supply shock

Positive supply shock

Monetary accommodation of negative supply shock

Real business cycles

Laffer Curve

Questions

1. Explain carefully the difference between the supply-side focus and the demand-side focus in trying to understand why the macroeconomy speeds up or slows down.

2. Do high and volatile interest rates interfere with supply-side economic policies? Explain and discuss.

3. What are some of the different things policymakers might do to try to attack inflation from the supply side? Which of these policies do you think would be most likely to be successful? Explain why.

4. Explain the logic of the Laffer Curve, and then explain why its use is somewhat limited as a guide to public policy.

5. Explain, and use an AD-AS diagram to illustrate why a supply side anti-inflationary program is not likely to be very successful in the short-run, even though it might be successful in the long run.

6. Following a negative supply shock, most Keynesian economists would recommend monetary accommodation, while most monetarist economists would not. Explain what all this means, and then explain why the policy recommendations of the Keynesians are so different from those of the monetarists. Use AD-AS diagrams to illustrate your answer.

7. Explain why the effect of monetary accommodation of a negative supply shock would depend on the slope of the ASsr curve. Illustrate with graphs.

8. Explain the effects of a new technological breakthrough, and illustrate in the AD-AS diagram.

9. Explain what is meant by "real" business cycles. What does the term "real" mean in this context? Do you thing there have been any indications of real business cycles in the American economy during the past two decades? Discuss.

Suggested Readings

Barro, R. H. "Intertemporal Substitution and the Business Cycle." in K. Brunner and A. H. Meltzer, eds., *Supply Shocks, Incentives and National Wealth.* Carnegie-Rochester Conference Series on Public Policy 144, pp. 237–68.

Burnanke, Ben S. "Nonmonetary Effects of the Financial Crisis in the Propagation of the Great Depression." *American Economic Review.* (June 1983), 257–76.

Froyen, Richard T., and Roger N. Waud. "Real Business Cycles and the Lucas Paradigm." *Economic Inquiry* 26 (2). (April 1988), 183–201.

Hansen, G. D. "Invisible Labor and the Business Cycle." *Journal of Monetary Economics* 16. pp. 309–27.

King, Robert G., and Charles Plosser. "Money, Credit, and Prices in a Real Business Cycle." *American Economic Review.* (June 1984), 363–80.

Kydland, Finn E. and Edward C. Prescott. "Time to Build and Aggregate Fluctuations." *Econometrica* 50. (January 1982), 1345–70.

Long, John B. Jr., and Charles I. Plosser. "Real Business Cycles." *Journal of Political Economy* 91. (February 1983), 39–69.

Lucas, R. E. Jr. "Understanding Business Cycles." in K. Brunner and A. H. Meltzer, eds., *Stabilization of the Domestic and International Economy.* Carnegie-Rochester Conference Series on Public Policy 5, pp. 7–29.

Manuelli, Rodolfo E., Edward C. Prescott, and Lawrence H. Summers each presented papers in: Federal Reserve Bank of Minneapolis, *Quarterly Review,* Fall 1986, 10 (4). This entire issue was devoted to real busines cycle theory. The titles of the papers:
Manuelli: "Modern Business Cycle Analysis: A Guide to the Prescott-Summers Debate."
Prescott: "Theory Ahead of Business Cycle Measurement."
Summers: "Some Skeptical Observations on Real Business Cycle Theory."
Prescott: "Response to a Skeptic."

Meltzer, A. H. "Size, Persistence and Interrelation of Nominal and Real Shocks: Some Evidence from Four Countries." *Journal of Monetary Economics* 17 (1). (January 1986), 161–94.

Solow: Robert M. "Unemployment: Getting the Questions Right." *Economica* 53 (supplement), pp. s23–s34.

Thurow, Lester L. *Dangerous Currents: The State of Economics.* New York: Random House, 1984.

Walsh, Carl E. "'Real' Business Cycles." Federal Reserve Bank of San Francisco *Weekly Letter.* January 30, 1987.

Zarnowitz, Victor. "Recent Work on Business Cycles in Historical Perspective: A Review of Theories and Evidence." *The Journal of Economic Literature* 23 (2). (June 1985), 523–80.

PART IX

International Banking and Financial Markets: Rapid Global Integration into a One-World System

Throughout this book you have been constantly aware of the international, "globalized" nature of the modern world's money-banking-financial system. By now, surely you have a "feel" for the one-world nature of the modern-world economy and of the global financial system which permits the world economy to function efficiently. So what is left to do in the area of international money-banking-finance? Just this: To take a more detailed look at this globalized financial system and how it works.

You need to know something about exchange rates and how they work and about the balance of payments and what we can see from that. You need to know about the markets in which the currencies of different nations are traded (by the billions) every day. And you need to know about the interlocking "spider-web network" of banks and other financial institutions which encircles the globe and provides for instantaneous asset exchanges and funds transfers twenty-four hours a day.

In Chapter 37 there's an explanation of the international balance of payments and its importance in understanding international financial flows. Also in Chapter 37 you will read about foreign exchange markets—what they are and how they function.

In the final chapter (38) you will see an overview of international banking—of the network which ties together all of the diverse and widely scattered units of the worldwide financial system. There you will be reading about multinational banking and international correspondent banking.

After you study Part IX you will have an understanding of the world's globalized financial system—how it is all tied together, and how it functions.

CHAPTER 37

International Trade and the Functioning of the Foreign Exchange Market

Chapter Objectives

During the 1970s and '80s the growth of international trade has been explosive. International finance has grown commensurately, and an efficient global money-banking-financial system has developed. That's what you'll be reading about in this chapter and the next. After studying this chapter you will understand and be able to explain:

1. How the American economic and financial system has become an integral part of the **worldwide system**.

2. Exactly what is meant by the **foreign exchange market**, how it functions, and how supply and demand influence exchange rates.

3. The idea of the **international balance of payments** and how this balance (or imbalance) influences the supply of and demand for each nation's currency.

4. Other factors which influence the supply of and demand for a nation's currency in the foreign exchange markets.

5. What is meant by **managed floating** exchange rates and how floating rates are "managed."

6. Spot and forward exchange rates, and the **interest rate parity** theory for explaining the difference between spot and forward rates.

7. The **purchasing power parity** theory of exchange rates.

EXPLOSIVE GROWTH OF THE "WORLD ECONOMY"

Recent growth in international trade truly has been explosive. In the early 1970s, the total value of U.S. imports plus exports amounted to less than 10% of GNP. By the early 1980s—only ten years later—that percentage figure had more than doubled. The actual dollar value of imports plus exports (in current dollars) had more than *quintupled*.

During the 1980s that explosive rate of growth has continued. By the late 1980s the annual value of sales to foreigners by American businesses plus purchases by Americans from foreign businesses was approaching *one trillion dollars*.[1]

The other nations of the free world—both highly developed and less developed countries (LDCs)—have been participating in this explosive growth of international commerce. And during the 1980s the so-called Communist nations—China, Eastern Europe, the USSR—were also rapidly expanding their trade with the free world.

This explosive growth of international trade and worldwide competition is having a profound impact on the U.S. economy and throughout the world. We now have in many respects an **integrated world economy**.

The "One-World" Money and Banking System

There is no aspect of the American economy which has not felt the impact of this new global economic integration and competition. But nowhere has the impact been more profound than in the area of money and banking and the financial markets.

You might say that the one most "one world" aspect of the world economy is the world's integrated financial system. Truly it's a global "spiderweb network" which reaches everywhere, links all places throughout the world, and provides instantaneous communications and billions of dollars of funds transfers every day, twenty-four hours a day.

Could the explosive growth in world trade have occurred without a highly efficient mechanism to perform the **international medium of exchange** function? Of course not. As trade was expanding, the exchange mechanism was expanding too—becoming much larger and more efficient in meeting the sophisticated needs of global finance.

Trade Occurs Between Buyers and Sellers

In international trade, do the flows of goods and services—and the flows of funds—occur *between nations*? Not really. It's more accurate (and clarifying) to think of it as flows of goods and services (and of funds) between buyers and sellers. The buyers want the products they want at the best deal they can get—and regardless of whether the seller is on the same block, across town, across the nation, or across the ocean. And the seller wants to sell the product. The geographical location of the buyer isn't important.

That's the basic economics of the situation. But an efficient **medium of exchange** mechanism is needed to permit it to happen. And there's a complication here: The kind of money (national currency) the buyer in one country has is not the kind of money the seller in the other country wants.

Suppose the buyer wants to pay in American dollars and the seller wants to receive payment in Australian dollars. What then? The next section explains that.

---

[1] Up-to-date figures on the volume of foreign trade can be found in recent issues of the *Survey of Current Business*, published monthly by the U.S. Department of Commerce. Summary statistics on foreign trade can also be found in the Statistical Tables in the *Federal Reserve Bulletin* (monthly).

Exchanging One Nation's Currency for Another: Buying Foreign Exchange

When an American buyer wants to buy something from an Australian seller, the buyer's American dollars must be exchanged for Australian dollars. Every day millions of American dollars are used to buy the currencies of other nations. People, businesses, and governments in the United States are buying goods and services from people and businesses in other countries. So they must buy the other countries' money to pay for all these things. How does it happen? Through the banking system.

The large American banks have deposits of francs in French banks, pounds in British banks, lire in Italian banks, Deutsche marks in German banks, yen in Japanese banks—in fact, deposits of local currencies in banks all over the world. And small American banks have correspondent relationships with these large banks so they can get any foreign money they want from them.

No matter where you live, chances are you can go to your bank and buy some foreign money—called **buying foreign exchange**. What happen is, your bank sells you a check drawn in any kind of foreign money you want. Then you can send the check to the foreign seller to pay for whatever you want to buy.

It's this need to exchange one kind of money for another that makes international trade different from domestic trade. And it's because of this minor complication that it's necessary to understand **international finance** and the **balance of payments**.

THE INTERNATIONAL BALANCE OF PAYMENTS

Every day, billions of U.S. dollars are being placed in the hands of foreigners by American individuals, businesses, and governments. Why? To pay foreigners for goods and services we want to buy from them, and to invest in assets—stocks, bonds, real estate, whatever—in foreign countries.

Also every day billions of dollars are being returned to American individuals, businesses, and governments to pay for goods and services foreigners want to buy from this country and for investments in U.S. assets. The U.S. international balance of payments records the dollar amount of all of these transactions.

The balance of payments is an accounting statement which shows the ultimate money-flow results of all the transactions between all of the buyers and sellers in one country and buyers and sellers located in all of the other countries throughout the world.

Whenever all of the dollars being paid out to foreigners are exactly equal to and offset by dollars being paid back, the U.S. balance of payments is in balance. But whenever the outflows and inflows of dollars are not equal, the balance of payments is out of balance.

Debits and Credits and Deficits and Surpluses

Each transaction which places American dollars in foreign hands is a **debit item** on the international balance of payments. Each transaction which causes foreigners to place the dollars back in Amercian hands it a **credit item**. When total debits are less than total credits then the balance of payments shows a **surplus**—more dollars coming back than going out. When total debits exceed total credits the balance of payments shows a **deficit**—more dollars going out than coming back.

Current Items and Capital Items

On the balance of payments, **current items** are transactions which do not create *future claims*. **Capital items** do create future claims. Examples:

Examples of current items:

a. buying goods from foreigners.

b. buying services from foreigners.

c. giving dollars to foreigners.

Examples of capital items:

a. investing in foreign assets.

b. lending to foreigners.

c. depositing dollars in foreign banks.

As you can see, all capital items create future claims, and will result in a future return flow of dollars.

What Happens When the Balance Doesn't Balance?

Suppose Americans are buying a lot more imported goods than foreigners are buying from the United States. Many more dollars are being pushed into the hands of foreigners than are coming back to buy U.S. goods and services. What happens?

Most of those dollars come back as investments in the United States. That's what has been happening throughout the 1980s when the U.S. trade deficits have been running in excess of $100 billion per year. Foreign investment in the United States has used up most of those surplus dollars. That's why so much property in the United States—and a sizeable portion of the U.S. government debt—is now owned by foreigners. And that's why the United States is now the worlds largest **net debtor** nation.

But what happens if foreign holders of dollars don't want to buy American goods and don't want to invest in U.S. assets? What if they want to exchange their surplus dollars for their own nation's currency so they can pay the rent, for example? And suppose everyone is already holding all of the dollars they want to hold. Then who is going to be willing to accept more dollars in exchange for local currency? You could guess: Nobody!—except maybe the central banks?

The Role of "Official Transactions"

The U.S. Fed and all other central banks hold "foreign currency reserves"—deposits of the currencies of other nations. When there's a surplus of dollars the U.S. Fed and the other central banks can enter the foreign exchange markets and buy up dollars and pay out their holdings of local currencies. These central bank transactions are called **official transactions**—undertaken from time to time to offset temporary surpluses or shortages of any one nation's currency.

The Fed's operations in the foreign exchange markets work very much like domestic open market operations in government securities. The Fed buys to hold prices up and sells to hold prices down. But there's one big difference.

When the Fed buys bonds in the domestic market it pays with its own credit (new bank reserves) which it can create in unlimited amounts. But it can't use its credit to buy dollars in the foreign exchange markets. It must pay out some of its foreign exchange reserves: foreign currencies, or gold, or its deposits of SDRs at the IMF. (SDRs are explained in chapter 22.) So the Fed can't buy any more dollars than it has reserves (or can borrow reserves) to pay for.

A Surplus of a Currency Will Push Down Its International Value

Suppose the U.S. balance of payments runs a big deficit year after year. A constant flow of surplus American dollars would be pouring into the hands of foreigners. Could the Fed and the foreign central banks buy up all of these billions of dollars? Year after year? And prevent the dollar's value from falling in the foreign exchange markets? Of course not.

When a nation runs a chronic balance of payments deficit, eventually the international value of that nation's currency must fall. Why? It's obvious. Too much supply of that nation's currency. And too little demand.

Exchange Rate Adjustments: The Automatic "Self-Equilibrating" Mechanism

When the international value of a nation's currency falls, then that currency will no longer buy as much in world markets. Suppose the international value of the U.S. dollar falls. That means we must pay more dollars to get British pounds or French francs, etc. Since we must pay more to get the foreign money, it becomes more expensive to buy imported goods. As a nation's currency depreciates in foreign exchange markets, that not only raises import prices. It also lowers export prices. The result: Imports are discouraged. Exports are encouraged.

When a nation's balance of payments is running a chronic deficit, the problem tends to solve itself automatically. Here's how:

a.   The surplus of that nation's currency pushes its value down.

b.   Imports tend to decrease and exports, to increase.

c.   Ultimately trade moves into balance and the deficit is eliminated.

The next section takes a closer look at the foreign exchange markets where all of this is going on all the time.

THE WORLDWIDE FOREIGN EXCHANGE MARKET

The foreign exchange market is the largest financial market in the world. It isn't unusual for a total volume of more than $250 billion to be traded in one day. The main centers of the market are London, New York, Frankfort, and Tokyo. But there are many other places where the buying and selling of different currencies is going on.

Currency Trading: Worldwide, Instantaneous, Around-the-Clock

All of these market centers, large and small, are electronically interlinked for instantaneous trading. The relative prices of the various currencies are changing in response to supply and demand conditions from moment to moment throughout the day (and night), just as the prices of stocks on the New York Stock Exchange rise and fall from moment to moment. The interlinked market centers keep the exchange rates between the different currencies "in sync" at all times and at all places throughout the world.

International Banks Are the Major Traders

The major traders in the foreign exchange market are the international banks, which operate both as dealers (holding inventories of different currencies) and brokers (buying or selling different currencies in response to customer orders).

The international banks sometimes accept some "risk exposure," taking either a long or a short position in one currency or another. But in general their revenues are generated by the difference between the price at which they buy a given kind of currency, and the price at which they sell it.

For example, suppose a bank is dealing in marks and someone wants to use dollars to buy marks. The bank might charge a rate of 1.8030 for the marks it sells. But when someone wants to sell marks to the bank (and get dollars) the bank might only pay 1.8020 for the marks.

That one-tenth of one cent spread between the buying price and the selling price doesn't seem to be a large commission. But consider this: The basic unit for trading foreign exchange is large. Usually for the pound it's £100,000 (that's about $180,000) and for West German Deutschmarks, DM 200,000 (about $120,000). Also several of these units frequently are traded at the same time. So a markup of one-tenth of a cent generates a significant return.

Foreign exchange trading is going on constantly. As North American markets are closing, the oriental markets are opening. As the oriental markets are closing, the European markets are opening, and before the European markets close, the North American markets are open again.

Every night at midnight people in New York are trading in Tokyo. And at 5 a.m. they're trading in London. And it all happens just as quickly and efficiently as if the traders were in Tokyo or London. That's the kind of financial world we're living in now. Mind boggling? For my generation, *truly*! For yours? Maybe not.

Exchanging a Demand Deposit from One Currency to Another

A transaction in the foreign exchange market consists of exchanging a demand deposit denominated in one national currency for a demand deposit denominated in another national currency. For example, suppose a major oil refinery wants to buy a tankerload of crude oil which is priced in German marks. The American refining company will exchange a dollar demand deposit (probably borrowed from either an American bank (borrowed dollars) or a foreign bank (borrowed Eurodollars) for a demand deposit in marks to pay for the oil.

In this example the foreign exchange market is "serving the needs of trade." But only about 10% of the transactions in the foreign exchange market are generated from trade. The other 90% are related to financial transactions—portfolio adjustments.

Investors are constantly shifting from one kind of currency to another when it appears profitable to do so. If interest rates rise in West Germany, investors will move their highly liquid assets into Deutsch marks where they can earn the higher interest.

Speculation and Arbitrage

Foreign exchange speculators watch for signals regarding the direction of change of exchange rates. They move very quickly out of one kind of currency and into another in response to these signals.

Also, arbitragers watch for slight differences—for example, a difference of one one-hundredth of a cent—in exchange rates between one market center and another. They take advantage of these differences by buying in the lower-priced center and simultaneously selling in the higher-priced center. So they immediately lock in a profit generated by the spread. Such transactions push the exchange rates in the two markets into precise equality.

Spot and Forward Exchange Rates

A spot foreign exchange transaction means that it is a "present time" transaction. However, the actual exchange of deposits occurs two business days after the date of the contract. A forward transaction results in an exchange of deposits at some specific future date.

Most foreign exchange transactions are forward, rather than spot, and involve a prearranged exchange of deposits—perhaps 30-days, 60-days, six months, or one year in the future. But a foreign exchange trader can arrange a forward contract for any number of days desired. These forward exchange contracts do not have standardized amounts or maturities as do the **currency futures** contracts which are traded on the futures and options exchanges.

The Forward Rate Is Influenced by Relative Interest Rates

The relationship between the spot and the forward exchange rate is influenced by the relative rates of interest for short-term funds between the two countries whose currency is being exchanged. In general (*ceteris paribus*) an investor would prefer to "stay for as long as possible in the currency which pays the most interest."

Suppose you know you are going to need to pay 2 million Deutsch marks to buy a shipment of oil 60 days from now. You would like to establish a definite price for those Deutsch marks to eliminate the risk of changes in the exchange rate. Should you buy marks in the spot market and hold them for 60 days? Or should you buy in the forward market for delivery to you in 60 days?

Suppose the spot and forward rates were identical. And suppose short term interest rates in both Germany and the United States were identical. Then it wouldn't make any difference whether you bought spot or forward marks.

But suppose U.S. short-term interest rates were 10% and German rates were only 5%. Then you would want to keep your money in dollars, earning 10% for the sixty days. On the day you need to spend the marks to pay for the oil, that's the day you want to exchange your dollars for marks. So you would buy 60-day forward marks. That's what you would do, and that's what everybody else would do.

When you and everyone else are demanding marks in the forward market, the forward price of marks is going to rise. And when nobody is demanding marks in the spot market, the price of marks in the spot market is going to fall. How far will the forward price rise? And the spot price fall? You know the answer: Until the spread between the spot price and the forward price is just great enough to offset the interest rate differential between dollars and marks.

The "Interest Rate Parity" Theory

Now you know what is called the **interest rate parity theory**. It says that the spread between the spot rate and the forward rate (*ceteris paribus*) will be exactly large enough to offset the spread between short-term interest rates in the two countries.

If interest rates on U.S. dollars are highter, then the forward price of marks will be higher than the spot price—enough higher to eliminate the profitability of remaining in dollars to earn the higher rate on dollars. Alternatively, if the interest rate on marks is higher, then the forward exchange rate for marks will be lower than the spot rate—enough lower to eliminate the profitability of shifting immediately into marks to earn the higher rate on marks.

Exhibit 37-1 shows an example which illustrates all of this. Study that exhibit and the explanations and you'll understand very well the distinction between spot and forward rates.

THE PURCHASING POWER PARITY THEORY OF EXCHANGE RATES

The idea of the **purchasing power parity** theeory is that exchange rates will tend to automatically adjust to where you can trade your currency for any other currency and still buy just as much goods as before. Here's an example.

Suppose I exchange my $10 for some other kind of national currency. Then I should be able to buy just as many goods and services in that foreign country with that foreign currency as I would have been able to buy with my $10 in this country. If the American dollar and the Canadian dollar are exchanging one-for-one, that means that (according to the purchasing power parity theory), $10 Canadian will buy exactly the same quantity of goods in Canada as $10 U.S. will buy in the United States.

Suppose the exchange rate happened to be $2 U.S. equals $1 Canadian. Then you have to pay $20 to buy $10 Canadian. But the theory says that you should be

Exhibit 37-1. The "Foreign Exchange" Table Published Daily in *The Wall Street Journal*

FOREIGN EXCHANGE

Monday, June 22, 1987

The New York foreign exchange selling rates below apply to trading among banks in amounts of $1 million and more, as quoted at 3 p.m. Eastern time by Bankers Trust Co. Retail transactions provide fewer units of foreign currency per dollar.

Country	U.S. $ equiv. Mon.	Fri.	Currency per U.S. $ Mon.	Fri.
Argentina (Austral) ..	.5817	.6013	1.7190	1.6630
Australia (Dollar)	.7215	.7220	1.3360	1.3850
Austria (Schilling) ...	.07740	.07782	12.92	12.85
Belgium (Franc)				
Commercial rate ..	.02624	.02646	38.11	37.80
Financial rate	.02607	.02641	38.35	37.86
Brazil (Cruzado)	.02372	.02369	42.16	42.21
Britain (Pound)	1.5895	1.6120	.6291	.6203
30-Day Forward .	1.5871	1.6097	.6301	.6212
90-Day Forward .	1.5816	1.6042	.6323	.6234
180-Day Forward .	1.5741	1.5983	.6253	.6257
Canada (Dollar)	.7503	.7467	1.3328	1.3393
30-Day Forward .	.7496	.7459	1.3341	1.3406
90-Day Forward .	.7478	.7443	1.3372	1.3436
180-Day Forward .	.7458	.7422	1.3408	1.3473
Chile (Official rate) ...	.004576	.004576	218.51	218.51
China (Yuan)	.2693	.2693	3.7128	3.7128
Colombia (Peso) ...	.004158	.004158	240.50	240.50
Denmark (Krone) ...	.1447	.1453	6.9125	6.8800
Ecuador (Sucre)				
Official rate	.005319	.005319	188.00	188.00
Floating rate	.006309	.006309	158.50	158.50
Finland (Markka) ...	.2243	.2254	4.4575	4.4375
France (Franc)	.1626	.1639	6.1500	6.1020
30-Day Forward .	.1625	.1637	6.1547	6.1070
90-Day Forward .	.1622	.1634	6.1670	6.1190
180-Day Forward .	.1617	.1629	6.1860	6.1370
Greece (Drachma) ..	.007288	.007326	137.20	136.50
Hong Kong (Dollar) .	.1281	.1281	7.8065	7.8060
India (Rupee)	.07726	.07776	12.94	12.86
Indonesia (Rupiah) ..	.0006079	.0006079	1645.09	1645.00
Ireland (Punt)	1.4610	1.4700	.6845	.6803
Israel (Shekel)	.6242	.6242	1.602	1.602
Italy (Lira)	.0007536	.0007570	1327.00	1321.00
Japan (Yen)	.006848	.006913	146.02	144.65
30-Day Forward .	.006867	.006933	145.62	144.24
90-Day Forward .	.006905	.006973	144.83	143.42
180-Day Forward .	.006963	.007033	143.62	142.18
Jordan (Dinar)	2.9499	2.9499	.339	.339
Kuwait (Dinar)	3.5474	3.5474	.2819	.2819
Lebanon (Pound) ...	.007828	.007828	127.75	127.75
Malaysia (Ringgit) ..	.3967	.3977	2.5210	2.5145
Malta (Lira)	2.8653	2.8653	.3490	.3490
Mexico (Peso)				
Floating rate	.0007559	.0007622	1323.00	1312.00
Netherland (Guilder)	.4826	.4859	2.0720	2.0581
New Zealand (Dollar)	.5950	.5955	1.6807	1.6793
Norway (Krone)	.1486	.1485	6.7275	6.7325
Pakistan (Rupee) ...	.05780	.5780	17.30	17.30
Peru (Inti)	.06293	.06293	15.89	15.89
Philippines (Peso) ..	.04890	.04890	20.45	20.45
Portugal (Escudo) ..	.00700	.007027	142.80	142.30
Saudi Arabia (Riyal) .	.2667	.2667	3.7500	3.7500
Singapore (Dollar) ..	.4715	.4719	2.1210	2.1190
South Africa (Rand)				
Commercial rate ..	.4935	.4955	2.0263	2.0182
Financial rate	.2950	.30	3.3898	3.3333
South Korea (Won) .	.001231	.001231	812.50	812.50
Spain (Peseta)	.007880	.007893	126.90	126.70
Sweden (Krona)	.1563	.1569	6.3975	6.3725
Switzerland (Franc) .	.6523	.6583	1.5330	1.5190
30-Day Forward .	.6537	.6598	.1.5298	1.5156
90-Day Forward .	.6572	.6634	1.5216	1.5073
180-Day Forward .	.6630	.6695	1.5083	1.4937
Taiwan (Dollar)	.03223	.03222	31.03	31.04
Thailand (Baht)	.03880	.03880	25.77	25.77
Turkey (Lira)	.001194	.001194	837.70	837.70
United Arab (Dirham)	.2723	.2723	3.673	3.673
Uruguay (New Peso)				
Financial	.004552	.004552	219.70	219.70
Venezuela (Bolivar)				
Official rate	.1333	.1333	7.50	7.50
Floating rate	.03390	.03390	29.50	29.50
W. Germany (Mark) .	.5420	.5472	1.8450	1.8275
30-Day Forward .	.5435	.5487	1.8398	1.8224
90-Day Forward .	.5466	.5519	1.8294	1.8118
180-Day Forward .	.5512	.5568	1.8141	1.7960
SDR	1.27872	1.28485	0.782031	0.778303
ECU	1.13022	1.13517	....	......

Special Drawing Rights are based on exchange rates for the U.S., West German, British, French and Japanese currencies. Source: International Monetary Fund.

ECU is based on a basket of community currencies. Source: European Community Commission.

z-Not quoted.

The two left columns show how many cents (or in some cases, dollars and cents) one unit of that foreign currency is worth in American money. The two right hand columns indicate how many units of that currency you could buy with one U.S. dollar. For example, the table indicates that you could have bought one West German mark on Monday for 54.2 cents. And it shows that on Monday, for one dollar, you could have bought 1.8450 German marks.

From this table you can see that not all currencies have actively traded forward markets. You can also see that for some currencies, the forward price is below the spot price, while for others it is above.

The British pound, for example, has a spot quote for Monday of $1.5895, and a 180-day forward value of $1.5741. So you could buy forward pounds for less than the cost of spot pounds. Does that mean the British interest rates are relatively higher, causing people to want to buy their pounds up front and earn the higher interest rates? Or does it mean that speculators are betting that the future value of the pound will be lower? It could be either.

For the French franc, the forward price also is lower than the spot price. But for the Japanese yen, the Swiss franc, and for the West German mark the forward prices are higher than the spot prices.

Note: When you're planning a trip and go to the bank to buy some foreign currency, you'll have to pay a little more than the prices indicated in this table. These figures represent "wholesale trades" involving $1 million and up. Foreign currency at retail costs a little more.

able to buy as much in Canada with that $10 Canadian as you could buy in the United States with the $20 U.S. That's purchasing power parity.

Does it work? In the short run, not exactly. But in the long run, it tends to. Here's how it's supposed to work.

The Exchange Rate Automatically Adjusts Toward "Parity"

Suppose the exchange rate between the U.S. and Canadian dollar is one-for-one, yet prices in the United States are twice as high as those in Canada. You know very well what will happen. A flood of people from the United States will go to Canada and buy Canadian dollars. Then they will buy the things they want in Canada instead of in the United States. And not only that.

Enterprising people will go to Canada and load up trucks, freight cars, and ships with those cheap Canadian products and bring them to the United States and sell them for the high U.S. prices.

As all of this is going on, the demand for Canadian dollars is very strong. But who in Canada wants to buy American dollars?—to buy those over-priced American goods? Nobody. So how long can the exchange rate between these two currencies remain at one-for-one? Not very long.

The exchange value of the Canadian dollar will rise. For how long? You know the answer. Until purchasing power parity is reached. Americans will keep paying more and more for Canadian dollars and Canadians will keep paying less and less for U.S. dollars, and the exchange rate will move into equilibrium.

Price Levels Automatically Adjust Toward Equilibrium

While the exchange rates are moving, another equilibrating adjustment is going on. The quantities demanded of Canadian goods are great, and of U.S. goods are small. So what happens to prices in Canada? And in the United States? Canadian prices tend to go up. U.S. prices tend to come down.

These price level adjustments continue until equilibrium in reached. And where is that? Where "purchasing power parity" is achieved.

In the final equilibrium, Canadian prices will be higher and the cost of Canadian dollars will also be higher. When the adjustment process is complete, the number of Canadian dollars you could buy with your U.S. dollars will buy exactly the same quantity of goods in Canada as you could have bought if you had spent your U.S. dollars at home.

Expectations Exert an Important Influence on Exchange Rates

The idea of purchasing power parity obviously has some truth. Common sense would tell you that. But if you look at the exchange rate swings which have occurred in the past (and are occurring all the time), you will see that there is much more involved in exchange rate determination than "purchasing power parity." This theory gives us a "basic level" or "basic range" within which exchange rates will fluctuate. But it certainly doesn't tell us where the exchange rate will be, or which way it will be moving on any specific day.

Expectations regarding future economic developments can have an important influence on exchange rates. And expectations are subject to change on very short notice. In a market in which hundreds of billions of dollars worth of units are being traded daily, small changes in the outlook can bring big changes in the price!

As you look at figure 37-1 you will see the very significant fluctuations which have occurred between the U.S. dollar and several other national currencies. As you look at the lines in these charts it becomes obvious that there must be something other than "purchasing power parity" involved in exchange-rate determination.

FACTORS WHICH INFLUENCE THE SUPPLY AND DEMAND FOR A NATION'S CURRENCY

Relative Interest Rates. Suppose interest rates available on financial instruments in Germany are moving upward. Or suppose interest rates in Germany are staying the same but interest rates in the United States are falling. Either way, the mark is becoming a more attractive holding because the returns on mark-denominated financial instruments are going up relative to dollar-denominated instruments.

Expected Exchange Rate Movements. What if you think the mark is going to appreciate (its value will go up) in terms of the dollar? Then you'll be more interested in holding marks and less interested in holding dollars. Nobody wants to hold any asset whose value is expected to decrease!

Relative Inflation Rates. Relative inflation rates are important, too. The currency of a country where inflation is high will be less desirable than a more stable currency. Inflation is another word for "currency depreciation." As the prices of goods go up, the purchasing power of the currency goes down.

What About the Desire to Spend? All three of the above factors—interest rates, exchange rate movements, and inflation rates—deal with portfolio choices—the desire to hold one national currency or another. Nothing yet has been said about the desire to spend any of this foreign money. But that's important, too.

Demand for a Country's Exports. Suppose people suddenly decide they like imported Volkswagens better than domestically produced Fords and Chevys. The demand for marks will increase. Anything that causes people to want to buy more goods from a certain country, will increase the demand for that country's currency. And that will tend to push up the exchange value of that currency.

The Supply of a Nation's Currency

The supply of one currency is the demand for another. Anything which increases the demand by Americans for marks, increases (by exactly the same amount) the supply of dollars in the "dollars-for-marks" exchange market. It's the same thing, looked at from the opposite side of the market. Therefore, all of the "demand increasing factors" for one currency are simultaneously "supply increasing factors" for the other.

Figure 37-1.   Exchange Rate Fluctuations: Weighted Average Values of Selected Foreign Currencies, Compared with U.S. Dollar Values of Those Currencies

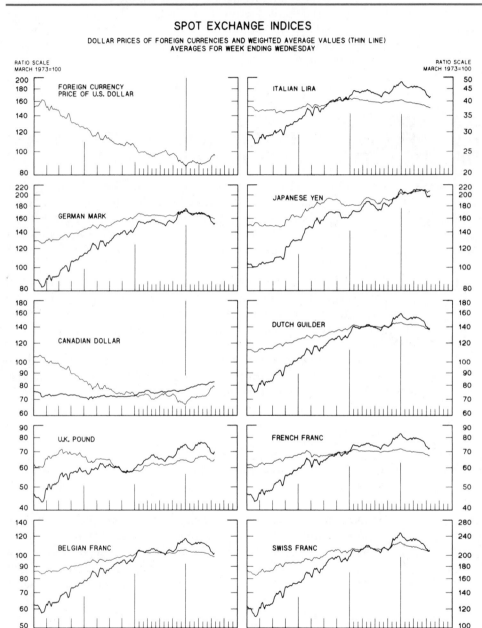

SPOT EXCHANGE INDICES
DOLLAR PRICES OF FOREIGN CURRENCIES AND WEIGHTED AVERAGE VALUES (THIN LINE)
AVERAGES FOR WEEK ENDING WEDNESDAY

Source: Board of Governors, Federal Reserve System, Selected Interest & Exchange Rates: Weekly Series of Charts (Washington, D.C., August 1, 1988).

How Supply and Demand Determine Exchange Rates

A system of **floating exchange rates** now exists among the currencies of the major trading nations. The international value of each nation's currency is determined by the supply of and demand for that currency, (relative to other currencies).

If any country's money gets in short supply, then the exchange rate (price) goes up. Foreigners must pay more to get it. If any country's money gets in oversupply its exchange rate (price) goes down. Foreigners can buy it cheaper.

Figure 37-2 uses supply and demand graphs to illustrate the exchange-rate effects of a decrease in the demand for dollars in the "dollars for marks" exchange market. There you see now the exchange rate moves to maintain equilibrium in that market.

Suppose prices go up in one country. Foreigners aren't going to want to buy those higher-priced goods! So people don't want as much of that country's currency. Its price (exchange rate) goes down.

But as the price of that country's money goes down, that country's goods get cheaper to foreigners. And that's what brings the country's trade back into equilibrium. The exchange rate must adjust enough to offset the effect of the inflation.

Figure 37-2.   Changes in Supply and Demand Alter Exchange Rates: The Case of a Decrease in the Demand for Dollars in the "Dollars for Marks" Exchange Market

A decrease in the demand for dollars is the same thing as an increase in the demand for marks.

Dollars

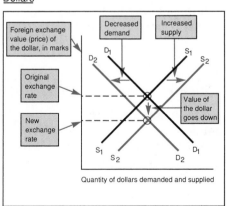

Marks

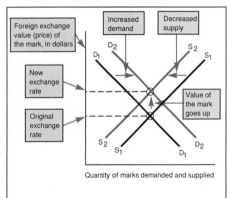

People begin trying to get rid of their dollars—to exchange them for marks. So the supply of dollars increases. But people are not willing to trade their marks for dollars, so the demand for dollars decreases. So the exchange value of the dollar goes down.

People try to use their dollars to buy marks. So the demand for marks increases. But people who have marks are less willing to sell their marks for dollars, so the available supply of marks decreases. So the exchange value of the mark (in terms of dollars) goes up.

Note: A decrease in the demand for dollars is the same thing as an increase in the supply of dollars. An increase in the demand for marks is the same thing as a decrease in the supply of marks.

With floating rates that's what will tend to happen—automatically. And as you know, that's how floating exchange rates tend to bring trade between nations into equilibrium.

HOW AND WHY ARE FLOATING EXCHANGE RATES "MANAGED"?

With floating exchange rates, the price of each nation's currency in the international exchange markets can move freely up or down. The price responds to changes in supply or demand. It works the same way as prices of stocks and bonds in the stock and bond markets.

People are buying and selling different kinds of national currencies all the time. Some are speculating, hoping to profit from future changes in rates. And this **speculation** brings an element of danger into the floating-rate system.

The Destabilizing Effect of Rumors

You know what would happen to the price of a stock if there's a rumor that the company is going broke—or that the company while digging for copper had struck gold! Stock prices are always "floating" up or down in response to supply and demand changes. When big rumors hit, prices plummet, or skyrocket.

With floating exchange rates, couldn't rumors (about inflation rates and such) push the value of the dollar way up? or way down? And then what would happen to the importers and exporters who are doing business between the United States and West Germany and Japan and everywhere?

How can trading partners carry out their business in an orderly fashion when the exchange value of the dollar is jumping up and down? They can't, of course. That's one reason why governments (mostly central banks) try to "manage" the floating rates.

Central Banks Can Stabilize Exchange Rates

Suppose there's a rumor that the inflation rate in the United States is speeding up—that is, the domestic purchasing power of the dollar is going down. Foreigners who hold dollars (and American portfolio managers too) start trading their dollars for marks, francs, yen, etc. So the dollar supply increases and the demand decreases and the value of the dollar starts going down. That's exactly the situation you saw illustrated in figure 37-2.

Setting a "Bottom Price" on the Dollar. How can the declining exchange value of the dollar be stopped? Like this: Let the central banks set a "bottom price" (exchange rate) for the dollar and agree to buy all the dollars anyone wants to sell, at that price. Maybe the Deutsche Bundesbank will offer to pay 1.8 marks for one dollar and will buy all the dollars anyone wants to sell, at that price. Then the value of the dollar cannot go below 1.8 marks.

And the central bank in Switzerland can set the "bottom price" of the dollar in terms of Swiss francs and buy all of the dollars offered at that price. So the price of the dollar (in Swiss francs) can't go any lower than that. The same thing can be done by the central bank of every other country. And if everyone is willing to buy enough dollars (big if!) then the policy can succeed.

It works the other way too. Suppose everyone suddenly gets the idea that the U.S. inflation rate will be low and that costs of production soon will be going up faster in other countries than in the United States. What happens?

Everybody wants to own U.S. dollars because everybody thinks dollars will be getting more valuable. People and businesses and banks begin to buy dollars in exchange for marks, francs, drachmas, etc. So the exchange value of the dollar goes up. The exchange value of the other currencies (in terms of dollars) goes down.

Setting a "Top Price" on the Dollar. It's obvious what the central banks can do to prevent the exchange value of the dollar from shooting sky high. Sell dollars!

The Federal Reserve can set a "top price" for the dollar in terms of each foreign currency—e.g., 2.6 marks, 1.30 Canadian dollars, etc.—and sell all the dollars anyone wants to buy at that price. The Fed would have to agree to accept unlimited amounts of all kinds of foreign currencies in exchange for dollars.

By supplying an unlimited number of dollars at a given price (exchange rate) the Fed (and the foreign central banks) can absolutely prevent the foreign exchange value of the dollar from going above the set rates—i.e., can prevent the foreign exchange value of the other currencies from going below the set rates. But remember, to succeed, this policy requires a commitment to sell *unlimited quantities* of dollars. And it may not be feasible to do that.

Exchange Rate Stabilization Involves Rigging Demand and Supply

From the above examples it is clear that stabilizing the exchange rate for a currency involves influencing the demand and supply of that currency. Usually it is not too difficult to "manage" the floating exchange rates if all of the central banks agree and cooperate with each other, and if the disequilibrium is only temporary and is not too serious. But suppose there is a serious disequilibrium. Or suppose the international financial community decides it's time either to "dump the dollar," or to "dump everything else and buy dollars."

An overwhelming flood of buy or sell orders would hit the foreign exchange markets—a much greater disequilibrium than the central banks could handle. The exchange rate would break free from the pegged rate and respond to the market forces of supply and demand.

Market-Rigging Can't Cure Chronic Disequilibrium

If Americans are buying a lot more foreign goods than foreigners are buying from the United States, then there will be a constant flow of surplus dollars into the foreign exchange markets. To keep the exchange value of the dollar from falling it would be necessary for the central banks to continually pour more other kinds of currency into the market—and buy up billions of dollars. Sooner or later, something has to give!

A chronic balance of payments deficit ultimately can be corrected only by a currency depreciation—lower international value of the dollar. A lower dollar will make foreign goods relatively more expensive and U.S. goods relatively cheaper, both to domestic and foreign buyers.

For short-term destabilizing influences, central bank stabilization policies can sometimes have significant success. But in the case of a chronic imbalance in the trade flows between one nation and the rest of the world, exchange rate management (rigging the exchange market) cannot solve the problem. A change in the exchange rate is the only answer.

THE U.S. DOLLAR IN THE 1980s: A ROLLER COASTER RIDE!

You already know about the Fed's money tightening moves of October 1979. One of the immediate reasons for that move was because the international value of the dollar was falling rapidly. Following the announcement of the Fed's "new operating procedure," nominal interest rates in this country rose to their highest levels in modern times. The dollar strengthened.

Throughout 1980 and '81 and on into '82, money was tight. Nominal interest rates were very high. In early 1982 the U.S inflation rate seemed to be slowing down. The international value of the dollar continued to increase. In fact, it increased by an unprecedented 45% during the two and one-half years between mid-1980 and the end of 1982. Then it stabilized for a while.

In midsummer of 1983 the U.S. inflation rate was low, real interest rates were high, and in late July and early August of 1983 the Fed and the central banks of Germany, Japan, Switzerland, and the Netherlands all sold millions of U.S. dollars in the foreign exchange markets to try to hold down the dollar's rise. But the stabilizing efffect was only temporary. Foreigners were demanding and holding dollars because of (1) the high real U.S. interest rates, (2) the low U.S. inflation rate, and (3) the economic recovery and healthy outlook for the American economy.

Throughout 1983 and on into 1984, many of the world's finance experts were talking about the "overvalued dollar." Some foreign countries were having to push up their own interest rates (and slow down their economies) to prevent further weakness of their own currencies.

American exporters were having difficulty selling in foreign markets because of the high cost of the dollar. And American buyers of automobiles, TV sets and many other products were finding it cheaper to buy imports. Some domestic producers were hard hit by this foreign competition. And the U.S. balance of trade deficits grew larger, year after year.

Throughout 1983 and 1984 and in early 1985 many finance experts were waiting for (and expecting) the international value of the dollar to fall. But that didn't happen until March of 1985.

The Dollar Begins Its Slide

In mid-March of 1985 there was a savings and loan crisis in Ohio. One S&L failed and thousands of S&L depositors began "panic withdrawals" of their deposits from other S&Ls. The Ohio govenor ordered the S&Ls closed until the crisis could be worked out—which it soon was. But this incident was enough to trigger sales of dollars by foreigners. So the dollar began going down. Many observers said that it was about time!

By mid-March of 1985 the U.S. dollar was worth about 3.4 West German marks—up from 1.8 marks in mid-1980; 2.9 Swiss francs—up from 1.6 in mid-1980; and 260 Japanese yen—up from 130 in mid-1980.

On an index using 1982 as the base year (1982 = 100), the dollar's value against the currencies of 15 other major trading nations was less than 90 in 1980. By March of 1985 it was up to 137. Then came the slide.

By the end of 1986 the index number was back down to 100—the same as in 1982, and by the end of 1987 it was below 90—the same as in 1980.

In December of 1987 the dollar's value against the currencies of several of our major trading partners dropped to the lowest levels sinced World War II. The dollar would buy only 120 Japanese yen—down from 260 in 1985; only 1.6 West German marks—down from 3.4 in 1985; and only 1.3 Swiss francs—down from 2.9 in 1985.

Such wide swings in exchange rates can have serious destabilizing effects on international trade and also on financial markets worldwide. The falling international value of the dollar was a contributing factor in the stock market crash of October, 1987. So why haven't the major trading nations taken action to stabilize exchange rates? The fact is that they have tried, but without much success.

The G-7 Nations Attempt to Stabilize the Falling Dollar

Finance ministers and central bankers of the so-called Group of Seven (G-7) nations (the U.S., Canada, Japan, West Germany, Britain, France, and Italy) agreed to cooperate in trying to stabilize the international value of the dollar. In February of 1987 at the Louvre in Paris the group declared their intention to work together to keep exchange rates near current levels.

During 1987 the central banks of the G-7 countries spent something approaching $100 billion in foreign exchange markets to try to keep the dollar in the agreed range. But in spite of this intervention, the dollar's value continued to slide downward to reach new lows in December.

The G-7 nations repeatedly reaffirmed their commitment to cooperative action for exchange rate stability. But it was clear that the massive size of the foreign exchange market—hundreds of billions of dollars in transactions every day—is much too great to be rigged by the central banks on a permanent basis.

By mid-year 1988 the international value of the dollar was trending upward again. Some observers were cautioning that the dollar might be poised to go too high, too fast again. By the time you are reading this, you probably already know what happened. If not, *The Wall Street Journal* will tell you.

SUMMARY

- When exchange rates are floating, the value of each nation's currency is determined by the demand and supply for that currency in the foreign exchange markets. A nation which is importing a lot more than it is exporting is likely to see the value of its currency begin to depreciate.

- The market for foreign exchange operates around the clock and around the world. It is interlinked by electronic communications, with the ability to execute transactions and to transfer funds worldwide, instantaneously.

- Foreign exchange is bought in the spot market and in the forward market. The **interest rate parity** theory says that the difference between the spot and forward rates will be just enough to offset differences in short-term interest rates between the two countries.

- The **purchasing power parity** theory says that exchange rates will automatically adjust to equate the purchasing power of the different currencies. Both **exchange rates** and **price levels** between the nations tend to adjust to bring about purchasing power parity.

- Factors which influence the supply and demand of a nation's currency include: Relative interest rates, expected exchange rate movements, relative inflation rates, and relative demand for a country's exports.

- Exchange rate stabilization requires rigging the demand and supply for the currencies involved. It can be successfully done only if the disequilibrium is relatively minor and short run.

- During the 1980s the international value of the U.S. dollar took a roller-coaster ride: from historic lows to historic highs and back to historic lows again. At midyear 1988 it was low, but trending upward again.

Important Principles, Issues, Concepts, Terms

Explosive growth of the world economy

International medium of exchange function

How foreign exchange is traded

Buying foreign exchange

International balance of payments

Debits and credits on the balance of payments

Surpluses and deficits

Current items and capital items

What happens when a nation runs a deficit

The role of official transactions

What happens to correct a chronic deficit

The automatic exchange-rate self-equilibrating mechanism

Role of international banks in currency trading

The procedure for trading currencies

Meaning and role of speculation

Meaning and role of arbitrage

Spot and forward exchange rates

The interest rate parity theory

Purchasing power parity theory

Why the exchange rate adjusts toward "parity"

The effect of price level adjustments on exchange rates

Effects of expectations on exchange rates

Factors which influence the supply and demand for a nation's currency

How supply and demand determine exchange rates

How and why floating rates are "managed"

How central banks try to stabilize exchange rates

Limitations on the effectiveness of exchange rate stabilization

The U.S. dollar exchange rate fluctuations in the 1980s

Questions and Problems

1. How is it possible for a person to exchange American dollars for Japanese yen? Describe the banking relationships which permit this exchange to occur.

2. What does it mean to say that the American economic and financial system has become integrated with the worldwide system?

3. Describe the foreign exchange market. What is traded there? And what influences supply and demand in this market?

4. What is the international balance of payments? What information can you find from it?

5. Explain the difference between a debit transaction and a credit transaction on the U.S. balance of payments, and give some examples of each.

6. What are some of the things which might cause the demand for dollars in the international exchange markets to increase? To decrease?

7. Mention some of the problems which arise in trying to operate a "managed floating" exchange rate system.

8. Explain as much as you can about spot and forward exchange rates, and factors which influence these, and the relationship between them.

9. Explain the "purchasing power parity" theory of exchange rate determination. Do you think this theory explains exchange rates in the modern world? Explain.

Suggested Readings

Aggarwal, Raj. "The Strategic Challenge of the Evolving Global Economy." *Business Horizons*. July/August 1987.

Aliber, Robert Z. *Exchange Risk and Corporate International Finance*. New York, NY: Halsted Press, 1979.

American Federation of Labor and Congress of Industrial Organizations. *The National Economy and Trade, AFL-CIO Policy Recommendations for 1986.* Washington, DC: American Federation of Labor, 1986, pp. 23, 31.

Balbach, Anatol. "The Mechanics of Intervention in Foreign Exchange Markets." *Review* 60. Federal Reserve Bank of St. Louis, February 1978, pp. 2–7.

Balbach, Anatol B., and David H. Resler. "Eurodollars and the U.S. Money Supply." *Review* 62 (6), Federal Reserve Bank of St. Louis, June/July 1980, pp. 2–12.

Bergstrand, Jeffrey H. "Selected Views of Exchange Rate Determination After a Decade of Floating." *New England Economic Review*. Federal Reserve Bank of Boston, (May/June 1983), 14–29.

Bilson, John F., and Richard C. Marston (eds.). *Exchange Rate Theory and Practice*. Chicago: University of Chicago Press, 1984.

Bordo, Michael D. "The Classical Gold Standard: Some Lessons for Today." *Review*. Federal Reserve Bank of St. Louis, May 1981.

Boyd, John H., David S. Dahl, and Carolyn P. Line. "A Primer on the International Monetary Fund." *Quarterly Review* 7. Summer 1983.

Chrystal, K. Alec. "A Guide to Foreign Exchange Markets." *Review*. Federal Reserve Bank of St. Louis, March 1984.

Coombs, Charles. *The Arena of International Finance*. New York: John Wiley & Sons, 1976.

Corrigan, E. Gerald. "Coping with Globally Integrated Financial Markets." *Quarterly Review*. Federal Reserve Bank of New York, (Winter 1987), 1–5.

de Vries, Rimmer, and Derek Hargreaves. "The Dollar's Decline and Trade: Mission Accomplished?" *Challenge*. (January/February 1987), 37–46.

Dornbusch, Rudiger, and Jacob A. Frankel (eds.). *International Economic Policy: Theory and Evidence*. Baltimore. MD: Johns Hopkins University Press, 1979.

Dufey, Gunter, and Ian H. Giddy. *The International Money Market*. Englewood Cliffs, N.J.: Printice-Hall, 1978.

Federal Reserve Bank of Boston. *Managed Exchange Rate Flexibility: The Recent Experience*. Boston, Mass.: Federal Reserve Bank of Boston, 1978.

Friedman, Milton. "The Case for Flexible Rates." in his *Essays in Positive Economics*. Chicago: University of Chicago Press, 1953, pp. 157–203.

———. "The Eurodollar Market: Some First Principles." *The Morgan Guaranty Survey*. (October 1969), 4–15.

———. "In Defense of Destabilizing Speculation." in his *The Optimum Quantity of Money and Other Essays*. Chicago: Aldine, 1969.

Glic, Reuven. "The Largest Debtor Nation." *Weekly Letter*. Federal Reserve Bank of San Francisco, Feb. 14, 1986.

Goodfriend, Marvin. "Eurodollars." *Economic Review*. Federal Reserve Bank of Richmond (May/June 1981), p. 14.

Humpage, Owen F., and Nicholas V. Karamouzis. "A Correct Value for the Dollar?" *Economic Commentary*. Federal Reserve Bank of Cleveland, January 1, 1986.

———. "The Dollar in the Eighties." *Economic Commentary*. Federal Reserve Bank of Cleveland (September 1, 1985), 1–4.

International Monetary Fund. *Annual Report on Exchange Restrictions*. Washington, D.C., yearly.

Johnson, Howard G., and James J. Lewis. "Keep Control of Foreign-Exchange Operation." *The Bankers Magazine*. (Spring 1975), 79–83.

Kemp, Donald S. "A Monetary View of the Balance of Payments." *Review*. Federal Reserve Bank of St. Louis (April 1975), 14–22.

Kohn, Donald L. "Capital Flows in a Foreign Exchange Crisis." *Monthly Review*. Federal Reserve Bank of Kansas City, February 1973.

Kubarych, R. M. *Foreign Exchange Markets in the United States*. revised edition, Federald Reserve Bank of New York, 1983.

———. *The New York Foreign Exchange Market*. New York: Federal Reserve Bank of New York, 1979.

Leontieff, Wassily. "Observations on Some Worldwide Economic Issues of the Coming Years." *Challenge* 21, (March/April 1978), 2–10.

Maldonado, Rita M. "Recording and Classifying Transactions in the Balance of Payments." *International Journal of Accounting*. Fall 1979.

Mayer, Martin. *The Fate of the Dollar*. New York: Times Books, 1980.

Metzler, Lloyd A. "The Process of International Adjustment Under Conditions of Full Employment: A Keynesian View." in his *Collected Papers*. Cambridge, Mass.: Harvard University Press, 1973.

Mundell, Robert A., and Alexander K. Swoboda (eds). *Monetary Problems of the International Economy*. Chicago: University of Chicago Press, 1969.

Murphy, J. Carter. *The International Monetary System; Beyond the First Stages of Reform*. Washington, D.C.: American Enterprise Institute for Public Policy Research, 1976.

Officer, Lawrence H. "The Purchasing-Power-Parity Theory of Exchange Rates: A Review Article." *Staff Papers 23*. International Monetary Funds (March 1976), pp. 1–60.

Schmidt, Wilson E. *The U.S. Balance of Payments and the Sinking Dollar*. New York: New York University Press, 1979.

Sobol, Dorothy M. "The SDR in Private International Finance." *Quarterly Review*. Federal Reserve Bank of New York (Winter 1981–82), p. 35.

Solomon, Anthony M. "Toward a More Resilient International Financial System." *Quarterly Review 8 (3)*.

Federal Reserve Bank of New York, Autumn 1983, pp. 1–5.

Solomon, Robert. *The International Monetary System, 1945–1976*. New York: Harper & Row, 1977.

———. *The International Monetary System, 1945–81*. New York: Harper & Row, 1982.

Sweeney, Richard J., and Thomas D. Willett. "Eurodollars, Petrodollars, and World Liquidity and Inflation." in Karl Brunner and Allan Meltzer (eds.) *Stabilization of the Domestic and International Economy*, a supplement to the *Journal of Monetary Economics*. Carnegie-Rochester Conference Series on Public Policy, vol. 5, 1977, pp. 277–310.

Tarshis, Lorie. "Disarming the Debt Bomb." *Challenge*. May/June, 1987.

Tew, Brian. *The Evolution of the International Monetary System, 1947–77*. London: Hutchison, 1977.

Thurow, Lester C., and Laura D. Tyson. "The Economic Black Hole." *Foreign Policy*. Summer, 1987.

Triffin, Robert. *Gold and the Dollar Crisis*. New Haven, Conn.: Yale University Press, 1960.

U.S. Department of Commerce. *Report of the Advisory Committee on the Presentation of Balance of Payments Statistics*, in *Survey of Current Business*. U.S. Department of Commerce, June 1976.

Wallich, Henry C. "A Defense of Fixed Exchange Rates." United States Balance of Payments Hearings before the Joint Economic Committee, 88th Congress, 1st session, Pt. 3.

Willett, Thomas D. *Floating Exchange Rates and International Reform*. Washington, DC: American Enterprise Institute, 1977, p. 50.

Wood, Geoffrey E., and Doublas R. Mudd. "Do Foreigners Control the U.S. Money Supply?" *Review 59*. Federal Reserve Bank of St. Louis, (December 1977), pp. 8–11.

Yeager, Leland B. *International Monetary Relations*. New York: Harper & Row, 1966.

———. *The Night We Floated*. International Institute for Economic Research, Ottawa, Ill.: Green-Hill Publishers, 1977.

CHAPTER 38

International Banking and the Worldwide Financial System

Chapter Objectives

In this chapter you will be reading more about the structure and functioning of the integrated worldwide financial system. After studying this chapter you will understand and be able to explain:

1. How the international **medium of exchange mechanism** works mostly through the international "spiderweb network" of **correspondent banks** and **foreign branches**.

2. How this international medium of exchange enables money to fulfill its **microeconomic role** on a global scale.

3. Some of the reasons why so many banks have established foreign branches in recent years.

4. How American banks conduct international banking operations—via **IBFs** and **Edge Act branches**—without having to locate outside the country.

5. The nature, extent, and effects of **foreign bank entry** into U. S. banking and financial markets.

6. The role of the **central banks** (the Fed and others) in the operation of the international financial system.

7. The **one-world nature** of both the *structure* and the *functioning* of the international money-banking-financial system.

THE VITAL ROLE OF THE INTERNATIONAL BANKING SYSTEM

In the previous chapter you read about the explosive growth of international trade since the 1960s. And you read about the growth of international financial mechanisms—the exchange mechanisms needed to support this growth of world trade.

The "international medium of exchange mechanism" exists only in, and functions only through the international banking system. So the international banking system plays a *vital role* in the functioning of the world economy.

The Microeconomic Role of the International Medium of Exchange Mechanism

It's the "worldwide medium of exchange mechanism" which performs the essential microeconomic functions of money on a global scale. All kinds of resources and products—inputs and outputs—flow away from places where they are more plentiful and less valued and to places where they are less plentiful and more valued. Worldwide supplies are brought into balance with worldwide demands. Prices of goods (worldwide) are constantly being moved toward equilibrium as goods flow from surplus to deficit areas.

This international medium of exchange mechanisms fosters **increasing specialization**. All people everywhere in the world can specialize in producing their **comparative advantage** products and then sell those products all over the world—anywhere they're demanded. The increases in productivity and in economic welfare which result from this kind of specialization couldn't occur without "the international money mechanism." And it's the international banking system which makes it possible for the money mechanism to work.

Overview of the International Banking System

The **international banking system** is the worldwide system of *interlocking relationships among banks and other financial institutions* located in different countries all over the world. The system is interlinked worldwide—tied together without much regard to national boundaries. It's this interlinked system which lets money perform its microeconomic (efficient resource allocation) function on a global scale.

This international banking system in effect integrates the economies and the financial markets of all nations, worldwide. Important? More than that. It's absolutely vital—not only in the functioning of the world economy but also in the functioning of the national economies which comprise the world economy.

What kind of "links," or "interlocking relationships" tie the international banking system together? Basically there are two kinds: (1) International correspondent relationships, and (2) international bank branching. You'll be reading about both of these in the sections coming up.

INTERNATIONAL CORRESPONDENT BANKING

You already know how correspondent banking works in the United States. Smaller banks keep deposits in larger banks, and the larger banks provide "big bank" services for the smaller banks. This correspondent banking network ties together all of the financial institutions in the country into a *nationwide banking system*. The worldwide banking system operates in much the same way.

Banks in London, Zurich, Melbourne, Amsterdam, Tokyo, Rome, Toronto, Mexico City, Bonn, Delhi, Montivideo (and all over the world) keep deposits in and have correspondent relationships with banks in New York City. And banks headquartered in New York City keep deposits in and have correspondent relationships with banks in all of those cities—and just about everywhere else around the globe.

International and Domestic Correspondent Banking Are Similar

International correspondent relationships are basically the same as domestic correspondent relationships. The big difference is that the international correspondent banks are dealing in (depositing, withdrawing, exchanging) several different kinds of money (national currencies)—not just one.

The international correspondent network is constantly involved in (1) the financing of trade flows among nations, and (2) the flows of different kinds of national currencies and financial instruments among the various financial markets all over the world.

Through this system, money and other financial instruments are always being changed from one form to another and from one place to another. Money and financial instruments move through the international banking system in response to the changing supply, demand, and price conditions in the various financial markets.

It's this international correspondent banking network which makes possible the instantaneous electronic transfer of funds (*in any kind of national currency*) from New York to Tokyo, from London to Sydney (or almost anywhere else). It's worldwide money, moving through the worldwide banking system performing its essential function: facilitating exchange.

Changing Financial Conditions Are Quickly Transmitted Worldwide

You can see that the banks in each nation are closely tied into the international banking network. So what happens when there's some change in market conditions in any one major nation? The changes are automatically and very quickly transmitted to all other financial markets throughout the world. Truly, it's a one-world money-banking-financial system.

A Bank's Choice of a "Foreign Correspondent" Is Very Important

Suppose you were a New York banker and you wanted to establish correspondent relationships with banks in London, Mexico City, Sydney, Paris, and Tokyo. Which bank (or banks) would you choose in each of those places?

You want to choose a bank which will offer you the "best-all-round deal." What services will they provide to you? And what payments, minimum balances, and services will they require from you? You will want to choose only banks which are unquestionably sound and which are well respected both in their locality and in the worldwide financial community.

Remember this: You're going to be shifting around and changing the denomination and ownership of millions of "national currency units." And you're going to be doing it instantly on the basis of a phone call, or a telex message or other electronic communication. And you're going to expect your correspondent bank to be doing the same. So you certainly want to have complete confidence in the bank you're dealing with!

Why Not Establish Your Own Overseas Branch?

There's one way to ensure your complete confidence in your foreign correspondent: Establish your own foreign branch.

In recent years, hundreds of banks have done that. In fact foreign branch banking has grown explosively during the 1970s and '80s. The next section explains why.

WHY DO BANKS ESTABLISH FOREIGN BRANCHES?

Maybe you have read or heard someone say: "Foreign banks are taking over the country!" If you lived in some other country you might have read or heard someone say: "American banks are taking over the world!" Neither statement is true, of course. But it is true that in recent years bank branching into foreign countries has been occurring at a rapid pace.

Suppose somebody asked you where the largest U.S. banks are located. Your answer would be the same as if someone asked you where Exxon or Ford Motor Company or IBM or DuPont was located. Where? All over the world! And it isn't just the largest banks. Many of the medium-sized (regional) banks have overseas branches too. And the large European and Japanese banks are all over the world too.

Banks Follow Their Customers Overseas

When Volkswagen decides to set up a factory in Pennsylvania, it makes sense for their bank in Germany to say to Volkswagen: "We will set up a branch near your new U.S. plant to help you in financing the flows of goods and services between Germany and the United States, and we will provide local financing for your U.S. operations as well." And when Exxon decides to set up a refinery in Rotterdam or IBM decides to set up an assembly plant in Paris, it makes sense for their American banks to set up branches in those countries to provide them financial services.

The growth of multinational corporations has played an important role in stimulating foreign branching. Obviously it's good business for banks to set up overseas branch offices to serve the overseas operations of their domestic customers—and to try to profit from doing so. But this isn't the only reason why banks establish foreign branches.

Banks Seek to Enter New Markets

Banking has become a very competitive industry and this competition is not constrained by national boundaries. In fact, because of U.S. laws regarding branch banking, it usually would be easier for a bank in New York or Los Angeles or Houston to set up a branch in London or Paris or Tokyo than to set up a branch in North Carolina or Oklahoma or Ohio.

Banks like to expand into, serve, and profit in new markets, both at home and abroad. When a bank establishes a branch in a foreign country, usually it makes services available to anyone who wishes to use them—not just to the foreign operations of its domestic customers. So it brings a new source of financial services—and new competition—into the local market. Usually the foreign branch will hire local people, follow local procedures and customs, and eventually become considered a "local bank" by the businesses and people in the area.

If you live near a large city in the United States the chances are good that there's a branch of a foreign bank nearby where you could open an account and/or borrow money. And if you travel to foreign countries, almost anywhere you go you'll find that you aren't very far from a branch of an American-owned bank.

Suppose you go to a place as remote as the Fiji Islands in the South Pacific. There you'll find branches of ANZ of New Zealand, Barclays of London, Bank of New South Wales of Australia—and, of course, Citibank of New York. Why? Mostly because these banks want to get part of the (hopefully profitable) Fiji Islands banking business! Private enterprise responding to the demands of the marketplace? Yes.

Foreign branches provide to the home office (and receive from the home office) many correspondent banking services. These networks of worldwide branches play a very important role in tying together and integrating the worldwide banking system.

American Banks Establish Branches Overseas to Escape Regulations

Banks like to establish offices in places where they can do the things they want to do. That's why Citibank of New York has established an office in South Dakota where there are fewer restrictions on some activities. Several banks have established offices in Delaware for the same reason. The point is that banks will establish offices in places where they're permitted to do what they want to do.

Much foreign branching by American banks has resulted from the desire (1) to participate in the less-stringently-regulated foreign banking business, (2) to escape from U.S. banking laws and regulations, and (3) to participate in the Eurodollar market—rapidly growing and already the largest money market in the world.

Most Foreign Countries Allow Banks More Freedom

In general, banks in the United States are more closely regulated than are banks in other countries. And the Fed's position has been for **mutual nondiscrimination** in bank regulation between U.S. and foreign banks. The idea is that the U.S. branches of foreign banks should be required to abide by U.S. banking regulations and the foreign branches of U.S. banks should be required to follow the regulations of the host country. "When in Rome, do as the Romans do."

As the result of this mutual nondiscrimination principle, foreign branches of a U.S. bank often are permitted to engage in activities and to adjust their asset portfolios in ways which would be illegal for the parent banks located in the United States. This gives U.S. banks an added incentive to set up overseas branches.

A special case in the mid-1960s stimulated overseas branching by U.S. banks. In 1965 the U.S. government placed restrictions on foreign lending by domestic banking offices. So what did the large, internationally involved U.S. banks do? They set up foreign branches which were not affected by these restrictions.

U.S. Banks Established Foreign Branches to Avoid "Reg. Q"

Prior to April, 1986, American banks and thrifts were under the Fed's "Regulation Q" which limited the amount of interest they could pay to attract deposits. As money market rates moved above the Reg Q rates, banks lost deposits and reserves. Some of these "disintermediated" dollars were deposited in banks located outside the United States—banks not subject to the Reg Q ceilings. So that means more Eurodollars were created.

Some banks began to replace lost reserves by borrowing Eurodollars—frequently from their own foreign branches. In fact many U.S. banks established foreign (so-called "offshore" or "overseas") branches for the specific purpose of attracting Eurodollar deposits (often from U.S. citizens) and then lending those deposits to the parent bank. An "end run" around Req Q? Exactly.

Foreign Branches of U.S. Banks Can Take Eurodollar Deposits

If your deposits and reserves are escaping to banks located outside the United States, what can you do? Set up an office located outside the country (an "offshore branch") and recapture some of those escaping dollars! When your depositors withdraw their money, sell them Eurodollar CDs (which always paid market interest rates, not Reg Q rates)—CDs issued by your offshore branch.

Any American bank which wants to participate in the Eurodollar money market—taking Eurodollar deposits and making Eurodollar loans—must establish an "offshore branch." Either it must have a banking office located somewhere outside the United States or it must establish an "International Banking Facility" (IBF—explained later in this chapter). When you think of the size and importance of the Eurodollar money market you won't be surprised that many U.S. banks have established offshore branches to be able to participate in this market.

In London—the center of the worldwide Eurodollar market—there aren't as many British banks as there are branches of American banks. In fact the Eurodollar market worldwide is dominated by foreign branches of American banks.

Are American banks taking over the world? No. Far from it. Large European and Japanese banks also are deeply entrenched worldwide, and are tough competitors. But American banks certainly are out there in the middle (and in all corners) of the competitive arena. These multinational banking corporations—U.S., and foreign—form the basic structure of the worldwide banking system and play the most important role in the functioning of the worldwide medium of exchange mechanism.

EXPANDING INTERNATIONAL ACTIVITIES OF AMERICAN BANKS

There are several ways in which American banks participate in international banking activities. One way is to establish one or more branches (and/or other kinds of banking offices) in foreign countries. Another way is to establish one or more subsidiary units (in the United States) to engage in international banking. In this section you'll be reading about both of these. First, international branch banking.

Foreign Branching by American Banks

In the early 1960s, less than a dozen U.S. banks had overseas branches. The total number of overseas branches was a little more than 100. The total assets of those branches amounted to less than $5 billion.

By the mid-1980s about 200 American banks had overseas branches. The total number of branches was almost 1,000. And total assets of those overseas branches? Over $400 billion! During the 1980s some of the large U.S. banks were earning between one-third and one-half of their income from their foreign operations.

Most of the foreign branches of U.S. banks are bona fide branches offering a range of banking services. But some of the overseas branches are called "shell branches" because they aren't really "branches" in the true sense of the word. A **shell branch** is a bookkeeping operation which is located outside the United States—usually in the Bahamas or in the Grand Cayman Islands in the Caribbean—where Eurodollar deposits and loans can be recorded.

The Location of Foreign Branches of American Banks

Where are these overseas branches of American banks? Everywhere in the world! In terms of value of overseas assets the greatest concentration (almost 50% of the worldwide total) is in Europe. More than 40% of the European total (20% of the worldwide total) is in Great Britain—mostly in London.

More than 20% of total overseas branch assets of U.S. banks are in Latin America and the Caribbean and almost 20% of the total assets are located in Asia—mostly Japan, Hong Kong, Singapore, and the Philippines. The remaining overseas assets of U.S. banks are located in Canada, in the various countries in Africa, and in Oceania—Australia, New Zealand, and the Pacific islands.[1]

Edge Act International Banking Offices

In 1918 the Congress passed an act (sponsored by Senator Walter Edge of New Jersey) which allowed U.S. banks to establish special subsidiaries (called Edge Act corporations) to specialize in financing international trade. Since that time, banks in the United States have been permitted to establish these "Edge Act" subsidiaries for the purpose of engaging in international banking operations.

These subsidiaries are exempt from the McFadden Act which restricts interstate branching. Several large banks now have Edge Act corporations in major cities throughout the country.

IBFs: Foreign Branches at Home

Is it possible for a bank whose home office is in New York City to have a foreign branch also located in New York City? In the home office building, in fact? Yes. The "foreign branch" is called an **international banking facility** (IBF). It operates with no more restrictions than would exist if it were located in a foreign country.

Transactions of the IBFs are considered to be "foreign" banking transactions. They are free from reserve requirements and deposit insurance payments and were never subject to "Reg Q" interest rate ceilings.

What's the logic of all this? Why permit banks to set up an IBF, to "pretend all the transactions of the IBF are carried out in a foreign country" and let banks

---

[1] Statistics on the locations and asset sizes of overseas branches of American banks are published in the *International Letter* of the Federal Reserve Bank of Chicago and in various issues of the *Federal Reserve Bulletin*.

escape normal banking regulations? Answer: Because banks were establishing "offshore branches" and getting around the regulations anyway. Might as well let them do it at home!

Banks were establishing overseas branches in London, the Bahamas, the Cayman Islands, all over Europe, Asia, etc. to escape regulations and to be able to participate in the Eurodollar market. So what happened? In December of 1981 the Fed decided to permit banks to establish IBFs so that they could escape the regulations and deal in Eurodollars without having to leave the country.

An IBF is really only a separate bookkeeping operation—like a shell branch. When the bank sets it up, it notifies the Fed. All of the assets and liabilities and all of the transactions of the IBF must be kept completely separate from all other operations of the bank. It is this "new set of books" which is, in effect, the IBF.

In addition to avoiding some banking restrictions and regulations, sometimes IBFs offer tax advantages. So why don't all banks set up IBFs and transfer all assets and liabilities into the IBF? And thus circumvent all of the banking regulations? They can't.

Here's the catch: IBFs can only transact *international* business—and that goes for both *sources* and *uses* of funds—i.e., they can't accept *domestic deposits*, and they can't make *domesic loans*.

The "IBF bookkeeping operation" in New York isn't very different from a "shell branch" bookkeeping operation in the Bahamas or the Cayman Islands. But it's more convenient (and a lot cheaper!) to have your "shell branch" located in the home office. That's why more than $100 billion in assets flowed into IBFs during the first six months after the Fed approved the establishment of IBFs in December, 1981.

FOREIGN BANKING ACTIVITY IN THE UNITED STATES AND WORLDWIDE

As U.S. banks have been establishing overseas branches, foreign banks have been doing the same—both in this country and all over the world. For example, by the mid-1980s about 15 percent of the total dollar volume of commercial bank business loans in the United States was accounted for by U.S. branches of foreign-owned banks.

Foreign Bank Offices in the United States

Foreign banks have been establishing and operating branches in this country for many years. In the mid-1980s there were about 400 foreign banking offices in the United States. Many of these offices are located in New York and California, but some are scattered all over the country. Most of the parent banks of these U.S. offices are in Britain, Canada, Germany, France, Switzerland, the Netherlands, and Japan. But many other countries are also represented.

Two of the 15 largest banks in the United States—Crocker National Bank of San Francisco and Marine Midland of Buffalo—are foreign owned. Several other large banks are foreign owned. Union Bank of Los Angeles and the National Bank of North America in New York are both British owned. California First Bank of San Francisco is Japanese owned.

When Franklin National Bank in New York failed in 1974 it was acquired by a consortium of six foreign banks based in Austria, Belgium, England, France, Germany, and the Netherlands. It now operates under the name "European-American Bank."

The Regulation of Foreign Bank Offices in the United States

There was very little regulation of foreign bank offices in the United States until 1978. Many American bankers complained of the unfair competition from the foreign bank branches: They were not required to hold reserves with the Fed. They were permitted to branch across state lines. They were not prohibited from engaging in nonbanking activities, as are American banks. In general, they were untouched by the restrictions limiting the actions of domestic banks. But the U.S. Congress passed the *International Banking Act of 1978* and changed all that.

The 1978 Act embodied the (previously explained) principle of **mutual non-discrimination**. Essentially the act extended the same federal regulations to foreign banking offices as apply to domestic banks.

The Worldwide Branch-Banking Network

The large banks of every major trading nation have branches in all of the financial centers in Europe, in the Americas, in Asia—in fact, all over the world. And some of these banks have branches and are providing both commercial and consumer banking services worldwide. Even in the Fiji Islands? Yes.

This worldwide branch banking network meshes with the highly developed system of correspondent banking to form the "spiderweb network"—the modern world's integrated money-banking-financial system.

THE WORLDWIDE MONEY-BANKING-FINANCIAL SYSTEM: AN OVERVIEW

Clearly, there is an intricate one-world international banking system. American banks have **branches** all over the world—in addition to their Edge Act offices and IBFs in this country. Foreign banks have branches all over the world—including several hundred in the United States.

Then there is the **correspondent banking** network which makes it possible (in fact very easy) for the smallest bank in the most out-of-the-way place to provide to its customers any kind of international banking service, reaching to anywhere in the world.

The **central banks** hold foreign exchange reserves and provide liquidity when necessary to facilitate exchange. If the banks are running short of some kind of foreign money, the central bank can provide that currency and make it possible for trade to continue.

At the center of this international money-banking-financial system is the **International Monetary Fund** (IMF). The IMF is a sort of "central bank for central banks" in dealing in foreign exchange.

Each central bank holds a deposit account in the IMF. These deposits are of different kinds of money, and of SDRs—"Special Drawing Rights." SDR deposits permit the central bank to withdraw (to "buy" from the IMF) the currency of any other nation. Example: Suppose the money center banks in New York are running short on Deutschmarks. They can buy marks from the Fed. Then the Fed can get more marks from the IMF in exchange for dollars and/or SDRs.

Money Flows toward the Highest Return

Alert money managers all over the world are constantly in touch with money market conditions, interest rates, and inflation rates (and projections) for the currencies of all different nations. Funds are constantly being changed from one national currency to another (marks for yen, yen for francs, francs for dollars, etc.) in response to the changing worldwide economic and money market conditions.

The eyes and ears of the banking structure are located everywhere throughout the world. And these eyes and ears are constantly watching for opportunities to direct the flow of funds toward the tight money markets where returns are higher and away from the easy money markets where returns are lower. Funds tend to flow out of the currencies of nations where inflation threatens and into the currencies of nations where inflation rates are low—where real rates promise to be highest.

If U.S. interest rates rise, investors throughout the world change other kinds of currency into dollars. Then they invest those dollars in Eurodollar CDs or U.S. T-bills or some other dollar-denominated asset which pays the higher rates. If the inflation rate in the United States increases, people will begin to get rid of their dollars—trade them for marks or yen or some other currency—one which is not being so rapidly eroded by inflation.

Suppose the U.S. government runs a large deficit. If this is expected to be inflationary, it will tend to weaken the dollar. But if it's thought that the "crowding out effect" of government borrowing will force interest rates up in the United States, then this may tend to strengthen the international value of the dollar.

Here's the point: Anything which happens regarding U.S. economic conditions, financial markets, or economic policies—either in reality, or in expectation—is transmitted throughout the world almost instantaneously. It happens through the intricate, interconnected worldwide money-banking-financial system.

The Impact on National Monetary Policies

Each nation has its own central bank with its own monetary policies, of course. But none of these policies can escape the rigid market discipline imposed by the free, one-world international financial market.

Neither the Fed in this country nor the central banks in foreign countries can take any significant monetary policy action without having an impact on the international value of the nation's money. You can see that the realistic monetary policy alternatives of the Fed (and of the central banks of all other countries) are significantly limited by the existence of this free, instantly responsive international financial system.

New York City—Center of the Worldwide System

The global money and banking system is centered in New York. Where are all of the Eurodollar reserves of all of the banks all around the world? They're in New York. That's where the foreign banks keep their Eurodollar deposits. Some economists like to say: "When Eurodollars are shifted from London to Tokyo, all they do is go across Wall Street from one bank to another." In fact, sometimes the dollars only change from one account to another within the same bank!

And where is the world's monetary gold? Most of it is down deep in the basement vault at the Federal Reserve Bank of New York. If England sells gold to Japan, what happens? Somebody at the New York Federal Reserve Bank picks up the gold bricks from the British pile and moves them across the room and puts them in the Japanese pile. (It isn't quite that simple, but almost!)

Yes, we really do have a worldwide money and banking system. And it really is centered in New York—the financial center of the world. There are other major financial centers—London, Tokyo, and several on the continent of Europe. But New York surpasses all the others. And the American dollar surpasses all other currencies in its importance as "the international generally acceptable medium of exchange." So nothing can happen to the U.S. dollar without a significant impact on the world's financial markets and on the money-banking-financial and economic systems of the world.

You have read quite a lot in this book about American banking and financial institutions and about domestic monetary conditions and policies. As you think about such issues as the effects of changes in the size of the domestic money supply on interest rates, about domestic monetary policies designed to influence economic conditions, and about other such domestically oriented issues, please try not to forget about these limitations imposed by the one-world nature of the global money-banking-financial system.

Everything that happens in this country's financial markets has a significant worldwide impact. And economic and financial conditions in other nations have a significant influence in this country. We're all tied together in this rapidly broadening and deepening **one-world money-banking-financial system.**

SUMMARY

- The microeconomic functions of the international medium of exchange permit resources and products to flow (worldwide) into their most productive, most demanded uses. The international banking system is what lets this medium of exchange function.

- The interlocking relationships of the international banking system consist mostly of (a) international branching and (b) correspondent relationships.

- The correspondent network lets any bank in any country exchange domestic currency for any kind of foreign currency.

- Important reasons why banks establish foreign branches are: (a) to follow their customers overseas, (b) to enter new markets, (c) to escape regulations, and (d) to participate in the Eurodollar market.

- The London-based Eurodollar market is dominated by the foreign branches of American banks.

- About 200 American banks now have overseas branches, the total number of branches is about 1,000, and total assets of those branches amounts to more than $400 billion.

- "Edge Act" branches and "international banking facilities" (IBFs) permit U.S. banks to conduct foreign operations without having to go overseas.

- The are about 400 foreign bank branch offices in the United States, and several major U.S. banks are foreign owned.

- The *International Banking Act of 1978* established the policy of **mutual nondiscrimination**—i.e., it extended to U.S. branches of foreign banks the same regulations as apply to domestic banks.

- The modern world has an intricate and highly developed **international money-banking-financial system**. The central banks of the various nations, and the International Monetary fund both play important "balancing roles" in this system. The center of the system is Wall Street in New York City.

- Through the worldwide system of money, banking, and finance, financial market conditions in any nation are quickly transmitted to the financial markets of all other nations, worldwide. So domestic financial and ecomic conditions and policies are inexticably interlinked, worldwide.

Important Principles, Issues, Concepts, Terms

The global nature of the world economic and financial system

The importance of interbank deposits in the Euro-currencies market

The vital role of the international banking system

The microeconomic role of "international money"

International correspondent banking

How to choose a correspondent bank

Why banks establish foreign branches

The influence of U.S. regulations on bank "offshore branching"

Extent of foreign branching by American banks

Location of foreign branches of American banks

Edge Act offices

International banking facilities (IBFs)

"Shell branch"

Extent of foreign bank branching in the United States

Regulation of foreign bank branches in the United States

Overview of the integrated worldwide money and banking system

Role of

—correspondent banking

—the central bank

—the International Monetary Fund (IMF)

Impact of global banking and finance on national policies

Impact of interest rate changes on international money flows

The importance of New York in the international banking/finance system

Questions

1. Describe the role of (a) correspondent banking, and (b) foreign branch banking in contributing to the global money-banking-financial system.

2. List some of the reasons for the rapid recent growth in the number of foreign branches, both by American banks overseas, and by foreign banks in the United States.

3. What are international banking facilities (IBFs)? Why are they permitted? What functions do they perform? And why have so many banks established them? Explain.

4. The chapter emphasizes the one-world nature of the global money-banking-financial system. Describe in as much detail as you can the characteristics of this global "spider-web" system.

5. Describe the role of the central banks in the functioning of the global financial system.

6. Describe the "international medium of exchange mechanism" which permits and facilitates the now-greatly expanded volume of world trade. What is it, and how does it work?

Suggested Readings

Abrams, R. K. "Regional Banks and International Banking." *Economic Review.* Federal Reserve Bank of Kansas City (November 1980), 3–14.

Aliber, Robert Z. *The International Money Game*, 4th ed. New York: Basic Books, 1983.

Baughn, William H., and Donald R. Mandich. *International Banking Handbook.* Homewood, Ill.: Dow Jones-Irwin, 1983.

Chrystal, K. Alec. "International Banking Facilities." *Review.* Federal Reserve Bank of Richmond, 1981.

Crane, Dwight B., and Samuel L. Hayes III. "The Evolution of International Banking Competition and its Implications for Regulation." *Journal of Bank Research.* (Spring 1983), 39–48.

Dale, R. S. "Country Risk and Bank Regulation." *The Banker.* (March 1983), 41–48.

Dale, R. S., and R. P. Mattinoe. *Managing Global Debt.* Staff Paper, Brookings Institution, Washington, D.C. 1983.

Daniels, John D., Ernest W. Orgram Jr., and Lee H. Radebaugh. *International Business: Environments and Operations.* Reading, Mass.: Addison-Wesley, 1982.

Davis, S. *The Management Function in International Banking.* New York: John Wiley & Sons, 1979.

Donaldson, T. H. *International Lending by Commercial Banks.* New York: John Wiley & Sons, 1979.

Dufey, Gunter, and Ian H. Giddy. *The International Money Market.* Englewood Cliffs, N.J.: Prentice-Hall, 1978.

Editeman, David K., and Arthur I. Stonehill. *Multinational Business Finance.* Reading, Mass.: Addison-Wesley, 1982.

Fieleke, Norman. *Key Issues in International Banking.* Boston: Federal Reserve Bank of Boston, 1977.

Fisk, Charles, and Frank Rimlinger. *Foreign Bank Competitive Analysis.* New York: Citicorp, February 1981.

Friedman, Milton. "Outdoing Smoot-Hawley." *The Wall Street Journal.* April 20, 1987.

Goodfriend, Marvin. "Eurodollars." *Instruments of the Money Market.* Federal Reserve Bank of Richmond, 1986, pp. 53–64.

Gray, Jean M., and Peter H. Gray. "The Multinational Bank: A Financial MNC?" *Journal of Banking and Finance.* (March 1981), 33–64.

Grennes, Thomas. *International Economics.* Englewood Cliffs, N.J.: Prentice-Hall, 1984.

Guth, Wilfried. "International Banking: The Next Phase." *The Banker.* (October 1981), 27–34.

Hector, Gary. "The Japanese Want to be Your Bankers." *Fortune.* October 27, 1986.

Hoffman, Stuart G. "U.S. Banks Expand Offshore Banking in Caribbean Basin." *Economic Review.* Federal Reserve Bank of Atlanta, (July/August 1980), 22–25.

Houpt, J. V. "Performance and Characteristics of Edge Corporations." *Staff Studies.* Washington, D.C.: Federal Reserve Board, January 1981.

Johnson, Manual H. "Reflections on the Current International Debt Situation." *Review* 72 (6). Federal Reserve Bank of Kansas City, (June 1987), 3–8.

Key, Sydney. "The Internationalization of U.S. Banking." in Richard Aspinwall and Robert Eisenbeis (eds.) *Handbook for Banking Strategy.* New York: John Wiley & Sons, 1985.

Key, Sydney, and J. M. Brundy. "Implementation of the International Banking Act." Federal Reserve Bulletin, vol. 65, October 1979, pp. 785–796.

Korth, Christopher M. "The Evolving Role of U.S. Banks in International Finance." *The Bankers Magazine.* (July/August 1980), 68–73.

Lees, Francis A. *International Banking and Finance.* London: The Macmillan Press Ltd., 1974.

Little, Jane Sneddon. *Eurodollars.* New York: Harper & Row, 1975.

Makin, John H. *The Global Debt Crisis.* New York: Basic Books, 1984.

Mathis, F. John, ed. *Offshore Lending by U.S. Commercial Banks.* Washington, D.C. and Philadelphia, PA: Bankers' Association for Foreign Trade and Robert Morris Associates, 1978.

Mills, Rodney. "Foreign Lending by Banks: A Guide to International and U.S. Statistics." *Federal Reserve Bulletin.* Washington, D.C.: Board of Governors of the Federal Reserve System, October 1986.

Park, Yoon, and Jack Zwick. *International Banking in Theory and Practice.* Reading, Mass.: Addison-Wesley Publishing, 1985.

Pecchioli, R. M. *The Internationalization of Banking: The*

Policy Issues. Organization for Economic Co-operation and Development, Paris, 1983.

Porzecanski, Arturo C. "The International Financial Role of U.S. Commercial Banks: Past and Future." *Journal of Banking and Finance.* (March 1981), 5–16.

Quinn, Melanie R. "A Selected Bibliography on the Topic of International Banking Supervision and Risk." Washington, D.C.: Comptroller of the Currency, Staff Paper, 1982.

Rodriquez, Rita, and E. Eugene Carter. *International Financial Management.* Englewood Cliffs, N.J.: Prentice-Hall, 1984.

Steuber, Ursel. *International Banking.* Netherlands: A. W. Sijthoff International Publishing Co., 1976.

U.S. Congress, House Committee on Banking, Currency, and Housing. *International Banking.* Washington, D.C.: Government Printint Office, 1976.

Veith, R. H. *Multinational Computer Nets.* Lexington Books, 1981.

Wallich, Henry C. "International Lending and the Role of Bank Supervisory Cooperation." Board of Governors of the Federal Reserve System, September 24, 1981.

———. "American Banks Abroad in 1985." Board of Governors of the Federal Reserve system, March 11, 1986.

Williamson, John. *The Open Economy and the World Economy.* New York: Basic Books, 1983.

APPENDIX 1A

A Guide to Information Sources

The study of money, banking, and the financial system is a very broad and important subject area. This appendix could not hope to cover all of the available information sources. But it can go far enough to get you started. And in research—in this field as in all fields—your first sources will lead you to others. The chain is endless. Also at the end of each chapter you will find sources of additional information listed under "suggested readings."

Current News Sources

On a day-to-day basis, current news sources are an excellent place to look for money, banking and financial information and statistics. *The Wall Street Journal* is an excellent daily source, as is *The New York Times*. And several of the big-city newspapers provide good coverage of this subject.

The **specialized banking daily**, the *American Banker*, carries day-to-day information on just about everything that is happening in banking and finance. If you ever want a blow-by-blow description of some development that occurred in banking and finance at some time in the past, you can find that in the back issues of the *American Banker*.

A subscription to the *American Banker* is expensive—about $500 per year. Also it's a bulky item for libraries to handle. So unless you are at a large college or university it isn't likely that you'll find it in your library. You may be able to get access through interlibrary loan. But a more direct approach would be to contact the home office of a large bank and arrange to use theirs. Or if you happen to be near Washington D.C., the **American Bankers Association** (at 1120 Connecticut Avenue) has a library with an unbelievable collection of information on banking and they are very friendly and helpful to members of the academic community who are seeking information on banking.

Current news magazines such as *Business Week, Fortune, Forbes, The Economist*, and several others are good sources. Also, the publishers of the *American Banker* now publish *Banking Weekly* which carries the banking and financial highlights of the week. And the same publishers also publish the *Banking Yearbook* in the spring of each year.

This *Yearbook* gives the highlights of banking and financial developments of the previous year.

There are several daily and weekly **business and financial news programs** on both radio and television. Both the number and the depth and accuracy of these programs increased significantly during the 1980s. An easy way to keep in touch with this fast-changing field is to watch the developments on TV or listen to the radio when you're driving. Consult your local radio and TV listings to find the times and stations where these programs are available.

Federal Reserve Publications

The **Board of Governors** of the Federal Reserve System in Washington has a large staff of economists and writers who investigate and report on every aspect of the money, banking, and financial scene. In addition, each of the 12 **Federal Reserve banks** has its own staff of economic and financial experts and writers. These research departments are constantly investigating and reporting on various aspects of money and banking and financial markets.

Weekly, monthly, quarterly and annual publications are constantly flowing out of the Federal Reserve System. The semiannual publication, *Fed in Print*, Federal Reserve Bank of Philadelphia, lists all of these publications. Several probably are available in your library. If not, the Fed Board and the Fed banks will supply these publications to college libraries (and to college professors) free of charge. Box 1A-1 tells you where to write.

The *Federal Reserve Bulletin* is the monthly publication of the Board of Governors. It is also free to college libraries and professors. It carries highlight articles on the money and banking system, statements to Congress by the Fed Board Chairman and other Board members, and detailed statistics on conditions and changes in the banking and financial system, domestic and international. For specific data on money, banking, financial markets, and the economy, the *Federal Reserve Bulletin* always would be a good first place to look.

Box 1A-1

Sources of Publications from The Federal Reserve System

Board of Governors of the Federal Reserve System
Publications Services
Washington, DC 20551
(202) 452-3244

FRB Atlanta
Research Department, Publications Unit
104 Marietta Street
Atlanta, GA 30303-2713
(404) 521-8788

FRB Boston
Bank and Public Services Department
600 Atlantic Avenue
Boston, MA 02106
(617) 973-3459

FRB Chicago
Public Information Center
230 South LaSalle Street
Chicago, IL 60690
(312) 322-5112

FRB Cleveland
Public Information Center
P.O. Box 6387
Cleveland, OH 44101
(216) 579-2048

FRB Dallas
Public Affairs Department
Station K
Dallas, TX 75222
(214) 651-6289 or -6266

FRB Kansas City
Public Affairs Department
925 Grand Avenue
Kansas City, MO 64198
(816) 881-2402

FRB Minneapolis
Office of Public Information
250 Marquette Avenue
Minneapolis, MN 55480
(612) 340-2446

FRB New York
Public Information Department
33 Liberty Street
New York, NY 10045
(212) 791-6134

FRB Philadelphia
Public Information Department
P.O. Box 66
Philadelphia, PA 19105
(215) 574-6115

FRB Richmond
Public Services Department
P.O. Box 27622
Richmond, VA 23261
(804) 643-1250

FRB St. Louis
Bank Relations and
Public Information Department
P.O. Box 442
St. Louis, MO 63166
(314) 444-8421

FRB San Francisco
Public Information Department
P.O. Box 7702
San Francisco, CA 94120
(415) 974-3234

Note: Look at the last few pages inside the back cover of the *Federal Reserve Bulletin* for a list of Fed Board Publications. Also, write to Publications Services for a list of Fed Board Publications. Also, write to Publications Services for a booklet listing all of the publications of the Board, and of all of the 12 banks. And for the latest items, see *Fed in Print*, mentioned previously.

Publications of the Other Bank Regulatory Agencies

Each of the agencies involved in supervising or regulating the banking or financial community or financial markets has a staff of economists and financial experts and writers. These experts are constantly doing studies and publishing results on conditions, developments, and issues in the financial system. These agencies include:

- the Comptroller of the Currency in the U.S. Department of the Treasury
- the Federal Deposit Insurance Corporation (FDIC)
- the Federal Savings and Loan Insurance Corporation (FSLIC)
- the National Credit Union Administration (NCUA)
- the Federal Home Loan Bank Board (FHLBB).

Each of these agencies publishes an annual report explaining their activities and findings, and including detailed statistics on conditions in their respective industries. Also, all of these agencies issue periodic reports, several of which might be available in your library.

In addition to the federal agencies, each of the 50 states has an Office of the State Banking Commissioner, or State Banking Supervisor. These state supervisory offices are joined in the "Association of State Bank Supervisors" which undertakes studies and publishes reports dealing with state-chartered banks.

The Regulators of the Financial Markets

The agencies which regulate the securities markets also employ economists and finance experts, undertake studies, and issue annual reports and special reports. These agencies include:

- the Securities and Exchange Commission (SEC)
- the Commodities Futures Trading Commission (CFTC)
- the Chicago Board of Trade (CBOT)
- the New York Stock Exchange (NYSE)
- the American Stock Exchange (ASE)
- and various others dealing with various segments of the financial markets.

Congressional Committees

Each house of Congress has a committee which is concerned with overseeing the banking industry and the financial markets. In the House of Representatives it's called "the Committee on Banking, Currency, and Housing." In the Senate it's called "the Banking, Housing, and Urban Affairs Committee."

Both of these committees have subcommittees dealing specifically with banking and with other segments of the financial system. These committees have economists and financial experts doing studies and issuing reports. Also, these committees and subcommittees hold hearings to gather detailed information on various aspects of the financial system. These hearings documents, committee reports, and other publications can be obtained from the committees. Several of these publications probably are available in the government documents section of your library.

Academic and Professional Associations and Banking and Finance Magazines and Journals

There are dozens of magazines and journals which focus specifically on banking and finance. Also, the many economics journals carry information and research results in monetary economics, and monetary theory and policy.

The several academic associations—the American Economic Association and the several regional economics associations, the American Finance Association and the several regional finance associations, the Financial Management Association, the National Association of Business Economists, the North American Economics and Finance Association (and there are several others) all publish their own journals. Some of the journals are likely to carry articles dealing more with theory and policy, others, more with the practical business of banking and finance.

In addition to the association-related journals there are many other academic journals in economics and finance which carry articles in this field. One which is aimed specifically in this direction is *The Journal of Money, Credit, and Banking*—an excellent source.

To search the other journals for articles in this field, *The Journal of Economic Literature (JEL)* is indispensable. If you aren't already familiar with *The JEL*, the next time you are in the library, go find it and spend a few minutes with it. You'll be amazed how much useful information you can find there, and how much time it can save you.

The strictly banking-related magazines you are most likely to find in your library are the *ABA Banking Journal*, *Banking*, the *Bankers Magazine*, perhaps the *Bankers Monthly*, the *Journal of Bank Research* and, if you're lucky, several others.

There are several banking magazines focusing on the various regions of the country—e.g., the

Southern Banker—and in most states there is a statewide organization of bankers and this organization often issues a magazine focusing on banking within that state.

There are journals dealing with specific segments of or functions within the industry—the *Journal of Retail Banking*, the *Journal of Bank Marketing, Commercial Bank Management*, etc. If you would spend an hour in your library with your friendly periodicals librarian you could quickly find out which of these sources are available to you. It would be an hour well spent.

Associations of Banks and Other Financial Institutions

There are a great number of professional associations involving bankers, thrift organizations, insurance organizations, investment organizations—all kinds of financial institutions. Each of these organizations issues an annual report. Several of them publish their own journals—e.g., the *ABA Banking Journal*—dealing with subjects of interest to their membership.

If you want to contact any of these organizations for a copy of their annual report and/or for lists of their other publications, you can find the addresses in:

* the *Encyclopedia of Associations*, or
* the *Encyclopedia of Business Information Sources*, or
* the *Executive Guide to Information Sources.*

At least one of these sources is sure to be available in the reference section of your library.

Banking Organizations

The most important banking organizations—the ones which have the largest membership and are most active in gathering and disseminating information—are:

* American Bankers Association (ABA)
* Bank Administration Institute (BAI)
* Bankers Association for Foreign Trade
* Independent Bankers Association of America
* Mortgage Bankers Association of America
* Robert Morris Associates (RMA: also "National Association of Bank Loan and Credit Officers").

Organizations of Thrift Institutions

The following organizations of thrift institutions (S&L's, mutual savings banks, and credit unions)

all issue annual reports and provide other information on their respective industries:

* American Savings and Loan Institute
* American Savings and Loan League
* National League of Insured Savings Associations
* Savings and Loan Foundation
* United States League of Savings Associations
* National Association of Mutual Savings Banks
* Credit Union Executive Society
* Credit Union National Association

Insurance Organizations

* American Society of Pension Actuaries
* National Association of Independent Insurers
* National Association of Insurance Brokers
* National Insurance Association

Investment Organizations

* Investment Company Institute
* National Association of Securities Dealers (NASD)
* Securities Industry Association

Additional Sources

In the securities industry, all of the hundreds of brokerage companies and investment advisors provide information on financial conditions, on market conditions and outlook, and on specific financial institutions and instruments. Each individual bank and other financial institution puts out its own annual report and provides other information on its earnings and financial condition.

The American Bank Directory and *The American Savings Directory*, produced annually by McFadden Business Publications (Norcross, Georgia) provide lists of all of the banks and savings institutions in the country and summary statistics on each. The *Moody's* and *Standard and Poor's* directories also provide detailed information on financial institutions.

Information on international banking and finance is gathered by the U.S. Department of Commerce and published in the *Survey of Current Business* and in other publications. Also the International Monetary Fund (IMF), the International Bank for Reconstruction and Development (the World Bank: IBRD), the Organization for Economic Cooperation and Development (OECD), the U.S. Agency for International Development (USAID in the Department of State), and several other international agencies publish international banking and financial information and statistics.

The *Economic Report of the President, together with the Annual Report of the Council of Economic Advisers* (published each February) is an excellent source of analysis of the economy. It's also a good place to find out the administration's position on economic policy. The *Report* carries detailed economic and financial statistics, both national and international.

The Statistical Abstract of the United States

The sources of information presented in this appendix are far from complete. But for most readers, I fear I already have told you more than you wanted to know. If at this point you haven't found enough appropriate sources, then my advice is that you should go to the *Statistical Abstract of the United States*. There you will probably find a lead on what you are looking for.

The full title of the *Statistical Abstract*—published by the U.S. Bureau of the Census—is: *Statistical Abstract of the United States: National Data Book and Guide to Sources*. It is just what its title says. It carries some statistics on almost anything you can think of. Then it tells you where to go for more. Whenever you need statistics on something and you don't know where else to look, go to the *Statistical Abstract*. It will seldom let you down. Box 1A-2 gives an example of some of the kinds of data you can find in the statistical abstract.

Statistical Abstract of the United States:
Table of Contents, Selected Sections

Future Value (Compounding) and Present Value (Discounting) Tables

Table 3-A-1. The Compounding Table. Future values of one dollar n years from now, invested today at compound interest.

($1 compounded at r% for n years)
(Future value = $1 $(1 + r)^n$)

n	1%	2%	3%	4%	5%	6%	7%	8%	9%	10%	11%	12%	13%	14%	15%	16%	17%	18%	19%	20%	24%
0	1.000	1.000	1.000	1.000	1.000	1.000	1.000	1.000	1.000	1.000	1.000	1.000	1.000	1.000	1.000	1.000	1.000	1.000	1.000	1.000	1.000
1	1.010	1.020	1.030	1.040	1.050	1.060	1.070	1.080	1.090	1.100	1.110	1.120	1.130	1.140	1.150	1.160	1.170	1.180	1.190	1.200	1.240
2	1.020	1.040	1.061	1.082	1.102	1.124	1.145	1.166	1.186	1.210	1.232	1.254	1.277	1.300	1.322	1.346	1.369	1.392	1.416	1.440	1.538
3	1.030	1.061	1.093	1.125	1.158	1.191	1.225	1.260	1.295	1.331	1.368	1.405	1.443	1.482	1.521	1.561	1.602	1.643	1.685	1.728	1.907
4	1.041	1.082	1.126	1.170	1.216	1.262	1.311	1.360	1.412	1.464	1.518	1.574	1.630	1.689	1.749	1.811	1.874	1.939	2.005	2.074	2.364
5	1.051	1.104	1.159	1.217	1.276	1.338	1.403	1.469	1.539	1.611	1.685	1.762	1.842	1.925	2.011	2.100	2.192	2.288	2.386	2.488	2.932
6	1.062	1.126	1.194	1.265	1.340	1.419	1.501	1.587	1.677	1.772	1.870	1.974	2.082	2.195	2.313	2.436	2.565	2.700	2.840	2.986	3.635
7	1.072	1.149	1.230	1.316	1.407	1.504	1.606	1.714	1.828	1.949	2.076	2.211	2.353	2.502	2.660	2.826	3.001	3.185	3.379	3.583	4.508
8	1.083	1.172	1.267	1.369	1.477	1.594	1.718	1.851	1.993	2.144	2.305	2.476	2.658	2.853	3.059	3.278	3.511	3.759	4.021	4.300	5.590
9	1.094	1.195	1.305	1.423	1.551	1.689	1.838	1.999	2.172	2.358	2.558	2.773	3.004	3.252	3.518	3.803	4.108	4.435	4.785	5.160	6.931
10	1.105	1.219	1.344	1.480	1.629	1.791	1.967	2.159	2.367	2.594	2.839	3.106	3.395	3.707	4.046	4.411	4.807	5.234	5.695	6.192	8.594
11	1.116	1.243	1.384	1.539	1.710	1.898	2.105	2.332	2.580	2.853	3.152	3.479	3.836	4.226	4.652	5.117	5.624	6.176	6.777	7.430	10.657
12	1.127	1.268	1.426	1.601	1.796	2.012	2.252	2.518	2.813	3.138	3.498	3.896	4.335	4.818	5.350	5.926	6.580	7.288	8.064	8.916	13.215
13	1.138	1.294	1.469	1.665	1.886	2.133	2.410	2.720	3.066	3.452	3.883	4.363	4.898	5.492	6.153	6.886	7.699	8.599	9.596	10.699	16.386
14	1.149	1.319	1.513	1.732	1.980	2.261	2.579	2.937	3.342	3.797	4.310	4.887	5.535	6.261	7.076	7.988	9.007	10.147	11.420	12.839	20.319
15	1.161	1.346	1.558	1.801	2.079	2.397	2.759	3.172	3.642	4.177	4.785	5.474	6.254	7.138	8.137	9.266	10.539	11.974	13.590	15.407	25.196
16	1.173	1.373	1.605	1.873	2.183	2.540	2.952	3.426	3.970	4.595	5.311	6.130	7.067	8.137	9.358	10.748	12.330	14.129	16.172	18.488	31.243
17	1.184	1.400	1.653	1.948	2.292	2.693	3.159	3.700	4.328	5.054	5.895	6.866	7.986	9.276	10.761	12.468	14.426	16.672	19.244	22.186	38.741
18	1.196	1.428	1.702	2.026	2.407	2.854	3.380	3.996	4.717	5.560	6.544	7.690	9.024	10.575	12.375	14.463	16.879	19.673	22.901	26.623	48.039
19	1.208	1.457	1.754	2.107	2.527	3.026	3.617	4.316	5.142	6.116	7.263	8.613	10.197	12.056	14.232	16.777	19.748	23.214	27.252	31.948	59.568
20	1.220	1.486	1.806	2.191	2.653	3.207	3.870	4.661	5.604	6.728	8.062	9.646	11.523	13.743	16.367	19.461	23.106	27.393	32.429	38.338	73.864
25	1.282	1.641	2.094	2.666	3.386	4.292	5.427	6.848	8.623	10.835	13.585	17.000	21.231	26.462	32.919	40.874	50.658	62.669	77.388	95.396	216.542
30	1.348	1.811	2.427	3.243	4.322	5.743	7.612	10.063	13.268	17.449	22.892	29.960	39.116	50.950	66.212	85.850	111.065	143.371	184.675	237.376	634.820
40	1.489	2.208	3.262	4.801	7.040	10.286	14.974	21.725	31.409	45.259	65.001	93.051	132.782	188.884	267.864	378.721	533.869	750.378	1,051.67	1,469.77	5,455.91
50	1.645	2.692	4.384	7.107	11.467	18.420	29.457	46.902	74.358	117.391	184.565	289.002	450.736	700.233	1,083.66	1,670.70	2,566.22	3,927.36	5,988.91	9,100.44	46,890.4
60	1.817	3.281	5.892	10.520	18.679	32.988	57.946	101.257	176.031	304.482	524.057	597.597	1,530.05	2,595.92	4,384.00	7,370.20	12,335.4	20,555.1	34,105.0	56,347.5	402,996

This compounding table is the "compound value interest factor" (CVIF) table. It tells you what the value of one dollar will be n years in the future if the dollar is invested today at interest rate r.

Example: The table shows that if one dollar is invested today at r = 10%, then 10 years from now that investment will be worth $2.594. So suppose you invest $1,000 at 10%. In 10 years that investment will be worth $2,594. You could calculate this using the formula $F = P (1 + r)^n$. But it's easier and quicker to look it up in the table. And these days you don't even have to do that. Financial calculators are preprogramed to give you the answer automatically.

Table 3-A-2.   The Discounting Table Present Values of one dollar, to be received n years in the future.

($1 discounted at r% for n years)

$$\text{Present value} = \$1 \times \frac{1}{(1 + r)^n}$$

n	1%	2%	3%	4%	5%	6%	7%	8%	9%	10%	11%	12%	13%	14%	15%	16%	17%	18%	19%	20%	24%
0	1.000	1.000	1.000	1.000	1.000	1.000	1.000	1.000	1.000	1.000	1.000	1.000	1.000	1.000	1.000	1.000	1.000	1.000	1.000	1.000	1.000
1	0.990	0.980	0.971	0.962	0.952	0.943	0.935	0.926	0.917	0.909	0.901	0.593	0.885	0.877	0.870	0.862	0.855	0.847	0.840	0.833	0.806
2	0.980	0.961	0.943	0.925	0.907	0.890	0.873	0.857	0.842	0.826	0.812	0.797	0.783	0.769	0.756	0.743	0.731	0.718	0.706	0.694	0.650
3	0.971	0.942	0.915	0.889	0.864	0.840	0.816	0.794	0.772	0.751	0.731	0.712	0.693	0.675	0.658	0.641	0.624	0.609	0.593	0.579	0.524
4	0.961	0.924	0.889	0.855	0.823	0.792	0.763	0.735	0.708	0.683	0.659	0.636	0.613	0.592	0.572	0.552	0.534	0.516	0.499	0.482	0.423
5	0.951	0.906	0.863	0.822	0.784	0.747	0.713	0.681	0.650	0.621	0.593	0.567	0.543	0.519	0.497	0.476	0.456	0.437	0.419	0.402	0.341
6	0.942	0.888	0.838	0.790	0.746	0.705	0.666	0.630	0.596	0.564	0.535	0.507	0.480	0.456	0.432	0.410	0.390	0.370	0.352	0.335	0.275
7	0.933	0.871	0.813	0.760	0.711	0.665	0.623	0.583	0.547	0.513	0.482	0.452	0.425	0.400	0.376	0.354	0.333	0.314	0.296	0.279	0.222
8	0.923	0.853	0.789	0.731	0.677	0.627	0.582	0.540	0.502	0.467	0.434	0.404	0.376	0.351	0.327	0.305	0.285	0.266	0.249	0.233	0.179
9	0.914	0.837	0.766	0.703	0.645	0.592	0.544	0.500	0.460	0.424	0.391	0.361	0.333	0.308	0.284	0.263	0.243	0.225	0.209	0.194	0.144
10	0.905	0.820	0.744	0.676	0.614	0.558	0.508	0.463	0.422	0.386	0.352	0.322	0.295	0.270	0.247	0.227	0.208	0.191	0.176	0.162	0.116
11	0.896	0.804	0.722	0.650	0.585	0.527	0.475	0.429	0.388	0.350	0.317	0.287	0.261	0.237	0.215	0.195	0.178	0.162	0.148	0.135	0.094
12	0.887	0.788	0.701	0.625	0.557	0.497	0.444	0.397	0.356	0.319	0.286	0.257	0.231	0.208	0.187	0.168	0.152	0.137	0.124	0.112	0.076
13	0.879	0.773	0.681	0.601	0.530	0.469	0.415	0.368	0.326	0.290	0.258	0.229	0.204	0.182	0.163	0.145	0.130	0.116	0.104	0.093	0.061
14	0.870	0.758	0.661	0.577	0.505	0.442	0.388	0.340	0.299	0.263	0.232	0.205	0.181	0.160	0.141	0.125	0.111	0.099	0.088	0.078	0.049
15	0.861	0.743	0.642	0.555	0.481	0.417	0.362	0.315	0.275	0.239	0.209	0.183	0.160	0.140	0.123	0.108	0.095	0.084	0.074	0.065	0.040
16	0.853	0.728	0.623	0.534	0.458	0.394	0.339	0.292	0.252	0.218	0.188	0.163	0.141	0.123	0.107	0.093	0.081	0.071	0.062	0.054	0.032
17	0.844	0.714	0.605	0.513	0.436	0.371	0.317	0.270	0.231	0.198	0.170	0.146	0.125	0.108	0.093	0.080	0.069	0.060	0.052	0.045	0.026
18	0.836	0.700	0.587	0.494	0.416	0.350	0.296	0.250	0.212	0.180	0.153	0.130	0.111	0.095	0.081	0.069	0.059	0.051	0.044	0.038	0.021
19	0.828	0.686	0.570	0.475	0.396	0.331	0.276	0.232	0.194	0.164	0.138	0.116	0.098	0.083	0.070	0.060	0.051	0.043	0.037	0.031	0.017
20	0.820	0.673	0.554	0.456	0.377	0.312	0.258	0.215	0.178	0.149	0.124	0.104	0.087	0.073	0.061	0.051	0.043	0.037	0.031	0.026	0.014
25	0.780	0.610	0.478	0.375	0.295	0.233	0.184	0.146	0.116	0.092	0.074	0.059	0.047	0.038	0.030	0.024	0.020	0.016	0.013	0.010	0.005
30	0.742	0.552	0.412	0.308	0.231	0.174	0.131	0.099	0.075	0.057	0.044	0.033	0.026	0.020	0.015	0.012	0.009	0.007	0.005	0.004	0.002
40	0.672	0.453	0.307	0.208	0.142	0.097	0.067	0.046	0.032	0.022	0.015	0.011	0.008	0.005	0.004	0.003	0.002	0.001	0.001	0.001	0.000
50	0.608	0.372	0.228	0.141	0.087	0.054	0.034	0.021	0.013	0.009	0.005	0.003	0.002	0.001	0.001	0.001	0.000	0.000	0.000	0.000	0.000
60	0.550	0.305	0.170	0.095	0.054	0.030	0.017	0.010	0.006	0.003	0.002	0.001	0.001	0.000	0.000	0.000	0.000	0.000	0.000	0.000	0.000

This discounting table is called a "present value interest factor" (PVIF) table. It tells you the present value of a dollar to be received n years in the future, at various interest rates.

Example: The table shows that if the dollar is to be received in 10 years and if the interest rate is 10%, its present value is only $0.386. So a 10-year $1,000 zero-coupon bond (for example, a government E-bond) would be worth $386. Here again you could calculate this using the formula

$$P = F \times \frac{1}{(1 + r)^n}.$$

But with PVIF tables and preprogramed calculators, who would do that? Nobody. The reason for learning the formulas is to gain **an understanding of compounding and discounting**. The tables and calculators can't give you that.

APPENDIX 8A

Explanations of Various Kinds of EFTS Functions[1]

When we talk about electronic funds transfer systems, we include several different kinds of functions, and in fact, several different "systems." But all of these systems are alike in that they transfer funds electronically rather than by the use of paper instruments, such as checks, drafts, certificates, etc. Each EFT system replaces manual processes, and transfers funds instantly. So an EFT system of any kind speeds up the transaction and reduces the amount of manual labor involved. The obvious advantage of any kind of EFT system results from the reduced labor cost and the increased speed.

The following sub-sections briefly describe eight different kinds of EFT arrangements. The first five of these involve EFT arrangements in which no direct "customer contact" is required. The electronic fund transfers are handled in "batches" by the interbank EFT networks. These are: wire transfers of funds, check truncation, automated clearing house arrangements, pre-authorized credit arrangements such as automatic payroll deposits, and pre-authorized debit arrangements such as bill-paying services. The last three of the EFT arrangements involve direct customer contact. These are: the automated teller machines (ATMs), point-of-sale (POS) terminals, and on-line telephone connections between the customer's telephone and the bank's computer.

NO CUSTOMER CONTACT EFT SYSTEMS

Wire Transfers of Funds

Banks have been using "wire transfers" for the instantaneous transmission of funds from one bank to another since the 1950s, on the "interbank wire."

Wire transfers amount to sending electronic messages (rather than paper documents) in order to move funds from one bank (or one account) to another.

The Federal Reserve System operates a major wire transfer network. This Federal Reserve Communications System network transfers large volumes of funds for member banks, for their correspondent banks, and for bank customers. The dollar volume of funds transferred through this system is several times as large as the amount of money handled by the Fed's check-clearing system. It is now possible to transfer funds to any place in the country, instantaneously. These transfers are going on in large volume, every day.

Check Truncation

The purpose of a check truncation system is to reduce the flow of checks through the banking system. The data from the check is entered into a computer, then sent back by electronic signals. With the usual design of a "check truncation" system, the customer who wrote the check never gets back the cancelled check. Once the data from the check is entered into the electronic system, the checks are stored for awhile and ultimately destroyed. All the customer gets is an accounting statement.

Technology now makes it possible to transmit the image of the check, not just the data. Perhaps this will speed the introduction of check truncation systems. There are also possibilities that nonpersonal checks—perhaps Federal Government checks—will someday be handled by check truncation.

Automated Clearing House (ACH) Systems

Automated clearing houses are arrangements for electronically settling debits and credits among banks. When checks are written on one bank and deposited in other banks, funds must be transferred

[1] Reprinted from: Elbert V. Bowden and Judith L. Holbert, *Revolution in Banking*, 2nd ed., Reston Publishing Co. (a Prentice-Hall Company), Reston, Va., 1984, pp. 175–180. Reprinted with permission of my co-author and the publisher.

from the banks on which the checks are written to the banks in which the checks are deposited. ACH systems permit the debit and credit items to be transmitted electronically, usually through a computer-generated magnetic tape.

Several ACH systems are now operating, handling a large volume of debit and credit items at various places throughout the country. For example, the California Automated Clearing House Association is called "CACHA," the North Carolina Automated Clearing House Association is called "NORCACHA," and other clearing house associations around the country have similar acronyms.

During the early 1980s, there were more than 10,000 financial institutions participating in these regional ACH systems. Since 1978 these regional systems have been linked together by the National Automated Clearing House Association. The Federal Government is the largest user of the ACH systems, through direct deposit of social security payments and other federal disbursements. These ACH systems are now playing a very important role in facilitating the flow of interbank settlements.

Preauthorized Credits: Automatic Payroll and Other Deposits

Preauthorized credit arrangements include such things as automatic payroll deposits by employers to the employees' bank accounts, automatic deposits of government social security and pension payments, and other kinds of recurring payments such as dividend and annuity payments.

Preauthorized payments are deposited automatically to the accounts of the recipients, and are distributed to the various banks through the ACH system. The employee (or other recipient of regular preauthorized payments) authorizes the employer (or other payor) to make direct payments, and then the payor prepares the data on a computer tape and sends it to the bank. Then the funds are automatically withdrawn from the payor's account and distributed to all of the payees through the ACH system. These preauthorized credit plans are now playing a significant and increasing role in the nation's payments system, and are significantly increasing the speed and reducing the cost of making these payments.

Preauthorized Debits: Automatic Bill-Paying

Preauthorized debit arrangements work very much like preauthorized credits except that the funds are being deducted from the individual customer's account and deposited into the company's account. Preauthorized debits are also cleared through the ACH systems.

Preauthorized debits are well suited for any case of regularly recurring bills, such as mortgage payments, insurance payments, and other payments of a definite amount. Bills which recur but which have varying amounts (such as utility bills) also can be handled through a preauthorized debit arrangement. But most customers have been unwilling to give their utility companies and others the authorization to automatically deduct bills from their accounts. So it isn't likely that all bills will ever be paid in this way. But preauthorized debits already are playing an important and increasing role in the payments system.

CUSTOMER-CONTACT EFT SYSTEMS

Automated Teller Machines (ATMs)

The most important and most rapidly expanding EFT arrangement involving direct customer contact is the ATM. Automated teller machines provide a broad range of banking services to the customer and provide 24-hour access to the bank's services. They are playing an increasing role in reducing the "direct customer-teller contact."

ATMs often are located at the bank itself. But many are located in remote locations such as shopping centers, airports, etc. Customer resistance to the use of ATMs was difficult to overcome at first. But customer resistance now seems to be a problem of the past.

There have been some legal problems with the use of the ATMs concerning such questions as *where* the machines can be located and *who* will be provided access to the machines, and questions about customer *safety* and *privacy*. These issues will be discussed later.

Point-of-Sale (POS) Systems

As the name implies, point-of-sale systems involve terminals located in places of business—usually retail stores—which permit the customer to pay the store by EFT. The amount of the purchase is automatically deducted from the customer's account and simultaneously added to the seller's account.

It works like this: The customer's card is inserted in the POS terminal, the amount is entered manually or through an electronic cash register or "products code reader," and the transfer of funds is made instantaneously. If the customer's bank is different than the store's bank, a "switching and processing center" (SPC) connects the computers of the two banks and completes the transfer.

Both the customer and the store receive a printed statement from the POS terminal at the time of the transaction. Then the customer's regular bank statement lists each one of the POS purchases individually.

POS systems have been introduced in a few cities, but there have been impediments to their expanded use. There has been customer resistance, and the cost of installing all of the POS terminals required is high. One clear advantage of such a system from the point of view of the seller is that the problem of bad checks is eliminated. These issues and the latest developments on POS will be further discussed later.

Telephone Bill-Paying Services

The technology now exists for customers with touch-tone telephones to use their own home phone to contact the bank's or thrift's computer to pay bills and perform other services automatically. A system like this was introduced in Seattle in 1973 by Seattle First National Bank, but the number of customers attracted to this service was so small that the service was withdrawn after only a few months.

Washington Mutual Savings Bank also introduced a telephone bill-paying service, with the belief that there will be a dramatic increase in acceptance of this service once people understand how it works. It appears likely that in the future these telephone bill-paying services will become an important kind of electronic banking in many places throughout the country.

Telephone Home Banking Services

During the early 1980s, as telecommunication technology continued its rapid development, "home banking" systems were introduced experimentally in several places in the country. These systems use either the TV cable or telephone line and are linked into the TV set. By 1984 this was beginning to look like "an idea whose time has come." You'll be reading more about that in a subsequent chapter.

CBCTs and RSUs

The ATMs and POS terminals and other terminals that serve as remote connections between customers and their bank or thrift institution are referred to in general as "CBCTs" and "RSUs." They are called "customer-bank communications terminals" (CBCTs) by the Office of the Comptroller of the Currency, which supervises National Banks. They are called "remote service units" (RSUs) by the Federal Home Loan Bank Board, which supervises most of the thrift institutions. Some CBCTs and RSUs are full-service ATMs. But others are less sophisticated terminals that do not provide the full range of services—such as receiving deposits, dispensing funds, transferring funds between accounts, making credit card advances, and receiving payments—that are provided by a full-service EFT terminal.

APPENDIX 11A

The Stock Market Crash of October, 1987

BACKGROUND

In 1982 the economy was in serious recession and stock prices were low. During 1983 and '84 as the economy recovered, stock prices began rising. They continued to rise until August 25, 1987. At that point the average stock was selling for about 3.5 times as much as in 1982. For example, if you paid $20 for a share of stock in 1982, on the average that share would be worth about $70 in August, 1987.

Stock Values Were Up 40% in 8 Months

By mid-August of 1987, average stock prices were about 40% higher than they had been in January— a 40% gain in less than 8 months. But then there were indications that inflation might be picking up. Interest rates began rising. Some investors became uneasy and began selling.

Between mid-August and mid-September, stock prices dropped fairly sharply. But this was regarded by many as a **normal correction** in a rising market—a good buying opportunity. By early October, stocks had recovered more than half of their September losses. Many analysts were declaring that the bull market (the upward trend in stock prices) was alive and well and heading for new highs. Then the downtrend began.

On Tuesday, October 6 the major industrial stocks lost about 3.5% of their value—all in one day. Then in the next week—Wednesday, October 14—stocks dropped sharply again, losing almost 4% of their value in that one day. Thursday, October 15 wasn't as bad, bringing a value loss of only about 2.4%. But then on Friday the 16th stocks lost another 4.6% of their value. Was this another normal correction? Another good buying opportunity in a rising market?

Many Investors Lost Confidence

Over the weekend, people had time to think things over and consider alternatives. Many of them de-cided that it was time to get out. The managers of billion-dollar-plus portfolios—pension fund managers, big mutual funds, others—decided to sell. Before the New York Stock Exchange and other U.S. markets opened on Monday, October 19, the handwriting was already on the wall.

When it's Sunday evening in New York it's already Monday morning in Tokyo. And long before daybreak in New York, the markets are already open in Paris, Frankfurt, London. And on the morning of Monday, October 19 what was happening? Stocks were under heavy selling pressure. Prices were dropping fast. Several American stocks trade in these foreign markets. Many portfolio managers and traders in New York were up all night selling stocks on the far eastern and European markets.

October 19, 1987: The Biggest One-Day Drop EVER!

When the New York markets opened, prices plummetted. When everyone is trying to sell and no one is trying to buy, prices must fall until someone is willing to buy. And prices did fall. How far? Until the total value of the major industrial stocks had dropped by 22.6%—the biggest one-day percentage drop ever.

More than 600 million shares were traded on that fateful "black Monday." The previous record number of shares traded in any one day had been 340 million—and that record had been set on the previous Friday (October 16). Before that there never had been a 300-million share day.

The following day (Tuesday the 20th) another 600 million shares were traded. Stocks were sharply up and down all day long. But at the close, some of Monday's losses had been regained. Then in the days and weeks that followed, stock prices jumped around a lot. But for the most part the trend was upward.

Throughout November and December, many forecasters were drawing parallels with the 1929 crash. Some were predicting the next *great depression*. But as the weeks and months went by the statistics on the economy kept looking better, not worse. In December and January unemployment

709

was at the lowest rate since the 1970s. And production, output, and income all were increasing at a healthy pace.

WHY DID THE MARKET CRASH?

There were many complex causes of the crash. It isn't likely that we'll ever know for sure all of the contributing factors.

The sharply falling prices generated panic selling. So the collapse tended to feed on itself. But also, it is generally agreed that prices had gone up too far, too fast. Most stocks were selling for more than their "fundamental values"—based on the assets, earnings, and dividends represented by each share. So the market was poised for a fall.

The Fundamentals: Stocks Were Overvalued

In mid-August, the stocks of major industrial corporations were selling at around three times the book value of each share. That means that the assets of the corporation, as valued on the corporations books, were only worth one-third as much as the value of the shares of stock outstanding.

To be sure, book value usually is not a very good measure of *the current market value* of a corporation's assets. For example, real estate holdings often are valued on the books at original cost, when the current market value may be many times as high. But in August of 1987 the stock value to book value ratio had become about twice as high as the past average for this ratio. That was one indication that stocks might be overvalued.

Another indication was the average dividend yield. The dividend yield on the major industrial stocks in the past has averaged a little more than 4%. In mid-August of 1987 it was down to only 2.2%. And the average price/earnings ratio—the relationship between the price per share and earnings per share—was also far higher than past averages. It was on the basis of these fundamental factors that some analysts were saying that the market was "riding for a fall."

The Breakdown of the "Specialist" System

The **specialist** is "the buyer and seller of last resort." The specialist is supposed to guarantee that whenever anyone wants to sell a stock, a buyer will be available. If no other buyer is available at the moment, then the specialist becomes the buyer.

But what happens when everyone is trying to sell and no one wants to buy? Can a specialist buy all of those billions of dollars worth of stocks? Obviously not. As a spokesperson for one specialist firm said after the crash: "It isn't our responsibility to buy the whole company!"

On Monday, October 19 specialist firms spent billions of dollars buying stock. Their funds were depleted. So what were they going to do when the markets opened on Tuesday? The values of the stocks in their inventories had dropped sharply. The bankers who lend money to these specialist firms saw the value of their collateral eroding. They seemed unlikely to want to lend any more.

The Federal Reserve Comes to the Rescue

On Tuesday morning the Federal Reserve banks pumped new money into the banking system and put pressure on the banks not to cut off credit to the broker firms. So the specialist firms were bailed out. This quick and decisive action by the Federal Reserve helped to keep the market "liquid" and to avoid a severe financial crisis. Still, there were times on Monday the 19th and Tuesday the 20th when trading was closed in many of the stocks of major U.S. corporations including: DuPont, Philip Morris, Dow Chemical, Kodak, Sears, IBM, and several others.

It's very critical in today's fast-moving financial world that the marketability of financial assets be maintained. What is the market value of a share of stock which you cannot sell? At that moment: zero! So it's extremely important that the Federal Reserve pumped new money into the banking system and urged the bankers to maintain the flow of money to the broker-specialists. It isn't unlikely that without the quick and decisive action by the Fed we would have had a "system meltdown"—a collapse of the financial system with far-reaching and disastrous consequences.

If the brokerage companies were forced to fail for a lack of available credit, then the banks which had been financing them, also could be forced to fail. And in our interdependent worldwide financial system when banks begin to fail there's a "falling dominoes" effect. The whole banking system could collapse as it did in the 1930s.

When the banks go, money goes. And when money goes, spending, and the economy goes. The economic system collapses. So in this case the Federal Reserve can be credited with playing a major role in averting a financial disaster.

Program Trading

There are all kinds of ways to program computers to constantly monitor the stock market and buy or sell stocks in response to changing market conditions. For example, suppose you had bought $10,000 worth of Chrysler stock when it was $3 per share, and suppose that the price of Chrysler is now $30 per share. Your $10,000 investment is now worth $100,000. And suppose you aren't in the mood to pay any capital gains taxes, and besides, you think Chrysler stock is likely to continue to go up. So you don't want to sell it.

But suppose you're wrong. If the stock begins to fall, you would like to keep some of those big gains. So you decide to enter a stop-loss order to sell at $27 or below and the broker's computer is programmed to sell your shares if the price ever drops to $27. Now you'll get to keep most of your gains.

But consider this. What if *everybody* who holds Chrysler stock does the same thing? Then if the price ever drops to $27 there will be an avalanche of sell orders! Nobody will be buying. The price will collapse. A significant amount of that was happening on October 19 and that contributed to the crash.

Portfolio Insurance

Another program-trading practice which contributed to the avalanche of sell orders was "portfolio insurance." This practice grew explosively in 1985—87. To understand this you first need to understand *stock index futures* and how they work.

Stock Index Futures. If you want to take a position in the market, you can buy a group of stocks and hold them. But you don't have to do that. You can buy a lot of little pieces of a large number of different shares of stocks by buying "stock index futures." You buy at a set price, fixed today. Then if stock prices go up, the value of your futures contract goes up.

Or if you want to, you can sell stock index futures. Then you're betting that the market is going down. You are, in effect, selling lots of little bits of stock at a price that is set now. When the future time come (the time specified in the contract) if stock prices have dropped by half, the value of your contract will have doubled.

Now suppose you are a portfolio manager of a large pension fund or mutual fund and you have a billion dollars worth of your assets invested in stocks. If stock prices begin to fall, you can't dump all those stocks on the market at one time. If you do, you will drive prices down and guarantee yourself some big losses! So how can you "insure against" falling stock prices? You can sell stock index futures!

When you sell index futures that gives you some "portfolio insurance" to protect your assets if stocks prices fall. Why? Because as the value of your stocks go down, the value of your index futures go up. But what if stocks go up? Then you enjoy the gains of the rising stock prices, but you will suffer losses on your futures contracts.

So what to do? Suppose you're pretty sure that the market is going up. Then you won't want to limit your gains by selling very many stock index futures. But suppose something happens to cause you to get really nervous about the market. Then you'll dash out and sell a lot of index futures to try to protect the value of your portfolio.

When the Market Looks Shaky, Sell Index Futures! Now you can understand why on October 19 there was a lot of selling of stock index futures. And what did this great supply of futures sales do to the futures prices? Pushed them down, of course!

The Role of Arbitrage

Suppose you are holding a portfolio of stocks worth $100,000 and you see the futures price go down to where you can buy this same basket of stocks (for future delivery) for only $80,000. What will you do? It's obvious. You'll sell your $100,000 worth of shares and with $80,000 you'll buy the stock futures. And you'll earn yourself a $20,000 profit on the deal! You're selling the stocks in today's market and buying them back in the futures market for a lower price.

What you just did is called "arbitrage." **Arbitrage** means simultaneously buying something in one market and selling it in another market. **Arbitageurs** make a profit on the price difference (the "spread") between the two markets.

There are arbitrageurs with their computers programmed to monitor both the stock markets and the futures markets—constantly looking for a divergence between the two prices. Whenever the futures prices get lower than today's market prices the computers automatically will sell the higher-priced stocks in today's market and buy them back in the lower-priced futures market. The arbitrageur will make a profit on the difference. Or if futures prices rise above today's market prices the computers will sell the higher priced futures and buy the lower priced stocks.

So now, *the bottom line*: When "portfolio insurers" sell stock index futures to reduce their risk in a falling market, this pushes futures prices down. Arbitrageurs (and their computers) immediately see the opportunity to sell stocks and buy futures and make a profit. But as the arbitrageurs sell stocks, they push stock prices down.

As stock prices fall, portfolio managers get more nervous and they sell more stock futures. Futures prices go down more, so arbitrageurs buy more of the lower-priced futures and sell more stock. So stock prices continue downward and trigger more futures sales by portfolio managers. And down, down, down we go. And, don't forget, all these things happen *very quickly*. The computers are programmed to send out all of the "buy" and "sell" orders in the wink of an eye!

Program Trading in the October 19 Crash

To what extend did all this "portfolio insurance" and "arbitrage" program trading contribute to the October crash? No one knows for sure. But for a time following October 19 some kinds of program trading were suspended. The purpose was to try to reduce the volatility—the ups and downs—of the market and bring more stability.

Several high-level investigations were initiated to try to better understand all of the contributing factors in the October crash. By midyear 1988 several institutional and regulatory changes were being recommended to try to reduce the likelihood that "it could happen again." But, realizing the global nature of the financial markets and the ease with which transactions can be instantaneously shifted from New York to Tokyo to London—there are serious limitations on what any one market can do to ensure stability. Some observers are saying that *international coordination* of financial market procedures and practices is the only answer.

WHY NO DEPRESSION? AND WHAT HAPPENS NOW?

The drop in stock prices from the August highs to the October lows wiped out about $1 trillion of wealth. That was expected to have a severe impact on the economy. But that didn't happen. Why not? Who knows? But don't forget that that trillion dollars in wealth had been created by increasing stock prices between January and mid-August. Maybe that had something to do with it. Maybe the stock owners were saying, "On well—easy come, easy go!"

The stock market crash didn't destroy the economy. But it was frightening. The financial system came dangerously close to a breakdown.

Since October of '87 studies of "the crash of '87" have been undertaken by the banking committees of both houses of Congress, by the President's "Brady Commission" by the Commodities Futures Trading Commission (CFTC), by the Securities and Exchange Commission (SEC), by the New York Stock Exchange (NYSE), by the Federal Reserve Board, by reporters for *The Wall Street Journal* and *The New York Times* and by many others. By the time you're reading this it's likely that much more will be known, and that some changes will have been made. Recent issues of *The Wall Street Journal*, *The New York Times*, and *Business Week* and the other news magazines would be good places to look if you'd like to find out about that.

List of Terms from the Appendix

Specialist

Market maker

Program trading

Portfolio insurance

Arbitrage

Stock index futures

Suggested Readings on the Crash of '87

Following the week of October 19, 1987, the news media were full of articles analyzing the stock market crash. Several articles appeared in all of the news magazines, and soon articles began to appear in the weekly and monthly publications of the Federal Reserve Banks, in publications of the SEC, the CFTC, the NYSE, as well as the special reports prepared on the crash. For anyone who wants to look at what happened and what the analysts have said, there is no shortage of information.

The Wall Street Journal carried a series of front-page articles dealing with *the crash of '87*. The last article in the series ran on December 30, 1987, but then another article ran on April 11, 1988 on *The crash of '87, 6 months later*. These articles provide an excellent blow-by-blow description of what happened and some analysis as to why. A few additional references are listed below.

Garner, C. Alan. "Has the Stock Market Crash Reduced Consumer Spending?" *Economic Review*. Federal Reserve Bank of Kansas City (April 1988), 3–16.

Roley, V. Vance, and Lawrence D. Schall. "Federal Deficits and the Stock Market." *Economic Review*. Federal Reserve Bank of Kansas City (April 1988), 17–27.

Stern, Gary H. "Achieving Economic Stability: Lessons from the Crash of 1929." *1987 Annual Report*. Federal Reserve Bank of Minneapolis, pp. 3–17.

APPENDIX 17A

Managing Interest Rate Risk: Gap Management, Duration, Swaps, Futures and Options

In "normal" times with low and stable interest rates there would be no great need to constantly manage interest rate risk. But when rates are high and financial markets are unstable—as they have been much of the time since the mid-1970s—managing interest rate risk is absolutely essential for the survival of a financial institution.

The very high and volatile nominal rates of the late 1970s and early '80s were unexpected. So the risk had not been "managed" by many financial institutions. As you know, most suffered severely and many did not survive.

The Basic Problem of Interest Rate Risk Exposure

The basic problem of interest rate risk exposure is illustrated by the situation of the thrift institutions. Thrifts lend mostly on long-term mortgages, yet their sources of funds are mostly short term. Here's an example.

Suppose a thrift obtains $100,000 from selling one-year CDs paying 7% and lends that $100,000 on a 30-year 10% fixed rate home mortgage loan. Then suppose short-term interest rates increase so that the one-year CD rate goes up to 10%. As the one-year 7% CDs mature, the thrift must sell new 10% CDs to get the funds to pay off the 7% CDs. Either that, or it must borrow $100,000 in the money market to pay off the 7% CDs. Either way the cost of its liabilities—its cost of funds—will go up. But its return on assets (the 10% return on the mortgage loan) will remain constant.

Then suppose money market rates go even higher—from 10% to 11% or 12%. Then the institution will be in serious trouble. If cost of funds is 12% while return on funds is 10%, it's just a matter of time before the thrift goes broke. That's what happened to many financial institutions—mostly thrifts—in the 1980s. The harsh lesson taught by

this experience has now been well-learned by the surviving institutions.

The need for effective techniques of interest rate risk management now has become universally recognized and several new techniques have been developed. The purpose of this appendix is to give brief, nontechnical explanations of some of the modern "state-of-the-art" techniques of managing (reducing) interest rate risk.

The Basic Objective: Arranging for Interest Rate Changes to Generate Offsetting Effects

The basic objective of interest rate risk management is to structure the balance sheet (hold just the right mix of assets and liabilities) to ensure that future interest rate changes will have offsetting (balancing) effects both on (a) the institution's income and expense flows (the profit and loss statement) and on (b) the values of its assets, liabilities, and capital (the balance sheet).

- In terms of the bank's **income (P&L) statement**, successful interest rate risk management requires that if *cost of funds* changes, *return on assets* will change in the same direction and by an equal amount. The balance sheet (assets and liabilities) should be structured so that if rising interest rates on liabilities (on CDs, for example) push up the cost of funds, then the rising rates also will apply to (and push up) the return on assets (on loans, for example).

- In terms of the bank's **balance sheet** it means that as interest rate changes cause some of the *asset values* to change, other balance sheet changes must also be automatically induced so as to offset these changing asset values. Either the value of *liabilities* must change in the same

713

direction, or the value of some *other assets* must change in the opposite direction—or some combination of both.

Here's a balance sheet example. Suppose a 10% increase in short-term market rates would result in a 10% decrease in the value of some of the bank's assets. If nothing else changed, all of this asset-value decrease would show up on the other side of the balance sheet as a decrease in the bank's capital account. Bad scene!

To be perfectly hedged against this risk the bank must hold either (a) an equal value of liabilities which will *decrease in value* by an amount equal to the asset-value decrease, or (b) other assets which will *increase in value* by an equal amount, or (c) some combination of a and b.

The concept in general is quite simple. But as you would guess, achieving the objective is no easy task. In the sections coming up you'll be reading about the specific techniques which financial institutions use as they try to protect both their income flows and their asset value (and their capital) from the potentially disastrous effects of unexpected interest rate changes.

GAP MANAGEMENT: BALANCING VARIABLE RATE ASSETS (VRAs) AND VARIABLE RATE LIABILITIES (VRLs)

Gap is a measure of the degree of imbalance between the institution's variable rate assets (VRAs) and its variable rate liabilities (VRLs). Suppose all variable rate liabilities are completely and exactly matched by variable rate assets. That's a **zero gap** position.

With zero gap, suppose market rates go up. Rates on VRLs (cost of funds) will go up. But return on VRAs (income from assets) also will go up.

Gap management focuses on the next few months during which maturing liabilities will need to be paid off and new liabilities acquired at the market rates existing at the time. If the institution has zero gap, then whichever way market rates move, both the cost of funds and return on assets will move in the same direction and (approximately) by the same amount. If cost of funds goes up by 10%, return on assets also goes up by about 10%. You can see that a zero gap position would remove most of a bank's worries about the effects of interest rate changes on its income flows—on its P&L statement.

Examples of Zero, Positive, and Negative Gap

Gap is measured as variable rate assets minus variable rate liabilities:

$$Gap = VRAs - VRLs.$$

When VRAs equal VRLs gap is zero. Whenever the dollar value of VRAs exceeds the dollar value of VRLs there will be **positive gap**. When VRLs exceed VRAs that's **negative gap**.

With Zero Gap the Earnings Flow is (Almost) Interest-Rate-Risk Free. Suppose a financial institution is holding a group of assets which will reprice in one year (say, term loans with rates adjustable annually). If it is also holding liabilities of equal value which will reprice annually (say, CDs with 1-year maturities) then its gap on these assets and liabilities is zero.

If market interest rates rise, earnings on loans will be below market rates. But cost of funds (the CDs) also will be below market rates. No problem.

If market rates fall, the institution will be paying above-market rates on its CDs but earning above-market rates on its loans. So it's covered. On this group of assets and liabilities it can neither gain nor lose from interest rate changes.

With Positive Gap, if Rates Fall You Lose. What if the institution has positive gap (VRAs > VRLs)? Then if market rates are rising, assets will be repricing upward faster than liabilities. Speculative profits!

But when interest rates are falling, positive gap can be disastrous. Liabilities (cost of funds) remain at the old, high rate while returns on assets continually reprice downward. Increasing losses!

With Negative Gap, if Rates Rise You Lose. Suppose the institution has negative gap (VRAs < VRLs). Then if market rates are falling, the institution will make speculative profits. Liabilities will be repricing downward sooner than assets. Cost of funds will be going down while return on funds remains constant. Great!

But for rising rates, negative gap can be disastrous. Return on assets remains the same while liabilities keep repricing upward. Cost of funds keeps going up. This is the situation which faced many banks and all of the thrifts in the late 1970s and early '80s. It destroyed a lot of them.

The Greater the Gap the Greater the Risk Exposure. If a financial institution really wants to minimize interest rate risk, then the objective is obvious: zero gap. If VRAs = VRLs then no matter which way market rates move, the financial institution's position is hedged. The greater the gap—either positive or negative—the greater the interest rate risk exposure.

If the maturities and/or repricing periods of all assets could be exactly balanced by liabilities having identical maturities and/or repricing periods, then all interest rate risk—both to the income statement and to the balance sheet (and to the capital account)—could be almost entirely eliminated. But such a balanced position is not easy to achieve and maintain. One reason is because of the "duration" complication.

DURATION: THE "AVERAGE EFFECTIVE TIME" TO MATURITY

One problem with trying to match the maturities of assets and liabilities is that the **effective time to maturity** of a financial instrument often is not indicated by the **maturity date** of the financial instrument. And this interesting fact leads us to the very important concept of **duration**—frequently called **bond duration** because much of the work on duration has been done with bonds.

The Duration of a Financial Instrument: A Definition

One way to define the "duration" of a financial instrument is to say that it is "the average effective time to maturity." Duration can be thought of as: *the stated time to maturity, minus something to account for cash flows from the instrument prior to maturity.* Here are some examples to show exactly what all this means.

Example 1: Asset A

Suppose you pay $10,000 for a zero-coupon 10-year bond (asset A). At the end of 10 years you will receive $10,000 plus all of the interest which has accrued over this 10-year period. In this case there's no question about the duration of the bond. It's exactly equal to the stated maturity: 10 years. You commit your $10,000 plus all earnings on those funds for a full 10-year period. Nothing comes back prior to the maturity date.

Example 2: Asset B

Now suppose you buy a $10,000 bond which pays a 10% coupon rate (asset B). You will receive $1,000

each year over the 10-year period. Ten years from now when you receive the principal payment of $10,000 you already will have received coupon payments of $10,000 ($1,000 per year for 10 years).

It's obvious that if the average effective time to maturity on asset A is 10 years, then on asset B it must be less than 10 years. With each coupon payment, $1,000 of your investment in asset B "matures." Each payment releases $1,000 for reinvestment. So $1,000 of your funds are reinvested and the reinvested funds are repriced at the interest rates existing at that time.

The point is that with asset B, all of your funds aren't totally "locked in" for the entire 10-year period. Some of your funds mature and can be repriced—reinvested at current interest rates—each year. And that's an important opportunity—to reinvest and **reprice the return** on some of your funds prior to the final maturity date of the bond.

It's this **repricing opportunity** which makes the pre-maturity cash flows important, and which causes "effective maturity," or "average maturity" to be shorter than stated maturity. And that's the key to the concept of *duration*. Duration takes into account the pre-maturity cash flows and the opportunity to reprice these funds prior to the maturity date of the instrument. Now, here's another example.

Example 3: Asset C

What about a home mortgage loan (asset C) which is amortized—paid off over the life of the loan? For a 30-year home mortgage, what is the average, or effective time to maturity? Certainly not 30 years! One month's interest and a part of the principal matures with the first monthly payment. The very last payment (30 years hence) completes the payoff. So what's the average maturity of a 30-year home mortgage loan? Less than 15 years.

The bottom line: For any asset which generates a flow of payments prior to the stated maturity date, duration will be a shorter period of time than the stated maturity. The greater this intermediate cash flow and the sooner it occurs, the shorter the duration.

How to Calculate the Duration of a Financial Instrument

For any instrument which carries a fixed flow of intermediate payments prior to maturity there is a formula which can be used to calculate the duration of the instrument. The formula requires

1.   the calculation of the discounted value of each of the future payments,

2. the weighting of each of these by the number of years in the future the payment is to be received,

3. adding all these together and then

4. dividing by the present market value of the financial instrument.

When these steps are taken, the answer will come out as a number (in years). That number is the *effective* or *average time to maturity*. It's the *duration* of the instrument. Box 17A-1 shows and explains the formula.

Other Ways to Define and Calculate Duration

In addition to what you've just been reading, and to the formula shown in box 17A-1, there are other ways to define and to calculate duration. One alternative approach focuses on the sensitivity of a bond's price (market value) to changes in market rates of interest.

Everyone knows that when market rates rise, bond prices fall, and that the longer a bond's term to maturity the more its price will fall. But, as you

---

Box 17A-1

Feature: **One Way to Calculate the Duration of a Financial Instrument**

This formula for calculating duration is similar to the present value bond formula explained in chapter 3. The only differences are that:

1. Each cash flow payment's present value is multiplied by the number of years in the future it is to be received (because the farther in the future, the greater the duration of the asset), and

2. The sum of all these weighted present values must be divided by the present value of the asset (PV).

Here's the formula, where D is duration, C is the annual coupon payment, Z is the face value, i is the interest rate, and the numbers 1, 2, 3 refer to the number of years in the future.

$$D = \frac{\dfrac{C1}{(1+i)^1} \times 1 + \dfrac{C2}{(1+i)^2} \times 2 + \dfrac{C3}{(1+i)^3} \times 3 + \dfrac{Z}{(1+i)^3} \times 3}{PV}$$

Example: Calculate duration (D) for a 3-year 10% bond with a face value (Z) of $1,000 and an annual coupon (C) of $100 when the current market rate of interest (i) is 10% (PV = Z):

$$D = \frac{\dfrac{100}{1+.1} \times 1 + \dfrac{100}{(1+.1)^2} \times 2 + \dfrac{100}{(1+.1)^3} \times 3}{1,000}$$

$$+ \frac{\dfrac{1,000}{(1+.1)^3} \times 3}{1,000}$$

$$= \frac{\dfrac{100}{1.1} + \dfrac{100}{(1.1)^2} \times 2 + \dfrac{100}{(1.1)^3} \times 3 + \dfrac{1,000}{(1.1)^3} \times 3}{1,000}$$

$$= \frac{\dfrac{100}{1.1} + \dfrac{100}{1.21} \times 2 + \dfrac{100}{1.331} \times 3 + \dfrac{1,000}{1.331} \times 3}{1,000}$$

$$= \frac{90.91 + 165.289 + 225.394 + 2253.94}{1,000}$$

$$D = \frac{2735.53}{1,000} = 2.74. \ D = 2.74 \text{ years.}$$

This calculation tells us that this 3-year bond has a duration of not 3 years, but 2.74 years. Why? Because the cash flow to the owner generated by the annual coupon reduces the average effective maturity of the bond from 3 years to 2.74 years.

This example calculates the duration of one financial instrument. But portfolio managers calculate duration for their entire portfolio of assets and for all of their liabilities. And they continually make adjustments to try to achieve a balance between the durations of their assets and their liabilities.

may have guessed by now, it isn't the bond's *stated maturity* which determines how much its price will fall. It's the bond's *duration*.

Think back to asset A (the zero-coupon bond) and asset B (the 10% coupon bond). If market rates begin to rise, the market values of both of these bonds will fall. But *equally*? Certainly not!

With asset A, none of the funds can be reinvested at the higher interest rates until the end of the 10-year period. But with asset B, each year some of the funds "mature" and can be reinvested. And the key to duration, remember, is this: "How soon can I reinvest my funds at the new rates?" The sooner the funds become available for reinvestment (and repricing), the shorter the duration of the instrument.

You can see that the larger and more frequent the coupon payments the more quickly the funds can be reinvested (and repriced). So the less the funds are "locked in" and the less the asset's price will fall when interest rates rise.

Another way to say it: The larger and more frequent the interim payments, the shorter the asset's duration will be. And the shorter the duration, the less responsive the asset's price to interest rate changes. And you can say it the other way around.

The less the interest rate sensitivity of the market value of the asset, the shorter the duration of the asset must be. So, Aha! Duration also can be calculated as *the sensitivity of a financial instrument's market price to interest rate changes!*

This leads us to a completely different way of measuring and comparing the duration of different financial instruments—say, bonds. Just compare the sensitivity of the bond prices to interest rate changes. It's this simple: When interest rates change, bond prices change. The more the price of a bond changes, the longer the duration of the bond.

This different approach to defining and calculating duration may seem to be conceptually different than the "stated maturity, as shortened by cash flows prior to stated maturity" concept. But it isn't. It's the same concept, but approached and measured in a different way.

In all cases, no matter how it is conceptualized or measured, the duration of a financial instrument is its *effective average time to maturity*, and the larger the intermediate cash flows and the sooner they occur, the sooner the funds can be repriced and the shorter the duration of the instrument.[1]

Duration Matching: A More Comprehensive Approach Than Gap Management

Now that you know about this more precise measure of effective maturity you can see that minimizing interest rate risk requires the matching of, not stated maturities, but the durations of assets and liabilities. If a financial institution can succeed in managing its assets and liabilities so as to achieve **matched durations** then its vulnerability to market rate changes can be largely eliminated.

If an institution's assets are of longer-term duration than it's liabilities, then the appropriate course of action is clear: either get some shorter-duration assets, or some longer-duration liabilities. But that isn't always easy to do.

During the 1980s, long-duration instruments have been convered into shorter-duration instruments through the introduction of variable rates—that is, frequent repricing. The sooner the funds are subject to repricing, the shorter the duration. Remember?

Today there are variable rate mortgages, floating-rate loans, variable-rate CDs and other deposits and several other kinds of VRAs and VRLs. Converting fixed rate instruments into variable-rate shortens their duration. But even so, these developments have not resulted in "the perfect interest rate risk hedge."

As liabilities and assets reprice, interest rates in some markets move differently than rates in other markets. So even if all assets and liabilities are repricing at the same time, rates on assets may be rising faster than those on liabilities, or vice versa. So some interest rate risk exposure still exists. So the *balance sheet restructuring techniques* discussed so far in this appendix cannot be relied upon to completely eliminate interest rate risk. But what more can be done?

---

[1] The concept of duration was originally derived by Professor Frederick R. Macauley in 1938 and presented in his book, *Some Theoretical Problems Suggested by the Movements of Interest Rates, Bond Yields, and Stock Prices in the United States Since 1865* (New York: National Bureau of Economic Research, 1938.). But it was not until the late 1960s that the duration concept began to be further refined and applied.

By the mid-1980s, duration had become an important technique of interest rate risk management by financial institutions. Joel L. Rosenberg, in his article "The Joys of Duration," *The Bankers Magazine*, March–April 1986, p. 63. says: "For providing financial managers with an indication of the potential gains or losses to their institutions based on future interest moves, duration is invaluable."

For an excellent explanation of duration and its various applications, see: Frank K. Reilly and Rupinder S. Sidhu, "The Many Uses of Bond Duration," *Financial Analysts Journal*, July –August 1980, pp. 58–72. This article presents in its footnotes a survey of the literature on duration up to 1980. For more detailed explanations of duration matching and techniques for minimizing interest rate risk, see Joseph F. Sinkey, Jr., *Commercial Bank Financial Management*, 3rd edition, Macmillan Publishing Co., New York, 1989, chs. 3 and 9.

Other Techniques for Managing Interest Rate Risk

During the 1980s several other interest rate risk management techniques have been developed. Three now-widely-used hedging instruments are: **interest rate swaps**, **financial futures**, and **options**. The remainder of this appendix explains briefly what each of these is and how it is used to hedge against the ill effects of changing interest rates.

INTEREST RATE SWAPS: EXCHANGING FUTURE INTEREST RECEIPTS ON ASSETS, OR PAYMENTS ON LIABILITIES

In an interest rate swap, the two parties agree to exchange future flows of interest payments. Either each takes on the payment obligations of the other, or each agrees to accept the income payments from assets of the other.

Interest rate swaps are a new wave of the 1980s. A few swaps were made in 1981. By the end of 1984 the outstanding volume of swaps was estimated to be over $50 billion. By the beginning of 1988 the volume had increased more than ten fold—to more than $500 billion. Why? Because swaps offer an opportunity for both parties to benefit, and because arranging and marketing interest rate swap instruments can generate significant income for the banks and other swap brokers, dealers, and market-makers.

One important use of swaps is to reduce interest rate risk exposure. Here's a simple hypothetical example to illustrate how it might work.

Swap Partner   1

Suppose there's a savings and loan institution (S&L) which is holding among its assets a group of home mortgages worth $10 million and on which the interest rate is fixed for 5-year periods—that is, these mortgages are repriced every five years. And suppose this S&L holds among its liabilities $10 million in one-year CDs. These liabilities reprice each year. These CDs are the source of the funds which have been invested in the mortgages.

This S&L faces serious interest rate risk exposure. If rates rise, its cost of funds will go up as the CDs reprice at higher rates. But the mortgages will remain at their fixed rate. The S&L's liabilities re-price much more frequently than do its assets. This institution has a large negative gap.

Swap Partner   2

Now suppose that there is a bank which has among its assets $10 million in one-year commercial loans. These loans will roll over or be replaced and repriced each year. And suppose this bank has funded these loans by selling 5-year fixed-rate Eurobonds. The Eurobonds will reprice every five years.

What will happen if the short-term commercial loan rate goes down? The bank will still be obligated to pay the fixed rate on its Eurobonds, but the interest income from its loans will be declining. The bank has a serious case of interest rate risk exposure!

The bank has exactly the opposite gap problem from the S&L: a large positive gap. Its liabilities are not rate sensitive, but its assets are.

The Swap Arrangement

In this hypothetical case it isn't difficult to figure out what could be done to eliminate the risk exposure of both institutions. If they would either swap assets or swap liabilities their risk exposure would be largely eliminated! One institution would have 5-year assets and 5-year liabilities; the other would have one-year assets and one-year liabilities. But there's an easier way to achieve the same objective: Swap either the payment obligations on the liabilities, or the income flows from the assets.

The more usual arrangement is for payments on liabilities to be swapped, although in recent years income flows on assets also are being swapped. Suppose they decide to swap payments on their liabilities.

The S&L agrees to make all of the interest payments on the 5-year Eurobonds at a fixed rate for a 5-year period. That way, no matter what happens to interest rates over the 5-year period, the S&L is not exposed. It is now paying a fixed contracted rate on its source of funds and receiving a fixed rate on its use of funds—the $10 million in mortgages. It has effectively eliminated the interest rate risk exposure of its income statement.

The bank agrees to pay interest on $10 million for a 5-year period, but at a rate determined by the one-year CD rate. So each year as the bank's $10 million in commercial loans turn over and are repriced, the bank's obligation on its liabilities will also be repriced. If rates on loans are rising, rates on CDs also will be rising, so the bank comes out even. If rates on loans are falling, rates on CDs also will be falling. Again, the bank comes out even.

The Swap Payments Are Based on a "Notional" Sum

Notice that in this case no actual principal is exchanged. The **notional amount** of the swap is $10 million. But the only funds which change hands are the interest payments.

The only actual transfer of funds is the balance: the difference between what the S&L owes the bank and what the bank owes the S&L. In this example, if interest rates go up rapidly, the bank, because it is obligated to pay the variable rate, will owe money to the S&L. If market rates fall, the S&L, which is obligated to pay a fixed rate, will owe funds to the bank.

In a swap of this kind, whichever institution would have lost because of its exposure, will receive funds from the other party to offset its would-be loss. Whichever institution would have gained by interest rate movements will be required to make payments to the other party to give away its would-be gains. Eliminating interest rate risk exposure, remember, not only wipes out the threat of unexpected losses. It also eliminates the chance for unexpected gains. Box 17A-2 gives an illustration of an actual case of a swap.

The Many Uses of Interest Rate Swaps

As the financial institutions and portfolio managers and the entire financial community have developed increasing expertise in creating swaps, many new uses of swaps have been developed. Swaps are used to adjust positions on different kinds of national currencies, to borrow in markets where rates are relatively lower and swap to achieve lower borrowing costs, and for many other uses.

As the swap market has developed rapidly, many of the financial institutions which initially arranged swaps between two parties, have become dealers in swaps. They will arrange swaps with a financial institution and will themselves take the opposite position. Then when the opportunity comes they will "sell" that position to someone else.

Now, with investment bankers, commercial banks and others "making a market" in different kinds of swaps, it's easy for anyone to enter into any kind of swap they wish. Any financial institution can find a swap to hedge whatever position they may find themselves in. Now you can understand why swaps have become such an important part of the modern financial scene. Box 17A-3 tells more about the growth of and different kinds of swaps.[2]

HEDGING WITH FINANCIAL FUTURES AND OPTIONS

As you know, the most usual cause of interest rate risk for depository institutions—especially S&Ls—has been the holding of long-term assets and shorter term liabilities. As already explained, one way to deal with this problem is to restructure the balance sheet. Moving toward zero gap and matched durations of assets and liabilities will help. Also, as just explained, interest rate swaps can help.

The swap approach is designed to protect the **income statement** from the risks of positive or negative gap. Using swaps, cost of funds can be balanced against income on investments. What about an approach designed to protect the **balance sheet** from the risks of positive or negative gap, or a duration mismatch? Is there an approach which will protect the **net worth** of the institution as interest rates rise or fall? Yes. It can be done using financial futures. Here's an example to show how.

[2] As the use of interest rate swaps has grown rapidly, the literature on the subject also has grown rapidly. Here are some recent examples:

Larry D. Wall and John J. Pringle, "Alternative Explanations of Interest Rate Swaps," Federal Reserve Bank of Atlanta Working Paper 87–2, April 1987; "The Fearsome Growth of Swaps," Euromoney, October 1985, pp. 247–61; Bank for International Settlements, "Recent Innovations in International Banking," prepared by a study group established by the central banks of the Group of Ten countries, April 1986.

Sylvester Johnson and Amelia A. Murphy, "Going off the Balance Sheet," Economic Review, Federal Reserve Bank of Atlanta, September/October 1987; Robert McGough, "Our Wildest Dreams," Forbes, July 30, 1984, pp. 53–57; A. Gregg Whittaker, "Interest Rate Swaps," Economic Review, Federal Reserve Bank of Kansas City, March 1987, pp. 3–13; International Swap Dealers Association, Inc. Code of Standard Wording, Assumptions and Provisions for Swaps, 1985.

Jan G. Loeys, "Interest Rate Swaps, A New Took for Managing Risk," Business Review, Federal Reserve Bank of Philadelphia, May/June 1985, pp. 17–25; Douglas T. Breeden and Michael J. Giarla, "Hedging Interest Rate Risk with Futures, Swaps and Options," in Frank J. Fabozzi, ed., The Handbook of Mortgage-Backed Securities, 2nd ed., Probus Publishing Co., Chicago, 1988.

T. S. Arnold, "How to Do Interest Rate Swaps," Harvard Business Review, September 1984, pp. 96–102; D. Bennett, D. Cohenfield, and J. McNulty, "Interest Rate Swaps and the Management of Interest Rate Risk," paper presented at the annual meeting of the Financial Management Association, Toronto, 1984.

Stuart M. Turnbull, "Swaps: A Zero Sum Game?" Financial Management, 16, 1, Spring 1987, pp. 15–21; C. R. Beidleman, Financial Swaps, Homewood, Ill.: Dow Jones-Irwin, 1985; J. Bicksler and A. H. Chen, "An Economic Analysis of Interest Rate Swaps," Journal of Finance, July 1986, pp. 645–55.

Feature: An Actual Case of a Swap

How a Swap Works

The following example is based on an actual transaction that was arranged by an investment bank between a large thrift institution and a large international bank; it is representative of many swaps that have been arranged since 1982. "Thrift" has a large portfolio of fixed-rate mortgages. "Bank" has most of its dollar-denominated assets yielding a floating-rate return based on LIBOR (the London Interbank Offered Rate).

On May 10, 1983, the "Intermediary," a large investment bank, arranged a $100 million,

7-year interest rate swap between Thrift and Bank. In the swap, Thrift agreed to pay Bank a fixed rate of 11 percent per year on $100 million, every 6 months. This payment covered exactly the interest Bank had to pay on a $100 million bond it issued in the Eurodollar market. Thrift also agreed to pay Bank the 2 percent under-writing spread that Bank itself paid to issue this bond. In exchange, Bank agreed to make floating-rate payments to Thrift at 35 basis points (.35 percent) below LIBOR. Intermediary received a broker's fee of $500,000.

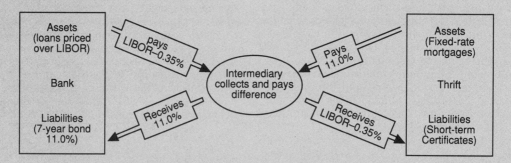

Twice a year, Intermediary (for a fee) calculates Bank's floating-rate payment by taking the average level of LIBOR for that month (Col. 2), deducting 35 basis points, dividing by 2 (because it is for *half* a year), and multiplying by

$100 million (Col. 3). If this amount is larger than Thrift's fixed-rate payment (Col. 4), Bank pays Thrift the difference (Col. 5). Otherwise, Thrift pays Bank the difference (Col. 6).

1	2	3	4	5	6
Date	LIBOR	Floating-rate payment 1/2 (LIBOR -0.35%)	Fixed-rate payment 1/2 (11%)	Net Payment from Bank to Thrift	Net Payment from Thrift to Bank
May 1983	8.98%	—	—	—	—
Nov 1983	8.43%	$4,040,000	$5,500,000	0	$1,460,000
May 1984	11.54%	$5,595,000	$5,500,000	$95,000	0
Nov 1984	9.92%	$4,785,000	$5,500,000	0	$ 715,000
May 1985	8.44%	$4,045,000	$5,500,000	0	$1,455,000

The swap allows both Bank and Thrift to reduce their exposure to interest rate risk. Bank can now match its floating-rate assets price off LIBOR with an interest payment based on LIBOR, while the fixed-rate interest payments on its bond issue are covered by Thrift. At the same time, Thrift can hedge part of its mortgage portfolio, from which it receives fixed interest earnings, with the fixed-rate payment it makes to Bank. However, the floating-rate payment that Thrift receives is linked to LIBOR while its

cost of borrowing is more closely linked to the T-bill rate. Since LIBOR and the T-bill rate do not always move in tandem, Thrift is still exposed to fluctuations in the relation between LIBOR and the T-bill rate.

Source: This box is copied by permission from Jan G. Loeys, "Interest Rate Swaps: A New Tool for Managing Risk," *Business Review,* Federal Reserve Bank of Philadelphia, May/June 1985, p. 19.

Box 17A-3

Feature: **The Rapid Growth of Different Kinds of Swaps**

From Zero to $80 Billion in Three Years

Interest rate swaps first emerged in the Euro-bond market in late 1981.[a] Large international banks, which do most of their lending on a floating-rate basis, were involved in the first swaps so that they could use their fixed-rate borrowing capacity to obtain lower-cost floating-rate funds. Initially, the swapping partners consisted mainly of utilities and lower-rated industrial corporations that preferred fixed-rate financing. During 1982, the first domestic interest rate swap occurred between the Student Loan Marketing Association (Sallie Mae) and the ITT Financial Corp., with Sallie Mae making floating-rate payments to ITT. Since then, the market has grown tremendously; in 1984 about $80 billion in swap agreements were concluded.[b] Any large corporation can now use interest rate swaps as an instrument for asset-liability management.

Both investment banks and commercial banks have been active in arranging interest rate swaps. These intermediaries earn fees by bringing the different parties together, by acting as settlement agent (that is, collecting and paying the net difference in the interest payments), and by serving as guarantor of the agreement. Most intermediaries have recently gone beyond their initial role of merely bringing different parties together and function also as dealers. As a dealer, the intermediary is also the counterparty to each swap it "sells." That is, each party has an agreement only with the intermediary and is totally unaware of who might be on the other side of the swap. This arrangement allows the intermediary to sell one leg of the swap before selling the other and to work with an inventory of as yet unmatched swap agreements. The existence of dealers also facilitates an informal secondary market in swaps, where parties to a swap can sell their position to the intermediary or to another party, thereby increasing the liquidity of this instrument.

A typical swap involves a bond issue for $25 to $75 million with a 3 to 10 year maturity on one side, a floating-rate loan on the other side. Initially, this floating rate loan was priced at a fraction over LIBOR, the London Interbank Offered Rate. Recently floating-rate loans have also been using the prime rate, the T-bill rate, or other indices of the cost of short-term borrowing.

The most common type of swap is the one described above: a dollar fixed-rate loan swapped for a dollar floating-rate loan, otherwise called the "plain-vanilla" swap. However, several variations on this basic swap have emerged in the market. One such variation is a floating-to-floating swap where parties agree to swap floating rates based on different indices. For example, a bank with assets tied to the prime rate and liabilities based on LIBOR may want to swap the interest payments on its liabilities with payments on a prime-tied, floating-rate loan. Another type of arrangement involves currency swaps such as a swap of a sterling floating-rate loan for a dollar fixed-rate loan. For firms whose assets are denominated in a different currency than are its liabilities, this type of swap may be more appropriate. Finally, rather than exchanging interest payments on liabilities, swaps can also be used to exchange yields on *assets* of different maturities or currencies.

The interest rate swap market has proven to be very flexible in adjusting its product to new customer needs. This innovativeness all but guarantees that swaps will remain a permanent feature of international capital markets.

[a] For more technical and institutional details on interest rate swaps, see Carl R. Beidleman, *Financial Swaps: New Strategies in Currency and Coupon Risk Management,* (Homewood, Illinois: Dow Jones-Irwin, 1985); and Boris Antl (ed.), *Swap Financing Techniques,* (London: Euromoney Publications Limited, 1983).

[b] Since there are no official reporting requirements on swaps, estimates of the size of this market vary tremendously. The amount of $80 billion, as estimated by Salomon Brothers (see *The Economist,* March 16, 1985, p. 30, Table 16), appears to be somewhere in the middle.

Source: This box is copied by permission from Jan G. Loeys, "Interest Rate Swaps: A New Tool for Managing Risk," *Business Review,* Federal Reserve Bank of Philadelphia, May/June 1985, p. 21.

Protecting the Balance Sheet by Short-Selling Financial Futures

Suppose you're operating an institution which has $10 million in mortgages on which rates are fixed for five years. If market rates go up, the market value of those mortgages will fall. How do you hedge against that? One way: Get some other assets whose market value will rise as interest rates go up. What assets? Short-sale futures contracts on financial instruments!

You could enter into a futures contract to sell $10 million worth of Treasury Bonds at some future date at a price which is set today (say, $10 million). Then if interest rates remain the same, the mortgage values will not change and the T-bond values will not change. The value of the futures contract will be zero. The futures contract obligates you to sell $10 million worth of Treasury Bonds for $10 million. But in this case the contract is of no value because the market value of those bonds is exactly $10 million. But what if interest rates go up?

Suppose interest rates rise so sharply that the value of your fixed-rate mortgages drops from $10 million to $7 million. That sharp rise in interest rates will also force down the market prices of T-bonds from $10 million to (lets assume) $7 million. Now the futures contract is worth real money!

The contract obligates its holder to sell for $10 million, T-bonds which are currently worth in the market only $7 million. The holder of the contract can buy T-bonds in the market for $7 million and then sell them for $10 million to fulfill the contract. So what's the value of the contract? Three million dollars! In this case the decreased value of one asset (mortgages) has been completely offset by the increased value of another asset (the futures contract).

What if interest rates had gone down sharply? Then the value of the mortgages would have gone up from $10 million to perhaps $13 million. That's a $3 million gain. But at the same time, the T-bonds represented by the futures contract would also be going up from $10 million to $13 million. And since the futures contract requires the sale of those T-bonds for $10 million, you are going to lose $3 million on the contract.

You must buy bonds in the market for $13 million and then sell them for $10 million to fulfill the contract. So in this case the $3 million capital gain on the mortgage portfolio is exactly offset by the $3 million loss on the futures contract.

This example illustrates the ultimate result of hedging interest rate risk by short-selling financial futures. And here it worked out perfectly! But in the real world it doesn't. Current prices and futures prices don't actually move in perfect lockstep. And there are other complications. However, to the extent that you can find "the perfect hedge," you can protect yourself so that you can't lose from unexpected rate changes. But this also means that you can't gain either.

But there is one way you can hedge against the losses, and still leave the opportunity for possible gains. Use **options contracts** instead of futures contracts.

With Options the Losses Are Limited

In the above example, there is a way that you could hedge against rising rates without being obligated to sell the $10 million worth of T-bonds. Instead of entering into a futures contract *guaranteeing* the sale of $10 million in T-bills, you could buy a **put option**. That would give you the opportunity—but not the obligation—to sell $10 million in T-bills for $10 million at any time over the period of the option.

Suppose you buy the put option and then interest rates fall sharply. The value of the loan portfolio will rise from perhaps $10 million to $13 million, and the value of the basket of T-bonds represented by your put option will rise from $10 million to $13 million. Will you exercise your option to sell that basket of T-bonds for $10 million? When the market value of those T-bonds is now $13 million? Of course not! You'll just let your options contract expire unexercised. So what do you lose? Only the cost of the contract.

But suppose interest rates had risen sharply and the value of your mortgage portfolio had dropped from $10 million to $7 million. The value of the basket of T-bonds represented by your put option also would decrease from $10 million to (let's assume) $7 million. Will you exercise your option to sell that basket of T-bonds for $10 million? You bet you will! Or what you probably would do is to sell the put option contract which now has a value of $3 million.

As you can see, an option contract is more like an insurance policy than is a futures contract. With an option contract all you can lose is the cost of the contract—you might call that cost the "insurance premium." In the event of a serious adverse move which would reduce the value of your assets (and therefore your net worth), you are covered. And the maximum cost of that coverage is known, and paid up front. Now you can understand why options are so widely used by depository institutions in their interest rate risk management programs.[3]

SUMMARY OVERVIEW OF MANAGING INTEREST RATE RISK

One important function of the management of every financial institution is the management of interest rate risk. The bank must arrange to protect its **stock values**—the balance sheet, and also its **funds flows**—the income statement.

If the average durations of all of the assets and all of the liabilities can be balanced and matched, then if interest rate changes are approximately equal in all markets, the interest rate risk exposure of the institution can be reduced to near zero. Both the income and expense flows will be balanced. Also, as interest rates change, the values of assets and liabilities will change in the same ways and by the same amounts. Both the balance sheet and the income statement are protected. But this ideal objective is not easy to achieve.

Whenever because of the nature of the business it is in a financial institution finds it impossible to achieve the objective of matched durations of assets and liabilities, there are other techniques of interest rate risk management which can be used to largely eliminate the risk exposure. Swaps can be used to protect the funds flows by matching the variability (or fixity) of cost of funds and return on funds over the term of the swap agreement.

Futures and options contracts can be used to protect the asset values on the balance sheet. Long positions on the balance sheet can be offset by entering into short-sale futures or options contracts.

The futures contract holder is obligated to make the future sale. But with a put option, the contract holder is not obligated to make the sale. So a put option is more like an insurance policy because the institution is hedged against adverse interest rate movements, while the extent of the loss is limited to the cost of the contract.

Now, take a few minutes to read box 17A-4 and see what *American Banker* columnist Sanford Rose has to say about some of the difficulties and pitfalls in managing interest rate risk. This column was published on October 12, 1987 as interest rates were rising, just one week before the stock market crash of October 19.

---

[3] The literature on financial futures and options is now voluminous. Here are a few basic and recent sources: M. Belongia, and T. Gregory, *Are Options on Treasury Bond Futures Priced Efficiently?* Federal Reserve Bank of St. Louis, 1984, pp. 5–13; M. Brenner, ed., *Option Pricing*, D. C. Heath, Lexington, Mass.: F. Faboozi, *Winning the Interest Rate Game: A Guide to Debt Options*, Probus, Chicago, 1985; M. Garman, "The Duration of Option Portfolios," *Journal of Financial Economics*, 14, 1985, pp. 309–15.

Bank for International Settlements, *Recent Innovations in International Banking*, Basle, Switzerland, April 1986; G. Koppenhaver, "Futures Options and Their Use by Financial Intermediaries," *Economic Perspectives*, Federal Reserve Bank of Chicago, 10, January/February 1986, pp. 18–31; Samuel L. Cramer, Lyn Miller Senholz, and Carl O. Helstrom, III, *Options Hedging Handbook*, Center for Futures Education, Inc., Cedar Falls, IA, 1985.

Anatoli Kuprianolv, "Short-Term Interest Rate Futures," *Economic Review*, Federal Reserve Bank of Richmond, 72, September/October 1986, pp. 12–26; Anatoli Kuprianolv, "Options on Short-Term Interest Rate Futures," *Economic Review*, Federal Reserve Bank of Richmond, 72, November/December 1986, pp. 3–11; Charles S. Morris and Thomas J. Merfeld, "New Methods for Savings and Loans to Hedge Interest Rate Risk," *Economic Review*, Federal Reserve Bank of Kansas City, 73, March 1988, pp. 3–15; Richard A. Followill, "Relative Call Futures Option Pricing: An Examination of Market Efficiency," *The Review of Futures Markets*, 6 (3), Chicago Board of Trade, December 1987, pp. 354–82.

Box 17A-4

Feature: **Some Problems and Pitfalls in Managing Interest Rate Risk**

BANKING WEEK/Viewpoints

Thoughts on Asset-Liability Management

By SANFORD ROSE

The following consists of excerpts from a speech on asset-liability management given by the author at the joint examination and supervision staff conference of the Federal Home Loan Bank of New York.

ASSET-liability management has been defined as the "controlled mismatching of maturities to maximize net interest earnings while taking reasonable business risk." Regal as this definition sounds, it is something less than useful. The focus on maturities is unfortunate. Interest rate risk does not arise from an imbalance in the maturity schedule of assets and liabilities. It comes from a cash flow gap.

Equal dollars in and out, and there is no rate risk. But if you get cash before you must disburse it, you are exposed to the threat of falling interest rates. Vice versa, you are exposed to the risk of rising rates.

Say that in the next few months, more of my liabilities than my assets will mature—or rather reprice, since it is the maturity of the yield not that of the instrument which counts. Am I necessarily liability sensitive? Perhaps not. Factoring in loan amortization and interest cash flows could conceivably change the calculation, rendering me asset rather than liability sensitive.

Popular ideas about asset-liability management also frequently ignore intraperiod differences in the timing of repricings. It is sometimes said that as long as the summary volume of assets being repriced equals the summary volume of liabilities being repriced in a particular period, there is no interest rate risk.

But if, on average, assets are being repriced earlier in the designated period than are liabilities, the institution is exposed to sizable reductions in net interest income if rates decline, even though, by the end of the period, the cumulative volume of repriced assets corresponds perfectly to that of repriced liabilities. Otherwise put, the traditional concept of a zero cumulative gap is an absurdity.

GOOD asset-liability management stresses the time value of cash. To what end? Is it to maximize net interest income, as was stated in the introductory quote? It is possible to maximize net interest income in the next couple of accounting periods while simultaneously laying the groundwork for the destruction of the institution.

Cast your mind back to the year 1978. Rates were rising, and the thrifts were long assets—liability sensitive. That is, they were liability sensitive from a composite balance-sheet viewpoint. Yet they were asset sensitive from a short-term income point of view because there was a lag in the repricing of liabilities with nonmarket-determined rates.

The rise in rates were eroding the market value of equity. Yet that same rise in rates increased net interest income because thrifts were able to invest amortizing principal and interest receipts at progressively higher yields. Thus the book value of equity rose at the same time as its market value was collapsing.

The very circumstance that was to plunge the industry into acute crisis temporarily created a roseate and entirely bogus aura of unprecedented prosperity. That prosperity abruptly terminated when nominally short liabilities became effectively short—that is, when the industry was forced to reprice liabilities at market-sensitive rates.

Presumably what the thrifts learned from this experience is the primacy of market over book values—that changes in market value foreshadow, are leading indicators of, changes in book value. So one must take steps to arrest the deterioration in market values despite any current buoyancy of book values. Yet one wonders how well this lesson has been learned.

Consider the current attitude toward risk-controlled mortgage arbitrages. Say that a thrift bought a current-coupon mortgage-backed security some months ago, funded it with a reverse repo, and hedged by lengthening the duration of the repo with rate swaps so that it more or less equaled the duration of the asset, provided that could be determined.

If rates had fallen sharply, prepayments

would have accelerated. The extra cash being received would have had to be reinvested at quite unfavorable yields. Thus the market value of the arbitrage would have fallen because the duration of the assets had declined relative to that of the liabilities in a period of falling rates. And the spread would also have fallen because asset yields were dropping relative to fixed liability costs. Hence, the thrift would have had to scramble to rebalance in an effort to minimize the damage.

But when rates rise, as they have in the past six months, the effect on market values and book values is not symmetric. The rise in rates raises the discount rate on future cash flows, which should lower the duration of the asset. Simultaneously, however, prepayments slow, which raises that duration. In most instances, the prepayment effect swamps the discount-rate effect, lifting overall durations.

Since the duration of the asset is now greater than that of the liabilities in a period of rising rates, the market value of the arbitrage falls. But this decline in market values is not immediately reflected in reduced spreads and book values, as would be the case if rates had fallen sharply and prepaid cash had to be reinvested at disappointingly low yields. Assuming a complete prior hedge, the income effects begin showing up only when the swaps start to mature, raising liability costs.

Thus, focusing on book values and ignoring market values, the thrift appears to have the leisure to do nothing, which is what many are now doing. Damage control is expensive, so it is easier to sit with a position, praying that reversals in rates will save the day. That didn't happen in the post-1978 period, and it may not happen now.

Source: Banking Week, October 12, 1987, p. 14. Reprinted by permission.

Basic Concepts: The Relationships Between Curves and Equations

Note: Most students will not need to read this appendix. Unless you need a review of these very basic concepts, please skip it. This appendix is included because I find that some of my students have not been exposed to any math recently and they need to review the basic concepts. If you need it, please take the time to *learn well* these basics.

A CURVE IS A SERIES OF X AND Y POINTS

Much of the mathematics used in economics consists of (1) translating the curves in a graph into equation form, and then (2) working with those equations. So it's necessary to understand the basic relationships between the curves and the equations which describe them.

After you draw a curve in a graph, if you choose the value of (number of units of) X, then you can look at the curve and see the value of (number of units of) Y. Once the curve is there, if you tell me the X value, I can tell you the Y value. So you can say that *the value of Y* depends on (is a function of) *the value of X*. That gives us a functional relationship:

$$Y = f(X).$$

This equation tells you that the value of Y depends on the value of X. But you can't figure out the value of Y from that.

An Equation Can Identify the Specific Y Value for Each X Value

An equation which identifies the value of Y that corresponds to each value of X describes a curve in a graph. The curve shows, for each value of X, the corresponding value of Y. So an *equation* which shows that tells you exactly what the *curve* must look like.

THE EQUATION OF A STRAIGHT-LINE CURVE

To see what all this means, here's a familiar example. Remember the 45-degree line in the Keynesian National Spending = National Income (NS = NI) Graph? The value of Y at any point along this line depends on the value of X.

Suppose the value of X is 5. What's the value of Y? It's 5 also. Suppose X is 12. What's Y? It's 12 also. The value of Y is always the same as the value of X. Here's the equation:

$$Y = X.$$

Now study figure 28A-1 which shows this equation on a graph.

The Equation of a Straight-Line Curve Which Begins at Zero

Suppose you are dealing with *any straight-line curve* beginning at zero—one where Y is not equal to X. For example, what if Y goes up only half as fast as X? Here's the equation:

$$Y = 1/2X, \text{ or}$$

$$Y = 0.5X.$$

Using this equation, suppose the value of X is 10. Then the value of Y is 1/2 of 10.

$$Y = 0.5(10)$$

$$Y = 5.$$

Figure 28A-1.   The Equation of a Straight-Line Curve Which Begins at Zero and Rises at a 45-Degree Angle

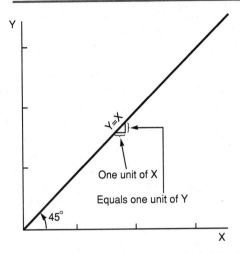

The equation "Y = X" tells you that whatever the value of X may be, that also will be the value of Y. Also, if the value of X increases or decreases, the value of Y will increase or decrease by exactly the same amount. (A look at the curve in the graph shows you that. The equation "Y = X" tells you exactly the same thing.)

Suppose X = 20. Again, use the equation Y = 0.5X.

$$Y = 0.5(20)$$

$$Y = 10.$$

The general form of the equation for a straight-line curve which begins at zero is:

$$Y = bX.$$

This says that the value of Y will always be equal to the value of "b" times the value of X. And what's the value of "b"? It's how much Y goes up when X goes up by one unit. This "b" term tells you how steeply the line slopes upward.[1]

_____

[1] Slope is sometimes defined as "the rise over the run." The rise is the increase in the Y value, and the run is the increase in the X value. For example, if the rise is one and the run is 5, the slope is one over 5, which equals 1/5. Suppose you're driving up into the mountains on a straight highway and you find that you've gone 5 *miles* and you're now *one mile higher* than when you started. Then the run was 5 miles and the rise was one mile. So *the average slope* of that highway is 1/5th. Steep highway!

If the "b" term happens to be *exactly one*, then Y will go up just as fast as X goes up. You will have a 45° line just as in the Keynesian NS = NI graph. But if "b" is *less than one*, then when the value of X increases by one unit, the value of Y will increase by *less than* one unit. So Y will not go up as fast as X. You can see that when "b" is *less than one* (b < 1) the straight line will not rise as steeply as when b = 1. Now if you will take a look at figure 28A-2 you'll see how all this looks on a graph.

The General Equation of a Straight-Line Curve

Suppose you have a straight-line curve which *does not* begin at zero. Then you must know how high up on the Y axis the straight line begins. So you need another term in your equation—a term to show you the "Y intercept" value—where the straight line meets the Y axis—a term to tell you the value of Y when X is zero.

Suppose you have a straight-line curve which is at 10 on the Y axis and goes up from there. Suppose the curve looks just like curve #2 which

Figure 28A-2.   The Equation of a Straight-Line Curve Which Begins at Zero

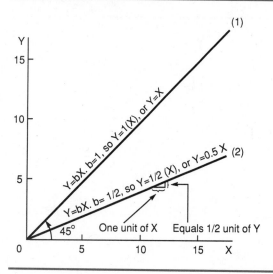

started at zero in figure 28A-2. The only difference is that now, when X is zero, the Y value is 10. So the Y value at each point along the curve is going to be *10 units larger* than if the curve had started at zero.

Suppose the "Y intercept" is 10 above zero, and for each unit increase in X, Y increases by half a unit. You find the value of Y for each value of X just as before, only you now must add the Y intercept value—in this case, 10. The equation for this straight-line curve is

$$Y = 10 + 0.5X.$$

Using this formula you can find the value of Y which corresponds to any value of X. Example: Suppose X = 10.

$$Y = 10 + 0.5 (10)$$

$$Y = 10 + 5$$

$$Y = 15$$

The Equation of a Straight Line: Summary Statement

The equation of a straight-line curve must include two terms. The first term tells you where the curve meets the Y axis. The second term tells you how much Y changes for each unit change of X.

The value of Y, at each value of X, is determined by

1. the value of Y when X = 0 (the "Y intercept" value of Y), and

2. the rate at which Y increases as X increases (the steepness of the slope of the line).

The generalized equation for the straight-line curve is

$$Y = a + bX.$$

The "a" term tells you the value of Y when X is zero. The "b" term tells you the rate of change in Y as X changes.[2]

Figure 28A-3 shows several graphic illustrations of the equation: $Y = a + bX$. After you study and practice working with the curves and equations in that figure I think you will have a good basic understanding of the relationship between curves and equations. And you'll be ready for the other math appendixes in this book.

---

[2] There are various ways of expressing the equation of a straight line. A frequently used form of this equation is

$$Y = MX + b$$

where:

M indicates the slope of the line (it's the "b" term in the $Y = a + bX$ equation) and b is the Y-axis intercept (the "a" term in the $Y = a + bX$ equation).

This $Y = MX + b$ equation is just a different way of expressing a straight line on a graph. It makes no difference which equation you use, just as long as you know what the terms mean. The form: $Y = a + bX$ is usually used in macroeconomic analysis.

Figure 28A-3.   The General Equation of a Straight-Line Curve

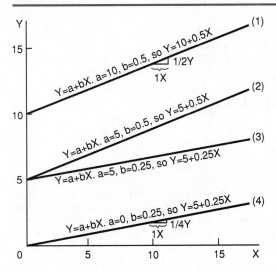

- the larger the "a" term, the higher the "Y intercept." If the "a" term is zero, the curve begins at zero.

- the larger the "b" term, the steeper the slope of the curve. If the "b" term is zero then the line will be *horizontal*.

APPENDIX 28B

The Simple Algebra of the Two-Spending-Sector Model

This appendix uses the equation of a straight line to calculate the equilibrium size of national income (NI).[1] The straight line we will be dealing with is the consumption function (C) in the Keynesian Cross diagram.

THE STRAIGHT-LINE CONSUMPTION FUNCTION: THE CURVE AND THE EQUATION

On the consumption function, the Y-value indicates the size of (rate of flow of) consumer spending (C). So in the equation $Y = a + bX$, the Y can be replaced with C: $C = a + bX$. And since the X-value is really the size of (rate of flow of) national income (NI), the X in the equation can be replaced by NI: $Y = a + bNI$. So, to express the (assumed straight line) consumption function the equation

$$Y = a + bX, \text{ becomes}$$

$$C = a + bNI.$$

This equation gives us a way to compute the level of consumer spending (C) for each level of a national income (NI). This equation says that the amount of consumer spending (C) is the sum of "a" (the amount of autonomous consumer spending which would exist at national income of zero) plus "bNI" (the amount of additional consumer spending induced by the size of the national income, above zero).

Stated differently, the equation $C = a + bNI$ says that the total level of consumer spending (C) is equal to (1) autonomous consumer spending (the "a" term) plus (2) induced consumer spending (the "bNI" term). The "b" term tells how much C goes up when NI increases by one unit. It indicates the upward slope of the consumption function curve.

When NI increases, the size of the induced increase in C depends on the marginal propensity to consume (MPC). And that's what the b term indicates: the fraction of each dollar of additional national income which would be spent for consumer goods—i.e., the "not-saved" fraction of an income increase. Since the consumption function is a straight line the b term is constant, indicating that MPC is constant. The steeper the curve the higher the constant MPC (=b).

In figures 28B-1 and 28B-2, the equation $C = a + bNI$ is used (with some assumed numbers—parameters—for "a" and "b") to illustrate the consumption function—that is, to illustrate the relationship between C and NI. The two graphs show the size of consumer spending at each level of national income. As you study the graphs you'll see that if consumers are the only ones doing any spending, macroequilibrium will be at NI = 50. If C is the only spending source, then 50 is the only size of NI where national spending (NS) equals NI.

But aren't there other spending sources in addition to consumer spending? Of course there are. So to find macroequilibrium we must know what additional spending injections are being added into the income stream.

The Size of NI Depends on Autonomous Injections Plus Induced Consumer Spending

Assume that in addition to consumer spending (C), the only injection is from investment spending (I)—no government spending and no injections

---

[1] The letter Y (not NI) is the usual symbol for national income both in this book and in writings on macroeconomics in general. However, to eliminate the possibility of confusion, I have chosen to use NI (instead of Y) as the symbol for national income in these appendixes. So in this and the other math appendixes for this chapter and the next, the letter Y will be used only to refer to the Y axis on the graph. The symbol "NI" will be used for national income.

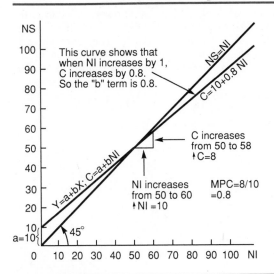

With the equation $C = 10 + 0.8\ NI$ you can figure out, for any value of NI, the value of C.

Examples:

If NI is 30, then $C = 10 + 0.8(30)$, or $10 + 24$.
$C = 34$.
If NI is 50, then $C = 10 + 0.8(50)$, or $10 + 40$.
$C = 50$.
If NI is 80, then $C = 10 + 0.8(80)$, or $10 + 64$.
$C = 74$.
If NI is 100, then $C = 10 + 0.8(100)$, or $10 + 80$.
$C = 90$.

The graph below illustrates these answers.

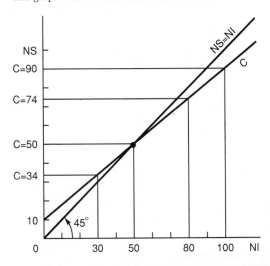

731

from foreign buyers. Then the size of NI is indicated by the following equation:

$$NI = C + I.$$

To solve this for NI we need to know the consumption function. Assume that

$$a = 10$$

$$b = 0.8$$

So the consumption function is

$$C = 10 + 0.8 \, NI.$$

So in the equation

$$NI = C + I,$$

we can substitute for C

$$10 + 0.8 \, NI.$$

So the equation becomes

$$NI = 10 + 0.8 \, NI + I.$$

Assume that the size of the investment injection will be 5, no matter what the size of NI may be. Then

$$NI = C + 5, \text{ and } NI = 10 + 0.8 \, NI + 5.$$

When we solve this equation we'll know the equilibrium size of NI when I = 5. To solve the equation, first subtract 0.8 NI from both sides to eliminate all of the NI on the right side of the equation. That leaves 0.2 NI on the left side. Here it is:

$$1.0 \, NI = 10 + 0.8 \, NI + 5$$

$$-0.8 \, NI = -0.8 \, NI$$

$$0.2 \, NI = 10 + 5$$

$$0.2 \, NI = 15$$

Divide both sides by 0.2

$$\frac{0.2 \, NI}{0.2} = \frac{15}{0.2}$$

$$NI = 75.$$

The solution shows that, given this consumption function, when I = 5, equilibrium NI is 75. Now study figure 28B-3 which shows this on a graph.

Without any investment injection, the equilibrium national income would be 50. That's what you saw in figure 28B-2. With an investment injection of only 5, equilibrium NI is up to 75. That happens because of the income multiplier. More on that soon. But first, here's another question.

Figure 28B-3.   The Effect of an Investment Injection

When the investment injection is 5, equilibrium NI is 75. The C + I curve is the C curve shifted upward by the amount of the investment injection. Here, I = 5.

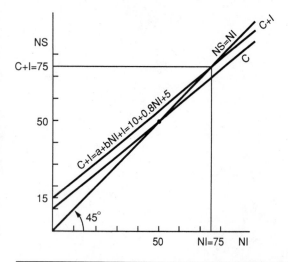

What If the Investment Injection Was Larger? Or Smaller?

Suppose the investment injection had been 2? Or 3? Or maybe 7? Or 9? You could figure out the equilibrium level of NI just as easily. Here's an example assuming that the investment injection is 3.

$$NI = C + I$$

$$NI = 10 + 0.8\, NI + I$$

$$1.0\, NI = 10 + 0.8\, NI + 3$$

$$-0.8\, NI = -0.8\, NI$$

$$0.2\, NI = 10 + 3$$

$$\frac{0.2\, NI}{0.2} = \frac{13}{0.2}$$

$$NI = 65$$

A decrease in the investment injection from 5 to 3 caused equilibrium NI to decrease from 75 to 65. That's the multiplier effect working in reverse.

What If the MPC Was Larger? Or Smaller?

Suppose the consumption function curve wasn't quite so steep. Suppose MPC was only 0.75. Then the multiplier would be smaller. Assume that I = 5 as in the first example and work it out and you'll see the difference when MPC is 0.75 instead of 0.8.

$$NI = C + I$$

$$NI = 10 + 0.75\, NI + I$$

$$1.0\, NI = 10 + 0.75\, NI + 5$$

$$-0.75\, NI = -0.75\, NI$$

$$0.25\, NI = 10 + 5$$

$$\frac{0.25\, NI}{0.25} = \frac{15}{0.25}$$

$$NI = 60.$$

A decrease in the MPC from 0.8 to 0.75 caused the NI to decrease from 75 to 60. Now look at figure 28B-4 which shows this on a graph.

Figure 28B-4.   The Effect of a Change in the MPC

When the MPC decreases from 0.8 to 0.75 that reduces the upward slope of the C + I curve and reduces the size of the equilibrium NI from 75 to 60.

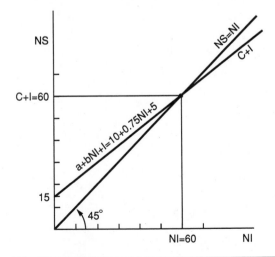

Now you know how to compute the size of national income for (1) different sizes of the investment injection, and (2) different slopes of the straight-line consumption function curve. The appendixes of the next chapter use these same equations to explain how to calculate the income multiplier, and more.[2]

[2] Note that the model we are dealing with is based on some simplifying assumptions. We are assuming (1) that the price level is fixed, (2) that the only spending sources are C and I, (3) that the investment injection does not change as national income changes, and (4) that the consumption function is linear so that the MPC is the same for all levels of NI. We could depart from these simplifying assumptions but that isn't really necessary. This simplified model illustrates the principles just fine.

Using Algebra to Derive the Income Multiplier

From the appendixes to the previous chapter you know that the equation for the consumption function is $C = a + bNI$. And to get the equation for $C + I$ you just add "+I."

$$C = a + bNI$$

$$C + I = a + bNI + I.$$

and since $C + I = NI$ we can substitute NI for $C + I$, and get:

$$NI = a + bNI + I.$$

This equation, like all equations, can be expressed in various ways. You should express it in the way that's most useful in finding what you want to find out.

What we are interested in finding out is the size of national income, and *what happens when the investment injection changes*—that is, we want to know about the **income multiplier** effect. So just watch this:

$$NI = a + bNI + I$$

Now subtract enough NI from both sides of the equation to get rid of all of the NI on one side:

$$-bNI = -bNI$$

And you get:

$$NI - bNI = a + I$$

Now factor out[1] the NI on the left side of the equation and you get:

$$(1 - b)NI = a + I$$

Divide both sides by $(1 - b)$ and you'll see another way of finding the size of NI.[2]

$$NI = \frac{a + I}{(1 - b)}$$

This equation tells you that "a" (the size of consumer spending when NI = 0) plus I (the amount of the investment injection) divided by $(1 - b)$ gives you the size of the national income. Neat! But what's the real meaning of $(1 - b)$?

The "b" term is the marginal propensity to consume (MPC), remember? So $(1 - b)$ is $1 - MPC$. It's the marginal propensity to save (MPS). The larger the "b" term (MPC) the smaller will be the $1 - b$ (=MPS) term and the larger NI will be.

Or you can say it the other way. As the "b" term (MPC) gets smaller, the "consumer respending effect" gets smaller. So the size of the equilibrium NI gets smaller.

Here's an example using the same numbers as before ($a = 10$, $b = 0.8$, and $I = 5$).

$$NI = \frac{a + I}{(1 - b)}$$

$$NI = \frac{10 + 5}{(1 - 0.8)}$$

$$NI = \frac{15}{0.2} = 75.$$

---

[1] In case you've forgotten how to factor a term like "NI − bNI" there are only two little rules you need to be reminded of: (1) a term such as NI which does not have a coefficient, really has the coefficient 1, so "NI" really means "1.0 NI" and (2) a term outside the parenthesis means that this term is to be multiplied by each term within the parenthesis.

Logical example: Suppose you have 1 orange + 3 oranges. You have, in fact $(1 + 3)$ oranges. Or suppose you have 1 box of graham crackers at home, and you know your little sister likes to eat graham crackers. If I asked you how many boxes of graham crackers you had at home you might tell me, "Let b equal the amount that my sister has eaten, and I have at home (1 box minus b boxes), or $(1 - b)$ boxes." That's factoring.

Now you see why NI − bNI says exactly the same thing as 1.0 NI − bNI, which means exactly the same thing as $(1 - b)$ NI.

[2] This is a neat and helpful little equation, but please be warned that it would only work for values of b ranging between zero and one—that is, for consumption function curves ranging between horizontal and sloping upward at an angle of 45 degrees. But that's the only kind of consumption function anyone is ever likely to encounter!

The answer comes out the same as when it was worked out the long way a few minutes ago. Here it is again with a smaller investment injection (I = 3):

$$NI = \frac{a + I}{(1 - b)}$$

$$NI = \frac{10 + 3}{(1 - 0.8)}$$

$$NI = \frac{13}{0.2} = 65.$$

And now, for a smaller MPC (say $\frac{3}{4}$ths, or 0.75)

$$NI = \frac{a + I}{(1 - b)}$$

$$NI = \frac{10 + 5}{(1 - 0.75)}$$

$$NI = \frac{15}{0.25} = 60.$$

The Logic of This Equation

In this equation the numerator (a + I) tells how big C + I would be when NI = 0. The numerator (a + I) gives *the size of the autonomous injections into the income stream*. None of this "autonomous injection" in induced by people receiving income.

Once you know the size of the *autonomous injection*, then you need to know how much *additional consumer spending* will be generated by the multiplier effect—the effect of the responding of income received.

As NI increases, C continues to increase until the savings withdrawal increases enough to withdraw all of the "autonomous spending." In this case, first the *negative savings* (10, when NI = 0) must be eliminated. Then *positive savings* must expand enough to withdraw all of the investment injection.

The smaller the marginal propensity to consume (MPC), the larger will be the marginal propensity to save (MPS). The larger the MPS, the sooner (1) the *negative savings* will be eliminated and (2) the *positive savings* will be large enough to offset the investment injection. So the smaller the MPC (the larger the MPS) the smaller the equilibrium NI will be.

The **income multiplier** is the "consumer respending effect"—the increase in consumer spending induced by an income increase. The larger the MPC the more consumers will spend out of an income increase. So the larger the income multiplier will be. The next section uses algebra to derive the income multiplier.

The Simple Algebra of the Income Multiplier

If you want to see the income multiplier working, you increase the size of the investment injection and then watch what happens.[3] We can *derive* the simple formula for the income multiplier as follows:

First start with the basic equation:

$$C + I = NI$$

So it is obvious that

$$C + I = C + I$$

You know that C = a + bNI, so for C you can substitute (a + bNI) and get

$$C + I = a + bNI + I$$

Then increase the size of the investment injection. If you change the "I" term to "I + 1" that will increase national income by 1, plus the additional income generated by the multiplier. So the next step is to change I to (I + 1).

$$C + I = a + bNI + I + 1$$

(Note that the C + I term in this case refers to the *new* NI, with the multiple effect of the new investment injection included.)

You know that NI = C + I. So you can replace the C + I term with NI, and the equation becomes:

$$NI = a + bNI + I + 1.$$

Now subtract bNI from each side of the equation:

$$-bNI = -bNI$$

And you get

$$NI - bNI = a + I + 1$$

which, when the left-side term is factored, becomes

$$(1 - b)NI = a + I + 1.$$

Divide both sides of the equation by (1 − b) and you get

$$NI = \frac{a + I + 1}{(1 - b)}$$

---

[3] Or you could increase the size of the "a" term—that is, shift the consumption function upward—increase the size of the "negative savings" injection when NI = 0—and it would work exactly the same. But in this example, we'll just increase the *investment injection* and watch what happens.

This last equation takes you right back to the equation you were working with a few minutes ago $NI = \left(\dfrac{a + I}{1 - b}\right)$ except that the numerator is changed by "+1." What's the difference between NI, as arrived at by our original formula, and NI as arrived at by this new formula which includes the "+1"?

This new equation tells us how big the national income will be *with the additional investment injection*. The former equation told us how big the national income would be *without* this new "+1" investment injection. So how much bigger is the new national income with the "+1" injection?

New NI (with + 1 Injection) Minus Old NI Equals the Multiplier Effect

Just subtract the size of NI *without* the new injection $\left(\dfrac{a + I}{1 - b}\right)$ from the size of NI *with* the new injection $\left(\dfrac{a + I + 1}{1 - b}\right)$. The answer will tell you how much NI will change as a result of a change in the size of the investment injection—that is, it will tell you the multiplier effect. Here it is:

$$\text{Change in NI} = \frac{a + I + 1}{(1 - b)} - \frac{a + I}{(1 - b)}.$$

Simplify the equation by combining the numerator over the denominator.

$$\text{Change in NI} = \frac{a + I + 1 - (a + I)}{(1 - b)}.$$

When you subtract the (a + I) in the numerator, you get:

$$\text{Change in NI} = \frac{1}{1 - b}.$$

Since "b" is the marginal propensity to consume, (1 − b) is the marginal propensity to save. This equation tells you that the income multiplier is "one divided by (that is, the reciprocal of) the marginal propensity to save."

In the example we have been using, "b" has been 0.8, so (1 − b) has been 0.2. Divide 0.2 into 1, and you find that the multiplier is 5.

If you prefer to work with fractions, when MPC is 0.8, that's 8/10 or 4/5, and 1 − 4/5 = 1/5 (the MPS). When you divide 1 by 1/5 (to divide a fraction, invert the divisor and multiply), again you see that the multiplier is 5.

Autonomous Injections, Times the Multiplier, Equals NI

Here's another shortcut way to calculate NI. A few minutes ago you saw how to calculate NI using this equation:

$$NI = \frac{a + I}{1 - b}.$$

This equation can also be expressed as

$$NI = (a + I)\left(\frac{1}{1 - b}\right).^4$$

You know that $\left(\dfrac{1}{1 - b}\right)$ is the income multiplier. So what this equation says is: *The autonomous injections* (a + I) times the *multiplier* $\left(\dfrac{1}{1 - b}\right)$ equals the size of the national income.

Appendix 29B goes further into all of this.

---

[4] If this second equation doesn't look the same to you as the first, consider this: What's the difference whether you say $\dfrac{10}{5}$ or $10\left(\dfrac{1}{5}\right)$, which is ten times one-fifth. No difference! You come out with 2 either way.

Calculating National Income When All Spending Sources Are Considered: The C + I + G + F = NI Equation

It's easy to include the other spending sources—government spending (G) and net spending by foreigners for our exports (F)—in the C + I equation. Then we can figure out everything in exactly the same way. Here's an example:

$$NI = C + I + G + F$$

You remember that C = a + bNI, so we can substitute this for C in the equation and we get

$$NI = a + bNI + I + G + F.$$

Subtract bNI from each side of the equation and you get

$$NI - bNI = a + I + G + F.$$

Factor the left side of the equation

$$(1 - b)NI = a + I + G + F$$

Divide each side of the equation by (1 − b) and this will solve the equation for NI

$$NI = \frac{a + I + G + F}{(1 - b)}$$

This equation can also be expressed as follows:

$$NI = (a + I + G + F) \left(\frac{1}{1 - b} \right)$$

Or as follows:

$$NI = \frac{a}{1 - b} + \frac{I}{1 - b} + \frac{G}{1 - b} + \frac{F}{1 - b}$$

Or as follows, to show that what you are doing is multiplying each one of the autonomous injections by the multiplier, and then adding all these together:

$$NI = \frac{1}{1 - b}(a) + \frac{1}{1 - b}(I) + \frac{1}{1 - b}(G) + \frac{1}{1 - b}(F)$$

Multiply Each Spending Injection by the Multiplier, Then Add Them Up

Suppose you wanted to use this equation to compute the size of the national income. You would need to know the values of a, b, I, G, and F. Once you know these values it's very easy to solve the equation. Assume that:

$$a = \$10 \text{ billion}$$
$$b = 0.8$$
$$I = \$5 \text{ billion}$$
$$G = \$2 \text{ billion}$$
$$F = \$1 \text{ billion}$$

Inserting these values into the equation we get:

$NI = \frac{1}{1 - .8}(\$10)$	$+ \frac{1}{1 - .8}(\$5)$	$+ \frac{1}{1 - .8}(\$2)$	$+ \frac{1}{1 - .8}(\$1)$	
$NI = \frac{1}{.2}(\$10)$	$+ \frac{1}{.2}(\$5)$	$+ \frac{1}{.2}(\$2)$	$+ \frac{1}{.2}(\$1)$	
$NI = (5)(\$10)$	$+ (5)(\$5)$	$+ (5)(\$2)$	$+ (5)(\$1)$	
$NI = \$50$	$+ \$25$	$+ \$10$	$+ \$5$	
$NI = \$90$ billion				

You can look at the above computation and see very clearly that the equation says: "Multiply each autonomous spending injection by the multiplier and then add all these together and you will find the size of the national income." Or you could add all of the autonomous injections together and then multiply by the multiplier. You get the same answer either way.

From this analysis you can see that it makes no difference where the autonomous injection comes from—I, or G, or F, or from C when NI is zero (i.e., negative savings), or from any combination of these—the multiplier effect is always the same. Those consumers who are spending 8/10ths (0.8) of their extra income on consumer goods don't care where the extra income came from!

To Find C at Any Level of NI, Use the Equation: C = a + bNI

In the calculation you just went through, NI turned out to be $90 billion. But that calculation didn't tell you the size of consumer spending. When NI = $90 billion, how big is C? To find out, just substitute the numbers into the basic equation for the straight-line consumption function curve:

$$C = a + bNI$$

$$C = \$10 + 0.8(90)$$

$$C = \$10 + \$72$$

$$C = \$82 \text{ billion.}$$

Then if you want to know how much is being pulled out as savings:

$$S = NI - C$$

$$S = 90 - 82$$

$$S = \$8 \text{ billion.}$$

Now compare total injections with total savings. The investment injection is 5, the government injection is 2, and the foreign injection is 1, for total injections of $8 billion. So equilibrium NI is where S = $8 billion—where the saving withdrawal is equal to total injections. That must be true in this case because we're assuming that saving is the only withdrawal.

What if there were other withdrawals? Taxes, for example? You can find out about that in appendix 29C. But before you go on, spend a few minutes studying and practicing with figure 29B-1. There you'll see a Keynesian NS = NI graph which illustrates the effect of *all of the injections*. And you'll see that the answers you got using equations will come out exactly the same on the graph.

Figure 29B-1.   Equilibrium NI When All Injections (I, G, and F) Are Considered, and the Only Withdrawal Is Savings

If there were no injections (I + G + F = 0) then equilibrium NI would be 50. But with the injections assumed in this example (5 + 2 + 1 = 8) equilibrium NI increases from 50 to 90—an increase of 40, induced by an injection of 8! The income multiplier must be 5 because 5 times 8 equals 40.

Also $\dfrac{1}{-\text{MPC}} = \dfrac{1}{1 - .8} = \dfrac{1}{.2} = 5$; and that's the multiplier.

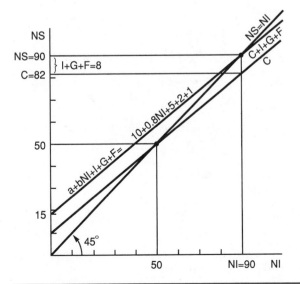

APPENDIX 29C

The Algebra of Tax Withdrawals and the Balanced Budget Multiplier

When the government pulls money out of the income stream by collecting taxes, that is somewhat like a "reverse injection." You know that if the income multiplier is 5, one dollar of new injections will result in a $5 increase in NI. Does it work the other way, too? If the government suddenly started pulling out an additional dollar in taxes, would that ultimately result in a $5 decrease in national income? No. Not exactly. This appendix explains why not.

Not All of NI Is Disposable Income

So far we have been going along the assumption that disposable income (DI) was the same as NI. But you know that when the government collects taxes, that isn't true. Not all of the NI flows to people and becomes disposable income. So DI is smaller than NI by the amount taken away by taxes. Now to be more realistic we'll say that *disposable income* equals *national income minus taxes*:

$$DI = NI - T$$

It's obvious that the consumption function really reflects DI—not NI. People can't spend for consumer goods the money they must pay as taxes! So the straight line consumption function equation really isn't:

$$C = a + b \, NI. \text{ It is}$$

$$C = a + b \, DI.$$

You know that DI equals NI − T, so let's substitute that in the equation and get

$$C = a + b(NI - T).$$

And multiplying out the b(NI − T) term, we get

$$C = a + bNI - bT.$$

This last equation tells us that the size of the consumer spending flow will be determined by (1) the size of the consumer spending flow when NI is zero, plus (2) the marginal propensity to consume times the size of the national income, and (3) *minus* the marginal propensity to consume times the tax withdrawal.

The "minus bT" term in this equation shows you that the tax withdrawal is going to pull down the size of consumer spending. The question now is, *by how much?*

How Much Will Taxes Reduce NI?

We begin with the same equation as in the earlier example:

$$NI = C + I + G + F$$

Again we substitute for C, but now instead of substituting "a + bNI" we substitute "a + bNI − bT" and get

$$NI = a + bNI - bT + I + G + F$$

Again, subtract bNI from each side of the equation

$$-bNI = -bNI, \text{ and get}$$

$$NI - bNI = a - bT + I + G + F$$

Factor out NI on the left side of the equation

$$(1 - b)NI = a - bT + I + G + F$$

Divide both sides of the equation by (1 − b) and you get

$$NI = \frac{a - bT + I + G + F}{(1 - b)}.$$

This equation is expressed in expanded form and then solved in box 29C-1.

740

Box 29C-1

Question: How Does a Tax Withdrawal of $2 Billion Reduce NI By $8 Billion?

$$NI = \frac{1}{1-b}(a) \quad -\frac{1}{1-b}(bT) \quad +\frac{1}{1-b}(I) \quad +\frac{1}{1-b}(G) \quad +\frac{1}{1-b}(F)$$

Insert the same figures used before, assume that T = $2 billion, and you get

$$NI = \frac{1}{1-.8}(\$10) - \frac{1}{1-.8}(.8 \times \$2) + \frac{1}{1-.8}(\$5) + \frac{1}{1-.8}(\$2) + \frac{1}{1-.8}(\$1)$$

$$NI = \frac{1}{0.2}(\$10) \quad - \quad \frac{1}{0.2}(\$1.6) \quad + \quad \frac{1}{0.2}(\$5) \quad + \quad \frac{1}{0.2}(\$2) \quad + \quad \frac{1}{0.2}(\$1)$$

$$NI = \quad 5(\$10) \quad - \quad 5(\$1.6) \quad + \quad 5(\$5) \quad + \quad 5(\$2) \quad + \quad 5(\$1)$$

$$NI = \quad \$50 \quad - \quad \$8 \quad + \quad \$25 \quad + \quad \$10 \quad + \quad \$5$$

NI = $82 billion

A tax withdrawal of $2 billion reduces NI from $90 billion to $82 billion.

When you work through the solution in the box you find that a tax withdrawal of $2 billion reduces NI to $82 billion. With no taxes, NI was $90 billion. Taxes of $2 billion reduced NI to $82 billion because of the income multiplier working in reverse.

This $2 billion tax withdrawal also reduced saving by $2 billion. So the size of total withdrawals is the same as before—savings withdrawals are $2 billion smaller to offset the $2 billion tax withdrawal.

NI had to decrease by $8 billion to decrease the savings withdrawal by $2 billion and reestablish macroequilibrium. Why $8 billion? Because when MPS is 2/10ths, NI must decrease by $8 billion to reduce savings by $2 billion. The next section explains more about that.

The Balanced-Budget Multiplier

Now consider this: When the government is spending $2 billion, that injection pushes up national income by $10 billion. A $2 billion injection times a multiplier of 5 equals $10 billion. But when the government collects enough taxes to balance the budget ($2 billion), that only pulls down NI by $8 billion.

What all this says is that the government can balance its budget and still have a stimulating effect on national income. How is that possible? You probably already know, but before you see the answer, first consider this question: With $2 billion now being pulled out in taxes, and with NI now $82 billion, how big is consumer spending? To find out, use the consumption function equation. But this time you must use the equation which includes the effect of taxes:

$$C = a + bNI - bT$$

Just substitute the numbers and work it out.

$$C = 10 + (0.8)NI - (0.8)T$$
$$C = 10 + (0.8)(\$82) - (0.8)(\$2)$$
$$C = 10 + 65.6 - 1.6$$
$$C = 10 + 64$$
$$C = \$74 \text{ billion}$$

Consumer spending is down to $74 billion. It was $82 billion when no taxes were collected, so it's down by $8 billion! So most of that reduction in consumer spending didn't result from the taxes ($2 billion) taken away from the consumers. It resulted in the *lower national income* (down from $90 billion to $82 billion). With lower NI, people have smaller disposable incomes so they spend less.

The initial *direct effect* of the $2 billion in taxes was to reduce consumer spending, not by $2 billion, but by only $1.6 billion. Why?

Look at it this way. When you receive an additional $100, the MPC says that you won't spend it all for consumer goods—only part of it. Suppose the government had taxed away that $100. Would that have reduced consumer spending by $100? No. It would only have reduced it by $100 times the MPC (in this case 0.8 times $100 = $80).

G Puts More Into the Spending Stream than T Takes Out

All of government spending (G) is a *direct injection* into the income stream. But *not* all of the tax withdrawal is a withdrawal from the income stream. A part of the tax withdrawal comes from what would have been *saved*. Only that part which comes from what *would have been spent for consumer goods* represents a withdrawal from the income stream.

If the marginal propensity to save (MPS) was zero, then there would be no "balanced budget multiplier." That multiplier exists because some of the taxes collected are pulled out of, not the spending flow, but the flow into savings.

If the flow into savings is zero, then all of the taxes will be collected from the spending flow. So the tax withdrawal will be as great as the government spending injection and T will completely offset G. But as MPS gets larger, more of the tax collection comes out of the flow into savings, while all of G is a spending injection. So the larger the MPS, the larger the balanced budget multiplier.

Now you understand why there is "balanced budget multiplier." Also I think you now can see how helpful it is to be able to use algebra to figure out such things.

Using the Algebra of IS-LM to Find Simultaneous Equilibrium in the Macroeconomy

In this chapter you found out how to put the IS curve and the LM curve together in a graph. Where the two lines cross that indicates the level of national income (Y) at which both the product markets and the money market are in equilibrium. So this intersection indicates the equilibrium rate of operation of the macroeconomy. Also from the graph you can see the interest rate which must exist for this equilibrium to be obtained.

You will not be surprised to know that we can use the equation for the IS curve and the one for the LM curve and put these two together and find this simultaneous equilibrium without having to carefully draw lines in a graph.

In this appendix you will see the simple series of steps required to develop the equation for the IS curve, then the LM curve, and finally to put the two together and find the simultaneous equilibrium rate of national income, and the interest rate at which this occurs.

In the appendixes to chapters 28 and 29 you read about and worked with the equations for finding the equilibrium level of national income when only the product market is considered. In those equations it was assumed that the interest rate was (for the time being) fixed and that the level of investment spending was the same, regardless of the size of the national income. In those appendixes you found that (assuming investment spending to be the only injection), equilibrium national income occurs where "a" (autonomous consumer spending when national income is zero) plus I (the autonomous planned investment injection which is not responsive to changes in the size of national income), multiplied by the multiplier $(1/1 - b)$—the reciprocal of the marginal propensity to save.

In the appendixes to chapters 28 and 29 you also found out how to calculate the equilibrium size of national income considering not only "a + I" but also autonomous spending injections

from government spending and from net sales of goods to foreigners. If you don't remember all this, it would be a good idea for you to go back and review the appendixes to chapters 28 and 29 before you go on into this one.

In this appendix we are going to assume that we're dealing with a closed economy (no foreign trade) and one in which there is no government spending or taxes. So the only autonomous spending injections will be represented by "a + I," and the size of national income will be determined by a + I times the multiplier $(1/1 - b)$.

The Equation for the IS Curve

Equilibrium real income (Y), as you learned from the appendixes to chapters 28 and 29, is determined by the size of a + I times the multiplier $(1/1 - b)$. The term a + I is autonomous—that is, not induced—planned spending and the multiplier is the reciprocal of the marginal propensity to save: $\frac{1}{1 - \text{MPC}}$.

Throughout this appendix we will assume that MPC equals 0.8, so that MPS $(1 - 0.8)$ is 0.2. The reciprocal of 0.2 $\left(\frac{1}{0.2}\right)$ is 5.

Also to simplify, for the purposes of this appendix we will use "k" to refer to the income multiplier. So k = 5. And also to simplify, we will refer to "a + I"—the rate of autonomous planned spending—as Ap.

Now, with these shorthand symbols, we can say that

$$Y = k(Ap) \qquad [1]$$

or using the number of the multiplier which we

have already decided on, we can say

$$Y = 5(Ap).$$

So now the only task is to get the size of Ap and we will know the size of Y.

But here's a minor complication. We know that the rate of investment spending (I) is responsive to changes in the interest rate (Δr). As r increases, I decreases. This relationship between r and I was ignored in the equations used in the appendixes to chapters 28 and 29. But in IS-LM analysis this relationship takes on significant importance. So the equation for the IS curve must show autonomous planned spending (Ap) to be responsive to interest rate changes.

This equation for the IS curve is developed assuming that this is a linear relationship. First we can assume a given size of Ap when the interest rate is zero. Then we can show that Ap gets smaller as interest rates rise because of the discouraging effect of higher interest rates on the investment spending component of Ap.

Suppose we asume that the level of autonomous planned spending when the interest rate is zero is represented by A. Then for any increase in the interest rate above zero we can find the size of Ap by subtracting something from $\overline{A}$ to reflect the magnitude of the interest rate, above zero.

Assume that "g" indicates how much Ap decreases for each percentage point increase in r. Then we get the equation

$$Ap = \overline{A} - gr. \qquad [2]$$

You can see that if r equals zero, Ap equals $\overline{A}$. But as interest rates rise above zero, Ap gets smaller than $\overline{A}$. The larger the g term, the smaller Ap will become as interest rates rise. So the larger the g term, the more responsive Ap will be to Δr, and the flatter the IS curve will tend to be.

Example: Suppose g equals \$5 billion. Then for each percentage point increase in r, Ap will be \$5 billion smaller than $\overline{A}$. If g happens to be \$10 billion then for each one percentage point rise in r, Ap will be \$10 billion less than $\overline{A}$.

Now we can substitute equation [2] into equation [1] and get the basic equation for the IS curve.

$$Y = k(\overline{A} - gr). \qquad [3]$$

Suppose we assume that g equals 10 and (as previously assumed) k equals 5. Here's what this equation says:

$$Y = 5 (\overline{A} - 10r).$$

Example: Suppose $\overline{A}$ is 200 and r is zero. Equilibrium NI will be NI = 5(200) = 1,000. So the IS curve will intersect the horizontal axis (where r = 0) at Y = 1,000.

If $\overline{A}$ is 200 and r is 20%, equilibrium Y will be

$$Y = 5 [200 - (10 \times 20)]$$
$$Y = 0.$$

So the IS curve will intersect the vertical axis at r = 20%. These two points locate the linear IS curve in the graph. Using equation [3] you can locate any point on the IS curve, because the equation tells the size of Y which corresponds to each interest rate. You can assume a series of different interest rates and for each, solve the equation for Y. That will give you a series of points on the IS curve.

The Equation for the LM Curve

The LM curve shows combinations of Y and r where the size of the real money supply (M) is exactly equal to the demand for (desire to hold) real money balances (Mqd):

$$M = Mqd.$$

For any given LM curve, M is fixed. So, the only variable is the quantity of money demanded (Mqd). Mqd tends to increase as Y increases (because of the increased transactions demand for money balances). Mqd tends to decrease as r increases (because of the increased opportunity cost of holding money balances, and the reduced Mqd for speculative balances).

The equilibrium in the money market which occurs where M = Mqd depends on the degree of responsiveness of Mqd to change in Y (ΔY) and to changes in r (Δr). So the equation for the LM curve must contain a term for the responsiveness of Mqd to ΔY and also one for its responsiveness to Δr.

- Let "h" indicate the responsiveness of Mqd to ΔY : h = the amount of the change in Mqd—change in the number of dollars of desired money balances—which results from each dollar of change in Y (assuming r constant). The h term represents a positive relationship: $\uparrow Y \rightarrow \uparrow Mqd$.
  Example: Assume that h = 0.4. Then if Y increses by \$1,000 (with r constant) Mqd will increase by \$400.

- Let "j" indicate the responsiveness of Mqd to Δr: j = the number of dollars of change in Mqd which results from each percentage point change in r (assuming Y constant). The j term indicates a negative relationship: $\uparrow r \rightarrow \downarrow Mqd$.
  Example: Assume that j = \$20 billion. Then if r increases by one percentage point (assuming Y constant) Mqd will decrease by \$20 billion.

Now, using these new terms (h, and j): Mqd = hY − jr. So in the money market equilibrium equation M = Mqd, hY − jr can be substituted for Mqd. When this is done the equilibrium equation becomes

$$M = hY - jr. \qquad [4]$$

Using the same numbers (parameters) assumed previously, money market equilibrium occurs where:

$$M = 0.4Y - 20\,r$$

Assume that Y = 500 and r = 5%.

$$Mqd = 0.4\,(500) - 20\,(5)$$

$$Mqd = 200 - 100$$

$$Mqd = 100$$

If M also equals 100 then that means that Mqd = M, and the combination Y = 500, r = 5% is a point on the LM curve.

Now it's time to assume a given size for the money supply (say $100 billion), and with our assumed parameters for h and j (and with a little algebraic manipulation), obtain the equation for a specific LM curve.

First, to obtain the general equation:

1. add jr to both sides of equation [4] and get

$$M + jr = hY$$

2. divide both sides by h and get

$$\frac{M + jr}{h} = Y$$

3. shift Y to the left side and you have the general equation for the LM curve

$$Y = \frac{M + jr}{h} \qquad [5]$$

Insert the previously assumed parameters (the "givens") into equation [5] and get

$$Y = \frac{100 + 20(5)}{0.4} = \frac{200}{0.4} = 500$$

So with these parameters and with the interest rate assumed to be 5% we find that Y = $500 billion, just as was previously assumed.

Equation [5] describes any straight-line LM curve. Given the size of the money supply (M) and the assumed numerical values of h and j, the equation tells you for each interest rate (r) the exact size of the national income (Y) required to bring equilibrium in the money market—where M =

Mqd. You can assume a series of different interest rates and for each, solve the equation for Y. That will give you a series of points on the LM curve.

Combining the IS and LM Equations

Standing alone the equation for the IS curve [3] and the one for the LM curve [5] can only establish "if—then" relationships between r and Y: If r is this, then Y will be this. Just as with the curves, to find the **unique combination** of r and Y which will bring equilibrium both in the product markets and in the money market it's necessary to put the equations together. Fortunately, that's easy to do.

The LM equation [5] can be rearranged to solve for r, as follows:

1. multiply both sides of equation [5] by h and you get

$$hY = M + jr$$

2. subtract M from both sides and get

$$hY - M = jr$$

3. divide both sides by j and get

$$\frac{hY - M}{j} = r$$

4. and move r to the left side

$$r = \frac{hY - M}{j} \qquad [5a]$$

You can see that equation [5a] is the general LM equation [5], only arranged differently. But now, since the right side of equation [5a] is equal to (has the same value as) r, it can be substituted for r in the IS equation [3]. And when that is done what we have is one equation which contains all of the functional relationships indicated by both the IS and LM curves. Here it is.

Into the IS equation [3]

$$Y = k\,(\overline{A} - gr),$$

substitute from the LM equation [5a] for r and get

$$Y = k\left[\overline{A} - g\,\frac{(hY - M)}{j}\right]$$

Multiply out the term in parenthesis and get

$$Y = k\left[\overline{A} - \frac{ghY}{j} + \frac{gm}{j}\right] \qquad [6]$$

To solve this equation [6] for Y, it's necessary to move all of the Y to one side. To do that, first multiply the terms in the brackets by k, and get

$$Y = k\bar{A} - \frac{kghY}{j} + \frac{kgM}{j}$$

then add $\frac{kghY}{j}$ to each side and get

$$Y + \frac{kghY}{j} = k\bar{A} + \frac{kgM}{j}$$

Divide both sides by k

$$\frac{Y + \left(\frac{kghY}{j}\right)}{k} = \frac{k\bar{A} + \frac{kgM}{j}}{k}$$

The k in each of the terms cancels out and you get

$$\frac{Y}{k} + \frac{ghY}{j} = \bar{A} + \frac{gM}{j}$$

Factor out the Y on the left side and get

$$Y\left(\frac{1}{k} + \frac{gh}{j}\right) = \bar{A} + \frac{gM}{j}$$

Divide both sides by the term in parenthesis and what you get is the general equilibrium income equation:

$$Y = \frac{\bar{A} + \frac{gM}{j}}{\frac{1}{k} + \frac{gh}{j}} \qquad [7]$$

This is the "master equation" which combines the IS and LM equations and lets us find the unique Y and r combination which brings both the product markets and the money market into equilibrium. This equation tells us the level of Y and r where investment injections equal savings withdrawals (I = S) and where the money supply is equal to money demand: M = Mqd, or L = M.

Solving the Equation to Find Equilibrium Y

So now, insert the previous parameters into the equation and solve for Y. The parameters:

MPC (=b) is 0.8, so the multiplier
(1/1 − b) = k   = 5

$\bar{A}$ = autonomous planned spending when r is zero   = 200

g = amount by which autonomous planned spending (Ap) decreases for each one percentage point increase in r   = 10

h = increase in Mqd when Y increases by $1   = 0.4

j = decrease in Mqd when r increases by one percentage point   = 20

M = the size of the money supply   = 100

Inserting these parameters we get

$$Y = \frac{200 + \frac{10(100)}{20}}{\frac{1}{5} + \frac{(10)(0.4)}{20}}$$

$$Y = \frac{250}{\frac{2}{5}} = \frac{250}{0.4}$$

$$Y = 625.$$

You can see from the solution that, given these assumed parameters, the equilibrium level of Y is $625. You know that this equilibrium Y is based on some specific equilibrium interest rate. But this equation does not tell you what that rate is. Why? Because the value of r has been replaced in the equation by the right side of equation [5a]. But once we solve for Y, it's easy enough to find r.

Now that we know the equilibrium level of Y, we can insert that together with the parameters, in any one of the equations in which r appears explicitly, and then solve for r. Equation [5a] is arranged to solve for r, so we'll use that one to calculate equilibrium r.

Equation [5a] is

$$r = \frac{hY - M}{j}$$

Inserting the numbers

$$r = \frac{(0.4)(625) - 100}{20}$$

$$r = \frac{250 - 100}{20} = \frac{150}{20}$$

$$r = 7.5$$

Now you can see that, given our assumptions, simultaneous equilibrium occurs in this economy when Y = $625 and r = 7.5%.

Now study figure 31A-1 and you'll see the curves described by these equations, plotted in the IS-LM diagram.

Figure 31A-1.   Graphic Illustration of the IS and LM Equations

These curves are plotted from the equations. The assumed numbers (parameters) are the same as used in the text. Here you see the same simultaneous equilibrium as calculated using the equations.

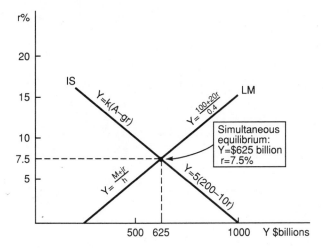

SUBJECT INDEX

749

NAME INDEX